The Means of Naming

The Means of Naming

A social and cultural history of personal naming in western Europe

Stephen Wilson

First published in 1998 by UCL Press

UCL Press Limited
1 Gunpowder Square
London EC4A 3DE
UK

and

1900 Frost Road, Suite 101
Bristol
Pennsylvania 19007–1598
USA

The name of University College London (UCL) is a registered trade
mark used by UCL Press with the consent of the owner.

British Library Cataloguing-in-Publication Data
A CIP catalogue record for this book is available from the British Library.

Library of Congress Cataloging-in-Publication Data are available

ISBN's: 1–85728–244–2 HB
        1–85728–245–0 PB

Typeset in Garamond by Graphicraft Limited, Hong Kong
Printed by T.J. International Ltd, Padstow, Cornwall

To my mother

"For love of unforgotten times"
Robert Louis Stevenson, *A Child's Garden of Verses*

Contents

CONTENTS

Preface

> A historian aware of the difficulties of his métier . . . does not decide readily to retrace in a few hundred pages an extremely long evolution, obscure in itself and moreover insufficiently known.[1]

Most historians have not been very interested in the names of those whose lives and activities they study. "These people are little more than names" is a typical dismissive comment.[2] Where more information about characters from the past is available, historians get names wrong; they modernize their spelling or translate them into their own language; they invent names that the people concerned never had. While convenient and familiar, such procedures in effect tamper with historical evidence in a way that would not be acceptable in other circumstances. Even historians of the family until very recently either ignored the fact that their subjects had names or interpreted the thinking behind their choice from a purely modern perspective.

However, the need for serious name studies has long been recognized and acted on by scholars in other fields, notably in philology and social anthropology, though comprehensive accounts are missing. "It is unfortunate", wrote Pitt-Rivers in 1976, "that there is yet no anthropological account of the history of naming systems in Europe."[3] This book seeks to meet that need, though it looks only at Britain, France and Italy, and it must be regarded as an essay in a field which still remains very patchily worked. Medieval names attracted a fair degree of scholarly interest earlier in this century; and Roman names have been adequately covered more recently. But investigation of early modern and modern names has only just begun, with the development of a special interest in the topic in France among historians (and some sociologists) from around 1980. Little work has been done in Britain. Though partly based on original research, this book relies mainly on the work done by others, which is acknowledged in the notes and bibliography. Its shortcomings are its own.

As its title indicates, the book is about the means of naming, that is the ways in which individuals were named rather than the meaning of names in the old-fashioned etymological sense. It is very much, however, about the meaning of names in a much broader sense, and it derives from the conviction that to elucidate this is essentially a task for the historian.

Linguisticians and philosophers have clearly separated words and names. For John Stuart Mill, proper names were "meaningless marks set upon things [or persons] to distinguish them from one another".[4] Or, as Camille Jullian put it in 1919, names are "sterilized words", words that have lost their original meanings and have come to be employed as simple labels.[5] Put yet another way, "words connote and names denote". A name "has no lexical meaning, or rather . . . whatever lexical meaning it may have had, or still retains, does not interfere with its denotative function". Thus Stella is the girl next door and not the Latin name for a star, when she is referred to; Baker is the name of her father, who happens to have inherited that family name, and who may be a chartered surveyor or a dustman. But Nicolaisen, whose exposition we follow, has rightly objected that this distinction is simplistic. Instead of an absolute contrast, there is a continuum: "Words which have become names never totally cease to be words, nor can names ever fully deny their lexical origins."[6] Were this not the case, for example, the vast repertoire of children's nicknames making word-play with other names would be impossible.

Moreover, there are meanings and meanings. One should not confuse the absence of lexical meaning in a name with total lack of meaning.[7] Names of all kinds have associations, flavours; they are evocative, and carry messages that are no less powerful for being ambiguous. Novelists, poets, advertisers, and creators of names for film stars and other performers are expert in these meanings of names. They know that Obadiah Slope or Smallweed is a suitable name for an unattractive character; that sonnets addressed to Pamela or Cynthia sound more serious than ones to Molly or Nell; that Parson's Mead or The Beeches will sell houses or attract elderly people more than Pigg Lane or The Four Winds; that Cary Grant has more appeal than Alexander Archibald Leach, and Mario Lanza than Alfredo Arnold Cocozza.

Nicolaisen also points out that there are onomastic fields, or sets of names appropriate in particular contexts. Thus "in the naming of children, parents depend on a conventionally accepted" repertoire of personal names, from which few depart.[8] This is largely different from the repertoire of names for animals or houses. Within the personal name repertoire there are names for boys and names for girls, few of which overlap; and all names have a penumbra of connotations. It is these which are significant in guiding choice and not the literal meaning of the name. How many parents calling their baby girls Cynthia in the 1930s to the 1950s in the USA and the UK wished to give them one of the titles of the Greek goddess Artemis?

How many had read the Elegies of the Roman poet Sextus Propertius relating to his mistress of that name? And, if they had, would they have named their dear ones after a woman presented there as both promiscuous and cruel?

As Zelinsky expressed it in 1970, "each forename is a one-word poem", but he added "in an undecipherable language",[9] which is not really true. The meanings are complex, multiple and shifting, as the example of Cynthia shows, but they are not totally obscure. Names, moreover, like other words, 'only have meaning . . . in relation to other names".[10] They are part of a system. First names or forenames are distinct from second or family names, which are distinct again from nicknames, though each also interconnects with the others. Different particular names have belonged to these different categories at different times. Indeed, the categories themselves have evolved. So names are connotative, but in a way that requires social and historical analysis to explain. And beyond individual names, naming systems must be described and analyzed.

Names identify individuals and are often the focus of a person's sense of identity, but the name also "defines an individual's position in his family and in society at large; it defines his social personality".[11] In other words, it classifies a person. Zonabend writes that the name is "a mnemonic tool whose function is to mark out the different fields of reference of the society in question: the kinship field, the social field, the symbolic field", placing the individual in each.[12] So, to take the modern European or North American name, the family name attaches the person to a family as a legitimate child; the first name or names may indicate place and roles within the family; a nickname may in addition say something about the status and past behaviour of the person or the family. Different functions may be more important in different kinds of society. In "traditional" societies individuation may be less stressed; in modern societies more. In some societies names may be more obviously central to and expressive of the total structure than in others. Among the Iatmul of New Guinea, for example,

> the naming system is indeed a theoretical image of the whole culture and in it every formulated aspect of the culture is reflected. Conversely, we may say that the system has its branches in every aspect of the culture and gives its support to every cultural activity. Every spell, every song . . . contains lists of names. The utterances of shamans are couched in terms of names . . . Marriages are often arranged in order to gain names. Reincarnation and succession are based upon the naming system. Land tenure is based on clan membership and clan membership is vouched for by names.[13]

The situation in Europe was not so far removed from this.

Names may also register progress through the life cycle, with appropriate changes of names at puberty, marriage, death of father and so on. In all societies, too, and more so in complex ones, a single individual is known by a variety of names depending on the role he or she is playing and the milieu of reference. So there will be one name used by close relatives of origin, another by spouses and lovers, another by children, another by friends, another in public, another at work, and so on. Again, names here serve as a kind of social map, placing individuals in the broader multi-dimensional landscape.

But, as we have stressed, naming systems and categories themselves change and develop and they must therefore be investigated historically and in the long term. We shall therefore begin with Ancient Rome and take the story through the Middle Ages, when the modern European system evolved, down to the present.

We have already implicitly broached questions of terminology, which are problematic given the long time-span. In this book we will use terms employed by contemporaries themselves, where these are appropriate or necessary, as with the Ancient Roman system. We will also use our own objective terms. The modern "Christian name" and "surname" will generally be avoided. First, we will be dealing with situations in which the modern dual-category name is not operative, where people have only single names or sometimes more than two. Secondly, we need to distinguish between names that come first and names that have a specific Christian meaning or origin. Where more than one name is given, therefore, "first name" will be used for the former, while "Christian" will be reserved for the latter. Then the other name, which becomes the family name, is best designated as the "second name" and then the "family name". The English "surname" can be confused with the French "surnom", which is a nickname. For second names that are not hereditary we sometimes use the established term "by-name", keeping "nickname" on the whole for unofficial names used in addition to official ones, which means in the modern context in addition to the first and the second or family name. For additional first names, we use "second first name" or later "middle name". All this will, it is hoped, be clear in practice. A glossary of other technical terms is provided.

We discuss the issues of documentation through the book, but a general point in this area may be made here. For much of the historical period, we only have access to official recorded names. These are themselves significant, but they may not be the names in everyday use. We have earlier glimpses but only in the modern period is name usage reasonably clear.

I have incurred debts in writing this book. For providing information and material I am grateful to Edward Acton, James Casey, Richard Gordon, Oliver Logan, Neil MacMaster, Jane Martindale and especially René Lévy. Norman and Sarah Crowder kindly supplied me with the Crowder-Woodward and Wylie-McDougall genealogies, which they have researched. David Harris and Sue Julier of the Inter-Library Loan department of the University of East Anglia dealt patiently and efficiently with my many requests for often abstruse items. Helena Spurrell word-processed a good part of the manuscript.

PART I

Ancient Rome

CHAPTER ONE

The name system: individual and family

We know more about the names of ancient Romans than those of many other historical societies as a result of what has been called their "epigraphic habit".[1] The Romans liked to place inscriptions on buildings, on statues, at shrines and on tombs, paying honour to or commemorating particular people. These individuals' full names were inscribed, and on monuments so were those of the persons who had erected them. Indeed the name of the commemorator was frequently more prominent that that of the commemorated, since it was the duty of heirs to put up tombstones and to show that they had done so. Monuments were usually in durable stone, and over 300,000 inscriptions are known from all over the Roman Empire and from most periods. Inscriptions have been widely and ingeniously used by historians to investigate different aspects of Roman society, starting with naming practices.

Of course, the evidence of inscriptions can be misleading. Most are from Italy and from the first and second centuries AD, leaving other places and times underrepresented. Again, some people, some classes of people, were much more likely to have inscriptions made than others, most obviously those with something to boast about and those who could afford to pay a stone-cutter. So the rich and famous are more likely to have their names recorded than the poor and the obscure; men more likely than women; Latins than Greeks. The upwardly mobile, as we should say, seem also to have been especially anxious to record their successful ascent of the slippery pole. Freed slaves and new provincial citizens particularly wanted to have their new names recorded, while those who had already made it, whether high aristocrats or ordinary free-born proletarians, were less interested. But with these caveats inscriptions are a marvellous source of information and may be complemented by literary material. What do both tell us about Roman names?

3

The *tria nomina*

As every schoolboy used to know, the Romans had three names, the *tria nomina*, for example Gaius Julius Caesar, the Dictator; Marcus Tullius Cicero, the orator; or Quintus Horatius Flaccus, the poet. All these three lived in the first century BC when this classic system was firmly established and legally prescribed. Roman citizens were officially registered in this style, together with the all-important filiation indicating their fathers and even grandfathers or great-grandfathers, and the tribe or voting district to which they belonged. So Cicero's full official name was Marcus Tullius Marci filius Cornelia Cicero, Marcus being also his father's name and Cornelia his tribe. This would all usually have been abbreviated to M. Tullius M. f. Cor. Cicero.

Of the three elements of the name proper, the first was known as the *praenomen* and was a man's personal given name; the second, known as the *nomen* or *gentilicium*, placed him in his *gens* or kinship group; and the third, the *cognomen*, was either a personal nickname or epithet acquired during a man's lifetime or an inherited name indicating a branch within the wider kinship group or clan. So by 200 BC the large *gens Cornelia* (distinct from the tribe of the same name) was divided into a number of branches, whose members were called Cornelii Cethegi, Cornelii Lentuli, Cornelii Scipii, and so on.

Much ink has been used to account for this supposedly unique Roman system of nomenclature. Where did it come from? When and why did the Romans adopt it? Given the paucity of evidence before about 200 BC, any answers to these questions must be mainly speculative, but some things one can say. First, other three-name systems have existed and do exist in other parts of the world. Secondly, it seems reasonably certain that originally Romans did have single names like other Indo-European peoples. "As to names", Appian wrote in the second century AD, "Roman citizens formerly had only one each; afterwards they took a second, and not much later, for easier recognition, there was given to some of them a third."[2] Livy's *Histories* and other evidence confirm that a two-name system of *praenomen* plus *gentilicium* predated the three-name system at Rome and in other areas of central Italy from the sixth century BC. It seems that the Romans developed a more complex nomenclature as their society became more complex and as they developed a powerful and expansionist state. Having two and then three names was a mark of social distinction, as it had been among the Etruscans from whom the Romans borrowed much, and it became a privilege of citizens. At the same time the *tria nomina*, carefully recorded by officials in five-yearly censuses, served the interests of the state, facilitating the task of recruiting soldiers, taxing and arranging elections among growing numbers of citizens. "Easier recognition" was essential to the functioning of Roman society, and nowhere more so than in the city of Rome itself, whose population grew rapidly in the last two centuries BC to reach around a million by the first century AD. One must add that the *tria nomina* were especially characteristic of the Roman Republic and its participatory political system and tended to die out when that was replaced by the authoritarian Empire.

The nineteenth-century German historian Theodor Mommsen believed that Rome's political bias was reflected in the uniform and limited style of Roman names (nearly all ending in *-us*) and their restricted stock, which he contrasted with "the luxuriant and poetical fullness of those of the ancient Greeks".[3] This restraint is never more obvious than with the *praenomen*.

Praenomina

Exhaustive trawls of literature and inscriptions have yielded 64 known *praenomina*, but in practice this total should be greatly scaled down. The unknown author of a book on names written in the first century AD said that there were about 30 and half this number were in common use. As we have seen, the commonest *praenomina* were usually abbreviated when placed with other parts of the name: A. for Aulus; M. for Marcus; T. for Titus; C. for Gaius; Cn. for Gnaeus, and so on. The last two incidentally show the great age of *praenomina*, since they refer to a time when these names were spelled with C.

There is no doubt that in the Republican period the *praenomen* was a real personal name. It was bestowed shortly after birth; it always came first in the order of a man's names; and it was used to address him and to refer to him either alone or in combination with one of his other names. Romans themselves, like Varro, believed that *praenomina* originally had a meaning and were chosen by parents for their children for this reason. So a Manius was born *mane* or in the morning; a Lucius *luci* or at dawn; while a Marcus was born in March. These sound like folk etymology, or explanations invented after the fact, though some *praenomina* clearly do refer to birth circumstances. Postumus was a child born after his father's death, for example; Vopiscus was the sole survivor of twins. Spurius had been a respectable *praenomen* used by consular families in the second century BC, but it acquired the meaning "illegitimate" in the first century, apparently because its abbreviation Sp. was so similar to that for "sine patre filii" or "without a father". Ordinals may once have indicated real birth order, though, if so, it is hard to see why Quintus and Sextus should have become the most common.

Other *praenomina* were wish-names or names aimed at giving protection. It has been argued that both Lucius and Marcus really mean "bright" or "renowned", while Gaius expressed the "joy" of parents at their child's advent. Servius, a name which later fell into disuse, meant "protected". Other names suggest a link with the ancestors, and perhaps the idea, common elsewhere, that the new-born replaced or reincarnated a past member

5

of the family. So Aulus may mean "little grandfather", and Manius may be related to the Maniae or spirits of the dead.

The choice of *praenomina* also had geographical and social dimensions. Many originated in particular areas of Italy, though they lost their ethnic flavour in time. Again, certain names /"belonged" to particular aristocratic families. So Caeso was used in the early Republic by the Fabii and then from around 200 BC became almost a monopoly of the Quinctii. Appius was especially associated with the Claudian *gens*, even being used to designate public works and monuments for which they had been responsible: the via Appia (Appian Way), the acqua Appia (Appian aqueduct), the forum Appii. Another rare aristocratic *praenomen* was Nero, of which only three examples appear in Republican inscriptions. The future emperor took the name when he was adopted by his uncle Claudius in AD 50. It had been the *praenomen* of his grand-uncle, consul in 9 BC, though it was also used as a *cognomen* by the Claudii. Such aristocratic *praenomina* were rarely abbreviated and some, like Appius, were not transmitted to emancipated slaves as most *praenomina* were.

Sometimes particular *praenomina* were avoided by families. Marcus Manlius, who saved the Capitol from being taken by the Gauls in 390 BC, was subsequently condemned to death on a charge of sedition and flung from the Tarpeian rock. According to Livy, following this disgrace to the family, "the Manlian *gens* made a decree forbidding anyone henceforth to bear the name Marcus" and no patrician member subsequently did.[4] Marcus was banned later for the Antonii and Lucius for the Claudii in similar circumstances.

Not only was the stock of *praenomina* in common use very small, but of those used an even smaller number greatly predominated over the others. Of the seventeen appearing more than ten times in Republican inscriptions, six or seven appeared over a hundred times and two, Lucius and Gaius, over five hundred times. Families habitually used only a few *praenomina* and the choice became more restricted over time. Under the Republic it was usual for the eldest son to have the same *praenomen* as his father but for other sons to have different ones. From the mid first century AD, however, the custom had developed of giving the same *praenomen* to several sons. This meant that uncles and nephews, cousins, and then fathers and sons and brothers, came to have the same *praenomina*. At the same time emancipated slaves and new citizens took the *praenomina* of their masters, patrons or sponsors. The first name therefore lost any distinguishing function it may have had.

One reaction to this situation on the part of great families was to adopt new *praenomina* from their stock of other names. Africanus Fabius Maximus and Paullus Fabius Maximus, brothers who were consuls in 10 and 11 BC, had famous family *cognomina* as their *praenomina*. The younger Pompey similarly had his father's *cognomen* Magnus. More generally, the *praenomen* tended to die out, being replaced by the *cognomen* as the significant personal name. The *praenomen* was less used in literature in the first century AD. It was omitted from lists of soldiers in the second century AD, and it began to disappear from inscriptions of the lower classes at the same time. Only the high aristocracy clung to the *praenomen* as a badge of rank, and some of them continued to do so down to the end of the Roman Empire.

Gentilicia

The *gentilicium* or *nomen* was a man's most important public name during the Republic and early Empire. *Gentilicia* took a number of forms but nearly all were adjectival in style, ending in -ius, for example, Antonius, Aurelius, Sempronius. Many had specific meanings and probably derived from nicknames: Cassius from *cassus* (empty); Fabius from *faba* (bean); Curtius from *curtus* (short); but such meanings were almost certainly not something that anyone was aware of after the name became established. Similarly some *gentilicia* indicate a particular geographical or ethnic origin. Oppius, Tittius and Tattius are Sabine; Caecina, Maecenas and Spurinna Etruscan. But these associations were again forgotten in time. There were about 150 *gentilicia* in use in the Republican period, but with the expansion of Roman rule and the extension of citizenship, thousands of new ones were added to the original corpus. A recent compendium lists over 10,000.

There is evidence that the *gentilicium* was originally a patronymic, that is a name taken from the father's name. By the classical period, however, it was an authentic hereditary family name and indicated membership of a *gens* or clan. Both men and women took the *gentilicium*, and it was trans-.mitted in the male line. The *gens* in turn derived its name from a real or supposed agnatic ancestor: "the Claudii are descended from a Clausus; the Caeculi honoured as chief of their race the hero Caeculus; the Calpurnii, a Calpus; the Julii, a Julus". [5] Fifty of the *gentes* were believed to be descended from the Trojans, though few of these survived into the historical period. Sixteen of the rural tribes had the names of *gentes*, for example Aemilia, Claudia, Cornelia, suggesting an ancient identity between them. Some of these ancient *gentes* remained undivided down to the time of the later Republic and they had many functions: religious, legal, social and political. They performed rites related to their clan founders. Livy relates, for example, that during the occupation of the Quirinal Hill by the Gauls in 390 BC a member of the Fabian *gens* still went there in ceremonial dress to sacrifice on the appointed day. Much later, according to Ovid and Macrobius, the cult of ancestors was confined to agnatic kin.

Gentes owned property in common, and intestate succession still devolved on the *gens* in later Roman law. The famed authority of the *paterfamilias* over his children was tempered by the requirement that he consult a family council before taking any drastic steps, particularly with implications for inheritance. This may indeed reflect an earlier situation in which he was the head of a co-resident family grouping, and there is evidence of agnatic relations living together much later on. Incest prohibitions and the pattern of marriage also reflect the strength of agnatic ties. Roman girls married young – in their mid to late teens – a phenomenon usually associated with extended kindreds. Restrictions on who could marry whom operated until the mid third century BC within the agnatic group to the seventh degree, that is all the descendants in the male line from the same great-grandfather; but they did not extend to maternal relatives to the same degree or to kin in the female line. Much later, a woman's male relatives retained some controls over her even after she married. Guardianship over women without immediate kin was entrusted to agnatic clansmen; and women could not make legacies without consulting the same relatives.

When Marcus Manlius was indicted in 384 BC, the fact that he was not supported by his kinsmen was much remarked upon, according to Livy. People recalled that in similar circumstances Appius Claudius had been helped by "all the Claudian *gens*".[6] Modern historians have followed in this track, analyzing politics in the later Republican period in terms of interest groups based on extended kinship ties. The importance of maintaining the *gentilicium* may also be seen in the prevalence of adoption among the childless, and the practice of making a son-in-law marrying an heiress take his wife's family name. The *gentilicium*, in short, reflected the general saliency of the *gens*. It defined the circle of kin",[7] and defined it widely.

The structure of Roman families changed from the later Republican period, and this changed the significance of the *gentilicium*. First, cognatic ties came to supersede the traditional agnatic ones. Most obviously the incest rules were changed, reducing their scope from the seventh to the fourth degree but extending them to all relatives in the male and female lines. *Gentilicia* from the maternal side of a family came to be used as *cognomina* or even as *gentilicia* proper if the in-laws were sufficiently prestigious. The first-born son of M. Crassus Frugi, consul in AD 27, for example, was called Cn. Pompeius Magnus, taking none of his father's names but all those of the great Pompey, who was his mother's great-grandfather. And much more than snobbery was involved in such ploys. A family might only be able to survive through the female line, as was the case with the Julio-Claudian emperors. Cognatic ties and the names that went with them also allowed the development of networks of influence and protection. This change is also evident in a switch in emphasis in ideology from the agnatic *gens* to the broader *domus*, which encompassed physical house, household with slaves and retainers, as well as the circle of cognatic kin and affines.

Secondly, especially among freedmen, there was a tendency for the nuclear family of couple and children to become the main social unit rather than the *gens*. As emancipated slaves, freedmen had no *gens* of their own and were attached as clients to the *gens* of their former masters, taking their *gentilicia* along with their *praenomina*. But neither of these was their real name, and they both tended to atrophy over the generations as close links with the patrons were lost. With emancipation, too, and the extension of citizenship to provincials, there was a proliferation of persons bearing the great Republican *gentilicia* and especially those of the emperors under whom they had been enfranchised. The devaluation of these *gentilicia* is indicated by the fact that the most common came to be abbreviated in inscriptions: Ael. for Aelius, Cl. for Claudius, and so on.

The third development was the hiving-off of branches of the *gens* through the device of adopting *cognomina*, which takes us to the third name.

Cognomina

The *cognomen* was the last element in the full Roman name to become established. The first definite example is found in a funeral encomium dating from around 300 BC, and the *cognomen* did not become common in inscriptions until a century later. But, since the man referred to in the encomium, L. Cornelius Scipio Barbartus, already has a double *cognomen*, it is clear that the process of name formation must have begun much earlier. Among the consuls recorded by Livy for the years 467–408 BC about two-thirds have *cognomina*, and among those for 400–357 BC, 85 per cent. *Cognomina* may have been interpolated here from a later period, but it is unlikely that all or even most of them were and the figures clearly indicate a trend. By the period 222–146 BC, when information is more reliable, over 85 per cent of consuls have one *cognomen* and around 10 per cent have two. Of censors over the same period, more than 90 per cent have one and 10 per cent two *cognomina*. Having long been customary and being "firmly established" in inscriptions by the mid second century BC, *cognomina* were, however, still omitted from official documents, and especially laws and decrees of the Senate, down to the second century BC. They began to appear in such documents around 120 BC, "becoming regular only in the age of Cicero",[8] when they also had to be registered with the other names.

Cognomina originated among the aristocracy and were for long confined to this group. Some plebeian *gentes* indeed, like the Antonii, made a point of not adopting them. At first they were personal nicknames. Many of the *cognomina* of the oldest families relate to individual attributes, moral and physical. Among the former, for example, are Cato (prudent), held by M. Porcius Cato, the censor of 184 BC; Pius, earned by one of the Metelli for his piety towards his father; and Severus (strict), borne by a tribune of the plebs, Q. Varius Severus, in 90 BC. Less pleasant characteristics were also preserved, for example Varro and Brutus, both of which mean stupid. Physical characteristics were more commonly alluded to, both neutral and complimentary like Cincinnatus (curly-haired), Pulcher (beautiful, noble) or Rufus

9

(red or red-haired), but more frequently uncomplimentary. So we have consuls from the Caecilii Metelli and the Cornelii Scipiones in 142 and 222 BC called Calvus (bald-head); members of the latter family called Nasica (big nose); an emperor called Galba (fat belly); and another called Nerva (sinew or penis). The list could go on: Crassus (fat); Scaevus or Scaevola (left-handed); Macula (with moles); Varus (bow-legged); Caecus (blind). The elder Pliny gives a long list of *cognomina* relating simply to defects of the eyes. Bad habits could also earn their special names: Aleator (dice-player); Bibulus (drunkard); Cunctator (ditherer). The paradox has often been noted that such pejorative names became in time a mark of noble birth, proudly adopted and passed on to descendants. This reverses the usual way that complimentary nicknames were given as a joke to those with the opposite traits, like the dwarf musician in an ode of Propertius called Magnus.[9]

Cognomina had a range of other derivations and meanings. A family might have its native place recalled or its foreign origin underlined; hence Camerinus from the town of Camerinum in Umbria (Sulpicii); Medullinus from Meduluum (Furii Camilli); Regillensis from Regillus, a *cognomen* of the *gens* Claudia, later abandoned. Some of these might later be confused, deliberately or not, with *cognomina* indicating victories won by family members over Italian cities in Rome's early wars. Residence in different districts of the city of Rome might also be indicated, for example Capitolinus borne by the *gens* Manlia; or Aventinensis borne by the *gens* Genucia. These also might be lent more fanciful meanings, as we shall see.

There were also occupational *cognomina*: Pictor (painter); Faber (smith); Pollio (polisher of arms); Metellus (mercenary), for example. Pliny the Elder claimed that

> the earliest *cognomina* were derived from agriculture: Pilumanus belonged to the inventor of the pestle for grinding corn (pilum pistrinis); Piso came from pounding corn (pisendo); and again families were named Fabius (bean) or Lentulus (lentil) or Cicero (chick-pea), if one of them was the best grower of some particular crop. One of the Junii was called Bubulcus because he was very good at managing oxen.[10]

All kinds of other objects and animals provided *cognomina*: Scipio (staff); Dolabella (pick-axe); and so on; and they were also derived from both *praenomina* and *gentilicia*.

Sometimes *cognomina* originated in a particular incident or event that seemed striking or representative. Livy relates that Titus Manlius fought in single combat with a Gaul in 361 BC, killing his opponent and taking the chain from around his neck: "Amidst the rude banter thrown out by the soldiers in a kind of verse was heard the *cognomen* Torquatus (the man with a chain or necklace), and thereafter this epithet was adopted as an honoured *cognomen*."[11] According to Suetonius, the later emperor Caligula gained his *cognomen* as a child "from an army joke, because he grew up among the troops and wore the miniature uniform of a private soldier, including the *caligula*, or half-boot."[12] In some cases, such explanations are clearly later rationalizations or legends placing a heroic gloss on a name more mundanely acquired.

Livy tells again, for example, how C. Mucius failed in an attempt to assassinate the king of Clusium in 508 BC. When arrested he placed his hand on the sacrificial altar, allowing it to be burned off "in order to show how cheaply Romans regarded their bodies" in warfare. He was thereupon freed and was "afterwards known as Scaevola, from the loss of his left hand".[13] As we have seen, Scaevola is more likely to mean simply left-handed. Similarly, tradition had it that M. Manlius received his *cognomen* Capitolanus for his exploit in saving the Capitol; but the name is found among the Manlii and other *gentes* before 390 and almost certainly refers to place of residence. Divine intervention was invoked to explain the *cognomen* Ahenobarbus, borne by a branch of the Domitii, from whom the emperor Nero was descended. The founder of this branch, L. Domitius, had a vision of Castor and Pollux foretelling the Roman victory at Lake Regillus in 498 BC. "As a sign of their divinity", Suetonius writes, "it is said that the gods stroked his cheeks, and turned his black beard to a ruddy hue, like that of bronze."[14] His descendants retained both red beard and the name that went with it. Syme shows that this story was invented much later, probably around 35 BC; far from being a very ancient Roman name, Ahenobarbus came from Illyria via the Abruzzi.

M. Manlius Torquatus was given his *cognomen* by the troops. This was not unusual. In a harangue before a battle in the Samnite Wars, M. Valerius referred to "my *cognomen* of Corvinus, which you men have given me with Heaven's sanction".[15] Later many generals were granted honorific *cognomina* related specifically to successful campaigns. The first authentic case seems to be that of Valerius Maximus, who was given the *cognomen* Messala after capturing the city of Messana in Sicily in 263 BC, though both Livy and Plutarch provide earlier examples. Plutarch states that C. Marcius who captured the Volscian city of Corioli in 493 was given the *cognomen* Coriolanus by a vote of the Senate. Later official sanction for such names became normal, and they came to refer to whole conquered nations. So P. Cornelius Scipio was formally granted the *cognomen* Africanus after his defeat of the Carthaginians in 201 BC. Many others followed over the next century and a half: Asiaticus, Macedonicus, Allobrogicus, Gaetulicus. A related practice was the adoption of the name of an office held with distinction. So M. Porcius Cato was given the additional *cognomen* Censorinus. C. Scribonius was known as Curio. The *cognomen* Flaminius used by the Quinctii derives from a member who was *flamen dialis* (a priestly function) in the mid third century BC.

All these *cognomina* were bestowed by other people, but, in exceptional cases, individuals chose their own. The mid-fourth-century dictator L. Manlius Imperiosus incurred widespread hatred, according to Livy, "on account of his *cognomen*, which offended a free state and had been assumed out of pride and ostentation".[16] Another dictator, Sulla, took the name Felix or the fortunate one, and the Senate ratified this in 82 or 81 BC. Similarly Gn. Pompeius (Pompey) gave himself the *cognomen* Magnus. This points forward to the grandiloquent names-cum-titles taken by the emperors, which we will discuss separately. During the Empire, too, emperors took over the function of bestowing honorific *cognomina*, and, in some, cases, of removing them.

New personal *cognomina* were still being coined among the élite in the late Republic and early Empire. Cicero refers, for example, in a letter in 45 BC to Ventidius Bassus adopting the *cognomen* Sabinus in the hope that such a name "with its connotations of ancient virtue" would help him in his canvassing for the quaestorship.[17] Sometimes such *cognomina* were what we would call nicknames, like that of Cicero's friend Atticus, who acquired his because he had lived for a long time in Athens and was a devotee of Greek culture. Cicero also indicates that people remained aware of the "meaning" of established *cognomina*. He often used them as the butt of jokes and attacks in his own speeches and advised others to do the same.

However, by this time most *cognomina* had long been family names. They became hereditary at an early date, in some cases indicating the demarcation and then the hiving-off of branches or segments within a *gens*. This point was well made by Fustel de Coulanges in 1864:

> The Cornelian *gens* was for a long time undivided . . . all its members alike bore the *cognomen* Maluginensis and that of Cossus. It was not until the time of the dictator Camillus that one of these branches adopted the further *cognomen* Scipio. A little later another branch took the *cognomen* Rufus, which it replaced afterwards by that of Sulla. The Lentuli do not appear till the time of the Samnite Wars, the Cethegi not until the second Punic War. It is the same with the Claudian *gens*. The Claudii remained for a long time united in a single family, and all bore the *cognomen* of Sabinus or Regillensis, a sign of their origin.

There were no branches over seven generations. Only in the eighth do "we see three branches separate, and adopt three *cognomina*, which became hereditary with them. These were the Pulchri, who continued during two centuries; the Centhones, who soon became extinct; and the Nerones, who continued to the time of the Empire."[18] Many other *gentes* went through the same process.

In some cases the careful preservation of a string of *cognomina* reflects a segmentation of a pure agnatic type, where the branches remain firmly and clearly attached to the trunk from which they successively spring. Among the Cornelii, for example, we have P. Cornelius Scipio Nasica Corculum, *pontifex maximus* in 150 BC. Corculum was a personal *cognomen*, apparently a tribute to his legal learning; actually it meant "little darling". Nasica was a family of the Scipio segment of the Cornelian *gens*. In other cases, the original *gentilicium* might be dropped, the *cognomen* effectively taking its place. So the Caecilii Metelli were always known simply as the Metelli, to which further *cognomina* were added; the Fabii Maximi as the Maximi; the Calpurnii Pisones as the Pisones. Both these cases should be clearly distinguished from the practice found later in the Empire of selecting or accumulating names from both one's father's and one's mother's families. Again, it is a contrast between agnatic and cognatic filiation, though it is true that in the earlier period people could be as selective about the transmission of *cognomina* as they were about other elements of their names.

The double *cognomina* of the Calpurnii Pisones Frugi had great social cachet and were passed on intact through four generations or more down to the mid first century BC. Then a son of L. Calpurnius Piso Frugi, praetor around 112 BC, was adopted by a certain M. Pupius. He took his adopted father's names as was usual but added to them the two famous *cognomina*. His son dropped the Pupius. Despite a further adoption in the next generation, the *cognomen* Frugi continued to appear in three further generations. A younger son in the fifth generation from M. Pupius reverted to the full ancestral name: L. Calpurnius Piso Frugi, adding Licinianus which came from his grandfather's name of adoption.

This takes us to another important function of the *cognomen*. Adoption was not uncommon among the aristocracy in both the Republican and early imperial periods. It ensured the perpetuation of lines among an élite that seems often to have been either unwilling or unable to reproduce itself. Syme comments that "sons of the blood enjoyed no kind of organic or mystical preference".[19] The rule if a child or a man were adopted was that he take the full name of his adopted father adding as a *cognomen* "the *gentilicium* of his natural father with the suffix *-anus* (or *ianus*)".[20] Thus the general L. Aemilius Paulus, who achieved the further *cognomen* Macedonicus after his victory over the king of that country in 168 BC, had two sons. One was adopted by Q. Fabius Maximus and took his names plus that of Aemilianus after his natural father. The other son was adopted by P. Cornelius Scipio Africanus, the elder son of the great Africanus, and he took the name P. Cornelius Scipio Aemilianus Africanus Minor. More simply, the future Augustus, originally C. Octavius Thurinus, became C. Julius Caesar Octavianus on being adopted by Caesar, though he soon dropped the reminder of his humble origins.

After the time of Sulla, the rules were less clear-cut or they were not closely followed. M. Valerius Messalla Appianus, consul in 12 BC, was a Claudius Pulcher by birth; adopted by M. Messalla, of an equally aristocratic family, he chose to emphasize his natural family's peculiar *praenomen* in his new *cognomen*. The original name of Cicero's friend Atticus was Q. Pomponius; adopted according to the terms of his will by his natural uncle Q. Caecilius, he became officially Q. Caecilius Pomponius Atticus, but he seems hardly to have used this name, continuing to be known as Q. Pomponius or Q. Atticus. Imperial adoptions could lead to especially complex transmissions of names. The emperor Hadrian, P. Aelius Hadrianus, for example, adopted as his heir in AD 138 T. Aurelius Goionius Arrius Antoninus, a man aged 52, who changed his name to T. Aelius Hadrianus Antoninus and succeeded as emperor in the same year as Antoninus Pius. He had in turn adopted his young nephew M. Annius Verus, who took the name M. Aelius Aurelius Verus and was known on becoming emperor as Marcus Aurelius.

Attractive *cognomina* could also become the object of competition among families. The Manlii, to whom the *cognomen* Torquatus "belonged", died out in the early Empire. Augustus granted the name to the Nonii Asprenas, but the Junii Silani also laid claim to it. It was borne by a D. Silanus, consul in AD 53, and by his nephew.

Much of this discussion applies exclusively to the Roman élite. However, from around 100 BC *cognomina* began to be taken up by other inferior social groups, though they did not become general for ordinary citizens and soldiers until the reign of Claudius. New citizens, whether enfranchised foreigners or emancipated slaves, adopted the *tria nomina*, including the *cognomen*, in ways that we will look at later. To a lesser extent free proletarians did the same. The result was a vast multiplication in the number of *cognomina*, and changes in their functions, shapes and meanings. A recent study has shown that under 10 per cent of *cognomina* are found in both the Republican and the late imperial periods. Ninety per cent of the later names are new. Already among the élite of the Republic, the *cognomen* could sometimes serve as the first name. Or the *cognomen* could become the family name, as we have seen in the segmentation process among noble *gentes*. For freedmen and other new citizens, the *cognomen* was usually their original personal name, to which the first two Roman names taken from ex-master, patron or sponsor were a somewhat formal attachment. These various tendencies made the *cognomen* the most important name element.

At the same time the form of *cognomina* changed. There always had been more variety in the style of *cognomina* than in that of the other names. Suffixes in *-a*, *-o*, *-io* and *-or* (e.g. Cinna, Galba, Seneca; Cato, Cicero; Buccio, Pollio; Nicanor, Pictor) are found alongside the more familiar in *-us* in the Republican period. Later there was even more diversity. A greater foreign element, especially Greek, was introduced; participle names like Clemens or Crescens appear; and a wider range of suffixes is found. The suffix *-ianus*, previously almost restricted to adopted persons, became very common, for example; also suffixes in *-lus*. In general shorter forms gave place to longer ones, especially diminutives. So alongside the older Fronto, one finds Frontonius and Frontonianus; alongside Firmus one finds Firminus, Firmianus and Firminianus; and so on. Kajanto lists 19 variants on Maximus.

In terms of meaning, the range also increased. Pejorative *cognomina* of the old type tended to die out, and there was an opposite preference for complimentary and/or protective names. Felix was by far the most popular *cognomen* among legionaries in the imperial period. Names referring to the body accounted for 35 per cent of the total in the Republican but only around 12 per cent in the imperial period. Names referring to mental or psychological qualities, by contrast, increased. Wish-names like Felix, Faustus, Fortunatus and Victor became much more popular, rising from 5 per cent to 20 per cent. Theophoric names or those giving religious protection, like Martialis or Saturninus, also increased from under 1 per cent to 5 per cent. There were also *cognomina* derived from other names; ethnic, geographical and occupational *cognomina*; ones taken from flora and fauna; ones taken from the calendar.

Women's names

Nearly all that we have written so far applies exclusively to men, who alone took part in public life and had full civic and legal rights. In the Republican period, women usually had only one name, a feminized version of the *gentilicium*, such as Caecilia, Claudia or Cornelia .

The absence of female *praenomina* has puzzled scholars. They are virtually unknown under the Republic, and only 70–80 exist in the 200,000-odd inscriptions from the Empire. It seems that female *praenomina* did exist in archaic times but that they fell out of use. One indication is the use of Gaius and Gaia as type names for husband and wife in the Roman marriage formula. Women retained *praenomina* in other parts of Italy, notably Umbria and Etruria, down to the early years AD, and the few *praenomina* from later times tend to be borne by rural provincial women and those of inferior status. Where they are used, *praenomina* are feminized versions of the male names, Lucia, Quinta and Gaia being the most common. They were also abbreviated.

The emphasis on the *gentilicium* as the female name par excellence was apparently specific therefore to the Roman élite, though the custom may then have been followed in other parts of society. "It is as if the Romans wished to suggest very pointedly", Finley wrote, "that women were not, or ought not to be genuine individuals but only fractions of a family."[21] This is made very clear where the *gens* has segmented, but the segment has not (yet) achieved its own appropriate female name. So one gets a woman called Cornelia Scipionum gentis. The *gentilicium* was a label placed on women to be used in the game of dynastic marriages and successions. Her link with her original *gens* could never be broken unless she changed her name, which was virtually unknown, and for the family into which she married she remained a permanent reminder and advertisement of their alliance.

By this means, too, daughters could perpetuate lines where male succession failed, as it often did among the late Republican aristocracy and most notably in the Julio-Claudian imperial house. Augustus, we have seen, was adopted by C. Julius Caesar, who had no son. Caesar's sister Julia (1) had married M. Atius Balbus, and their daughter Atia married C. Octavius, Augustus' father. So Caesar was Augustus' uncle in the maternal line. Augustus had one child, a daughter, Julia (2), who was married off three times in succession. From one of her marriages – to M. Vipsanius Agrippa – there were children, two boys called Caesar, a daughter, Julia (3), and two named after Agrippa. After the two Caesars died, Augustus eventually adopted Tiberius as his heir. Tiberius was the son of Augustus' second wife Livia Drusilla and of Ti. Claudius Nero and had his father's name. He was forced to divorce his wife and marry Julia (2), but this marriage produced no children. Immediate succession to Tiberius went to a grandchild of Julia (2), however. Her daughter by Agrippa, Agrippina (1), had married Germanicus Caesar, the son of Nero Claudius Drusus and Antonia Minor, who was the daughter of Octavia (1), Augustus' sister and her second husband M. Antonius. The child of Agrippina (1) and Germanicus, Gaius Caesar Caligula, was thus doubly descended from Augustus' father in the female line. Caligula was succeeded by his uncle, Ti. Claudius, the brother of Germanicus. Claudius had two daughters, Claudia Antonia and Octavia (2), and was succeeded by his stepson, Nero, whom he had adopted. Nero was the natural son of Cn. Domitius Ahenobarbus and Agrippina (2), who was Germanicus' daughter and Claudius' niece and fourth wife. Nero married Octavia (2), Claudius' daughter by his third wife and cousin, Messalina, and they in turn had a daughter, Claudia. The rules of succession were not fixed, and actual succession as emperor depended on circumstance, intrigue and violence, as any reader of Suetonius and Tacitus knows. But it is clear that attempts were continuously made to bind together and to perpetuate the Julian and then the Claudian lines by adoptions, serial polygamy, endogamy and by using and reinforcing succession in the female line. Naming played an important part in these procedures and particularly in the last.

This still leaves the question of individual identification. Numbers of Julias, Antonias and Octavias were as potentially confusing to contemporaries as they are to historians. First, it is clear that the *gentilicium* was in the Republican period also the primary name for address and reference. In his letters Cicero addresses his first wife as Terentia and his second as Publilia. His beloved daughter is Tullia or Tulliola, a pet version. If he wants to identify other women more closely, he uses their relationship to fathers or husbands; for example, Annia, "the daughter of C. Annus, the senator"; Auria, "your brother's wife"; "the two Lucretias, daughter of Tricipitinus and wife of Conlatinus". Within families a number of descriptive distinguishing names were used: Major and Minor, as for boys; ordinals: Secunda, Tertia, and so on; and pet names. Here Posilla and Paulla, Paula or Polla, seem to have been especially common as names for little girls.

Some women in the late Republican period did have more than one name. The daughter of Q. Caecilius Pomponianus Atticus was called both Caecilia and Attica. Varro mentions a woman with large breasts called Mammosa, which sounds like an equivalent of male corporeal *cognomina*. But the use of *cognomina* proper by women, whether inherited or personal, was virtually unknown at this time, and we are dealing here with privately used alternative names or nicknames. So the mistress of M. Antonius, the triumvir, was an actress called Cytheris, whose "real" name was Volumnia, as an ex-slave of Volumnius Eutrapelus. Stage-names were obviously not typical, but slaves and freedwomen, like their male counterparts, did at this time often take the master's or patron's name, usually in addition to their own individual name. The order of these names was quite frequently inverted, for example Euclesis Cestia, Danais Annia, Grata Plotia.

From the time of the early Empire, upper-class women began to be given and to inherit *cognomina*, for example Aemilia Lepida and Corellia Hispulla; and women with two or three names become frequent in inscriptions and literature. On birth registers mothers and female children are "always designated by two names", the *gentilicium* plus a personal name "used like a *cognomen*".[22] Women in Pliny's letters nearly all have two names, and he refers to them by their *cognomina* alone or their *gentilicia* plus *cognomina*. In the later Empire, women joined in the accumulation of names that characterized the upper classes.

In the Republican period it is obvious that a woman did not change her name at marriage; it remained the *gentilicium*. She might, however, add her husband's name in the genitive; for example, Caecilia Metelli Crassi was the wife of M. Licinius Crassus. There are a few cases also of wives' names preceded by their husbands' *praenomina*. Under the Empire, adding the husband's to the wife's name became more usual. In a late example, a provincial woman of the *gens* Liguria married to C. Albucius Menippus was called Liguria Procilla quae et Albucia. In another case, three of her husband's names, the *gentilicium* and two *cognomina*, were inserted between the wife's own two names: Valeria Tossia Pia Sabina Euhemeria – all in the feminine.

This leads to a final general point in this area: there was a very strong tendency in Roman nomenclature for female names to be derived from male ones. This is true of *praenomina* and *gentilicia*, where there are no distinct female names in the historical period, and also of Latin *cognomina*, most of which are formed by feminizing male exemplars, often with diminutive suffixes as well: Petronilla, Priscilla, Saturnina, Felicitas. Very few *cognomina* were given to men and women in the same form; and very few female names were without male equivalents. Kajanto lists Amabilis, Elegans, Suavis and a few others. Some names with apparently feminine endings were in fact exclusively male names, like Aquila, Catalina and Pica.

Transmission of names

Under the Republic and the early Empire, the conventions for transmitting names were comparatively simple and reasonably well followed.

As we have seen, the eldest son usually inherited his father's *praenomen*, while the other sons were given different names from the family stock. So Marcus Aemilius Lepidus, consul in 285 BC, had two sons, Marcus Aemilius Lepidus and Manius Aemilius Lepidus. The first had three sons called Marcus, Lucius and Quintus. The eldest in the line of both brothers had the names Marcus and Manius respectively over at least three generations. Where this rule was in operation, there could be a break in the use of the eldest son's *praenomen*, where an eldest son was childless. This was overcome in some cases by giving the name to a nephew or other relative. Lucius and Quintus Volusius Saturninus were the elder and younger sons of Lucius Volusius Saturninus, consul in AD 3. The former was, it seems, unmarried and certainly without offspring, so his brother called his eldest son Lucius, giving his own name Quintus to his second son. M. Aemilius Lepidus, son of the consul of 46 BC, similarly, had no children. His brother Quintus had children, but they were probably named before their uncle died in 30 BC. Whatever the reason, the next Marcus Aemilius Lepidus was the son of the first's cousin Paullus.

In some families, the eldest son's name was less distinctive, or was given to the sons of younger sons when their first-born uncles did have offspring or the prospect of it. Gaius Licinius Varus, consul in 236 BC, a younger son, gave his son the name Publius, the name of his father, his elder brother and the latter's eldest son, Publius Licinius Crassus Dives, consul in 205 BC. His brothers Marcus and Gaius both called one of their sons Publius, although the consul had a son of the same name. This tendency led eventually to the custom of giving all sons the same *praenomen*. For example, seven members of the immediate family of the emperor Vespasian (AD 69–79) had the *praenomen* Titus: himself, his brother, their four sons and one of their grandsons. As we have noted, this led to the withering away of the *praenomen* as a useful name.

In some families a different convention can be detected: the alternating of *praenomina* from one generation to the next. The rare *praenomen* Caeso occurred in every other generation of the Quinctii Flamini. Another example is found in the family of the emperor Nero, the Domitii Ahenobarbi. Nero's name was originally Lucius; his father, consul in AD 32, was Gnaeus; his grandfather, consul in AD 16, was Lucius again; and so on back for at least another two generations.

The *gentilicium* was of course the family name and was inherited from the father by all legitimate children. The rule was very rarely departed from. Syme mentions a senator of the Augustan period, Postumius Sulpicius, who had his grandmother's *gentilicium*. She belonged to a family otherwise extinct. L. Nonius Asprenas, consul in AD 6, was married to Calpurnia, and they had three sons. The first was called after his father, but the other took the names Nonius Asprenas Calpurnius, thus adopting the *gentilicia* of both father and mother. This became a much more common practice later on.

As we have seen, the *cognomen* was increasingly inherited also, becoming among the aristocracy another family name. The practice of giving different brothers different *cognomina* did survive however. The three sons of Q. Metellus Macedonicus, consul in 143 BC, were called Balearicus, Diadematus and Caprarius. The son of Q. Metellus Balearicus was Q. Metellus Nepos, consul in 98 BC. He gave the name Nepos to his younger son, but the elder was called Celer. Macedonicus had a brother L. Metellus Calvus, consul in 142 BC. His sons were Delmaticus and Numidicus, while the latter's son had the *cognomen* Pius.

From the end of the Republican period, while hereditary *cognomina* became more predominant, selectivity in the transmission of *cognomina* is also evident, and derived *cognomina* began to be used, influenced perhaps by popular usage. So the son of M. Messala Corvinus was called Messalinus from his father's *gentilicium*, and his daughter was Messalina, the notorious wife of the emperor Claudius.

Cognomina were also taken from the mother's side of the family. The best-known example from the early Empire is that of the emperor Vespasian or Vespasianus himself, whose name derived from his mother Vespasia. He handed on his *cognomen* to his elder son, the future emperor Titus, while the younger again derived his *cognomen* Domitianus from his mother's name Domitilla. Both these *cognomina* passed in the next generation to the elder branch of the Flavian family. Here the saliency given by the imperial role overruled patrilineal descent. But again this represented a more general trend, too, with *cognomina* being chosen more generally from both sides and not necessarily passing in the main male line — all indicative of a weakening of the sense of lineage.

19

CHAPTER TWO

Name and status

Rome was a society of legally constituted ranks or orders. First, there were citizens and non-citizens. Citizens were registered by the censors in five classes according to wealth below which were the propertyless proletarians. There were three distinct grades within the first class: senators, equestrians and decurions. Although membership of these grades was not legally hereditary, in practice it was. A tiny élite monopolized power, wealth and high culture. But there was a degree of social mobility which varied from period to period without ultimately upsetting the overall framework. The élite did not reproduce itself biologically, and "new men" had therefore to be recruited. Factors countervailing the hereditary tendency in the Republican period were the need to get elected to office and generally the requirement that high office be maintained in a family for it to retain high rank and this was not a foregone conclusion. In the imperial era, emperors often favoured those from outside the élite who were more dependent on them, but they were unable to do without the aristocracy. Below the citizens were free-born non-citizens and a large number of slaves. Rome was peculiar among slave-owning societies in that emancipation was readily granted, and there was a constant flow therefore of ex-slaves into the citizen body. This body was also greatly increased as Rome expanded its frontiers. At all levels, status was expressed in nomenclature.

Aristocratic names

Members of the old aristocracy were very conscious of their ancestry. Masks of the dead were kept in family shrines and these embodied the family names. Livy refers to generals acquiring "glorious *cognomina* for their illustrious families and inscriptions for their funeral masks".[1] An aristocrat was also clearly recognizable to others by name. "I have only to read the list of candidates' names", Cicero declared in a speech, "and I shall say: This man is of consular, that man of praetorian family."[2] A century and a half later Tacitus refers to "the great names" of Scipio, Silanus and Cassius, and of Faustus Cornelius Sulla, implicated in a plot against Nero.[3] Attacks on the power of ancient names were a further tribute to that power. Cicero, who was a new man, the first in his equestrian provincial family to hold the consulate, remonstrated in a letter in 50 BC to Appius Claudius Pulcher, who had preceded him as governor of Cilicia, about constructions being put on the fact that he (Cicero) had not gone to meet Appius on taking over from him. It was being suggested that an Appius Claudius deserved such a courtesy from a mere Tullius, but Cicero objected: "Why, even before I had attained the honours which are most magnificent in the eyes of men [i.e. the consulate], those names of yours never excited my admiration as such; no, it was the men who bequeathed them to you that I thought great."[4] The same point is made more fully, explicitly and savagely in Juvenal's *Eighth Satire*, written at the end of the first century AD: "Why should someone be called noble, who is unworthy of his ancestry and distinguished in nothing but his famous name?"[5]

There were divisions within the aristocracy or nobility, also marked by names. The early history of the Republic had been dominated by a conflict between the patricians and the plebeians. Not only were the *gentes* in each grouping labelled by their *gentilicia*, as we shall see, but only the former at first had *cognomina*. Of consuls and military tribunes, offices held by patricians, 68 per cent had three names in the period 467–408 BC, but only 10 per cent of tribunes of the plebs. In the period 400–357 BC, the percentages were 61 per cent and nil respectively. The plebeians broke the patrician monopoly of power and high office in the fourth century BC, and also adopted the *tria nomina*. Indeed, this was one means together with intermarriage by which plebeian *gentes* were incorporated into the patrician élite. All this blurred the original division and there could be genuine uncertainty by the time of the late Republic as to whether a family were patrician or plebeian. This did not mean, however, that the distinction had lost all significance. Patricians still had exclusive control of certain priesthoods and new patrician *gentes* were being created in the time of Augustus. In his speech *Pro Sulla*, Cicero felt obliged to defend himself against the reproach that he was not of patrician origin: "Not all men are able to be patricians and, to tell the truth, they do not even care about it; nor do men of today think that they are your inferiors because they are not patricians."[6] The status, moreover, of most families was obvious from their names. There were two groups within the patriciate: the *maiores* and the *minores*. The former comprised the Aemilii, the Claudii, the Cornelii, the Fabii, the Valerii and possibly the Manlii; among the latter were the Quinctii, the Servilii and the Sulpicii. Leading plebeian *gentes* included the Antonii, the Aquilii, the

21

Caecilii, the Calpurnii and the Flavii. Some *gentes* had both patrician and plebeian branches; others transferred or claimed to have transferred from the one to the other, usually so that members could become eligible for plebeian posts, notably the tribunate.

All elements of the aristocratic name had cachet, but none more so, after *praenomina* and *gentilicia* had been broadcast via emancipation and enfranchisement, than the *cognomen*. For long, of course, it had been a privilege of the aristocracy, and at first of the patriciate. We have seen that early plebeian office-holders can be distinguished by their lack of *cognomina*. Indeed, these were later interpolated in the *fasti* (lists of major office-holders) to bestow retrospective high status. Several leading plebeian *gentes*, for example the Antonii and the Fufidii, still had no *cognomen* in the late Republican period, though by this time that peculiarity had itself become a distinctive sign.

Usage is most significant, too. In Cicero's time, aristocrats were "in formal contexts . . . both referred to and addressed by *praenomen* plus *cognomen*, and in less formal circumstances by *cognomen* alone". So, in writing, Cicero refers to C. Cotta for C. Aurelius Cotta, to P. Dolabella for P. Cornelius Dolabella, and so on. By contrast, men of lesser status were referred to by *praenomen* plus *gentilicium* or by *cognomen* alone, if familiar. A man of inferior standing could be admitted within the circle of the highest social class by naming him in the aristocratic manner. This is something that Cicero, himself, ardently desired and earned by his fame as an orator and his achievement of the consulate. In his letters, he nearly always refers to himself as M. Cicero and not M. Tullius, unless he is writing to close friends and family, and in the later part of his career he was usually addressed as M. Cicero also by other upper-class men. As Adams concludes, "the regular use of *cognomina* was . . . a mark of aristocratic society rather than of reciprocal address between equals of other classes."[7] This mode of naming was characteristic of a relatively small, relatively informal, unprofessionalized élite, most of whose members knew each other. It was also a relatively open élite, absorbing new men so long as they conformed to its customs. And the new men, like Cicero, could usually hardly wait to do so.

Nevertheless, uncertainties about status were present and never more so than in the period of "revolution" around the end of the Republic and the start of the Empire. The old aristocracy lost its independence, though it retained social prestige and some political power in the new order. Many families had been decimated in the purges of Tiberius, Caligula, Nero and Domitian. The last emperor of noble stock was Galba in AD 69. But the process of biological wastage and rapid turnover of political personnel were longer-term and more decisive factors. Only two-fifths of consuls in the last two centuries of the Republic had a consular father, "only a third of consuls had a consular son."[8] During the Empire there was a similar movement, extending further down the scale of the élite. Senators lost their monopoly of high civil and military offices to equestrians and others. At the same time geographical expansion opened up the élite, and an international aristocracy emerged. In these circumstances, the old naming conventions were profoundly affected in ways that we will examine more generally later. Immediately, two phenomena may be briefly pointed out.

First, aristocratic names were usurped. Cicero refers to "men of lower rank forcing their way into another family of the same name".[9] Occasionally such men may have been related to the noble houses whose names they used, but often the name was simply assumed without any justification though a fraudulent genealogy might be constructed to go with it. Another ploy used by those on the ascent was to drop the *gentilicium*, which betrayed their humble origin. M. Vipsanius Agrippa, a soldier of obscure beginnings, was a friend and associate of Octavius and rose with him. He became consul three times and married first a Claudia Marcella and then Octavius', now Augustus', daughter Julia. His son was called M. Agrippa, before being adopted by Augustus with the name Agrippa Julius Caesar. Such procedures were far more prevalent in the imperial period, when legislation was fruitlessly introduced to ban them.

Titles are an extension of or a substitute for names, when the name alone does not sufficiently proclaim or indicate a person's function or high status. They had not been prominent in the early Republic, but their importance increased with the enlargement, formalization and changing role of the élites. *Vir nobilissimus* or *vir clarissimus* was used for nobles or consulars in the time of Cicero; *splendidus* for senators and equestrians related to them. The title of *equus romanus*, originally purely functional, became an honorific sign of rank. In the Empire titles multiplied, both as adornments of hereditary élites no longer associated by right or in fact with power, paralleling the accumulation of names, and as adjuncts of a much more bureaucratic administration. Senators had the title *clarissimus*, which was extended to their wives and children; equestrian civil servants were rewarded with the titles of *vir inlustris, vir egregius, vir perfectissimus*; praetorians were called *vir eminentissimus*; and so on. By the second century AD, all such titles had become fixed.

Imperial names and titles

The nomenclature of the emperors developed from that of the late Republican aristocrats. We have seen that when C. Octavius was adopted by C. Julius Caesar, he took the latter's name. He later called himself Imperator Caesar and when the Senate voted him the honorific *cognomen* Augustus, he used the three names: Imperator Caesar Augustus. Imperator was a title given to generals between the time of their victories and their triumphs, and in the time of the Civil Wars some like Caesar and Pompey had taken it permanently. It conveyed the idea of authority and could also be used by magistrates. Its use as a *praenomen* was a novelty but one in line with contemporary aristocratic taste.

Caesar, of course, was a *cognomen* of the *gens* Julia, and substitution of the *cognomen* for the *gentilicium* was an extension of élite emphasis on this part of the name. Augustus as a *cognomen* was also in line with a more general tendency to take grandiose names, for example Pompey's Magnus. Augustus, in effect constructed a new name for himself that was both revolutionary and a development of existing trends, all couched in the traditional framework of the *tria nomina*. This symbolized his general policy of conservative revolution.

Nearly all subsequent emperors used these same three elements with variations. Imperator, abbreviated as Imp., became the prime imperial title from the time of Vespasian. Caesar was always used, being also given to the heir to the throne from the time of Hadrian. Augustus, too, was abbreviated. The emperor's personal names were also incorporated into his official name. In some cases, for example, Imp. Caesar Vespasianus Aug. and Imp. Nerva Caesar Aug., the personal name was the *cognomen*; both *praenomen* and old *gentilicium* were dropped or rather replaced by the Augustan imperial *praenomen* and *gentilicium*. Here the old *gentilicium* remained in use as the name given to freedmen and new citizens under imperial aegis: Julius for Augustus and Tiberius; Cocceius for Nerva; Ulpius for Trajan; and so on. With Marcus Aurelius a different option began of retaining the old *tria nomina* and inserting it within the imperial triad.

The early emperors retained the filiation. The fuller version of Augustus' name was Imp. Caesar Divi Juli f. Augustus, i.e. son of the deified Julius. But this form was soon replaced by taking the name of one's predecessor in lieu of real or adopted father, which was a way of claiming and proclaiming legitimate right to the throne. So Trajan took the name of Nerva; and Antoninus Pius of Hadrian. Septimius Severus, who came to the throne in AD 193 after a power struggle, used both the name of his immediate predecessor Pertinax, killed by the troops in that year, and those of a string of earlier rulers, reputable and disreputable, from whom he thus alleged descent: "son of the deified Marcus Aurelius, brother of the deified Commodus, grandson of the deified Antoninus Pius, great-grandson of the deified Hadrian, and great-great-grandson of the deified Trajan".[10]

Emperors also accumulated *cognomina* or pseudo-*cognomina*. These could derive from real military victories like those of Republican generals, but they were not always actively earned. So Marcus Aurelius became Armeniacus, then Parthicus, Germanicus and Sarmaticus. Diocletian had Germanicus and Sarmaticus four times conferred on him; Britannicus and Persicus twice; and Armeniacus, Medicus, Adiabenicus and Carpicus once each. Some of these names or titles were inherited. There were also general laudatory names like Augustus. Trajan received the epithet Optimus in 114;

and it was also given to Hadrian, Antoninus Pius and Marcus Aurelius. Pius and Felix were used by Commodus, Septimius Severus and Caracalla; Invictus by Commodus and Caracalla. Marcus Aurelius began the custom of adding Maximus to his triumphal epithets, for example, Parthicus Maximus. The Augustan title Pater Patriae was held by nearly all emperors, and 56 emperors were deified, which meant that they were referred to in posthumous inscriptions as Divus, as we have seen. The title *Dominus Noster*, abbreviated to D.N., was used by Caracalla around 200 and then regularly by Diocletian and his successors, who placed it in front of or instead of Imp.

A number of emperors were known at the time and/or since by nicknames. So C. Caesar Augustus Germanicus was Caligula; and Imp. Caesar M. Aurelius Antoninus Augustus was the proper name of both Caracalla and his successor Elagabolus. These names did not appear in inscriptions, though they are found in literary texts.

Slave names

Rome was a society in which a high proportion of labour was provided by slaves. They performed a great variety of tasks, working in mines, quarries, galleys and other public works and on large agricultural estates but also in households as personal servants, providers of sexual and medical services and secretaries. They acted too as business agents, factors and farm bailiffs for their masters, and as private and public entertainers. Some had considerable independence and were "highly skilled and cultured". Slaves belonged to individuals but also to towns and other bodies and to the State (later the Emperor); some belonged to other slaves. These different activites and positions meant that there was an internal hierarchy of slavery, which gave some a large degree of privilege and power and could lead out eventually to freedom. Slavery was not necessarily thought of as a permanent degrading status. Slaves were obtained in the wars of imperial expansion which continued over centuries from the early Republic to the early Empire; by trading, often exploiting or taking over existing trading structures managed by Greeks, Phoenicians and others; and increasingly in the Empire, when these external sources of supply dried up, by breeding. "Slaves were concentrated in Roman Italy, the heartland of the empire", where there were 2 million at the end of the first century BC out of a total population of 6 million.[11]

In general slaves had a single name, which was followed in inscriptions by that of their owner, either in the genitive case or in adjectival form; for example, Martialis C. Olii Primi or Martialis the slave of C. Olius Primus; Eros Aurelius or Eros belonging to the Aurelii. Surviving slave collars follow the same pattern, reading like the identification tags attached today to pet dogs: "I am called Januarius, I am the slave of Dextrus"; or the slave's name might be omitted: "I am a slave; my master is Scholasticus", in this case followed by the master's address.[12] An early form of slave name was similarly anonymous for the slave: Marci puer, Quinti puer, i.e. Marcus' boy, and so on. These names, often contracted to Marcipor or Marpor, Quintipor, etc., died out towards the end of the Republic. Varro associated slave anonymity with actual practice and its decline with the expansion in the numbers of slaves: "In a house where there is only one slave, there is need for only one (generic) slave name, but in a house where there are many slaves then particular names are needed."[13] The stress on the master's name and hence on the slave as his or her possession was continued later when slaves were accorded more than one name. Successus Valerianus Publicus, for example, was Successus, formerly the slave of Valerius, now the slave of the State; Anna Liviae Maecenatiana was Anna, slave of Livia, formerly slave of Maecenas. This form followed the usual rules of nomenclature with reference to the owner replacing the filiation and mention of the previous owner following that for adoptees. The slave was clearly placed and his servile status indicated. This was sometimes further emphasized by inserting s. or ser., abbreviations for "servus", after the owner's name.

Certain special categories of slave had distinctive nomenclature. Public slaves belonging to the State or to cities had the status indicator "servus publicus", from which "servus" was frequently omitted: for example, Herodes publicus; Laetus publicus populi Romani. During the Empire, two names were more common, with the second name referring usually to the previous owner who had sold the slave to the State, for example, Fortunatus publicus Sulpicianus; or Bithus publicus Paullianus. The names of slaves of towns and cities could take the same form, but there were several variants. The terms "colonorum" or "coloniae", often abbreviated in the inscriptions and referring to the status of the town, could be used; the name of the town could be added to the slave's name; and the term "vilicus" might be preferred to "servus". So we have Priscus colono. Aquil. s., from Aquileia, or Zosimus municipium Vercellensium vilicus, from Vercelli. Similar reference could be made to previous owners. Both types of public slave could also have their often important occupations attached to their names, something also found among the imperial slaves who were to some extent their successors. Diodumenus publicus aquae Annesis and Laetus publicus populi Romani . . . aquarius aquae Annionis Veteris both worked for the water services of Rome; Felix arcarius republicae Neapolitanorum was municipal cashier of Naples.

"To the single personal name, . . . the emperor's slaves added the distinctive mark of status 'Caes(aris) ser(vus)' or 'Aug(usti) vern(a)', or simply 'Aug(usti)' or 'Caes(aris)' " with the "servus" understood. From the Flavian period the form Caes. n.(ostri) ser. became predominant, for example: Victorinus Caes. n. ser.; or Maximus Caes. n. vern.. Since slaves belonged to individual emperors rather than to the imperial household, reference to individual reigning emperors was retained in slave nomenclature (unlike that of imperial freedmen) until the time of Trajan at least. "With the Flavians [too,] the *praenomen* 'Imp(eratoris)' appeared in the slave indication for the first time" and then became regular.[14] Caesaris came to predominate also in slave status indication, with Augusti being used for freedmen. This again reflects a difference in the position of the two, slaves being attached to the emperor via his private family name, freedmen via his public title or *cognomen* The distinction was never water-tight, however, and Augusti tended to prevail later with increasing institutionalization of imperial slaves, and with the introduction from the end of Hadrian's reign of the use of Augustus for the reigning emperor and Caesar for the heir. Public and imperial slaves sometimes had second names proper, often names in *-ianus* derived from previous masters but also chosen at will. Public slaves called Aemilianus or Cornelianus seem to have had no links with the noble families concerned, but rather to have been displaying rank by abandoning the single slave name and imitating the nomenclature of the free-born.

The usual status indicator for the slave of a slave was "servus vicarius"; while "liberti servus" signified the slave of a freedman. So the Stoic philosopher Epictetus, the slave and then freedman of a freedman of Nero, was formally Ti. Claudius Epaphroditus lib. servus Epictetus.

How did slaves obtain their personal names, and what kinds of name were they given? Little direct information is available about name-giving. Varro, however, relates that "when three men have bought a slave apiece at Ephesus, sometimes one derives his slave's name from that of the seller Artemidorus and calls him Artemas; another names his slave Ion, from Ionia, the district, because he has bought him there; while the third calls his slave Ephesius, because he has bought him at Ephesus".[15]

Obviously traded or captured slaves would have had names before they became slaves and these might sometimes be retained. Dealers would also bestow names, often ones indicating desirable qualities in their merchandise. Purchasers of slaves might find it convenient to keep a name that a slave already had, so long as it was not too alien or hard to pronounce, or, as Varro suggests, they might wish to exercise their power of possession by imposing a name of their own choice. Slaves bred by owners might be named by them, though again liberality or laziness might leave naming to the natural parents of the child, to the slave family. In all this there would be the constraining element of what was thought to be a suitable slave name.

Some of the principles lying behind the naming of slaves may be inferred from the names themselves, about which we are much better informed, though inevitably it is privileged household slaves, slaves on their way to emancipation about whom we know most. A very few slaves bore original "barbarian" names, such as Banobal, a Phoenician temple slave mentioned by Cicero; or Tiridas; Bargates; Bithus; Lullu. Though slaves often came from the Middle East, especially in the later Republican period, oriental slave names are rare. Often these "real" exotic slave names were translated into Latin names that sounded similar, for example Dorimachus from the Thracian Drimachus or Acme from the Syrian Hacma. More commonly, slaves were given "ethnic" names indicating their real or supposed origin. Names could also be indicative of the slave markets at which slaves were bought, like Varro's Ephesius. Ethnic names refer to "almost every part of the empire and beyond": Gallus, Germanus, Baeticus, Maurus, Cilix, Persicus.[16] In general they tended to emphasize places thought to produce good rather than bad slaves, so names referring to Sardinia, Egypt and Cappadocia, for example, reputed to produce poor slaves, were avoided. Certain areas of origin were also believed to be best for certain slave roles. Thracians made good gladiators; Gauls and Spaniards good stock farmers; Cimbri and Teutons were fit for hard agricultural, Greeks for intellectual and cultural work; and this too might be reflected in naming.

In general slave names indicated good character traits: Celer, Vitalis, Modestus, Hilarus, Laetus, Pudens. Such Latin names often took the form of participles, with past participles preceding present ones chronologically. Donatus, Datus, Extricatus were common in Africa; Exuperatus, Mandatus, Expectata in Cis-Alpine Gaul; Acutus, Cogitatus and Inventus in Rome itself. Some of these names are hard to account for as Latin names and it has been suggested that again some of them may relate to original names, Cogitatus to Celtic names in Cogi-, Dubitatus to names in Dubo-, for example. In contrast to earlier aristocratic *cognomina*, slave names were rarely pejorative and names indicating physical traits were usually avoided. An exception is Rufus or Rufio, a possible reference to the supposed red hair of Thracians and/or the red wig worn by slaves in Roman comedy.

Certain slave names were associated with particular occupations. "Actors often assumed the names of famous predecessors, or names in some way appropriate to their profession." Asclepiades was a common name for a medic, as were Erasistratus and Themiso, after well-known practitioners. The same names also recurred among gladiators: Pugnax, Celadus (crowd's roar), and Spiculus (from spiculum, a javelin or dart).

More generally, religious or theophoric names were very common among slaves. These include Parthenius, Eleutherius and Nicephor, one of the favourite early slave names, as well as Dionysius, Apollonius, Aphrodisius and Epaphroditus. Some of these may have been derived from ethnic or local cults. The very popular Fortunatus and Primigenius were probably originally inspired "by the name of the great goddess Fortuna Primigenia of Praeneste" near Rome.[17] Some slaves showed dedication to their native gods via Latinized religious names: Saturninus for Baal in Carthage; Mercurius, Martialis and Silvanus for equivalent Celtic deities. On the whole, however, and certainly once they were well established, such names lost any religious significance they may have had, being used rather for their variety (compared with Roman names proper) and at first for their distinctiveness.

Many scholars have compiled lists of the most common slave names. For the imperial period, these include in rough order of popularity the Latin names: Felix, Hilarus, Faustus, Salvius, Fortunatus, Primus, Secundus, and their female equivalents; and the Greek names: Eros, Pamphilus, Antiochus, Hermes, Alcxander, Philomusus and Onesimus. Greek names were especially common and more varied than Latin names, reflecting the more fertile nature of Greek nomenclature generally.

This brings us to the vexed question of Greek *cognomina*. The fact that slaves and ex-slaves often had Greek names led some scholars to assume wrongly that the bulk of Roman slaves came from Greek-speaking lands or the "Orient" and to see a Greek *cognomen* as a sure sign of servile origin. Moreover, studies of inscriptions, especially in Italy, Spain and Gaul, suggest that a high proportion of the population as a whole had Greek names: 40 per cent in the Port of Ostia, for example; and over 70 per cent in Rome itself in the first three centuries AD. This led to the further conclusion that the population of the empire was in process of being swamped by servile and alien elements, an echo of modern ethnocentric phobias.

Roman slaves, we have seen, tended to have either Latin or Greek names, mainly because these were the only two languages known to Romans. Names in other languages were usually changed or translated. Many slaves did come from the East, though of course the East was only Hellenized to a limited extent, and many would not have been Greek-speaking. More significant, as Gordon emphasized in 1924, such slaves passed through the hands of Greek slave-traders. In some cases, it is known that Greek-named persons were not Greek, for example a man, presumably a doctor, noted as Asclepiades natione Cilix, or the German guards to whom the philhellene emperor Nero gave Greek names like Gnostus, Chloreus or Nereus. Sometimes by contrast in some provinces those with Greek *cognomina* were either free-born Greeks, like the immigrant architects, sculptors and others at Leptis Magna in the time of Septimius Severus; or free-born non-Greeks who assumed Greek names because they had high status locally like the upper-class natives in Ptolemaic Egypt.

In choosing or retaining Greek names for their slaves, Roman slave-owners were reflecting their acquaintanceship with Greek culture and language – many upper-class Romans could speak Greek by the late Republican period – as well as perhaps their uneasy sense of superiority towards them. Rome had conquered Greece but had to recognize, defer to and absorb its culture. Many free-born Romans, of course, were given Greek names themselves. "The first two Greek *cognomina* in Roman onomastics belong to two consuls" of the late fourth century BC, Q. Publilius Philo and P. Sempronius Sophus.[18] Much later during the Empire, there were distinct vogues for certain kinds of Greek names among Romans. For example, female names taken from abstract qualities, such as Hedone, Helpis, Nike, Homonea, were either adopted straight, or, more significantly, in Latin versions: Voluptas,

Spes, Victoria, Concordia. Though Greek names are therefore not definite signs either of Greek ethnic or of servile origin, in a study of nine important Italian towns Kajanto does establish "that Latin and non-Latin *cognomina* were not used indiscriminately".[19] There were important differences in the incidence of Greek *cognomina* that are correlated to differences in the incidence of slavery and to patterns in the recruitment of slaves. There was a strong tendency also for parents with Greek to give their children Latin *cognomina*, a further indication of the perceived social superiority of a Latin name. Change over time as slaves became freed and freedmen absorbed can also be seen elsewhere. In Tarragona in Spain, Greek names were "most widespread among those of servile origin", but the proportion of slaves and freedmen among those with Greek names declined from nearly 100 per cent in the Republic to 50 per cent in the first and second centuries AD and to under 10 per cent in the third century.[20]

Some names remained distinctively servile in connotation, whether Greek or Latin, but lists of exclusively servile and non-servile names, such as those drawn up by Duff for the early Empire, become increasingly short and qualified. Most of Duff's names reserved to the free-born were actually borne by slaves and by the second century Crescens, Maximus and Secundus, all on his free-born lists, were among the commonest servile names. "The barriers between the personal nomenclature of the upper classes and of the slave and freedmen classes, which were still felt more or less keenly in the early and mid-1st century, broke down", mirroring a general "interpenetration of classes in Roman imperial society".[21] One of the main means by which both linked processes occurred was the emancipation of slaves.

Freedmen

A high proportion of Roman slaves were emancipated, especially in Italy. Manumission became so common indeed that legal restrictions were introduced by Julius Caesar and Augustus. Slaves could not normally be freed under the age of 30, and owners were only permitted to free a certain proportion of their slaves, half of them if they had less than 10, a quarter if they had 100, and so on. Manumission could be granted by owners while they were alive or by testament, and it could be more or less formal. "Latin" status was conveyed by informal manumission "inter amicos" or before witnesses, or if a slave were under age. Full Roman citizenship came only via formal manumission which had to be done by a magistrate.

Manumission involved a change of name. In the oldest inscriptions freedmen adopt a *praenomen* and the *gentilicium* of their former master with an indication of their status, for example P. Petronius libertus. The last element was usually abbreviated to lib. or l.. Around 100 BC, freedmen began to have their own *cognomina*, nearly always their original slave names. An example of the then "classic" freedman nomenclature is found on the famous monument of M. Caelius, the centurion, killed in the massacre of the legions of Varus by the Germans in AD 7. On it are found the busts of his two freedmen, who had added to their simple slave names Privatus and Thiaminus, the *praenomen* and the *gentilicium* of the master who had granted them liberty, and who called themselves from then on: M. Caelius Privatus and M. Caelius Thiaminus.[22]

This was indistinguishable from the free-born citizen's *tria nomina*, but in its full form the freedman's name did differ, with reference to the master or patron replacing the free-born person's filiation. So, in contrast to Cicero's son M. Tullius M. f. Cicero, his freedman was M. Tullius M.l. Tiro, that is not Marcus Tullius Cicero the son of Marcus but Marcus Tullius Tiro the freedman of Marcus.

Where the owner or patron was a woman and hence without a *praenomen*, the symbol Ɔ (for Gaia) was used to indicate the connection and the freedman took her father's *praenomen* and her *gentilicium*; for example, M. Arrius Ɔ l. Diomedes was Diomedes the ex-slave of Arria, daughter of M. Arrius. Under the Republic and early Empire, the *gentilicium* or *cognomen* of the patroness could replace Ɔ, for example Titinius Titiniae l. Antiochus. Freedwomen of course did not take the *praenomen* but only the *gentilicium* of their former owners; so Aurelia l. Nais was Nais the freedwoman of C. Aurelius.

Freed State or city slaves commonly took the *gentilicium* Publicius or Poblicius from Publicus. State slaves might alternatively be called Romanus and city slaves after their city, "for example Faventinus from Faventia or Reatinus from Reate".[23] Complex names could be formed in this and other ways. Q. Publicius Tergestinorum libertus Felix was Felix who was a public slave of the town of Tergeste, now emancipated. Fabricius Centonius collegiorum lib. Chresimus was Chresimus the freedman of the colleges of the smiths and garment-makers, with a pseudo-*praenomen* and a *gentilicium* being formed from the names of the Fabri and the Centonarii. Especially later in the Empire, freedmen and freedwomen of private persons might incorporate the latter's full *tria nomina* in their own name, and they also retained the names of previous owners.

So, although the freedman's name proclaimed his new citizenship and his escape from slavery, both of which he was proud to record in inscriptions, it also pointed to his inferiority vis-à-vis the free-born. In full form it labelled him as a "libertus"; in short form, the *cognomen* often advertised his servile origin, while the *gentilicium* linked him permanently with the man or woman who had freed him and who often for all intents and purposes remained his master or mistress. The letters of Cicero and Pliny often refer proprietorially to household servants, secretaries and agents who were freedmen: "Cilix your freedman"; "My freedman Philotimus"; "your Phylargus".[24]

Freedmen usually became the legal clients of their ex-masters, now patrons. Building up a following of clients indeed was one of the motives for manumission. Clients owed patrons reverence and courtesy and could not sue them at law. Patrons owed protection and tutelage and had a right to a share of clients' inheritances. Often such a relationship was amicable, if uneven. Freedmen, we have seen, could be devoted retainers, erecting funeral monuments to their masters. When Pompey was murdered in Egypt, it was his freedman Philippus who buried him. As more generally, involvement in funeral rites and monuments was the business of an heir, and freedmen sometimes inherited estates from their patrons, especially when they were childless. A well-known example is that of C. Caecilius Isidorus who inherited a fortune from the noble Metelli famly towards the end of the first century BC.

Freedmen did not share in the full rights of citizens. For example, they were normally precluded from joining the equestrian order, the praetorian guard and certain priesthoods. They were also the victims of social snobbery, as the literature of the first and second centuries AD makes clear. Juvenal, himself the grandson of a wealthy freedman, is especially vicious, ridiculing "Crispinus, that Delta-bred house-slave, silt washed down by the Nile", who had achieved equestrian rank through the favour of the emperor Domitian; or another freedman pushing aside nobles by birth at a grandee's levée, "born out East, on the Euphrates", with pierced ears, but the owner of five shops and again winning equestrian status through wealth and influence.[25] In a letter, Pliny reports news of the murder of Larcius Macedo by his own slaves, suggesting that it was perhaps deserved: "He was a cruel and overbearing master, too ready to forget that his father had been a slave, or maybe too keenly conscious of it"; and he recounts an anecdote in which Macedo had been struck in one of the public baths by an equestrian after one of Macedo's slaves had lightly touched the man to ask him to let them pass.[26] There was no legal ban to intermarriage between freed persons and the free-born, "but in aristocratic circles, the prejudice against such marriages was strong".[27]

In these circumstances it is not surprising to find that some freedmen sought to conceal their origins by altering their names. Dropping the lib. or l. from the full name was an obvious recourse, which became very general in inscriptions from the early Empire onwards except for imperial freedmen. Two-thirds of inscriptions from this period in Rome itself have no status indicator and most of these probably relate to freedmen. Then a new *cognomen* could be taken. A number of examples appear in the literary sources. The grammarian L. Crassicius Pasicles fom Tarentum changed his third name to the consular Pansa, according to Suetonius. An epigram of Martial ridicules a Cinnamus for wanting to be called Cinna. Nero made a law confiscating the bulk of the property of deceased freedmen who had taken "the name of any family without good reason", which suggests that the practice was quite common.[28]

In some cases the further change of name came with a further change of status. Especially in the period around the end of the Republic and the early Empire, the position of freedmen was fairly fluid, with good opportunities for social ascension. There were many categories of freedmen, depending on their origin, skills, and the status of their patrons. Some remained menial if familiar servants, as we have seen. Others made successful independent careers as actors, artists, doctors, teachers, civil servants, manufacturers and traders. Many, especially in the last category, became wealthy enough to qualify for equestrian status or more. These men were the primary targets of the satirists, together with court favourites.

For most freedmen, climbing the social scale would be gradual, occurring over several generations. This was reflected in nomenclature. Sons of freedmen had the right to use filiation in their full names, replacing and not simply omitting the libertus-patron tie. So L. Asellius L.f. Mamilianus of Puteoli was the son of L. Asellius L. lib. Hermes and of Mamilia Lyris. This example also illustrates two other significant changes. As we saw in discussing Greek *cognomina*, freedmen with these names, indicative perhaps of their servile origins, often picked Latin *cognomina* for their children. A son might also take his mother's name, especially if she were not of servile stock, like Claudius Etruscus, to whom Statius wrote a poem of condolence on the death of his father, an ex-slave from Smyrna, whose name remains unmentioned and hence unknown. Only at the next generation could the hereditary taint of slavery be finally thrown off. Grandsons of freedmen "rejoiced in full filiation" with citizen fathers and grandfathers.[29]

Imperial freedmen were always a special case. The prestige conferred by serving the emperor is well conveyed in an anecdote recounted by Epictetus, who was a slave of Nero's freedman Epaphroditus. The story belongs to a time when Epaphroditus' position was shaky. He

> owned a certain cobbler, whom he sold off as being no good at his job. Then by some chance the man was bought by someone in the imperial entourage and became the emperor's cobbler. You should have seen how Epaphroditus paid court to him. – "What is the good Felicio doing, I pray you?" And then if anyone asked us, "What is Epaphroditus doing?" he was told: "He is in consultation with Felicio."[30]

Some freedmen wielded enormous power as individuals under the early emperors like Claudius and Galba. Weaver has shown how later emperors used freedmen to run their secretariat and financial offices, developing a regular bureaucracy from around the second century AD. Freedmen also held senior posts administering the emperors' estates and properties throughout the empire, and they served as chief assistants to equestrian provincial procurators or governors or even as procurators themselves. "Felix, the procurator of Judaea, who judged St Paul, was an ex-slave".[31] Emperors in effect used men whom they fully controlled as agents of government in preference to members of the old or new élite, or as foils to them.

The names of imperial freedmen clearly expressed their peculiar and elevated status. The usual rule followed was to add the status element Aug. lib. or Aug. l., i.e. Augusti libertus, to the *tria nomina*. This they continued to do "even when the freedmen of private citizens were ceasing to use any form of freedman indicator at all",[32] and even when they achieved high office. Imperial freedmen at first took their *praenomen* and *gentilicium* from the emperor who manumitted them, for example Ti. Claudius from Claudius and Nero, T. Flavius from Vespasian. Later the very frequency of such names led to their being dropped, or the *gentilicium* might be retained in only abbreviated form: Fl. for Flavii, Aur. for Aurelii. The status indicator was usually placed between the *gentilicium* and the *cognomen* but could be placed last. There was a general trend towards standardization of the nomenclature of imperial freedmen, reflecting their attachment to the imperial family or household as an institution rather than to individual emperors.

Two additional elements in the naming of imperial freedmen should be mentioned. Some indicated in their names that their masters' names had changed or that they had been inherited by one emperor from another. Much more common was having two *cognomina*. The second *cognomen*, usually in -*ianus*, referred to a previous master and to a transfer of authority analagous to adoption and thus using the same onomastic form. It was acquired by the person as a slave but was kept after manumission. At first such names derived mainly from noble families, for example Antonianus, Cornelianus; or from members of the imperial family, for example Agrippianus, Germanicianus. But from the time of Claudius or Nero names taken from prominent imperial freedmen appear: Epaphroditianus, Primigenianus. The latter greatly increased in importance from Augustus to Trajan, while the former declined. Most of those with names derived from imperial freedmen were slaves or freedmen of those freedmen. They assumed or retained the second *cognomen* which advertised this fact, because it indicated at the same time they had moved up the ladder. They were no longer *vicarii*, slaves of mere slaves or freedmen, but now imperial slaves or freedmen.

Another element frequently present in the nomenclature of imperial freedmen (and slaves) is their occupational title. This was nearly always placed at the end of the name. A full example is provided by a high official in Britain in the reign of Tiberius, who was still legally a slave: Ti. Claudius Augusti Scurranus dispensator ad fiscum Gallicum.

As slaves had slaves, so freedmen could have freedmen. This was most likely for freedmen of the highest position and notably imperial freedmen. Here the status indicator "liberti libertus" was used, often abbreviated; for example Ti. Julius Anthi Aug. l. lib. Hilario was Tiberius Julius Hilario, freedman of the imperial freedman Anthus. Since the *gentilicium* of both persons was the same, it was not usually repeated. Sometimes the name of the immediate patron was entirely left out, for example C. Julius Augusti l. l. Priamus, that is C. Julius Priamus, freedman of an imperial freedman. All that mattered here was the connection with the imperial household.

Children of mixed marriages

Status is never more exactly highlighted than for the offspring of "mixed marriages" between slaves and non-slaves. Roman law laid down "that children born "in conubio", i.e. proper marriage, inherited the status of their father at the time of conception, and that children of any other union inherited the status of their mother at the time of birth".[33] The status in question here was indicated by the *gentilicium* and by the absence, presence or peculiar form of the filiation. So M. Amulius Epinicus, the son of L. Acolius Sosus and Amulia Maximilla, from Southern Italy, who had his mother's *gentilicium* and no filiation, was almost certainly illegitimate, though free-born like his parents. It was not uncommon for masters to marry slave women, whom they then emancipated. Marriages between free-born women and slaves were much rarer. Unions of this kind were most frequent between relatively high-status imperial slaves and free-born or freed women, and it is about this group that we have most information. Imperial freedmen usually married while they were still slaves. Their wives might be slaves also, or freedwomen or free-born, and the status of either spouse might change during the marriage. Most commonly, one or both spouses would be manumitted. It seems that slave families were particularly anxious to concentrate on freeing the wife, since her status was passed to her children. Some examples will make all this clearer.

Children of slave mothers were slaves, whatever the status of the father. Similarly, children of freedwomen born before their emancipation had slave status and took their mother's *gentilicium*. So Clodia Regina of Portus was the daughter of Terentius Reginus and Clodia Domitia. L. Ceionius Fructuosus was the son of Clodius Fructuosus and Ceionia Helias; he again took his mother's *gentilicium* and servile status, though he also took his father's *cognomen*, a not uncommon practice. Once the mother was freed, her children still took her *gentilicium* if the father remained unfree, but they also acquired her free citizen status. So the child of Lydus Caesar Aug., a slave, and Flavia Macaria, a freedwoman, who died aged 3 years, was T. Flavius Petalus. Once the father was freed, the children could take his *gentilicium* and the filiation. So Aelia T. f. Perpetua, who died as an infant, was the daughter of T. Aelius Aug. lib. Amphiatus and Flavia Aphrodisia. The importance of the newly acquired free status can be seen in the care taken to attach *praenomen* and filiation even to one dying so young. Children born before the father's emancipation could also be legitimized later, which involved changing or adding to the name.

All this could lead to complicated situations, in which children of the same parents had different *gentilicia*. So P. Aelius Aug. lib. Telesphorus and Naevia Tyche had three children. One, Naevius Successus, was a stepson, offspring of a previous marriage of the wife; a second, Naevius Telesphorus, with mother's *gentilicium* and father's *cognomen*, was the son of the couple born before his father's manumission; while a third, P. Aelius Telesphorus, with all his father's three names, was the youngest, born after his father's manumission.

CHAPTER THREE

Roman expansion

Roman citizenship

The manumission of slaves was only one avenue into Roman citizenship. Much more important in terms of numbers and hence social and political structure was the extension of citizenship to foreign subjects. The process began in the fourth century BC, when Rome, only one among other powerful states in central Italy, began to grant citizen rights to the inhabitants of allied cities. At the same time colonies of Roman citizens were established in many parts of Italy and later beyond. By the end of the Republic, the inhabitants of nearly the whole of Italy were full Roman citizens. Then under the early Empire citizenship extended into the provinces: Southern Gaul, Spain, then further afield.

It was still associated at this time with Italian birth and origin and with Latin culture, and some emperors granted it very sparingly. It was a valuable and much sought-after privilege conveying important rights. Under the Republic full citizenship had been the qualification for participation in political life. Later and for provincials access to legal rights was the important thing. These included *conubium* or full marriage, making a will, freedom from torture and other corporal punishments, as well as fiscal and commercial advantages and wearing the toga. Citizenship could be granted to individuals or whole cities, and there were at first different categories of citizenship, some of which did not convey full rights. It could be given later automatically to those holding certain offices. It was also granted as a reward for services to the community, such as building a ship or having three children. Increasingly under the Empire, citizenship was granted on petition. Pliny's letters to Trajan are full of such requests.

However acquired, Roman citizenship became an important means by which local populations, starting with their élites, were incorporated into the new Roman state, a means by which the vast empire could be unified. Under the Flavian emperors and then the Severi, citizenship spread well outside the Graeco-Roman world as the empire itself spread. Finally in 212 the famous Edict of Caracalla granted Roman citizenship to "all those who are in the Roman orbit". There has been much scholarly debate about the exact terms of the application of the decree, but it seems to have applied to virtually all the free population.

The new Roman citizen took a new Roman name: the *tria nomina* plus filiation and tribe. In addition, as late as the second century, it was not uncommon to "add the description 'Romanus' "[1] to make the new status quite clear. All this marked the new citizen off from slaves and freedmen, and from foreigners or *peregrini* without the citizenship who might have some kind of Latin name. Given the prestige of the citizenship, there was an incentive to try to usurp it by assuming the appropriate denomination. The earliest known case is that of M. Perperna, an Etruscan who achieved high office and whose son actually became consul in 130 BC. In 126 BC M. Perperna was charged with illegal usurpation of Roman citizenship and expelled from Rome. His son meanwhile had died. Later, Claudius brought in more severe punishments for foreigners who used the *tria nomina* without authority and by implication assumed the citizenship. Some safeguard against such usurpations was provided by the censuses of the Republican period, by the tablets or certificates issued to some new citizens, and by the public recording of births established by Augustus.

The new citizen took the name of the person to whom he owed the grant of citizenship. The most significant element here was the *gentilicium*, but the *praenomen* might also be adopted. The new citizen's *cognomen* was his original personal name, suitably modified as required. Under the Republic, the grantor might be a local governor, a magistrate, a general, or an important Roman acting in the capacity of a patron. So Caesar informs us that Gaius Valerius Caburus, a leader of the Gauls and an ally of Rome, was "presented with the citizenship by Gaius Valerius Flaccus", proconsul in the area around 80 BC.[2] In Spain in the first century BC, new citizens' *gentilicia* were taken among others from Q. Fabius Aemilianus, a governor; from Q. Caecilius Metellus, a general; and from M. Porcius Cato, who had connections with the region. The magnates of the late Republican revolutionary period made much use of the power to grant citizenship, which is reflected in the numerous Antonii, Claudii, Julii and Pompeii found especially in the Eastern provinces.

Pliny the Younger recommended the emancipation of slaves in provincial towns on the grounds that by "increasing the number of citizens" the interests of the town were advanced.[3] The same argument applied to the enfranchisement of free foreigners, both as far as their native places were concerned and also their sponsors and patrons. For enfranchisement was a means of building up useful clientèles. "It was a matter of pride and also of real advantage in various ways for a Roman noble to have clients and connections in . . . provincial cities; he aided and acted for them in Rome, while they added to his dignity . . . and furthered his interests in their respective countries."[4] Very often such a patron would have procured the citizenship for his clients, and their taking his name made known and cemented the link between them. In Southwestern Gaul, for example, Pompeius, Licinius, Domitius and Caecilius are among the commonest *gentilicia* taken by provincial citizens, and "all of them [are] *gentes* whose representatives . . . not only served in the province [as officials and magistrates], but actually [took] a political interest in it."[5] The high incidence of Clodii and Caecilii in Sicily similarly reflected the fact that members of these *gentes* had lands and interests in the island.

Very occasionally under the Republic a new citizen took the *gentilicium* of the consul for the year. The same principle seems to have underlain the adoption of the imperial *nomen*: the reigning emperor was the personification of the State. Most new citizens under the Empire took the imperial name, including the *praenomen*: for example Ti. Julius after Tiberius; Ti. Claudius after Claudius and Nero; T. Flavius after Vespasian; and M. Ulpius after Trajan. The Edict of Caracalla flooded the empire with Aurelii, both new citizens and existing ones who added Aurelius to the names they had already. As we have noted, the adoption by so many people of the same *praenomina* and *gentilicia* led to the devaluation of these parts of the name and a new emphasis on the *cognomen*, and the special form of the citizen name came to be lost.

Soldiers' names

Soldiers' names overlap with those of citizens, but they are really a distinct category deserving separate treatment.

The Roman army was originally a wholly citizen body, but, in addition to troops provided by the Latin allies, foreign auxiliaries were used from the second century BC. Legionaries were still citizens under the early Empire, though by the end of the first century AD some had probably not been citizens for very long before their enlistment. Well before this indeed, some of them were made citizens on enlistment. It appears that a number of these were issued with names in military fashion, usually including the imperial name, while others were allowed a degree of choice. Legionaries enrolled under Augustus, for example, have *gentilicia* like Antonius, Domitius and Livius as well as Julius. Some "crack" units remained the preserve of established citizens. The Praetorian Guard was recruited almost entirely in Italy before the time of Septimius Severus, and from countrymen and the sons of soldiers. This is reflected in the tiny proportion of non-Latin *cognomina* found among its members – far less than the Italian average.

There is some evidence that legionaries exchanged "foreign" *cognomina* for Latin ones on joining up. Similarly auxiliaries were given Roman names when they enlisted. From the first century AD, these included the *gentilicium*, filiation and *cognomen*. Again, recruits often took the name of the reigning emperor as their *gentilicia*. The rosters from Dura-Europos on the Euphrates show that after the Edict of Caracalla, the name Aurelius was added to soldiers' existing *gentilicia* in a forced show of loyalty. More spontaneous attachment many have been shown by taking the imperial name as a *cognomen*. Here Antonius was the most popular, but other emperors were also recalled including Commodus, Nerva and Septimius. But equally often *gentilicia* were not imperial but borrowed from Italian names or adapted from native ones, for example, Sex. Memmius Clearchi f.; C. Valerius Annaei f.; or Q. Panentius Quintianus, all soldiers of the fleet. Names were also borrowed from commanders or more junior officers.

An example of a name change often cited is that of a young man called Apion from Philadelphia in Egypt, who was recruited into the Roman fleet in the first half of the second century, and two of whose letters home have survived. In the first, written to his father Epimachus, he explains that his name is now Antonius Maximus, though he still signs the letter Apion. In the second, written some years later to his sister Sabina, he calls himself by his Roman name only and refers to his son and nephew, both called Maximus too.[6] Another conscript wrote "to my relations I am called Tarachus, but with the military I am called Victor."[7] Such dual names appear to have been quite common, and they sometimes figure as such in inscriptions, for example, C. Julius Victor qui et Sola Duni f.; and Ravonius Celer qui et Bato, both from Dalmatia.

As a rule auxiliaries did not obtain full citizenship before the mid second century AD, until they were honourably discharged at the end of their service. Then of course they took the full citizen name. It was possible to anticipate the grant of this privilege. Claudius Lysias, the military tribune who supervised St Paul's flogging at Jerusalem, according to Acts Chapter 22, told the apostle that it had cost him "a large sum of money to acquire the citizenship", and his case cannot be unique.

Two other features of military nomenclature may be noted. First, reference to geographical origin is found in inscriptions relating to soldiers more often than in those relating to other groups. So the full inscribed name of a man already mentioned was: Sex. Memmius Clearchi f. Mannes Oniandus ex Lycia. Presumably the military authorities wanted to know and record soldiers' place of origin, and it was probably significant to the soldiers themselves if they were serving away from home. The indication was given for both discharged men and recruits and seems to have become permanently attached to the name.

Soldiers' *cognomina* also had special characteristics. Epithets denoting suitability for the military role were common: Acer, Dexter, Ferox, Martialis,

Victor. Some of these were the most popular of all soldiers' names. Military positions or ranks also appear as *cognomina*: Pequarius, Princeps, Tribunus. Some names were reserved to common soliders and were not borne by centurions, for example, Datus and Donatus, both with generally servile or lower status connotations. Despite the odd exotic exception, the nomenclature of a Roman military unit must often have been monotonous. The list of members of a cavalry squadron, the Equites Singulares Imperatoris, has survived from the mid imperial period. Its decurion was Julius Moscellus; its NCOs Nonius Severus and Julius Victorinus; and its troopers Aur. Mucatral, Aur. Lucius, Ael. Crescens, Aur. Victor, Ael. Victor, Cl. Victorinus, and so on.

Romanization

At its greatest extent in the second century AD, the Romans ruled an empire that stretched from Hadrian's Wall, the Danube and the Crimea in the north to the Sahara and the middle Nile in the south, from Portugal in the west to the borders of Armenia and Persia in the east. Nearly all these territories had been acquired by military conquest. In many areas, especially in the early stages of expansion, native populations were killed, dispossessed or enslaved, land was confiscated, colonies of settlement were established, annexed territories were plundered, and local cultures attacked. Latin became the official language. In this sense there is no denying the imposition of Romanization. But in the longer term the Romans could never have acquired, still less governed the empire by themselves.

Until the mid third century AD, the Roman system was largely one of "government without bureaucracy",[8] of indirect rule, incorporating a widening circle of territories and communities into the Roman State by granting them Roman or quasi-Roman status but allowing them to retain a considerable degree of autonomy and self-government. As we have seen in connection with manumission and citizenship, the Romans had from the start pursued a policy of absorbing foreigners into their ranks, and this policy was simply extended to the whole of the Mediterranean world.

Crucially important here was the behaviour and attitude of local élites. Those conquered by her or on the edges of her influence frequently indicated a positive admiration for Rome. In the second century BC, the Greek historian Polybius compared the Romans favourably with their great rivals the Carthaginians, celebrating the former's moral superiority, bravery, pride in ancestry, piety and scorn for wealth. As Momigliano commented, he "identified himself with Roman success" and was only the first of Greek intellectuals to accept Roman rule and to collaborate with it.[9] It was very often in the interests of local élites to follow this path. Their prestige was enhanced and their privileges guaranteed via access to Roman citizenship. Roman law strengthened their property rights. Roman peace frequently put an end to social struggles and threats to their power. In many ways therefore

41

one can say that provincial aristocracies "Romanized themselves".[10] They adopted Roman lifestyle, language, dress and religion, and of course Roman names. They had admission too to the centres of power, for members of local élites were recruited into the Senate, into the imperial civil service, into the army, and finally to the imperial throne itself. Trajan came from "the Italian diaspora in the provinces"; Septimius Severus, who succeeded as emperor in 193, came from Leptis Magna in Africa.[11] In effect, an empire-wide élite was created having a common education and culture.

All this left most of the population untouched or only superficially influenced by Roman rule, and especially those in the peripheral recently annexed provinces and those living outside or away from towns, which were the main forums and agents of Romanization. Furthermore, there was always a huge variety of circumstances across the empire, which meant that Romanization could only be uneven from place to place and from time to time. Nomenclature was part and parcel of the process and has been used by historians to try to measure the degree and nature of Roman impact in different provinces. Two examples may be taken as illustrations: Greece and North Africa.

The Greeks are a very special case. As we have seen, the Romans had an ambivalent attitude towards Greece. Militarily and politically, they had the upper hand, but they recognized Greek cultural superiority. Indeed in the first two centuries AD, Roman culture was really a bilingual Graeco-Roman culture. From their side, Greeks admired Rome, as Polybius did, but there was also some incomprehension and disdain. It is significant that few Greeks bothered to learn or use Latin. These ambiguities were expressed in nomenclature.

From the first century AD onwards, some Greeks had "utterly Roman names [which] revealed nothing of their Greek origin".[12] So we have Q. Pompeius Macer, appointed to the Senate under Tiberius; or Cn. Cornelius Pulcher, procurator at Epirus around 110, "the descendant of a distinguished family at Epidaurus".[13] These examples come from a time when Roman citizenship was still rare among Greeks and went with the highest status. Even so the change of name seems to have occurred often over one or two generations. Theophanes of Mytilene was made an equestrian at the time of Julius Caesar; his son took the name Pompeius Macer; and his grandson added the crowning *praenomen*, as we have seen. Often, too, individuals seem to have employed alternative names, reserving the Roman or Roman-style name for relations with Romans. So from Sparta, Xenophanes was also called Ti. Claudius in the reign of Trajan. An inscription at Salonica listing magistrates from the first century gives their names in both Greek and Latin form. It should also be noted that Greek inscriptions were usually in Greek with names transliterated as required.

Much more common was the option of adopting the proper Roman name form but with a Greek *cognomen*, the style adopted by freedmen. So the Eurycles, the ruling family of Sparta, granted the citizenship by Julius Caesar, produced successively C. Julius Eurycles, C. Julius Laco and C. Julius Spartiaticus. Among later senators we have T. Flavius Phaedrus, M. Aurelius Asclepiodotianus Asclepiades, and C. Julius Antiochus Philopappus.

As some of these examples show, once Roman names became more widespread they tended to depart more and more from classical forms. The Greek and Roman systems of naming were in effect at odds, and the Greeks frequently misunderstood the Roman system or forced Roman-style names into their own frameworks. Greek nomenclature did not have the practical, status orientation of the Roman. In it a person was known by a single name plus patronymic, with an additional name or nickname sometimes for further identification. On first acquaintanceship with Roman names, Greeks took the *praenomen* for the significant name, ignoring the *gentilicium*, which they themselves did not have. Polybius follows this practice, causing much potential confusion. When Greeks later adopted Roman names, the *cognomen* was the significant individual name, and the *praenomen* and *gentilicium* tended to become purely formal, anticipating a more general trend in Roman naming. Daux comments that the first two parts of the name, which were frequently transmitted from generation to generation unchanged, became decorative titles, "like Herr, Professor or Sir".[14] In the great Hellenistic cities, it seems that the complete Roman names were only used in formal legal situations and on occasions when full honours were required. None occur in the everyday usage of the New Testament. The Greeks had special difficulties with filiation, which they expressed via the *cognomen* but which the Romans designated by the *praenomen* and separate filiation.

Roman Africa comprised several provinces, differently organized in different periods. The Carthaginians (Punic-speaking) had represented the only serious threat to Roman power, and at first after the defeat of Carthage in 146 BC, Rome's policy was one of repression and settlement. By the time of the Empire, if not before, the usual pattern of selective assimilation and indirect rule was established. This was very uneven. The cities founded or developed on or near the coast and the corn-growing central plateau became Romanized, while the interior and particularly the nomadic pastoral populations were little touched. The earliest evidence of the introduction of Roman names comes from the agreements made between African cities and Roman patrons, to whom they looked for aid and protection. The oldest is from the time of Julius Caesar for Curubis. The names of the representatives of the city were Punic: Himilconis son of Zentuc; Ammicaris son of Lilua. One of its officials, a Roman citizen, was called L. Pomponius Malchio, taking the name of the patron C. Pomponius but adding his personal Punic name as a *cognomen*. Another agreement made a century later by the town of Gurza shows considerable progress in the Romanization of names. The signatories were Herennius Maximus Rustici f. and Sempronius Quartus

Iafis f. But though Roman names are used, they are used incorrectly. There are no *praenomina*; filiation is indicated by father's *cognomen*; and Iafis is an African name.

By the end of the first century AD, many Africans, and particularly those occupying the highest local offices or recruited into the administration of the empire, had the *tria nomina* in proper form. A study of Africans, who became equestrian officers, provides many examples: L. Julius Crassus from Thugga; C. Augidius Maximus from Cirta; and M. Sempronius Liberalis from Acholla, for example. At the other end of the scale were those who retained single African names, such as Baric, Mattan, Melek or Zebag, even in inscriptions, though these might sometimes be transcribed into Greek or Latin. Baric, for example, could become Baricio or Bariciolus; Melek Malchius or Malchio; Zebag Zabacius.

Most Roman African names came somewhere between these two poles; they were a blend of African and Roman names, either inserting Roman names into the Punic/Libyan formula of single name plus patronymic or bringing native elements into the Roman formula. The former was very common. Of 65 members of a youth militia from Mactar, according to a list dating from AD 88, only two had names not in patronymic style. This form could be more or less Latinized; it could involve single or dual names; and filiation could extend to the grandfather. So Masac Alurusae f., Candidus Balsamonis f., and Crescens Sullae were all single names in the "son of" style. Balsillec Imilconis Tituris f. and Nahanius Saturninus Januari f. were sons with dual names, whose fathers had single names.

If the Roman formula were adopted, there were often significant omissions and peculiarities. Although the *tria nomina* predominated over the first two and a half centuries AD, the *praenomen* was fairly often absent. Mention of the tribe was rare, and filiation was misplaced or took unorthodox forms. "Native" *gentilicia* are found alongside the usual imperial or patronal ones. They were most often formed by adding -*ius* to the father's or the grandfather's name, and were being used as a form of patronymic. One inscription makes this very obvious. It is for "Tossunia Saturnina Tossunis fil., where the Tossunia and Tossunis fil (ia) are clearly synonymous".[15]

Most significant was the treatment of the *cognomen*. As neglect of the *praenomen* indicated, the *cognomen* was the main personal name in Africa. It was therefore used in the filiation very often rather than the *praenomen*, even where the father had this. So Maximus son of L. Volusius Saturninus was designated as L. Volusius Saturnini f. Maximus, where the proper Roman form would have been L. Volusius L. f. Maximus. As we have seen, too, the *cognomen* was frequently African, for example M. Furius Mamonicus; Q. Julius Baliaho; and ethnic names were used: Africanus, Maurus, Numidianus. Even when they were in good Latin, moreover, *cognomina* in Africa were often distinctive. Religious theophoric names were common. These included the very popular Saturninus, linked originally to the cult of Saturn but then becoming a Latinization of the Carthaginian Baal. It was almost certainly used as a substitute for Punic names such as Abdbaal, Ammatbaal and Baalsillac, which meant servants of Baal or those dedicated to the god. Also common were names conveying the notion of dedication more generally: Datus, Donatus, Optatus; names of good augury: Faustus, Felix, Fortunatus; and names conveying the idea that the birth of a child had been wished or prayed for: Donosa, Precarius, Votivus. It has been noted that this indicates a contrasting attitude towards naming on the part of the Romans and the Africans. While Roman *cognomina* originated in physical or moral traits or remarkable events in a person's history or that of his ancestors, African *cognomina* express "an individual relationship with a divinity chosen as a privileged protector. Africans charge the name with a religious and moral aura and also give it the quality of an omen."[16] As Bénabou concludes, "the Latin name penetrated Africa without a doubt, but it did not succeed in eliminating the traditional native name nor did it eclipse the spirit of native nomenclature."[17]

There was also a class differential in the process of cultural assimilation represented by names. In the first place, as always only a minority could afford or were inclined to follow the Roman custom of having their names inscribed on monuments. And then there were great contrasts within this minority.

> The municipal magistrates, aediles, quaestors, duumvirs, the priests of the official religion, and the richest citizens of each town generally bore the *tria nomina* in proper form . . . The little people, on the other hand, those whose names were inscribed, not on public buildings, or at the base of statues or on mausolea, but on modest tombstones and on humble votive columns, small landowners, farmers, share-croppers, workers in the fields and in the towns, these people were far less inclined to take the socially ambitious step of choosing a string of foreign names for themselves or for their children.[18]

Given the African attitude to names, they may also have seen breaking with traditional names as a potentially dangerous course. It was among this group that native names were preserved, or where Latin forms were adopted in the hybrid styles that we have discussed.

Bénabou also detects another phenomenon. After an initial eagerness to become Roman by changing one's name, there was sometimes a reaction in a later generation and a reversion within a family to African names. Once Roman names became normal among the élite, they tended to lose some of their prestige. The social structure, moreover, with a tiny group at the top of society, itself absorbed in part into a wider imperial élite, meant that there was a continuous process of upward movement, a progressive Romanization of new aspiring strata, whose attitude towards their nomenclature differed. Once sure of Roman status over more than one generation, too, families could perhaps afford to be more relaxed, to admit African names without fear of losing that status.

Romanization thus had a miscellaneous impact on and via names. For much of the population native names must have survived in native forms and languages. For the rest a degree of Romanization of names occurred. Some adopted full and proper Roman names, but commonest perhaps was taking a Roman or Roman-style *gentilicium* with or without a *praenomen* together with a *cognomen* that preserved a native personal name, suitably Latinized. *Gentilicia* were borrowed, but they were also invented, again by Latinizing native names. Dictionaries yield some most un-Roman-sounding examples: Bapsenna, Fumusilleaticus, Congonnetius, Miogmius, Pompuleddius, Zazgius, Zmertuccius. Roman homonyms could be assumed, like Seneca for the Celtic Senaca. Names could be translated or transliterated. The native patronymic form could be obtruded into the Roman formula.

Within the Roman system, there were provincial preferences for particular names or name forms. We have seen that there was an African vogue for theophoric names, often in adjectival form, while Spaniards "fancied animal names like Lupus or Taurus".[19] Provincial usage frequently differed from that of Rome, mainly through stress on the *cognomen* rather than the *praenomen* – a preference which prevailed – and through attachment to the patronymic which distorted or excluded the Roman filiation. Provincials also showed a lack of concern for or perhaps defective knowledge of proper forms. The Spartans, for example, in the second century AD "observed no rigid rule in the recording of proper names in the published lists of magistrates", and private documents were even more irregular. Only in very important situations, as when a statue was set up by the State to honour a citizen, was care taken to observe the correct Roman form.[20]

Some have seen this process in terms of more or less resistance to Romanization. Clearly people were attached very often to their old nomenclature and what it stood for in terms of family, religion, perhaps ethnic identity. But at the same time members of the élites especially were anxious to become Roman and to accede to the advantages and prestige which this brought. Becoming Roman was symbolized by adopting a Roman name. However, the operation of acquiring new names and of general assimilation was bound to be patchy, uneven and incomplete, and like all culture contacts it was a two-way process. Rome had achieved hegemony over Italy and then the Hellenistic world and beyond, but in so doing Rome had become Italianized, Hellenized and then provincialized. Once again here nomenclature is paradigmatic. As Rome expanded and its system of naming spread over the empire, that system itself was fundamentally changed.

CHAPTER FOUR

Late Roman names

The typical names of the late Roman Empire were very different from those of the Republican period or the early Empire. The classical *tria nomina* broke up, and naming moved in two opposite directions. Much of the population came to have a single name, the old *cognomen*, sometimes supplemented by new additional names. Members of the old aristocracy by contrast developed long strings of names, which proclaimed their ancestry. Both groups used new kinds of names with new meanings and forms.

The emergence of the single name

We have seen that the *praenomen* lost ground from the time of the early Empire. In Lyon, for example, all names on inscriptions had the *praenomen* until AD 70; between 70 and 140 15 per cent had no *praenomen*; between 140 and 250 over 50 per cent; and by the start of the fourth century over two-thirds. In Africa similarly, the *praenomen* declined significantly. By the fourth century, it was very rare anywhere, even among those exercising power. Less than a fifth of the prefects of Rome after Constantine had a *praenomen*. Of the consuls, Eastern and Western, between 260 and 400 only 11 per cent had a traditional abbreviated *praenomen*, and a further 16 per cent the first name Fl. for Flavius, which was really a *gentilicium*. Between 400 and 527 only one consul had a traditional *praenomen*, though over half were called Fl. The *praenomen* did survive among the old Western nobility, but even among them it had become "exceptionally rare" by the fifth century.[1] Q. Aurelius Memmius Symmachus, consul in 485, was very unusual. The decline is reflected in changes in terminology and style. In the fourth century, the *gentilicium* was often called the *praenomen*, which it had actually become, while the *cognomen* was called the *nomen*,

47

which it effectively was. Traditional *praenomina* like Gaius or Marcus were used as *cognomina*, and where an abbreviated first name did continue to be used, it was the ubiquitous Fl., deriving originally from the enfranchisements made under the Flavian emperors.

The significance of the *gentilicium* also changed. In Lyon again by the late third century, a growing proportion of the élite had *gentilicia* that were not borrowed from those of Italian families but invented instead from *cognomina*, for example Firmius from Fermus, Vitalius from Vitalis. Le Glay sees this as the sign of a "social mutation", the weakening of the old Latin oligarchy of colonists and their entourage and the rise of new native strata.[2] Developments in the newer provinces were even more radical. For new citizens, as we have noted, the *gentilicium* was not a personal or even a family name. The universalization of citizenship after the Edict of Caracalla meant that thousands of individuals had the same imperial *nomina*. Among Christian inscriptions and taking *gentilicia* that appear more than twenty times, 51 per cent of persons shared eight such names, and of these nearly half were called Aurelius. These very common *gentilicia* were abbreviated and then later dropped or transformed into personal names. Former imperial *gentilicia* were still extremely common in the late third and fourth centuries but as single names or new-style *praenomina*. Flavius, Aurelius and Claudius were the three most common names, together with derivatives such as Aurelianus and Claudianus. Flavius retained its position as the most common name in the fifth century, but the others had declined considerably.

By the end of the fourth century, the *gentilicium* as such had become almost extinct among the mass of the population. Where it was retained, this was because it had some meaning in terms of status. No longer needed to proclaim a person's citizenship, it could still mark social distance or indicate membership of an important family. Some of the epitaphs in the Generosa cemetery outside Rome dating from the fourth century are in the form *gentilicium* plus *cognomen* in contrast to the mass in single name form. It has been suggested that the *gentilicium* was used here by a small group of "respectable" families to distingish themselves from "a miserable population of slaves and workers".[3] Magistrates and members of the élite in Italy still used the dual name at this time, and it was rarely omitted from official documents.

The attachment of aristocrats to the *gentilicium* was a direct reflection of their claim to high status based on ancestry. So in fourth-century Italy, the Anicii, the Ceionii, the Petronii and so on carefully preserved their family names. The *gens* in effect still had a tenuous existence for such people and was directly referred to by writers such as Claudian and Ausonius. However, even in this milieu, the old *gentilicium* lost its clear position as the middle name and thus its saliency. Some great families placed it first. In other cases its position seems to have been random. Three brothers belonging to the *gens* Decia held the consulship in the 480s. Their names were Fl.

Caecina Decius Maximus Basilius Junior; Decius Marius Venantius Basilius; and Caecina Mavortius Basilius Decius. The *gentilicium* had become one among many names, conveying old family. By the fifth century, it was optional "even on important public documents".[4]

All of this meant that for most people the *cognomen* had become the significant and increasingly the sole name. The progress of the single name can be seen all over the empire. Among Christian inscriptions in Rome itself, just over half the names were in single form before the pax or official recognition of Christianity in 313. Over the next century, the proportion of single names rose to 90 per cent, and in the fifth and sixth centuries to over 95 per cent. In the provinces single names are found earlier than in Italy, though dual names held on in some places surprisingly late. In Gaul at the time of the pax, the dual form still predominated. In Africa single-name epitaphs are found from the first century, but at Caesarea Mauretania all names on funeral inscriptions were in dual form down to 590.

The evidence of the names of holders of high office is very telling. Among consuls from the late third and fourth centuries (AD 260–400), 5 to 10 per cent had a single name; but among those from the fifth century (395–527), the figure is 35 per cent. The figures for prefects of the city of Rome over the same period rise from 13 per cent to 38 per cent. Of praetorian prefects in the fourth century, 32 per cent had single names; in the fifth century 49 per cent of praetorian prefects for Italy and Africa, 67 per cent of those for Gaul, 76 per cent of those for the Eastern provinces, and 82 per cent of those for Illyria. Single names were much more prevalent among the military leadership and in the east rather than the West. Already in the late third century 72 per cent of military commanders in the West had single names, while 83 per cent of military commanders in the East had single names in the fourth century (284–395). The proportion of governors and proconsuls in the West with single names in the late third and fourth centuries ranged from 21 per cent in Italy to 26 per cent in Africa; those in the East from 42 per cent in Thrace and Macedonia to 77 per cent in Syria and Cyprus. Among prefects of the city of Constantinople, 84 per cent had single names in the fourth century, and 91 per cent in the fifth.[5]

Those with single names ranged across the social and political spectrum. They included the early Christians mentioned in Acts and with whom greetings are exchanged by St Paul in his letters to those occupying the highest offices of state in the last centuries of the Empire. Though more prevalent in the East and among those of humble origin, the single name was by no means confined there. Aginatius, vicar of Rome 368–70, for example, was of noble family. Of the 32 professors of Bordeaux referred to by Ausonius in the fourth century, 24 had single names, and all were addressed by single names in his poems.

There were important changes, too, in the style and incidence of these single names. The *cognomina*, of which old Roman families had been so proud, disappear from epitaphs in Rome itself from the fourth century onwards. But many of the once servile or low-status *cognomina* dating back to the Republic, such as Faustus, Felix, Hilarus and Maximus, retained their popularity. Increasing emphasis on the *cognomen* as an individual and individualizing name led to a proliferation of names in this category. The municipal "album" of Timgad in North Africa, dating from the late fourth century, contains around 200 names, none of which was borne by more than three people. One way of diversifying *cognomina* was to add a range of suffixes. The old suffix *-ianus*, originally denoting adoption or manumission, remained important in the fourth and fifth centuries, but a great range of other suffixes was introduced alongside it: *-antius, -entius, -osus, -inus, -illus*, and so on, each with feminine equivalents. Secundus, for example, gave rise to Secundianus, Secundinus, Secundina, Secundio, Secundius, Secundosa, Secundula and Secundilla; Ursus to around twenty such derivatives. Such names were propagated in part via the habit of giving children suffixed variants of their parents' names.

Apart from these names derived from other names, there was a huge repertoire of new names taken from a great variety of sources. They included names of animals and plants (Leo, Lupus; Amaranthus, Floris); of rivers, seas and places (Marinus, Jordanis, Tuscula); of months and times of the year (Decembrina, October); of moral qualities (Benignus, Casta, Sophia); of corporal qualities (Crispinus, Formosus, Longina); from astronomy (Phoebe, Lucifer). Especially characteristic of the period were religious names: names, often dedicatory, relating to the gods; theophoric names like Theodotus and Theodosius; and names expressing religious ideas like Anastasius (resurrection) or Irene (peace). It is clear, too, that names were still being more officially conferred that were in origin personal nicknames. Ausonius relates that his grandmother acquired her name Maura from her dark complexion, while an aunt "gained the [male] *cognomen* Hilarus in the cradle, because, bright and cheerful, you were the very picture of a boy".[6]

However, while "some of the population sought after originality"[7] in these different ways, others stuck to old favourites and some names were used again and again. We have seen that Flavius, Aurelius and Claudius were very common in the third and fourth centuries, as were Maximus, Julianus, Severus, Theodorus and Rufinus. Again, in the fifth century, there was a clear group of very common names, including, in order of popularity, Flavius, Ioannes, Theodorus, Felix, Eusebius, and Maximus.

All this has been seen as part of a levelling-down process, reflecting general changes in social structure. The old status indicators built into the *tria nomina* and filiation became obsolete. Official controls over nomenclature, practicable when the numbers involved were small, were inevitably relaxed. More significant was the persistence and influence of non-Roman forms of naming in the provinces.

Status, ancestry and polyonomy

There was a crucial divergence between the evolution of names of the lower orders and relative outsiders and that of members of the traditional aristocracies and those who imitated their style. While the former usually had only one name, or at most two, the latter had an accumulation of names (polyonomy), of which one might be used in everyday contexts.

Late Roman society retained two features which had always been present to a greater or lesser degree: an obsession with status and rank, and limited upward mobility. These were not conflicting but complementary. So in the late fourth century, the Theodosian Code elaborated a rigid social hierarchy at the same time as "spectacular promotions" actually occurred "from son of a bath-attendant [or] . . . son of a sausage-maker to consul . . . ; from manual worker to praetorian prefect".[8] As citizenship had become nearly universal, so new distinctions had been introduced, notably between "honestiores" and "humiliores". The *honestiores* "comprised the top three privileged groups (or orders), senators, equestrians and decurions, and all legionaries of whatever rank".[9] The relative standing of the different orders varied from period to period but their collective hegemony remained, and the prestige of the old nobility was never really eclipsed, especially in the West. There indeed the political power of the senatorial aristocracy was revived from the fourth century. High positions tended to be monopolized by a few great families with a strong group ethos underpinned by intermarriage.

Belonging to these élites was signalled via their names but in ways that differed from the classical system. A few men retained the *praenomen*. More commonly, certain names were exclusive or nearly exclusive to particular families. Paulus was used as a *praenomen* or *cognomen* by the Fabii or those alleging connection with them; Gallus and Cerealis were *cognomina* of the Neratii; and Auchenius and Nicomachus of the Anicii – all old Roman families. Such names were also claims to ancient ancestry. In a poem addressed to Acilius Glabrio Junior, Ausonius referred to "Glabrio a name drawn from a line of famous forbears",[10] and the family could trace its descent back to a "consul of 191 BC, victor over King Antiochus III of Syria".[11] Many such links with great names from the Republican past were spurious, but the fact that they were used to earn status is very significant.

However, the main distinguishing feature of the nomenclature of the late Roman élites was polyonomy. This development must be related to others, which we have discussed: the disappearance of specific status indicators in the name, and the relative lapse of the *gentilicium*. To these should be added the end of filiation in the old manner. Filiation, which occurs in 70 per cent of Republican inscriptions, rapidly declined under the Empire and was very rare in the fourth and fifth centuries. Behind all this lay a new emphasis in the tracing of descent. The stress on patriliny represented by the *gentilicium* gave way to a more selective and inclusive system using both lines. Taking names from the mother's side, where they were prestigious or perhaps linked to material inheritance, was not new, but systematically combining names from the mother's and the father's side was. Taken to extremes, such a policy led to accumulation. A person's full formal designation was a declaration of his or her family tree, a collection of prestigious names.

Examples of polyonomy can be found from the late first and second centuries in Italy. Indeed the longest name found on an inscription, comprising 38 elements, belonged to a consul of 169. But such names, usually considerably shorter, are most common in the late third and fourth centuries, for example, Amnius Manius Caesonius Nicomachus Anicius Paulinus Junior Honorius, prefect of Rome in 334; or M. Maecius Memmius Furius Baburius Ceacilianus Placidus, consul in 343. Polyonomy also spread to the provinces. L. Silius Plautius Amicus Haterianus Gavilianus Proximus and T. Fl. Umbrius Antistius Saturninus Fortunatianus were African senators of the third and fourth centuries. Women also accumulated names, for example, L. Septimia Pataviniana Balbilla Tyria Nepotilla Odaenathiana, of senatorial rank and descended from the third-century kings of Palmyra. By the fifth and early sixth centuries, such names were rarer, though still found among the Roman and Gallo-Roman aristocracy and the entourage of some Eastern Emperors.

In some cases the ancestry contained in the polyonomous name can be detailed. Amnius Manius Caesonius Nicomachus Anicius Paulinus Junior Honorius took Amnius and the *gentilicium* Anicius from his father and agnates. Paulinus was also a patrilineal name, a *cognomen* belonging to the African proconsul who was his grandfather or great-grandfather. Nicomachus, too, derived from the paternal side, but Caesonius was the distinguished *gentilicium* of his mother's family and Manius one of their *cognomina*. Q. Fl. Maesius Cornelius Egnatius Severus Lollianus Mavortius, a fourth-century praetor, took Cornelius and Severus from his mother's relatives, but all his other names from his father, prefect of Rome in 342 and consul in 355. Both Maesius and Egnatius were derived from consular families further back in the male line, while Lollianus was probably acquired in the female line. Cornelius suggests links with the Scipiones.

In composing these sets of names, different principles of selection seem to have been employed. Sometimes names of relatives were incorporated wholesale, for example, C. Antius A. Julius Quadratus, consul in 105; or L. Pompeius Vopiscus C. Arruntius Catellius Celer. Sometimes choice was more deliberately restricted. Ausonius wrote that "some people like names taken from the outside; but we (in our family) like names taken from the main family tree, not from cognates either but from the male line".[12] As we have seen, many Roman aristocratic families carefully preserved the *gentilicium*, against the general trend, and handed it on from generation to generation. Acilius was borne by members of that family, male and female, consistently from the first century to the fifth. Transmission of the *cognomen* in the male line was also common in the same milieu. Paulinus, with one deviation to Paulinianus, occurred in five generations of the Anicii from the mid third century. Among the Ceionii Rufii, Albinus or Albina occurs in five generations again from Ceionius Rufius Albinus, consul in 335, to Caecina Decius Aginatius Albinus, prefect of Rome in 414. Sabinus and Volusianus were also hereditary *cognomina* in the same family. There seem to be two patterns in the inheritance of names here, though neither was strictly adhered to. Either the name follows from father to son, often the eldest, or it jumps a generation. Among the Turcii, Apronianus and Secundus alternated in the late third and fourth centuries, though the names were also given occasionally in successive generations. Transmission of names from fathers to sons and from grandfathers to grandsons was also a more general phenomenon, as one might expect.

Among the polyonomous élite, variation of the transmitted name was also quite common, a grandfather's Probus becoming Probinus, Probianus, etc.. This was sometimes an indication that the name belonged to an adoptive parent, for adoption was another source of name accumulation. People also added to their own names those of "well-known persons in whose wills they had figured".[13] This reflected the custom of leaving minor legacies to a wide circle of friends, a kind of post-mortem gift exchange.

A problem in writing about these persons with such lengthy names is how to refer to them briefly and how to avoid mixing them up. It is one that contemporaries shared and devised ways of solving. Polyonymous individuals might be given all their names on some inscriptions, but on most and more generally in practice their names would be shortened. Fl. Anicius Probus Faustus Junior Niger, consul in 490, is called variously Anicius Probus Faustus, Probus Faustus, Fl. Faustus Junior, Fl. Faustus, Faustus Niger and simply Faustus in documents. Many other examples could be cited. Use of the single name for a person with many names was in fact quite common, reflecting the general fashion for single names as well as convenience. In a lengthy account of his proconsulship in Africa in 366–7, the historian Ammianus Marcellinus refers constantly to Hymetius, and we only know from other sources that the person concerned had the full name Julius Festus Hymetius.

But which name was chosen as the significant single name? Which was the so-called "diacritical" name? We have seen that sets of names were not composed according to any strict rules, though once a person had a set the order was adhered to, for example when they were shortened. Although we have referred to *praenomina*, *gentilicia* and *cognomina* in the context of polyonymy, in many ways these terms no longer fitted. The early-fifth-century grammarian Pompeius declared indeed: "You would have been laughed at, if you had asked a man which of his names was his *cognomen*."[14] The general rule seems to be that the last name was the significant name, though this was not always the case, and it was usually a personal and not a family name. The uncertainty means that medieval and later scholars have made mistakes here. The writer whom we call Macrobius was Macrobius Ambrosius Theodosius, known for short in his own time as Theodosius. Similarly Flavius Magnus Aurelius Cassiodorus Senator was called Senator by his contemporaries and not Cassiodorus.

There has been little or no attempt to study women's names in the late imperial period. As always the overwhelming emphasis in the sources is on males. Among the most popular names taken from comprehensive collections for the fifth century, only one out of 55 names is female: Maria; and it figures at the bottom of the list for frequency. It is possible to make a few observations, however. First, the formal distinction between male and female names, characteristic of the Republic and early Empire, tended to disappear with the lapse of the *praenomen* and the *gentilicium*'s loss of prominence. Women have names of varying length depending on their status much like men. Some upper-class women have large accumulations of names, as we have seen. Many have three, like Faltonia Betitia Proba, the Christian poet of the mid fourth century; or Munatia Abita Susanna, a child who died aged five in 391. More common of course were dual names or single names, as with men. Women still bore the *gentilicia* of their fathers, though there seems to have been no absolute rule about this. Some had two *gentilicia*; some had none – again like men. For women as for men the *cognomen* had become the significant name, and seems to have been bestowed in much the same way, either as a name in the family, like Proba, or as a more particular name with religious or other significance, like Susanna or the nicknames given to Ausonius' aunt and grandmother. Wives did not normally take husbands' names – Faltonia Betitia Proba was married, for example, to Clodius Celsinus Adelphius – but adding the husband's name to the wife's is found: Liguria Procilla quae et Albucia was married to C. Albucius Menippus. More generally, women had become more important as transmitters of names. We have seen that this was the case among the polyonomous élites, but the practice of inheriting names from mother and father seems to have been more widespread, though never predominant. Where the *cognomen* was taken from the mother, this was in some sense to balance the paternal *gentilicium*. So, from Gaul, Flavius Maximinus was the son of Flavius Mascellus and Maximinia Marsa; M. Justinius Marcellus of M. Justinius Secundinus and Primania Marcellina.

As other marks of status disappeared, titles received new emphasis in the later Empire. The full names of leading people included titles appropriate to their rank, for example, C. Matrinius Aurelius Antoninus vir perfectissimus from Hispellum around 335, a higher equestrian civil servant; or Macrobius Ambrosius Theodosius vir clarissimus et inlustris, the fifth-century author with both senatorial and equestrian titles. While these old titles continued in use, new ones were introduced. *Amplissimus* appears in the second century for those who had been consuls. This was often combined with *consularis* or *vir consularis*, which became a title in its own right for those of consular status (provincial governors, etc.) From the early third century *vir consularis* began to replace *vir clarissimus* for ex-consuls. It seems that the old title "was no longer felt to be elevated enough, and a more glorious epithet was sought in order to distinguish former consuls and those of equivalent status from mere senators".[15]

A similar process occurred in the other orders. Among equestrians, *vir perfectissimus*, reserved at first for the highest grades and offices, spread further and lower down the administrative hierarchy. A new title was therefore introduced at the top. *Vir egregius* was used from the time of Marcus Aurelius for procurators with a salary of 200,000 sesterces. This in turn came to be more widely used, at first alongside *vir perfectissimus* but then, from the third century, instead of it. While *clarissimus* applied to all members of a senator's family, equestrian titles were strictly individual. To compensate for this, *honesta* began to be used for wives of equestrians from the third century onwards, for example Ancharia Luperca honesta matrona, the wife of Laberius Gallus primus pilus (chief centurion) egregius vir. Later the title *honestus* was used by local municipal aristocrats, men and women, to be inflated further to *honestissimus* in the fourth century. A range of other titles is found in late inscriptions: *spectabilis, devotissimus, laudabilis*, etc. There was a similar inflation in the imperial titles. *Dominus Noster*, generally used from the third century onwards, stressed the emperor's absolute authority, while designations such as *Rector orbis, Restitutor generis humani, Aeternitas Augusti* and *Perpetuitas* proclaimed his divine status.

Pflaum saw the proliferation of titles as a sign of "a solidification of the social structure" and the closing off of avenues of social ascension.[16] It seems rather that, while mapping the hierarchy more meticulously and reinforcing it, they precisely allowed for mobility within it and the introduction of new recruits to the élite. Titles also reflected the increased importance of the bureaucracy as such and of the court that provided and sanctioned them.

Office and occupation also continued to figure with names on inscriptions. Those of important people were like entries in *Who's Who*, listing all posts held or at least the most prestigious. The humbler would record or have recorded their profession: *magister, scholasticus, ortolanus, tinctor.*

Supernomina

Further elements were sometimes added to names in the later Roman empire, elements that scholars have called *supernomina*. They were of two kinds. First was the *agnomen* or added name, which began to appear in Latin inscriptions in the second century. The first dated example from Rome is C. Julius C.1. Ephesius qui et Mascutius in 136. The "qui/quae et" is a direct translation of the Greek expression "o/e kai" as bilingual inscriptions confirm. Other forms in Latin were "qui vocatur", "qui dicetur", "qui appelatus" or "sive", all meaning "also known as". *Agnomina* were especially common in Rome, Campania, the Balkans, Africa and Egypt, that is in areas of Greek influence and settlement. They are also characteristic of freedmen, as the first example suggests, and of soldiers.

Kajanto has investigated the types of *agnomina* and the circumstances in which they were acquired. They were often nicknames, differing from the regular nomenclature in their informality, and/or late additions to a person's names. Here the name might refer to place of origin or ethnicity, for example T. Claudio Niceroti qui et Asiaticus. Then there were pet names, found especially on epitaphs for children, for example: C. Julius Alexio Vitulus sive Alexandrus, aged six from Lyon, where the pet form was actually one of the *cognomina*. A Christian African inscription read: "Because of my manners I earned the name of Mater but otherwise I was only called Damula, also Inbidiosa".[17] One of these *agnomina* was a nickname, the other bestowed at birth. Names given at birth were often grandiose ones, like Alexander or Scipio. *Agnomina* could also be inherited like other name elements. Volusia Longina quae et Dionysiodora was the daughter of Dionysiodorus Longinus; Candidia sive Martinia Dignilla of C. Candidius Martinus. Wives could take *agnomina* from their husbands, as we have seen.

New citizens, whether freedmen or free provincials, could also adopt *agnomina*, either to preserve old native names or to show off their new Roman status. So we have, from Africa, Sempronia Peculiaris quae et Anpamilla, and Q. Lollio Satunino qui et Bicchari; or, from Aquileia, C. Julius Epictetus qui et Fato. In many of these cases the *agnomen* was little different from the *cognomen* or the *gentilicium*, "and it often depended upon individual choice whether or not a connecting expression like 'qui et' was used".[18]

But the use of the *agnomen* is also linked to the Greek and Eastern custom of employing extra or alternative names, which became a means of accommodating both Roman and native names. From the New Testament, for example, we have "Joseph, who was known as Barsabbas, and who bore the added name Justus", who was put forward to replace Judas as one of the Twelve or "Simeon called Niger", a teacher at Antioch.[19] By the fourth and fifth centuries, the *agnomen* seems to have become mainly an alternative non-Latin name, for example Eusebius qui et Pittacas, an orator from Emesa in 354; or Theodotus qui et Colocynthius (pumpkin-man), who was prefect of Constantinople in 522–3. But for the last, all these are relatively humble people and all are from the Eastern half of the Empire.

The second kind of additional name was the *signum*. This was either attached to the other names with the connecting term *signum*; or it appeared on inscriptions as a detached name. While *agnomina* seem to have been an Eastern tradition brought "to the West with slaves, immigrants and soldiers, *signa* were a genuinely Latin innovation".[20] Attached *signa* began to appear in the late second century, becoming more common later. Like *agnomina*, they were often nicknames: for example, Delmatius signe, prisco denomine Laetus, or Delmatius, formerly called Laetus; and M. Aur. Sabinus cui fuit et signum Vagulus inter incrementa coequalium sui temporis, or "who was also known as Vagulus among his contemporaries when he was growing up" – Vagulus was a pejorative name meaning vacillating. *Signa* could also be names of good augury, given to babies at birth or added to their names if they died in infancy, though the two categories are difficult in practice to distinguish. So C. Martus Valerius qui et Viventius vana signo cognominatus, on the epitaph of a child of six, indicated that "he had been called Viventius in addition to his regular names", in the hope that his life would be long but "in vain".

The detached *signum* appeared on inscriptions at around the same time as the attached one. On epitaphs the detached *signum* was usually in the vocative case and might be an epithet coined for the gravestone, for example, Telephi Dulciti, O sweet Telephus, a kind of special death name. By far the most common detached *signum* of this kind is Gregori, meaning "to be awake" and expressing "a wish for life after death".[21]

Like *agnomina*, *signa* were mainly used by the lower classes. However, they were found also among the Roman aristocracy of the fourth and fifth centuries. So we have L. Turcius Apronianus signo Asterius; and Memmius Vitrasius Orfitus signo Honorius, both prefects of Rome in the mid fourth century. Here the *signum* appeared on honorific and votive inscriptions. It appears to have been a kind of nickname, primarily for informal use. Two other prefects of Rome in the mid fourth century, C. Ceionius Rufius Volusianus signo Lampadius and Q. Flavius Maesius Egnatius Lollianus signo Mavortius, were known as Volusianus and Lollianus in official contexts, but the historian Ammianus called them Lampadius and Mavortius. But sometimes the *signum* achieved more general official currency. Yet another prefect of this time, Lachanius, is known solely by his *signum*.

Presumably, too, the *signum* served to distinguish those with the same or similar names or to provide an everyday name to use for the polyonomous. Valerius Maximus, prefect from 319 to 323, with two common names which he shared with a consul of 327, his father or uncle, could be identified as signo Basilius. But identification cannot always be adduced from the *signum*. L. Turcius Apronianus' *signum* Asterius distinguished him from his father of the same name, but he shared it with a brother, L. Turcius Secundus.

In some cases the *signum* had the same religious significance for members of the highest élite as it did for the lower classes. Ceionius Contucius vir clarissimus, governor of Flaminia and Picenum around 400, and belonging to an old noble family, had the familiar *signum* Gregorius. The emperor Maximian (286–305) attached the religious title Herculius to his names as a *signum*.

Supernomina (like some *cognomina*) provide a welcome insight into nicknames that must have been as common among the Romans as among other peoples. Independent evidence of nicknames is rare, but some exists, mainly for important figures. Emperors had always received nicknames, as we have seen in the case of Caligula. Suetonius also relates that Vespasian was called Mulio (mule driver or dealer) because of his business affairs; and that the soldiers called Tiberius Claudius Nero, Biberius Caldius Mero (drunkard who drinks warm wine or wine with no water added).[22] This tradition continued in the later Empire. Courtiers called Constans (337–50) Capella (the goat – because of his goatee beard), or Loquax talpa (the loquacious mole), or Purpurata simia (the monkey raised to the purple). Romulus Augustus (475–6) was known as Augustulus or little Augustus, because of his youth; while Anastasius, emperor in the East (491–518), was called Dicorus from the fact that one of his eyes "was black and the other blue".[23]

Officials were given nicknames too. Meletius, bishop in the Pontic province in the third century, was known as the Mellifluous, according to Eusebius, a pun on his name as well as referring to his oratorical skills. Strategius, Eastern praetorian prefect (354–8), received the nickname Musonianus from Constantine, a tribute to his literary talent. These were laudatory, but names bestowed by the populace were more likely to be pejorative. In the second century in *The Golden Ass*, Apuleius has an old woman say to a miller's wife: "You know Barbarus, don't you? decurion of our city, whom the people call Scorpio because of his cutting manner?"[24]

We should also mention the habit of using shortened versions of names or hypocoristics. We have seen that suffixes, often diminutive, were very common in late Roman names. Abbreviations of names in everyday use must also have been usual. Some idea of this usage may be gleaned from the New Testament. St Paul "uses the formal names Silvanus and Prisca, but Luke always speaks of Silas and Priscilla".[25] Similarly St Paul uses Epaphrus to the Colossians who knew him but the full Epaphroditus to the Philippians who did not.

Names of Christians

Older scholars liked to think that once Christianity began to win adherents in the Roman empire, it must have had a great impact on nomenclature. The abandonment of filiation and status indicators, the advance of the single name, were attributed to Christian egalitarianism, other-worldliness and humility. Surely too Christians must have wished to repudiate names associated with hated paganism and to take new names that reflected their special religious beliefs? The evidence does not support this view.

A special category of insulting or humiliating name was particularly linked here with being a Christian. These were names such as Calumniosus (insolent),

Exitiosus (pernicious), Injuriosus (acting unjustly), Projectus (cast out, contemptible), and Stercorius (excremental). Of these Projectus and Stercorius were by far the most common. These names were not exclusively Christian, however, and, if they are found more often on Christian than on pagan inscriptions, this simply reflects the fact that they are "late" names which were in general more Christian than pagan, given the progress of the former and the decline of the latter religion. Exitiosus came into use so late that it is only found in Christian material. Some writers have suggested that Projectus and Stercorius were names given to abandoned children, but the grounds for this are slight. It seems more likely either that all these humiliating names began life as uncomplimentary nicknames like the old Republican *cognomina*, or that they were protective names aimed at diverting evil influences away from children.

More generally, there was no properly Christian nomenclature anywhere before the fourth century. Christians named in the New Testament have ordinary Jewish, Greek or Latin names, and the early Church seems to have been "indifferent about the names of the faithful, leaving them to conform to received custom". In the cemeteries of Rome itself Christians are rarely distinguished by their names until well after the pax. It was not thought appropriate to change one's name on conversion or at baptism. Baptism never implies a change of name in the New Testament or for many centuries afterwards. Even the clergy hardly ever had specifically Christian names at this time. All the bishops of Rome down to the start of the fourth century except three had standard Roman names. Most telling is the use of the names of pagan gods by Christians. Apollos, Apollinaris, Cupido, Jovianus, Mercurius, Saturninus, Venus: "all of Olympia is found in Christian nomenclature".[26] Even bishops found no incongruity here. There were third-century bishops called Dionysius at Alexandria, Rome and Paris. The list of bishops of Antioch included Eros, Hero and Asclepiades.

Only gradually did the situation change and a Christian nomenclature become established from the mid fourth century, but even this was largely a development of existing practice. A few converts had changed their names before this time. St Cyprian, a third-century bishop of Carthage, is supposed to have taken the name Caecilius "from a feeling of gratitude to the person who had converted him",[27] though the name is an old Republican *gentilicium*. Eusebius was a friend and disciple of Pamphilus and added his name to his own after the latter was martyred in 309. "The first example of a 'spiritual name' taken at baptism is provided by St Ignatius of Antioch (in the first century), who chose the name Theodorus"[28] but this also was not a specifically Christian name and the story may be legendary. The first firm examples of adults adopting new Christian names at baptism date from the sixth and seventh centuries. However, it seems very likely that, with the introduction of infant baptism from the third century onwards, some Christian parents did associate the ritual with the conferring of a name on their child that had some religious significance. There is indirect evidence too that some adult converts did assume extra or alternative religious names. These are people who had double *cognomina* or *agnomina* with one name being pagan and the other Christian: for example, Lixinia Aeliodorus Adeodata, Alfinia Narcissa signo Martyri, Optatina Reticia sive Pascasia. It is significant that these are the names of women, for Christian nomenclature seems generally to have become established among women before men.

Christian names fall into a number of categories, the largest being that of theophoric names. As we have seen, such names were very popular among pagans. These were either dedicatory, "derived from the name of the deity with a suffix and bringing out the idea of a human being belonging to, or supposed to enjoy the protection of the deity",[29] for example, Apollonius or Saturninus; or they made direct use of the name of the deity, like Hermes or Mercurius. Christians continued pagan practice here and took over some of "the existing theophoric names like Theodorus, Theodosius and Theodotus, linking them with their own God".[30] But most Christian names in this category were new and they were exclusively of the dedicatory type. Most contained the name of God (Deus, Theos) in sentence form: Adeodatus/-a, Deogratias, Deusdedit, Quodvultdeus, Theodulus. These names express an idea also found on inscriptions in the form "servus Dei" or "ancilla Dei", servant of God. One of the commonest *cognomina* in the inscriptions of Rome is Cyriacus or Cyriace, meaning "belonging to the Lord (Kyrios)". Also common are names derived from the Latin equivalent Dominus, for example Dominicus, Domna, Domnula, though these are not exclusively Christian.

The second category is that of names deriving from significant religious times. Pagans had been named after days and months; so again Christians were following precedent. Some Christian date names, moreover, were direct borrowings from pagan names. Natalis and Epiphanius/-a were pagan names, and the Christian festivals to which they were later related do not predate the late fourth century. The most common and most obviously Christian name in this category is Pasc(h)asius/-a. It was given primarily to children born at the appropriate time, as an epitaph for a child dying in 463 indicates: "Pascasius with the name Severus born during the Easter period". Sabbatius was also used, probably "a Jewish legacy".[31]

The third category comprises "names expressive of Christian ideas".[32] Here again a Christian meaning could be given to pagan names, "Felix evoking hoped-for beatitude, Victor the victory over sin, Vitalis eternal life and so on".[33] The most important of these names was Anastasius/-a, derived from the Greek term for the resurrection of the dead, "anastasis". Originally a Jewish name, it became an exclusively Christian one. A group of names implied the idea of redemption: Redemptus, Renatus, Renovatus and Reparatus. Only the last two were mainly Christian. Similarly Refrigerius/-a, a name expressing the wish that a child will "enjoy heavenly bliss", was a pagan name, adopted by Christians. Agape had been used as a pagan name but took on a Christian connotation; Agapetus and Agapius were also used. Innocentius/-a was also a mainly Christian name.

Fourth are Biblical names and the names of saints. This was the only category to be mentioned or explained by the Fathers of the Church. According to Eusebius, Bishop Dionysius of Alexandria referred in the third century to the adoption of the names of the Apostles by early Christians, mentioning John, Paul and Peter in particular. The reasons given for the practice were "love, admiration and esteem" and the "wish to be loved by the Lord" in the same way as one's namesakes had been.[34] Old Testament names were very rare. The only one that was at all common was Susanna, who was seen as "a symbol of the soul saved from the machinations of Satan".[35] Among New Testament names, in addition to those cited, only Maria and Nazarius were important, and only the last was exclusively Christian. Ioannes or Iohannes "was employed in the East from the Apostolic Age", but was rare in the West until the end of the fourth century.[36] The names of martyrs were used from the mid fourth century, but only a few became really popular: Agnes, Hippolytus/-a and Laurentius/-a in the West; Cosmas, Damian, George and Thekla in the East; and Cyprianus, Perpetua and Mercurius in Africa. Martyrius/-a had some currency. As some of these examples show, martyrdom could change a pagan into a Christian name. "The cult of the protomartyr, introduced in the fifth century, completely Christianized Stephanus."[37] Saints' names became increasingly important from the fifth century, tending to oust the other categories.

We should also mention quasi-titles or religious status terms given to Christians on their gravestones. These included reference to the status of neophyte: Naeophyta in Cristo. Benedictus was also often used to indicate either a neophyte or a full church member. It was added to epitaphs as a kind of *signum*, sometimes abbreviated to BD. Ranks within the Church might also be given: Lector, Diaconis, Acolythus, Sacerdos, Episcopus, Virgo Sancta or Sacra. Though found from the fourth century, these mostly belong to the fifth and sixth centuries.

By the end of the Roman Empire, names that were specifically Christian never made up more than 10 to 15 per cent of the total names in any place. There were also significant variations in the incidence of Christian names generally and of particular types, which must be related to the size, saliency and religious life of local churches. Christian names, for example, were generally more common in Carthage than in Rome, and theophoric names predominated there, while Biblical ones did in Rome. Theophoric pagan names were popular in Africa, we have seen, and Christians there presumably adopted this preference from their cultural environment. But most of the Christian names used in Carthage were also exclusively Christian, which suggests by contrast that Christians there formed more of a distinct community than they did in Rome, where names were more open.

PART II

The Middle Ages

CHAPTER FIVE

Germanic names

The Roman Empire came to an end in the West in 476. The mainly Germanic tribes, who set up kingdoms in its place, had often been clients of Rome, and they progressively adopted the ways of their more "advanced" former patrons. They became Christian; they maintained some form of centralized government, though this was more obvious in Italy than in Gaul.

Latin survived as the language of the Church and by extension in most parts of Western Europe for many centuries as the language of administration and documentation. Inscriptions did not immediately cease, but they do gradually disappear, and historians have to rely on other written sources: charters recording grants or exchanges of property, estate surveys, tax registers, lists drawn up for religious purposes. Such documentation is very sparse before the eleventh century.

Although, in the medium or long term, historians now play down the disruption involved in the fall of the Roman Empire, disruption there certainly was in the short to medium term, especially in Gaul. There was often a brutal exchange of power, and confiscation of property. There was also a revolution in nomenclature. We have seen that the single name had become predominant in the late Roman Empire. Here there was no change, but that single name came to be Germanic rather than Latin.

Latin to Germanic names

Germanic names existed in Gaul before the fall of the Roman Empire, but they were rare. Immigrants adopted Roman names; natives were Romanized Celts. However, after the "great invasions" of the fifth century, the situation changed fairly quickly and dramatically, although the numbers of invaders, Burgundians, Visigoths, and Franks, did not exceed around 200,000 by most recent estimates. About a quarter of names on monuments dating from the late fifth to the late sixth century were Germanic, not Latin, as were 12 per cent of signatures to the acts of ecclesiastical councils. Some estimates put the proportion of Germanic names at the end of the sixth century at half, and by the ninth century it was Latin names that had become exceptional.

But there were geographical and "class" variations to this pattern of onomastic revolution. Latin names survived better in the southern half of Gaul and especially Aquitaine and Provence, where there were fewer Germanic settlers and where Roman culture was more deep-seated. In the Toulouse region, Greek and Latin names still formed 27 per cent of the total in the seventh and 20 per cent in the eighth century, and before the tenth century in Gascony as a whole the commonest names (Aner, Donatus, Forto, Garcia and so on) were all Latin in origin. In neighbouring Catalonia, names on Christian inscriptions were mainly Greco-Latin from the fourth through to the eighth century, and in judicial documents of the early ninth century, there were still two or three times as many Latin as Germanic names. It was not until the tenth century that Latin names seriously declined, and even then they still showed considerable vitality.

The clerical élite seems to have been especially attached to Latin names, and the best-documented names in Gaul are those of bishops. They also reflect the geographical pattern. Germanic names appeared earliest, as one might expect, in the north and east. Metz had a bishop called Gunsolinus, a hybrid name, and Tongres, one called Monulfus, before 500. In most dioceses in these regions, Germanic names became definitive in the course of the seventh century, and Latin names rarely persisted beyond 650. At Reims, for example, we have Flavius (c.535), Mappinus, and then Egidius, deposed in 590 – all Latin; then Romulfus (hybrid), Sonnatius (Latin); then, from around 640, all Germanic names: Leudegisilus, Angelbertus, and so on, except for Abel in the mid eighth century. In the centre and west, Latin names came to an end in over half the dioceses in the course of the sixth century, and in the rest in the seventh. At Angers, for example, the run of purely Latin names ends with Albinus and Domitianus around 570. Then there is about a century of mixed names, some hybrid, some Latin, some Germanic. Lupus, with a Latin name, was succeeded around 700 by Aiglibertus, and all his successors had Germanic names except Benedictus around 815. In some cases, here and elsewhere, the transition came more quickly. For example, at Le Mans, Principius, Innocentius, Domnolus around 570–80, are followed by Batechisilus, Bertechramnus, and so on – a run of Latin by a run of Germanic names.

Latin names persisted longer among bishops in the south-west: in two-thirds of dioceses into the seventh century, but in a few cases into the late eighth and even ninth centuries. The situation is much the same in Provence and the south-east generally. Gap had bishops named Donadeus and Symphorianus in the eighth century, for example; Carpentras had Licerius in the late seventh and Amatus in the late eighth century; while the first Germanic names appear in the list for Arles only in the early ninth century with Notho and Rotlandus. In general in this region, German names only became definitive from the eighth and ninth centuries.[1]

The nomenclature of the secular élites seems to have followed a similar pattern, though the evidence is more slender. The genealogy composed at the end of the eleventh century in Limoges of Carissima, a woman living in the seventh century, contained 45 names over ten generations, all Gallo-Roman. Over half the Merovingian counts had Latin names. And in the tenth century, several "aristocratic families in Provence . . . still boasted of their Roman or Gallic descent, and still gave almost exclusively Roman names to their children . . . though in Provençal forms, such as Pons, Honorat, Maïeul and Amelius."[2] There was also some traffic the other way. Until the late ninth century, the Frankish counts of Toulouse had Frankish names; then they began to use the Latin-derived name Pons "as though the taking of an illustrious Gallo-Roman name by a Frankish family might enhance their influence in a region where the prestige of things Roman never disappeared".[3]

Among the peasantry, the switch to Germanic names was definitive much earlier, though we find the same discrepancy between north and south. In a seventh-century list of dependents of the important monastery of Saint-Martin at Tours, 90 per cent of names were Germanic, and the same proportion is found among the serfs of Saint-Germain-des-Prés around Paris, in Abbot Irminon's famous *Polyptique* of about 800. But in a comparable survey of the serfs on the estates of the abbey of Saint-Victor at Marseille a little later over half the names were of Latin or Greek origin.

Several features of this remarkable change suggest that it represented a real and rapid assimilation of the invaders and their amalgamation with the Gallo-Roman population, though things moved more gradually in the south. This in turn indicates cultural continuity across the divide of the Dark Ages. Gallo-Romans would tend to be those who stuck with Latin names, while the invaders bore Germanic ones. Ethnic indicators added to names in early Frankish documents support this. Among mayors of the palace in the early seventh century, listed in Fredegar's *Chronicle*, we find, for example, Claudius genere Romanus and Bertoaldus genere Francus. But Romans also adopted Germanic names and vice versa, and there are mixtures of names within families. Gregory of Tours' maternal uncle, a man of senatorial class, was called Gundulfus, a common Germanic name. The Austrasian duke Lupus, with a Latin name, had two sons, Johannes, whose name was Latin by adoption, and Romulfus whose name was Germanic. Nor was this pattern confined to the élite, at least in later centuries. Among the serfs of Saint-Germain-des-Prés we find parents called Petrus and Scupilia with children called Agembaldus and Agembalda; or, the other way about, parents called Aclcharius and Girberga with children called Stadius and Benedictus. There are also people with alternative names, one Latin and one Germanic.

Another indicator of fusion was the development of hybrid names. All names were given Latin endings in the documents, and they were even given Latin declensions. But beyond this "a fairly important part of Gallo-Frankish nomenclature was made up of names created by the Romance population in imitation of names imported into Gaul by the barbarians".[4] Most commonly, the first part of a popular Latin name was given a Germanic second part. For example, on the analogy of Christianus or Christophorus, one has Christohildis or Christomerus.

The same process of adopting Germanic names occurred in Italy, but there the victory of Germanic names was neither so rapid nor so complete as in Gaul. This is hardly surprising, given the fact that Italy was the home of the Latin language and that Germanic (Ostrogothic, then Lombard) settlement was more limited there. Only five Germanic names occur on Roman monuments between 476 and 589, and only one among signatures to the acts of ecclesiastical councils over the same period. At Ravenna, then capital of Italy, over half the names recorded over the period 445 to 650 were Latin and the proportion did not decline over this time. Gothic names accounted for only 10 per cent of the total, the rest being Greek or Biblical. At Rimini, the proportion of Latin names fell from 51 per cent to 43 per cent between the late seventh and mid tenth centuries, while that of Germanic names rose from 14 per cent to 25 per cent. The pattern is similar elsewhere, for example in Latium and at Piacenza.

One also finds in Italy the same growing mismatch between ethnicity and name that existed in Gaul. At Ravenna in the sixth century, Gothic names were reserved to Goths, but by the mid tenth century the choice of name was independent of ethnicity and influenced more by fashion. Within families, too, names might be heterogeneous, while in Ravenna and elsewhere there was much coining of hybrid forms. Germanic suffixes were added to Roman roots (Cristopertus, Forteramnus), or vice versa (Baldemia, Hrodemia, or Aimerianus for the son or descendant of Haimerich).

Though Germanic names did eventually become predominant, Latin names were never entirely displaced in Italy, some surviving without a break down to the Renaissance period and beyond. In Latium in the twelfth and thirteenth centuries, for example, one finds Nero, Sallustius, Jugurtha and Tiberius. Even far from the ancient capital, in the Canavese, it is not difficult to discover classical Latin names in the eleventh and twelfth centuries or later: Aurelius, Augustus, Balbus. Serra's studies provide a host of examples of the continuity of whole names like these, but also of word elements and suffixes (-entius, -inianus, -issima, etc.), and of what he calls "semantic frameworks".[5] In the last category, he cites opprobrious names given to protect children, such as Nontevoluit (Ravenna, 1197), or Maloncontro (Lucca, 1156); or the related names of good augury, like Benati, Bonaguro and Orobona. He also notes the persistence of Latin names referring to birth circumstances (hour, day, month, season, religious feast). The names of the pagan gods were hére preserved as names of the days or months: for example, Martius and Venerius. Though the Latin naming system was dislocated, Latin names also continued to show some creativity. New names were invented, like Ambra, Anima, Gemma and Rosignolus; and old names were given new forms, like Crescebonus and Crescimbene from Crescens.

What was the role of Christianity in this survival of Latin names? It is certainly the case that some Greco-Latin names did have a Christian resonance, and particularly those, often of Greek origin, which referred to abstract qualities or religious ideas; and those related to thé cults of saints. Among surviving names in Northern Italy in the first category are Anastasius, Benedictus, Desiderius, Gratus and Peregrinus. Some of these names came to be associated with saints and martyrs, as did other kinds of names. Names of the old pagan gods even entered the Christian repertoire by this route, for example Mercurius, Flora, Victoria, Diana, all saints of the early Church. At the same time, the names of Biblical saints, many of them Greco-Roman, became increasingly popular. But this leaves many names, probably most, which were simply traditional and had no Christian meaning. As we have seen, classical Roman names were retained, and people were named after cities (Siviglia, Parma), after abstract qualities as such (Concordia, Felicitas); and after flora and fauna (Rosa, Liliosus; Agnus, Falco, Leo).

Lazard's case-study of Ravenna in the tenth century attempts to settle the issue on a less impressionistic basis than older accounts. She places Latin names in three categories: traditional Latin names like Magnus or Romanus; clearly Christian names (names of apostles and theophoric names); and classical names which had become the names of saints, like Vitalis or Laurentius. She decided that if a name in this third class was already popular in the sixth century, then it was essentially classical and secular; but, if not, then it had probably been adopted under Christian influence. On this basis, she concluded that between 56 per cent and 70 per cent of Latin names were "Christian" and survived for that reason, leaving at least a sixth that were just Latin names, perhaps reflecting an attachment to the Roman past.[6] This is probably, however, to make distinctions that are too hard and fast, and to make assumptions about the meaning of names and naming that are not valid. Latin names could be preserved for traditional, mainly family, reasons, and many names may have proved popular precisely because they were both Latin (secular) *and* Christian.

A similar situation seems to have existed in southern Gaul. Some names borne by the serfs of Saint-Victor at Marseille in the ninth century and later were not borne by any saint prior to the eighth century, for example, Aprilis, Aquilo, Expectada. About 30 per cent of Latin names fell into this category. Bergh concludes that "not all the Graeco-Latin names . . . owe their survival to Christianity; the persistence of a profane tradition of Latin onomastics in Provence . . . is indubitable".[7] Most Latin names surviving in Catalonia into the tenth century and beyond – Abundius, Cristianus, Felix, for example

– are Christian in tone, but this may be misleading. As in Italy, Christian and classical or pagan names were inextricably mixed. There were bishops in Gaul called Claudius or Aurelius in the seventh century and later, and some of the sainted founders and early administrators of sees had names derived from pagan gods, like St Saturninus of Toulouse and St Dionysius of Paris.

Earlier historians sometimes imagined that they could trace the path and pace of the Germanic invasions and the settlements which followed them via the personal names enshrined in place-names. Even in Northern Gaul, place-names are taken from Roman personal names. So Antony, near Paris, was Antoniacus, or the place of Antonius (using a Romanized Celtic suffix); Orly was Aureliacum; Crépy-en-Valois was Crispiacum after Crispus. Later, places were named after people with Germanic names, most often with the suffixes "*villa*" or "*ville*", meaning village, or "*curtis*" or "*court*", meaning estate. So Ajoncourt (now in the Moselle) was Agnaldi curtis in 777, or Aginald's estate; Roubille (now in the Oise) was Radulfi villa around 1200, or Radulf's village. The switch from Latin to Germanic personal names is significant here, though one should note the use of the place-name elements in Latin, another hybridization. It is also clear that most of the personal names involved in such place-names were not original founders of settlements but subsequent owners. The late date at which many of them are first recorded is a pointer here. The names belong to the élite and not to the peasantry, and they are not a guide to the pattern of early settlement.

The Germanic name system

The Germanic name system was very different from the classic Roman one. A person had a single individual name. In the earliest times, it seems, this name was indeed individual, which means that, as with the ancient Greeks and Hebrews, names were not repeated and there was an enormous variety of them. Germanic languages spoke not "of giving a name but of creating one".[8] Of Gothic names recorded from the fourth century only a tiny number belonged to more than one person, and at Ravenna in the sixth century, the proportion of names to persons was still roughly one to one.

Names fell into two categories. Most were in compound form or dithematic, that is they were composed of two name elements. A minority were not compounded, but many of these were shortened versions of compounded names. There was a restricted or closed range of elements used to make names. These were selected from the normal vocabulary and to some extent retained their meaning. Specific elements were used to indicate gender and, more ambiguously, status. Though names were individual, various features were employed to indicate attachment to family or kindred. These were alliteration, passing on of the name elements, and later repetition of names. All of this will become clearer if we look in more detail at naming among two Germanic peoples: the Franks and the Anglo-Saxons.

The Franks

The Franks established independent kingdoms in Northern Gaul from the later fifth century. They annexed the Visigothic kingdom of Aquitaine in 507 and took over control of Provence in the 530s, but few Franks settled in Southern Gaul, as we have seen. In the eighth century, under Charles Martel, Pepin and then Charlemagne, they greatly extended their power beyond Gaul into western Germany and Italy, founding the Carolingian Empire. This relatively sophisticated and centralized political structure lasted until the end of the tenth century.

Early recorded Frankish names are mainly dithematic. First elements included: *Adal-* (noble); *Am-* or *Amal-* (active); *Bald-* (bold); *Bert-* (bright); *Child-* (fight); *Chlod-* (celebrated); *Sigi-* (victory); and *Theud-* (folk). Second elements included: *-ger* (lance); *-man* (man); *-mund* (protection); *-ric* (powerful); and *-sind* (road). Many elements could serve in either first or second position. Typical Frankish names, combining these elements, are those of the first royal kindred, the Merovingians, for example Childebert, Childeric, Chlodobert, Theudebald and Theuderic. The same kinds of dithematic name are found much later among the serfs of Saint-Germain-des-Prés: Adalbert, Adalsind, Amalric, Baldebert, Sigemund. Some elements were especially common and figure in large numbers in distinct names. Morlet, for example, lists 40 male and 33 female names with *Adal-* as their first element; 34 male and 29 female with *Child-* or *Hild-*; and 31 male and 15 female with *Sigi-*.[9] Similar concentrations are found of popular second elements. Among the serfs of Saint-Germain, there were 52 distinct names ending in *-ric*, 65 in *-hard*, and 104 in *-bert*.

By the ninth century, if not before, uncompounded names had become much more common in the sources. These were often short versions of the dithematic names, starting life perhaps as pet names: Adda, Adzo and Atto from *Adal-* names; Berta or Berto from *Bert-* names, and so on. The second element could also provide the short name. Gregory of Tours mentions an inhabitant of Saintes called Chardegysil, "who had the alternative name Gyso".[10] Syllables or consonants of the longer name could be doubled. So one has Gundegisil, Count of Saintes, who was called Dodo, *Gunde-* giving Dedo, then Dodo. Similarly, the archbishop of Rouen, Ardoin, who died in 683, was also called Dido. Names in *Sigi-* provided Siggo. Such names could be further altered by adding suffixes, sometimes Latinized. So Berto or Bert- names could give Bertilo, Bernico, Bertinus, etc. All kinds of such hypocoristic forms are found in the ninth-century polyptiques and other later documents. Among the serfs of Saint-Germain were Abbo, Boso, Ello, Ringo, Tonto, to name but a few. Place-name evidence provides many more such names, for example: Arpo, Batto, Bekko, Bippo, Dozo, Faffo, Gibbo, Scatto, Swifo, Tatto, Wizzo. Some of these may well have been independent simple names or may have become so.

71

Gender was always and status could be indicated by the form of the name. For female names the suffix -*a* was often added to a male second element: Sigibranda/Sigibrand. But there were also a number of specifically female second elements, for example: -*burg* (fortress, protection); -*gard* (dwelling-place); -*gund* (combat); -*hild* (combat); -*lind* (gentle); -*swind* or -*swinda* (strength); and -*trud* (power). It will be noted that, while some of these elements refer to what might be regarded as feminine qualties, others belong to the same warrior idiom as the male elements. They clearly suit the forceful and often quarrelsome and bloodthirsty queens and princesses who appear in the pages of Gregory of Tours: Berthegund, the daughter of Ingitrude, who despoiled the convent at Tours, of which she had once been, though married, the abbess; Fredegund, the wife of King Chilperic, who had a succession of relatives tortured and killed; her great rival, Brunhild; or Clothild, the daughter of King Charibert, who led a revolt in another convent at Poitiers. But names in the same style are also commonplace later among the serfs of Saint-Germain.

There is some evidence that dithematic names were originally reserved for those of high status. They are generally more common earlier on than uncompounded names because names of serfs are not then available; but, where the proportion of dithematic to simple names can be measured from a fair sample, that proportion decreases over time. In the Toulouse region, for example, dithematic names rose from 9 per cent of the total in the sixth century to 50 per cent in the seventh and between 60 and 70 per cent in the eighth to tenth centuries, suggesting the levelling-down of an élite custom. What is more, certain name elements were restricted to important and especially royal kindreds. *Chlod-*, for example, was a special mark of the Merovingian kings, 23 members of the royal house bearing names with this element. Chlodovech (Clovis) evolved through Chlodovius and to Hluodovicus to the medieval and modern royal Looys or Louis.

This shows, too, that shared name elements were signs of family solidarity and common descent. King Theuderic I in the early fifth century had a son Theudebert, who in turn had a son, Theudebald. King Guntram, who died at the end of the sixth century, had a brother called Gunthar and a son called Gundobad. His other children were Chlothar, Chlodomer and Chlotild, named after Guntram's own father Chlothar. The first element in Guntram's name and that of his brother derived from their mother Ingund. Taking elements from the mother's name was, however, rare at this time, especially among the royalty, and there was no clear rule for the transmission of name elements. The same use of name elements is found later in the polyptiques. Among the serfs of Saint-Victor, for example, Wiliberta, Roobertus, Ingilbertus, Maganbertus and Isinbertus were all children of Maurobertus; Rigomaris and Gomaris were the sons of Tudomaris. There are also many cases of children's names composed of elements taken from each parent, reflecting the cognatic and nuclear nature of the serf family in contrast to the patrilineal royal kindreds. On the estates of Saint-Germain, Teutberta was the daughter of Teudulfus and Ercanberta; Erboardus the son of Frodoardus and Erbedildis.

Repetition of ancestral names had been an important mode of family identification for the Merovingians early on. Between the fifth and eighth centuries, Childebert and Theudebert were used three times, Childeric and Chlodovech four times, and Chlothar and Theuderic five times. Later, repetition of names became much more common. Morlet provides many examples of Frankish names, of which over 25 instances are preserved in the sources. Some were very much more popular. There are 38 instances of Leutgardis; 58 of Chrodobertus; and 80 of Charibertus. Among the serfs of Saint-Germain, 14 names belonged to more than 25 persons each, though none reached 40 attributions.

Family transmission was at work here, but the end-result was a departure from the tradition of individual names. This is related to another development. Like other Germanic names, Frankish names were single: each person had only one. But, from the sixth century onwards, there is evidence that some people had additional or by-names. Gregory of Tours relates that a certain Sigibert was known as "the Lame because in a fight against the Alamanni, he was wounded in the knee so that he limped". This is what we would call a nickname. Others had short names taken from their full names, as we have seen; and a few others seem to have had distinct alternative names. Queen Austrechild, third wife of Guntram, was "also known as Bobilla"; "a citizen of Tours, Wastrimund, was also named Tatto"; and another Guntram was called Guntram Boso.[11] As the last example shows, as names came to be repeated and some names to be quite popular, then second names became necessary to distinguish those with the same name or homonyms. At this stage, it should be stressed, this was only a minor phenomenon.

The name elements used to compose dithematic names were either nouns or adjectives, originally with lexical meaning. They were characteristically words evoking and celebrating excellence and especially prowess in battle. The meaning of the names was presumably at first transparent, and the names had a descriptive, but more an augurative, function. The Latin writer Fortunatus addressed a poem around 570 to a Merovingian king: "O powerful Chilperic, the name you bear could be translated as 'vigorous helper' ['powerful protector' would be more accurate]. It is not in vain that your parents named you thus: it was the annunciation of your glory; it was at the moment of your birth the indication of what you would become one day; and the words spoken then have been justified since by your merit."[12] As D'Arbois de Jubainville notes, this already indicates a certain veil between the name and its meaning, and he suggests that names increasingly lost their meaning over the course of time, as they were adopted by non-Germans, as they changed their forms, and as they became established as names with their own autonomy. Smaragdus, abbot of Saint-Mihiel, significantly felt the need to supply the meanings of a number of Gothic names in a treatise written at the start of the ninth century. More significantly, he got many of the meanings wrong.

The Anglo-Saxons

Angles, Saxons and Jutes arrived in Britain in the fifth century gradually subduing the Romano-British or driving them to the western fringes. In England, this British substratum is little reflected in the nomenclature of places or persons. Local English kingdoms were established by the sixth century in Wessex, Mercia, Kent, Northumbria and so on. These came under the general supremacy of Mercia in the eighth century and then of Wessex in the ninth century.

The bulk of early recorded Anglo-Saxon names are dithematic or compound. As with the Franks, the compound names were formed of name elements with lexical meaning, for example: *aelf* (elf); *berct* or *beorht* (bright); *ead* or *ed* (riches); *heri* (army, host); *mer* (renowned); *os* (divine power); *sig* (victory); *wald* (to rule, hence ruler); and *wine* (friend, protector or lord). Many of these elements were the same as or similar to those found among other Germanic peoples. They could be combined in a variety of ways, but, while some elements could come first or second in names, others tended to be restricted to one or the other function. Among names recorded by Bede, for example, *Berct-* figures as the first element in five names (Berctfrid, Berctgils, Bercthun, Berctred and Berctwald), but as the second element in sixteen names (including Eadberct, Heriberct, Ricberct and Sigberct). *Ead-* figures as a first element only (Eadbald, Eadberct, Eadgar, etc.), as does *Os-* (Osfrid, Osric, Oswald, etc.). *Wald* appears as a first element in one name, but as the second in twelve. The less common uncompounded or simple names again fall into two categories: shortened versions of compound names, and original short names. Examples of the first are Cutha or Cudda for names in *Cuth-* or *Cud-*; Wulfa for names in *Wulf-*; Beoffa for names in *Beorht-*. Occasionally it can be shown that the same person was known by both the short and the full version of his name, for example, Cutha and Cuthwine in the sixth century; Sicga and Sigefrid as well as Sigehelm in the eighth; and Aelle and Aelfwine in the tenth. The commonest form of such names ended in *-a*, and the final consonant was often doubled: Eadda, Godda, Wuffa. There were also forms in *-i* : Ecgi, Ini, Tidi.

The independent names took the same forms. Some could obviously have been nicknames: Biga (big), Bucca (buck), Horsa (horse); but most seem to have been pet or affectionate names with no particular meaning, for example: Abba, Cissa, Tigga, for men; or Dudde, Tibbe, for women. Only one of these names, Offa, became at all common. Either kind of short name could have a suffix, usually a diminutive: Duddel (from Dudda),

Baldic, Taetica (from Tata), and so on. The suffix *-ing*, originally a term indicating a kin relationship, could also be used to make a pet name, for example, an eleventh-century Exeter monk called Swottinc (from "swot", meaning "sweet").

Anglo-Saxon names of all kinds reflected gender. In compound names, the second element was the gender indicator, and the main female second terms were *-burh, -flaed, -gifu, -hild, -lufu, -swith, -thryth* and *-wynn*. From the *Anglo-Saxon Chronicle*, we may cite Aethelflaed, the sister of King Edward, who died around 920; or Herelutu, abbess of Shaftesbury, and Wulfwynn, abbess of Wareham, who both died in 982. From place-names, Goodwood in Sussex was Godgifu's wood; while Dennington and Alpheaton in Suffolk were Denegifu's and Aelfhild's tun or manor respectively. As these examples show, "male second elements could normally be used as first elements of female names"[13] and, by the same token, female second elements could serve as first elements of male names. It was the placing of the element and not the element itself which conveyed gender. Female short names usually ended in *-e*, while male names ended in *-a* or *-i*, as we have seen. So Dudde, Tate and Tibbe are names of women, and Bibury and Tetbury in Gloucestershire were "burhs" (places of defence or perhaps convents) belonging to Beage and to Tette.

Uncompounded names seem to have been widespread before 700. They are common, for example, in the early parts of the *Anglo-Saxon Chronicle*. "In this year [477]", we learn, "Aelle came to Britain and his three sons Cymen, Wlencing and Cissa . . . In this year [488], Aesc succeeded to the kingdom of Kent . . . In this year [501], Port and his two sons, Bieda and Maegla, came."[14] They became progressively less common in later centuries and they virtually disappear from charters in the first half of the tenth century. The changing frequency of such names is related, it seems, as among the Franks, to their social standing. Later Anglo-Saxon society was hierarchical with specific ranks, whose status was measured by the wergild or compensation that had to be paid for injury or death. Beneath the kings were the nobles, whose wergild in most eighth-century kingdoms was six times that of the free peasants. In the century or so before the Norman Conquest, distinctions were made between higher and lower nobles or thegns, and a class of peasants owing labour services – serfs or virtual serfs – developed. The clergy occupied a special position, and there was a tiny "bourgeois" grouping of merchants and moneyers. In the early period, kings, bishops and members of the élite generally had simple names. In the later period, however, compound names came to be associated with noble and simple names with lower status. The latter were most numerous among moneyers and serfs. Eleventh-century manumissions yield Hwatu, Dudde, Tottel, Tulling, for example; and names of this kind were quite common among Anglo-Saxon names that survived the Conquest – again among serfs. The correlation between status and name appears loose, therefore, rather than strict and does not match the exactness of wergild tariffs, but other factors come into the picture. The Anglo-Saxons also used personal names and their elements to indicate kinship and to proclaim family solidarity and prestige. Certain name elements were preferred by certain important families. The East Anglian royal family, for example, favoured the first elements *Aethel-* (as did those of Kent and Wessex) and *Ead-* (also favoured in Wessex). The second element -*weald* was also characteristic of this house: Raedweald, Eorpweald, Aethelweald.

Names indeed were transmitted across the generations according to the three principles of alliteration, passing on of name element, and repetition of whole names. Alliteration was especially marked among the kings of Essex, all but two of whom reigning between the early sixth century and around 800 had names beginning with S. But there are many other examples. The early Kings of Wessex had names in C, like Cerdic, Ceadda, Coenred, Cuthwine; early Northumbrian kings had names in S. Alliteration was also important among non-royal families. Bede provides the example of Cedd, bishop of the East Saxons from 653, who had three brothers Cynibill, Caelin and Caedda. Alliteration was a feature of Old English poetry and may have served the needs of verse celebrating and perhaps inventing genealogies. Scholars disagree about the last, but there is a good case for seeing alliteration of names as a mnemonic device, a means of tracing real descent.

Passing on of name elements can again be seen in the royal genealogies. Ten of the 21 Essex royal names in S, for example, begin with the element *Sige-*. Among non-royal families, this practice seems to have become progressively more significant. It was relatively unimportant in the eighth and ninth centuries, but by the tenth, around half of recorded names were connected in this way. Generally, name elements were passed from father to children and/or shared by siblings, but in some cases it can be shown that elements were taken from each parent. St Wulfstan, Bishop of Worcester in the eleventh century, "was the son of Aethelstan and Wulfgifu" and his biographer records expressly that he "was given a name composed of the first part of his mother's and the last part of his father's name".[15] Where a couple had a number of children, this principle could not be applied to all of them. In another eleventh-century example, Wulfgyth and Aelfwine had seven children. One was called Aelfgyth, taking one element from each parent; two others were Aelfcytel and Wulfcytel, one taking one element from the father and the other one from the mother; there was a fourth child Kytel, using an element from two siblings' names; and two of the others were paired, though sharing no element with either parents or other siblings: Gode and Godric.

Where transmission of elements was consistently carried out within a family over time, it led to name repetition. Among the Wessex royals, for example, there were three Aelfgifus, four Aethelstans, four Eadgars, and six

Eadweards. In the family of the ealdormen (high royal officials) of Mercia in the tenth century, not only is the first element *Aelf-* repeated, as well as alliterative second elements, but whole names recur. Aelfwine, killed at the Battle of Maldon in 991, shared his whole name with a maternal uncle, while Ealhhelm, ealdorman 940–51, gave his name to a great-grandson.

Transmission of elements and whole names could indicate close ties from father to children or among siblings, but it was not restricted to this function. Woolf repeatedly comments that in the royal genealogies "repetition or variation of names does not indicate closeness of kinship".[16] Cousins or second cousins, great-grandfathers and great-grandchildren could share the same name. Occasionally, it seems that a child was named to replace a deceased relative, but on the whole there were no clear rules about passing names or name elements to particular relatives, say grandfather to eldest grandson or father to son. Instead name association appears to have the effect of linking persons vertically with the ancestors (obvious in the royal genealogies), and with a wide range of fairly distant kin horizontally. Does this mean that there were large kindreds operating as clearly delineated groups?

Those who have investigated this question have reached a largely negative answer. Significant circles of kinsfolk varied from person to person: they were ego-centred. Although there was an emphasis on patrilateral kin and on agnatic descent, most marked among royal and other important families, descent was broadly bilateral, traced through both father and mother. Place-name evidence among other things shows that women could and did inherit land. The nuclear family was important, not least in the ownership and bequeathing of property. Wider kinship terms were limited and sometimes vague, suggesting that such ties were not of major social significance. The strength of other institutions – kingship, lordship, church – militated against the formation or persistence of organized agnatic kindreds. On the other hand, name transmission shows that agnatic ties were very strong. Daughters often inherited name elements from fathers. They belonged to the paternal kindred and remained part of it even after they were married. Obligations to exact blood-vengeance and to pay wergild, the right to receive such support, duties towards orphans, and so on indicate that ties beyond the immediate family should not be ignored. Personal naming customs again suggest a loose but not negligible sense of identity with quite distant relatives.

Place-names indicate that in some cases such groupings resided in particular locations. Charles-Edwards points to the existence of clusters of farms held by agnates in the same area, which might be known by "the name of the kindred whose members owned the farms".[17] Lancaster asserts quite wrongly that there were no names for kin-groups in Anglo-Saxon society; but Bede quite specifically states that members of the East Anglian royal house were known as Wuffingas and of the Kentish royal house as Oiscingas, after their eponymous ancestors Wuffa and Oisc. Such collective names were used to designate places and have been thoroughly studied by Ekwall and Gelling. Examples would be Blickling or Blikelinges in Norfolk, and Lancing or Wlaecingas in Sussex. Nottingham was Snotingeham in Domesday Book or the meadow of Snot's people.[18]

There was little apparent change in the naming practices of the Anglo-Saxons from the time of the migrations down to the ninth century, apart from the increasing popularity of compound names among the élite. But in the tenth century and the first half of the eleventh, changes become evident. A few alien names begin to infiltrate from the Continent. The range of name elements narrows, and certain of them become very common. By dint of repetition, certain names become very frequent, with a consequent depletion of the name stock. In Searle's *Onamasticon*, which has most names from this later period, there are 42 names beginning with A borne by more than ten people and these account for over half the total number of persons with A names. Eleven names in A are borne by more than fifty persons. Among these are 97 Aelfrics, 76 Aethelstans, 72 Aelfsiges, and so on. This is a far cry from the classic individual Germanic name.

This situation probably encouraged the use of secondary or by-names. A few by-names are recorded from the earlier Anglo-Saxon period. In the royal families, we hear, for example, of Aethelburg "otherwise called Tata", a Kentish princess who married King Aedwin of Northumbria in 625;[19] of two other Kentish princesses in the mid seventh century called Eormenburg and Eormenburg Domneva respectively; and of Aethelwold Moll, King of Northumbria in the mid eighth century. Some early non-royal cases can also be found, but on the whole such names are rare before the tenth century. When they do become more frequent it is significant that they are often attached to the commonest existing names: Wulfhere Cydding, a Wiltshire witness (902); Wulfric Spot, the founder of Burton abbey (*c*.990); Wulfnoth Cild (1009); Aelfric Puttoc, Bishop of Worcester (1040). The commonest types of by-names were local names and nicknames. Patronymics are not characteristic of Anglo-Saxon nomenclature, as they are, say, of the Celtic. They figure in the formal royal genealogies in the form Athelberht Uihtreding, Uihtred Ecgberhting, and so on, but were hardly used outside this context. The oldest patronymics added *-ing* to the father's name. A later form employed the word "suna" or son with variants after the father's name: Eadweard Accan sunu; Aelmaer Aelfrices sunu. The term "cild" or child designated the youngest son, the heir where descent was governed by Borough English or ultimogeniture, a custom found in the south of England.

Finally we must return to the meaning of Anglo-Saxon names. Most authorities agree that the names and their elements did have lexical meaning in the earliest times. As with other Germanic name-systems, the elements evoked the warrior virtues in particular and/or good fortune, and very probably had an augurative and magical function. Later on, however, as the names became established as names, and as they were repeated, their original meaning was no longer taken literally. It has been pointed out that some combinations of elements produce names that are nonsensical, like Frithwulf (peace-wolf) or Wigfrith (war-peace). It also seems that the original meaning of names was sometimes not obvious and had to be pointed out by scholars as it does today. In his biography of St Guthlac, written in the mid eighth century, Felix explains the meaning of his subject's name in a way that suggests that it was not common knowledge. Changes in the form of names and their elements over time could also obscure their meanings. Whereas in the tenth century the name *Aethel-* usually appeared as such and was readily identifiable with the adjective "aethele", meaning "noble", by the eleventh century the form *Aegel-* was much more common and forms in *Ael-* had begun to appear, masking any such identification.

Against this, attention has been drawn to the Anglo-Saxon love of etymology, of word-play with names, and of kennings and riddles. A well-known example is provided by the prophecy of Pope Gregory the Great about the conversion of the Anglo-Saxons reported by Bede. Not only did Gregory supposedly associate the name of the Anglian slave boys, whom he saw in Rome (Angli) with angels (angeli), and the province from which they came, Deira, with "de ira" or the wrath of God from which they would be plucked by Christ's mercy, he read the name of their king Aella to say: "Alleluia! the praise of God the Creator must be sounded in those parts".[20] Another well-known but later example is the addition of the epithet "unraed" (no counsel) to the name of King Aethelred II. This could only have been done in a context in which the meaning of his name – "noble counsel" – was obvious.

Redin tried to distinguish here between names that were intelligible to the Anglo-Saxons themselves and ones that were not. But, as Barley argues, this puts things too simply and to some extent begs the question. He takes Lévi-Strauss's contrasting categories of "motivated" and "unmotivated" names, for example Dartmouth (on the mouth of the Dart) and London (no lexical meaning), and refines them. "Lévi-Strauss does not seem to clearly distinguish 'motivated' in the sense of 'formed and assigned by rules' from 'motivated' in the sense of 'reflecting a relationship between *signans* [the signifier or name] and *signatum* [what is signified]'. They may amount to the same thing . . . but . . . not necessarily . . ." Barley introduces a further distinction therefore between "internally" and "externally" motivated names. Internal motivation means following the demands of the naming system; external motivation means means reflecting a link with the outside world.

> The ordinary Anglo-Saxon bithematic names are internally motivated, firstly in that they are formed from a restricted set of elements and in accordance with rules of a regular systematic nature, secondly in that the model to which they conform is structurally isomorphic with the Anglo-Saxon model of kinship.

However, motivation, reference and meaning are all different. The elements "of which the bithematic personal names are formed are linguistically meaningful and were generally intelligible to the Anglo-Saxons that bore them . . . [but the] actual linguistic meaning [of their elements] plays no part in the motivation of the name". The elements are culturally predetermined and are combined in the ways and for the reasons that we have described – to mark status, to trace descent and to express family solidarity. Hence the production of nonsense names. However, in some circumstances, the linguistic meaning of names could be brought into play, as in the cases just cited. Here internally motivated names were being treated as if they were externally motivated, like modern children's nicknames derived from given family names.[21]

Leading names and kinship structure

Names provide important evidence on early medieval family structure on the Continent also. The trail starts with a particular kind of document, from an era when any documents were rare.

Monasteries kept books of remembrance, known as Libri Memoriales or Libri Vitae. They recorded the names of the living and the dead and in the earliest centuries were read out during mass. At first the names were just those of the monks themselves, but then the names of patrons and benefactors, of monks from other monasteries, of visitors were added. It became impracticable to read out all these names, and instead the books were simply left on the altar. The names of those in the books were thus associated with the prayers of the monks and with the spiritual benefits that the latter brought especially after death. It was hoped that the names would also be enrolled in the Liber Vitae or Book of Life referred to in Scripture.

The Libri were mainly found in northern Europe and a few have survived. The oldest date from the eighth and many from the ninth century, and they were added to through the medieval period. They provide valuable compendia of personal names and changes in name style. The Durham book contains over 3,000 names, that of Remiremont over 11,000. But historians have concentrated on the evidence that they provide for the early medieval period and particularly on kinship. The earliest entries are classified by social type – abbots and bishops, monks, kings, dukes and so on – but this was later abandoned as the names grew in numbers. Among the consequent lists of undifferentiated single names, Schmid and other German historians were able to detect patterns. "We find groups of names separated from each other by changes of script and ink", and these groups recur. They also had other things in common. They might be monks from elsewhere formally associated in confraternity with the monastery of the book; they might be guests and pilgrims who arrived together; these or other groups might be linked by kinship and the last "can be recognized from the repetition of name-elements (or names) within the group".[22] These kinship groups, moreover, were large and fluid, overlapping with others, recognizing both matrilineal and patrilineal ties, and their solidarity owed little to any dynastic sense. Their cohesion was often focused on persisting rights over a monastery, a bishopric or a secular public office such as a countship, and they gathered round the occupants of such positions. The kin-groups found in the Libri Memoriales of the monasteries around Lake Constance and of Brescia, for example, are centred around the Salomons, successive bishops of Constance, and the Waldos, bishops of Freising and Cher.

Leading names "are names which occur over and over again in lines of descent either completely, when children are named after their ancestors, or in part, when children receive one half of the Germanic name".[23] We are already familiar with these procedures, and we know that repetition of whole names had generally replaced transmission of name elements by the end of the ninth century. Certain names belonged to particular family groups; they were their "moral property". This is most obvious and probably appeared first in royal families. We have seen that the Merovingians had a reserved repertoire of names. "The Carolingians were so jealous of their dynastic names that one finds absolutely no one bearing them outside their kindred from 780 onwards."[24] The "Robertians" at first restricted Eudes and Robert or Rotbert to their immediate kin. In Germany similarly, Konrad and Heinrich (Chaganric) were borne almost exclusively by the kin and descendants of the Salian kings. The same phenomenon is also found among other leading families. In northern Italy, the so-called Aldobrandeschi centred in Lucca used the names Ilprando, Ildebrando, Eriprando and Rodolfo. The "Bernardinghi", counts of Pavia, used Bernard, Ugo and later Umberto; the "Oberthenghi" Oberto, Adalberto and Berta. Among comital families in Francia or France in the Carolingian period, Baldwin was a leading name of the counts of Flanders; Raginharicus or Renier of those of Hainaut; Teutbaldus or Thibault of those of Toulouse.

The name indicated in effect the kin-group to which an individual belonged, since those outside the group would not and could not use it, and names outside the ancestral repertoire would only be drawn on very exceptionally. An anecdote from the Life of John, Abbot of Gorze, in Lorraine, who died in 977, shows how carefully names for children were chosen.

> Count Teutbert came to the abbot to ask heaven for a son. The abbot promised that the count would have a son but claimed him for the Church, imposing on the child in advance the monastic name of Benedict. When the child was born, therefore, the count took him secretly to Gorze where the abbot baptized and named him. At the end of the mother's confinement, she reminded the

count, her husband, that it was time to christen the child and "to give him a name of his ancestors". When the count confessed that he had already had this done and that the child had been named Benedict on the orders of the abbot, she was upset and lamented "the great insult done thereby to our kindred".[25]

The name "was a kind of programme. One family member would be scheduled for an ecclesiastical career; another might be destined to receive an estate coming from the mother; and in each case a specific name was given to the child".[26] When Charlemagne's first son by Himilfrude, for example, was called Pepin, after his paternal grandfather, and a previous king, this "implied that he was destined to succeed his father as king of the Franks".[27] And where events upset such calculations, names might be changed. A younger son of Hugo the Great had been intended for the Church and had been given the appropriate name Eudes. "When he became Duke of Burgundy in 965 on the premature death of his elder brother Odo, he took instead the name Heinrich or Henricus belonging to the house of Saxony, from which his mother came."[28] This was a more prestigious name and one suited to a secular ruler. Some ancestral names lost their standing and were either discarded by kindreds or could be used as ecclesiastical names or as names for bastards.

Cases of transmission from grandfather to grandson and from father to son can be found in the Carolingian period in France, Germany and Italy, but these patterns were not consistently followed. In the pedigree of the Frankish "Nibelungen", established by Levillain, for example, the leading name Childebrand or Hildebrand goes from paternal grandfather to eldest grandson and then reappears with a great-nephew. Theobertus is the name of the youngest son of the first Nibelung, which is transmitted to an eldest son. Theobertus then disappears but is linked to Theodericus, the name of two nephews. Bernard III, count of Parma and Pavia at the end of the tenth century, took his name from his paternal great-grandfather; his brother Ugo had his paternal grandfather's name. Bernard III's father and his eldest son were called Maginfredo, and Bernard was transmitted to his second son, Bernard IV, who eventually succeeded his brother Maginfredo II as count. Bernard also went to a cousin of Bernard IV and to his second son. Among the counts of Bergamo, there was a neater transmission of Giselberto in alternative generations in the tenth and eleventh centuries. Other leading names, Maginfredo, Arduino and Lanfranco, were used in the intervening generations and for collaterals, some of whom did succeed to the office. There are suggestions, too, that naming after an ancestor was seen as in some way "reviving" that person and that this notion was of particular importance where agnates were concerned. It was said at the end of the tenth century of the Carolingian Arnulf, nominated to the archbishopric of Reims by Hugh Capet, that he had been "endowed with an honourable dignity being the only survivor of the royal line, in order that the paternal name should not be forgotten".[29]

Though patriliny tended to be predominant, matrilineal descent was also important and thus ties via marriage as well as by blood. This has been demonstrated by Duby's and Vercauteren's studies of genealogies from the period. These show that relations by marriage could be given great prominence where they were of higher status than agnates. Marriage with socially superior women was, it seems, an established custom in both France and Germany, and a means by which the nobility renewed itself or expanded. Moreover, in southern Europe especially, men were not infrequently designated by matronymics. In a contract sworn before the court in Catalonia in 1,000, for example, Hug of Cervelló declared himself as the "son of Rechildis", despite the fact that his father, an important person, was a co-witness.[30] Herlihy suggests that this phenomenon, which was most prevalent in the late tenth and early eleventh centuries, reaching maybe 10 per cent of all naming after parents, reflects the importance of women as property holders. Of course, in most parts of Europe, women could inherit estates and frequently did so where there were no male heirs.

Names both reveal and reflect these features of early medieval kindreds. They could be taken from both maternal and paternal lines, depending often on which was regarded as the most important and on lines of property inheritance, and this practice survived into the era of stricter patriliny which followed. For example, "two of the sons of Richard the Justiciar and his wife, who was the daughter of Rodolph I of Burgundy, bore the Welf names Rodolph or Raoul and Hugo. Gisla, wife of Adalbert of Ivrea, introduced the name of Berengar into the family from the house of Friuli."[31]

So far we have considered only male names, whether inherited in the male or female line, but female names were themselves of course significant both as indicators of the status of women and as markers of kin relationships. As we have seen, in the Germanic naming systems, men's and women's names were similar, though they had distinct suffixes, and women could inherit name elements from male relatives, mainly their fathers. Among the Frankish nobility, including the royal house, however, women were named mostly after other women by the ninth century, usually older relatives. In the Carolingian royal family, daughters were named almost exclusively after their father's rather than their mother's kin, and fathers named their daughters after "quite close relatives: their own mothers, paternal (not maternal) grandmothers, sisters, and paternal aunts". Of Charlemagne's legitimate daughters, for example, "the oldest, Adelaide, was named for [after] his sister; the second . . . , Rotrudis, for his paternal grandmother; the third, Bertha, was named for his mother; the fourth, Gisela, was named for another of his sisters; and the fifth, Hildegard, was named for her mother, Charlemagne's wife", that is, four after paternal relatives and one after her mother. "The same pattern was followed by Charlemagne's sons", and by the Capetians later, as well as by the Ottonian kings in Germany.[32] To some extent the practice reflected the superior status of the royal fathers and the early and special emphasis on patriliny in royal houses, but it was also found among Frankish noble families.

At first Bouchard saw this as a sign that kindreds were more patrilinear than Schmid and others supposed, but she later revised her view. Women's names, she realized, migrated from one lineage to another, as women married, and this pattern persisted in the face of strengthened patriliny in the eleventh century. There was a greater willingness in the eleventh and twelfth centuries, moreover, to name daughters after their mothers' relatives. So women's names that began as royal names, like that of Beatrix, the wife of King Robert I of France in the early tenth century, or of Hadwidis, Henry the Fowler's mother, "began to spread through the ducal and comital lineages of France and Germany as Capetian women began to marry" men from that background.[33] It seems that this communication of female names may not have been such a novelty. In unsuccessfully opposing the proposed marriage between the German ruler Henry III and Agnes of Poitou in 1043, Abbot Poppo of Stavelot explained that consanguinity between the two could be traced through recurring female names. "The descent of the genealogy is achieved", he wrote, "through Mathildas and Gerbergas, in such a way that Mathilda, the daughter of Gerberga (with the same name as her grandmother) called her daughter by her mother's name, and she left her own name as an inheritance to her granddaughter."[34]

The appropriation of names was as much a part of the system of leading names as burglary is of the consumer society. The example of William is a case in point. It was used by the counts of Auvergne and dukes of Burgundy in the Carolingian period. The counts of Poitou, later dukes of Aquitaine, seem to have borrowed the name from the counts of Auxerre in the ninth century; and the counts of Provence took it from the dukes of Burgundy. In southern France, it then spread further downwards to the lords of Montpellier in the late tenth century and to the viscounts of Provence in the eleventh. Meanwhile, the name first appeared among the dukes of Normandy with William Longsword, who died in 942. It went on to be one of the commonest names among all classes in the central Middle Ages and after.

Names could travel with brides, as we have seen. They could be simply usurped; but more often a material reason was involved. Dependents were named after patrons or superiors. The "Aimon" family at Montpellier, for example, vassals of the Guillems in the eleventh century, were also called Guillem. Godparenthood may have been a means of transmission in some cases, as it was later. Depoin notes that the French royal names were sometimes given to godsons, but only as a special privilege, and such names could never be handed on. Until the eleventh century, royal names were similarly guarded in Germany, but after that Heinrichs and Konrads proliferated like

Williams. Perhaps alternative policies were being pursued here. On the one hand, keeping the royal names exclusive bolstered the aura that surrounded French kings, as did the rituals of sacred monarchy; on the other, the names were used to percolate royal power and influence through society in a way that parallels the broadcasting of the relics of saints by ecclesiastical authorities.

Names were also used to claim property and office or to reinforce claims to both. "If a particular lordship was held by a man with a particular name, then later claimants might indicate their claim by use of the same name."[35] Genealogies could be "massaged" for this purpose. Such procedures were used to legitimize usurpations at the highest level. Grimoald, son of Pepin of Landen, wanted to substitute his own son for the Merovingian heir to the throne, so he gave him the name of Childebert. Later, when Grimoald's descendants did manage to obtain the Frankish throne, they also took over Merovingian names: Chlodovech (Clovis or Louis) and Chlothar or Lothar.

It was an essential feature of the Germanic systems that individuals had single names. No family names existed and wider kin-groups were indicated by their use of particular single names. Most of the names given to these groupings are therefore "modern constructs"[36] that give a misleading impression of cohesion. A few kindred names were used in early medieval texts, but they characteristically generalize a single ancestral name. So the Frankish royal houses were the Merovingii or Clodovei and the Karoli or the Karolingi; the German royal houses the Welfi or Welfones and the Henrici. A Frankish family with the leading name Agilulf was known as the Agilofinga, and the kindred of the count of Le Mans executed by Charles the Bald in the ninth century were referred to as the Gauzberti. Only with changes in the kinship structure around 1,000 and the advent of feudalism did a different kind of second or family name begin to establish itself.

CHAPTER SIX

Christian names

The advent of Christian names

We have seen that only a small proportion of names were specifically Christian by the end of the Roman Empire, and Christian names continued to be uncommon in the early medieval period, when Latin names were replaced in western Europe by Germanic ones. However, during the central medieval period there was a fairly rapid and progressive Christianization of names, and more and more people were given names of the saints. This process may be followed in more detail by looking at Italy, France and Britain.

In sixth-century Ravenna, only 6 per cent of names were Biblical and only 17 per cent of the population bore them. Most were names of the Apostles, led by Johannes and Petrus. By the tenth century in Ravenna, Christian names were more important. Among the élites, they exceeded all other kinds of non-Christian name (Latin, Greek or Germanic) put together. Again New Testament names stand out and also some theophoric names: Deusdedit and Dominicus; and those of more recent universal saints: Martinus, Gregorius, Leo. The picture is similar for nearby Rimini. Of names recorded between around 700 and around 950, 20 per cent were Biblical, with Johannes, Petrus and Maria the most popular. The story could be repeated with evidence from Latium, Tuscany and the north-west. Only in the tenth century and more so in the eleventh was the predominance of Germanic names ended. And in some regions this development came even later. In Latium, old Latin names retained their vogue till the twelfth century and beyond, while the castellan and knightly classes kept Germanic names. In Genoa in 1150, Guillelmus was by far the commonest name, and only two Christian names figured in the top eight: Johannes and Bonifacius.

The process of "Christianization" of names has been most thoroughly studied for the cities of Tuscany and the north. It involved the adoption of two kinds of names: "mystical" names both augurative and theophoric, and saints' names, of which the former were at first more popular. Auguratives became widespread in the twelfth century, which also saw the introduction of "new" saints' names from Byzantium: Bartholomeus, Jacobus, Matheus, Tommasus and Nicolaus, the last being the only non-apostolic example. In Florence at the end of the thirteenth century, 18 per cent of names were saints' names, led by Jacobus, Johannes, Petrus and Philippus; and 34 per cent were mystical, mainly auguratives. Among the latter, such names as Benvenutus, Donaguida, Dictiguardi, Datus and Donus were popular. They were mainly neo-Latin in form and were implicitly rather than explicitly Christian like their ancient models. In the Florentine *contado* (hinterland), between 1240 and 1280, auguratives were similarly important, though saints' names were less common. In Siena around 1270, auguratives were again paramount; Bonaventura was the commonest male and Benvenuta the commonest female name, and there were a host of others. The most frequent saints' names were Jacobus, Johannes and Pierus, and Maria and Jacobina. Auguratives were less popular outside Tuscany. In a sample of citizens from Cremona in 1283, 43 per cent had saints' and only 11 per cent augurative names. In Milan at about the same time, Jacobus and Petrus were the commonest male names, and the list of ten most popular names contains no augurative. By the end of the fourteenth century, saints' names had made great progress. In Florence, Johannes or Giovanni was well in the lead, and Antonio and Francesco were also very popular. Auguratives had declined, though Domenico was still commonly given to children born on Sunday. In Genoa, seven out of the eight most popular names in 1368 were saints' names, led by Jacobus, Johannes and Nicolaus, and all seven accounted for 40 per cent of all male names. Over the course of the fourteenth century among the élite, the proportion of those with saints' names of all kinds rose from 65 per cent to 80 per cent.

The Christianization of names in Italy and especially the adoption of saints' names was much more marked among men than among women. In Siena in the mid to late thirteenth century Germanic names like Berta and Aldobrandesca were still very popular, together with Latin names, like Fiore, Gemma and Bianca, and auguratives. With the exception of Maria, saints' names were not common. In Perugia similarly in 1285, Germanic historical names were still important, along with names referring to ideal feminine qualities: Bella, Bona and so on. Saints' names were uncommon, and Christian names were mainly represented by auguratives.

Much more information is available for France. Among the peasants of Saint-Martin of Tours in the seventh century, where Greco-Latin names were under 10 per cent, "names drawn from Scripture were absent, except for Peter . . . The Christian names that did appear were theophoric, such as Amadeus, Donatus, or augurative, like Benenatus".[1] Names of local saints were not used. The picture is much the same in the ninth-century polyptiques.

At Saint-Germain-des-Prés, probably less than 10 per cent of persons had Christian names. The commonest category related to dogmas, festivals and rituals, for example Benedictus, Dominicus, Natalis, Deodatus. Biblical names were comparatively rare, with Johannes, Stephanus and Petrus the most common. At Marseille Latin and therefore Christian names were much more frequent, and the pattern was rather different. Mystical names were important, but so were saints' names, accounting for at least 12.5 per cent of persons mentioned. These were mainly New Testament saints or those whose cult was widespread, like St Martin. "The influence of local saints was much weaker or often nil."[2] Old Testament names appeared in all these sources, but they were very rare.

Between the ninth and the twelfth centuries, the proportion of Christian names grew, until it became predominant. For France as a whole over half the male population had Christian names by the mid thirteenth century. The process of Christianization seems to have begun in the south. In the Toulouse region, Christian names became significant in the tenth century, comprising 14 per cent of the total. This rose to 24 per cent in the eleventh century and 27 per cent in the twelfth. The commonest names included Johannes, Petrus and Stefanus. In Poitou, Christian names also advanced after 1000. Only 2–3 per cent of names in charters came from the New Testament at the start of the eleventh century but nearly a quarter by 1200. Petrus became especially popular after 1050, while Johannes and Stephanus were also common again. Mystical names declined, and local saints were unimportant. In Languedoc, the proportion of men's Christian names rose from 10 per cent in 880 to 25 per cent in 1150, with the growth strongest in the half-century each side of 1000. During this time some Germanic names became Christian through being associated with saints, and the stock of names expanded after 1050, but a few names were still predominant and especially Petrus or Peire. Christian names progressed further in the thirteenth and fourteenth centuries, and they were almost exclusively saints' names. By around 1300, over half the names of peasants of the Albigeois were Christian, and by 1400, 53 per cent of men at Rabastens bore Christian names. There is evidence from both Languedoc and elsewhere in the south that the Christianization of women's names lagged considerably behind that of men's. At Albi in 1450 only one-third of women had Christian names compared with 60 per cent of men.

The picture is much the same in northern France, with the process of Christianization being somewhat delayed compared with the south. Constable comments on "the comparatively small number of Christian names"[3] in the Liber Memorialis of Remiremont in Lorraine over the period from the ninth century to the end of the eleventh century. At Gorze, only 16 per cent of names were Christian over the period 1000–1200. In Alsace, Christianization of names did not get under way seriously until the twelfth century, when it occurred "both by introducing Mediterranean names and by Christianizing

Germanic ones".[4] At Metz, however, 57 per cent of men and 58 per cent of women had Christian names by the late thirteenth century. Christian names were unusual in French-speaking Flanders or Wallonia until the mid twelfth century. Even as late as the 1270s, less than one-third of the names and persons in the charters of Saint-Lambert were Christian. In Flemish Flanders, Christian names were virtually unknown before the tenth century and very rare before 1100. However, in Flanders generally Christian names became steadily more common after 1100. New Testament names were by far the commonest, but Old Testament ones are also found, together with some names of saints of the early Church (Laurentius, Eustachius, Agatha, Agnes) and eastern names probably introduced via the Crusades (Georgius, Nicholaus, Margaretha). The names of more recent saints were not generally used. A few French saints like Dionisius, Martinus and Remigius are represented, but more local saints are not, at least not before 1225. In the period 1100–1225, Johannes became one of the most popular names, rivalling the Germanic Heinricius, Walterus and Willelmus.

The Christianization of women's names seems to have begun after that of men both in Alsace-Lorraine and in Flanders and Picardy but then to have overtaken it. Whereas only around 30 per cent of men's names in Flanders were Christian by 1300, 50 per cent of women's were. At Calais at the end of the thirteenth century, 59 per cent of men but 84 per cent of women had a non-Germanic name. By 1260–1360 at Arras, five of the ten commonest male names were Christian, and they accounted for 44 per cent of attributions; the top five women's names were all Christian and they accounted for 59 per cent of attributions. For both men and women, Christian names by this time meant saints' names.

With nuances, we find the same story in Burgundy, Normandy and the Ile-de-France, including Paris. A slight exception is Brittany. Old Testament names were in use here in the early medieval period – to such an extent that Samson, Salomon, Daniel and so on were regarded as Breton names. The "universal" saints' names that prevailed elsewhere came to the region quite late and then spread slowly. Johannes was the first to become popular – from the mid twelfth century – joined by Peter in the second half of the thirteenth century. But the Christianization of names in Brittany was still only beginning around 1330. Among the witnesses to the canonization process of St Yves at that time there were only 10 Christian as against 55 non-Christian names.

The situation in England was rather different from that in Italy and France. First, Christian names were virtually unknown in the Anglo-Saxon period, and, secondly, the late introduction of Christian names was complicated by the circumstances of the Norman Conquest. Christian names came into England along with continental Germanic names.

Searle's *Onamasticon*, which includes names down to Domesday Book, has only 28 Christian names among hundreds of non-Christian. Nine were

New Testament names, seven Old Testament, seven mystical, four names of post-Biblical saints, and one, Biscop, a nickname. Only Benedictus, Biscop, Daniel, Martin and Petrus had five or more attributions. Nearly all these names were borne by clerics. The first local study we have relates to names in Winchester. At the Conquest, the proportion of persons with Biblical, Greek or Latin names was 2.6 per cent. By the start of the twelfth century, it was 9 per cent, by the mid twelfth century 13 per cent and by around 1200 31 per cent. Around 1200, 15–22 per cent of taxpayers listed on the Lay Subsidy rolls across the country had Christian names; by the end of the thirteenth century, the proportion was 24–39 per cent. But this was mainly the result of the great rise in the popularity of John. In several counties, John was the second most popular name by around 1300. Thomas was the second commonest Christian name, with Hugh, Nicholas, Simon, Stephen and Peter appearing some way behind. In contrast to the situation in parts of Italy and France, in England Germanic names were not pushed below 50 per cent of attributions in the thirteenth century. But there was a further advance of Christian names from that time, as a sampling of names of peasants from Holywell-cum-Needingworth from the late thirteenth to the mid fifteenth century illustrates. Forty-one per cent of men and 67 per cent of women then had Christian names, of which the commonest for men were John, Nicholas and Thomas, and for women, Johanna, Margaret and Agnes. By this time, Christian names were almost exclusively saints' names.

The Norman Conquest of England was followed by an extensive and fairly rapid change in personal naming. At first among the élites, then among townspeople, peasants and women, Anglo-Saxon and Scandinavian names were replaced by continental Germanic ones. By the start of the thirteenth century, native names had virtually disappeared. Christian names were among the new names introduced at this time, but their prestige at first in no way matched that of the West Frankish and Norman names of the conquerors.

These of course ousted native holders of office, secular and ecclesiastical. The line of bishops with Anglo-Saxon names, for example, petered out with the appointment in the 1070s and 1080s of William, then Maurice, of London, of Remigius of Dorchester, of Walter of Hereford, and so on. By the start of the second quarter of the twelfth century, only Sigefrith of Chichester remained. The same change of name and personnel affected the great abbeys. At Abingdon, the last abbot with an Anglo-Saxon name was Ethelhelm (1071–83). Aethelnoth, abbot of Glastonbury, was deposed in 1077/8, and Ulfketel, abbot of Crowland, in 1085. They were succeeded by continentals with continental names.

In women's houses, Aelfgyva was the last Anglo-Saxon-named abbess of Barking; she was followed in 1087 by Agnes, Alice and Mary. Abbess Aelfgifu of Romsey was succeeded by Christina, then Athelitz and Matilda; abbess Leofgifu of Shaftesbury in 1066 by Eulalia and then Cicely.[5]

Local studies provide some quantification, especially for towns. Among the tenants of St Paul's cathedral in London by around 1130, 57 per cent had continental names. At King's Lynn in 1166 about half the names of citizens were continental. At Winchester in 1066, native names accounted for 85 per cent of attributions; by around 1110 for 30 per cent and by around 1200 for 5 per cent. In the Thorney Liber Vitae, Anglo-Saxon names were 45 per cent in the immediate post-Conquest period, falling to 26 per cent in the first half of the twelfth century, to 16 per cent in the second half, and to 4 per cent by around 1300. With some delay, the same process affected peasants. The names in pedigrees of those claimed as villeins in a number of Eastern and Midland counties in the early thirteenth century were mainly Norman like those of their lords. In East Anglia, more generally, native English names were 10–20 per cent of total names in the twelfth century, falling to around 2 per cent in the later thirteenth century and to under 2 per cent in the fourteenth. Similar figures are found elsewhere.

There is much evidence that women retained native names later than men and that both peasants and "humbler" townspeople retained them longer than members of the élites, suggesting that the change in naming spread downwards through society. Native names became names of low standing and were thus not passed on to children. Many instances may be cited indeed, in which parents with Anglo-Saxon names gave Anglo-Norman ones to their children.

A few Anglo-Saxon names did retain some popularity into the thirteenth and fourteenth centuries, for example Saemann and Eadmund, Edith and Etheldreda. It is most significant that most of these were the names of saints, and it seems that that was the key to their survival.

Here we should mention a special category of theophoric name found in Ireland and Highland Scotland. "With the introduction of Christianity, a new expression of service was coined from the tonsure practised by the priests. The adjective 'mael' or 'maol', meaning 'bald', was used to denote 'bald one' or servant of a particular saint."[6] Ten such names occur in the Scottish Book of the Deer of around 1100. They include Maol-Brigde (servant of St Bridget), Maol-Colum (St Columba), and Maol-Mori or Maol-Moire (St Mary). Other common names in the medieval period were Maol-Phadraig (St Patrick) and Maol-Micheil (St Michael). Maol was also attached to Jesus in the form Maol-Iosa, later Malise, Mellis or Miles; and Maol-domnaich (servant of the Lord) was a preferred name among the earls of Lennox in the thirteenth century. From the twelfth century, Maol names began to be replaced by ones using Gille or Gil, meaning "servant" or "boy", though this process did not occur in some districts, for example the Western Isles, until much later. Gille names occur in the Book of the Deer, though they are less frequent there than Maol names; examples include Gillebride (St Bridget), Gillendrias (St Andrew), and Gille-Crist. Further Gille names found in the twelfth and thirteenth centuries include: Gillecallum or Gilcolmus (St Columba), which was very common; Gille Fhaolaon (St Fillan); Gillemur or Gille Moire; and Gillis or Gillies from Gille Iosa (Jesus). Gille was used almost exclusively before saints' names, though there are a few exceptions. The commonest was Gilleasbuig or Gillespie (servant of the bishop).

The names of the clergy

Before considering the reasons for the arrival and spread of Christian names in the general population, we should say something about the names of the clergy. Were they perhaps pace-setters? Were boys destined to become clerics given special names? Did they come from pious families who used Christian names precociously? Did they change their names on becoming priests? Though the evidence is largely indirect, the answer to most of these questions is: no.

In the early medieval period, the secular clergy seem on the whole to have had and to have retained the same kinds of names as the laity, and only a few were given or adopted specifically Christian names.

In northern Italy, the archbishops of Ravenna between the late seventh and the late tenth century all had Latin or Greek names, but only seven of the seventeen were clearly Christian and five of these were called Johannes. A little later, among the kindred of the priest Anselmus of Besate, active in the early eleventh century, we find Arnulfus, Archbishop of Milan; Landulfus, Bishop of Brescia; Rotefredus, Archdeacon of Pavia; Mainfredus, Archpriest of Vercelli; Sigfredus, Bishop of Pavia, all with Germanic names, like Anselmus himself; but also two Johannes, Archbishop of Ravenna and Bishop of Lucca, and a monk called Simeon. We have seen that in noble kindreds in Italy and elsewhere in the early medieval period, particular names could be given to those destined for ecclesiastical careers. A few of these were Biblical, like Salomon, borne by three bishops of Constance in the ninth century, but most were Germanic. Some Christian names were, however, mainly reserved to the clergy in this period. For Tuscany before the twelfth century, Brattö mentions Jacobus, Leone and Tommasus.

The picture is much the same for France, though again, information is largely restricted to bishops. Before 1000, Christian names were not at all common among them. Of those listed in Duchesne's *Fastes Episcopaux*, only just over 100 had Christian names. Of these about half had "old" Christian names of the mystical type, for example, Felix (6), Desiderius (4), Eusebius (3), Optatus (2). These are found over the whole period. There were 28 bishops with New Testament names, with Johannes being by far the most popular with 9 attributions, followed by Petrus (4), Stephanus (4) and Paulus (3). Eleven New Testament names in all were in use, and they are mainly found in the sixth and seventh centuries. Twenty-eight bishops had Old Testament names, of which the commonest was Elias or Helias with 5 attributions; others were Jonas, Joseph, Isaac, Samuel and Salomon. Old Testament names were almost exclusive to the late eighth and ninth centuries and were almost certainly related to the Carolingian reform movement of this time.

Little seems to have changed before the twelfth century, even among the most pious. Among the promoters of the Peace of God movement, we find Bishops Guy of Le Puy, Garin of Beauvais, Berold of Soissons and Aymon of Bourges. Among French bishops appointed in the reign of Louis VII (1137–80), 20.5 per cent had Christian names and 79.5 per cent non Christian names. There are significant differences from province to province. Sens has the highest proportion of bishops with Christian names (37.5 per cent), followed by Lyon (33.3 per cent) and Bordeaux (28 per cent). Those with the lowest percentages are Auch and Narbonne (each with 12 per cent) and Rouen with 14 per cent. There seems to be no north–south divide here, though Auch and Narbonne are both in the south-west. Of the Christian names used, 79 per cent were New Testament names; 11 per cent were from the Old Testament; and under 5 per cent each mystical or later saints' names. So there was a clear switch in the style of Christian names between the pre-1000 period and the twelfth century. Among the New Testament names, Petrus was well in advance with 19 instances, followed by Stephanus with 9 and Johannes with 8. The non-Christian names were overwhelmingly Germanic, with a few Breton names in the west and a few Latin in the south.[7]

The situation seems to have been much the same among the lower clergy. Among the senior educated clergy, French, Italian and English, mentioned by John of Salisbury in his *Historia Pontificalis* of the mid twelfth century, three-quarters had Germanic names. A study by Bourin and Chareille, based on charters from Touraine, Berry, Burgundy, Dauphiné and the Mediterranean south of France between 1000 and 1250, concludes that there was no significant difference between the names used by clerics and laymen.

St Augustine, his entourage and his immediate successors came from the Continent and had Latin names, some of which were clearly Christian. Augustine's successor as archbishop of Canterbury in 605 was Laurentius; Paulinus became archbishop of York in 625; and Deusdedit, an Englishman, who died in 663, was also archbishop of Canterbury. But this vogue for Christian names was minor and short-lived. Nearly every cleric mentioned in the sources from the later seventh century to the time of the Conquest had an Anglo-Saxon name, with a few Scandinavians later in the period. In the early-ninth-century Liber Vitae of Durham, out of nearly 250 priests' names, there are only two Christian ones: Tobeas and Abniau; among the lesser secular clergy there is one John. Again, among the witnesses to the charter establishing the Liberty of Oswaldslow in 963 are the two archbishops, Dunstan and Oscytel; Bishops Oswald, Osulf, Wynsi and Wulfric; and Abbots Aescwi, Osgar, Aelfstan, and Kineward. Moreover, such prominent churchmen often had martial and pagan names, like Wulfsige or Aelfgar.

Two countervailing factors should be mentioned. First, though so rare even among the clergy, Christian names in Anglo-Saxon England do seem to have been confined to this social group. Secondly, some clergy in the early period took new Christian names, though they did not always discard the old ones. The missionary Willibrord was named Clement by the pope when consecrating him as archbishop of the Frisians in 695, and he was subsequently known by both names. Similarly Boniface was originally called Wynfrith and was again given his new name by the pope on being consecrated a bishop around 720. He used and was known by both names after this. Berctgils, a Kentishman, who became bishop of Dunwich in 658, "also had the name Bonifatius", according to Bede; while Aeddi, who taught sacred music in the 660s, "had the name Stephanus".[8] But there are also cases of bishops and other clerics having alternative names that were not Christian, like Aelfheah, "who was also known as Godwine", who became bishop of Winchester in 984.[9]

Anglo-Saxon names were replaced among the clergy after the Norman Conquest, as we have indicated, but by Norman French and not Christian names. Christian names did progress later among the secular clergy but no faster than among the population at large. Among those promoted to holy orders in the diocese of Lincoln as late as 1291, 38 per cent had Christian and 62 per cent non-Christian names.[10]

Was the situation any different for those especially dedicated to the religious life, that is for monks and nuns, and later friars? Did they take new religious names as is the modern practice? There was precedent in both the Old and New Testaments for changes of name with religious significance, and profession as a monk or nun was specifically regarded as a "new baptism". Yet, despite this, monks and nuns in the early Middle Ages nearly all had non-Christian names, and they rarely changed their names on profession.

From Italy, we may take the example of the abbots of Monte Cassino, founded by St Benedict in the sixth century. Through the eighth and ninth centuries, non-Christian names predominated over Christian by 12 to 5. The Christian names used were mainly mystical and not Biblical (Apollinaris, Deusdedit, Optatus). In the tenth and eleventh centuries, non-Christian names again predominated over Christian by 12 to 6. But now Christian names were nearly all from the New Testament (Johannes and Petrus). In the twelfth and thirteenth centuries, non-Christian names were still twice as frequent as Christian, but the repertoire had become more diverse. New Testament names were the commonest (Pietro, Stefano, Tommaso), but some new names were used (Domenico and Nicola). Only in the fourteenth century did Christian names overtake non-Christian and then only just, by 9 to 8.[11] By the later medieval and Renaissance periods, Christian names were normal for religious in Italy, as they were for the population at large, but religious do not appear to have taken new names.

More information is available for France. Of the monks of Saint-Germain-des-Prés in the early ninth century just under 10 per cent had Christian names. There were seventeen Christian names in use, of which nine were Old Testament names, three New Testament, three mystical, and two later saints' names (including Balthasar attached in the medieval period to one of the three Magi). This pattern is found in other monasteries at this time and later. At Saint-Martin-du-Canigou in the Pyrenees, for example, in the eleventh century a few Benedictus, Elias, Johannes, Petrus and Stephanus stand out among the mass of Germanic names. Among the 71 monks in the linked houses of Stavelot-Malmédy in Flanders in the mid twelfth century, "only nine had non-Germanic names".[12] These included two Johanneses, a Bonifacius, a Mayricius and a Symon. Again, all the abbots and priors of Mont Saint-Michel had Frankish names from the ninth to the late twelfth century, when a Martin and a Jourdain appear. On the list of abbots of Saint-Amable in Riom, Christian names do not being to predominate until the thirteenth century and not definitively until the fifteenth. The sole Christian name in the twelfth century was Eustachius, that of a saint of the early Church, but from the thirteenth century New Testament names were the only ones found.[13]

There are hints that in the central medieval period monks may even have been less likely to have Christian names than secular clerics. Among Louis VII's bishops, whereas the proportion of Christian names among those known to come from the secular clergy was 32 per cent, that for those known to be from the regular clergy was only 12 per cent. Further there is virtually no evidence over the whole medieval period to suggest that those becoming monks as adults or entering monasteries as oblates changed their names. "It is not impossible that monks inside their monasteries bore a religious name, but there is no trace of this in the written documents."[14] By the later Middle Ages in France, religious including friars usually had Christian names, but in this they were no different from the population outside the cloister.

French nuns' names followed the same pattern as monks'. There is some evidence from the Carolingian period that females like males were programmed to the religious life by choice of name at birth, but the name used was a Germanic kindred name, not a religious one. At the Cluniac house of Marcigny at the start of the twelfth century, about 20 per cent of nuns had Christian names. Seventeen such names were in use, of which eight were mystical (Beatrix, Benedicta, Constantia, Sofia and so on); four were New Testament (Anna, Helisabet, Petronilla and Stephana); three were Old Testament (Eva, Sara and Susanna); and two were names of later saints (Agnes and Cecilia).[15] The situation was similar at other convents at this time. An apparent exception is provided by the community of canonesses at Schwarzenthann in Upper Alsace between around 1150 and 1300. Here changing one's name on entering the religious life seems to have become quite common by the twelfth century. This name could be Christian, and names such as Benigna, Claricia, Genia, Johanna and Susanna were still exclusively nuns' names at this time. Or Germanic names, new or original, could be adapted. In a way paralleling the Christianization of late Roman names, "a new Christian sense was injected into old German names, whose original sense had been lost".[16] So Guta, who wrote the manuscript containing the convent's necrology, asked the Virgin to indicate to her what her name signified and was told: "she who is provided with high qualities". Similarly, Diemuede was taken to mean "servant of God", and Germanic names in *engel* were interpreted to mean "angel". Another factor was the Christianization of Germanic names through their being borne by a saint. So there was a vogue for the name Adelheit among the nuns of Schwarzenthann and elsewhere, stemming from veneration for St Adelheit or Adelaide, wife of Otto the Great. But all this was really a development within the Germanic name system, and it was not until the thirteenth and fourteenth centuries that Christian names proper came to predominate among nuns in France as among monks.

With very few exceptions, English monks before the Conquest had normal Anglo-Saxon and not Christian names. Examples may be cited from the seventh and eighth centuries: Botulf of Icanhoh, later canonized; Berhtwald and Tatwine, successive abbots of Reculver; Botwine, abbot of Ripon; Seaxwulf, abbot of Medestamstead, later Peterborough. In the Durham Liber Vitae of the early ninth century, only one out of nearly two hundred abbots listed had a Christian name, and none of the thousand-odd monks. Many monks' names, like bishops', were in overtly pagan or martial style. So the Bury monk, made abbot of Abingdon in 1048 and later bishop of London, had the un-Christian name of Spearhafoc. In the Thorney Liber Vitae between around 1050 and 1110, the proportion of Christian names among monks had risen to 23 per cent. But, against this, there were no Christian names among those of the monks of Winchester cathedral on the roll to commemorate the death of Matilda, abbess of La Trinité, in Caen, in 1113. Figures over a longer period are available for the monks of the New Minster at Winchester. The proportion of those with Christian names was under 3 per cent in the period from the tenth century to 1078; it was 19 per cent over the subsequent century, and 41 per cent over the next. Only in the fourteenth and fifteenth centuries did more than half the monks have Christian names, and this proportion remained below 60 per cent. The names used were overwhelmingly from the New Testament; the only other name to be at all popular was Nicholas in the fourteenth and fifteenth centuries.[17]

We have more comprehensive country-wide information on the heads of religious houses between the mid tenth century and the late twelfth century. In the independent Benedictine houses, there were no Christian names for abbots until the mid twelfth century, and they were still in a distinct minority by 1200. Of the names used, eleven were from the New Testament, led by John, Peter and Thomas; nine from the Old Testament, with four Adams and four Eliases; and two mystical, with six Benedicts. Twelve were names of later saints, with six Nicholases and three Lawrences. Christian names were also introduced into Cluniac houses in the twelfth century. At the important house of Lewes, the first Christian name, Stephen, came only in 1218. Petrus or Peter seems to have been especially popular with Cluniac heads, reflecting their close ties with the papacy. Other and later orders follow the same pattern. Cistercian heads came to have Christian names from the late twelfth century; New Testament names predominated and especially John. Christian names were not the rule among the Augustinian canons, though they became more common in the later twelfth and thirteenth centuries. Among the Gilbertines and the Premonstratensians the same is true, with non-Christian names continuing into the thirteenth century.[18] By this time, however, some Germanic names had acquired Christian connotations. St Robert, for example, was a Cistercian saint; Hugh the name of a line of Cluniac abbots.

Among those promoted to holy orders in the diocese of Lincoln in the 1290s, there was no difference between those from religious orders and others; around 40 per cent had Christian names. It may be significant, however, given their involvement in pastoral work, that 45 per cent of ordinands who were friars had Christian names, a figure that rose to 51 per cent for Carmelites and Franciscans. Out of 33 Franciscans with Christian names, 21 were called John, four Thomas and two Nicholas.

The nuns mentioned by Bede all have Anglo-Saxon names, for example: Ercongota, a nun at Faremoutiers-en-Brie in the late seventh century; Begu and Frigyth at the convent of Hackness near Whitby; Heriburg, abbess of Watton near Beverley, and her daughter Quoenburg. Much later, among the nuns of St Mary, of Winchester, on the death-roll of Matilda, abbess of La Trinité, all the names but four are non-Christian. To judge from the names of heads of houses, Christian names were not introduced until the later twelfth century. At the Benedictine house of Barking, only two or three of the ten abbesses between the tenth century and 1242 had Christian names, the first being Mary in 1173. At Wilton, two out of the eleven abbesses over roughly the same period had Christian names, starting again with Mary around 1195. More generally, among the nuns mentioned by Elkins from the twelfth century, Anglo-Saxon names are still in evidence (Edit, Thydit, Godit) and new names tend to be secular Norman ones (Alice, Avice, Maud) as much as if not more than saints' names (Agatha, Anne, Margaret).

Though there are exceptions, religious in England, like their continental counterparts, do not seem to have changed their names on profession as a rule. Both Willibrord and Wynfrith retained their original names on becoming monks, only adopting alternative names when they were consecrated as bishops. Moreover, when a name change did occur, it was not necessarily from an obviously non-Christian to a Christian name. The twelfth-century recluse Christina or Christian of Markyate had originally been called Theodora.

Conclusive evidence is provided here by the visitations of the early Tudor period. At Glastonbury in 1526 several monks had "uncouth 'religious' names in the new fashion"; while at Bardney in 1530 "the younger half of the community had taken up with the new and not yet common fashion of taking a 'religious' name, that of a saint of ancient times".[19]

In conclusion, secular and religious clergy across western Europe seem to have been part of the general trend towards adopting Christian names – mainly from the New Testament – rather than the initiators of it, though the friars may have played a more active role in the thirteenth and fourteenth centuries. Before exploring the reasons for this general trend, we should complete our account of clerical names with a brief excursus on papal names.

From the tenth century, if not before, it was usual for those elected to the chair of St Peter to adopt a new papal name. So Gerbert elected in 999 became Sylvester II; Suidger, Bishop of Bamberg, elected in 1046, took the name Clement II; and Cardinal Guido was "raised to the papacy as Celestinus II" in 1143.[20] Some writers suggest that where a man already had a "clerical" name, there was no need to change it. Leo VIII, who became pope in 963, was already called Leo – though, in fact, he was a layman – but Desiderius, Abbot of Montecassino, who became pope in 1086, nevertheless changed his name to Victor III.

Writing of the twelfth century in particular, when the practice seems to have become systematized, Ullmann declared that the change of name pointed to the change of role and was seen as being analagous to the rebirth that occurred at baptism. The choice of name could also have "political" significance. The reforming popes of the later eleventh century "aimed at the restoration of ancient discipline" in the Church.

> The names which they took when they became popes show this more clearly than many words: they abandoned names such as John and Benedict, which had been common in the tenth and early eleventh centuries, and took those by preference which had not been used for many centuries – Clement, Damasus, Victor, and so on. These names contained a challenge.[21]

In a similar way, Nicholas Brakespeare, elected pope in 1154, chose the name Adrian IV, a name not used since the ninth century. Adrian I had been a man of action, a defender and extender of the papal state; he also had a special connection with England, being "the pope from whom [the abbey of] St Albans claimed its earliest privileges."[22]

Though a repertoire of names became established early on as proper papal names, they were not necessarily Christian in origin. Chiming in with current fashion, New Testament names were not used at first – no pope was ever called Peter – and early popes often had standard Roman names: Julius, Sixtus, Vigilius, Vitalian. From the sixth century, Christian names did come to be used, but among them Biblical names were comparatively rare. The high-point for these was in the eighth and ninth centuries, when about half the Christian papal names were Biblical, and the tenth and eleventh, when about a third were. The names were all from the New Testament, with John well in the lead, followed by Stephen. The first Pope John was chosen in 523; nineteen popes had had this name by 1100. Over the same period there were ten Stephens. But the most favoured Christian papal names down to the end of the eleventh century were mystical names: Adeodatus, Victor, and especially Gregorius, Benedictus and Boniface. It is ironic that the eleventh-century reformers regarded the Biblical names as somehow corrupt and preferred those from the late antique period.

Over the last four medieval centuries, the proportion of Biblically-named popes fell dramatically. In the twelfth and thirteenth centuries, there was only one, another John; and in the fourteenth and fifteenth centuries two, yet another John and a Paul. There were also five popes with the names of later saints: two Martins and three Nicholases. The commonest papal names in the twelfth and thirteenth centuries were either mystical Christian or secular: there were four Innocents, four Celestines, two Clements, but also two Alexanders and two Urbans. In the fourteenth and fifteenth centuries, the same trend continued, the commonest papal names being Innocent (3), Benedict (3), Clement (2) and Pius (2), but also Alexander and Urban again (2 each). Clearly certain names had become firmly established as papal names, indicative of programmes and attitudes, but also transmitted in families. Francesco Piccolomini took the name Pius III in memory of his uncle Silvio, who had been Pius II (1458–64). Some papal names were names in general use; a few acquired a special cachet and were rarely used by others, viz Innocent, Pius, Urban, Callixtus. They are a final example of the preservation of Latin names in the later Italian context.[23]

The reasons why

The Christianization of names was Europe-wide and represented a radical departure from the old Germanic name system. There was a break in the transmission of names within families and "a new religious value" was attached to the name.[24] Various explanations have been offered for what was in effect a revolution.

Abbé Duffaut suggested in 1900 that the clergy were able to impose "the names of saints as protectors and models" thanks to the establishment of infant baptism.[25] But infant baptism was already a very old custom by the eleventh and twelfth centuries, and what is critical here is the precise linkage between name-giving and baptism and whether the Church wished to lay down the law in this area. Originally, of course, baptism was not a naming ritual, though it does seem that naming was incorporated into the ritual perhaps as early as the eleventh century in parts of the Continent and from the early thirteenth century in English dioceses. However, though some clerics may have had ideas on the subject – Archbishop Pecham of Canterbury ordered his parochial clergy in the late thirteenth century not to allow "improper" names to be conferred at baptism, especially on girls[26] – the child's name was given by the godparents not the priest, and the Church had no general rules about personal names until the late sixteenth or early seventeenth centuries. It was only then that "obscure, fabulous or ridiculous names of either so-called gods or of impious persons" were proscribed and the faithful enjoined to give their children the names of saints.[27]

A number of examples may be adduced from the early Middle Ages of adults who changed or took new Christian names at baptism. Gregory of Tours relates that when the Arian Visigothic prince Hermangild married the daughter of King Sigibert and became an orthodox Catholic, he was at the same time baptized and given the name John; while according to Bede King Caedwalla of Wessex was "named Peter by the pope at his baptism" in Rome in 688.[28] However, there are more examples of such name changes at baptism where the new name was not Christian. Guthrum, the Danish king of East Anglia, who died in 890, was a godson of King Alfred, who had given him as a baptismal name one of the royal names of Wessex: Athelstan. Duke Rolf or Rollo of Normandy took the name Robert in around 900. In these cases the name change took place in a context of lay patronage and acculturation to English and Frankish society respectively. In a later case from Catalonia, a man "formerly called Bonus, son of Petrus, was baptized and then called Arnallus".[29] Here the baptismal name was non-Christian, but the man's father had a saint's name and his own pre-baptismal name was a mystical one.

Other liturgical influences would seem to have been much greater: first the general incidence of saints' names in religious services; and then special devotions, and especially those encouraged by the friars. "Through the exertions of the friars, it became possible, from the middle of the thirteenth century onwards, for laymen to focus their . . . worship on saints with whom they felt a social and emotional affinity."[30] The Mendicants promoted saints' cults via sermons, and especially in Italy via pictures in their churches. The saints were presented as mediators, intercessors and patrons, and emphasis was placed on the "great" saints of the New Testament and on "new" saints from among the ranks of the friars themselves. La Roncière has shown how the spread of Francesco and Domenico in the region north of Florence went hand in hand with the activity of the Orders which these two saints founded. One should note, however, that there is no necessary connection between the promotion of saints' cults and hagionymy or naming after saints. Saints may be venerated without people taking their names and particular cults may not include name-appropriation. Indeed, in some cases there may be a feeling that saints' names should not be used by mere mortals, except perhaps in the "servant of" form.

The vogue for augurative names that preceded that for saints' names does suggest, however, that names were already being used as protective devices. The names wishing luck to the new-born or giving thanks for their arrival were taken literally. This may be gauged perhaps from the late fourteenth-century and early fifteenth-century diary of the Florentine, Gregorio Dati, which often followed a birth entry with an augurative comment: "God grant he turn out well"; "God grant her good fortune"; God make him a good man" – all of which could well have been augurative names.

The names of the saints and especially of the "great" or "universal" saints took over the role of auguratives, since they were believed to be such effective protectors in this life and beyond, a belief fostered by the friars and others. Children came to be named after a saint whose feast fell on or near their birthday, or in accordance with a vow, or to honour a saint regarded as a special patron by a family. Some of Dati's children were named after saints because they were born or baptized on the feast-day. A son born in 1402 was called Antonio because of his wife's "special devotion" to the saint; another was called Girolamo "from devotion St Jerome" since it was on his feast-day "that her pains began".[31] The devotion could predate the birth; the vow be for the child itself after a period of infertility. According to his canonization process, a childless couple who had a son after Gilbert of Sempringham had slept in their bed called him Gilbert in gratitude. St Colette (Nicoleta) of Corbie, born in 1381, was so named because her aged parents believed that her birth came in answer to a prayer to St Nicholas. The dislocations of the later medieval period, especially from around 1330 with the Black Death, almost certainly reinforced the appeal of protective saints' names, as well as promoting the popularity of specific guardians against the plague such as Sebastian and Anthony.

Augurative names in Italy and probably elsewhere were mainly plebeian. In Tuscany they were more characteristic of the *contado* than of Florence and other towns, and of the lower orders in Florence rather than the élites. The vogue for saints' names had the same "class" bias. In Latium at the end of the eleventh century it was peasants and artisans who tended to use them, while the nobility held to Germanic names. And the same contrasting pattern is found in northern Italy from the eleventh century, if not before. In Genoa between the mid twelfth and mid thirteenth centuries, saints' names were more prevalent among non-nobles than nobles, which led Kedar to suggest that the progress of hagionymy may have been related to the "advent of the popolo" or "middle class" to greater power and influence in the city.[32]

The same situation is found in some, though not all, parts of France. In Poitou before the twelfth century "a Christian name normally implied that its bearer was not a noble but a peasant".[33] Jean and Jacques were found among the nobles of Brabant in the twelfth and thirteenth centuries, but they were rare and Germanic names predominated in this class. There was no clear distinction between noble and non-noble names in Burgundy before 1200, but once the nobility had adopted Christian names they tended later to maintain their social distance via a preference for the less popular names of warrior saints like Michel or George or for names relating to the Crusades like Jourdain and Damas. It is hard to know how to interpret this evidence, but it seems certain that hagionymy either derived from the interaction of clergy and people, not clergy and élites or secular élites and people, or it was an autonomous feature of popular piety.

This brings us to the significance of the type of saints' name that was most popular. Everywhere, we have seen, the popular names were those of "universal" saints, mainly from the New Testament. Local cults and church dedications rarely had much impact on naming. St Victor had few namesakes in Marseille, St Sernin in Toulouse, or St Rémi in and around Reims. The cathedral of Genoa was dedicated to St Lawrence but Lorenzo was a very rare name in the city. There was the same neglect of parish patrons, as detailed studies of Paris and Florence have demonstrated. In Paris around 1300, for example, there were three parishes under the patronage of St Germain with a population of nearly 2700 taille-payers, but only 35 of these were named Germain or Germaine: of the 1400 in the parish of Saint-Merri only 7 had the patron saint's name. In Paris, Florence, Ghent and elsewhere, only when a saint was a universal saint is there a strong correlation between dedication and naming. Here the dedication often predated the naming fashion and may well have influenced it, but that leaves a host of dedications to local saints that had no such impact, which suggests that church dedication *per se* was probably not the crucial factor.

Important shrines appear to have had some effect locally, though this was patchy. In England the continuing popularity of the Anglo-Saxon name Edmund in East Anglia does seem to be a reflection of the importance of his cult there, radiating from Bury. In Normandy, Michel was common in the vicinity of Mont Saint-Michel; while Nicolas became common in Lorraine in the wake of the establishment of a pilgrimage to St-Nicolas-du-Pont, where an arm of the saint had been brought after the First Crusade. But in these two cases the local factor only reinforced a general trend for the names, operative elsewhere. There could also be some odd time lapses in this field. The cult of St Michael was associated with the cave-shrine on Monte Gargano in Apulia, where he first appeared in the fifth century, and over 800 churches in Italy were dedicated to the saint by the end of the seventh century; but his name only became common from the twelfth century. Local factors seem to have been less important than the role given to the archangel as the protector at the hour of death and the weigher of souls at the Last Judgment, themes illustrated in church art.

La Roncière shows that, in the case of the abbey of Settimo in Tuscany in the fourteenth century, naming in the local population was not affected by the influence or example of the lordly monastery itself. He does point, however, to the importance of a confraternity dedicated to San Lorenzo in 1288, and confraternities may have acted more generally as channels for the spread of saints' names, as they did of their cults. A more diffuse monastic influence may be detected also in the way in which Benedictus/a and Dominicus and their equivalents – both monastic names – survived the general eclipse of mystical names all over Europe in the later medieval period.

Paradoxically, therefore, hagionymy was both a popular custom stemming from popular piety and a reflection of "the importance of the universal Church",[34] coinciding here with the papal reform movement of the eleventh and twelfth centuries. Did it mark, as Bloch supposed, "the firmer and firmer grip taken by the Church over family life" in this period?[35] Or is this anachronistic, assuming means at the Church's disposal which it did not possess until the time of the Council of Trent or later? And there was a civilizing process involved too. For northern Europe – England, Flanders, Normandy – acquiring Christian names was part of a general involvement in expanding Romance culture, of an incorporation into a common society and culture. And this took place despite the extreme localization of society and economy, despite limitations on any centralizing authority, despite the lack of modern communications and media. Together with the related development of second names, the advent of hagionymy represents a vast cultural change taking place in circumstances with which we are very unfamiliar.

Once saints' names had been adopted for whatever reasons, they then became part of the established name system and were transmitted within it. Secular patronage, imitation and fashion would build on what was initially a religious impulse. What had an individualizing aspect at first, became a vehicle for "the consolidation of family solidarities".[36] The very process of Christianization via naming proved a two-way process. Names used at baptism and taken largely from saints' names became "Christian names" and are dubbed so still, but Christian religious names in the course of time became purely secular.

Name fashions and name stock

We have discussed some of the specific names used in the central medieval period, but there is more to say. Which names were most common and why? How well did other names survive the advent of Christian names? How did men's names compare with women's? What happened to the overall stock of names as the names of the saints became more frequent?

By far the most popular medieval Christian names were those of the great New Testament saints. The Apostles were especially favoured: Andrew, Bartholomew, Matthew and Thomas. The name of the proto-martyr Stephen was also very common, and, in the later Middle Ages, Philip. A few names stand out from the rest. The first of these in time was Peter (with its variants Petrus, Pierre, Pier, etc.). The name was already established in the late

Roman period and it was common through the early Middle Ages, especially for clerics. The prime reason for using the name was, of course, its association with the first of the Apostles, the holder of the keys to Heaven, and with his successors, the popes. Petrus spread out over Europe, like relics from the shrine of St Peter, like church dedications, as signs of the veneration in which he was held. Naming after Peter was reinforced by the Church reform movement of the eleventh and twelfth centuries, emanating from Rome. In Languedoc, the lesser nobility adopted the name precisely at the time that "they were using the Gregorian movement as a weapon against the high aristocracy in order to force them to give up their monopoly of senior ecclesiastical posts"; and it was never used by the latter group or the counts. Peter continued to be very common through the later medieval period, when it was joined also by Simon.

In the central and later medieval periods, John in its various forms became the most popular name, displacing Peter and other names from the first position. Like Peter, John was not a novelty. It was not uncommon in the late Roman period and the early Middle Ages, but it did not really take off until the twelfth and thirteenth centuries, first in France. It was already well in front in Paris, the Lyonnais, Burgundy, Normandy and Flanders by 1300. Its triumph came later in southern France – from the later thirteenth and early fourteenth centuries. In Italy and England John really came to the fore in the fourteenth and fifteenth centuries. Once arrived, the predominance of John was far greater than that of any other name. Across Europe from Warboys in Huntingdonshire to Nuits in Burgundy up to one man in three was named John. The vogue for John stems from the fact that it was the name of two great saints, whose cults were both officially sponsored and popular. "Naming a child John was to place him under the double sign of the Precursor of Christ and the Visionary of the Second Coming, of baptism and resurrection."[37]

Another "multiple" name was Jacobus or James, belonging to the Old Testament patriarch and two Apostles. This was not a common name in the early medieval period, but it became popular in the twelfth and thirteenth centuries, especially in Italy and northern France. Brattö attributes its Italian vogue to Byzantine influence. Further west, the pilgrimage to the shrine of St James at Compostela, which attracted devotees from all over Europe from the eleventh century, must have been decisive. Another New Testament name received reinforcement from a later cult. The importance of Thomas in Normandy and elsewhere in Northern France as well as in England was boosted by devotion to St Thomas of Canterbury, canonized in 1173.

A number of "new" saints joined the Apostles as name models. St Nicholas was a fourth-century bishop of Myra in Lycia. The name is found in early medieval Europe, but "the diffusion of this name became much more important after the translation of the body of the saint to Bari [in Southern Italy] in 1087".[38] It became more common in different parts of Italy from this time, and was one of the most popular names in Genoa and Tuscany by the thirteenth century. It seems to have been introduced to France via Norman influence and was particularly common in the north. It was the second commonest name at Metz by 1300 and the fifth commonest in Paris. It was among the top five male names at Evreux, Soissons and the Artois in the fourteenth and fifteenth centuries. Already by 1300, the full name was tending to be eclipsed by hypocoristic variants, especially Colin. Female forms of the name were also popular.

Antonius and Antonia were of course Latin names and may have survived as such at a very low level. Antonia occurs in the ninth-century polyptique of Saint-Victor. Two saints bore the name Antonius, St Anthony of Egypt, whose relics were brought to France in the eleventh century, and the Franciscan, St Anthony of Padua, who was canonized in 1232. The former seems to have had little impact on naming, except locally in France near his shrine, but the latter attracted an important cult, with naming. Antonio does not appear in thirteenth-century lists of names in Florence and Genoa, but it jumps to second place by the late fourteenth century in Florence and is borne then by one in twelve Genoese.

Most of the popular great saints' names for men had their feminized equivalents. Of these, Johanna and its variants was the commonest. Jehanne headed the list of women's names in Paris in 1300 and came second at Amiens. At Evreux in Normandy, Jeanne rose from third position in the twelfth century with 6 per cent of bearers to the head of the list between 1250 and 1350 with 21 per cent, rising again over the following century to 27 per cent. A similar rise is found in Burgundy and the Forez.

Only one or two independent female saints' names achieved a similar popularity: Elisabeth or Isabel from the Old Testament; and Agnes and Margaret, martyrs of the early Church, both with later cults. Agnes or Anes was quite common in France in the tenth and eleventh centuries but did not take off until the twelfth century and after. It was in third place among women's names in Flanders in the twelfth century and in Evreux and Paris around 1300. It remained popular in northern France into the fourteenth century, but was never so common in the centre and the south, or in Italy. In England, it seems to have been the commonest Christian name for women in the early thirteenth century among the peasantry and the élite. At Warboys, it was the second commonest female name in the first half of the fourteenth century and the commonest in the second half, when nearly one in three women bore it. Margaret was even more popular than Agnes in France, coming first or second on the list in the Forez, Metz, Calais, Nuits and Arras in the fourteenth century and in Paris in the fifteenth. The name was used in Gaul in the early medieval period but did not become at all common until the thirteenth century. In England, Margaret was among the top five names at Warboys through the fourteenth and fifteenth centuries, which seems to have been typical.

Maria was used in the late Roman period – the wife of the Emperor Honorius around 400 bore the name – but it was rare. It occurred more frequently in the early medieval period in Italy, France and elsewhere. Maria was the commonest Biblical name for women in tenth-century Rimini, and it was fairly common among the peasants of Latium in the tenth and eleventh centuries. There are 15 Marias among the peasants of Saint-Victor of Marseille in the ninth century. But at this time as earlier, the name may not necessarily have been connected with the Virgin Mary. It was a feminized version of the Latin Marius, which was popular in Provence. There, too, girls may have been named after St Mary Magdalene, associated with the region from the seventh century. It has often been suggested indeed that there was a kind of taboo on naming after the Virgin Mary. She was too sacred for humans to imitate. However, increasing use was made of Mary from the central Middle Ages, which parallels the development of Marian devotion in the same period. Around 1300, 3 per cent of women in Metz, and 6 per cent in Paris, bore the name. In Amiens Marie or Maroie was the commonest female name. By around 1400, between 20 and 30 per cent of women bore the name in the Limousin, Picardy and Flanders. The name was less popular in the west of France and in the south, where its vogue only came from the later sixteenth century. The name enjoyed far less of a vogue too in late medieval Italy: it was rare in fifteenth-century Florence, for example. It was also less common in England. As with other names and perhaps more so, Mary appeared in hypocoristic forms. In the Forez, for example, between 1250 and 1400, three Marias are recorded, but 31 Marionas and 115 Marietas.

We have seen how important leading names were to the family identity of noble families in the early medieval period. It is not surprising therefore that many of them clung to these names in the face of the wave of Christianization, though not all such names were old or noble. Germanic names retained an important position all over Italy in the thirteenth century. About a quarter of the names in the Florentine Libro di Montaperti of 1260 fell into this category, while Aldobrandino, Guido, Raniero and Ugo were among the commonest male names in Siena in 1285. Some of these names were "historical" family names – the Guittoni in Florence used Berlingerius, for example – but some had become quite plebeian, like Albertus. Some had been introduced fairly recently. Aldobrandinus appeared in Lucca and in Arezzo in the mid eleventh century. Arrigus or Arrigo arrived in Tuscany about the same time, in imitation of the German emperors called Heinrich or Henricus, while Fredericus only appeared in the early twelfth century in the wake of the "Hohenstaufens". Both were still aristocratic names in the thirteenth century.

Germanic names were better established in France on the whole, but their survival as very common names was uneven. Willelmus, Bernardus, Raimundus and Arnaldus remained the commonest men's names (with

Petrus) in Languedoc through the twelfth century, and Willelmus or Guilhem was still advancing at this time. These names were also common elsewhere in the south-west, together with Bertrand and Guiral or Girard, and remained so into the fourteenth century and after. In the Forez, the Lyonnais and Burgundy, Germanic names fared less well through the thirteenth and fourteenth centuries, save for William. William or Guillaume was the second commonest name around 1300 in Paris, where three of the top ten male names were Germanic. Guillaume was still the second name in Paris in the early fifteenth century with Pierre and behind Jean. In the Vendômois in the twelfth century, all five of the commonest names had been Germanic: Hugue, Geoffroi, Renard, Robert and Guillaume; by 1355 Guillaume and Geoffroi survived, though outstripped by Jean, Pierre and Mathieu. In Picardy, Raoul, Robert and William retained their popularity into the later medieval period, as did Heinricius, Walterius, Wilhelmus and Baldinus or Bauduins in Flanders and Artois.

Germanic names also held up for women in France. In the early fourteenth-century Lauragais, Guilhama was the commonest name, followed by Ramunde, Azalais and Ermengarda. In the Forez, Guillelma appeared in the top six names through the thirteenth and fourteenth centuries, while at Nuits, in Burgundy, in the fifteenth century, Guillette was the third commonest name and Girarde the fifth. Two other names were especially popular in the north and centre: Ameline and Alis. Alis took a variety of forms (Alisia, Aalis, Aileit, etc.) and derived from the Germanic Adalheidis or Adalhaid. It was the second commonest women's name at Evreux by 1250, and at Metz and in the Artois around 1300. It was also very common at this time in Paris, Picardy, Flanders and the Forez.

In England, as we have seen, the significant transition in the post-Conquest period was from Anglo-Saxon to Norman secular names, and Christianization came late. At Winchester, Newark and Warboys, through the twelfth century, William, Robert, Richard, Roger, Walter and so on were the predominant names, and especially the first three. John, Stephen, Thomas and Nicholas find their place among the commonest names in the thirteenth and fourteenth centuries, but the old Germanic names were not eclipsed. Similarly, for women, Alice, Emma and Maud remained popular alongside the new Christian names.

Two other factors are relevant in explaining the survival of Germanic names. First is the influence of the French epics or *chansons de geste*. These were established in written form around the late eleventh and early twelfth centuries but must have circulated earlier orally. In 1904, Langlois compiled a list of all the names in the French *chansons*. The most frequently used names, mainly for knights, were, in order: Gui, Guis or Guion; Gautier; Huon, Hugon or Hugues; Girart or Gerart (all with over 100 mentions); Thierri or Tieri; Henri; Renier or Rainer; Milon or Miles; Bernart; and Garnier (all from 50 to 70 mentions). Frequency of mention and of different characters with the same name is not of course always the best guide to the importance of a name. Guillaume, the hero of the Guillaume of Orange cycle, who has under 50 mentions, is an obvious case in point, as are the names of the heroes of *The Song of Roland*: Roland and Olivier. Only 11 other characters are called Olivier, and only one other Roland: the giant in *Fierabras*. However, the popularity of these fictional names almost certainly reflected and had an impact on naming practices among the nobility in France from the eleventh century, and later among townspeople. Poly and Bournazel suggest that epic names were perhaps "the knightly equivalent of a clerical name, given at the time of baptism . . . to a child promised by his parents, if not to the crusade, then at least to an ideal type of Christian knight".[39] Certainly the trend for epic names ran parallel to Christianization and to the rise of chivalry, though the names involved were Germanic. Some Germanic names had their vogue reinforced, notably Guillaume. Other names rose to prominence with the epics, for example Huon and Girart.

"New" Germanic names taken from the French epics also enjoyed a vogue in Italy. Brattö attributes perhaps 4 per cent of names in the Libro di Montaperti to this influence. Roland, Hrodlandus or Orlandus existed in Italy before the epics became popular there, but became more widespread from the eleventh century. Orlando was "widely spread among [all] classes" in Siena in 1285,[40] and was also quite common in Florence. Oliviero or Uliverius was rare in late thirteenth-century Florence, but quite common in Siena and apparently in Padua and the Veneto, where the hypocoristics Liviéro, Viéro and Vero are found. Two brothers at Pavia in 1145 were called Rolando and Oliviero. Though Roland and Oliver were the most popular, examples of most of the epic heroes can be found among Italian names from the mid eleventh century onwards: Rinaldo, Viviano, Ospinello and so on. Women's names were also taken, for example, Drusiana from Josiana, Fiaramont and Blancaflora; and even the names of villains and pagans. A Ganellone or Wanelloni is recorded near Turin in 1040; and Saraceno, Turco and Pagano all became fairly common from the mid eleventh century. Epic names were borne first by members of the nobility, but by around 1200, if not before, peasants had them too. Rajna suggests that naming after an epic hero may have been regarded in a similar way to naming after a saint.

A little later there was a related vogue for names from the Arthurian romances. Artu or Artusius (Arthur) appeared in northern Italy from the late eleventh century and is found in most cities. Galvano (Gawain) is also found around this time. Both became more common in the thirteenth and fourteenth centuries as the general vogue for Arthurian names grew: Lanzalotto or Lancelotto, Percevali, Erecco, Ivani, Isolda, Ginevra. Probably the most popular of all these names was Galasso, Galeotto or Galeazzo (Galahad), which was adopted in the later medieval period by both the Montefeltro and the Visconti families.

A second factor making for the spread and then the survival of Germanic names was the influence of the names of lords and rulers. In France, there was a zone where royal names were important: Picardy, Burgundy, the Vendômois, Berry with Robert, Hugues and Eudes. William, Richard, Robert and Raoul were followed in Normandy; Geoffroi in areas of Angevin power; Baudouin in Flanders; Bernard, Raimond and Guillaume in Gascony and the south-west. More locally, the commonest men's names in the Mâconnais in the eleventh century were those borne by the family of the count and by castellans. Duby argues, moreover, that such names were not just imitated out of social deference. Taking the superior's name indicated a tie, of vassalage, of godparenthood and, in some cases, of marriage, and, being political, it was much more likely for men than for women.

Contemporary with these developments in the central and later medieval periods was another: the reduction of the name stock and the sharing of fewer names by more people. Bourin and Chareille have distinguished here between "concentration", where there are a few dominant names leaving a large number of rare names, and "condensation", where the stock is reduced but there are no very dominant names. The former situation seems to have been more characteristic of Italy, the latter of France, though they are hard in practice to distinguish.

There is no doubt about the decline in the name stock in Italy. In Lombardy in the seventh and eighth centuries, there were two persons per name; in tenth-century Ravenna 2.4. In the Florentine *contado*, there were still two persons per name on average in the period 1240–80, but the rate rose considerably over the next century or so. By 1370, the three commonest names were borne by about a quarter of the population, and only 20 per cent of names were not shared. In Florence itself there were four persons per name in the 1260s, and 80 per cent of men bore names appearing five or more times. Still there was a large number of names in existence, many of which were little used, and it took 41 male names to cover half the population. Put another way, the five commonest names accounted for only 17 per cent of men, and the ten commonest names for under a quarter. There was a big reduction in stock again by the early fifteeth century, when the eleven commonest names covered half the male population. The picture in Genoa was similar but perhaps more stable. By the mid twelfth century there were three persons per name on average, and this was still the rate at the end of the fourteenth century. The number of names required to cover half the population also stayed put at 13. The great popularity of a few saints' names went along with the retention of a large stock of names that were not frequently used.

The reduction of the name stock was slower to get started in France but then became more sharp and more comprehensive than in Italy. Among the charters of Stavelot-Malmédy around 900, there were still 1.2 persons per name; in the polyptique of Saint-Rémi, at Reims, there were 1.4; and in the

Mâconnais around 1000 1.3. But already in some places, the stock of names used had begun to decline and name repetition had grown. There were three persons per name in the polyptique of Saint-Germain; and among the peasants of Saint-Victor, the ten commonest names accounted for 16 per cent of persons. Further diminution of the stock and further repetition occurred from the eleventh century. In a sample of names from the Mâconnais, 35 names were shared by 47 men around 1000, and by 150 around 1100. In the cartulary of Saint-Cugat in Catalonia, there were three persons per name around 1070 and over six by the end of the twelfth century. In the Lauragais by 1245, there were 9.5 persons per name. In the thirteenth and fourteenth centuries, comparable figures of 10, 20 or more are found in Normandy, Paris, Metz and elsewhere. At Cluny around 1300, the four commonest names accounted for about half the men, and only 28 per cent of names were borne by only one person. Nine names accounted for half the male population at Metz in 1300; and five in Paris and Metz. By the end of the Middle Ages, all these trends were further accentuated. In the Forez, among men in the fourteenth century, there were 25.9 persons per Old Latin name, 24.4 per Germanic name and 97.2 per Christian name. Among women, the figures were 6.3, 17 and 37.2. At Nuits, in Burgundy, the six commonest names accounted for 58 per cent of men in 1317, but 71 per cent in 1470.

A number of features of this "crystallization"[41] of the name stock should be remarked. It does seem to have begun among Christian names, but it soon became an independent trend affecting all names. At Evreux between the twelfth and the fourteenth centuries, the percentage of men with the five commonest Christian names rose from 57 per cent to 73 per cent, while that of men with the five commonest Germanic names rose from 59 per cent to 74 per cent. The crystallization of women's names lagged behind that of men in Normandy, but then became more marked. A similar trend is found elsewhere in France, and it seems to be linked to the feminization of masculine names. There is some evidence also, for example from Burgundy, that the commonest names were used by the established and better-off members of society, while the poor and incomers used the less usual names. "Marginal people had marginal names."[42]

The name stock also declined in England, though the process is less well documented than for France. In the Thorney Liber Vitae in the tenth and eleventh centuries there were two persons per Scandinavian name and three persons per Anglo-Saxon one. At Bury around 1100, there were between three and four persons per name. By the thirteenth century, much higher figures are found in some counties, and these rose further later. At Warboys in the first half of the fourteenth century there were 14.2 men per name and 8.3 women; and in the first half of the fifteenth century 19.8 men per name and 8.1 women. There was a temporary increase in the repertoire of names immediately after the Conquest, and the narrowing of the stock began during the later twelfth century, accelerating thereafter. There was also a considerable degree of concentration on a few names. According to Postles, the top two names accounted for between 25 per cent and nearly 50 per cent of attributions in selected counties around 1300–30; while at Thornbury in Gloucestershire in the mid fourteenth century, the six comm-onest men's names accounted for around 80 per cent of attributions and the five commonest women's names for the same proportion. There was signifi-cant regional variation in the breadth of name stock. In the Lay Subsidy Rolls for Derbyshire, for example, there were only 46 male names, while in Northumberland there were 93, and in East Sussex 100.

An important consequence of the growing frequency of certain names was the use of distinguishing hypocoristic forms. Hypocoristic forms became extremely common in official sources in Italy from the thirteenth century and were almost certainly in everyday use well before this. Half the persons in the Florentine Libro di Montaperti had such names, and over half those in similar documentation from Siena in 1285.

Hypocoristics took two basic forms, the abbreviated and the suffixed name, though combinations of the two were possible. The name could be shortened to the first part, for example Stroza for Strozzafico, Strozzalino and so on, or Vinci for Vinciguerra, Vinceforte and so on. But use of the second part of the name was far more frequent. So Baldus, Bardus, Ding(h)us, Neri derived from names ending in -*bald*, -*bard*, -*ingus* and -*erius*, a familiar Germanic procedure but one which was applied to non-Germanic augurative and saints' names also. In the Libro di Montaperti, Corsus, Giunta, Ventura were all much more common than their parent names Bonaccursus, Bona-giunta and Bonaventura.

In the Biccherna records from Siena in 1285, "there are 84 entries of Ventura . . . to 17 of Bonaventura", with a similar emphasis for several other common names.[43] Among saints' names, Filippus gave the more common Lippus or Lippo, Tommasus Masus, and Nicola Cola. Another way to form the hypocoristic was to remove letters and/or syllables (syncopis). So, among Germanic names, Alberico gave Berico, hence Bico; Aldobrandinus gave Bindus or Bindo. Two very famous Italian names derived from Latin ori-ginals via syncopis: Dante from Durante; and Giotto via Giolotto from Angiolotto, a suffixed version of Angelo. The augurative Bencivenni gave Cenni via Civenni; while the very common saints' names Jacopus and Giovanni gave Lapus or Lapo and Gianni. Consonants might also be doub-led or changed. Arnolfus became Nolfus then Noffus; Guillelmus Lemmo or Memmo; while Maffeo was an alternative for Matteo in Florence and elsewhere.

Italian suffixes were legion. To take a simple example from the Libro di Montaperti, alongside 44 Albertus, there are three Albertescus, 35 Albertinus, one Albertinuzzus, one Albertonicius and five Albertuccius. Altogether, Brattö has identified 25 different suffixes in this source alone, not counting minor variants and compounds. The most frequent were -*ellus*, -*ettus*, -*inus* and

-uccius –, in the vernacular *-ello* or *-cello*, *-etto*, *-ino* or *-cino –* and *-uccio* or *-occio*, with female equivalents. Suffixes later acted as diminutives, pejoratives or terms of endearment, and it is hard to believe that they did not do so in the medieval period also, alongside their differentiating function. Sons were certainly known by hypocoristic versions of their fathers' names. This was common practice in Siena in 1285; Malatestino, lord of Rimini from 1312 to 1317, was the eldest son of Malatesta da Verruchio; and Grifoneto was the son of Grifone degli Baglioni of Perugia around 1500.

Suffixes themselves could be taken as short names, on the analogy of the use of second name elements. So Lottus derived from Arlottus, Ugiolottus, etc.; Fuccius from names with the *-uccius* suffix, like Grifuccius or Ridolfuccius. It also became common to add suffixes to shortened forms of names. So Cola from Nicola could become Colello, Coletti, Colaci, Coluzzi and so on; Ventura from Bonaventura could become Venturelli, Venturini, Venturazzi, then Tura, Turatti, Turazzo and so on. Going into the modern period, Fucilla lists 38 suffixed full forms of Francesco and 133 short or short suffixed forms. He gives comparable numbers of variants for Domenico, Giacomo, Giovanni and Pietro. Giovanni – to provide only a selection – gives Vanni, Nanni, Nannini, Nanuccio; Giovannini, Vannini, Ninni, Ninnoli; Giannico, Nico, Nicchini; Zanni, Zannetti, Zanussi and so on.

In addition to acting as nicknames and serving to distinguish homonyms, it seems that hypocoristics acted in Italy in the same way as alliteration and repetition of elements in the old Germanic systems: to indicate family relationship. Indeed they were a form of alliteration and repetition. Fucilla cites some lines from a sixteenth-century Bolognese satire to make this point: "I am from Bertagnana; my name is Bertoldo. Bertolazzo my father is called, or was called, for he has laid down his earthly burdens . . . Bertin, Bertuzzo and Bertolino were my grandfathers."[44]

Hypocoristics were also important in France, where they multiplied in the thirteenth and fourteenth centuries. Their spread in the official documents coincides with that of the vernacular and almost certainly reveals a situation that had been masked earlier by the use of Latin.

Lorraine seem to have been one of the first areas to experience the trend. Of the 110 male names in use in Metz around 1300, 92 had hypocoristic variants, and over half the population, male and female, bore such names. They were formed in a variety of ways. For example, from Jehan came Jennat, Jennass, Jennin, Jennel, Jennetel, Hanelot, Hanekins and so on; from Nicolle, Colin, Collart, Colignon and Colinat. The commonest suffixes here and elsewhere were *-in*, *-at* and *-ot*. As the examples show, both first and second parts of the name could be taken for the root.

Hypocoristics were also common quite early on in Flanders. Haket from Johannes and Collard were found in the first half of the twelfth century; Clais from Nicolais, Monin from Simon, Bele from Isabele and Nela from Petronela from before 1225; all testifying to the popularity of these Christian names. Such names became even more popular and more varied in the thirteenth and fourteenth centuries. Further examples from among the tax-payers of Calais around 1300 are Baudin, Baudet and Boidekin or Bodekin from Baldwinus; Stas and Stasekin from Eustasse; and Margrie, Margrietekin, Grite, Griele and Grielekin from Margareta. The suffix -*kin* was a character-istic Flemish and northern French one. Using suffixes and other devices, sometimes in combination, meant that some common names could have many variants. There were 14 forms of Stephen among the confraternity of jongleurs of Arras in the first half of the thirteenth century, for example, and 12 forms of James.

The same picture is found elsewhere in northern France. In both Picardy and Normandy the frequency of hypocoristics increases from the end of the thirteenth century. Both Germanic and Christian names were affected, and both Germanic and Romance suffixes were used. The commonest were again -*et*, -*in*, -*on* and -*ot*, and they were mainly attached to the commonest names. In some cases the hypocoristic form eclipsed the original name altogether. At Reims in the fourteenth century, Ponsart, Ponsot, Poncelet and Poncinet were common, but Pons itself never occurs in the sources.

The fullest study of hypocoristic names in medieval France is Berganton's of Béarn around 1400. By this time, hypocoristics were widely used there in the official documents, though there was some resistance to them from among the clergy. In Béarn, proper, 39 per cent of persons had such a name, and in Bigorre 15.5 per cent. Their usage in official documents declined in the fifteenth century and then died out with the imposition of the collective family name. It continued, however, at the unofficial level.

A large number of suffixes and their combinations are found in the sources. Including double and triple suffixes, Berganton counts 114, which comprise 22 different basic elements. To take an example, 60 derivatives of Arnaud are recorded. These start with the shortened versions of the main name: Auda and Naude. Then there are suffixed versions of the main name unchanged: Arnaudat, Arnauto, Arnautuc; suffixed versions of the short name: Audine, Audote; short versions of the suffixed name: Nauto, Nautuc. Then there are versions with double suffixes: Arnautolet, Arnautucat, Audinot; and short versions of these: Tolet, Tucat, Dinot. Similarly, there were 52 derivatives from Raymond or Ramon; 55 from Garcia or Garsia; 74 from Guilhem; and 129 from Petrus.

There is little doubt that hypocoristics were used to distinguish hom-onyms and especially sons from fathers of the same name. In the Forez in the second half of the thirteenth century, we find Guillerminus, a son of Guillelmus de Cenosche, knight; and Johannetus, son of Johannes Bauduins. It is also the case in France that different forms of derivative had different implications. In Béarn, for example, masculine -*et*, -*in*, -*ot* and -*uc*, and feminine -*ete*, -*ine*, -*ote* and -*uque* were all diminutives; but, whereas -*et*, -*in*, -*ete* and -*ine* were affectionate or tender, -*ot*, -*ote* and -*ou* could be almost derogatory, and *-uc* and *-uque* were uncomplimentary and were later dropped for this reason. The suffixes *-as* and *-asse* were augmentative and also depreciative.

Hypocoristics were generally more prevalent among women than men. The main reason for this seems to have been that women were frequently given male names. At Evreux in the fourteenth century, women used male names without change, for example Eustache, Eudes, Guillaume and Philippe, but usually a female ending was attached: Chrétienne, Denise, Martine; and very often a female hypocoristic suffix: Eudette, Gilwette, Guillotte, Philipotte. At Paris around 1300, Perronnelle was very common and also Jehannete, in addition to Jehanne. At Metz at the same time Jaikemate was the seventh most popular woman's name, and Martenate and Mathiate both figured in the top forty. In the Forez in the fourteenth century, women had both Germanic and Christian hypocoristic names. Guillelma and Guillelmeta were the most popular in the first category. In the second, Johanetta was common, alongside Johanna, and also Stephana and Stephaneta, Andreva and Petronilla.

Hypocoristic names are not very evident in later medieval English sources. At Holywell-cum-Needingworth, for example, between around 1300 and around 1450, there are no such forms among men's names and only two among women's. But the documentary evidence conceals the situation as far as everyday usage is concerned. As we shall see in discussing family or second names, shortened name forms must have been common among the peasantry by the thirteenth century, since they figure so largely in patronymics. There is also some literary evidence. Langland refers in *Piers Plowman* to "Cesse [Cecilia] the sonteress . . . , Watte the warner . . . , Tymme the tinker . . . , Hikke the hackney man . . . , Dawe the dyker" and so on; while Gower provides a list of stereotyped participants in the Revolt of 1381, including Symme (Simon), Bat (Bartholomew), Gibbe (Gilbert), Colle (Nicholas), Hobbe (Robert), and Jacke (John).[45] It is significant that such hypocoristics rarely bear suffixes (*-kin* is the commonest), that they derive from continental and not Anglo-Saxon names, and that they are associated with the peasantry.

CHAPTER SEVEN

Second names: I

The introduction of the second name

The single name predominated in the early Middle Ages, and what had become the baptismal name remained "the main denomination"[1] right through the medieval period and beyond. But increasingly from the eleventh century onwards, a second name was added. At first "an accessory and transitory addition",[2] this second name in time became an integral part of an individual's name. This was a slow and irregular process. Meanwhile, the second name also became the family name, transmitted from generation to generation. This whole development was Europe-wide.

In France, the acquisition of second names began among the noble élite and is first recorded as a significant trend in the south. Second names constituted around 3 per cent of names in charters from Languedoc in the ninth and tenth centuries; 36 per cent in the eleventh century; and 72 per cent in the twelfth. By the eleventh century the second name was usual among witnesses to charters in Béarn, that is among the élite, but it was also becoming common among the peasants. On lists of tenants of the monastery of Saint Mont from around 1050, only four out of thirty names were single ones. By the twelfth century, townspeople in Béarn also had second names. In the Lauragais under 2 per cent of men questioned by the Inquisition around 1250 had only one name. A recent study concludes that "the triumph of the new system was total in southern France by the second half of the twelfth century".[3]

Turning to central France, we find that the proportion of double names increases in the Forez from the eleventh century onwards. By the first half of the thirteenth century, 83 per cent of men's names were double, and by 1300 95 per cent. A similar picture emerges for the Lyonnais, where nearly all names were double by 1300. Those taking an oath of allegiance to the

abbot of Cluny in 1309 nearly all had second names. In Burgundy generally the single name predominated in charters until the second half of the
eleventh century, but by 1250–80 nearly 90 per cent of persons had two
names. In the Dijon area, women still had single names in the first half of
the thirteenth century, but from the second half they too nearly all had a
second name.

Most Paris taxpayers had two names by 1300. At Metz second names
remained rare among patricians until the early thirteenth century, when
they were quite rapidly adopted. By the second half of the twelfth century
in Picardy around 40 per cent of names were still single, but this percentage
dropped quickly to under 10 per cent by around 1225. An entry in the
necrology of the Confraternity of Jongleurs of Arras from 1275 indicates that
the absence of a second name was worthy of remark by then even for a
woman: "Sans sournom Maroie", or Maroie without a second name.[4] All
taxpayers and tenants of the bishop had two names at Amiens by 1300,
while only 20 people listed in the account books of the Hôtel-Dieu at
Soissons in the fifteenth century had one name, that is around 3 per cent of
the total. They were mostly servants or nuns. In Brittany the introduction of
the second name came comparatively late. Around 75 per cent of names in
charters were single in 1000, the rest being by-names or patronymics. The
second name proper reached 20 per cent in the later twelfth century and
only overtook the single name around 1250.

Single names were still the rule in England in the eleventh century. Most
subtenants in Domesday Book, for example, do not have a second name;
while Whitelock comments on "the rarity" of second names in the Thorney
Liber Vitae for this period.[5] By the twelfth century, however, most of the
élite, clerical and lay, did have second names, though there were exceptions in remoter areas. Nearly all those mentioned in Giraldus Cambrensis'
Speculum Duorum of around 1200 had two names, though quite often the
second "name" was simply the office a man held. All ordinands in the
diocese of Lincoln in the 1290s had two names. By the later thirteenth
century, too, the great majority of names in the Durham Liber Vitae were
double. The single names that still appeared were almost certainly those of
children or religious.

Second names were also established among townspeople and peasants.
At the old capital Winchester, 55 per cent of the citizens had only one name
before the Conquest. By 1100–50 the balance had been sharply reversed
with around 70 per cent having two names; a survey in 1285 revealed only
one person with a single name. The picture is much the same at Newark, a
less important town in the Danelaw: by the late twelfth century, 75 per cent
of men and 60 per cent of women had second names. For peasants, we
have a list of tenants of the abbey of St Edmund (Bury) from around 1100,
in which "more than half had a single name only".[6] A century later, the split
among St Edmund's peasants was 31 per cent with one name and 69 per

cent with two. Studies of families of serfs and those claimed as serfs, mainly from East Anglia and the Home Counties, in the early thirteenth century indicate that they had mainly single names at this time. Most of the tenants of the bishop of Lincoln around 1225, however, had a second name, as did the tenants at Warboys in 1251. About 95 per cent of the latter were designated by a second name, though this was often a family tie. Matthews has summed up this process: 45 per cent of all men recorded in printed sources had second names by around 1100; 90 per cent by around 1200; and 99 per cent by around 1300.

Second names first came into use in Lowland Scotland in the early twelfth century. Witnesses to the foundation of the abbey of Selkirk around 1125 included Robertus de Brus, Robertus de Umfraville and Galterus de Lyndeseia. Such names were first used by the great nobles, often incomers of Anglo-Norman origin. Second names spread to other classes during the thirteenth century. They were normal in the so-called "Ragman Roll" of 1296, listing the landowners and burgesses who paid homage to Edward I of England on his military progress through Scotland. A few Highland chiefs bore second names from this time also, but second names generally were not used in the Highlands even by the seventeenth century. Similarly, in Wales, only shifting patronymics were in general use by the end of the medieval period.

"In Ireland the adoption of hereditary surnames began in the tenth century",[7] and the bulk of second names became fixed in the eleventh and twelfth centuries. Second name formation, according to Woulfe, was generally ended by the fourteenth century, though there were "a few surnames that originated only in the 16th [century]".[8] Patriotic pride in this precocious Irish development has perhaps exaggerated its significance. For though most Irish people may in theory have had second names available to them before the end of the Middle Ages, they did not use them.

Second names can be found in documents in Italy from the eighth century, notably in and around Venice, and examples become more common from the end of the ninth and into the tenth centuries just about everywhere. Most of the élite in Genoa had second names by the eleventh century, and second names were adopted by the middle and lower classes by the end of the twelfth. In Latium, the second name began to spread in the last quarter of the twelfth century, and in Bologna from the start of the thirteenth. In Cremona in 1283, a significant minority of citizens had single names but most had two. At Perugia in 1285 nearly all taxpayers were identified by patronymics. In Florence and Tuscany generally, most members of the élite had two names by the mid thirteenth century, if not earlier, though examples of important men designated by single names are not hard to find into the fourteenth century, for example, Ciaccio, the Florentine, found among the gluttons in the Third Circle of Dante's *Inferno*, or the painter Giotto (1261–1337). Second names became normal in Piedmont, the County of Nice and the Trentino in the late thirteenth and fourteenth

117

centuries. So in Italy also, the process of adopting second names was slow and patchy, and it was not complete in remoter rural areas or the south until the sixteenth century or later.

Types of second name

Students of the subject have largely agreed in identifying four main categories of second name: (i) names deriving from by-names or nicknames; (ii) names deriving from first names, often with patronymic prefixes or suffixes; (iii) names deriving from places or topographical features; and (iv) names deriving from occupations and offices. As we shall see, there are sub-categories within these, and it is not always possible to ascribe every name to a particular category, either because its exact meaning is unknown or because it is ambiguous.

Second names from nicknames

The category of second name taken from nicknames was usually one of the smallest, ranging in France in the twelfth to fourteenth centuries from 10 per cent to 24 per cent of all second names. Only in Arras in the twelfth century did just over half the second names derive from nicknames. Figures for England in the thirteenth century were around 15 to 20 per cent. This almost certainly does not reflect the general incidence of nicknames, which we know was high in later centuries. For the early medieval period inevitably we have information only for the élite.

We have seen that by-names were occasionally used in the mainly single-name systems of the Franks and the Anglo-Saxons. Kings, clerics and nobles bore nicknames throughout Europe. For example, "the great magnates of Gascony often bore a nickname, which served to distinguish them from others in the same dynasty with the same first name".[9] So the count of Bordeaux around 930 was Guillelmo comite qui vocatur Bonus; and lesser eleventh-century lords included Arnardus cognomine Ursus and Bernardus miles dictus Contrarius. Some writers believe that such names, often pejorative, were given by nobles to each other: they were the signs of belonging to an exclusive group, like Roman *cognomina*. Others have supposed that names such as Escorche Vilain (Champagne, 1172) or Deffie Dieu (1249) could only have been bestowed by disgruntled peasants. The former seems more likely. In Catalonia, alternative nicknames were especially important in the tenth and eleventh centuries for women of the élite, and they expressed ideal feminine qualities: Elegancia, Miravella, Fidela, Onorata.

Initially nicknames were individual, but they could be inherited. Examples of such names becoming family names in eleventh-century Normandy and

England are Giffard (fat-cheeked), Malet (evil), and Crispin. A later family chronicler claimed that the first Gilbert Crispin was so called because he had hair that stood on end like "a bristly pine (crispus pinus)".[10] The great Poitevin castellan of the early eleventh century known to historians as Hugh of Lusignan was called Hugonis Chiliarchi or commander of a thousand, a name that was handed on for four generations. In the Mâconnais, the lords of Uxelles used the name Grossus through the twelfth century, and 7 of the 31 noble second names in use there around 1100 were hereditary nicknames. Again, there were families of knights in the Auxerrois in the twelfth century called Crassus, Strabo, Bailledart and Li Chat, all originally nicknames.

From the end of the eleventh century nicknames are quite often expressed in the vernacular, and the range and number of second names deriving from nicknames in the documents is greatly expanded. It becomes possible to distingush between different kinds of nickname belonging to all classes. One of the fullest studies is that by Carrez for Burgundy mainly in the fourteenth century, and we shall take it as a case-study, referring to others as necessary.

Names relating to physical traits were always very common. Size in height or girth is an obvious distinguishing feature. A small person might be called Cristianus Li nains. If "petit" were used in Burgundy, it was usually in suffixed form; hence Biatrix Petitot. Various other words were used, including figurative terms; hence Estienne Milley and Hugonis dicti Grain d'orge. There was a similar range of names for a thin person, for example Perrenot Maigrot, Odo Mal norriz and Perrenot Poul de char (peu de chair). Next to the big fat and strong. From "carré" (four-square) derive Odot Quarey, Perrin Quarrenet or Carnet, and, Carrez argues, the later important family from the region, the Carnot. Roundness is conveyed in Petrus Boulez and Oudenote la Boulle.

Names indicating colour of skin or hair were also frequent, especially those referring to red or dark tones. So we have Estienne Le rous, Agnote fille au Rosseaul and Martin Le noir. "Brun" and its derivatives were also common, as was "maure", the one applying to hair and the other to skin. Blond, grey or white hair was also labelled. Jehan Malchenu had gone grey early. An excess or lack of hair was also liable to be remarked, examples being Humberdas Le pelley and Phelibert Chaulve.

Parts of the body might be singled out, if they were unusual in any way. From Reims around 1300 we have Gullaume Yeux de buef, Gilles Bouche de lièvre, Rose La cuissarde, and Baudessons culdoie. References to bottoms, thighs and genitals were not uncommon. Again, infirmities or odd physical traits could be signalled. From Burgundy again, we have: Martins Bote avant, for a person who bends his head and shoulders forward; Jehannot Petit pas; Jehan Boiteux; and Jehan Baubaul, a stutterer. Carrez found sixteen nicknames for hunchbacks, ten for those with bad eyesight, and so on.

Estienne Put villain smelled badly. Ironically the modern family name Pubel or Poubelle, borne by a nineteenth-century Paris Prefect of Police and hence attached to French refuse bins, originally meant "smells sweet".

References to moral or behavioural traits were sometimes but not usually complimentary. In the first category, from Reims around 1300, we have Bourie La bone ouvrière; from elsewhere, Probus Homo, Bonefoys, Costanz, all used as second names. In the second category, from Picardy from the thirteenth to the fifteenth centuries, Morlet garnered Bécart or Béchart (too talkative), Dolle (sad), Froissart or Froisset (fighter, from the word for wound), Quenoille (distaff, i.e. effeminate man), and Tricart (tricky), among many others.

The use of animal names was very common and could have a variety of meanings. Among domestic animals, names for ox or bull, such as Le Buef, Bouvet, Thorel, all from Picardy, almost certainly indicated strength and heavy build. Names for the goat, such as Le Bouc, Boucquet, Bouquin, suggested lechery. Aignel or Laniel (lamb) meant meek and mild; Pourcel and Porchelet, like Cochon (pig), meant dirty and greedy. The dog was commonly used, examples being Le Quien, Caignet and Cagnet, and could mean either faithful or dirty and of low status. Naming after the cat seems to have indicated slyness. Among domestic birds, the cock (Coquart, Coquel, Coquelin) indicated vanity, the exercise of petty authority, maybe virility; the hen (Pouillé, Poulet) domesticity and stupidity. Among wild birds, only the crow was very common (Corbel, Corbin, Corbaut, etc.). Wild animals provided some complimentary names like Lionnet, but mainly pejorative ones. The fox (Li Renars) was sly; the hare (Le Lièvres) was timid. The commonest animal names in this class came from the wolf (Lupus, Louvel, Lutre). The wolf was also most common where parts of the animal furnished the nickname, for example Peslupi, Pideleue (wolf's foot), Queue de Loup (wolf's tail), and Coue de louf (wolf's testicle). Some animal names may also derive from house, inn or shop signs.

Second names referring to titles or offices could be descriptive, as we shall see, but many seem to have been nicknames. The Le Roy, Daufin and Le Duc among the leading citizens of Eu between 1250 and 1400, and Li Marchis, Castellania and Levesque among the citizens and the tenants of the bishop of Amiens around 1300, either had actual regal or noble bearing or put on airs, or their names may have been ironic. This kind of name could also have other origins. At Cluny in the fourteenth century, Li Reis, Reyars, Reyaz and so on seem to have been names given to those born at Epiphany, the Feast of Kings. In a number of places, such names derived from the leading role played by a person on a particular festive occasion or in a society. The owner of the victorious cock in the cock-fighting at Soissons at Mardi Gras, like the cock itself, was known as the Roi des poules. At Auxerre and Dijon the man who hit the popinjay in the annual archery contest took the title of Roi de l'oiseau, and if someone won three years in succession then he was called Empereur. The leaders of guilds, youth groups and other organizations might also be called "rois". Levesque or Archeveque could refer to the role played by a boy or a man in the Feast of Fools. Names of characters played in the mystery plays could also adhere to people, like the Caiaphas and Judas found in Poissy in the twelfth and thirteenth centuries.

A whole range of other, mainly obscure, nicknames is recorded, relating to objects, clothes, plants, etc. Sometimes a phrase was used. Phrase names from Burgundy relating to food include Jehannot Semesau (a person who scatters or wastes salt, a wastrel); Perrenot bait les aux (one who beats garlic, probably implying poverty); and Johannes dictus Tue pain (one with a keen appetite). Other phrase names remain less transparent, for example those taken from the liturgy: Salve Domino, Amen, and Diex le bénie, all from Amiens; perhaps the last was a favourite expression.

There was a similar range of types of second name from nicknames in Italy and Britain, and we will only mention examples of special interest. Second names taken from animals were especially common in Italy. In the Trentino in the thirteenth and fourteenth centuries, for example, domestic and wild animal names were used as well as those of birds and insects: Ser Bartolo detto Gatta (cat); Odorico de Vulpesino (fox); Martino Cicogninus (stork); Giovanni detto Gazza (magpie); Odorico detto Grillus (cricket); Thomasius Scorpione. Patrician families in Venice at the same time included the Dolfin, the Lion, the Volpe, the Stornello (starling) and the Galina (hen); while the Capponi of Florence derived their name from capon. Animal names usually had metaphorical meanings. Henricus Paparotus from the Trentino was a little goose in the English figurative sense. A huge variety of regional variations and shades of meaning existed, however. As Fucilla explains for the modern period, calling a person a horse generally implied that he was a hard worker, but in some districts it was applied to a restless or flighty person, in others to an ignoramus, and in yet others to a person with a loud and insistent voice like a neigh.

Nicknames from the animal kingdom could be acquired for reasons other than some supposed similarity to the creature in question. The Florentine painter Paolo Uccello (1396–1475) acquired his second name, meaning "bird" or "of the birds", according to Vasari, "because he loved birds most of all' to watch and to paint.[11] Heers suggests that once such names had become the names of families or kindreds they were especially well suited to serve as totemic representations of those groups. He cites, for example, the four clans "which evolved out of the great Monaldeschi confederation" at Orvieto in the 1320s,[12] and which took the names of the stag, the viper, the dog and the eagle. This was analagous to the use of such emblems by confraternities and guilds.

Title nicknames were found in England and in Italy. The name King existed in most English villages in the fourteenth-century subsidy rolls and earlier sources, together often with Abbot and Lord. Among those with lay title names in the Trentino were Ser Antonius dictus Baronus, Benvenuto detto Comes and Ioannis dicti Marchesi; and with ecclesiastical: Vivaldi dicti Prioris, Alberto detto Episcopus and Martino detto Papa. "Pageant" names were also found in both countries, for example English peasants or artisans called Thomas Cardinal, Thomas Le Emperor and Robert Le Pope. Caifas, Herode, Angel, Death and Dragon must also derive from parts played in plays or shows.

All the days of the week occur as nicknames (or first names) in Italy, and by derivation as second names, and the same is true of the months of the year, though Gennaro, Maggio and Agosto were by the far the commonest. A more restricted range was used in England and in France, suggesting that they did not necessarily refer simply to birth circumstances. Days of the week in England were mainly restricted to Monday and Friday. Some manors had Mondayland and Mondaymen, who worked it on that day, and the nickname may refer to those who performed this labour service. Friday was an unlucky day and a fast day, through its association with Good Friday, and may have referred to a gloomy or unfortunate person. In France, the first six months of the year are much commoner as second names than the rest, though no reason for this is obvious. The second name could also refer to being born on or near a particular festival. In England we have Candlemas, Plouday (Plough Monday), and, much more commonly, Cristemasse, Nowell, Midwinter, and probably Jolyf and Jolliffe from "jolo" or Scandinavian Yule. Easter gave Pask, Pash, Paish and Pascoe from Pasques. In Italy, we have Epifani, Annunzio, Natale, Pasquale, Carnovale. An unusual example from the Trentino is naming after San Paol Revers or the Conversion of St Paul, hence Iohanis Roversii and Franciscus Reversi.

Phrase names were particularly common in Italy. We have come across auguratives as first names and many also became second names: Amedei (love God); Bentivenga (may good befall you); Tornabuoni (be good). The name of the painter Mantegna is short for Dio ti Mantegna (God keep you). Imperatives of the "Shakespeare" type could be nicknames recording a personal habit or an event: Basadonna (kiss woman); Bevilacqua (drink water); Scannagatta (kill cat). Sometimes they were associated with occupations: Battilana (wool beater); Spezzaferro (break iron, i.e. a smith); Tagliapietra (stone cutter). A follower of the Baglioni of Perugia chosen around 1500 to carry their banner was called Stracciabandiere (bear the flag) or Straccia for short.[13]

Such names were less common in England. From Domesday Book, we have Aluricus Chacepol (hunt fowl) and Radulfus Tailgebosc (cut wood, probably an occupation). Later examples are Brunild Prichelous (1148, Winchester), a woman good or fond of delousing her relatives and friends, and Galfridus Traillewinge (1202, Yorkshire), probably a man with a limp. A number of English phrase names derive from oaths, though a few may have been auguratives: for example, Cristiana Deubenie (1194, Yorkshire – God bless), and Roger Agodeshalf (1222, London – for God's sake). Pardew, Pardoe and Purdy, from par or pour Dieu, were quite frequent.

Among second names from miscellaneous nicknames, there was an Italian penchant for names referring to plants. From the Trentino again, we have Bartolo detto Ceueoleta (onion – elsewhere Cipolla); Pelegrino dicto Fasolo (kidney bean – otherwise Fagiolo); Antonio Pavarino (poppy); and Antonio detto Ravica (turnip). Such names were usually figurative, but sometimes indicated a liking for, the growing of, or trading in a food plant.

Generally the meaning of all these nicknames must be inferred, though sources do occasionally explain how a name came to be given. Orderic Vitalis wrote that a certain Edricus "was called Streone because he was a miser".[14] The much disliked tutor of Giraldus Cambrensis' nephew was called Willelmus Capre sive Capelle. He got his second name originally from a chapel which he acquired, *capella*, which by a play of words and given his character led to his being called Capra, which in turn meant both "goat" and one with supposed goat-like sexual appetites and behaviour.[15]

In addition to describing individual traits, nicknames as second names could be used to distinguish family members with the same first name. In Wales, Bach or Vach originally meant small and was later used in a variety of circumstances "ranging from endearment to contempt".[16] It was also used to distinguish son from father and younger from elder brother. The same is true of the comparative Bychan or Bechan, commonest in the form Fychan, Vachan or Vaughan. So in a sixteenth-century example, the two sons of Philip Goch of Glamorgan were called Philip Vychan and Philip Vychan Vach.

Second names from first names

In much of France in the twelfth and thirteenth centuries, second names from first names were also a small category, in many places comprising between 10 and 20 per cent of the total. In England at the same time the proportion seems to have been higher on average at around 25–30 per cent, with some places exceeding this by some margin. Among the peasant tenants of St Edmund around 1200, 51 per cent had patronymics or names relating to family ties. In Italy patronymics were even more prevalent: 40 per cent in the Venezia Euganea; and over 90 per cent among the taxpayers of Perugia in 1285 and in the mainly plebeian Libro di Montaperti of 1260 for Florence. Patronyms were also preponderant in Celtic areas.

First names used as second names are found in the early Frankish period but only become at all frequent from the late ninth or tenth century. In some cases, they are clearly additional or alternative names. From Catalonia, for example, we have Sabado que vocant Mirone (962), and Bona dona que vocant Ermegot (1057). But in most cases second names of this type were patronymics, sons being designated via the names of their fathers, or more rarely of other relatives. This practice is best documented for

France in the south-west, which was probably one of the places where it first began.

It was the rule among the nobles in much of Gascony by the tenth century for a man to take the first name of his father as his own second name. The custom was imitated by other classes with some delay. In the north of the region, the practice was abandoned by leading families from the start of the eleventh century, being superseded by naming after the fief and other forms, but it was retained by the great feudal lords of what is now called the Basque country and by other classes more generally. The second name was usually in the nominative not the genitive case, and it was an integral part of the denomination. After the "patronymic rule" had been abandoned, the trace of it survived in the region in the form of double first names. These were frequent in Gascony down to the end of the Middle Ages.

A similar pattern is found in Catalonia, but the forms of the patronymic were different. In the eleventh century, the predominant style was with the Latin "filius", for example Guiscafredus filio Mocione, or less commonly Guilelmus prolis Seniofred; but from the mid eleventh century putting the father's name in the genitive was introduced and became the main form, for example Bernardus Guifredi, or Sendredus Leopardi. Placing the second name in the nominative case is also found, but may refer to an alternative name as well as that of the father. Second names were occasionally taken from other relatives. A Berengarius Pucululli seems to have acquired his name in the early thirteenth century from an uncle called Puculul de Vila nova, from whom perhaps he inherited.

The same evolution took place in the Fribourg region as in Catalonia, though perhaps later in time. The form Anselmus filius Gonradi, still recorded in the thirteenth century, gave way to more direct forms based on vernacular practice. Aebischer cites examples with prepositions in the genitive (Mermerius de Member) and in the dative (Perrerius à l'Egmonet), as well as the simple juxtaposition of nominatives (Willelmus Achardus). This pattern is repeated all over France with variations. In Brittany the "filius de" formula accounted for 50 per cent of names between 1050 and 1100, a transitional form. An example from the Vexin illustrates the switch from the "filius" form to the elided genitive. Hugo filius Gervasii in 1155 was later called Hugo Gervasii.

The change from Latin to the vernacular in documents confirmed the abandonment of the "filius" forms. Declension of the second name also tended to disappear, though not immediately. At Arras in the fourteenth century, second names in French were usually in the nominative, though sometimes preceded by the article: Tumas Guifrois, Maroie Martine, Ansiaus le Adan, Marges le Golis; second names in Flemish were in the nominative or the genitive: Monart Helbode, Lipin Boudins. In Flemish documents of the thirteenth and fourteenth centuries, where patronyms are in the genitive, they are usually followed by "sone" or "dochter", though these could be omitted and just implied. Similarly "fils" and "fille" were omitted in French documents. These terms of relationship never became attached to the name as they did in England, in Scandinavian countries and elsewhere. There is no French (or indeed Italian) equivalent on the -son, -s, ap or Mac names of Britain.

In many areas of France it was the least common first names, often Germanic, that were most likely to be used as second names, ostensibly because they could best perform the distinguishing function required. In the Vexin from the eleventh century to the thirteenth, names of Germanic origin were the most frequently used for this purpose but "the commonest, like Gautier, Guillaume and Eudes, were not represented".[17] At Eu in Normandy, two-thirds of the first names used as second names were again Germanic. In Paris around 1300, only five of the sixteen first names most frequently used were themselves common as second names, and none of the five exceptions was very common. And where Christian names were used as second names, it was the comparatively rare Old Testament names that were favoured, for example Adam and Daniel. All of this suggests that logic may have ruled the choice of second name. If one's father's name was a common one, then a different kind of second name would be chosen rather than the patronymic. Or is the bias simply an accidental function of the coincidence in time of the adoption of second names and the switch from Germanic to Christian names, of the fact that there were in this period and temporarily a large number of persons with Christian first names, whose fathers had Germanic ones?

A related feature is the use of hypocoristic forms of first names to make second names. There was no preference for this form in Paris around 1300; but in the Forez, as Christian first names were increasingly used in the course of the thirteenth and fourteenth centuries, there was a tendency to use hypocoristic forms; and in fifteenth-century Soissons over half the second names of this type derived from them. The phenomenon seems to have occurred all over France in the later Middle Ages, and is often in retrospect one of the main testimonies to the importance of this first-name style. Names involved were both Christian and Germanic. At Amiens in 1300, for example, we have Foukete, a feminized Fouket from Fouke and Folco; Monnequin from Simon via Monet; and Turel or Turele from Artur. At Calais around the same time we have Lai or Lais from Wilhelm via Willai; Lammes, Lammin and Lammekin from Lambert; and Lips, Lippin and Lippinni from Philippus.

In England second names formed from the first name, usually of a person's father, are found quite early and take a variety of forms. The father's name may simply be added unchanged, or in genitive form, or the filial relationship may be spelled out in Latin, English or French.

Direct use of an existing first name as a second name was found in the eleventh century and earlier, examples being Dodda Aethelmaer, Aelfweard Dudd, and Ulfstan Eudlac. A few examples are alternative names, but most

seem to have been patronymics. They became more numerous in the following centuries, and it has been plausibly argued that as Anglo-Saxon
names lost ground as first names their value as distinguishing second names
grew, which parallels developments in France. Around 20 per cent of all
second names from first names in East Anglia were Anglo-Saxon still in the
fourteenth century. In 1907 Skeat listed over 350 Anglo-Saxon names preserved in this way as modern family names: Darwin from Deorwine, Stannard
from Stanheard, Woolsey or Wolsey from Wulfsige, and so on. The same
process occurred to a more limited extent with Scandinavian first names in
the north and east. Though attention has thus been focused on the old
vernacular first names that were transformed directly into second names,
more of the latter ultimately were "new" Christian or Norman names. In
Norfolk by the early sixteenth century, among the commonest second names
deriving from first names, one-third were old vernacular but two-thirds
were Christian or Norman.

The oldest genitive form was in -*ing*. We have seen that it was used in
the Anglo-Saxon royal genealogies, and it is found in place-names, referring
sometimes to collective kin-groups. Patronymic examples are found from
the eighth to the twelfth centuries: Eadolf Bosing (from Bosa); Wulfric Cufing
(from Cufa); Ceolla Snoding. Another old vernacular form was in -*en*, for
example Otten from Odo or Otto. There were 72 names of this kind in the
1332 Warwickshire subsidy roll.

The Latin -*i* form is found, especially in the twelfth and thirteenth centuries: we find Goduin Aluini, Stannard Lefstani and Galfridus Ordmeri, all
from Suffolk. Here "filius" must usually have been understood, for the "filius'
form was the usual patronymic style from the eleventh century to the fourteenth all over England among all social classes. The "filius" could be placed
between or after the two names: for example, from Domesday Book, Osgot
Aedrici filius or Goduine filius Edric; but the latter was more common. The
form was used with names in all languages and, though most common with
other first names, it is also found with other types of second name: nicknames and occupations.

In French, there were two patronymic devices. The preposition "de"
could be employed, as with, for example, Robert de Wlfun and Petrus de
Sewall, from thirteenth-century Suffolk. The meaning of the term is sometimes made quite explicit, as in the case of a Norfolk man called Simon de
Turlac in 1200, but also Simon Turlac and Simon filius Turlac. "Fitz", preceding the father's name, was the Anglo-French equivalent of "filius". Short for
"fils de", it was used in Normandy but not in the rest of France. It was
introduced to England by the Norman élite, and some early hereditary
noble names took this form: Fitz Alan, Fitz Gerald, Fitz Walter. But it did
spread to other classes, and remained current till around 1300. Some Fitz
names are found among London burgesses. Gilbert le Fitz Kew in 1297 was
the son of a cook. Giraldus Cambrensis used "fitz" around 1200 as an

alternative for "filius". The idea that "fitz" indicates illegitimacy is a popular misconception, as far as the medieval period is concerned, though sometimes the term followed by a title, like Fitz Count, may have been used for bastards. Henry Fitzroy was the name of Henry II's legitimate heir, and the first royal bastard called with this name was, it seems, another Henry Fitzroy, son of Henry VIII and Elizabeth Blount, born in 1519, later Duke of Somerset and Richmond.

Two English patronymic forms in -son and in -s eventually became predominant. The -son form derived from the Anglo-Saxon "suna", "sune" or "sunu". The earliest recorded instance is Hering Hussan sunu from the early seventh century, mentioned in the *Anglo-Saxon Chronicle*. Tengvik found over a hundred Old English personal names linked with "sune" and variants down to around 1100, plus 24 with Scandinavian names. As this shows, though second names of any kind were not the rule at the time, the "sune" patronymic was not a great rarity, and it became commoner in the eleventh century. A few examples continue to crop up in the sources in the early twelfth century (and later), but the "sune" form was generally eclipsed from this time, and -son forms do not begin to appear until the late thirteenth century. In the interval, the Latin "filius" form was used in the documents. At the level of everyday usage it seems that there must have been a large degree of continuity with "filius" acting as a translation of "sune" and then -son.

The patronymic in -son does not become common until the fourteenth and fifteenth centuries. It was more often found in the north than in the south, where the -s form was more frequent, but neither was regionally exclusive. Though mainly found with personal names, -son second names could also be formed with occupational names and nicknames, for example le Clerkson, le Taillorson and Spynksone (finch). The personal names used were nearly all post-Conquest ones, and they were very often the most popular of these: John, Richard, Robert, William, etc. The consequent second names had no pronounced distinguishing functions as their equivalents may have had in England and France earlier on. Names ending in -son were also "initially characteristic of the poorer social groups, such as small free tenants and labourers";[18] they were very rare among the names of substantial landowners.

Ultimately the commonest of all forms was the English suffix -s. Mainly a genitive, it could also stand for -son. A few examples are found in the late twelfth and thirteenth centuries: Edricus Kettles; Stephen Paynes; Mabil Wulmers; but it did not become at all common till the later fourteenth century. It seems to have been most frequent in the Midlands and rare in the north and at first in the south-east. Like -son, the -s form went with lower status and was used with the commonest first names: Robert, Richard, William, Roger, John. It spread from England to Wales, becoming a characteristic Welsh form from the late medieval and Tudor periods. It began as an alternative form to the native patronymic in "ap" among the urbanized and anglicized parts of the population, and down to the eighteenth century the -s was added or detached at will. The -s was attached both to entirely "foreign" names, for example Andrews, Edwards, Watkins and, of course, Jones from John; but also to Welsh forms of such names, for example Davys, Davis and above all Davies, all found from the later Middle Ages and deriving from the hypocoristic form of David: Davy; Hughes from Hugh substituted for Hywel; and Evans from Ieuan or Evan for John; as well as Jennings and Jenkins from hypocoristic forms again. Examples from authentic Welsh names, for example Onionas from Einion, were rare, emphasizing that the style was a form of anglicization. The avoidance of common first names seems not to have operated at all – quite the reverse – and the second-name evidence for Wales and England suggests a most severe reduction of the first-name stock itself during or just prior to the period of second-name formation.

The genitive -s form was by no means exclusively patronymic. It could signify other relationships. A high proportion of those with such names in fourteenth-century East Anglia were women, often widows, whose -s names refer to their relationship to husbands or former husbands, for example Alice Thomys (widow of Thom) and Katherine Wilkyns. Others were servants, for example Adam les Prestes, Diot del Daykins, or Thomas at Adamys. Here the inserted article or preposition makes the relationship clearer. Some in this category may also have occupied land belonging to other named individuals: Alice Prioures, or William atte Personnes, for example.

As in France, many patronymics in England were formed not from the full formal first name but from a hypocoristic version of it. Among simply juxtaposed names, one has Daw, Dick, Hodge and Hobb, for example, from David, Richard, Roger and Robert respectively. A range of hypocoristic suffixes could also be attached to names or their shortened versions, and these in turn produced a range of second names. Given the paucity of direct references to such names in the sources, second names provide valuable evidence of them. From around 1250, there were names in -kin, borrowed originally perhaps from Flanders, such as Atkin or Adkin from Adam; Dawkin or Dakin from David; and Simkin from Simon. Again, there were names in -cock, such as Adcock, from Adam again; Hitchcock, from Richard; Laycock, from Lawrence; and names using the common French suffixes, such as Parrot, Perrott, Perrel and Perrin from Piers, or Willett, Willott and Wilmot from William. Some individual first names thus gave rise to a large number of different second names. Reaney lists 14 modern family names from Hugh and over 90 from its derivatives; and similar numbers stem from Nicholas, Richard, Thomas and William.

Names in -s and -son made particular use of hypocoristic forms. In a sample from Norfolk in 1330, 70 per cent of names in -s stemmed from hypocoristics. This is all confirmation of the great popularity or currency of these endlessly repeated and varied names, and also of their popularity in the sense of being names of the people, of the lower orders. Hodge, Dob and Robin were proverbially and in fact the names of peasants and then of their descendants. Very few members of the élite has such names before the end of the medieval period, or very few used them in public. Robert Dobes, a London sheriff in 1293–4, was unusual, but he also employed the grander name Robert de Rokesle.

Second names using first names were especially common in Italy, as we have noted. All varieties of first name were chosen, but there are indications that the less common names prevailed before the later medieval period. Fucilla emphasizes the very large number of modern Italian family names which derive from Germanic first names. From names in *-aldo*, there are, for instance, Garibaldi, Grimaldi, Rinaldi, and – in the Piedmontese variant – Einaudi, Rinaudi; from names in *-berto*, Aliperti, Ghiberti; from names in *-olfo* or *-ulfo*, Arnolfini, Gandolfo, Mondolfi. Epic names and Old Testament names are also surprisingly well represented, with Olivieri, Bramante, Danielli, and so on, but also a range derived from hypocoristic versions: Sacco and Sacchetti from Isacco; Vitti and Vitelli from Davide or Davite. Christian and saints' names are common in some areas. Cesarini-Sforza lists 25 modern family names in the Trentino deriving from variants of Peter. But in other areas they were infrequent. In documents relating to a number of places in the County of Nice in 1157, Nicolaus was the only saint's name to figure as a second name, and saints' names were still in a distinct minority in similar material from 1295.

A variety of patronymic forms was used. At first the Latin "filius" formula was used, as it was elsewhere: for example, Johannis filii Calmoli (760, Setteponzio di Sabina) and Leo filius Marini (931, Amalfi). This could show that the father was dead: Teodarci filii quondam Leotari (720, Lucca). The "filius" formula had become common in most parts of Italy by the tenth and eleventh centuries in formal documents. From Gubbio, for example, in the eleventh century, we have Cafarello filio Rustico, Ingo filio Urso, and so on; and also the variant Guelfulo Martini filius, or Ubaldus Ugonis filius. Occasionally other formulae were used. According to the inscription on it, the pulpit at Pistoia was made around 1300 by "Johannes . . . Nicoli natus".[19] The "filius" form continued to be used into the later medieval period, but it was generally superseded by other vernacular types.

The "filius" could simply be dropped, leaving the name of the son followed by that of the father in the genitive. This type predominated, for example, at Modena in the tenth and eleventh centuries: Liuzo Loperti; Bonizo Lupi. This type also proliferated in Tuscany and Umbria from the start of the eleventh century and was the form taken by many of the earliest élite family names in these regions: Alberti, Medici, Strozzi.

The alternative was the "de" or "di" form, which sometimes preceded the other or co-existed with it. This form is found in the Campania and Latium from the late tenth century: Iohannes de Stephano, Urso de Bibenzo, and so on; and it became usual, it seems, in most of central Italy during the eleventh and twelfth centuries. This formula was predominant in Tuscany by the Renaissance period. The élite had adopted fixed family names by this time – a point to which we will return – but individuals were still designated by the patronymic. Members of the Alberti family in the early fourteenth century, for example, were known as Agnolo di Neri, Benedetto di Nerozzo, and Cipriani di Duccio. Among the middle and lower classes, the patronymic alone was used, examples being Antonio di Tome, "a man of low condition", condemned for incest in Florence in 1413; Bartolomeo di Lorenzo, a pimp; and Biagio di Niccolò, a woolcarder.[20] Florentine building workers and artisans in the fifteenth and early sixteenth centuries had names in the same form. Aebischer claims that the directly juxtaposed genitive form of the father's name ultimately triumphed in Tuscany and elsewhere in northern and central Italy – hence the frequency of modern family names in -*i*. This process seems to have taken place by imitating the élite, and it was only completed in the post-medieval period.

The doubling of names is found in Latin onomastics, and of course alliteration was a principle in the transmission of names in Germanic naming systems. Both perhaps contributed to the Italian fashion for using the same appellation as both first and second name. The phenomenon is most evident in Tuscany and thereabouts. Many examples may be cited: Antelminello di' Antelmino, a patrician of Lucca (1173); Cavalcante Cavalcanti, who died before 1280, the father of Dante's friend Guido; Ubaldino degli Ubaldini, whom the poet places among the gluttons in Purgatory. By the fourteenth and fifteenth centuries, the style was very common, and it has survived down to the present. The practice clearly stressed the continuity of the family and the importance of the person concerned in it. He would usually be the heir, sometimes taking his first name from his father and sometimes from his grandfather and beyond, as with Alberto di Giovanni Alberti, or Giuntino di Guido Giuntini, both from Florence in the early fifteenth century. The custom existed elsewhere and the alliterative double name could become a second name in itself, as with the noble family of Ravenna, called Pasolini de Pasolini. Elsewhere, however, for example in England at the same time, the practice of sons using fathers' names if they were homonymous seems to have been specifically avoided.

Second names taken from first names were the predominant form in Lowland Scotland in the Middle Ages and after; in the Gaelic-speaking Highlands the patronymic *was* the second name. Occasionally, the Gaelic first name was used directly. Farquar (from Fhearchair), Forsyth (from Fearsithe), and Kinnoch or Kynoch (from Coinneach, now Kenneth) are recorded, for example, from the medieval period. But the essential form was that employing the Gaelic prefix meaning "son": Mac and its variants Mc, Mhic, Vic, Vc and so on. So Gileskel McLachlan (1292) was the son of Lachlain; Malcom Macpadene (1304) the son of Paidean or little Patrick;

Huchon McConzochquhy (1505) the son of Dhonnchaidh or Duncan. Lowland or English first names could also be used in hybrid forms. A Dolfinus mach Adam witnessed a charter around 1160. Other examples include: Raynald Mac Alyschander (1398); Johannes M'Lern, or Maclaren (1466) from Lauren or Lawrence; Mac Phetrius or Macfetridge (1503) from Peter. Sometimes hypocoristic versions of the first name were used: Macdicken, Macgibbon, Macjock. Many such names were characteristic of the Highland districts bordering on the Lowlands, but some non-Gaelic first names were borrowed early in the Highlands and more fully Gaelicized, like Támhais from Thomas, giving the second name Mac Támhais or Mactavish. Special mention should be made too of Norse names, such as Macmanus (son of Magnus), Mackettrick or Mac Shitrig (son of Sitrig), or Macaulay (son of Óli), testimony to Scandinavian immigration and settlement, especially in the Islands.

Patronymics were also the essential form of second name in Ireland. As an early Latin tag put it, "By Mac and O you can tell the true Irishman".[21] We will return to the distinction between the two prefixes in discussing name and family. Women were also designated by patronymics. In Ireland "ni", meaning "daughter of", was used; hence Maire ni Ó Briain, or Maire Nic an Goill.

We have seen that in Ireland and the Scottish Highlands, a first name might indicate that a person was the follower, devotee or servant of a saint or of Christ himself, using the terms Maol- or Gille- and Giolla. Each could produce second names via the patronymic, but those formed from the latter were much more common. Some derived from nicknames using the term in its secular mode, for example, from Ireland: Mac Giolla Arraith, son of the prosperous boy (later Mac Alarry, Macleary and so on); or Mac Giolla Bhain, son of the fair boy (later Mac Gilvane, MacIlwaine and so on). Others expressed an original and perhaps continuing devotion to a saint, for example, from Ireland again: Mac Giola Adamnain, son of the servant of St Adamnan (later Mac Alonan, MacLennan); or Mac Giolla Cheallaigh, son of the servant of St Ceallach (later MacKilkelly and so on). The Scottish Maclean derives from Mac Gille Eoin or Mac Ghill'Eathain (St John); and Maclehose comes from Ma Gille Támhais (St Thomas).

The same type of name was found in the Isle of Man. Here some of the names at least were also territorial in origin, deriving from "the name of the saint to whom the church in their treen or quarterland was dedicated". So in the parish of Kirk Bride, there is a quarterland called Ballavarkish, that is the farm of St Mark's church. The holder of the land would have been called Guilley Varkysh, servant of St Mark, a name corrupted over the years to Macvark, Macwrak or Macquark. In 1515, the land was held by William Mac Quark, and his family still held it in 1937.[22]

The Welsh second name was also predominantly patronymic. In the lay subsidy lists of 1292–3 for Merioneth, 53 per cent of taxpayers bore patronymics. The son's first name was followed by "mab" or "ab", meaning

131

"son of", and then by the father's name, for example Adda mab Einion. Where the father's name began with "h" or "rh", "ap" was used. A large number of Welsh second names derive from this formation by a process of agglutination. The final "b" or "p" of "ab" or "ap" became attached to the front of the father's name. Some of these names, deriving from the commonest first names, themselves became very common, for example Bevan or Bivon from Ieuan or Evan; Bowen from Owen; Parry or Parris from Harry or Harris; and Price, Preece and so on from Rhys. "Ab" or "ap" did not agglutinate with first names whose initial letter was not suitable, for example Gruffydd, Llewellyn or Morgan. Here (and in other cases), the father's name could become the second name unchanged, as it did elsewhere: for example, John, Owen, Rees, Thomas. Less common second names in this category from Welsh first names include Elliss from Elisedd or possibly the Biblical Elias; Yarworth or Yarwood from Iorwerth; Lodwick from Lodowicus or Ludovicus, a substitute for Llewellyn; and Maddox from Madog. The term for daughter was "merch", "ferch" or "verch", which was used in much the same way as "ab" or "ap" in, for example, Tanno verch David ap Ithel, or Morfudd Ferch Gruffyd ap Rhys, both from the fourteenth century.

Second names from places

Second names derived from places fall into three main categories: names after estates or fiefs; names after topographical features; and names after places of origin. The incidence of each type was related to social milieu. In England from the twelfth to the thirteenth century, the great landowners and knights had "a much higher proportion" of names "derived from place-names than did any other class".[23] For example, of those holding land by knight service in East Anglia in 1166, 58 per cent had second names taken from places; and among those making payments to a feudal aid in Norfolk in 1242–3, that is the most important landholders, 70 per cent had such names. These were in the main names of estates. In other cases, a locally high incidence of second names from places, for example 60 per cent in the Forez in the twelfth century and around 75 per cent at Capdenac (Lot) at the end of the thirteenth century, can be attributed to a preponderance of names after topographical features. These served as second names in rural areas, where they related to places of residence and/or land-holding. Naming after places of origin was a mark of immigrants, and this explains the high proportion of toponyms in cities like Amiens or Milan around 1300.

If we return to the origin of second names among the nobility, it will be recalled that some noble second names were by-names or nicknames, and some were patronymics; but the characteristic and ultimately prevailing noble second name derived from the land. Whereas earlier, lords gave their names to manors and villages, from the eleventh century they began to take their names from the villages, fiefs and castles which they controlled.

In Normandy, "the most important barons (or leading nobles) were nearly all called by the name of one of their principal lordships" by the mid eleventh century, and this practice spread to their knightly vassals after about 1060. For example, the name of the Tosny (de Todeniaco) first appears in a charter of 1014, and among their twelfth-century vassals were Robert de Romilly, Gilbert de Cleres and Roger de Mussegros, all named after their fiefs.[24] The names of Beaumont and Montgomery appear around 1035–50; of Warenne around 1040–50; and of Mortimer in 1054. In Flanders, Canon Lambert only gave second names to five out of the thirty people who figure in his family tree. These were his two noble grandmothers de Nechin and de Menin, and his two grandfathers of lower knightly status and one of their cousins, who were all designated de Wattrelos, from the village in which they had lands. All flourished in the later eleventh century. In the Mâconnais, at the end of the eleventh century, "family groups are clearly distinguished by a *cognomen*, a surname borne in common by brothers and cousins [and] . . . of the 31 surnames in use, . . . 27 are place names, that is [names] of a landed patrimony, an inheritance".[25] By the twelfth century, nobles all over northern and central France, including Brittany, had such names. Even the urban patriciate of Metz by the thirteenth century had second names taken from nearby villages and estates. In southern France, one finds the same story. "Denomination with a name taken from the land appeared very distinctly in the mid eleventh century" in the Bordeaux region.[26] In Languedoc by the eleventh century 63 per cent, and by the twelfth 80 per cent, of noble second names were territorial. In Catalonia territorial names had replaced patronymics by 1120–30, while in Béarn by the same time second names usually comprised patronymics plus the names of fiefs and castles.

In Italy similarly, nobles had territorial names. In the County of Nice, from the late tenth and early eleventh centuries, "the holders of fiefs had names in the form: Isnardus de Castronovo, that is first names followed by that of the fief".[27] The same custom was found then and later all over central and northern Italy. The great noble families, for example, who had settled in Pisa by the twelfth century, often kept the names of their rural properties, sometimes in addition to other names, for example the Buonaccorso di Cicogna, the Nobili di Caprona, and the Ripafratta. The last "took their name from their original castle which stood on the bank [ripa] of the Serchio river".[28] In the same way, the first lord of Rimini, from the Malatesta family, took the name da Verruchio after a castle of that name.

In England, the adoption of territorial second names by the élite coincided with the Norman Conquest. Among the Anglo-Saxons, names linking individuals to places had been rare and were personal by-names and not inheritable. They usually referred to villages and seem to be indications of residence. By contrast the Normans made frequent use of family names deriving from places. Of the tenants-in-chief in Domesday Book, 27 per cent had names relating to places in France. These names were usually the names of lordships or castles and they were hereditary. Many subtenants also had such names. Hugh de Bolebec, for example, a subtenant of Walter Giffard, was also a subtenant at Bolbec (later Seine-Inférieure), where he donated a quarter of the church to the abbey of Bernay around 1070. Ernald de Bosco, who held land from the Earl of Leicester in 1130, confirmed gifts to the abbey of Lyre from his ancestors, including half the tithe of Bois-Arnault (later Eure). The custom was carried over to England, and "Norman and other French lords used English toponymics in the generation in which they acquired their new estates",[29] for example Baldwin of Exeter, Robert of Stafford, and Roger of Berkeley. By the twelfth and thirteenth centuries landowners at all levels and of all ethnic origins tended to use the names of their estates as second names.

The custom also spread with the Norman conquerors to Scotland and Wales. Naming after fiefs or principal estates dates in Scotland from the twelfth and thirteenth centuries. Examples include Hugh de Aberbothenoth or Arbuthnot (a barony in Kincardineshire), Richard de Cunningham (Ayrshire), and Duncan de Forbeys (Aberdeenshire). The use of the term "of that ilk" or "of that place" to designate the estate-named noble appears to date from the mid fourteenth century, when Philip de Arbuthnott was referred to as "dominus eiusdem".[30] As the selection above indicates, this naming practice was mainly a Lowland phenomenon, though it was adopted in some parts of the Highlands. The Campbells used the designation of Lochow, Argyll and Breadalbane from the fifteenth century. Some well-known Scottish second names from places were brought by Norman barons from France or England. Balliol, Bruce, Fraser, Gordon and Menzies were all derived from places in France. The founder of the great house of the Lindsays, later Earls of Crawford, was Walter de Lindsey, so named after the district in Lincolnshire, where he held land; while William de Graham, founder of another great house, later Dukes of Montrose, also held land in the same county, at Grantham.

The same process is observable, though on a lesser scale, in Wales. The Norman conquerors had names like de Turbeville, de Umfraville, de la Mare; and the practice of using territorial names became transferred to Welsh estates among Welsh and non-Welsh owners. So the son of Madog Fychan ap Madog ab Iorwerth Goch of Creuddyn was known as Madog Gloddaith, his seat after he married the heiress Morfudd Ferch Gruffydd ap Rhys in the early fourteenth century.

Noble second names were not at first definitive or strictly inherited. The Tosny, in Normandy, also used de Conches after another of their estates, and, following the Norman Conquest, de Stafford was also employed. Though the name Beaumont first appeared in a ducal act of 1035/40 with Roger de Beaumont, he was also called Roger son of Humphrey. In the Auxerrois, the lords of Seignelay "were often designated by the *cognomen* de Siligniaco" in the twelfth century, but not all members of the family used the name, while some non-members did so. Again, "both the lords of Toucy and another noble family living at Toucy were called de Tuciaco, and the members of the second family were sometimes called de Narbonia as well".[31] In Béarn similarly naming did not clearly attach a particular family to a particular fief. Possessors of several fiefs might have different designations from each or they might be named after more than one fief, as with for example, Bernardus d'Urgossa et de Laborda (c.1085), or Raimunda de Big et de Guron (1201). In the case of the great, the name of the fief was often omitted "in their own region of domination, since the name plus the title could only apply in that region to one person".[32] So the Viscount of Béarn was Vicecomes Gasto in the Cartulary of Lescar, but away from his home territory he would be Gasto Centullus de Bearno.

The nature of the linkage between a noble second name and the land varied considerably. The place could simply be a birthplace or place of origin. Where it was land in the possession of the family, it could be ancient ancestral land, or land more recently acquired. Where ancestral land was involved, the name might refer to land from which descendants had subsequently moved, as it often did in Flanders and Normandy. Again, the family lands might be consolidated, forming a definite seat of interest and power, or they might be dispersed through accident or design. Before 1000, nobles like kings tended not to have stable residences but moved across scattered possessions. This pattern continued in later centuries, for example in Normandy, where the dukes and great vassals deliberately acted to prevent the building-up of local power-bases by their dependents. In some regions too the tradition of partible inheritance proved very resistant. This, together with gifts to the Church and the provision of gifts and dowries at marriage, all served to fragment estates and thus inhibit the adoption of family names taken from them.

Cadets could take the main family name, as they often did in post-Conquest England "presumably because their fortunes too depended on the success of the founder's line on whose lordship and patronage they depended and to whom they might succeed in default of heirs".[33] But more commonly at this time cadets adopted new and different names, linked to their lesser holdings. So in Béarn, one finds brothers bearing the names of their different fiefs: Ainardus de Maur and Arnaldus de Malmuzon. In Brabant, "the Berthout were a branch of the Grimberghe, and themselves hived off into Berthout de Malines, de Berlaer, de Ghrel or de Duffel".[34] In northern Italy, the "Obertenghi" divided in the twelfth century into four distinct lineages, most of which took their names from the main places where they exercised lordship. The same process was also occurring in England well after the Conquest. Around 1200, a cadet branch of the St Leger family, named after a place in France, acquired land at Socknersh in Sussex and adopted the name de Sokernerse. Similarly, when Sir Richard de Trafford gave lands at Chadderton in South Lancashire in the late thirteenth century to a younger son, that son assumed the name de Chadderton, the elder branch continuing to use the well-established name de Trafford.

Most telling, names could change in this formative period to follow the land in the female line. Stephen, a younger son of Aswalo I, lord of Seignelay, "was called de Siligniaco only until his marriage with the heiress of Pierre-Pertuis; thereafter, he was designated de Petra-Pertusa . . . His own son was not called Stephen of Pierre-Pertuis until after his father's death; until then . . . he was called Stephen of Brive."[35] The first Stephen was called de Seignelay presumably because he was born or came from the place and lived in the lord's castle. When he assumed control of lands of his own via marriage, he adopted his wife's second name that went with those lands. The second Stephen had a second name of his own, origin unknown, until he in turn assumed control of the family lands, when he again took their name.

Another Anglo-Norman example may be cited. The name of the Mowbrays derives from the Norman fief of Montbrai. It was acquired by Nigel, younger brother of William d'Aubigny, through his marriage to Maud, who had been the wife of Robert de Mowbray, Earl of Northumbria, whose estates were forfeited in 1095. When Nigel in turn divorced Maud, he retained Montbrai, his earliest Norman estate with a prestigious name, and passed the name to his children. "But it did not come to them through human generation. It came with the land."[36]

Naming after a castle controlled by a noble or noble family was not uncommon. This could be "the kernel of their family patrimony",[37] as Este was for one branch of the "Obertenghi", for example. But whether this was so would depend on the status of the castle and its castellan. As early as 990 in Catalonia, castellans were using second names, and this second name was usually the name of the castle which they held. But these castles were firmly under the control of the central authority and castellans were public officials. In Poitou, a century or so later, by contrast, naming after castles was also common, but the situation was quite different. The proliferation of castles there had come at a time of weakening central power, of centrifugal feudalism, and the castle was the centre of a quasi-independent fief or an allodial family estate. In England again after the Conquest, one finds yet another situation. "Title to castles was markedly less secure than title to lands"[38] as a result of royal strength not royal weakness, and they were therefore rarely the origin of long-lasting second names. An exception is Clifford on the Welsh border, acquired around 1150 by Walter Fitz Ponz or Poins, and taken by him and his descendants as their second name. Great magnates in the region of Clifford over four generations, they moved their power-base and their name to Yorkshire in the late thirteenth century.

In time names from castles and estates became hereditary. In England, according to Holt, there were three stages in the adoption of the toponym.

"First, the land was acquired. Secondly, the son inherits it and begins to be called or to call himself by the appropriate toponymic. Thirdly, both land and title pass to his son so that the surname becomes hereditary, not just a personal but a family name."[39] This process depended in turn on a fundamental switch to patrilineal inheritance and primogeniture, and on the establishment of a feudal system of land tenure in which fiefs were regularly inherited.

We are all familiar with second names derived from topographical features, since they have given rise to some of the commonest modern family names: Dubois, Duval, Rivière; Hill, Green, Wood; Monti, Poggi, Valle. They made use of any feature of the landscape, natural or man-made, that could distinguish. Carrez's study of such names in Burgundy again gives a good idea of their range. They might refer to the terrain or configuration of the ground, hence Hugon Montenot (hillock), Lambelin de la Vau (valley), and Henriot Daveal (slope). Woods and heaths gave names like Estevenin dou Bois, Wachiers Boissons, and Andreas la Bruere. Reference might be made to isolated trees or groves of a particular variety, for example Thevenin du Freigne (ash), or Perrenetus Fraigneaux. Very common, too, was reference to plots and fields, for example Simonet de La Borde (house or farm), Rosselot dou Chesant (plot or house held in servile tenure), Villemot du Cloux (enclosure), or Perrel du Mesnil (peasant house and plot). Spots in the village might also be used to identity a person, for example Thibault des Barres (referring to the barriers or defences of the village), Coloth de l'Eglise, and Grimouhart Demartrois (from martres, referring to the cemetery).

The same kinds of topographical second name were found in England and Italy. In England, location within the village or its vicinity could be indicated via the four points of the compass. Nearly 200 such names (North, South, East and West) are found for example in the Lincolnshire subsidy rolls around 1330. In the old Danelaw, forms in -by were also used: Martinus Oustiby, Willelmus Northiby and so on. Other forms are Norris, Southerton or Sutton, and Westaway.

Such formal classifications tend to obscure the social and cultural significance of these names. Here three main categories may be identified, though the first two are not absolutely distinct. First, peasants were designated by the name of the land which they cultivated. Originally this holding may have been named after some obvious feature, but this soon became its proper name, the name of a farm. Secondly, both these names and names conveyed on people directly from landscape features relate to the habitat concerned. Thirdly, people were named after places within towns.

In Béarn peasants were designated by the names of the lands which they held and cultivated from the mid eleventh century. This might be the name of the *villa* or village, as with, for example, Ane Fuert de za Costa or Sanz Garsias de Badas. Such a designation in monastic lists may not have been a name used of and by the person so described within the village, and it would not have allowed individuals to be distinguished clearly unless lordship and estates were very dispersed. Note that double first names or patronyms were also used. More precise was designation by the *mansus* or holding within the village, such as Barbaru, Limalonga, or Porcus Mortuus; or by a landscape feature such as Petra, Montaia, or Ozeral, which may well have been the name of the *mansus*. "It was natural that the name of the tenure should become that of the man who cultivated it."[40] This mode of designation is found all over France throughout the medieval period. Once *terriers* or land-registers are available, this can be clearly shown. A *terrier* of the late fourteenth century from the Forez lists peasants thus: "Johannes de l'Aera . . . pro tenemento de l'Aera; Petrus de Bargiis . . . pro tenemento de Bargiis" and so on.[41] The name of the holding and of the holder were the same.

The identification of person and property could also be expressed by giving the person's name to the holding, for example, again from fourteenth-century Forez, Andreas Jaqueti de la Jaquetary, or Stephane Columba . . . apud la Columbari. The same person could then bear either his original second name or that transferred to his property; for example, Johannes Benevens de la Beneventeri was also Johannis de la Beneventeri. Other family members might share the name; so Petrus Chabrols had a sister Duranne de la Chabrotia; Johannis Chalvet an heir called Petrus de la Chalvia. Use was also made of other possessives, which varied from region to region. "In the west the suffix -*ière* was commonly added preceded by the feminine article, for example, La Richardière, La Menardière; in parts of the centre and south, the family name was in the plural with a plural article, for example, Les Richards, Les Menards." Finally, in a band in the middle of France from the Charentes to the Jura, one finds the family name preceded by the preposition Chez, for example Chez Richard, Chez Michaud.[42] A study of a village in the Charente finds examples from the early fourteenth century onwards and associates the custom with a period of demographic expansion, which accentuated the clearing of woodland and the division of existing tenures.[43]

Peasants also went by the names of their places of residence and their holdings in England. A number of tenants of the bishop of Lincoln around 1225, for example, bore the name of the vill in which they actually held land: Petrus de Bukeden; Ricardus de Karleby; Walterus de Milnethorp. Conversely, the names of a person and then of a family could become attached to a holding or farm. Homans writes for the thirteenth century that "a yardland might have descended from father to son for several generations. It would [then] be called by the name of the blood which held it", and he cites an example from a Hertfordshire manor, in which a virgate belonging to the Eywodes was called "Eywodeyherd".[44] Similarly at Elmley Castle, Worcestershire, in 1412, a messuage and half yardland surrendered by William Dyring for the use of his heir was called 'Dyring's place".[45] Small places or hamlets could be called after families, too, following the same principle.

Naming after the land could be a means of securing it. A certain John Culpon gave 12 pence in 1308 "for licence to take half an acre of land [in the manor of Wakefield] . . . from another man who had taken it in from the waste. The court roll records this and his right to hold the land for himself and his heirs on condition of certain services for the lord." Culpon (modern coupon) means "a piece cut off" and almost certainly refers specifically "to the new piece of land cut out from the waste. In purchasing the land, John reinforced his heirs' claim to it by passing on his surname [taken from it] to his descendants."[46] This example is probably not untypical, for second names taken from topographical features and places where families resided and held land were the first to become fixed in Yorkshire and elsewhere. Much more generally this aspect of the "naming revolution", which affected the peasantry from the twelfth century if not before, signals and expresses "the new establishment of lineages, whatever the social level, on the land, which come from their ancestors and which would be transmitted to their descendants".[47] The relationship with the land had become stabilized for both peasant and lord.

In the Forez, names derived from topographical features predominated and later survived in the poorer upland areas rather than in the richer, more open plains. Here, and more generally too, topographical features were more likely to be used where the habitat was scattered. Where villages were nucleated then certain features might be used to designate those living away from the centre: millers, forest workers, marginal people. Deschamps, Ducamp, Campin, and Campi referred to those living in the fields, incomers, squatters, those too poor to live in the centre. Names like Dumoulin, Chabannes (cabin), Postel (boundary post), Delacroix (crossroads) and Dou Raffor (lime-kiln) would also fall into this category. Other names reflect a different habitat and the process of colonization that was going forward in the central medieval period. In regions of Burgundy

> where the habitat was dispersed over the whole area of the village and where fields had so bitten into the forest that there remained only a few scattered copses, one can see how people would have given farms and remote spots – and hence their inhabitants – a name relating to the vestiges of wood saved from the clearance process. To this type, it seems, belong Joffroy dou Boichat, Jehan du Boisson, Guillemin des Brosses . . . A person like Guiot du Bois could be an itinerant worker in the forest: a woodcutter or a specialist in land clearance.[48]

Names like Ouche or Deloche, referring to recent enclosures, must have originated in the same way, as did very specifically the modern family name Lesserteur, from "l'essarteur" or land-clearer. Many farms or holdings named after persons were thus attached to new clearances made from the thirteenth century onwards.

Naming after place of residence in towns or cities was found all over Western Europe. From Exeter in the late eleventh and early twelfth centuries, for example, we have Ricard a Paules Stret, Morin aet Gestgate (Eastgate), and Ascetill buta Port (outside the gate); from fourteenth-century Norwich, Henry atte Barreyates (Ber Gate). From Amiens around 1300, we have de l'Abeie (abbey of Saint-Jean), de Baiart (a mill), de la Bare, Cokerel (an area in the Saint-Germain quarter), and du Four. In Paris, there were reference to churches, hospitals, parishes and streets, for example de Cordeles (a street), de l'Ymage (referring to an image of St Katherine in the street where this innkeeper lived), de Navarre (College de Navarre), de Petit Pont, and de Nostre-Dame. An anecdote recounted by Vasari shows how such a name might be acquired. The painter later known as Fra Bartolommeo was born in the country around 1475 and was "known as Baccio for short according to Tuscan custom". He was sent to Florence as an apprentice "and lodged with some of his relations who were living at Porta San Piero Gattolini, where he stayed many years; so he was never called or known by any other name than that of Baccio della Porta".[49]

Naming after features within the city (as well as sometimes outside) is found among several Italian patriciates, where it has a particular significance. Among the noble families of Venice from the thirteenth and fourteenth centuries, we have the Da Camino, Da Canal, Da Molin, Da Ponte and Da Riva. A branch of the Roman Orsini was called the Orsini of Monte Cardinal. Genoese patrician families similarily took names from places in the city, in this case very clearly quarters which they dominated. The Fieschi di Carignano, for example, had several palaces and other property in that district, while the Fieschi di Canetto had a presence and a power-base in that more popular area. The reverse process occurred, too, with districts and urban features being named after the great families associated with them. This happened, for example, in thirteenth-century Siena and in Genoa again.

In towns and cities, second names deriving from places were usually the names of other towns or villages, and one may presume that they were nearly always places of origin. At first they may have been scribal labels or addresses, but by the thirteenth century, if not before, they were clearly names. Some French examples will serve as illustrations. In the small town of Rabastens, now in the Tarn, at the end of the fourteenth century, about half the second names were from places. Some of these were topographical features, brought from villages probably, though a small agro-town may have generated its own. Quite a few names came from villages in the immediate district, but many were from towns further afield, for example d'Albi, de Cordoas (Cordes), Marmanda, de Barssalona, and de Ric Estar (Requista). The second example is that of Paris in the early fourteenth century, when about 30 per cent of second names derived from places. Michaëlsson's list of the towns and villages concerned runs over several pages and includes such names as Yve de Mantes, Henri du Mans, Thomas de Marli and Guillot de Montpellier. Names of regions and countries were also attached to immigrants. At Rabastens, we have Albeges (Albigeois), de Lemozi (Limousin), Tolsa or Tholsa (Toulousain), and lo Bascol (Basque); in Paris, De Henaut (Hainaut), De Gascoigne and De Hollande, as well as the adjectival Alemande, Le Champenois and La Flamange.

As Quantin notes in connection with fourteenth-century Reims, the size of a town or city was important in determining which kinds of place-name were commonly used.

> In Paris, the names of little towns (let alone villages) meant nothing; in Reims, the smallest localities were known. People were attracted to Paris, moreover, from every province, whereas the field of attraction of Reims was above all local.[50]

So broader naming categories like ethnic adjectives were more prevalent in Paris, while more specific references to actual places, often quite small, were commoner in Reims. This contrast clearly applies to big cities and small towns generally.

Names of origin are a valuable guide to population movements, in the absence of other evidence, but they are a difficult source to use. Place-names may change and be hard or impossible to locate now. Orthography was variable then and has varied since. Unfamiliar names were often assimilated to familiar ones. Latin forms confused very different places. The Latin names of villages in the Narbonne area, for example, were the same as the names for Aix, Antioch, Arras, Cahors, Marseille and so on. Guillelmus de Valencia in Limoux could come from Valencia or Valence; a person called de Londris in Montpellier could be from London or from the nearby village of Londris. Again, many place-names were very common – McClure has calculated that only about 40 per cent of English place-names in the Middle Ages were unique – which means that the actual place of origin of a person often remains uncertain. Then, for purposes of analysis and comparison regular and optimally-sized units should ideally be devised, and this is not at all easy to do. The whole operation, moreover, is only viable during the short period while such second names were being given to individuals and before they became inherited names, that is, generally speaking, during the thirteenth and fourteenth centuries. Nevertheless, a number of interesting studies have been made.

At Reims in the fourteenth century, the bulk of immigrants came from the immediate vicinity. Beyond this was a second circle of neighbouring provinces: Picardy, Brie, Lorraine, Burgundy, Flanders, providing fewer but still significant numbers. A third circle of remoter places – Auvergne, Limousin, England, Brabant, Germany, Spain – supplied a final thinnest recruiting ground. With variations, this pattern is repeated at Cluny, Amiens and elsewhere, and some historians have attempted to quantify. Morlet suggests that

75–80 per cent of immigrants into the towns of Upper Picardy (Laon, Soissons, etc.) came from the province itself; 10–15 per cent came from a second circle around the province; and 5–10 per cent from further afield. Within this third circle, specific places stood out: Bourges, Paris, Reims, Ghent, Namur, all of which had special trading or other links with the area.

Higounet used names of origin to investigate various population movements to, from and within south-west France. First, he looked at immigration from the region into Spain. The oldest names are from the eleventh century and the first half of the twelfth, and belonged to pilgrims, merchants and artisans found along the pilgrimage route to Compostela. A larger wave of immigration is evident in the twelfth century in the lands newly conquered from the Moors. "The names of origin of French people in the different Spanish towns are nearly always the same: Morlass, Gascon, Toulouse, Cahors, Limoges."[51] These names very often stood for the districts around the towns named and not just the towns themselves; so Morlass meant Béarn; Cahors and Limoges stood for Quercy and all of the Limousin respectively. The main areas of emigration to Spain at this time were clearly the Toulouse region, Quercy and the Albigeois, with other areas like the Rouergue, the Aude and Périgord hardly involved.

French emigration into Spain at this time was paralleled by a more general movement of surplus rural population within the region into existing towns and into the new settlements that were being founded. The latter recruited locally but also over long distances. In the twelfth and thirteenth centuries, too, established towns and cities extended their areas of attraction. Montpellier recruited in the twelfth century mainly from lower Languedoc, but in the thirteenth century also from the Rhône valley and the Cévennes, the Aude and the Carcassonne area. Carcassonne itself continued to recruit mainly locally. This typifies a general pattern, smaller places having limited catchment areas, while the larger towns and cities, like Narbonne, Montpellier and Toulouse, attracted people from over a much wider area. But recruitment operated within a firm social and cultural framework. Migrants seem to have followed established commercial and religious routes, sometimes rivers like the Garonne. And twelfth- and thirteenth-century population movements within France did not cross linguistic frontiers. Very few migrants from northern France went south or vice versa.

English studies have found similar patterns. Most immigrants to villages and small towns in Nottinghamshire in the early fourteenth century, for example, did not move "further than three parishes away".[52] Between 30 and 40 per cent came from places up to five miles away, and 60 per cent from within ten miles. In West Sussex in the fourteenth century one finds a similar picture, with many immigrants coming from the immediate north and east. but very few came from the immediate west – Hampshire and the Isle of Wight – suggesting that mere proximity was not the determining factor here. There were cultural and natural barriers to migration in some cases; propinquities which fostered movement in others. In early sixteenth-century Norfolk, about a third of places in second names were from within the county. They were mainly villages, but there was some unevenness in their distribution. The area around Aylsham and North Walsham provided an unusually large number, for example, something related perhaps to the textile industry located there. Of the remainder, the bulk were from Suffolk and Lincolnshire, adjoining counties. Locative second names of this type were commoner in the county of Norfolk than they were in the main towns of Norwich and Great Yarmouth, and names from outside the county were more prevalent in the North Walsham region again and around Walsingham and its shrine, both places with "pull" factors. In Norfolk on average immigrants had moved around fifteen miles. McKinley concludes that "the distribution of locative surnames indicates that . . . there was a great deal of local movement amongst the population of Norfolk in the later Middle Ages, movement over fairly short distances".[53] This confirms other evidence from other parts of rural England, derived from the turnover of family names, that peasant populations were not so immobile as has sometimes been supposed. At Holywell-cum-Needingworth, for example, of just over a hundred known family groups residing in the village at some point between 1250 and 1370, only about half stayed put. But, as the second-name evidence shows, most of these migrants never went very far.

In the towns the situation was different. In the East Midlands in the fourteenth century, there were significant contrasts between the rural areas where migration was short-distance and the towns where it was longer-distance. In the larger towns of Norwich and York, the catchment area to obtain half the relevant names stretched to 20 miles. For York, an important chronological change may be detected, coinciding with the period of the Black Death which was paradoxically one of overall expansion in the city's size. Around 1300, 51 per cent of locative second names of freemen were from 1 to 20 miles away, and only 7 per cent from between 21 and 40 miles away. By the 1360s, 34 per cent came from up to 20 miles away and 35 per cent from between 21 and 40 miles away.

London was a special case. It drew larger numbers of immigrants and from all over the country, but certain configurations are marked. In the thirteenth and fourteenth centuries, 44 per cent of immigrants came from the Home Counties; 29 per cent from East Anglia and the East Midlands; 15 per cent from the south and south-west; 6 per cent from the West Midlands; 5 per cent from northern England; and 1 per cent from Scotland. Over 12 per cent of all immigrants came from Norfolk and Suffolk, with some towns and districts especially well represented, for example Bury St Edmunds and Norwich. Within Norfolk, there was a large contingent from the Aylsham area that we have already encountered, with names like Aylsham itself, Cawston, Corpusty, Marsham and Worstead. By the early fourteenth century many of these immigrants were members of London's merchant élite. One family from Suffolk must stand for all of them. There was a succession of three Geoffrey de Cavendyssh (the spelling varied), with property in St Lawrence, Jewry. The first, who died around 1299, was probably the original immigrant. Four Cavendishes are recorded in the early fourteenth century, three girdlers and a mercer or draper. It was an apprentice of the last, Thomas de Cavendych, taking his master's second name, who founded the dynasty of aldermen and mayors, which rose later into the ranks of the nobility.

Second names from places of origin were comparatively rare in Italy, which makes studies of migration based on them scarce too. We have seen that the use of second names was established early in Genoa, and immigrants to the city conformed to the Genoese custom in this respect. But while first generation immigrant workers in the thirteenth century had names taken from their birthplaces outside Genoa, "the second generation [often] abandoned the foreign surname for the name of the father or that of the street where the shop was located".[54] Lopez argues that those who had become established and perhaps obtained full citizenship, which was not hard to acquire, wished to keep their distance from and avoid confusion with fresh incomers. By comparing different territorial districts within the city, Hughes provides another line of explanation. Immigrants in the central medieval period came mainly from Liguria. They tended to settle in the hillier areas away from the old noble-dominated settlements near the sea, and did not form new ties within the city. They kept property in their villages, made donations to their village churches, and so on. These people were much more likely to be known in Genoa by names linking them to their places of origin therefore, while those who lived in the old parts of the city (perhaps second or third generation immigrants themselves) would use nomenclature that placed them within the urban milieu.

Second names from occupations

The final category of second names is that deriving from occupations and functions. This was most prominent in towns, as one might expect. In eleventh-century Winchester, 37.5 per cent of second names were occupational; at Newark in the late twelfth century, 59 per cent of those with Anglo-Norman and 35 per cent of those with English first names. Similar or higher proportions are found for the towns of Flanders and northern France for later centuries. The most striking thing about names in this category is their sheer range and variety, testimony to the extreme division of labour in the medieval urban economy.

One of the fullest studies, taking France as a whole in the thirteenth and fourteenth centuries, is by De Beauvillé, whose classification we follow. First, there were occupations relating to agriculture and the countryside. These might have to do with the type of holding, overlapping to some extent with locative names having the same significance. From *mansus*, one has Mansier, and, in the south, Mazier or Mazereau; from *borde* derives Bordier or Bordager (Normandy), Bordalier (south), and Bordereau (west). Mestayer or Métellier was a sharecropper, and Menager a man with a large farm in the south. Augagneur, Le Wagnieur and so on were cultivators of small holdings. Agricultural jobs were represented: Moissonnier, Meissonnier; Laboureur; Faucheur; Batteur; and other rural tasks: Bocheron or Bosqueron (woodman); Quarrier; Marnier; Fossier. Producers of particular crops might have names derived from them. L'Avanier, Delorgey, Bladier and Fromentin all referred to cereals; Cressonnier to cress; Aillier to garlic; though some of these might also be retailers. Vignerot, Vignard and so on were also common.

Then there were raisers of livestock. De Beauvillé lists over fifty names for shepherds, half from the Latin *pastor* (Pastre, Lapâtre, Pasquier, etc.) and half from *berger*. There were 20 regional and other variants for the ox-man: Boyer, Boué, Bouvier, Bouvard and so on; 24 for the cowman; and 30 for the pig-keeper. There were also keepers of goats and of poultry (Poulailler, Poulié, etc.), and of pigeons (Colombier, Colomié). There were those involved in hunting: Briqueur, the man in charge of hounds; Fauconnier; Perdiguier; Taupier or mole-catcher; and many others. Among rural artisans, the commonest was Charron, with 30 variants, the maker of carts and cart-wheels. The wheelwright also gave rise to Royer, Roudiez, and so on. Also very common were names deriving from milling: Meunier, Mousnier, Moulier, Molinier, and so on, with over thirty variants. Basket-making provided Le Corbusier, Vannier and Coffinier.

In general, however, agricultural and rural occupations did not produce second names to nearly the same extent that urban ones did. Many of them were broad terms, reflecting the unspecialized nature of peasant work, that would not therefore have singled persons out within the agricultural community. As we have seen, second names deriving from the land and the landscape were more characteristic.

Within towns, by contrast, occupation was a more obvious means of identification. All trades are represented, both general and particular. From building, for example, we have Maçon, Machon, Massonet (masons); Charpentier, Chapuis, and Fustier and Fustel from the Latin *fusterius* (carpenters); L'Ardoisier (slater); Thuillier, Thiollet (tilers). From metal-working (not necessarily all urban), we have many names for smith, stemming mainly from the latin *faber*, for example Fabre, Febvre and Faure. We have workers with the hammer: Martelier, Martelli; blacksmiths, using the term for a man in charge of horses: Le Mareschal, Manescal; iron-workers: Ferrier, Ferron; tin-workers: Estaignier. Much more specialized were spit-makers: Hastier; markers of pen-knives: Canivenc; makers of spurs, buckles and stirrups: Lormier, Lorimey; makers of hauberts: Hauberger, Aubergier; and of sieves or griddles: Cribier, Cribellier. Workers of leathers and skins provided Escoffier, Tanneur, Sellier and Pelletier. Beside general terms for potter – Potier, Pouthié, and so on, – there were many more specialized terms: Toupinier, from "toupin", a vessel made in Provence; Chanier, a maker of "chanes" or "cruches" (jugs); Gattier, a maker of "gattes" or "jattes" (bowls); and Pichonnier, of "pichons" (jugs); the last two both in Normandy.

Makers and sellers of food and drink were an important group. For bakers Fournier and its variants was found alongside Boulanger and its variants, the first being more common in the south and the second in the north. There were also other terms: Panetier, Panassier; Gastelier, Oublier, Watellier; Pastaier, Pestre. Tartier, Foassier, and so on were associated with special kinds of confectionery. Cook gave Cusenier, but also Lequeux, Lecoq, Coquin and so on. Brewers gave Lebrasseur, Gambier and Goudaillier or Goudelier, presumably from the English "good ale". The old name for butcher was "macelier" or "maskelier"; hence Maislier, Masoulet, Massacrier, etc. Carnier, Viandier, Mangon and Boucher are also found.

Even more second names derive from the textile trades. There are many names from the Latin for weaver, *textor* or *texarius*. From the maker of cloth from hemp ("chanvre") comes Chenevier; from the maker of linen, Lingier. Then we have combers: Peigneur, Peigné, etc.; carders: Cardeur, Chardaire; fullers: Battandier, Batanié; spinners: Le Filandrier, Philandrier. Those making clothes provided the general Tailleur, Taillandier; Sartor, Sartre, Sarthou, from the Latin *sartor*; Costuruer, Couturier; Parmentier; and the particular Boutonnier (button-maker); Chaucier (maker of hose); Gantier (glover); Guimpier (wimple or shirt maker). From the Latin for shoemaker, *sutor*, came Lesueur, Surier, Suriau; while Cordonnier, Corvisier and Courvoisier derived from the worker in Cordoba leather. Until the fifteenth century the "sabatier" was also a shoemaker (and not a clog-maker); hence Savatier, Sabaton, and so on. The clog-maker was "groullier", hence Grollier, Grolier, Grosley. Hatmakers in general provided Chaperonnier or Chapelier and variants. Very specialized was Laumucier, a maker of "amusses" or fur capes for canons.

Merchants received names such as Le Marchand, Marquand and Marcadet. Retailers were Cossandier, Le Regrattier, Eschoppier. Terms for moneychangers provided names, such as Changeur, Cange and Du Cange. L'Orfevre was a jeweller; Dorier or Lorier a gilder or goldsmith. Courailler was a Provençal coral merchant.

From the later service sector or liberal professions, we have terms for medics. From the Latin *medicus* came the general term "mire" or "mière" in northern and "mège" in southern France; hence names like Lemire, Miève, Mirot and Mège. Latin *scriba* gave Scribe, Scrive, and so on. There were many names from clerk, meaning either a cleric or a literate person, for example Leclerc, Leclercq and Clergue, the last from the south. Servants might be Ancel, Vallet, Varlet or Walet in the north; Naquet or Ramonnet in the south.

Among officials, Portier, Portalis and so on were concièrges or keepers of town gates; Mesureur and Mitterand (from "mitier", a measure) were measurers of grain; Dimier, Deymé, Daumier, etc. were collectors of the "dîme" or tithe. Bedel, Greffier, Chartrier, and Le Sergent were judicial officials. Higher legal officials or judges provided further names: Viguier, Vigié and Bègue in the south; Prévôt, Prévôtat and Léchevin in the north. Bail, Baille, Bayle and Baillard derive from "bailli", usually the agent of a lord.

Feudal status could also provide a second name, like some of the instances of Sergent. Chevalier and Chaballier were knights; Escuyer, Scudery, Bachelici and Challier squirees; Levasseur and Le Vavasseur vassals. The courtly household offices were also represented: Le Seneschal; Le Bouteiller, Bouthillier; Chambellan or Camberlanc. These were either honorific by this time or were used as nicknames among those of lesser status.

Monks seem to have had second names sometimes derived from the offices which they held in the monastery, for example Cellerier (cellarer), or Clavelier (keeper of the keys). The sacristan was "costre" from the Latin *custos*; hence the second names Costrel, Cousteau. The chaplain was Chapelain, Chaplin, Caperan. Moine, Lemoine and Monge, all meaning monk, were almost certainly nicknames, like the names deriving from high ecclesiastical offices.

As these examples have already shown, names from occupations took a great variety of forms deriving from Latin, French and dialects, and within a broad division between the north (langue d'oïl) and the south (langue d'oc), the incidence of particular names was very localized. Another formal feature was that the occupational name was very often preceded by the definite article, as with Mathei dicti lo Verer and Humbertus le Coudurers. This confirms that initially the name referred to an actual occupation.

In addition to direct use of the occupation itself, reference might also be made to the product being made or sold. From Reims, for example, we have Ysabel le Pastelle, Jehans Froument and Marie la Cauchonne; from Cluny, Fourno for a baker and Grasse Oye for a goose-keeper. Sometimes the name took the "Shakespeare" form: for example, Fille saie (Paris, 1292), literally, Spin silk; or Brise tartre, fornerius (Burgundy, 1323). The latter was keeper of the public oven, with a reputation presumably for spoiling the pies given to him to cook. One senses that there were stock nicknames that went with and stood for certain occupations, like Chips for carpenter in the UK today. Jehan Pincegrain, Phelipe Sauvegrain, Huguenin Moillefarine and Humbert Moille Avoyne were all Burgundian millers, the former owing their names to a supposed proclivity in the profession to keep more than their proper share of the grain and the latter to the practice of wetting it to make it weigh more heavily. Occupational names could also be used metaphorically as nicknames for others. Guillaume Carpentier, in the epic *Raoul de Cambrai*, is a knight not a tradesman, whose nickname indicates that he can split the skull of opponents like a carpenter splits wood.

It would be tedious to repeat this description for Britain and Italy – which could easily be done – for it would reveal much the same picture.

Occupational names derived from agriculture were again comparatively rare, and most derived from urban occupations. Such names were also rare in less developed countries or regions, like Ireland, Wales and the Highlands of Scotland. A partial exception is found with the Gaelic patronymics in Mac which use the father's occupation rather than his first name, for example Maccaig or Mackaig (son of the poet), Macintyre (carpenter or wright), Macnokard (smith) and Mactaggart (priest). One also finds in England and Italy the same great variety of names and intense specialization. Fransson, for example, found 165 English second names relating to textile trades. The relationship between the incidence of names and of the trades themselves is problematic. Scholars have sometimes found that leading urban occupations, like the common rural ones, were avoided as second names. For example, "the cloth-trades so prominent in [King's] Lynn's economic life are sparsely represented among the twelfth- and thirteenth-century by-names",[55] presumably because names taken from these occupations would not have been good identifiers.

Linguistic variety was again an obvious feature of these names. In England, parallel English and French terms existed for the same occupations: Nayler, Cluer; Roper, Corder; Flesher or Fletcher, Butcher; and these were carried over into second names. These variations were also regional. For example, Miller was found all over England in the medieval period, as occupational term and name, but it was not the commonest in either category. Milner predominated in the north and east, as well as in Lowland Scotland; while Millward or Millard prevailed in the south and west.

In England, too, occupational names were nearly always preceded by the definite article, indicating again that the name referred to the person's real job. In *Piers Plowman* we learn "Rose the regratere was her right name".[56] A range of suffixes and compounds were used, and their incidence has been analyzed. The commonest suffixes were in *-ier* or *-er*, and in *-ester*, the most frequent of the last being Bakestere, Litester, Webbester and Brewster. This seems originally to have been a feminine suffix, which later lost this character, at least for the commonest occupations. The leading English compounds were *-man*, *-makere*, *-herde*, *-ward* and *-monger*.

There are also English and Italian nicknames associated with occupations. Among names of the "Shakespeare" type in England, we have William Pluckerose (1275, Suffolk), a gardener; Johannes Rakedew (1353, Suffolk), a farm- or garden-worker; and Walterus Waggestaff (1275, Norfolk), a beadle. From the Trentino, we have a number of names referring to objects associated with professions, for example Ianes cui dicitur Cariolus (little cart or wheelbarrow); Enrico Cazola (trowel); Boninsegna detto Barzella (vessel to carry butter, etc. on muleback); and Ongelmano detto Zaramella (bagpipes). There were also nicknames associated with the supposed malpractices of particular occupations. Ognibene detto Malafarina was a miller, and Benevenuto detto Malacarne a butcher.

England also provides some evidence – rare elsewhere – for women. As Henrietta Leyser has observed, married women "derive[d] their work identity from their status as wives rather than from any other jobs they may [have] take[n] on".[57] So the occupational names of women would more often than not be those of their husbands, alongside whom they probably worked and whose enterprises they might continue as widows. Ten per cent of those on the 1319 tax rolls for London were women, most of whom were "identified by name with a trade",[50] for example Elena La Juelera, Alic la Stocfysshemonger, Petronella la Brewere and E. Scolemaystresse. Of these only the last two were likely to have been independently employed. Brewing and selling food as hucksters were two of the commonest female occupations in towns. We have seen that the -ester suffix probably indicated originally a job done by women, which suggests perhaps a higher incidence of independent female work.

CHAPTER EIGHT

Second names: II

Transitional forms

The switch from the single to the double name system culminated in the adoption of hereditary second or family names, which we still use. But there was a more or less long interval in which a variety of intermediate forms was employed.

The second name was sometimes linked to the first by terms in Latin or the vernaculars meaning "also known as". These were found in all countries. From France, we have, for example, Ermemgardus qui vocatur Vassadello (977, Narbonne), Walterius cognomine Fugans lupum (1061, Chartres) and Lisa dicta Honrecop (1070, Flanders); from England, Willelmus de Percy dictum Wyseman (1312, Durham) and Johannes de Blakeden alio nomine Bendebowe (1334, Durham). Common vernacular forms in France were "dit" and "alias"; in Italy, "detto". These were all usually found with alternative names or nicknames. We have seen that a distinct range of patronymic forms was used, such as "filius de".

Another indicator of the immediate and personal nature of the second name and of its recent coinage and literal meaning is the use of copulatives, either the definite article before a person's occupation or nickname, or a preposition attaching him or her to another person or to a place. In England, the article was nearly always in French in the sources – French was the language of the élite between the Conquest and the fourteenth century – though there is some evidence that "the" was used in vernacular speech. In the early documents, the article regularly agreed by gender, examples being Johannes le Dyare and Juliana la Dyare, both from Warwickshire around 1300. The article lasted longest in some northern counties, such as Lancashire where it is still found in the fifteenth century.

"Aet", "atte" or "atten" had been the prevailing English preposition linking place-names, but it was generally supplanted by the French "de" after the

Conquest for names of villages and towns. "Atte" and variants were still in common use before names from topographical features in the fourteenth century and occasionally beyond. "A" was sometimes used here, though whether it was an abbreviation of the old English or a French form is unclear. Hugh a Fenne was a correspondent of John Paston in 1456. Thomas More's servant, who was with him in the Tower in 1535, was John A Wood. In London, "de" began to disappear after 1300 but was mostly preserved until around the end of the fourteenth century. "De" was in general use in Warwickshire in the thirteenth and fourteenth centuries, and in Lancashire and Yorkshire until the early or mid fifteenth century.

In France, names with the definite article seem to have been commonest in the north and the south-east (Beaujolais, Lyonnais, Berry). The article was attached to occupational names – Humbertus li Coudurers – and to nicknames – Magister Petras li Bissons – both from the Forez. Dialect forms such as "li" and "lo" were used as well as "le" and "la". Sometimes the preposition "a" was attached to the article: Luce a la Broaleri; Johannes a la Ferrere. In many cases, these attachments became incorporated into later family names, examples being Lavocat, Lenoir and Augagneur. As in England, place-names were attached to the first name with the preposition "de" (or its dialect equivalent): for example, from fourteenth-century Rabastens, Peyre de Guachas and Johan de Palhars. This preposition could also be incorporated in the final version of the name: Dubois, Deschamps, Dérive. In some parts of France, patronyms also employed "de" as a linking term. One also finds suffixation of second names in France. In the Forez, the only region for which a chronology is available, this developed in the second half of the thirteenth century and was at its height in the last two-thirds of the fourteenth. Here it involved second names from first names: Guillelmus Girardot, Philippus Girardel, and so on, some of which may already have been in hypocoristic form. Elsewhere the practice was extended to occupations: Clergier, Clerget, Clergeot, Clergeon, from "clerc" or "clergue", for example; and to nicknames, for example Brunot, Brunet, Brenot and Breneau from "brun".

The use of copulatives was also fairly common in Italy and continued through the Renaissance period. They were used with all types of second name again, and they became incorporated into modern family names.

Two other stylistic signs of instability in second names should be mentioned: the frequent lack of capitalization of names in the sources, and wide spelling variations. Indeed, the idea that there was a single standard version of a name barely existed, and, like the royal scribe Louis in the time of King John, people "even varied the way" they wrote their own names. This situation was slow to change. In the Forez, for example, we find both Johannes Fornerii and Johannis Fournerii; Bons Vis and Bonvin; Servona and Selvona. A London grocer, five times alderman between 1372 and 1384, was variously recorded as John Philpot, Filpot, Philipot and Phelipot; while another aldermanic family was variously Gisors, Gisorz, Gisorcio and Jesors. Scottish second names displayed a high degree of orthographic variety in the medieval period and afterwards. Among non-Gaelic names, Black lists 22 spellings of Home or Hume in the fifteenth and sixteenth centuries; 32 of Fraser between the thirteenth and sixteenth centuries; and over seventy of Strachan from around 1200 into the seventeenth century. With Gaelic names, inherent lack of uniformity in spelling was compounded by transliteration, often by Lowland scribes ignorant of the language. The record in variety appears to be held by Maclean with over seventy versions of the name from the thirteenth century onwards. In England, there was also linguistic variation of the name. In earlier documents, Latin and French forms might alternate: Boscus and Bois, De Bello Marisco and Beaumarsh, and so on. Later there might be French and English versions, or different English versions, such as the Waterer and Atwater "used interchangeably" at Woking as late as 1550.[1]

Another feature of the transitional phase was the designation of a person by more than one second name. All combinations of types of second name were possible, as can be seen in the Paris tax rolls around 1300, though in this large city they usually included the occupational name. So one has place of origin plus occupation: Eude le Bourgueignon Regratier; or, placing the terms the other way round, Richardin l'Esmailleur de Londres. First name plus occupation gave Jehan Benoiet le Cordouanier; nickname plus occupation Mahy Bec-de-Coc Cavetier. In the Forez, where third-term denominations became abundant from the mid thirteenth century, the place-name was the commonest addition, reflecting the general importance of this mode of designation here. One could have first name plus place-name, for example Petrus Rollandi del Verney; occupational name plus place-name: Johannes Baiuli de Nigro Stabulo; nickname plus place-name: Petrus Bastardi de Dorola; or two place-names: Stephanus Rochafors de Aera, a man originally from Rochefort now with a holding at L'Aire. Sometimes a fourth term might even be introduced, examples from Paris being Jehan l'Englais Roussel Tavernier and Guillaume le Normant Pie-d'Ours Buffetier.

Such multiple designations were also found in Italy and England, especially in the thirteenth and fourteenth centuries. From King's Lynn, for example, we have Cecile Kineman de Dersingham, Thome Pistoris de Geywude and Iohannes de Vallibus de Westacre, a variety of combinations. Such names were frequent, too, in London: William atte Vine de Bekles; Roger de Clare Cormonger; William de Causton Mercenarius. They were also found in rural areas. Folco Walterus Elyot was a wealthier peasant tenant of St Edmund around 1200; Robertus Revel de Cokfeld and Mile de Hastinges de Hoccetone were minor landholders in the same area.

The third or other name was sometimes a means of distinguishing homonyms. Two men called William de Albini, members of a leading family in the reign of Henry I, were called Pincerna (the King's butler) and Brito (the Breton) respectively. In a village in the Lyonnais around 1300, there were

two men called Johanne de Poysaz or Peysaz, one of whom was differentiated as Johanne Bergerii de Poysaz. This mode of identification was important in rural France generally and remained so well after the end of the
Middle Ages at the unofficial level. Multiple designation in the medieval
period may have been a scribal way of identifying a person clearly. Such
formulae as Joseph frater Roberti cognomento Angeli, or Jordanus qui habet
filiam Reginaldi, from twelfth-century Canterbury, were not really names.
But other modes were more standardized, as we have seen. Scribal descriptions could also be related to "probable colloquial usage". So Elena uxore
Radulphi de Suthmer apud Wigehall manent, from thirteenth-century King's
Lynn, was, in the vernacular, "Helen, Ralph from Southmere's widow, the
one who lives over at Wiggenhall".[2]

Further evidence of the fluidity of the second name in this period is
provided by the fact that the same individual might be referred to by different names or by different variants of his or her name. In eleventh-century
England, a certain Ricardus was known as de Tonebridge "from his lordship
of that name in Kent", as Ricardus de Clara "from his Suffolk lordship", as
Ricardus de Benefacta "from his French possession of that name", and as
Ricardus filius Gisleberti "from his father's first name". Again, in thirteenth-
century Norwich, Seman le Agulyer or le nedler (needlemaker) was 'also
called Seman Wrynek (presumably from a deformity) and Seman de Blythburgh,
from his own or his family's place of origin". As late as 1442, an ancestor of
the dukes of Bedford was referred to in an official pardon as "Henry Russell
of Weymouth, otherwise called Henry Russell of Weymouth merchant, otherwise called Henry Gascoigne of Weymouth gentleman or by whatsoever
name he may be styled".[3] These are extreme cases, and two variants were
much more common. Alternative names were quite frequent in London in
the thirteenth and fourteenth centuries. A local or other second name was
often combined with an occupational one; so Adam de Bydik, the king's
tailor at the end of the thirteenth century, was also called Adam le Tailleur;
John de Totenham was also John le Poter. Such variants continued into the
later medieval period, but they became rarer.

The Paris tax rolls around 1300 provide many examples of persons des-
ignated by different names at about the same time. A person might be Lucas
Cochin or Cochin le Marinier; Jehan Agogue, Jehan Agogue Tavernier or
Jehan le Saunier dit Agogue; Genevieve la Piz-d'Oë or Dame Genevieve la
Flamange. Similar variations are found elsewhere. In the Forez, for example,
we have: Peros Moreuz le Basters, Peron Morel, or Peron Baster (1290), and
Jaquemetus alias Jacons del Boysson or Jaquemons del Boysson alias
Jacon (c.1350). The poet known to modern readers as François Villon, was
"originally known as François de Montcorbier". He was placed by his poor
mother in the care of a priest, Guillaume de Villon, whose name he took.
When charged with homicide in 1455, he was referred to as "Maître François
des Loges alias de Villon".[4]

Inconsistent use of second names was also common in Italy. Even in Genoa, where, we have seen, the practice of using second names was precocious, "additional names and second names proper were not yet clearly distinguished among the élite" in the thirteenth century. The same man was referred to as Guglielmo Negro Embriaco, Guglielmo Negro di Ravecca, Guglielmo Embriaco, Guglielmo Negro del quondam Embriaco, and Guglielmo quondam Ugone Embriaco; and many other examples could be cited. Varied name forms were still being used elsewhere in the fourteenth and fifteenth centuries. Artists' names provide some well-known cases. One of those who submitted plans for the Baptistery doors in Florence in the early fifteenth century was Simone dal Colle, also called Simone de' Bronzi. Fra Angelico (c.1400–55) was known by that name but also as Fra Giovanni Angelico, while a contract he entered into in Rome in 1447 refers to Frate Giovanni di Pietro Dipintore dell'Ordine di San Domeniche. Tommaso di Ser Giovanni di Mone Cassai, born in 1401, acquired the pejorative nickname Masaccio, according to Vasari because of his distracted personality and behaviour. He was referred to in the fifteenth century and later as Tommaso da Firenze detto Masaccio or by the nickname alone.[5] Such uncertainty persisted among the élite into the sixteenth century and among the lower classes for much longer.

Second names also changed from one generation to another; they were not inherited. This is an obvious feature of true patronymics; they are shifting. Filippo Brunelleschi (1377–1446), the Florentine architect, was the son of Brunellesco di Lippo Lapi. When Filippo was elected to the Signoria for a stint in 1423, he was entered in the register as Filippo di Ser Brunellesco Lippi, and Vasari comments that the father was more properly called da Lippo after his father.[6]

Second names of other types also varied from one generation to the next and among siblings. At Amiens around 1300, for example, Jehans Moniiers was the son of Simon le Fruitier, and Pierre de Pas of Huibert le Carpentier. In the Fribourg region, Johannes dictus Cullieroz was the son of Willelmus de Mollon (1322), and Uldricus Chedel of Mermetus dictus Fraschibos (1404), while Nicoletus dou Ru and Johannetus Cartier were brothers (1406). From England, we have Walterus le Swein, father of Willelmus le Paumer (1221, Worcestershire), John le Tundur of Peter le Chaucer (1287, Norfolk), and Gilbert le Tannere of William Marchant (1320, Somerset). Such variation and diversification was usual in all classes until the thirteenth century, and survived longer in the north.

The standardization of second names

However, the second name did over time become fixed. It ceased to be purely personal and became an inherited family name. Among the nobility in some parts of France, this process began as early as the eleventh century. It seems to have been more advanced generally in the south than in the centre and the north and in the towns than in the countryside. By the end of the fourteenth century most second names were fixed all over France, though a minority continued to float into the fifteenth century and beyond. Prat shows that in the Quercy second names from first names and from place-names and some from nicknames became fixed in the fourteenth century, while those from occupations followed later, and it is very likely that this pattern was more general.

The process of stabilization also followed "class" and geographical lines in Britain. Some Norman lords had inherited names by 1066: Tengvik lists just over fifty examples from Domesday Book. More great landowners adopted family names in the course of the twelfth century, and most noble and knightly families had them by around 1250. Some wealthy Londoners used hereditary second names in the later twelfth century and they were common, if not universal, in London by the second half of the thirteenth century. Most townspeople elsewhere acquired hereditary names in the first part of the fourteenth century. The rural population, free and unfree, also seems to have acquired fixed second names by around 1350. As Matthews sums it up, the upper classes took on stable second names between 1066 and around 1200, the rest of the population between around 1200 and 1360 or later. There were, however, important regional variations. The process described above applies to southern England in general. In some advanced regions, like East Anglia, stabilization occurred earlier, while in remoter, less "developed" regions the process was considerably delayed. In Lanca-shire most "landowning families had hereditary surnames by about 1300, but as late as the sixteenth century there were still some sections of the population without stable hereditary surnames". In Yorkshire, most names were not settled till around 1425 and the stabilization process continued until 1500 or beyond. In Wales, second names had become fixed in gentry families by around 1550, but the rest of the population employed a variety of styles including the shifting patronymic, the attachment of "ap" or "ab" to the father's name, and the fixed surname, well into the early modern period.[7]

In Britain as in France certain types of second name seem to have be-come fixed before others. Those indicating place of residence and those from nicknames generally achieved stability before those from personal names or from occupations. For example, of the many Yorkshire second names which became hereditary before 1250, most were place-names, taken from farms or holdings; some were nicknames and first names. Only later and mainly in the period 1350–1450 did occupational names become fixed, together with patronymics, especially in -*son*.

In Italy, the trend towards stabilization and heredity also began among the nobility and the urban élites. Some Venetian families are reported to have had hereditary names from the tenth and eleventh centuries. In Rome

155

by the twelfth century a few great families had stable names, for example the Frangipani and the Malabranca (names taken from nicknames); the Pierleóni and the Boveschi (patronymics). A long time after this, however, the later Orsini were still called "gli orsatti" or the "figliuli dell orsa" in Dante's *Inferno*. In Latium generally, the fixed family name began to spread among urban élites from the end of the twelfth century, using either a nickname or a patronym, "breaking the patronymic chain at some point and attaching all descendants to the same eponymous ancestor".[8] In Genoa, second names became transformed into hereditary family names during the twelfth and thirteenth centuries, while in Tuscany, Umbria and the Marches, the nobility had fixed names from the twelfth century and the merchant élites from the thirteenth. In the Trentino, this process seems not to have occurred until the mid fourteenth century. In the south and among the lower classes generally, stabilization was even further delayed.

The documents allow one to see the second name becoming hereditary. A Parisian charter of 1178–9 refers to Guiardus Herbodus, son of the late Gislebertus Herbodus; three generations of Fribourg citizens between around 1180 and 1230 were called Willelmus Achar, Petrus Achar and Willelmus Achardus. Such examples become much commoner in France in the course of the thirteenth and fourteenth centuries. From Saint-Quentin, we have Simon Carbonee, fils Tumas Carbonee (1248); Huart Cornet, le fill Jehan Cornet (1270); from the Marne, Giraz li Maires de Rouguel, filz de Jehannet qui fu mayres de Roguel, where "the son has inherited the name but not the office of his father".[9] In some cases, the father's name was at first passed on to only one son, presumably the heir. In 1340, Giroldus dou Pasquer of the Fribourg district was reported to have three sons: Mermetus Bachelars, Johannodus Corbos, and Franciscus later called dou Pasquier. This suggests, too, that a son or sons might not adopt or be given the father's second name while he was alive or perhaps for some time afterwards. At Metz in 1285 we hear of Colins li filz Matheu Drowat ki fut. It was not until 1290 that the patronymic was dropped and he was called Collignon Drowat. The sharing of the second name by siblings clearly marks a further stage in the "crystallization" of the family name. The 1296 Paris tax roll provides, for example, Jehan de Paci, Jehanot de Paci, and Colin de Paci, son fuiz, that is a father and two sons with the same second name. In the Forez in the fourteenth century, not only was the inheritance of the father's second name by a son quite common, but Vallet is able to trace groups of persons with the same second name in the same village, with the strong presumption that they belonged to the same family.

Similar evidence exists for England and Italy. The sources reveal sons taking fathers' names. For example, Ricardus filius Fyn (*c.*1160, Yorkshire) was later called Ricardus Fyn; Ricardus filius Nicolai Ode (thirteenth century, King's Lynn), Ricardus Ode. Then one finds sets of brothers with the same second name, an indication that all children (for sisters might be included) and not only the heir were inheriting the name. In the Durham Liber Vitae, for example, there is a thirteenth-century entry listing Elias de Stapultone, Willelmus de Stapletone and four other "fratres" with the same second name.[10] Less direct indicators also exist for England. Several people in the same village with the same second name are probably related, especially if the names are nicknames or first names. Fransson cites, among many examples, four men called Duffary in a Staffordshire village, and three men and a woman called Partrych in a Sussex village, both in 1327. At Warboys in the first half of the fourteenth century, there were 23 Bondes, 19 Pilches, 17 Ravens, 13 Aubyns, Albyns or Albinis, and so on.

In a typical example from the élite of Genoa, Zaccaria de Castro or de Castello, a name probably referring to his residence in the "castrum" district, had five sons called Zaccaria de Castro and Fulcone, Ogerio, Giovanni and Amigone, all with the second name Zaccaria. "While Ogerio's son was called Zaccaria de Castro like his uncle and his grandfather, Ogerio's brother – the second Zaccaria de Castro – had a son called Fulcone Zaccaria, who was in turn the father of Benedetto Zaccaria, the famous admiral", who died around 1310. "Thereafter the name Zaccaria was transmitted to all male descendants of all branches." Many examples may be cited, too, from thirteenth-century Tuscany of sons with the same second names as fathers: Tegrimi de Campi quondam Bernardi de Campi (1269); Brunetto Latini, son of Buonaccorso Latini; or Buonconto da Montefeltro, "son of the famous Ghibelline captain Guido da Montefeltro", killed in 1289. Brothers also shared the same second name at this time, for example, Teste et Gentilis Tornaquinci . . . dai Gianni Tornaquinci (1269), or Ugoccione del Cassero, podestà of Macerata in 1268 and Martino del Cassero, professor of law at Arezzo. By the fourteenth century, the fixed hereditary family name was usual among the Florentine élite. This can be seen from the example of the Ginori family, which acceded to this class in the mid fifteenth century. The brothers Gino and Piero, sons of Giovanni, used the name da Calenzano in the early fourteenth century. Towards the end of the century, the descendants of Piero were called Di Piero di Ser Giovanni da Calenzana, while those of Gino adopted the second name di Ser Gino. By around 1430, however, "the more durable and aristocratic forms Ginori and Ginoli" began to be used, Ginori ultimately prevailing.[11]

Another indicator that the second name had become fixed is provided by persons with occupations that are different from those indicated by their names. In some towns and cities it was possible to exercise more than one skilled métier at once and people changed jobs, but neither practice seems to have been very common. By the thirteenth and fourteenth centuries in France, the separation between name and actual occupation is evident in Paris, Picardy, Burgundy, the Forez and elsewhere. From Cluny, for example, around 1300, we have Stephanis Textoris presbyteri; from Eu in the early fourteenth century, Watier le barbier dit Marchand; and from Laon,

Jehan Potier, frepier (1380). Particularly telling are the examples of those occupying leading positions in their guilds, for example, from Paris around 1300, Jehan le Pastrier, juré tisserand; Oudin le Maçon, maître chaussier; and Nicolaus Bouchier de Verberie, juré epinglier.

Similar examples may be found in England from the later twelfth century, but they do not become common until the thirteenth and especially the fourteenth. From Norwich, we have Roger le Parcheminer, a butcher (1294), and Joannes le Combestere, piscenarius (1315); from York, Hugo le Biller, a pelter (1296), and Johannes le Carpenter, de Thresk, a cordwainer (1308). Among the Suffolk parish clergy in the first half of the fourteenth century were Peter le Mareschal, John le Mustarder, Richard Pottere and William le Smythe. At Warboys in the first half of the fifteenth century, the list of butchers included Chapman, Soper, Shepherd, Sperner and Mercator. The correlation between name and actual occupation still existed to a degree for other workers, but here both name and job were inherited together. There are no studies establishing disparity between second name and real occupation in Italy, but odd examples are not hard to find in the sources, for example, Nicola Pellipario (skinner), a potter at Urbino around 1500.

In addition to and alongside the inheritance of second names in the thirteenth and fourteenth centuries, there was a general process of standardization. Most obviously, copulatives began to be omitted. In the necrology of the Jongleurs of Arras, the "de" was being left out before names of origin by the early thirteenth century, and the article was going from occupational names. Similarly at Rabastens at the end of the fourteenth century, Peyre de Guachas became Peyre Guachas, Johan de Palhars became En Palhars (using the customary honorific title for men), and so on. In the Quercy, occupational names appeared at first alone or attached with the article. "At this stage, the second name was still only the simple designation of a worker. It required two or three generations for the name to become fixed", and this involved dropping the article. So lo molinier found in 1232 had become Molinier by 1317; lo pelhicier became J. le pelhicier and finally G. Pelhissier.[12] In England, the article began to be omitted in the twelfth and thirteenth centuries, but this did not occur generally until well into the fourteenth. Similarly "de" began to disappear from the early fourteenth century. At Stow Langtoft in Suffolk, in the Poll Tax returns of 1381, only the lord of the manor had "de" attached to his name. Among the Florentine élite, prepositions began to be dropped from patronyms and collective names from the late thirteenth century, and one finds individuals with modern-style first and second names from the early fourteenth century, though they are still in a clear minority.

Other procedures making for uniformity and the highlighting of the second name included the use of capitals, which clearly marked the name off from its context. These were not used in the earliest sources but become more common in the central medieval period. For England, they are used in the Newark survey around 1200 for most first names and some second names. By the thirteenth century, all names in the Durham Liber Vitae have capitals, as do most in the Hyde Abbey Liber by the end of the fourteenth century. Some standardization of spelling occurred in the later medieval period, but this was essentially a later development. We should also mention the end of the declension of names, though the variants N. Machiavelli or Il Machiavello, F. Guiccardini or Il Guicciardino, and so on, were still found in fifteenth-century Italy.

A particularly interesting development is the introduction of initials. In France this practice began in the south, it seems as a convenient way for scribes to indicate the commonest first names. So the first names on the twelfth-century lists of officials at Montpellier are nearly always indicated by initials, for example B. Lambertus and G. Raimundus, with the B. standing for Bernardus and the G. for Guillelmus. Selected persons are found with initials in other documents. At Capdenac, for example, on notaries' registers in the thirteenth century "certain first names are always indicated by an initial, while for others one finds more or less abbreviated forms".[13] So B. stood for Bernard or Bertrand, D. probably for Daorde or Dorde, the local version of the Latin Deusdedit, S. for Steve (sic), while Dur stood for Durand. Examples are harder to find from this period from the north, though a charter from Lisieux in 1321 lists Ricardus, Colinus and G. les Potiers, the G. presumably standing for Gui. Though the initial was used as shorthand for common and repeated names, its use did have the effect of emphasizing the second name. The same effect is achieved by another device used in the necrology of the Jongleurs of Arras from 1196. Here the first name was written after the second name, for example Grumeliers Robers li, Paris Jakemes de, and Barbica Enme li Barbiere. This was a revolutionary procedure for the time. Following the logic of the new system of naming, it pointed forward to bureaucratic methods of listing and reference that only became dominant much later.

Initials were very occasionally used in English documents from the later thirteenth century, for example H. de Durnegate and W. Speciario (1285, Winchester); J. de Swerdeston (1289, Norfolk). But even much later this practice was rare; only a small number are found in the Durham Liber Vitae, for example, in the fifteenth century. Again, initials designated only the commonest first names like John or William. The move towards recognizing the second name as *the* name was very slight.

Second names in context

Several reasons have been adduced for the introduction of the second name. In France and England, scholars pointed to the need for clarity in identifying individuals. This aspect was stressed for example by Aebischer in his important studies in the 1920s. The diminishing stock of single names and the increasing number of homonyms meant that further qualifiers had to be introduced in order to distinguish people clearly. This can be seen in charters recording land and other transactions from the late tenth century onwards. If there were two witnesses called Arnulfus, as for example in an act transferring land from the abbey of Stavelot-Malmédy in 1033, then one had to be distinguished as Arnulfus de Iasno (Aisne) from the other, Arnulfus de Verino (Verenne). In another example, from the Kalendar of Abbot Samson of St Edmund's around 1200, there were at least five tenants in Thedwestry Hundred named Wuluricus or Wluric. For the convenience of the abbot and his agents as well as for the security of the tenants themselves, they needed to be differentiated; and they were: as Wuluricus alone, and as Wuluricus filius Ricardi, Pelliparius, Tunge, and Kereford respectively. Nor is this just a fair assumption from the evidence being made by historians. Homonymy was a real problem for contemporaries. The sheriff of Essex was ordered by a writ of Henry III in 1230 to hold an enquiry into

> whether a loan of 60 shillings which is demanded by summons of our Exchequer . . . from Richard son of William in the time of lord John the king our father, was made to Richard son of William of Stapleford or to Richard father of Robert of Tilbury; and if the same Richard, the father of Robert . . . was called Richard son of William or Richard son of Robert?[14]

With the increasing use of written documentation of all kinds from the eleventh century onwards, this need for clear identification affected more and more people lower and lower down the social scale. The English *Song of the Husbandman* (probably dating from the early fourteenth century) "depicts the beadles collecting taxes from the peasants . . . by the authority of an Exchequer writ", and they tell the peasants: "You are written in my list, as you know very well." At some stage, it is assumed, what had perhaps been a purely scribal or notarial device became the actual name of the person concerned. This probably lends too much weight to the logic of the system. Those drawing up documents did use their own descriptions of people that were not names as such, but it seems likely that, where possible, scribes would have used unofficial second names already in use rather than inventing and then managing to impose their own denominations. What was going on in the documents in effect reflected broader changes in society. It is clear, moreover, that in some regions homonymy *per se* was not the trigger to second naming. In Catalonia, for example, by-names do not seem to have been used to make identification easier, since they do not occur especially with the commonest names. Indeed, Zimmermann argues that "far from leading to the phenomenon of double naming, the impoverishment of the first-name stock seems to have been a consequence of it".

More generally perhaps one can accept that what was happening was "a self-generating process: homonymy required the complementary designation, and this complementary designation permitted the reduction in the corpus of what now became first names".[15]

Reference to broader social change introduces the second main line of explanation for the introduction of second names, put forward mainly by scholars in Germany, Scandinavia and Italy. Reichert summed up their views. "The second name", he wrote, "was the immediate product of civic life." It developed in towns, in urban societies where people moved about, where large numbers were gathered together, and where designation by a single name was not merely an administrative inconvenience but a fundamental social disadvantage. This argument would account for the precocity of second-name use in Venice and then in the cities of Lombardy, Emilia and Tuscany, and it would explain the rapid spread of second naming in the later medieval urban environment, but it fails to account for the origins of the practice among the nobility. The same is true if the argument is given a more political slant. It suits centralized governments if people have fixed family names, since it facilitates such operations as tax-raising and conscription as well as bureaucratic rule generally, and such considerations played an obvious role in the encouragement and then prescription of fixed second names in later times. But in the eleventh and twelfth centuries such notions are premature. More plausible is a link between second naming and a looser "wish to structure public life shared by the Church and by lordships",[16] but even here a social and cultural movement seems to have been primary. People needed and used second names within their communities before the practice was enforced in any way by the authorities. But trends such as more formalized landholding, the replacement of oral by written agreements, the growth of towns and of trade, more sophisticated government generally, all characteristic of the central medieval period, amplified and encouraged the process. The linkage with class, status and gender is significant here. In most areas, the second name began among the nobility and percolated downwards or outwards later. It penetrated the laity before the clergy and was used by men before women. In other words, it was associated with public life and certain functions within public life; and it had cachet and might be imitated by burgesses and those with social pretensions for this reason. Once the process began, it spread geographically and socially because the underlying reasons repeated themselves but also through emulation. Once second names became the norm, they ran out single names and invaded even the lists of religious donors and beneficiaries, where they were not needed, because that had become the way that people were described and saw themselves.

All this is confirmed by the fact that in the later medieval period and long afterwards, "persons without autonomous social situations" as well as members of low-status groups or out-groups "continued to be designated by their first names alone, even in official documents".[17] In the first category would be children, women to some extent, servants and religious. In the parish of Saint-Germain-l'Auxerrois in Paris in 1292, for example, among male servants, 60 per cent had only one name and 10 per cent were listed after their masters as "son vallet" with no name at all. Among female servants, 61 per cent were listed with one name and 32 per cent with none. Designating servants by reference to their masters was common. From the Forez, we have Archimbaudo servienti meo (1180); Verjuz le valetz al conto (1288); and Johannete ancille Mathei Bois (1350).

The lack of autonomy of the poor was also reflected in their naming. In Paris around 1300, those with only one name were nearly all among the poorest. In fourteenth-century Ghent, the old-shoe makers or cobblers were a low-prestige profession; "several of them were identified only by a [single] given name . . . suggesting a mobile and rootless group". Monks and nuns, who had espoused voluntary poverty, also retained single names. Among outsiders, those of illegitimate birth, Jews and lepers were marked by the lack of a second name. From the Forez, again, typically, we have dicto Joce judeo (1292). A mid-twelfth-century charter from Béarn refers to "our lepers, Donatus, Wilhelmus, Poncet", and so on. Lepers depended on the Church and were under its jurisdiction. The so-called "cagots" or descendants of lepers, fairly common in Béarn, lived apart from the rest of the population and did not intermarry. Their residence in each vicinity was called "l'ostau deu chrestiaa", and they took their names from this, for example Johanot deu Crestiaa. Not until the fifteenth century did cagots acquire other second names, like the rest of the population, and ones that did not simply advertise their difference. This signalled their general assimilation.[18]

The second name and the family

The introduction and crystallization of second names was not just a question of logic and changes in public life. "To explain the birth of family names", Marc Bloch stressed in 1932, "it is to the internal history of the family itself that one must look." In the old single-name system, belonging to and place in the family or kindred was denoted via leading names, alliteration, and transmitted name elements. These practices, particularly in the form of the transmission of particular first names to go with particular familiar roles determined by gender and birth order, did not disappear, as we shall see, but their signifìcance did change. They remained markers within the family or kindred, perhaps within the narrow community, but for society at large the family was now designated by an unchanging family name.

Both the old and the new systems expressed the continuity of the family, but while the old one proclaimed that unity from the inside, from the point of view of members of the family, and which one had to know the genealogy of the family to understand, the new one . . . announced it from an external and social perspective.[19]

There was also a mutation in family structures involved with the new nomenclature, a mutation which took time to accomplish and which had conflicting tendencies within it. First, there was a strengthening of the sense of lineage. We have seen that in the early medieval period kinship groups tended to be loose and lacking in this sense. Around the year 1000, these shifting groupings gave way to agnatic lines or dynasties tracing descent firmly in the male line. Women, daughters and widows, began to be excluded from inheritance; patrimonies were consolidated, often around castles; marriage of males was restricted to the eldest, who became the principal heir. Office-holding often became hereditary too. The process obviously had social, regional and chronological variations. The model was provided by the royal houses, both German and French. The Carolingians showed strong patrilinear traits from the late eighth century, and the Capetians practised primogeniture from the ninth. The new structures were adopted next by the higher nobility, then by castellans, and finally by knights. According to Duby, this happened in northern France for the first in the early tenth century; for the second around 1000; and for the third in the early eleventh century. In southern France and northern Italy, the process occurred a little later. All this involved a reordering of the social and political structure also, which historians have called the advent of "feudalism".

Primogeniture was stressed in the first instance among royalty and nobility by the use of leading names, as we have seen. Certain names were used within families successively or alternately to designate the heir. A striking example of the first is provided by the Guillems, castellans of Montpellier. Nine holders of the office and heads of their family between 985 and 1204 bore the same leading name. In northern Italy, three Ildebrandos were counts of Pisa in the eleventh century with only one break; while five counts of Parma in succession used the name Umberto between 1067 and 1152. Many examples of alternation may also be cited from the ninth century onwards. In France, in the tenth and eleventh centuries, "the hereditary counts of Tonnerre were all Milo or Gui", "the counts of Nevers were all Landric or Bodo", and the lords of Seignelay in the next century were Aswalo or Daimbert.[20] The next stage, as we have seen, was for the noble family to adopt a second name, which was either a patronymic or a name linked to the castle or fief.

The true shifting patronymic was an important mode of naming in all classes in the first phase of second naming. It used the idiom of patrilineal descent in its pure form without reference to land or occupation. It could exist in a variety of social and familial milieus, among nobles and peasants, in small two-generational families or in larger "clans". The simple "son of" formula was more characteristic of the small family, and it was here also that patronymics first became "frozen": the father/son linkage as a continuing process was ended and one particular link became perpetuated as the family name, sometimes with an appropriate prefix or suffix. This happened for external and internal reasons, either because the authorities required a fixed name and simply chose the current second name, or because the family itself lost interest in the chain of ancestry. This was more likely to happen where families were smaller, vertically and horizontally – the situation probably of most medieval peasants and townspeople in England and France. Here the patronymic might be or have become largely a convenient community and family label and whether it fluctuated or was fixed mattered little.

Elsewhere the significance of the patronymic is different. An indication of this is the use of longer patronymic chains to identify individuals. These are found in English sources from the twelfth century to the fourteenth in different parts of the country but they are not common, and they seem to have been means of exact identification rather than the reflection of a strong genealogical sense. An example from Lincolnshire in 1219, Robertus filius Jalf patris Muriellis uxoris Roberti filii Roberti, shows this with its stress on horizontal and affinal relations rather than vertical patrilineal ties.

Patronymic chains were much more important in Italy, in the Trentino and Tuscany for example. Reference to father and grandfather was the commonest form, but longer chains were employed on more formal occasions. A maternal ancestor of Dante was designated as Durante di Scolaio di Rinieri di Rustino degli Abbati. Buonaccorso Pitti referred to himself in his diary in 1412 as Buonaccorso di Neri di Buonaccorso di Maffeo di Bonsignore d'un altre Bonsignore de' Pitti. Perhaps the record goes to the chronicler Galeotto de' Cei, who listed 12 forbears in the direct male line in the full version which he gave of his name. Here the name does indicate the importance of lineage within the wider kindred.

The patronymic chain was also a characteristic feature of Welsh nomenclature. It was satirized in the anonymous play, *Sir John Oldcastle*, of 1600. The judge asks, with reference to a defendant, "What bail? What sureties?", and is told "Her cousin Ap Rice ap Evan ap Morice ap Morgan ap Llewellyn ap Madoc ap Meredith ap Griffith ap Davis ap Owen ap Shinkin Jones." "Two of the most efficient are enough", he replies, to be told again by the sheriff "An't please your lordship, these are all but one!" Triple, quadruple and longer chains are common in the medieval sources and were still "in popular use" in Glamorgan and elsewhere down to the seventeenth century and beyond. This system of living genealogies is explained by the Welsh system of tenure and inheritance, where land was partitioned among a wide group of male relatives. Those "belonging to families with any landed possessions, even quite modest ones" might expect to inherit from distant kinsmen. Hence it was necessary "for a man to ensure that his ancestry and relationships were kept in mind constantly", and, in the absence of written records, keeping "the memory of descent" alive in the name itself was vital.[21] It was also important in such systems to know which relatives were alive and which were dead. This explains the custom, found for example in the Trentino, of referring to deceased fathers: Bertolucio q(uondam) Henrici (1348); Valentino fu Ser Pietro detto Crema (1391).

So genealogical depth implies breadth of kinship ties, which brings us back to the question of family structures. How far does the hereditary second name reflect a contraction of the family, the advent not only of patriliny but also of a new emphasis on the nuclear or conjugal unit? First, names join other evidence gathered by historians to show that the larger kinship group or "clan" was an important presence in some parts of Europe down to the end of the medieval period. In France, collective names for groups of kin are found in Languedoc, the Forez, the Lyonnais and Metz in the thirteenth and fourteenth centuries. John of Salisbury refers in the 1150s to Archdeacon William of London "of the kin-group (*gens*) which take their name from Bellus Mansus".[22] This was a Norman family.

The earliest Irish "family" names are collective names attached to clans or such-like groupings. Various terms were used to indicate the kin-group, but the prevailing formula in the historical period was Ui or O, meaning grandsons or descendants. This was attached to an eponymous ancestor. The history and age of O names is uncertain, but many can be traced back, it seems, to real forbears in the tenth, eleventh and twelfth centuries, for example to O'Boyle of Tirconnel, who flourished around 900; to O'Connor of Offaly, who died in 977; or to O'Callaghan of Desmond, who flourished around 1090. O names were probably in use collectively well before this; what happens from the tenth century is that they become attached to individuals, first perhaps to clan leaders and then to their descendants and followers. Clan or "sept" names – a sept was a subdivision of a clan – are also found using the patronymic Mac, for example MacArdle, Mac Cormack, MacConmara or MacNamara. There was a constant process of hiving-off of septs from the great clans, and very often the sept took the Mac form, while the clan or larger grouping retained the O form. The name of the Mac-Gillycuddy of the Reeks in Killarney "only dates from the sixteenth century". Before this

> they were O'Sullivans, a branch of O'Sullivan Mór, which at that comparatively late date became established as a sept distinct from the parent stem. At first the name MacGillycuddy was only used by the chief's family, the others still calling themselves O'Sullivan; for a while they were often described as O'Sullivan alias MacGillycuddy, but eventually the latter was adopted by the whole branch.

This must have been a common process usually at an earlier date. Clans and septs were territorial groupings. Some groups were displaced, especially by the Anglo-Norman invasions, but despite such displacements and later migrations "Gaelic surnames" were still, in the 1950s, mainly to be found "in the part . . . of the country to which their sept belonged",[23] testimony to the importance of these names and the kin-groups to which they referred.

The situation was similar in the Highlands of Scotland. The Scottish clan was a social grouping based on the idea of blood descent, led by a hereditary chief. "The power of the chief", wrote Burt in 1745, "is not supported by interest as they are landlords, but by consanguinity, as lineally descended from the old patriarchs or fathers of the families." This was reflected in the clan name which attached it to its founding father. So the Macdonalds or Donalds descended from an eponymous Donald, the Gunns from Gunni; while the Macleans were Clann 'ic 'ill Eathain, descendants of the servant of John. Though other forms were used in the medieval period, that using the patronymic Mac was predominant. As in Ireland, clans in Scotland were also territorial groupings. For example, the Sinclairs predominated in Caithness; the Campbells occupied Argyll and surrounding districts; the Macleods, Macdonalds and Mackinnons shared Skye.

Clan names "took definite shape in the 15th century",[24] but they seem to have retained a great deal of fluidity well beyond this time. There are several reasons for this. Septs developed within clans, with cadet branches taking new or additional names. The name Macpherson, for example, was borne by a small sept of the Campbells in Glassary, Argyll, from the fourteenth and fifteenth centuries. One of the three main Henderson families was a branch of the Clan Gunn, supposedly taking its name from a younger son of a fifteenth-century chief called Henry. A modern list drawn up by Martine gives 129 sept or family names belonging to the Macdonald clan, 79 belonging to the Campbell, 30 belonging to the Buchanan, and so on. At the same time, clan names and allegiance were assumed by tenants, neighbours and followers. On the one hand, clients sought the protection of the great families, old or new, like the Campbells in Argyll, the Macdonalds in the Western Isles, and the Gordons in Strathbolgy; on the other hand, the clans and their leaders sought supporters and fighters. Much later, "it was by this means that Clan Mackenzie was so rapidly enlarged in the sixteenth and seventeenth centuries", taking in Macraes, Murchisons, Maclays, Maclennans, Macaulays, Macleods, etc.[25] A written document of 1569 shows John McAchopich and his sons placing themselves under the chiefship of Campbell of Cawdor and taking his name.

Historians are by no means agreed on the connection between the establishment of the family name and the development of family structure and solidarity in Italy. Herlihy argues that "family solidarity, at least among the aristocratic classes, grew in the eleventh and early twelfth centuries, but it was thereafter subject to powerful pressures [especially the development of city government], which worked to loosen its cohesiveness". So larger kindreds began to split up. But the disasters and insecurities of the later

Middle Ages brought a reversion to older forms of family organization, for the sake of protection. Though "common ownership of property" by "consortial" families was not restored, "the moral and cultural bonds holding relatives together grew in strength". Against this, Goldthwaite played down the importance of wider family solidarities in fourteenth- and fifteenth-century Florence. The "sense of family" of Filippo di Matteo Strozzi (1428–91), for example,

> was far removed from the clan-like loyalties which had been such a cohesive social force in the medieval commune. His family pride only incidentally reached out laterally to embrace all the Strozzi; it was, rather, sharply focused on his own lineal descendants and extended vertically . . . through time to bind them into a single line.[26]

There is always an element of subjectivity in such debates. Some see the chessboard as white on black and some as black on white; for, of course, all family structures are both large and small. It all depends on whether one or the other receives more emphasis in social and cultural terms, and here names can be important signs and pointers.

Large families or clans are referred to by name from the early medieval period, often in connection with the lands which they owned: terra Isaffiliorum (757, Tuscany); terra Gherardinga (tenth century, Lucca); terra de illi Pantaleoni (963, Naples). Reference was also made to the clan: gente Leoniana (1150, Rome); to the "house": casa de li Ferrari (1075, Gubbio); or directly to family members: homines qui nominatur li Gaidoni (1046, Modena). The group could also be designated as sons or heirs: I figli Pernicis; or Heres Barucii (thirteenth century, Trentino). Collective names in -inga or -enga derived from the Germanic -ing. Other suffixes were also used to indicate descent groups or consortia, for example -esco or -eschi in Tuscany and elsewhere, giving Lamberteschi and Aldobrandeschi. The -i suffix, so common in northern and central Italy, was also used, though it was more frequently a simple patronymic.

According to Herlihy, such groupings accounted for between 10 and 20 per cent only of landowners in the tenth and eleventh centuries, and they were most characteristic of the feudal nobility or those later called magnates. By the twelfth century, the large family was found in the towns and cities of the centre and north. At first its overriding concern was defence and protection and it found its expression in tower societies, associations focused on fortified places within cities. Later, as communes tamed magnate violence, large families continued as economic, political, social and cultural entities.

All group members shared the same name, and this was an important element in their sense of solidarity. Venice had its "great sprawling clans" at this time: the Morosini, the Contarini, the Venier, the Giustinian. Though not tightly organized, they maintained a strong feeling of community which centred on the name. In a court case in 1364, Naufusio Morosini recounted that a fight, in which he had killed another man, began when the latter delivered an insult against the Ca' Morosini, or the Morosini house. The significance of the name emerges even more strongly where violent collective factionalism was still current, as in Perugia in the later fifteenth century. In a battle in the city in 1495 between the ruling Baglioni and a coalition of exiled families, the participants each began to shout "the name of his family and his party, for one cried . . . Feltro! Feltro! and another Savel Savelli! another Colonna! Colonna! others shouted Staffa! and Oddi! Renna! and Ranieri! and many other names", and the pro-Baglioni faction shouted "Bagliona! Bagliona!".[27]

Such kin-groups are found all over northern and central Italy, but they are best documented for Florence and Genoa. From the thirteenth century, if not before, the leading families of Florence, noble and non-noble, formed large kindreds with common names. The Cavalcanti comprised 82 adult males in 1316; the Medici 50 in 1373. By 1351 there were 28 Strozzi households and by 1427 there were 31. Nomenclature took two main forms. The house, line or family might be referred to in the singular. So in *I Libri della Famiglia*, written in the 1430s, Leon Battista Alberti refers to "la nostra famiglia Alberta" or "la casa nostra Alberta". But the custom prevailed of using the plural form: "nostri Alberti", "il legnazzio degli Adimari", and so on. By the fourteenth and fifteenth centuries, individuals were nearly always designated as degli Alberti, dei Bardi, de' Medici, and so on. "The public and formal badges of membership" of such a large family group or *consorteria* "were its surname and its coat of arms: by their use men linked themselves to the past and established themselves as part of the family continuum and community". Possession of a family name was itself "a sign of antiquity, of honourable ancestry. It established a man's right to share in his family's political patrimony . . . and social position." The functions and structure of such groupings changed in the Renaissance period, as collective defence became unnecessary and collective property and co-residence declined, and there was some fission into smaller families with different names. The ancient Tornaquinci, for example, split into the Popoleschi, the Giachinotti, the Marabottoni and the Tornabuoni. But many of the larger families remained in existence, continuing to live in "residential enclaves",[28] acting in concert politically and re family matters, especially marriage, and exercising patronage and jurisdiction over family churches, chapels and burial places.

The Genoese *alberghi* were similar in function and structure to the *consorteria* of Florence, though they were not confined to strict relatives. The first to be mentioned is the Spinola *albergo* in 1267. Most date from the late thirteenth and fourteenth centuries and some continued into the sixteenth. Around seventy existed in the 1370s; about a hundred in 1400; and

28 in 1528. *Alberghi* were a response to renewed insecurity and factionalism in this period, "a restructuring of the feudal kindred". They were often of rural origin but quickly became established in the city. The first were noble, but *alberghi* of "popolani" quickly followed. A few *alberghi* comprised one family only, like the *popolano* Maruffo; a few families, like the Scotti, split into two or three *alberghi*; but in general *alberghi* were formed by the fusion of a number of families, possibly distantly related. They entered into pacts of solidarity and agreed to use the same arms and the same collective name. This was either the pre-existing name of the leading family in the group, as, for example, with the Adorno, the Fornari and the Sauli; or a new name was adopted. For example, "the Marabotti, Ghisolfi, Piccamiglio, Savignone, Cibo and Pansani took their new names from the del Campo *contrada* or ward: de Campionibus", or Campioni. Abandoning the ancestral name was a serious step and an indication of the strong desire to form a new unit with the same solidarity as the old kindred group. Some statutes of *alberghi* required members "to act and comport themselves in all things as if they were born of the said name".[29] It was a commonplace to identify *albergo* and name, and the formation of *alberghi* contributed to the fixing of the second name in Genoa. However, some families continued to refer to themselves by their own names within the *albergo*. Members of the Giustiniani, for example, were Giustiniani olim de Banca, olim Longo, olim Castro, and so on. Fission also occurred, with families reverting to their old names without difficulties, for example the families belonging to the Scipioni *albergo*, which broke up in the mid fifteenth century.

Alberghi occupied particular neighbourhoods over which they generally had control. We have seen that quarters took their names from *alberghi* and vice versa. In 1463, 95 per cent of houses belonging to *alberghi* were situated "in their own quarter, along their own street, or around their own square".[30] For example, the Giustiniani, formed in 1362, all lived near the Platea Longa, a street leading to the old port, and they were still living in the same district a century later; the Doria occupied the San Matteo quarter, and the Scipioni the Porta Nuova. *Alberghi* also engaged in common economic activity and had patronage of churches and chapels. There was great variation in the size of *alberghi*, ranging from one or two households to over a hundred. In 1455, there were 95 Lomellini and 104 Spinola di San Lucca on the tax rolls. The Spinola at this time comprised at least 134 heads of household, that is about 600 persons; while the Fieschi in 1310 had only ten heads. *Alberghi* could be swollen by the inclusion of clients and servants, who all might take the *albergo* name.

Individual members of large Italian families were designated in various ways. A man could be called by his first name plus a singular version of the collective name, for example Matheus Cerutus, a member of the Ceruti kindred from the Canavese around 1300. Again, he might have both a personal second name and a singular version of the collective name, for example

Andreas Starna vocatus Nappaio, a member of the Nappari kindred (1160, Volterra). This form was sometimes used in Genoa for members of *alberghi*. Fifteenth-century statutes refer to Segundinus Vignosus (of the Vignoso or Vignosi family); Batistis Luxardus (of the Luxardo). But more often the collective name in the plural was used preceded by "de": Franciscus De Magnerri; Batistus De Vignosiis. The patronym was frequently added, especially if the father was dead: Joannis De Goano qd. Bartolomei; Manuel qd. Deserini de Cataneis.

In Florence, the patronym followed by "de' ", "dei" or "degli" and the collective name was one of the favoured forms from the thirteenth to the early sixteenth centuries: Galgano di Bonagiunta de' Medici (1240); Lorenzo Cione degli Ghiberti (1400); Giovanni d'Agnolo de' Bardi (1485). This form was also common elsewhere in central Italy, for example in Pisa, Siena and Bologna. According to Heers, "the name of the father was systematically given [in official documents] whenever a family of high social position was involved", which means a large extended family. In Genoa, the father's name had been "optional" at the end of the fourteenth century in notarial deeds, but it became "absolutely necessary half a century later . . . for the powerful, the noble and the rich". In Florence, the three-part name was not used for the middle classes and below; in Genoa it was not granted to "foreigners, the rustics of the Rivieras or the modest *popolani*".[31]

More elaborate forms are found, incorporating titles or further links in the patronymic chain, for example Nofri di Pagno di Messer Andrea degli Strozzi, or Tommaseo di Messer Guccio di Dini Gucci, both from late-fourteenth-century Florence. But the general trend over time was towards simplification. The patronym could be omitted, as with Chiarissimo de' Medici (1240). Then there was a tendency, resisted by some important Florentine families, to drop the preposition before the collective name: Gino di Donato Velluti (1267); Lorenzo di Bartolo Ghiberti (1300). This form also seems to have prevailed in Venice during the fourteenth century, if not earlier, and it is common elsewhere. The preposition could also fall from the patronymic, as with Piero Saccone de' Tarlati (1300, Florence). By the late fourteenth and early fifteenth centuries, therefore, we have some individuals, from large as well as small families, bearing simple first and second names: Orlanduccio Orlandi; Rosso Sassetti; Banco Corsi. This nomenclature signals the effective decline of the "clan" as a significant social grouping.

Nomenclature also indicates that it had always been a minority, though in some ways a dominant form. From his study of medieval Latium, Toubert concluded: "It is very important for the history of family structure that the family name should have been born in the narrow framework of the two-generational family and not that of a vast agnatic community." He is writing here mainly of the peasantry. Any extended families in this milieu referred to in early texts were either informal and unstable aggregates of small families already structured by marriage (joint families), or conjugal families occasionally enlarged on their edges by taking in ascendants, adult children, even in extreme cases, widowed or celibate collaterals.[32]

This observation can probably be extended to much of the rural and urban population of France and England in the central and later medieval periods. An interesting touchstone is provided by the landowners and well-to-do townsmen who subscribed to the Durham Liber Vitae. The explicit family groupings which occur in this document from the twelfth to the fourteenth century are like those described by Toubert. They include parents and siblings as well as spouses and children of the principals, for example, Thomas de Amundau, Willelmus pater ejus, Emme mater ejus, Helewis uxor ejus et filii ejus et filiae. By the fifteenth century, the purely nuclear family is more frequent, though the wider form survives. At the same time, the family name becomes more obvious. There are entries like "Dompnus Christophorus Wyllye; cum parentibus Ricardo Wyllye et Elysabeth uxore ejusdem; cum fratribus et sororibus Rolando, Thoma, Roberto . . . ; cum Willelmo Wyllye et Alicia uxore ejus, Roberto Kaye et uxore ejus", and so on.

Naming could also emphasize the importance of the household rather than the family of blood. In Italy, the term *casa* sometimes clearly applies to household rather than dynasty, for example, La casa Iohanini speciarij (apothecary) (1392, Trentino). In Béarn in the late medieval period, the family patrimony centred on the "*ostau*" or house, which usually remained in a family over many generations. The *ostau* had its own name, usually a place-name but possibly that of a founding head of family/household. The second name of later heads was nearly always that of their *ostau*. The name of the *ostau* was also given to children of the head and to other resident family members. But "the name was attached to individuals only so long as they occupied the house and the land that it designated". When an *ostau* was divided up, the new divisions received new names. Where an *ostau* was abandoned and later repossessed, its name would be likely to change also, a new name coming from the new occupant. So

the name of the house was not absolutely linked to the family, nor was it indissolubly linked to a particular house; it could pass from one house to another following a family that moved; it could pass from one family to another family inhabiting the same house. In general, the name stuck more to the house than to the family.[33]

In the urban context, we find pupils, apprentices and servants taking names of their masters. This seems to have been fairly common practice among Italian artists in the Renaissance. "Piero, the son of a certain Lorenzo, a goldsmith", born around 1460, was "the pupil of Cosimo Rosselli", Vasari relates, "after whom he was known, never being called other than Piero di Cosimo". He adds that Cosimo loved and treated him as a son. Again, Jacopo, the son of Antonio Tatti, was apprenticed to the sculptor and architect, Andrea Contucci, known as Il Sansovino. Their relationship, too, was filial, so "Jacopo began in those early years of his to be called not Tatti but Sansovino". In a slightly different instance, Francesco, the son of Michelagnolo de' Rossi, became the protégé in Rome of Cardinal Salviati, in whose household he lived. As a result, "he began to be called Cecchino Salviati, and he kept that name until he died". The custom of more ordinary apprentices and employees taking their masters' names was found in York, Norwich and elsewhere in England, but seems to have been especially prevalent in London. Thomas de Cavendish, son of William atte Watre de Ewelle and late apprentice of Walter de Cavendish, mercer, was admitted to the freedom of the city in 1311. "Hamo de Dene, an immigrant from Essex, . . . served as factor to Richard de Chigwell", an important fishmonger and alderman in the reign of Edward I, and later "assumed his master's surname".[34] Sometimes the name was taken from the widow after the master's death. Sometimes the apprentice married the widow. When Robert le Chaucer, grandfather of the poet, died in the early fourteenth century, his widow remarried, and her second husband was called Richard le Chaucer. He was presumably an apprentice taking over his late master's business, wife and name all in one go. This practice is also found in France. On the Paris tax rolls, for example, we have listed Perrenele, fame Jehan Augier (presumably dead), Jehan Augier son fuiz and Perrot Augier, son vallet.

Women and names

Women's names are much less common in the sources than men's, especially in the early medieval period. In French documents from the eleventh to the thirteenth century, for example, 10–15 per cent only of names belonged to women. Women's naming was also more conservative than men's. After the Norman Conquest in England, women were more likely than men to keep the old Anglo-Saxon and Scandinavian names. More generally, women retained single names longer than men, as we have seen. Second names for women were rare in France in the twelfth century: 1 per cent in Burgundy; 5 per cent in Lower Languedoc; rather more in Gascony. "Bearing a second name was a man's affair; it was the sign of personal responsibility for managing something." So, women only bore second names at this time when "they were exercising the functions and following the lifestyle usually reserved to men".[35] This was most likely to occur among noble women: heiresses, widows, those whose husbands were away fighting. Only during the thirteenth century did the use of second names spread to non-noble women, in the wake of the development for men and for the same reasons. The situation was similar in England and Italy, though the second name was established later. Most women in the Trentino, for example, were referred to by more than one name by the fourteenth century.

In the early stages of second naming, women might have independent names. As with men, these names were of several types. In the Trentino, nicknames were probably the largest category: Adelaide Bruascroua (1280 – scratch spot on the skin); Simona dicta la Charogna de Carzan (1554 – jade). Names from places or occupations were rarer: Una donna nomine Triuixana (1333 – from Treviso); Adeleyta Lavandaria (1351). In Paris around 1300, 60 per cent of women with second names had names of this kind. Independent names seem to have been more characteristic of large towns and cities. Later on, especially, they were likely to be attached to marginal women. In London, Alice Blerheg (blear-eye or hoodwinker) was indicted for manslaughter in 1276, and Elena le Haluedeuel (half-devil) owned a house, perhaps a brothel, in Fleet Street in 1279.

Women with independent names were probably always in a minority, and their proportion seems to have been reduced over time. In a list of 55 women's names from Ahuy, a small town in Burgundy, in 1331, only three second names were nicknames and two place-names, and all the rest referred to their kinship or marriage ties. Sometimes a woman was not even given her own first name. At Winchester in 1148, we have tenants called uxor Giffardi, filia Gupill, and so on; from Burgundy in the early fourteenth century, la fille Jaquet de Champaigne, and relicta dicti Saichot.

In general women were classified by reference to their fathers or their husbands. Naming placed them firmly within the family and in a dependent position. Like sons, unmarried daughters took their fathers' second names as a rule, though girls' names might be feminized. From the Lauragais in 1245, for example, we have Alazaisia Barrava from Barravus; Eslarmunda Engilberta from Engilbert; from Amiens around 1300, Maroie le Bourderresse, fille Jehan le Bourdeur. In Florence, women were named in this respect like men, for example Cilia di Gherardo de' Caponsacchi (late thirteenth century), a member of the élite; or Buona di Rossi (1356), a pauper. Sometimes in Italy women were referred to directly and independently as members of large family groups: Adeleita degli Alberti di Mangona (1125, Romagna); Maddalena degli Oddi (1500, Perugia).

The naming of married women followed two patterns. With the first, the woman kept her premarital name, like Cilia di Gherardo de' Caponsacchi, when she married Folco Portinari. This custom seems to have been more characteristic of the élites in Italy, where a wife's family might be very prominent, but it was not confined there. The same is true of France. Ysabelli de Chazeles and her husband Helyotus, from the Ile-de-France around 1300, were both serfs. From the Forez, as late as 1395, we have Johannes Textor and Marcelline Chainigni quondam uxor sue, and Symonis Arentz and Agnetis Ponsarde uxor dicti Symonis, rural craftsmen and peasants. Retaining the patrilineal name was much commoner in some regions than others. In Gascony in the twelfth century, 86 per cent of married women had second names referring to their fathers or other blood relatives, while only 14 per cent had names referring to their husbands; but in the Toulouse region, the percentages were 40 and 60 respectively.

There is some evidence also that retaining the name of origin became a noble trait in the later medieval period. This is certainly the case for the women whom the Lisles came to know while Lord Lisle was Lord Deputy of Calais in the 1530s. So the wife of Thybault Rouaud or Rouault, Sieur de Riou, and an heiress, always signed herself Jeanne or Jenne de Saveuzes, the name of her father, though she was sometimes called Madame de Riou. Similarly, Rouaud's sister Anne, married to Nicholas de Montmorency, Seigneur de Bours, signed Anne Rouaud, though again she was also known as Madame de Bours.

Married women with their original names are found in English sources but they are rare. In Wales on the other hand "the wife continued to be known by the name she had before marriage,"[36] and this custom persisted well after the end of the medieval period, since it was in the logic of the patrilineal family system.

The alternative pattern, emphasizing the conjugal unit, was for the wife to take the husband's second name. In Italy from the thirteenth century onwards, women were referred to via their husbands: Temporina uxor Petri Fabri; Donna Benvenuta moglie Jacobi Stramaioli. These examples are from the Trentino, but the custom is found in Tuscany and elsewhere. Another less common mode was for the wife to take a feminized version of the husband's name, for example, Margherita detta La Vanzina (1504, Trentino), who was the wife of Vanzin; or Mona Lisa, wife of Francesco del Giacondo, known as La Giaconda (late fifteenth century, Florence). As this instance shows, it was quite common to designate married women by reference to both her husband and her own kin. The daughter of Bernardo de' Bardi, who married Lorenzo, son of Palla Strozzi around 1430 – both leading Florentine families – was known variously as Alessandra de' Bernardo de' Bardi, Alessandra de' Bardi, and Alessandra Bardi negli Strozzi. It seems to have been very rare in Italy before 1600 for a married woman simply to take her husband's second name as her own, though cases may be found.

Conjugal ties were much more important in naming in France and England. By the thirteenth century, if not before, Frenchwomen exchanged their fathers' for their husbands' names, when they married. In a sample from the eleventh to the thirteenth century, only 13 per cent of married women retained the patronym. The simplest and perhaps the earliest form was to follow the woman's first name by "wife of" and the husband's full name. So, from the Lauragais in 1245, we have Bruna uxor Bernardi Fogassa; from the Lyonnais around 1300, Johanne uxore Bartholomei de Bosco. Quite often a feminized version of the husband's second name was also included in the denomination, for example, from Amiens around 1300, Ysabiau le Goreliere feme Thumas le Gorelier; or, from Arras in 1226, Belle fille feme Jehan, the wife of Bel fil Jehan.

Simple feminization of the husband's name – which probably reflects everyday usage – seems to prevail from around 1300, though it does not oust other forms. From Arras, in this category, we have Maroie li Camberesse, and Crestiiene li Prestresse, using occupational second names; or Mahaus li Blondele, wife of Jehans Blondiaux, and Agnes li Noire, of Jakes li Noirs, using nicknames. Sometimes "dit" or its equivalents was used, for example Catherine dite Cokelette, femme Jehan Cokelet (1316, Saint-Quentin). The simple juxtaposition of the wife's first name and the husband's second is found but seems to have been rare throughout the medieval period, as it was in Italy. Widows usually kept on their husbands' names and did not revert to their earlier premarital names, though their status as widows was noted: Cecilia uxor quondam Jordanis de Peite (1245, Lauragais); Gile fame feu Robert le Petit (1296, Paris). The genderization of second names, whether independent or derived from males, is very striking. As Nègre noted for Rabastens at the end of the fourteenth century, "even names of origin take the feminine form: Na Murela is the feminine of de Murel".[37] Nicknames were treated in the same way. A girl named Liejarde from the Vexin in the mid thirteenth century belonged to a family with the name Rex or Le Roy; her second name was La Reine.

The same range of denominations of wives via husbands is found in England, but simply taking the husband's second name was more common there and even became the rule after 1400. Here (and probably elsewhere) there is a discrepancy between the way in which wives were referred to in legal documents and everyday usage, which favoured the simpler form. This can occasionally be detected in the sources. A King's Lynn survey of around 1280, for example, refers to the widow Matildis que fuit uxor Reginaldi Wiz but also calls her Matilda Wiz. In another Norfolk document of 1315, Mabilla uxor Rogeri Norman de Fileby also appears as Mabilla Norman de Fileby.

As nomenclature underlines, medieval family structures, large and small, were firmly patrilineal. Property that went to daughters was lost to the family and to the name, and great efforts were made to avoid this eventuality. This is well expressed in an agreement made in 1452 by members of the noble Vergy family, seneschals of the County of Burgundy, to ensure that their main patrimony passed down in the male line. Their predecessors, it stated,

> were ever mindful to maintain the estate and honour of their name
> . . . by leaving their principal lordships successively to those bear-
> ing their name and arms . . . without allowing that . . . their lands . . .
> should go to daughters . . . or any not bearing the said name and
> arms, even if they ought to be their heirs. . . .[38]

However, where male heirs were not available and the estate went to an heiress as a result, the name could nevertheless be preserved by passing it to the man who married her and/or their children. This occurred in some of the greatest English families. Robert Fitz-Maldred, a descendant of the old earls of Northumberland, who died around 1245, married "Isabel . . . heir of the Norman house of the Nevils", and their children took that name. Among peasants, it was more likely for the husband of an heiress to change his name for hers, and the linkage with the transfer of property was clear. Among the tenants of Chertsey Abbey in the fourteenth century, one heiress took her husband's name at marriage, but when her father died and she inherited his property, they both changed to the father's name.[39]

The custom was also fairly widespread in France. At Metz around 1215, for example, Cunon du Neufchatel, a knight and descendant of a powerful family of feudal lords, was also called Cunon Bazin "because he had married the daughter of Jacques Bazin".[40] In the Forez, sons-in-law took or were given the names of their fathers-in-law, when they were established on the latter's land, that is where the wife was an heiress. The name was often that of the estate, and the adoption of the name was more likely where the father-in-law also had superior social status. Giving up one's own name was a kind of derogation and a price that only those of lower standing, or perhaps younger sons, would pay.

In some cases, a man might inherit through his mother and thus take her name. The mid-thirteenth-century Northamptonshire lord, Wischardt Ledet, was the namesake of his maternal grandfather, whose lands he inherited via his mother. Transfer of the maternal second name also occurred in towns. Cristiana de Evre, of London, who died in 1316, was the daughter of Roger de Evre and the wife of Giles le Qylter. She left the bulk of her property to her son, who was called Walter de Evre.

Herlihy has charted the incidence of naming after mothers (matronymics) in Europe between the eighth and twelfth centuries. Rare until the mid tenth century, matronymics then became more common, reaching a peak in the eleventh century and then declining. They were never more than a small proportion of all second names after parents, and they were more common in southern than in northern Europe. The highest incidence was in southern France, where between 9 and 12 per cent of second names after parents were matronyms between the late tenth and the twelfth centuries. Matronymics continued to be significant in the later medieval period though at a lower level. In France, they seem to have been commonest in Normandy and least common in the south, except for Gascony. In England, over the whole medieval period, Matthews calculated that they comprised 10 per cent of all names referring to a kin relationship. It has been suggested that they were rarer in Italy, though some sources indicate a fairly high incidence. In a list of emancipated serfs from Bologna in the 1250s, 52 per cent of second names were patronyms, 34 per cent matronyms, while 2 per cent used the names of both parents. In all three countries, matronyms have survived as not uncommon modern family names. From Italy, for example, we have La Cecilia, La Bianca, Della Bella; from England, Beatty and Beaton from Beatrice; Maude, Mawson and Mowatt from Matilda; Marriott, Malleson and Mallett from Mary.

The matronym was used in a variety of circumstances. First, as we have seen, it might imply inheritance via the mother. She could be a landowner in her own right, or, which was more likely, she could be filling in within the inheritance system for a missing male. But it is significant that in the early stages of second-name formation some heirs inheriting via heiresses took the latters' names (usually first names). Later, as we have seen, they would take the heiresses' fathers' second names, preserving their patriliny. Overlapping this case was the one in which the mother's family was more prominent than the father's. This seems to have been common among the élite in south-western France in the eleventh and twelfth centuries. It can be detected too in Italian examples which include the mother's title in the son's name: Guido de Madonna Ostia (1240, Bologna); Gerozzo di Monna Venna Dini (1500, Florence). Then the matronym might be used to distinguish between children of successive wives, as in a French example from 1138 referring to "Petrus Vilelmi, son of Dulciana and his brother Bertrand, son of Lucia". Here the matronymic element is really only a qualification of the patronym. Children of widows might also be known by their names. The painter Piero della Francesca, who was born around 1410 in Borgo San Sepolcro, "was given the name Francesca, after his mother, because his father died while she was pregnant, and it was she who brought him up". Posthumous birth was an additional significant factor. Mothers might also be unmarried and the children illegitimate. Children of priests might come into this category. Simple affection or attachment, linked to any of these reasons, may also have played a part. In the Chester Mystery Plays from the early sixteenth century or before, one of the shepherds is summoned as "Tudd, Tibby's son", and another shepherd explains that, if he is so called for, he is sure to come, "for in good faith, it is his custom/to love well his dame's name".[41]

Titles

Medieval society was hierarchical and titles were important in it as social markers. In the property registers at Rabastens from the fourteenth century, for example, names

> are nearly always preceded by an honorific title: Mossenh for the priests and sometimes for the nobles; Frayre for the only religious listed; lo Senh, lo Senher, lo Senhor for some nobles; Dona for some noble women; Maestre for the notaries and the master-artisans; En

for the great majority of men, from nobles to poorer peasants; Na for nearly all the women.[42]

With variations, linguistic and otherwise, this could apply to most other places in Europe.

The noble title was at first unspecific. A range of polite honorifics was used in the sources, of which *nobilis*, on the ancient Roman model, was only one. In the Mâconnais, 'the adjective *nobilis* (or its equivalents *clarissimus*, *illustris*, etc.) was used in the mid-tenth century to show that an individual belonged to the aristocracy". In the course of the eleventh century, *nobilis* declined and the term *miles*, meaning "knight", replaced it.[43] In eleventh-century Normandy, *divites*, *nobiles et divites*, and *magnates et proceres* were used of the highest nobles; *nobiles* alone of the less important; and *milites* of simple knights. In Brabant, *nobilis* was used generally in the eleventh century. In the twelfth, the clergy referred to *nobiles*; the Duke of Brabant to *milites*; while nobles themselves used the terms *liberi homines*, *milites* or *domini*.

Dominus was a more specific term, indicating the possession of lordship. Reserved at first to the great, it spread to petty lords in France in the twelfth and thirteenth centuries. In England, *dominus* was given to peers, knights and senior clerics. In a Newark survey of about 1230, we have Dominus John de Lisures, Dominus Hugo Bussy, and so on, all holding knights' fees. In the Durham Liber Vitae, *dominus* is used for knights from the thirteenth century to the fifteenth, but also for more senior nobles, for example Dominus Johannes de Gaunt, dux Loncastriae (sic). The title was not, however, given to all knights and nobles. *Dominus* was also used for clergy. In the Hyde Abbey register for 1467, for example, we find Dominus Willelmus, Comes de Aryndell (sic); Dominus Thomas Dowdale, Miles; and Dominus Jacobus Bowre, vicarius sancti Bartholomei.

Domina was the equivalent title for noblewomen: Domina Elizabetha comitissa de Westmerlande (sic) (*c*.1500, Durham); and for nuns (who may also have been noble): Domina Joanna Yonge; Domina Isabella Wymfolde, moniales de Wyltone (fifteenth century, Hyde).

From being a feudal title, *dominus* also extended its scope in Italy. The inscription placed outside the main gate to the Campo Santo in Pisa refers to Domini Federigi, the archbishop, and to Domini Tarlati, the podestà. In Perugia, Siena and more generally in the later thirteenth century, "the title *dominus* was always given to members of great families; but it did not only indicate seigneurial descent; it was used also to qualify any landed proprietor, patron, leader or person in control of the destiny of others".[44] In London, too, at this time, *dominus* was used for aldermen, leading members of the urban élite. "Dominus", shortened to "Dom", was also used later as a title for Benedictine monks, but this does not seem to have been medieval practice. The term in use was "Frater" for monks of all kinds, as well as friars.

"Sire" from the Latin *senior* was the French term for lord or seigneur. Down to the end of the twelfth century, it was mainly used for kings, and then for nobles. In the thirteenth and fourteenth centuries, it was a formal title, but it was also employed as a form of address to nobles from inferiors. "Sire" was added to other titles, for example Sire Rois, Sire Cuens (count); Sire Esvesques; Sire Prestre. Sire Chevaliers was common for nobles of all ranks. The forms "Mes Sire" and "Mon Seigneur" distinguished a particular king or lord (or husband). "Mes Sire" soon lost this meaning to become a general title of respect, used as early as the twelfth century by bourgeois, like "Monsieur" later. "Mon Seigneur" kept its specific meaning until well into the fourteenth century. "Dame" was originally a title for women in authority and mainly restricted to queens. Then it spread to the milieu of feudal lords and to other classes. "Ma Dame" like "Mes Sire" was at first a form of address to a particular person.

In England, too, the main terms of address and referral for nobles and knights were "dame" and "sire" or "sir", with "lord" also being used. In the Chester Mystery Plays, all those of high status are called "Sir"; so one has Sir Caiaphas, Sir Pilate and Sir Caesar, as well as Sir Colphram and Sir Grimbald Lanchedeep, fighting knights sent to guard the tomb or to massacre the Innocents. Sir Caiaphas reflects late medieval usage for the lower clergy.

In Italy, *Dominus*, in the abbreviated form "Don", became a mainly ecclesiastical title. Don Antonio of Pisa was a monk at the Angeli in Florence around 1500; Don Vincenzo Borghini, the governor of the hospital of the Innocenti at around the same time. "Signor" was the vernacular equivalent to *Dominus*, but it is very rarely found before 1500. It was then used for those of the highest family as well as those of lower status. The preferred title for men of noble and élite families in the late medieval and Renaissance periods was "Messer". This was used for members of ruling houses, like the Montefeltro, dukes of Urbino; for old nobles; and for the urban élites of Venice and Florence. It was often originally an indication of knighthood and, as we have seen, might be proudly preserved in patronymics.

"Messer" was also extended to lawyers, scholars and clerics. Machiavelli relates that a member of the noble Castracano family of Lucca "became a priest of the order of San Michele [in the mid thirteenth century] . . . , and for this reason was honoured with the title of Messer Antonio".[45] "Ser" may sometimes have been an abbreviation of "Messer" and was used in the same way, for example among the Venetian and Florentine patriciates. But generally in the thirteenth and fourteenth centuries in Tuscany and elsewhere, "Ser" was the title of a notary. In the Trentino, however, the title was being used more widely from the fourteenth century onwards. So we have Ser Bertoldo Scribano, a scribe; Ser Nicolai Merçadri, a mercer; Ser Benvenuto detto Malacarne, probably a butcher. Other men with the title "Ser" had pejorative nicknames also, not an indication of high status. It seems that "Ser" had become a courtesy title used by those of the artisan class. This almost certainly occurred elsewhere and is another example of the depreciation of titles.

Women in medieval Italy seem to have been given titles more regularly than men, and the general courtesy title, deriving from what had originally been a sign of noble superiority, took root among them earlier. *Domina*, then "Donna", "Madonna" and the abbreviated "Monna" or "Mona" were all very commonly used from the thirteenth century onwards, and they were applied to women of all classes at least in the towns. Monna Veronica, Mona Tita and Madonna Fiora di Lapo were all paupers in Florence in the 1350s, but they are referred to in the same way as the respectable wives of well-to-do citizens or nobles. "Signora" was a later development.

Magister seems originally to have been a title reserved to academic clerics. John of Salisbury in the twelfth century applied it to Gislebertus, Bishop of Poitiers, for example, and to Magister Ernaldus, a canon of the same place. Giraldus Cambrensis referred around 1200 to Magister David Oxoniensis, to Magister Albinus Herefordensi, and so on. Both the Durham and Hyde Libri Vitae also use *Magister* for clerics. The vernacular "Master", "Maistre", "Maestro" and so on were used more widely, but still for those with some authority over persons or property (ships, falcons, castles); with learning and skills; or with some social superiority. In *The Merchant of Venice* in the late sixteenth century still, when Old Gobbo is asked "Talk you of young Master Launcelot?", he replies "No 'master', sir, but a poor man's son."[46] Like others, however, the title became depreciated with further extension. In Italy, "Maestro" was given in the fourteenth and fifteenth centuries to teachers, senior clerics, doctors and master craftsmen, but by the period 1450–1550 in the Trentino we find it applied to a bath-keeper and a bombardier.

In England similarly, "Master" or "Maister" spread well beyond the ranks of those exercising a mystery or craft and took on a more general usage. In the Paston letters of the mid fifteenth century, "Master" seems to be used functionally by wife to husband, by servant to employer and by client to patron. By the sixteenth century, it is used to address or refer to nearly all men of any standing. The female "Maistris" or 'Mistress" followed a similar evolution. Another development, confirming the importance of the second name, is the use of the title with the second name alone. This seems to date from around 1500: Master Wyllde, Meister Babyngton, Mrs Leversshame. The abbreviated form had begun a little earlier. Some apothecaries and most doctors employed at Westminster Abbey in the fourteenth century were called "Mr".

Graded titles among the nobility did not exist in the early medieval period. The terms "count", "duke", "earl", "marquis" or "margrave" and "viscount" belonged to offices held from the king, the first two becoming titles used by rulers of quasi-autonomous territories in the post-Carolingian period. "Baron" derived from the Latin *vir* or *ber*, and was applied in general terms, usually in the plural, to the higher nobility. In England, graded titles date from the fourteenth and fifteenth centuries, when the House of

Lords became clearly established. The term "baron" lost its wider meaning to become attached to the lowest rung of the peerage. Above barons were viscounts, earls, marquesses and dukes in ascending order. Esquire or Squire had been a descriptive term for apprentice knights. By the later medieval period, like "knight" itself, it had lost its military functional association, and was applied to important men below the ranks of the nobility. John Paston, for example, a lawyer and important Norfolk landowner, was addressed as Squire or Esquire. In 1580, the Somerset Herald noted that it was the sign of "the first degree of gentry".[47] Noble titles existed in other countries but they were not widespread until well after the end of the medieval period; nor did they form so strict a hierarchy as in England.

A final point to make in this section is that kinship terms were very often used in address in the medieval period. In the Paston letters, Margaret Paston habitually addressed her spouse as "Right worshipful husband"; Agnes Paston addressed Edmund as "mine well-beloved son" and signed "By your mother Agnes Paston"; John Paston, the elder son, addressed a letter to "my right worshipful father", and signed "By your older son, John Paston". Younger brothers addressed elder brothers as "Right worshipful brother". Daughters and sisters, cousins, and uncles and nephews all, too, used kinship terms in address and signature. This custom, was to prove very long-lived.

PART III

Modern times

CHAPTER NINE

First names 1500–1900: I

The repertoire of names

The "Old Régime" in France was characterized by a limited stock of first names and a heavy concentration on a few very common ones. The situation began to change in the eighteenth and nineteenth centuries but only slowly and unevenly. This can be illustrated by a geographical tour of France, using case-studies, starting in the south.

At Saint-André-des-Alpes in Haute-Provence, in the first half of the seventeenth century, four names were borne by two-thirds of the men. Female names were less numerous overall though not so "bunched". By the mid eighteenth century, the stock of male names had risen significantly, while that of female names nearly tripled between 1630–50 and 1720–35 and doubled again by 1750–65. There was a similar development in the villages of the Barcelonnette, "a small handful of single first names, with a few very dominant ones" in the seventeenth century, giving way in the eighteenth and nineteenth to a far larger repertoire.[1] In two villages in the Hautes-Alpes in the eighteenth century, the general stock was quite large but most names were little used. At Chanousse, one boy in four was named Jean, and twelve names covered three-quarters of the male population. Nine names covered three-quarters of the women and girls. By 1830, the choice had become even more restricted. At Chanousse, half the boys bore the six commonest names; at Montjay, one-third. At Chanousse, half the girls bore the five commonest names; and at Montjay, ten names covered half the girls. The trend towards concentration seems to have continued down to the 1870s, though it was relieved here and elsewhere by the use of composite or multiple first names. At Chanousse in the mid nineteenth century, half the boys were called Jean or had Jean as part of a composite name.

In the south-west, at Lormont, in the seventeenth century, there is the same concentration. The ten commonest male names account for about three-quarters of the men, and the number of first names in use actually falls here over the century for both men and women. The disappearing names were those least frequently used. At the start of the nineteenth century still, in Saint-Emilion, 60 per cent of boys were called Jean or Pierre, and 53 per cent of girls Marie or Jeanne. In the Forez in the seventeenth and eighteenth centuries, the five commonest names represented just over half the population. In the seventeenth century, half the female population shared just three names. The concentration was somewhat mitigated in the eighteenth century, with nine names accounting for five-sixths of the population. The stock of female names also rose from 43 in the seventeenth century to 73 in the eighteenth.

Next, we turn to western France. Around 1500 in Nantes, there were 14 boys and 13 girls per first name, but the stock was significantly lower in neighbouring rural parishes: 20–30 for boys and 17–23 for girls. In Nantes, 20 first names were borne by 82 per cent of boys and the top ten by 70 per cent. In the villages, for the period 1480–1600, ten first names were borne by 75 per cent of boys and 84 per cent of girls. Overall, one child in four or five was called Jean or Jeanne, and one in twelve Pierre or Perrine. The story can be taken forward with a study of male names at Caen. The name stock fell by about half between 1570 and 1670 and again by a third between 1670 and 1770. At the same time there was a high and increasing concentration on just a few names. The five commonest accounted for half the instances in the mid sixteenth and mid seventeenth centuries and for 57 per cent in 1775. Those covered by the ten commonest names rose similarly from nearly two-thirds to three-quarters; and the 25 commonest from four-fifths to nine-tenths in 1775.

From the Paris region, at Noisy-le-Sec, for the period 1600–1800, five names accounted for 56 per cent of men, and four names for 53 per cent of women. One-third of women were called Marie. At Amiens, there was a considerable movement of concentration between the early sixteenth and early seventeenth centuries. At the earlier time there were 6.5 persons per male name and 5.5 per female; at the later 12 persons per first name for both genders. At Namur, between the fifteenth and seventeenth centuries, there was again a high degree of concentration, the ten commonest male names usually accounting for over 60 per cent of persons. Jean was borne by one-quarter of the male population. Concentration was even higher among female names and it intensified. The five commonest female names accounted for 63 per cent of females in the 1590s but for 90 per cent in the 1650s. The ten commonest female names accounted for 80–85 per cent of the female population through the two centuries.

Turning east to Strasbourg, in the sixteenth and early seventeenth centuries, 15 per cent of boys were called Johann. In five villages in Alsace between 1737 and 1837, there were 8.5 persons per name. At Vallorbe, in French-speaking Vaud, there were 6.5 persons per male name between 1569 and 1599; and the ten commonest names accounted for 77 per cent of boys. In the first two decades of the seventeenth century, there were four persons per name, and the ten commonest accounted for about two-thirds of persons, representing a slight decline in concentration. For girls, the ten commonest names covered 70 per cent at the start and 74 per cent at the end of the seventeenth century.

Finally, we have figures calculated from samples for France as a whole in the nineteenth century. The seven commonest male names in first position named 44 per cent of boys, and the seven commonest in first or second position named 64 per cent. The concentration was even greater among girls' names, thanks to "the triumph of Marie".[2] For girls, the five commonest names in first position named 44 per cent of individuals, and in first or second position 59 per cent. To name half the boys in first position, ten names were required; and to name half the girls in first position, eight.

Comparable information hardly exists for the other countries. In England, in five London parishes in the 1540s, the ten commonest men's names accounted for 75 per cent of the male population; and for four London parishes in the 1640s for 72 per cent. In a Bristol parish in 1696, there were 9 males per name and 14.5 females. The ten commonest male names accounted for 71 per cent of males; the five commonest female for 64 per cent of females, and the ten commonest for 78 per cent. In a West Cumberland parish around 1600, nearly half the boys baptized were called John, and 17 per cent Nicholas; but the stock of lesser-used names was quite high. Analysis of a Manx manorial roll of the early sixteenth century indicates an average of 25 persons per first name; 88 per cent of men bore names that were held by more than ten others; and 23 per cent of men were called John. In a smaller sample in 1611, 93 per cent of men bore names shared by at least ten others; and 25 per cent of men were called John.

There are some suggestions that the name stock was more extensive and less concentrated in Italy than in France or Britain, at least in the remoter areas. At Quenza, in Corsica, in 1622, there were three males and two females per name; and in the second half of the eighteenth century, four persons of both genders.

Which names predominated within this limited repertoire? Again, we may consult our case-studies. At Perpignan in the sixteenth century, the commonest male names were Joan (45 per cent); Antoni (19 per cent); Pere (13 per cent); Jaume and Miquel (19 per cent each); and Francesch – after St Francis of Assisi (8 per cent). There was some change in the period 1596–1685. Joseph became the favourite name, leaping from 3 per cent previously to 50 per cent, with combinations. This was followed by Joan; Francisco (after St Francis of Paola); Anton or Antoine; Pierre; Jacques; and Francesch. In the period 1686–1738, when French forms began to predominate over Catalan or Spanish ones, Joseph remained the commonest name (40 per cent), followed by Jean, François, Antoine, Pierre and Jacques. Over the whole period, most of the commonest male names remained in vogue, but certain new names did appear, notably Joseph.

The commonest female names in the first period were Joana (27 per cent); Anna (23 per cent); Elisabet (13 per cent); Caterina (12 per cent); and Margarit, Angela and Antonia (with 9 per cent each). Maria was a very rare name at this time. In the second period, however, Maria jumped to first place (60 per cent – with combinations). It was followed in popularity by Francesca (St Francis of Paola), Anne, Theresa (a new name), Jeanne or Joana, Caterina, Margarit and Elisabet. In the third period, Maria remained ahead with nearly 60 per cent of instances again and followed now by Theresa, Françoise, Jeanne, Catherine, Margarit and Josepa or Josephine (relatively new). Over the whole period only five female names remained constantly in vogue: Joana or Jeanne (never below 20 per cent); Anne (never below 16 per cent); Caterina or Catherine (never below 12 per cent); and Margarit and Elisabet (never below 9 per cent).

At Saint-André-des-Alpes in the mid seventeenth century, the commonest male names were Jean, Antoine, Honoré and Pierre; and the commonest female, Marguerite (well in front), Catherine, Jeanne, Honorade and Marie. By the mid eighteenth century, the four most popular boys' names remained the same, but Joseph and Jean-Baptiste had been introduced and were chasing them. Similarly, for girls, roughly the same names were in the lead a century later, but only Marguerite and Catherine were still very popular. Honorade had almost disappeared, while Anne and Marie had become more important. For children born between 1750 and 1765, there were further changes. The old favourites continued to decline. For boys, Jean only remained important in combinations. Joseph's popularity continued to grow. Hyacinthe, Célestin and Hippolyte appeared. For girls, the old names were largely eclipsed. Marguerite and Marie survived but in double combinations. There were many new girls' names, for example Emilie, Justine, Adélaïde and Delphine.

At Nogent-l'Artaud, a village in the Aisne, between the late seventeenth century and 1800, by far the commonest girls' name was Marie, nearly always, however, in combination with another name, the most popular being Marie-Madeleine. Next came Marguerite (also used for boys); then Anne (ditto); Françoise and Jeanne, both usually in combinations, as were Madeleine, Louise and Catherine. The commonest boys' name was Pierre, followed by Jean (mainly in combinations), then François, Louis, Nicolas, Claude and Antoine. Among names used singly, Nicolas was well ahead for both genders. Some names declined gradually, like Nicolas, Jeanne, Anne, Catherine and Françoise; others diappeared more abruptly, like Barbe around 1760. Marie and its combinations rose constantly, as did Jean with its. Louis and Louise both rose in the later eighteenth century. Some names remained stable throughout, like Pierre and François. A few names had sudden vogues. Twenty-six new names appeared over the period 1668–1727, but 86 from 1727 to 1787, that is three times as many. Some names became popular very quickly, like Victoire, which appeared first in 1729 and was in the top seven or eight names by the time of the Revolution.

Most of the names mentioned belonged to a "traditional" repertoire and were among the most popular names elsewhere in early modern France. Jean and Pierre were the commonest male names in most places that have been studied. Jean usually accounted for between 20 per cent and 35 per cent of instances; Pierre ranged from 12 per cent to 24 per cent. Names whose popularity grew included François, Louis and Joseph. Louis was already popular in the Ile-de-France in the sixteenth century, but its vogue spread to other parts of the kingdom, especially in the eighteenth century. In the Vexin it rose from third to first place. Joseph "exploded" in Caen in the eighteenth century.[3]

The repertoire of common girls' names was also found across France. Jeanne or Jehanne led at Lormont, for example, with 22 per cent of persons. In the Forez "Jeanne remained constantly in the lead [through the seventeenth and eighteenth centuries]; but Marie, which occupied the 17th rank in the seventeenth century, reached the second place in the eighteenth."[4] Marie also gained ground elsewhere, at first on its own and then massively in combinations. Marie was in the lead with 25 per cent of attributions at Amiens at the start of the seventeenth century. With combinations, it reached 60–70 per cent in the Vexin, at Noisy-le-Sec and elsewhere by the time of the Revolution. Marguerite was also very common – in Provence, the Vexin, Nantes – together with Anne and Catherine. Some formerly popular names disappeared, like Peyronne at Lormont in the late seventeenth century. New names were introduced, like Thérèse and Joséphine.

Though there are some indications that the traditional repertoire was beginning to move from the later eighteenth century, the old names were very resilient, particularly those which were most popular. A sample of nine parishes from all over France in 1836 indicates that the commonest men's names were Jean, Pierre, François, Antoine, Claude and Joseph; and the commonest women's, Marie, Jeanne, Françoise, Catherine, Anne and Louise, both extremely traditional lists. New names, like Victor, Alexandre, Edmé, for boys, and Eugénie, Julie, Rose, for girls, had come in, but at a lower level of frequency. Again, the commonest first names for boys in first place over the whole nineteenth century were, in order, Jean, Pierre, Louis, François, Joseph, and Antoine; and in second place, Joseph, Marie, François, Louis, Baptiste, and Pierre. For girls, the commonest first names in order were Marie, Jeanne, Louise, Anne, Marguerite and Françoise; and as second first names, Marie, Louise, Joséphine, Françoise, Anne and Jeanne. New names were rare and again not at the top of the lists. Jean or Jean-Baptiste in first position was borne by nearly 16 per cent of boys, and in first or second position by 18 per cent. Marie in first position was borne by 30 per cent of girls, and in first or second by nearly 36 per cent.

Withycombe declared in 1945 that the three commonest English names for men between 1550 and 1800 were William, John and Thomas, and for women Elizabeth, Mary and Anne. There are very few detailed studies to check this, but it does not seem far wrong. In five London parishes in the 1540s, the five commonest men's names were John (25 per cent); Thomas (13 per cent); William (12 per cent); Richard (7 per cent); and Robert (6 per cent). In four London parishes again in the 1640s, the same four names were in the lead, though in a slightly different order, and Samuel had ousted Robert. Among the noble Willoughbys and their in-laws between 1530 and 1670, the preferred male names were Thomas, Robert, John, Francis, Henry, Edward and George; and the commonest female names were Elizabeth, Catherine, Brigitt, Dorothy and Mary. In Bristol in 1696, among adults and children, the leading male names were John (21 per cent); William (13 per cent); Thomas (9 per cent); Richard and Edward (5 per cent each). The commonest female names were Mary (21 per cent); Elizabeth (18 per cent); Ann (12 per cent); Sarah (8 per cent); and Margaret (5 per cent). At Myddle in Shropshire in the late seventeenth century, the commonest names were, in rough order, for men: John, William, Robert, Thomas, Richard and Edward; and for women: Elizabeth, Alice, Jane, Mary, Joan(e), Margaret, Margery and Martha. The commonest names in Edinburgh marriage registers in the sixteenth and seventeenth centuries were, for men: John, James, William, Robert, Thomas and Alexander; and for women: Margaret, Janet, Agnes, Marian, Isobel and Catherine.

This consistent pattern of names persisted into the nineteenth century. The leading English boys' names in 1800, in order, were William, John, Thomas, James, George, Joseph, Richard, Henry and Robert. This list was little changed by 1875, by which time Frederick and Arthur had replaced Richard and Robert. Thereafter change was more rapid and extensive. The leading English girls' names in 1800 were Mary, Ann, Elizabeth, Sarah, Jane, Hannah, Susan, Martha and Margaret, a mainly "traditional" list. Eliza, Ellen and Emma entered in 1850, ousting Susan, Martha and Margaret, and the repertoire was radically changed in the second half of the century.

Names and religion

Saints' names

Most first names in France in this period continued to be saints' names. At Perpignan in the sixteenth century only about 7 per cent of first names in general use were secular names, and by around 1700 only 2.5 per cent. From the sixteenth century to the nineteenth in the Vexin, most people were named after "the saints of the liturgical calendar".[5] Here saints' names reached a high-point in the 1690s, when pagan, other Biblical and historical names virtually disappeared. A similar situation obtained elsewhere in France. The proportion of saints' names was made even higher by the fact that by this time many erstwhile secular or Germanic names had become those of saints.

In a traditional Catholic society, naming after the saints had obvious religious meaning. After the Council of Trent, the Church laid down that children should be given the names of canonized saints, so that those saints might act as models and as special protectors and advocates before God. Diocesan regulations in France reiterated this prescription from the late sixteenth century onwards, and repeated the reasons for it. As we have already seen, most people were called after the saints well before this. The Church was merely confirming the practice and its value to the individual. There is some evidence, however, that the clergy or some sections of it did influence the choice of particular names in the early modern period. Marie, Joseph, Anne and Madeleine were saints whose cults were promoted generally in the Counter-Reformation period. That of St Teresa was promoted by the Jesuits, for example, at Perpignan. Other religious congregations had an impact, too. The vogue for François and Françoise, after St Francis of Paola, was fostered at Amiens, Perpignan and elsewhere by the Minims, the order of friars which he founded. At Perpignan 13.5 per cent of saints' names in use from the sixteenth to the eighteenth century were loosely "monastic".

The vehicle for this clerical influence might be a confraternity. At Ussel in the Limousin the proportion of cases of Marie rose from 8 per cent around 1640 to 22 per cent around 1740, a rise coinciding with the spread of Marian devotions and especially the Confraternity of the Rosary. But confraternities could also be "traditional" and local. A village in the Forez, where 20 children, male and female, were named after St Pantaléon between 1484 and 1504, had a confraternity dedicated to him. Local cults and shrines had some impact. Diocesan saints could be influential, for example Domnain at Digne; Hilaire and Césaire at Arles; but many had no following. Claude, Clauda and Claudine were all popular in eastern France, within the ambience of the saint's shrine in the Jura; while the Honorés and Honorats of Provence were linked to the popular pilgrimage centre of St Honorat-de-Lérins. In some regions – the Vexin, Normandy, Alsace – the impact of local saints seems to have been very small. Elsewhere, for no obvious reason, it was higher, for example in the Limousin, where between 40 and 50 per cent of saints' names were local in the early modern period.

But, in general, the bulk of saints' names used continued to be those of the "great" saints. At Fronton, for example, between the mid sixteenth century and the mid eighteenth, 60 per cent of men were named after the Apostles. Another popular and enduring custom was to name the child after the saint on whose day it was born or baptized. It was followed at Perpignan, and also in Provence and in Burgundy. Jeanne Frémyot, second daughter of a councillor at the Parlement of Dijon and later Mme de Chantal, was born in 1572 on 23rd January and named accordingly after St John the Almsgiver, whose feast falls on that day. Lutherans in Strasbourg retained the custom into the seventeenth century, which suggests that it was deeply embedded in the culture. Divination could also be practised. Abbé Thiers in the early eighteenth century condemned the custom of "giving the names of the Twelve Apostles to twelve candles that were then lit, with the candle which burned the longest indicating the name to be given to the child".[6]

Naming after saints survived the dechristianization campaigns of the Revolution and the slower erosion of religious practice and belief in the nineteenth century, but its meaning changed. No longer a religious act, it reflected rather "tradition" and the passing on of "family" names.

The use of saints' names was well established in Italy by the late medieval period and continued through to modern times. Augurative or mystical names went into further decline. Only Domenico/a survived as an important name but this could also be regarded as a saint's name. On the whole, there was surprisingly little change in the stock, and the names of the "great" saints were preferred. The only significant innovation was the adoption of the names of the Holy Family.

We have seen that Maria had been a rare medieval name in Italy. In the Nice region, the name of the Virgin was virtually tabooed until the sixteenth century – "people thought that no creature was worthy to bear it"[7] – but from the seventeenth it became almost *de rigueur*. In the village of Sauze by the end of the eighteenth century, all the women had two first names, of which the first was invariably Marie. At Quenza in Corsica there was a similar development from Maria being almost unknown around 1600 to its becoming a name held by all women by the later eighteenth century. These examples are typical of what was happening all over Italy (and France) at this time. The name was also adopted from the sixteenth century by Italian men, a custom that did not spread to other countries till the eighteenth and early nineteenth centuries.

After a strong avoidance of the name, Maria also took off in Spain, often in the form of particular designations of the Virgin. Southern Italy, long under Spanish rule, followed this custom with names such as Assunta, Annunziata, Carmela, Concetta and Immacolata. Consolata was popular in Turin. In the south, some of these names were masculinized: Rosario, Concetto, Nunzio. Nunzia was a very common female name in eighteenth-century Corsica, and Regina and Signora were also used.

Joseph or Giuseppe was the other main novelty of the Counter-Reformation era. It appeared, for example, in Florence at the start of the sixteenth century. By the seventeenth and eighteenth centuries, it was very common there and elsewhere, often in combinations. The name of Jesus was not used in Italy (unlike Spain), but variants of Saviour were. Salvayre, Sauvaire or Sauveur were quite common in the Nice region; Salvatore in other places.

As in France, a variety of factors could play their part in the choice of particular saints' names. Sometimes the day of birth or baptism was decisive. At San Fedele in the seventeenth and eighteenth centuries, where multiple first names had become the rule, the first was the "family" name, transmitted from a relative; the second that of the patron saint of the parish; while the third could be that of the birthday saint. Again, naming could follow a particular vow. St Charles of Sezze explained that in 1665 he had prayed many times to the Franciscan St James of Alcala on behalf of a woman who wanted the child she was carrying to be a boy. When a boy was born, he was named Giacomo "out of devotion to the saint". In Renaissance Florence, "children baptized under conditions of urgency . . . were often called Giovanni or Giovanna" to give them special protection.[8]

Local cults and devotions could influence naming. So Rosalia was common in and around Palermo; Vitaliano in Catanzaro; and Gennaro in Naples. In the Romagna, for some reason, it was customary to give children one of the names of the Magi. But other cults far transcended their localities. Michele was very common all over southern Italy and in Sardinia in the sixteenth and seventeenth centuries, not just in the vicinity of his shrine at Monte Gargano. Similarly St Anthony of Padua was on the way to being a "universal" saint. In Corsica, for example, Anton-Padova, Anton-Padovano or simply Padovano were very common names by the eighteenth-century if not before.

The Irish were late converts to hagionymy. We have seen that the Maol or Gil formula was preferred in the early medieval period to direct naming after saints. Patrick, "the name of the national apostle", was first used in the thirteenth century, and its vogue was the result, it seems, of English influence. The old Celtic names persisted generally down to the end of the sixteenth century, and Christian or saints' names were only then very slowly adopted. Michael, and Maire, Muire or Mary, the commonest modern first names, were little used before the seventeenth century. Ireland also seems to have been distinctive in the weight attached to local cults. The patron saints of dioceses were "in frequent use . . . in that diocese but not elsewhere",[9] for example, Ciaran or Kieran in Clonmacnois and Ossory; Brendan in Kerry and Clonfert; Colman in Cloyne; and Phelim in Kilmore.

Protestantism

The Reformation left its mark on personal naming practices. Few converts to Protestantism in its various forms changed their names, but Protestant parents were influenced by their faith when they came to name their children. Calvinists and Puritans especially rejected both non-Christian and later or Catholic saints' names and preferred those taken from the Bible. Hypocoristic versions of Scriptural saints' names, like Monet for Simon, were also deprecated. The English Puritan divine Thomas Cartwright advised in 1565 that "the names of God, or of Christ, or of angels, or of holy offices, as of baptist or evangelist" should be avoided, and also all 'such as savour of paganism or popery"; instead names should be taken from "the Holy Scriptures" choosing especially "those who are reported . . . to have been godly and virtuous". Another English Puritan minister declared in 1654 that "a good name is a thread tied about the finger, to make us mindful of the errand we came into the world to do for our Master".[10] Such advice was repeated and reinforced throughout the sixteenth and seventeenth centuries and had more or less force, depending on the status and power of the ministers concerned. This ranged from an established ascendancy in Calvin's Geneva, Scotland, New England and the English Protectorate to a situation of merely local influence in England throughout most of the early modern period and in France. The habit of Bible reading must also have been a decisive influence. The vernacular liturgies may also have familiarized certain names. The traditional prayers in the marriage ceremony, invoking the virtues of Rachel, Rebecca and Sarah, were not dropped from the English Book of Common Prayer until 1662.

Contemporaries particularly associated Protestants with Old Testament names. Montaigne in the 1580s, for example, asserted that the Reformed religion "had peopled the world with Methusalems, Ezechiels and Malachis"; while Camden noted in 1614 that "in our late Reformation, some of good consideration have brought in Zachary, Malachy, Josias, etc., as better agreeing with our faith".[11] But Protestants had no objection to the established New Testament names – except for Peter and Paul, associated with Rome and the papacy. They did, however, introduce "new" names from the New Testament, for example, in the English-speaking world, Dorcas, Martha, Priscilla and Tabitha for women, Nathaniel and Timothy for men.

Another style of Puritan naming that caught the attention of both contemporaries and later scholars is that of names referring to moral qualities, or "grace names". They were probably a continuation or a revival of the personified abstractions of late medieval literature, like *Piers Plowman*. From sixteenth- and seventeenth-century England, Bardsley lists Patience, Grace, Faith, Hope, Charity, Mercy and Prudence among others, and these were probably the most popular. Such names were also used in New England, often in an imperative or hortative mode: Believe, Increase, Remember. Some of these names soon became gender specific. Increase was mainly a male name, while Comfort, Hope and Mercy were female. A few of the names also acquired pet forms, despite the Puritan aversion to hypocoristics, for example Prue for Prudence.

Hortative names could be shorthand for specific slogans or texts, for example Believe in Christ, Hope for Salvation, Remember now thy Creator. Hortative and other phrases were also sometimes given as names. A Puritan preacher at Cranbrook in Kent in the 1580s called his children Freegift and Morefruit, Faintnot and Wellabroad. Safe-on-High Hopkinson, baptized at Salehurst, Sussex, in 1591, was an infant rightly not expected to live. Other examples from the same county around the same time include Search-the-Scriptures, Fight-the-good-fight-of-faith, and The-Peace-of-God. Such names of course were grist to the mill of satirical playwrights like Beaumont and Fletcher, Cowley and Ben Jonson. "Tribulation Wholesome, our very zealous pastor" is mocked in Jonson's *The Alchemist* of 1610; and Zeal-of-the-land Busy, who names a baby Win-the-Fight instead of Winnifred in *Bartholomew Fair* of 1614.[12] The latter play was one of the first to be revived at the Restoration. Grace and phrase names were not evident in France, but they were found in Lutheran Germany.

The few local studies that exist suggest that this broad view is substantially correct, though "new" Protestant names took some time to get established and were never very prevalent, except perhaps in New England.

Among English Puritan ministers and preachers from the mid sixteenth century to the time of the Civil War, Old Testament names were quite rare. Ezekiel Culvernel, Job Throckmorton, Jeremiah Burroughs and Sidrach Simpson were in a clear minority among a host of Richards, Johns, Henrys and Williams. In five London parishes in the 1540s, none of the ten commonest male names were "new" Protestant ones, though the twelfth, Timothy, was. Nine Old Testament names were used, with David, Adam, Samuel and Abraham being the most popular. Among Biblical names, only 10 per cent came from the Old Testament, however. A century later, in the 1640s, in four London parishes, the situation had shifted significantly. The "old" names, like John, William and Thomas, were still predominant, but two Protestant names, Samuel and Joseph, had entered the top ten, Samuel as fifth with 5 per cent of attributions and Joseph as ninth with 2.5 per cent. Other Old Testament names occurring quite frequently included Benjamin, Daniel, Isaac and Jeremiah. Sixteen Old Testament names were used in all.

In a Bristol parish in 1696, 14 per cent of male names were Protestant (either Old Testament or "new" names from the New Testament). Of these, only Samuel and Joseph were in the top ten. Female names were substantially more Protestant at 24 per cent and included those in the "grace name" category. Four Protestant names for women were in the top eleven. In Bristol, Protestant names tended to go in families, with both parents and children, but more significantly both husbands and wives having them. So Matthew Court was married to Martha and their children were Mary, Patience, Elienor and Virtue; Jonathan and Susanna New had children Susanna, Joseph, Jonathan and James. Presumably spouses came from religiously likeminded milieus.

New Protestant and Puritan names in England seem to have spread geographically from south to north. They were not common in Lancashire and Yorkshire until the seventeenth and eighteenth centuries, being taken there by waves of non-conformity which lasted into the nineteenth century. They appear never to have reached Scotland in any force, which is a puzzle, given the fact of Presbyterian establishment. Perhaps their adoption was a function of minority status, a sectarian trait. Here we may mention the substitution on Orkney and Shetland of Old Testament and also classical names for the traditional Norse ones, regarded as signs of paganism by Protestant ministers from the mainland.

A number of Protestant names had become generally popular in England by the early seventeenth century. These included Dorcas, Judith and Phebe, and also Susan, Esther and Hannah, whose popularity lasted into the nineteenth century. Joseph, Samuel, Daniel, Isaac and Benjamin were among the top twenty boys' names through the eighteenth century; and Joseph and Samuel remained among the commonest names through most of the nineteenth century too.

Though a few such names predominated, the habit of picking names from a wider Biblical repertoire, especially in the Old Testament, was not lost. To begin with this reflected a knowledge of the Bible and possibly the selection of names by opening it at hazard, though most authorities are sceptical about this. Use of the less common Old Testament names, like that of grace or phrase names, had always been a sign of militancy. By the late seventeenth and eighteenth centuries, they were definitely sectarian if not eccentric. At Myddle, for example, Habbakuk Heylin was "a bastard son of Mr John Heylin", who also had a daughter called Golibra. John Wilkes commented in 1776 on the last City-Poet of London: "Now Elkanah Settle sounds so queer; who can expect much from that name?" Later, once Protestant names had been generally adopted, the unusual Biblical name was a means of being different that had no necessary religious connection. The Victorian editor of Camden's *Remains* noted that "the poor very often give their offspring names with the worst possible associations: I have known, for example, an Esau, a couple of Absaloms, an Ananias, and several Dinahs". According to Winstedt, Old Testament and grace names were commonly used by English gypsies, names "derived from texts which [they] certainly do not know, or commemorative of virtues which they do not esteem". Names of supposed Biblical provenance were even invented. In March 1870, Kilvert baptized "Mrs Jones the jockey's baby . . . The name selected was as far as I could make out Mahalah, which Mrs Jones declared to be the name of one of Cain's wives, on the authority of a book she had read called *The Life of Abel*. She called her elder child Thirza, which she says was the name of Cain's other wife. Not a happy allusion!"[13] And if the profane came to use religious names, the pious also in the course of time tended to abandon them, especially in circumstances of affluence and social success. The Rowntrees, a Quaker business family from York, for example, used clearly Protestant names in the first half of the nineteenth century, but by the second half such fashionable novelties as Agnes, Julia, Oscar and Winifred had been introduced.

New England names were not at first distinctive. In a broad sample of seventeenth-century male first names, only three of the twelve commonest names were from the Old Testament: Samuel, Joseph and Benjamin. The list was headed by John, Thomas and James, traditional names, albeit those of New Testament saints. Half of the twelve were non-Biblical. Dodge concludes that New Englanders "chose names not as Puritans but as Englishmen". A smaller sample suggests that Biblical and especially Old Testament names were rather more common among women. A study of Massachusetts freeholders between 1630 and 1640, who must have been strongly Puritan, also reveals that they "bore an average set of English names".[14] The ten commonest names were almost the same as in the London parishes at a comparable date, and only one was an Old Testament name. Only 16 Old Testament names were used.

The change came with those born in America. In another sample, of boys born in Plymouth Colony between 1640 and 1699, John, Thomas and William were still prominent in the list of commonest names, but their proportion had fallen, and the list also contained six new Protestant names: Samuel (7 per cent of instances), Joseph (6 per cent), Nathaniel, Ebenezer, Isaac and Jonathan. Overall 57 Old Testament names were used, in addition to "new" New Testament ones like Nathaniel, Cornelius and Theophilus. At Hingham, Massachusetts, after 1640, 95 per cent of boys had Biblical names, and the formerly popular traditional English names virtually disappeared. Similarly, 90 per cent of Boston-born males in the mid seventeenth century had Biblical names, 40 per cent from the Old Testament. Among girls born in the Massachusetts Bay Colony between 1630 and 1670, the top ten names were all Biblical, with the traditional Mary and Elizabeth topping the list but followed by Sarah, Hannah, Abigail, Rebecca and Ruth. Half the girls' names came from the Old Testament.

In general, if the Massachusetts freeholders are compared with the Plymouth Colony and Boston boys, "Old Testament names increase more than fourfold, English traditional [names] fall to less than one third, and the non-Biblical saints' names approach vanishing point".[15] What names were used within this new repertoire and why?

First, English traditional names decreased but they remained important largely because they were family names to which people were for that reason attached. Among New Testament names, Peter and Paul were regarded as "papist" and were therefore shunned; Mary and Maria escaped this proscription. The names of Christ were never used. As a minister explained in 1629, "Emmanuel is too bold. The name is properly to Christ and therefore not to be communicated to any creature" – an echo of medieval bans on Mary. The names of angels were also avoided. Among Old Testament names, those of the great patriarchs, lawgivers and kings were rarely used. "Moses was exceedingly uncommon. Adam was virtually unknown [and] . . . comparatively few children were named Abraham or Solomon or David." Among female names, similarly, Eve was not used, while Judith and Miriam were rare. Positively, names were favoured "primarily for their associated moral qualities – for character, virtue, decency, integrity and inner strength", which explains the vogue for John, Joseph, Samuel, Josiah, Benjamin and Nathan. There was a similar pattern for female names. Mary was "humble and devoted"; Elizabeth, Sarah and Rebecca all maternal figures; Ruth "industrious and obedient". But although New England's female name models "were all firmly anchored in a domestic role", they were also notable, many of them, for intellect, courage, spirit and strength of character. Anne, Hannah and Deborah, for example, were prophets; Abigail and Rachel resisted authority. Attention to the meaning of Biblical names also accounts for the popularity of Ebenezer, which does not seem to have been used in England at all at this period. The name was especially appropriate for the colonists, being the name of the landmark set up by Samuel and signifying "Hitherto hath the Lord helped us".[16]

In time the new Protestant names became family first names like the traditional names that they often displaced. So Samuel Sewall, the Boston diarist of the late seventeenth century, called one son Joseph after the Old Testament figure "and not out of respect to any relation"; but one of his daughters was named Judith "for the sake of her grandmother and great-grandmother", and another Sarah after his wife's sister.[17]

Protestant first names became quite common elsewhere in colonial America, though they were never so predominant as in New England. As in the old country, a sign of their familiarity was the use of hypocoristic forms. These were common by the later eighteenth century, especially for women: for example, Sally for Sarah, Patty for Martha, Nabby for Abigail, Hitty for Mehitabel, Tenty for Content. An Aunt Tribby, whose death was reported in *Harper's Magazine* in 1855, had the full name Through-Much-Tribulation-We-Enter-Into-The-Kingdom-of-Heaven Crabb.[18]

Studies of Protestant first names in France present a rather different picture, reflecting communities (mainly Reformed or Calvinist) that were in the minority and at times persecuted, and as a result leaving patchy and dispersed evidence of themselves. Synods recommended Biblical and particularly Old Testament names, but they were often not heeded.

French and Walloon ministers attached to exiled groups in England did not as a rule have Old Testament names in the 1560s and 1570s. The practice began among the second generation, sometimes sons of ministers or elders, like Aaron Cappel, minister at Norwich and then in London, or Samuel Le Chevalier, minister at Canterbury at the end of the sixteenth century. At Caen, in Normandy, Old Testament names rose and fell from around 1 per cent of persons in 1568 to 4.5 per cent in 1666, a high-point, to 1 per cent again in 1775. But this oscillation does not match the fortunes of the Reformed community in the town, which was important on the eve of the Revolution, despite the regression of names. This suggests that Protestants were perhaps deliberately avoiding "Protestant" names in the period following the Revocation of the Edict of Nantes in 1685. The behaviour of the Carpentier family of the Pays de Caux confirms this. Their stock of first names in the eighteenth century included Marthe and Suzanne for girls but no names of Protestant resonance for boys. They "did not wish to advertise themselves with curious names".[19] When the Revolution brought formal toleration, there was some return to Protestant names, especially from the Old Testament.

Among Protestants in Brie and Provence in the sixteenth and seventeenth centuries, over half the male names in use were Biblical, with more from the Old Testament than the New. But less than a third of female names were Biblical, and proportions of actual instances of names for both genders were much lower. Moreover, medieval saints' names remained fairly common and classical names were quite popular for men.

In German-speaking Alsace, first names chosen from the Old Testament were rare in Protestant (Lutheran) milieus. In five villages between 1737 and 1837, only 10 per cent of names were "Protestant". The situation was different, however, in Strasbourg. Here, there was a more fundamental "mutation" in naming practices. Medieval saints' names disappeared, and Abraham, Daniel, Jacob, Sara and Esther became very common. However, as we have noted, the old Catholic custom still persisted in the sixteenth and seventeenth centuries "of giving children the name of the saint on whose day they were baptized".[20]

A general sample of five Protestant parishes from all over France before 1685 shows Biblical names rising to reach 25 per cent for men and 16 per cent for women. The commonest Protestant names for men were Isaac, Daniel, Barthélemy and Abraham; and for women, Suzanne and Sarah. But they were by no means the commonest names in use. These continued to be the traditional names like Jean, Pierre, Jacques, Marie and Jeanne that French Protestants shared with French Catholics. Protestant notables also showed a minor but significant penchant for classical names. Three per cent of men and 6 per cent of women had names such as Annibal, Agrippa, Lucrèce, Diane and Olympe.

Another broad view may be obtained by looking at immigrants to Geneva from the sixteenth century to the eighteenth. The city was the headquarters of Reformed Protestantism and a haven for refugees. "By 1570 sixty per cent of its inhabitants were foreigners, mostly French."[21] Among immigrants to Geneva in the sixteenth century, two main samples have been selected, one from 1572, following the Massacre of St Bartholomew and largely made up of refugees from Burgundy, the Lyonnais and the Dauphiné; and one from 1585, made up of French refugees again but with a greater admixture of those fleeing persecution in nearby Savoy.[22] In the 1572 sample, only 3.6 per cent of immigrants had Protestant names. Most of these were from the Old Testament. Nine names were used, with David and Abel the most common. Classical names such as César and Hector were also found, as were "Catholic" names such as Ignace and Toussaint. In the 1585 sample, the proportion of instances with Protestant names is much higher: 13.6 per cent. Most names again were from the Old Testament, the commonest being Isaac, Samuel, Abraham, David, Esaïe or Isaïe, Daniel and Jacob. Again, classical and "Catholic" names were found. "Protestant" first names also seem to have been rare among ministers and trainees for the ministry at Geneva through the sixteenth century. Possibly Protestants avoided conspicuous names in times of persecution. More likely, the Protestant name as such was relatively unimportant at this time. Protestants could share in names generally used by Catholics, which were often those of New Testament saints.

Further samples indicate that Protestant names were more common in later centuries. The first is from the period 1684–1701, which saw a large-scale immigration mainly from southern and south-eastern France and mainly involving artisans and traders following the Revocation of the Edict of Nantes. Now 17.2 per cent of immigrants had what may be regarded as Protestant names. Some were New Testament names not generally used by Catholics, like Céphas, Timothée, Théophile, Christ; but the overwhelming majority were from the Old Testament. In all, 26 of these names were used, of which Daniel was the most popular, closely followed by David, Abraham and Isaac. The second sample in this period is from 1769–92, by which time patterns of migration had changed. The French element among migrants had fallen from around 75 per cent to around 25 per cent, and French migrants were coming from the north-eastern quarter of France closest to Geneva rather than from the south. At the same time, the share of Swiss immigrants, mainly from the Canton of Vaud, had risen considerably, and there was a significant current from Germany. Protestant first names had risen to around 30 per cent, of which 5 per cent were from the New Testament. Here eight names were used, including Christ again; Gabriel was well in the lead, followed by Emmanuel. The commonest Old Testament names, either borne singly or in accordance with the new fashion as part of combinations, were Abraham, David, Daniel, Samuel and Isaac; that is, they had changed very little.

This pattern in Geneva is repeated in the Pays de Vaud. At Vallorbe in the period 1569–99, only around 10 per cent of boys had Old Testament names. In Lausanne, the proportion was higher at around a quarter. Even fewer girls' names were Protestant. But by the second quarter of the seventeenth century, around 40 per cent of both boys and girls at Vallorbe had Old Testament names. One girl in five was called Suzanne. Figures were rather lower for Lausanne. Hubler concludes that the Reformation did bring a new mode of personal naming but it took a long time to do so. The transmission of names within the family and via godparents, regional fashions, cultural inertia all acted to brake the expansion of Biblical first names. The clergy probably acted as pioneers and proponents of the new names, aided by catechizing and a better general knowledge of the Bible. Protestant names were adopted in the towns before the countryside. Interestingly, once they were established in the region, Old Testament names came to be used in significant numbers by Catholics as well as Protestants. Local fashion was more important than religious affiliation.

The Protestant minority in France remained distinguished in its names into the modern period. Balzac, in *La Rabouilleuse*, written in 1842 but referring to events twenty years before, notes of Baruch Borniche that "his Old Testament name was a sign of the lingering remains of Calvinism in Issoudun".[23] Jérémie, Moïse and Jacob remained common through the nineteenth century in the Jura.

Other perennial styles

Beyond religion, a variety of other factors entered into first-name choice and style. These can be roughly divided into those which operated over a long time-span, and shorter-term fashions.

A long-standing custom was to name a child according to its birth circumstances. Most simply a successful birth could be celebrated. Deliverance, Thankful and Preserved, used among English Puritans, belong to this category. Unhappy events surrounding a birth could also be recorded. Posthumus/a was used for babies whose fathers had died before their arrival. Where a mother had died in childbed, Puritans used the name Benoni, "son of my sorrow", bestowed by the dying Rachel. The name was still being used in the nineteenth century. Diana Holman-Hunt recalled deploring the fact as a child that her Uncle Cyril had "that horrid second name" Benone, which registered the fact that "poor great-aunt Fanny" had expired while bringing him into the world.[24]

Twins were often named with a pair of related names. Gough noted that a man in Myddle in the late seventeenth century called his twin boys Moses and Aaron; while Parson Woodforde related in 1765: "I christened two children (twins) . . . this afternoon . . . by the names Joseph and Mary, being born on Lady Day last",[25] names that were also an indication of the date of birth. The day or season of birth gave such names as Pascall, Paskey or Pasco; Easter, later conflated with Esther; Pentecost; Nowell or Christmas – all found in England in the early modern period. Epiphany gave rise to Theophania, shortened to Tiffany, Epiphan or Ephin. Days of the week were not used after the medieval period.

In Catholic France and Italy, the main connection between birth circumstances and naming was the practice of using the names of birthday saints, to which we have referred. Children were also named after major festivals, as in England: Noël or Natale for Christmas; Pascal or Pasquale for Easter. Frédéric Mistral's mother had wanted in 1830 to call him Nostradamus because he was born on Assumption Day or the day of Notre Dame, but both priest and mayor associated the name rather with the sixteenth-century magician and astrologer and refused to allow it.

Birth events were also occasionally alluded to via names. Benvenuto, Providenza and Desiderio were used in eighteenth-century Siena. After a mother died in childbed in the Guiccioli family of Ravenna in 1819, her child was called Faustina. In Italy and France, too, twins were quite often given pairs of names, for example Isaac and Jacob or Adam and Eve in seventeenth-century Strasbourg; Louis and Louise or Paul and Paulette in modern Burgundy. Ordinal names were also sometimes used. A couple from the Auvergne, married in 1807, had four girls who were all given ordinary names, but the fifth, another girl, was called, presumably in exasperation, Quintienne-Ultime-Virginie. Besides referring to the number five, Quintienne was a saint's name used in the region.

Place of birth could also be recalled, if it were unusual. Catherine Willoughby had a son in 1555 at Wesel in the Duchy of Cleves, and "because he was born in a strange country, she therefore called his name Peregrin". Pericles in Shakespeare's play of 1606–8 names his daughter Marina "for she was born at sea".[26] Oceanus Hopkins and Peregrine White were both born on the *Mayflower* in 1620.

The use of classical names was another perennial minority style, which was related to the ongoing importance of the classics in the education of the élites. We have seen that Roman names had never been eclipsed in Italy. But classical names, Roman and Greek, were revived at the Renaissance, particularly in Humanist and aristocratic circles, as Burckhardt observed.

> When the enthusiasm for the ancient world was so great . . . , it was simple and natural enough that noble families called their sons Agamemnon, Tydeus, and Achilles, and that a painter named his son Apelles and his daughter Minerva.[27]

The future pope Pius II, born in 1405, was named Enea (Aeneas) Silvio Piccolomini after his father and grandfather.

There was also a vogue for giving or taking classical names as nicknames or new names. Humanists in Italy and elsewhere had been affecting classical pseudonyms since the thirteenth century and before. Accorso da Bagnolo, for example, who died in 1260, was known as Accursius; the Bolognese poet Fabruzzo di Tommasini de' Lambertazzi as Fabrutius; Angelo Ambrogini (1454–94) as Politian. The architect born in 1508 and called Andrea di Pietro or della Góndola was renamed Palladio by his noble patron to signify both his role in the revival of the building styles of ancient Rome and his access to higher social status.

Classical names persisted and spread in areas of Italian culture, despite the disapproval of the Counter-Reformation Church. In remote and rural Corsica, for example, among soldiers who served with the Genoese in the 1560s, one finds names such as Camillo, Octavio, Orazio, Ettore; and names of this kind remained quite common in the island in the seventeenth century.

In modern times, on the Italian mainland, old Latin names were especially popular in Lazio and Umbria, and they received a general boost from the Risorgimento's regard for them as symbols of past grandeur.

We find the same Latinizing fashion among scholars in northern Europe, who still of course wrote in Latin. Names were translated from the vernacular, like Melanchthon, Osiander or Paracelsus; they were also transliterated, like Grotius from De Groot and Vesalius from Wesel. Humanist names were also used in Britain. Dr John Kay, who refounded Gonville College, Cambridge, in 1557, gave it the name that he was known by in scholarly circles: Caius. The first president of King's College, Aberdeen, was Hector Boece or Boethius. Boswell referred in a letter to Dr Johnson in 1778 to "a book written by Wilson, a Scotchman, under the Latin name Volusenus, according to the custom of literary men at a certain period".[28]

Classical names were also used as given first names in England. The old Roman Christian names, like Donatus and Desiderius, were revived by Puritans. More generally, from the seventeenth century, we may cite almost at random Lucius Carey, Lord Falkland, patron of scholars at Great Tew; Leander Jones, a Benedictine monk; Sir Hannibal Baskerville; and Narcissus Marsh, Archbishop of Dublin in Swift's time. And the vogue affected women equally. Already at the start of the century, Camden was deploring that "Diana, Cassandra . . . Venus, Lais . . . are as rife . . . as even they were in Paganism". Our examples are from the educated and upper classes, but classical names penetrated into "popular" usage too. Villagers from Westbury, Buckinghamshire, in the early modern period were called Anastasius, Cicero, Hercules, Scipio and so on. Latinized girls' names enjoyed a widish vogue in the eighteenth century: Laetitia, Maria, Amelia, Camilla. But, on the whole, classical names were a minority taste, and they became even more unusual in the nineteenth and twentieth centuries. The London print maker and seller, Joseph Dickinson (1782–1849), who named his sons "out of Plutarch" was an eccentric.[29] The Cromer butcher, Icarus Hines, still going strong in the 1990s, is perhaps the last of his kind.

France, too, experienced a revival of classical names in the Renaissance period. Names from antiquity were in use among the élite in Languedoc in the fifteenth and sixteenth centuries, and the lords of Foix had adopted the name Phoebus before this. The sixteenth- and seventeen-century vogue for classical names among the "grands" was ridiculed by La Bruyère, and many actual nobles did use such names, for example César de Vendôme, Annibal d'Estrées, Hercule de Rohan. Classical names had also percolated lower down the social scale by the seventeenth century to judge from local studies of Caen, Brie and Provence. We have seen that some Protestants favoured such names. Classical names are found also among the official by-names given to soldiers in the French army in the eighteenth century. There was a further revival of classical names in the period of the French Revolution and the Empire. At Saint-Emilion, for example, in the 1800 decade there was a rash of Achille, César, Félicité and Sabine. The legislation governing first names in France from this time reflects this vogue, since it allows the use of names from ancient history alongside those from Church calendars, that is the saints. As Dauzat remarked in 1925, however, this had become a virtual dead letter as far as classical names were concerned, except for a few very popular names.

"In a society of estates, there are also estates of names . . . The personal name is a password denoting that its bearer belongs to a given social milieu."[30] This comment about pre-Revolutionary Russia applies also to pre-Revolutionary France, indeed to early modern Europe generally, and the "class" or status dimension of first-name choice is still significant. Out-groups like gypsies and Jews also had distinctive names.

At Perpignan in the sixteenth and seventeenth centuries, there were not aristocratic and plebeian names as such, but certain names were more commonly used by the upper classes, for example Galcerand, Hugues and Violande, all medieval names. In the Loire, too, social status and choice of first name were correlated, with César, Geoffroy and Melchior, for instance, being reserved to notables. In rural Alsace in the eighteenth century the same situation was found, perhaps even more sharply. Luc, Joseph and Valentin were used only by peasants; Abraham and Marie-Elisabeth by arti-sans. At Quenza in Corsica in the early modern period, there were two distinct social groups: the proprietors on the one hand and on the other the herdsmen and peasants. They did not intermarry and they had distinct first-naming patterns. The proprietors were more innovative. They used Anton Padova, Francesco Saverio, new saints' names first; and they adopted the custom of placing Maria in front of all girls' names. By contrast, the herds-men and peasants were conservative, preserving archaic names much longer, and they had the exclusive use of certain names like Pasquale, Stefano, Lucia and Santa.

The proclamation of social superiority via first names was most obvious in France and elsewhere among the nobility. In the late sixteenth century, Montaigne contrasted the supposedly "magnificent" names used by the nobility with names, such as Pierre, Guillot and his own Michel, used by ordinary folk. The point was reiterated by La Bruyère in the next century. "It is already too much to have to share the same religion and the same God with the people", he imagines the great nobles saying. "Do we also have to call ourselves Pierre, Jean or Jacques, like a tradesman or a peasant? Let us avoid having anything to do with the vile multitude; let us affect all the distinctions that separate us from it." Thus the common saints' names were disdained and the nobles had recourse instead to the names of ancient gods and heroes or of their own medieval ancestors.[31] And many nobles of course took this hypothetical advice, as we have seen, and gave their children classical names or ones from the tales of chivalry. The same snobbery vis-à-vis common names persisted into the eighteenth and nineteenth centuries, while Proust testifies to the distinctiveness of noble names in the Belle Epoque.

The situation was never static. New names and new modes of naming, like multiple first names, were usually introduced by the élites, as at Quenza, and then spread downwards via godparenthood, imitation, and so on. But once names became too popular, they would begin to be discarded by the upper classes. Dauzat cites the example of diminutives like Marion and Madelon. "Current in the best society in the seventeenth century, they were then taken up more generally by the rural population; by the nineteenth century they had a peasant flavour and were therefore dropped in the towns."[32]

The phenomenon of common names losing status may also be seen in England. It happened, for example, in the post-medieval period to Joan. A very popular name in the sixteenth century and already used by Shakespeare as a servant's name – "greasy Joan" in *Love's Labour's Lost* – it was still borne by members of the higher gentry like Lady Joan Barrington – an old women – in the 1620s. But Camden noted in 1614 that "in latter years some of the better and nicer sort, misliking Joan, have mollified the name . . . into Jane . . . [a name] never found in old records". Joan then became a lower-class name and was declared obsolete by Bardsley in 1880. Jane followed the fate of the name which it replaced. It "went out of fashionable use in the middle of the 19th c[entury] and came to be regarded as a typical maidservant's name". Another servant's name was Pamela. The success of Richardson's novel of 1740 is said to have ensured that the name remained one for servants and the lower classes until after the Second World War. More generally, Lady Mary Wortley Montagu wrote to her daughter in 1757 to welcome the name she had chosen for a new grand-daughter: "I am fond of your little Louisa; to say truth, I was afraid of a Bess, a Peg, or a Suky, which all given me the ideas of washing tubs and scouring kettles."[33]

Foundlings and illegitimate children might also be given names which signalled their marginal status. In Protestant London in the late sixteenth and seventeenth centuries, they could be named after the saint of the parish church where they were baptized, for example Peter at St Peter, Cornhill; Denis at St Dionis, Backchurch. This was not a general custom in England at the time. Other appropriate English names were Relictus and the Puritan Repent, Forsaken and Fly-Fornication. A study of Siena in the eighteenth century shows that there were significant differences between the first names of foundlings and of other children. The former were more likely to receive names alluding to birth circumstances, happy or not; they were also less likely to be given the double or triple names that were in general fashion. In France of the Old Régime, too, foundlings could receive only one first name, thus singling them out from respectable children with two or more.

Within countries, there were names that were clearly regional in their incidence. So, in France, among men's names, Yves was found from the sixteenth century onwards, if not earlier, in western Brittany but very rarely elsewhere. Léonard, which dates back to the fifteenth century, was largely restricted to the Limousin and became indeed a generic nickname for men from that region. Philibert belonged to the later Saône-et-Loire and the Côte-d'Or; Martial to the Haute-Vienne and the Corrèze, both from the late medieval period down to modern times; while Marius was confined to Provence, Languedoc and the Rhône valley. Among girls' names, Perrine was a Breton name; Léonarde was Limousin, like its male counterpart; while Bertrande was found mainly in the Hautes-Pyrénées, and Solange in the Paris region. Except for Marius and Solange, these regional names originated with local saints' cults, which they then transcended.

There were also regional preferences within the repertoire of national or universal names. In the nineteenth century, at least 16 common boys' names had this regional character. Pierre, for example, was most common in the west and south-west; Joseph in the east and in Brittany; Nicolas in Lorraine; René in Anjou; Antoine was "resolutely Southern".[34] Among girls' names, Anne was more prevalent in Brittany, the centre and the east; Madeleine in the south-west; Catherine in the south-west and north-east. These preferences seem to have deep historical roots, though their nature is not always known. Again, religious associations are sometimes involved. Naming after local ruling dynasties was also a factor. The royal Louis, for example, was especially common in the Capetian heartlands around Paris.

Regional first names were even more salient in Italy, which was only unified into a single country in the later nineteenth century. Among the commonest modern names, for example, Salvatore and Rosalia were especially common in Sicily; Roberto and Elena in Tuscany; Sergio and Paola in the Veneto. Among the less common names, Battista was commonest in Lombardy and Piedmont; Domenico, Gaetano and Filomena in the south. Corsica too maintained distinctive names down to the modern period, for example, Leone and Orso for men; Fiordispina for women.

Its smaller size meant that regionalism and regional names were less important in England, but some local names are found, albeit confined mainly to élite families, for example Marmaduke in Yorkshire and Kenelm in the Midlands. More significant variety is found in other parts of the United Kingdom. Among especially Scottish names, some are Gaelic: Alasdair, an early form of Alexander; Iain, a form of John; Finlay or Fionnlagh; Gilchrist; Malcolm; Morag. Sometimes an English phonetic rendering was used, for example Hamish for Seumas or James; sometimes a similar-sounding English name was substituted for a Gaelic name: Colin for Cailean; Ludovic for Maoldomhnnich. Other modern names found mainly or originally in Scotland include Alison, Annie, Chrystal, Donald, Duncan, Gavin (for Gawain), Griselda or Grizel and Kenneth. Norse names survived on Shetland – despite clerical disapproval – down to modern times, for example Olie, Hakki, Shuard from Siguthr for boys; and Inga, Hilda and Osla from Aslaug for girls.

Distinctive first names on the Isle of Man were also Gaelic or Norse in origin. Among the first were Ean or Juan (forms of John), Fingal, Mungo, Teig, and a number of Gil- names such as Gilbrid and Gilcolm; among the latter were Allow from Olafr; Magnus; and Mold, very common in the fifteenth and sixteenth centuries, from the Norse Moldi (of the earth). Alister, Cristal, Illiam and Sharry (Geoffrey) were local versions of continental names.

First or single names in Wales were mainly Welsh until well after the end of the Middle Ages. Among the commonest names in the late medieval period were David, Madoc, Iorwerth, Ieuan and Wln or Gwin for men, and Angharad, Tangwistel and Wentliana for women. A process of translation and substitution was also evident, with native names being replaced by English or French equivalents. "The obvious examples are Lewis for Llywelyn/Llewellyn; Hugh for Hywel/Howell; and Edward for Iorwerth." Hugh displaced Hywel in parts of north Wales in the sixteenth century, but had little impact in the south. Except for John, David and later Thomas, the standard Christian names made little headway in Wales at this time. There was a further anglicization of first names in the course of the sixteenth and seventeenth centuries, though some Welsh names held their own in large parts of the country, for example Gruffydd, Morgan and Owen. Wales also showed a special penchant for the names associated with "seventeenth century puritanism and eighteenth- and nineteenth-century evangelism",[35] so that Abraham, Elias, Jeremiah, and Moses and so on came to be in a sense Welsh names.

The custom of feminizing masculine and mainly saints' names was widespread in the later medieval period, as we have seen. Wishing to promote the notion of patron saints as exemplars, the Catholic Church after the Council of Trent banned the use of names not proper to the gender of the saint concerned. Abbé Thiers in the early eighteenth century included giving girls names like Michelle, Gabrielle and Philipotte among the "superstitions" which he wished to extirpate. The French secular law of the Year XI, the basis of modern legislation on names in France, also implicitly forbade the use of feminized masculine names.

But despite all this, they continued to be extensively used. At Perpignan in the sixteenth and seventeenth centuries, out of 143 male names, only 31 were not feminized, while the 48 commonest male names were all given to girls unchanged. Of the 119 female names in general use, 63 were feminized male names. At Perpignan, the usual mode of feminization was to add -a as a suffix, for example Rafel, Rafela; Nicolau, Nicolava; Martí, Martina. Elsewhere, a great variety of forms, including diminutives, were employed. For example, at Mirande in the seventeenth and eighteenth centuries, one finds Bertrande, Vincence, Antonie, Andrea, Simona, Simonetta; at Lormont in the seventeenth century, Sebastienne and Sebastianne. Two conflicting trends seem to have been at work in feminization. "Feminized first names were both more prone to archaisms and to new fashions than their male originals."[36]

"Traditional" feminization seems to have derived from the wish to give girls the names of their godfathers, and more broadly from a desire to procure the benefits accruing from the protection of the important saints concerned. Fashion is more obvious later. Among the Tesnière family in Normandy, for example, there was a flourishing in the mid nineteenth century of many new and invented names for girls, including feminizations, especially in -*ine*, like Albertine, Alphonsine, Léopoldine.

Feminized names were similarly common in Italy and in Britain, and they continued to be invented down to the modern period. According to Charlotte Yonge in 1884, the two feminine names from Charles, her own name and Caroline, were both fairly recent introductions. Caroline had come from Italy via Germany and particularly George II's queen, "by whom it was much spread among the nobility, and [it] is now very common among the peasantry".[37] Feminized names seem to have been especially common in Scotland, where the suffix -*ina* was readily attached to common male names: Adamina, Andrewina, Douglasina, Hughina, Jamesina, Malcolmina.

Giving female names to males was far less common. Indeed, in France it seems to have been restricted to Anne and Marie. Anne was a genuine male name in the sixteenth century; Marie was quite often used as a second name for males in the eighteenth and nineteenth centuries. We have seen, too, that female names associated with the Virgin Mary might be given in male form in Italy. On the whole, however, first names were clear gender distinguishers. Only a very few crossed genders unchanged. Where genderization via suffixes occurred, it was significantly a virtually one-way traffic. Females could and did benefit from the virtues inherent in male names, but not vice versa. Indeed, giving a man a female name was a way of insulting or depreciating him. In France, female names were used as generic nicknames – Cathelaine in the Walloon region, Jeannette in Anjou and elsewhere – for men who were effeminate or who fulfilled female roles, for example by doing the housework.

Politics and fashion

The role of fashion in determining first-name choice was limited in the early modern period. Religious considerations and the need to transmit names within families were paramount. Croix calculates that for Nantes and its region in the sixteenth century, for these reasons, only 10–20 per cent of names were subject to fashion at all. Innovation became more important in subsequent centuries, but, as we saw in discussing the commonest names or the impact of Protestantism, change was very slow. There was, however, some acceleration beginning in the late eighteenth century. In France, this encompasses the period of the Revolution, which deserves special treatment.

The French Revolution saw the rejection by some people of the old Christian first names and the adoption of new Revolutionary ones. This was part of a wider movement of reconstruction and renewal and only one of many iconoclastic measures "directed against the cultural Old Régime of monarchy, feudalism and Church". But while most of these measures – the new calendar, the metric system, the attack on the Church – were directed by legislation, the laicization of first names remained unofficial and "spontaneous". This means that it is in some ways a better guide to popular involvement in the Revolution than most of the other manifestations.

The practice of giving or taking Revolutionary names was confined by and large to the most militant stage of the Revolution. It began in a small way from January 1793, when the "état-civil" or registration of births, marriages and deaths was secularized, but only became important from September 1793 "with the advent of the Revolutionary calendar and the official campaign of dechristianization".[38] After November 1794, Revolutionary names declined without disappearing. Before September 1793, they reached at most 10 per cent of all names given; from September 1793 to September 1794 (the Year II), they were up to 25–30 per cent.

There were also important geographical and sociological variations in the incidence of Revolutionary names. Proportions ranged from a high of 62 per cent at Corbeil, a small town near Paris, and 47 per cent at Beauvais, through 12–17 per cent in the towns of the Seine-et-Marne, to 10 per cent in Poitiers and less than 5 per cent in the Pays de Caux. As one would expect, places further away from Paris and other centres of Revolutionary government were least affected, and loyal Catholic areas in or close to centres of resistance to the Revolution least of all. This is confirmed by looking at the social class of those choosing secular names. They were primarily those in the local Revolutionary administration, the Jacobin intelligentsia, together with their militant *sans-culotte* following, artisans and skilled urban workers. But in some small towns and even in some rural areas over half the population demonstrated its commitment to the Revolution in this way, though there were different modes and degrees of doing this.

Some adults changed their names – "militants, generals, members of the revolutionary armies". The Duc d'Orléans became Philippe Egalité; Bathilde, Duchesse de Bourbon, changed her name to Vérité. At a lower level, a member of the *comité de surveillance* at Mirande in the Year II adopted the name Germinal Léonidas Dubedat; an ex-religious from Anjou changed his name from Jean-Baptiste to Horatius Cocles Coquille. In most cases, militants simply adopted nicknames – Marat was particularly common – only occasionally going through the full legal and ritual procedures of civic naming or renaming. A rare example of ritual renaming occurred at Noyon on 30th Pluviôse Year II (July 1793), when Citizen Hennon dit Dubois took the opportunity, when registering and naming his new-born son Voltaire, to have his four other sons officially renamed. He "declared that it was repugnant to a Republican like himself to have children who bore the names of *ci-devant* saints, well-known only as a result of superstitious rituals, and that it was more suitable to use the names of great men who had either defended the Republic or had promoted it when no one else believed in it". The boys were presented, each accompanied by his two godparents; and Jean Victor or Jean Denis became Rousseau; Just Victor, Brutus; Agathon Gabriel, Marat; and Jean François Claude, Lepelletier.[39] Much more common of course was the giving of Revolutionary names to the new-born.

Various types of name were given, conveying different degrees of Revolutionary commitment. Indicating the highest level of militancy – like that of Citizen Hennon – were the names of Revolutionary heroes and martyrs: Marat, Le Pelletier, Chalier, Rousseau, all of whom were objects of cult in the period. At Corbeil, martyrs were more popular than thinkers. Then there were heroes of antiquity: Scaevola, Horatio, Gracchus, and above all Brutus. Also indicative of a high degree of commitment were civic concepts and Revolutionary virtues: Egalité, Unité, Espérance, Montagne, and above all Liberté. At Corbeil, these three categories, about evenly balanced, made up around a quarter of Revolutionary names. A further quarter comprised names taken from the Revolutionary calendar months, and these were common elsewhere. Autumn and Winter months, like Brumaire or Nivôse, were rarely used, which shows that the actual time of birth was not necessarily guiding the choice of name. Most of the rest of the names used were those of flowers, fruits and vegetables. Many of them: Jasmin(e), Hyacinthe, Myrtille, Narcisse, Rose, etc. were the names of days in the new calendar – each day of the Revolutionary year had a distinct name. But some of these, notably Rose, by far the commonest, were already in use as girls' names taken directly from flowers. Some bizarre names were used in this category. Foundlings at Auxerre received the names Cyclamen, Persil, Tulipe and Rhubarbe.

Names like Rose or Victoire were ambiguous. They might demonstrate active support for the Revolution, or simply going along with the new "politically correct" fashion by using a name that could be new or old. Marius, which remained a very common name in Provence, could recall the Roman general or act as the male equivalent of Marie. Another ploy here was to mix old and new names. Pierre Liberté and Elisabeth Maratrice were found in Compiègne; Jean-Baptiste Laurent Fédéré and Marie-Anne Gracieuse Pluviôse at Fronton. Did this reflect prudence or a genuine syncretism, accepting at least part of the Revolutionary culture and adapting it to older frameworks, as was done for example with the cults of Revolutionary "saints" and martyrs? Some force is lent to the latter idea by the fact that some of the popular Revolutionary fashions seem themselves to derive from naming practices current during the Old Régime. Eighteenth-century *noms de guerre* used by soldiers, for example, frequently borrowed names from flowers and vegetables; they also made use of classical names and names of qualities, such as La Liberté.

It has been asserted that Revolutionary names made little long-term impact, and that many bearers of them had abandoned them by 1815. At the same time, continuities in naming crossed the Revolutionary period. In some areas, like the Vexin, Louis remained popular or even reached its high-point in the 1790s, despite its close association with the discredited and then disbanded monarchy. Conversely, the adoption of the new names had not been forced, and a few Revolutionary names did persist or were revived well into the nineteenth century among left-wing families. In the remote south-western *département* of the Aude, Marceau, Marianne, Danton and Kléber were still in use around the time of the First World War.

However, there is little doubt that the militant Revolutionary names were a short-lived vogue on any scale. But the onomastic significance of the Revolution was nevertheless very great, if one takes a wider view and a broader time-scale. In many different parts of France in the half-century or so after 1789, a "quiet revolution" occurred in first naming.[40] The old pre-dominance of a few saints' names was diminished, and the stock of names in use greatly expanded as new names were introduced. In the Pays de Caux, for example, so resistant to French Revolutionary names as such, this half-century was the period of greatest change in the choice of names before the middle of this century.

These changes have been charted by a team led by Dupâquier for the nineteenth century as a whole. First, there was a fall-off in the use of traditional names. They revived in the decade 1810–19 after the Revolutionary eclipse, but they then went into definitive decline. Guillaume disappeared from the top ten male names in the decade 1810–19, André in the 1820s, Etienne in the 1830s, Jacques in the 1850s, and Antoine in the 1860s. Jean fell steadily from around 25 per cent in the 1810s to 9 per cent in the 1890s. Marie rose to 35 per cent in the 1850s, but then fell off. Marie and Maria together accounted for 36 per cent of girls in the 1850s, but only 24 per cent in the 1890s. Among traditional names, some lost ground constantly like Guillaume, Etienne, Catherine and Anne. Others fluctuated in popularity like Antoine and Madeleine. Still others fell for most of the century but then revived. René, for example, was quite popular in the 1810s, then fell steadily to rise very quickly again at the end of the century. Suzanne fell but was similarly resurrected very quickly in the 1890s.

Overall, the 11 traditional first names for boys fell from accounting for 66 per cent of individuals in the 1810s to accounting for 33 per cent in the 1890s; and the comparable percentages for the nine traditional names for girls were 63 per cent in the 1810s and 40 per cent in the 1890s. The decline was not a rout, and many traditional names still retained a leading position. Then there was the phenomenon of revival, though this tended to reclassify traditional names as "new" ones.

The second main trend in the nineteenth century was the introduction of new names both generally and among the most popular. For boys, for example, Auguste came into the top ten names in the 1850s; Henri and Jules in the 1860s; Emile in the 1870s; Georges, Paul and Léon at the end of the nineteenth century. For girls, Rosalie appeared in the top ten names in the 1800s; Rose in the 1820s. Josephine supplanted Elisabeth and rose to become the fifth commonest name in the 1850s. In the same decade, Julie and Augustine pushed out Madeleine. Eugénie's success began with the Second Empire but remained for twenty years, along with Eugène. Nearly all the "new" names were in fact old names revived after some elapse of time. But they had lost the quality of traditional names passed on from generation to generation without a break.

The names that ousted traditional names among the most popular ones usually had a fairly short-lived vogue. From the early nineteenth century, Joseph, Jean-Baptiste, Philippe, René, Augustin and Frédéric did not last as leaders beyond 1840. Claudine, Rose, Sophie, Victoire and Adèle did not last much longer. Again, of the 18 male names (Alphonse, Gustave, Victor, Ernest, and so on) and the seven female names (Pauline, Léonie, Berthe, and so on) which became leaders in the decades after 1840, most had gone out of fashion again or were in serious decline by the 1890s. There was a marked acceleration in the time it took for a name to achieve popularity (and then to lose it). Early in the nineteenth century, Sophie rose rapidly over two decades by 139 points on Dupâquier's scale, but Suzanne rose in the 1890s, a single decade, by 279 points.

The question of what determined or determines fashion in names is one of the most difficult to answer. A variety of factors may be adduced for nineteenth-century France. First, there was naming after important persons. We have seen that Eugénie, the name of the Empress, was particularly popular during the Second Empire. Joséphine and Pauline were also Bonaparte names. In some cases, very local political influence may be detected. After an influential local politician from a village in the Puy-de-Dôme called his daughter Germaine, a name unknown there before, "in the very same year, 16 out of 22 girls born in the village were called Germaine".[41]

Then there were literary names, like Adolphe from the novel by Benjamin Constant, René from that of Chateaubriand, and so on. Taine noted snootily in 1878 that the Ossianic names "Oscar, Malvina and company toured Europe and ended up around 1830 providing first names for grisettes and hairdressers".[42] But this was certainly a two-way process, with poets and novelists choosing names for their heroes and heroines that were "in fashion" or had a certain air.

In a sense to look for reasons behind fashions is reductionist. Fashion is *sui generis*, and fashion by itself became an increasingly significant factor in naming (and other spheres of life) in the course of the nineteenth century. In general, fashion was made in the urban centres and notably Paris, and among the élites, and then spread outwards and downwards. But as we saw in discussing noble names, once a fashion was generally taken up, it ceased to be "fashionable" as far as the élites were concerned. The system had an in-built dynamic and a tendency towards ever more rapid turnover as the means of social and cultural communication expanded.

One of these was migration, on which an interesting sidelight is provided from the Limousin. Here there was a clear contrast in the early nineteenth century between the sedentary section of the population and that engaged in seasonal migrations. The latter had a far larger stock of first names. Within this second group, moreover, there was a further distinction between those who migrated to other rural areas or to towns within the region, and those who went to Paris. It was the last that was most open to modernity in all its forms: new reading habits, dress, political ideas and personal names.

Other countries did not have the experience of the Revolution. Otherwise the history of their naming practices in the late eighteenth and nineteenth centuries must have paralleled that of France, though developments in Italy and Britain have not been systematically studied.

Some further insights into the general picture may be obtained from England. In a famous passage in Sterne's *Tristram Shandy* (1795), we learn that the narrator's father believed that "there was a strange kind of magic bias, which good or bad names, as he called them, irresistably impressed upon our characters and conduct". Some he regarded as "neutral names . . . Jack, Dick and Tom were of this class . . . Andrew was something like a negative quantity in Algebra with him; – 'twas worse, he said, than nothing. – William stood pretty high . . . But of all the names in the universe, he had the most unconquerable aversion for Tristram." Writers before and especially after this played on and drew attention to the penumbra of association surrounding first names, which became an increasingly important element in their being chosen. In Sheridan's *St Patrick's Day* (1775), Mrs Bridget Credulous tells her husband, when their daughter persists in an unsuitable attachment, "Lauretta! ay, you would have called her so; but for my part I never knew any good come of giving girls these heathen names: if you had called her Deborah or Tabitha, or Ruth, or Rebecca, or Joan, nothing of this had ever happened; but I always knew Lauretta was a runaway name." Later, in Jane Austen's *Mansfield Park* (1814), Fanny Price declares "there is a nobleness in the name of Edmund. It is a name of heroism and renown – of kings, princes, and knights; and seems to breathe the spirit of chivalry and warm affections."[43] Many more examples could be cited, including many where the "meaning" of the name depends on a host of factors that cannot be grasped. This is the essence of the modern first name.

England too experienced the same decline of old and traditional names, though there was a current of continuity. In the West Cumberland parish studied by Williams, the same names – John, Thomas, William, Elizabeth – recur in the registers down to the 1950s.

New names stemmed from the same kinds of sources as in France. Names of rulers and famous people were followed. Caroline and Henrietta or Harriet, common in the eighteenth century and after, were Stuart royal names. The Hanoverians provided the models for Fredericks, Georges and Augustuses, and for Amelias, Augustas, Charlottes and Sophias. By contrast, Queen Victoria's name was little used in her reign, though Prince Albert's was. Among other leading figures, we may cite Flora Macdonald, whose name was common in Scotland in the nineteenth century, and Florence Nightingale (1820–1912), whose fame helped to spread a virtually new female name.

Literary influence may also be inferred. Amy, Brenda, Edith and Fenella, all new names later in the nineteenth century, were heroines in Sir Walter Scott's novels. More significant perhaps are names associated with movements, literary and otherwise. An obvious example is the medieval revival of the eighteenth and especially the nineteenth century, which had a considerable impact on naming. Alfred, an Anglo-Saxon and royal name, was "restored to favour" in the later eighteenth century. Gerald and Norman were popular a century later. Some of the considerations underlying such choices are indicated by a letter of Lady William Russell in 1829, explaining to a friend why she had decided to call her third son Odo:

> Thomas [her correspondent's own name], begging your pardon, was not romantic enough nor William either [the father's name] & Leopold was too much so – so I took refuge in the Middle Ages & the family annals and found the first Norman adventurer of the Roussels who came over with the Conqueror was Odo de Roussel, so here is his name revived . . . 800 years after an ungrateful forgetfulness of his posterity.

Her brother-in-law, Lord John Russell, did not approve, declaring that the name would "look ridiculous in the Morning Post".[44]

What began as an aristocratic fad later became a more general fashion, particularly for girls. Edith, another Anglo-Saxon royal name, became very popular from 1875. Ethel, a shortened version of the Anglo-Saxon Etheldreda, used for the heroine of Charlotte Yonge's *The Daisy Chain* (1853–6), was also in vogue from the 1870s. Hilda, Mabel and Mildred belong to the same group of name, while Enid, popularized by Tennyson's *Idylls of the King* (1859), and Gladys, used for romantic heroines in several later-nineteenth-century popular novels, added a Celtic flavour to the basic medievalizing tendency. A classic example of the switch to these new names is provided by the children of the Manchester baker James Crowder and his wife Susannah: four of them, born in the 1870s and 1880s, were called Walter Clarence, Edith Adelaide, Mabel Annie, and Minnie Ethel.[45]

CHAPTER TEN

First names 1500–1900: II

Multiple names

For centuries individuals had only one first name, but by 1900 they nearly all had two or more. How were double, multiple or "middle" names introduced, and why?

The custom probably began in Italy. Persons with two first names are found there from the late thirteenth century, if not earlier. Such double names were already common in fourteenth-century Florence. Of Gregorio Dati's 24 children, born between 1391 and 1431, 18 had two first names. By the late fifteenth century double naming was frequent among the élites of Florence, Perugia, Venice, Rome and elsewhere, and there was a further progression of the custom in the sixteenth century. It also spread geographically and socially. Of Corsicans serving in the Genoese army in 1564, 18 per cent had double names. At the end of the sixteenth century also "two or more first names were given to all babies in the Fiesole, Chianti and Casentino regions of Tuscany, though it took a further century for the practice to reach the [more backward] Mugello".[1]

Double first names are found in Gascony in the eleventh and twelfth centuries – without second names proper. They were originally patronymics, as we have seen, though they became independent names. In 1385, 13 per cent of first names in the viscounty of Béarn were double ones. These names were composed with the old regional names, and only one of them, Arnaut-Guilhem, survived beyond the Renaissance.

Elsewhere in France, double first names make their appearance much later, in the sixteenth century, and then only among the élites and/or in selected regions. The custom was almost certainly introduced from Italy and Spain. It was adopted in the Franche-Comté, when it was under Spanish control, and two first names were the rule at Perpignan by around 1570, when Spanish (or Catalan) influence was again predominant.

Double first naming was introduced more generally in the seventeenth century – at Lormont in the south-west, in the Forez, in the Aisne, in Normandy – spreading rapidly from the later 1600s and into the eighteenth century. Among the élite Tesnière family in Normandy, the double name arrived around 1680 and the triple name around 1720, and by 1780, most members had at least two names. Similarly among the Breton nobility, the double name appeared from the seventeenth century for women and from the eighteenth for men. At Saint-André-des-Alpes, among the general population, there are no double names in the period 1630–50 save the odd Jean-Baptiste; by the mid eighteenth century double names made up one-third of instances; and by the 1760s over half. In the Vexin, double names were almost unknown in the sixteenth and early seventeenth centuries; by the 1690s, 13 per cent of boys and a higher proportion of girls had them, and triple names had appeared; by the 1790s, 66 per cent of boys and 62 per cent of girls had double and 16 per cent of boys and 30 per cent of girls triple names. In Nogent-l'Artaud, 25 per cent of children had two or more names at the end of the seventeenth century; 60 per cent by 1730; and 97 per cent by 1800.

In places where double names had been introduced early, there was sometimes a further proliferation of names. At Perpignan, the average number of names per child rose from three at the start of the seventeenth century to five around 1660, falling back to two or three in the eighteenth century. In some areas progress was slower. In the Calvados, only 25 per cent of persons had double names before the Revolution, a figure rising to 75 per cent for men and 62 per cent for women by around 1820.

"There was a general tendency over the nineteenth century in France for the number of first names to multiply." In the decade 1800–9, 55 per cent of boys had one first name, 37 per cent two, and 8 per cent three; by the 1890s, the figures were 31, 46 and 23 per cent respectively. The figures for girls' names were very similar. But these overall figures still conceal considerable regional differences. Single first names remained important, especially for boys, in the centre and south-west, while multiple first names were commonest in the Paris region and the north-east. The vogue does seem to have been urban in inspiration, reaching the rural parts of remoter regions with some delay. In the Barcelonnette, single first names were almost unknown for girls by the mid nineteenth century, Marie having become "an almost obligatory first name element", but boys' names lagged behind. Around 1840, 40 per cent were still single. At Fronton, the "crushing majority" of first names were single until the nineteenth century, and multiple names did not predominate until this century. Similarly, at Minot, in Burgundy, the single name prevailed until the mid nineteenth century, as it did in rural Alsace. In the Haut-Limousin, it was reported after the Second World War that "in general, a child receives only one name".[2]

Camden noted in 1605 that "two Christian names are rare in England", citing only a couple of royal examples and the same "among private men":

Thomas Maria Wingfield and Sir Thomas Posthumus Hobby. Indeed Lord Chief Justice Coke asserted at about the same time "that a man cannot have two names of baptism".[3] Bardsley suggests that the custom spread among the nobility and gentry in the seventeenth century through imitation of royal example or via royal godparenthood. The Wingfields had acquired the Maria from Queen Mary who had acted as godmother to an Edward Maria prior to her accession. Continental example may also have played a part.

However, the custom remained a minority one and one confined to the élite, and most children through the seventeenth century and later received only one name at baptism. In the parish of St Augustine in Bristol in 1696, there are only three examples of persons with two first names, that is under 0.5 per cent. There are virtually no double names in Gough's Myddle, and among the noble Willoughby family and its circle, there are none. This remained the case through the eighteenth century, too. Only about 10 per cent of the population had more than one first name around 1800, and many English nobles in the late eighteenth century still had only one first name.

The change only really came in the nineteenth century, and not till the second half did the custom spread to the provincial middle classes and further down the social scale. The Rowntrees of York, for example, gave most of their children, born from 1868 onwards, two names, though the fact that both Joseph's wives were of German immigrant origin was a special factor here. In a West Cumberland village, perhaps more typically,

> the use of more than one Christian name . . . became common during the latter half of the nineteenth century. The only people with more than one . . . name before this time were members of the "gentry", which suggests that the idea spread downwards from the uppermost social level to the remainder of the community.[4]

A few double names in Italy were classical, but the overwhelming majority were saints' names, as one would expect, and they usually included the name of one of the most popular saints. Among Corsican soldiers in 1564, the commonest double names all included either Giovan or Giovanni, Anton, Francesco or Piero, or more than one of these. At Siena in the late eighteenth century, there were 80 combinations with Giuseppe, of which the commonest was Giuseppe Maria. Among women, the commonest style by far was Maria in combination with another name. In Corsica generally in the second half of the eighteenth century, 92 per cent of women's names were of this kind. A distinction should be made here between the commonest double names, which became in effect composite single names like Gianandrea, Gianpaolo or Marcantonio, and double or multiple combinations proper. Giovanni Battista is a special case, where a double name in fact uses the name of a single saint.

The same distinction applies in France between composites, in which two names are treated as a single name, like Jean-Baptiste or Marie-Madeleine, and multiple names, where single names are simply strung together with or without hyphenation, though the two cannot always be differentiated. The composite name was often the first to appear, and in some areas students have seen the composite name as characteristic of the seventeenth and eighteenth centuries and the multiple name of the nineteenth. Composite names were nearly always made up of the commonest single names: Jean, Pierre, Marie, Jeanne, Françoise and so on. Among French immigrants to Geneva in the eighteenth century for example, most multiple names involved Jean, Pierre, François or Jacques. At Nogent-l'Artaud in the eighteenth century, the commonest composite names were Marie-Madeleine and Marie-Anne, Jean-Baptiste and Jean-Pierre. Some names came to be used only or mainly as second elements in combined names, for example Ignace and Thérèse at Namur – both names promoted by the clergy. These patterns remained in place in the nineteenth century. Composite names in France as a whole were nearly all formed with Jean or Marie. Thirty-nine names were combined with Jean, the commonest being Baptiste (well in front), Marie, Pierre, Louis and François; 120 girls' names were combined with Marie. Louise was well ahead of the others, followed by Anne, Françoise, Josephine and Rose. By the 1920s, however, the composite first name had become an archaism, associated with backward rural regions like Brittany and the Vosges. Only one or two names, like Marie-Thérèse or Marie-Louise, had survived in the more sophisticated urban areas.

Composite names were never so common in England. Odd examples may be cited from the seventeenth century, such as Lady Georgi-Anna, daughter of the Earl and Countess of Exeter, baptized in 1616. In the eighteenth and nineteenth centuries, Mary Anne and Anne Maria were fairly common in the middle and lower classes. Both had probably begun, like Georgiana, as fashionable names. Sarah Jane also acquired a certain vogue. Charlotte Yonge wrote in 1884 that "the habit of calling girls by both [of two first names], now so common among the lower classes, . . . is very recent". A few pockets with a high incidence of composite naming have been identified in the British Isles, which are probably areas of Catholic religion. Double names were quite common, for example on the island of Lewis. They were either "pronounced in full, as Mary Ann, etc., or are slightly blended so that John Norman and John Neil become J' Norman, J' Neil".[5]

In practice, only one of a person's multiple first names was in everyday use. Gregorio Dati explained, in connection with his daughter Antonia Margherita, "and we shall call her Antonia", and with his son Jacopo Filippo, "and we shall call him Filippo". In seventeenth- and eighteenth-century Italy, it was common, where a person had two names, for only one to be used in the burial register. It was the same in France. In Alsace, for example, in the eighteenth and nineteenth centuries, multiple first names were used in the baptismal register, but they did not reappear in subsequent personal documents, and, unless they were composites, they were not used in everyday life. Especially later on, an element of choice might be exercised. George Sand explained that her mother, Antoinette-Sophie-Victoire, used each of her first names in succession through her life.

> When she was a child she was usually addressed as Antoinette, because it was the name of the Queen of France. During the successful wars of the Empire, Victoire naturally prevailed. After their marriage [in 1804], my father always called her Sophie.[6]

How do we explain this new fashion in naming? First, multiple naming was a response to the poverty of the name stock and the consequent frequency of single-name homonyms. It allowed more people to be differentiated, while using the same number of names. Over time, multiple first names came to replace hypocoristics as distinguishers. Ultimately, too, multiple naming increased the repertoire of names by allowing a growing body of new names to be grafted on to the traditional corpus.

A more explicit motive was religious. It was common in Italy, according to Camden, "to adjoin [to the first name] that . . . of some saint, in a kind of devotion". In fourteenth-century Florence, the middle name, in half the cases studied by Klapisch-Zuber, was the name of the saint whose festival coincided with the child's birthday or day of baptism. "According to family journals in Lucca and Bologna, this middle name was given at the door of the church and the principal name at the font." The middle name was thus deliberately selected and bestowed, and kept distinct from the "family" first name, and it "sought to attract over the child the protection of a patron saint".[7] Thus the future Jesuit cardinal and saint, Roberto Bellarmino, born in 1542 at Montepulciano on the feast of St Francis of Assisi, received Francesco as his middle name. The second or other religious name continued to be chosen and regarded as a religious name in later centuries. Byron's mistress, the Contessa Guiccioli, born in 1800 in Ravenna, had three names: Teresa, the name she was known by; and Domenica and Gaspara, both of which were religious names.

In France, there is a correlation between multiple naming and religious denomination. Whether in Alsace, Normandy or Provence, in French-speaking Switzerland or among immigrants to Geneva, Protestants were less likely to have multiple names than Catholics and/or adopted them later. This suggests again that Catholics had a specific religious reason for bestowing the extra name: to gain the patronage of a saint; and the overwhelming popularity of Marie and Jean, the most powerful intercessors, only confirms this. The attitude of the clergy was also contrasting. Some Protestant clergy condemned the practice. Some Catholic clergy, like Abbé Thiers in the early eighteenth century, were suspicious of it, but no synod attacked it. Other

Catholic priests encouraged it, adding saints of their own predilection to names chosen by parents or godparents, especially if they were doubtful about the proper sanctity of the latter. Catholics might also be given additional names at confirmation.

Multiple naming also had a "class" dimension. It began among the élites and spread down the social scale. In later centuries, élites maintained their social distance by further multiplication of names. Nobles in Naples and Rome in the seventeenth century could have ten or more names; one of the Colonna had 25. Nobles continued this polyonomy into the nineteenth century in Italy, especially in the south. At the other end of society, we have seen that foundlings in Siena at the end of the eighteenth century were deprived of names. Poverty in name signalled poverty in general – and possibly disgrace.

In France, too, multiple first naming was an "élite" cultural trait, "an affirmation of social superiority". Mère Tournebroche in Anatole France's *Rôtisserie de la Reine Pédauque* (1893) noticed that "persons of quality have many more names than common folk",[8] reflecting both historical and contemporary reality. Indeed, the Lutheran clergy of Strasbourg condemned the new trend in the seventeenth century as an example of pride.

Local studies confirm this general picture. In the Limousin in the seventeenth and eighteenth centuries doubling first names was primarily a custom of the nobility and bourgeoisie. At Besançon in the same period among magistrates and judicial officials, those with the highest status were more likely to have double names. "Over half the court bailiffs and ushers had only one first name, but under one in five of the members of the Parlement". In the Bas-Quercy in the eighteenth century, the use of more than one first name was "at first the apanage of the highest social classes". It began to be adopted by artisans in the 1830 and 1840s, but did not reach the peasantry until the 1860s. Multiple naming at Namur in the seventeenth century was above all a noble phenomenon, especially the mode for triple and quadruple names.

There is much evidence from elsewhere in France of the enthusiasm of the nobility for strings of names through the eighteenth and nineteenth centuries. Nearly all the members of the Burgundian Saulx-Tavannes family in the eighteenth century, for example, had three names. Five or more names were not uncommon among the princely aristocracy of the Belle Epoque. In the later twentieth century still "wealth in first names was strictly correlated to social status; for example, in Paris, those registered in the (wealthy) 16th *arrondissement* had more first names than those in the (poorer) 13th".[9]

Apart from social emulation and snobbery, a very important vehicle for the spread of multiple naming from the élites to the middle and lower classes was the institution of godparenthood. The double first names that appeared in Lormont at the end of the seventeenth century were "always the consequence of godparenting by a noble or bourgeois".[10] Similarly at Minot much later the first peasant children to receive more than one name did so because their godparents had them. Here one of the godparent's names could be combined with another from other sources, or a whole multiple name could be borrowed.

Finally, multiple naming provided a more flexible system. It allowed a child to be given a traditional family name and that of a new patron saint; or names could be given from both sides of the family, from a relative and a godparent, or from both godparents, without having to make difficult choices in this area that might cause offence. Then later, families could meet the demands of family tradition and those of fashion. It is significant here that nearly everywhere girls had multiple names earlier than boys, and that girls were more likely to have more names than boys. This suggests that boys' names were more closely ruled by the demands of family and patrimony than girls' where more leeway was permitted. All this will become clearer if we look at the rules governing the transmission of names.

Transmission

Not much information is available on the transmission of first names in the medieval period outside the nobility. Examples suggest, however, that names were passed on within families in a deliberate way. Things are much clearer in the early modern and modern periods, especially for France. The second or family name was transmitted from fathers to all their legitimate children, but first names also were regarded as "a symbolic patrimony" to be passed on, according to more or less strict rules, to new members of the family. Each name in the set both formed "a link in a chain of dead ancestors"[11] and also represented a programme for the future, designating a role, perhaps an inheritance, for its bearer. Different rules applied in different milieus.

In many parts of France, for example Burgundy and the Pays de Sault, names recurred in alternate generations.

> The eldest son received the first name of the paternal grandfather, the eldest daughter that of the maternal grandmother, the second son and the second daughter receiving respectively the first names of the maternal grandfather and the paternal grandmother; as for other children, they bore the names of collaterals chosen alternatively from the two lines.[12]

This was also the pattern among the Ashkenazi Jews of Alsace-Lorraine. First and second sons were named after paternal and maternal grandfathers respectively, and first and second daughters after grandmothers, provided that these relatives were dead. If they were still alive, the names of great-grandparents were chosen.

Elsewhere, for example at Lormont in the seventeenth century, at Préty in the eighteenth, in rural Alsace in the nineteenth and the Bigouden in the twentieth, names were transmitted from fathers to sons and to a lesser extent from mothers to daughters. The "robe" family, the d'Aligres, who supplied two Chancellors of France in the seventeenth century, reserved the name Etienne for eldest sons from the mid sixteenth century through to the eighteenth century. Again, in the Honnorat family at Saint-André-des-Alpes, the name Antoine occurred through six succeeding generations between 1630 and 1770, latterly in composite names. In Old Régime Canada 72.5 per cent of unions transmitted the father's name to a child and 56 per cent the mother's. Nearly everywhere those bearing the paternal or maternal name were eldest children.

Another much rarer strategy was to use one "leading name" for all children, which was only possible once multiple naming had been established. Most children in the Saulx-Tavannes family from the mid seventeenth century to the early nineteenth century, for example, were given the names Charles or later Charlotte for girls. So the Comte de Tavannes (1649–1703) was Charles-Marie; his sons Léon-Charles, Henri-Charles, Charles-Nicholas and Charles-Henri. The children of Charles-François-Casimir (1739–92), who became first Duc de Saulx-Tavannes, included Charles-Marie-Casimir, Gabrielle-Charlotte-Eléanore and Catherine-Charlotte-Clémentine.

One also finds the idea that a new-born baby "replaced" and "revived" a dead relative. Here it was inappropriate for more than one living person in the family to have the same name, so naming after living elders was avoided. Positively a child would then be given the name of the last relative to die before its birth. Those who died by violence or prematurely were often "revived" or "completed" in this way. For example, at Minot in 1905, a girl was given the name of her mother who had died while giving birth to her. To underline the point, the child was "baptized on the day of the mother's burial", and in practice she grew up to be a little mother, looking after her father, acting as godmother to her nieces, and so on.[13] She took on the social role of the mother. Relatives killed in the two World Wars were quite often replaced in this traditional manner. The notion of replacement was also important among Ashkenazi (but not Sephardic) Jews. For this reason, children could not be named after living relatives.

The rules were closely related to patterns of family structure and inheritance, which explains why boys' names show far less innovation than girls', and why the names of the eldest were most strictly controlled. In the Pays de Sault from the eighteenth century to the twentieth, naming after the grandfather was part-and-parcel of a stem-family structure, in which the son could not be head of the household and the farm while his father was alive, and so could not share his name, which designated that headship. Both name and position thus leapfrogged the generations. The heir was very often the first-born or eldest grandson born in the grandfather's house, but the grandfather had the right to name all his grandchildren and could thus designate the heir. All this seems to have been a comparatively recent phenomenon. In 1740, 35 per cent of first-born males had the grandfather's name, but 50 per cent by the mid nineteenth century. Higher life-expectancy increased the likelihood of cohabitation between head of household and eldest married son and encouraged the custom of transmitting names from grandfather to grandson. And, of course, it was only "the emblematic names" conveying headship that were passed on in this way. Younger sons received names from their godparents, who were usually uncles and aunts.[14]

Where the name went from father to eldest son, this often signified that the latter was the privileged heir, as in the Pays de Caux. Here the heir first received his father's name and when the father died succeeded to the family property. Other siblings had no share in it. A similar situation obtained in rural Alsace, where over half the eldest children in the eighteenth and nineteenth centuries had their parents' names and where the eldest son again inherited the undivided property. A different and unusual system was found in the Bigouden. Here the eldest son was given the father's first name but would leave the household on reaching maturity to seek his fortune in a neighbouring village or further afield, while the youngest or next to youngest son would inherit. Rather than programming and reinforcing the pattern of property and role transmission within the family, naming here complemented it and acted to ensure a degree of continuity and solidarity in the face of migration.

Within the framework of the rules, there was room or need for flexibility. There was often a gap between the ideal model of naming and what could actually be achieved. Individuals died; there were no sons to take the name; there were conflicting demands (which multiple naming helped to resolve); other pressures intervened. Children might be named after relatives who were or had become especially important, either as the mark of a received or an expected favour. A cousin of the third Etienne d'Aligre, for example, was given the same name "in honour of the former's father, the Chancellor", who had paid for his education at the University of Orleans.[15] Names could travel circuitous routes in order to survive. At Fronton, the first name Jean-Blaise passed down the related Danjoy, Baville and Assanis families of notaries and surgeons from a maternal grandfather via his heiress daughter to his grandson; from this man, who was childless, to his nephew; and from the nephew, who was childless in his turn, to his sister's daughter's son.

The existence of rules did not mean either that decisions were automatic. The rules had to be applied by those responsible for choosing children's names, and they had different degrees of conscientiousness, competence and individuality. And the rules themselves always allowed some freedom of choice. Who chose the name varied from place to place. In the Pays de Sault, we have seen, it was the paternal grandfather. In eighteenth- and nineteenth-century Normandy, it seems that the names of the elder children were picked by the father, while mothers chose those of younger children. In Flaubert's *Madame Bovary* (1856), however, set in small-town Normandy, everyone has ideas about naming the Bovary child: father, grandmother, family friends, but the final choice of the fashionable Berthe is made by the mother. Jolas points out in connection with Minot that choosing the right name required a certain amount of genealogical knowledge, which was usually the province of older women. In some places, for example the Bigouden, names were not definitely chosen in advance of the birth since this might be tempting fate as far as the safety and survival of the child were concerned. Elsewhere, the names were ready in advance.

The same kinds of rules about naming are found in Italy. In Renaissance Florence, the requirement to "replace" or "remake" relatives seems to have been uppermost. Palla di Bernardo Rucellai wrote in 1521 to his brother, for example, to announce the birth of a son who had been named Bernardo: "And thus we have remade our father and God willing we hope to do the same for Madonna Nannina and Cosimo and Piero and the others."[16] Here it was a paternal grandfather who was being remade, but others would have their chance. The name of a dead father was usually reused, especially where a child was born posthumously, or, as we shall see, when it was orphaned in infancy.

Another special case was "the virtually automatic transfer of the name of a man's first wife to the first daughter born of a second marriage. This took precedence over any ancestral name that might otherwise have been destined for the child." For example, in 1512, Biagio Buonaccorsi named his eldest daughter by his second wife Alessandra "to remake Alessandra, who was my wife and who well deserves that I have her name eternally remembered". This did not happen with the sons of widows who remarried and their first husbands.

Otherwise, it was nearly always the close relative who had most recently died before a child was born whose name was then bestowed on it, and there was here an idea of placating the dead with the promise of revival. So Francesco di Tommaso Giovanni noted in October 1449 that his son-in-law Giovanni Arrigucci had named his third son Bernardo "because of his cousin Bernardo di Pagolo Baroncelli, who died in September 1449". Where a significant relative, and especially a father, died while a child was still an infant, the latter's name might be changed to accommodate the fact. So "Filippo di Filippi Strozzi had been baptized as Giovanbattista in 1489, but when his father died three years later, the widow renamed the child Filippo 'to renew the memory of his father'." The same might be done where children died, thus dropping the names which they were remaking. The eldest son of the jurist Giovanni Buongirolani had been named Bernardo in 1500 after his paternal grandfather. But he died in 1505, and the name Bernardo was then passed to his brother, born in 1504, the fourth son, who had originally been named Girolamo after a paternal great-uncle. The name

Girolamo was temporarily suspended, without a home, but was then given to a sixth son, born in 1507.[17]

Replacement was also important in Corsica.

> Each lineage disposed, at all stages in its history, of a patrimony of baptismal names which it was its duty to transmit. It was a sacred store that one had at all costs to maintain, for the name was identified with the person. Letting a name disappear was to let die a second time the person who had borne it. From this obligation flowed the rule of replacement. Every deceased person had to be replaced in his name. Priority went to the paternal grandfather (whose name went by preference to the eldest grandson), but, if he were still alive or if this first duty had been accomplished, it could be the great-uncle or the brother.

In much of Corsica, the system was overwhelmingly patrilineal, with names of mothers' relatives only being used, as at Quenza, when other names were not available. In the Niolo, however, while the eldest son took the paternal grandfather's name, the second took the maternal grandfather's. But everywhere "the replaced person had to be dead: to replace a living person would draw upon him a terrible threat". Often a child was given the name of the relative who had died most recently. Naming after a person who had been killed could carry special obligations in a feuding society. In a case before the Assize Court in 1840, it was explained that Pietro-Francesco Tomasi of Gavignano, who had shot and killed another man, had been given the name of an uncle killed in an ancient feud and had thereby been designated to avenge him, which he had felt obliged to do on attaining his majority.[18]

Elsewhere, transmission might be directly from one generation to the next. Parents' names were given to children, for example, in Bologna and the Trentino in the seventeenth and eighteenth centuries. In the Nice region, too, this custom is found. Asked what name to give a baby, the priest of one village was told: "My grandfather was called Méou [a diminutive of Barthélemy], my father was called Méou, my name is Méou, so I want my son to be called Méou." Here one may assume that the name was going in each case to the eldest son. By contrast, at Quenza in Corsica, "every time that a child bears the name of its father or mother, one knows that this is a posthumous son or daughter, whose mother has died in childbed".[19] Elsewhere in Italy, too, one finds attention being paid to the notion of a balance between both sides of the family, in contrast to the single-minded stress on patriliny found in much of Corsica. Whatever the rules, they were deeply entrenched, and religious and other interests came second to them. Their force may also be gauged by the fact that they crossed both the European continent and the Atlantic with nineteenth- and twentieth-century emigrants and survived in Italian expatriate communities in Britain and the USA into the 1950s and beyond.

The situation was similar in Britain, though it has been less studied. Families had sets of names that were transmitted according to certain rules or conventions. As Macfarlane observed of the Josselin family of Essex in the seventeenth century, in a sense "the names were present before the children who were afterwards fitted to them". So when a girl was born in 1645, her father wrote that she was "intended for a Jane".[20] Certain first names were especially associated with particular families like medieval leading names. So, in England, Fulk was a Greville name from the early sixteenth century; Oswald belonged to the Moseleys; Kenelm to the Digbys; while, in Scotland, Gavin was a name of the Dunbars, Sholto of the Douglases, and Simon of the Frasers.

As on the Continent, different rules could be followed, particularly where the heirs were concerned. Transmitting names in alternating generations seems to have been characteristic of nobles, gentry and landowners generally, including some humbler farmers. This custom tended to emphasize ancestry, continuity of the line and replacement of the dead and was more congruent with an extended family structure. Naming after the father (and the mother) was found among the élite, but it was more characteristic of the middle and lower classes. In Gough's Myddle, for example, in the seventeenth century, such transmission seems to have been normal among all classes. Six males ascending from Gough himself were called Richard, and he named his first son – who died as an infant – by the same name. The practice persisted in the rural and urban working classes into the mid twentieth century. Naming after the immediately previous generation, that is after living persons, was more congruent with the nuclear family and solidarity within the smaller group.

But whatever the rules, they had to be flexible, given the vagaries of mortality, premature deaths of first-borns, failure to marry or to produce children or children of the right gender. Quite often it seems that a combination of the two main systems was being used, or there might be a switch from one to another. Among the Cecils in the late sixteenth and seventeenth centuries, for example, William went from Lord Burghley (grandfather) to the eldest son of his second but most important son, Robert, Earl of Salisbury. Robert passed from the first Earl to his third paternal grandson and then to a great-nephew of the second Robert. But by the later seventeenth century, principal names were no longer alternating, and there were four Jameses in a row, father to son, from the time of the third Earl.

In both systems, other children were named after other grandparents and after uncles and aunts. Sometimes, especially in the more distant past, the father's side of the family predominated in the choice of names, but in more recent times an attempt to balance the two sides of the family is evident. So the future writer, born in 1850, was "given the names of both his grandfathers, together with the surname of his mother's family – Robert Lewis Balfour Stevenson".[21] Robert Alfred Hardcastle Collier, born in 1875, the eldest son of the Monkswells, received Robert from his father and paternal grandfather and Alfred Hardcastle from his maternal grandfather. As we have noted, the practice of multiple first names facilitated this balancing procedure, which was focused more often on individual children rather than on whole sets of siblings as families grew smaller.

A further factor can sometimes be glimpsed in the modern period and that is the wish to preserve in a child the name of a dead relative, usually a sibling, with whom the namer had a close and affectionate bond. The poet Thomas Gray wrote to his sister in 1747, referring to their sibling "poor Lizzie", who had just died, "You did right to call your daughter by her name; for you must needs have had a particular tender friendship for one another, endeared as you were by nature, by having passed the affectionate years of your youth together."[22] Similarly, the actress Dora Jordan named one of her daughters after her own sister Lucy, who had died in 1778 aged 14.

Yet another element must be woven into the pattern by which first names were transmitted, for in many parts of Europe children were named after godparents. Baptism and naming had become even more closely identified in the late medieval and early modern periods. The first name came to be called the "Christian name", and it was given at the font, as part of the baptismal ritual by the godparents. In Dante's *Paradiso*, Cacciaguida declares: "And in your ancient baptistery [in Florence], at once a Christian I became and Cacciaguida." Naming at the font was also established in France and England by this time, and it survived the Reformation. The English Prayer Books of 1552 and 1662 both bring name-giving and baptism together. In the latter, the priest says to the godparents just before baptizing, "Name this child"; and the rubric continues: "And then naming it after them . . . he shall dip it in the water."[23] By the time of Parson Woodforde, in the eighteenth century, the term "naming" was commonly used to mean baptism. Naming by godparents often became in this context naming after godparents.

The custom developed in France "towards the end of the Middle Ages and reached its height from the sixteenth to the mid nineteenth century".[24] Like other naming practices, it probably originated among the nobility and bourgeoisie and percolated downwards. Some statistics will indicate the importance of the custom, which seems to have spread to most parts of the country. In Nantes in the sixteenth century between 80 and 90 per cent of boys were named after godfathers. Figures of over 90 per cent were found also in the Morvan, in the Jura, in Flanders and in parts of the Limousin. So pervasive was the custom that it was also followed by Protestants. But there are significant variations in its incidence. In the Pays de Caux around 1690, only 65 per cent of boys and 50 per cent of girls had the names of their godparents. The rate in some villages in the Limousin in the nineteenth century was around 40–50 per cent.

As this demonstrates, the child usually received the main first name of the godparent of the same gender, but there were exceptions. Godparents' other first names could be used; names could be regendered; and in some cases godparents chose names other than their own. In an early example, Joan of Arc replied to questions at her trial in 1431 that she had "raised several children at the font . . . and gave boys the name Charles in honour of the king; and to girls Jeanne [after herself]; and sometimes as the mothers wished".[25] In the Pays de Caux in the early nineteenth century, an Edouard Tinel recalled being taken on the knees of his godfather Leroy as a boy and asked what his name was. If he answered Dominique, a name given him by the godfather but which his family did not use, the godfather gave him a sou. Second names might also be bestowed. At Lormont in 1695, Pierre Grégoire, for example, gave his family name, which was also a first name, to his godson rather than his very common first name. In Béarn, the second name might be a house name and its transmission a sign of inheritance. Jean de Bidet in 1680, the legitimate son of Arnaud de Chiron and Catherine de Latapie, had the second name of his godfather, Isaac de Bidet.

Two alternative models were used in the choice of godparents and hence of their names. In one – the commonest – godparents were selected from among relatives. In the Hautes-Alpes in the eighteenth and nineteenth centuries, the godparents "who normally gave their first names to the godchildren, were usually chosen from the close family: often an uncle or an aunt; sometimes grandparents . . . sometimes siblings of sufficient age". Often the rules were stricter, running parallel to and reinforcing those for the transmission of names from kin that we have already encountered. At Minot in recent times, for example, "one takes for the first child the paternal grandfather and the maternal grandmother, for the second the elder brother of the father and the elder sister of the mother".[26] Here balance between the paternal and maternal kin was carefully maintained.

In the Pays de Sault, where two-thirds of godchildren in the eighteenth century had the names of their godparents, godfathers were chosen according to birth order from grandfathers, paternal uncles and maternal uncles; and godmothers from grandmothers, maternal aunts and paternal aunts; and then from elder siblings on either side. Again, there was a strict regard for balance, which was only waived where one side of the family was missing or lived too far away. Extreme social distance might also cause imbalance. In general, godparents were more appointed *ex officio* as it were than asked or chosen, and the role could not be refused. There were only two important exceptions to the rule by which godparents named children. The first was where "a godchild was born after the death of a sibling of the same sex; here the name of that dead sibling supplanted that of the godparent". The second was more significant. Godparent-naming in the Pays de Sault only involved *cadets*. The name of the eldest son and/or heir was derived from the paternal grandfather, who was only sometimes also the godfather.[27]

Two reasons have been advanced for the adoption of the first model. Since the idea developed from baptismal ritual that the godparents "name" the child, it was a natural step, where the intention was to transmit sets of family first names associated with roles and property, to choose as godparents the appropriate relatives, who would then give their own names to the children. Transmission within the family was thus reinforced and given some kind of religious sanction. Fine suggests a further reason, associated with the idea that the godparent was the special protector of the child both in this world and in the next. Close relatives among the dead were particularly dangerous to the living for they harboured the wish to take their nearest and dearest with them. The protective role of the godparent countered this tendency and explains above all the choice of grandparents and the placating promise of "revival" via their names.

The second model was to choose godparents from outside the circle of relatives. This was a way of providing children and families with a wider network of contacts and especially with patronage in higher social strata. At Vallorbe, for example, at the end of the sixteenth century, Vincent Vallotton, a rich forge master, was godfather to several sons of poorer Protestants, who took his name. At Lormont in the seventeenth century, 20 per cent of godparents were outsiders to the parish, mainly better-off people from Bordeaux. The practice was also found at higher social reaches. The noble robe family of Froissard-Broissia of Dôle, for example, during the sixteenth and seventeenth centuries, pursued a policy of choosing godparents who were not kin. For this rising family "the wish to please a friend or obtain a useful ally and to enlarge and consolidate a network of alliances" overrode any concern to preserve a patrimony of family names",[28] and indeed the corpus of first names used by the family was almost totally renewed in the period. Choosing outsiders as godparents was clearly an important means by which onomastic innovation occurred.

Naming after godparents was also important in England. Among the gentry and nobility in the fourteenth and fifteenth centuries, around 90 per cent of children bore the name of a godparent, and the same proportion is found in some later parish registers. Among the late medieval élite, godparents were not usually relatives, and this seems to have been the case lower down the social scale in towns. At Bury St Edmunds in the fifteenth century, the preference for upper-class or clerical non-kin sponsors led to a few individuals having a very large number of godchildren. At Bury, too, a clear distinction was made in wills between less favoured godchildren who were not namesakes and more favoured ones who were.

It seems as if in general naming after godparents became less important in the post-medieval period, partly as a result of the Reformation, though the evidence is only impressionistic. Of the eight children of John More and Anne Cresacre, born between 1531 and 1546, only one, the eldest, was named after a godparent – his grandfather Sir Thomas More. Godparents were chosen from kin and non-kin, and they might or might not share names. Lady Joan Barrington of Hatfield, for example, who died in 1641, stood as godmother to the children of the family chaplain, the agent and of neighbouring minor gentry as well as to grandchildren and great-grandchildren. Only some of the latter received her name and they were favoured in her will. Names were especially likely to be taken from high-status godparents, if this were allowed. Both Philip Basset, son of a Gentleman of the Privy Chamber, and Philip, Earl of Arundel, were godsons of Philip II of Spain; while Caroline Robert Herbert (1751–1814) owed his unusual first name to the fact that he was the godson of Queen Caroline.

Existing but very partial evidence suggests that naming after godparents was relatively unimportant in Italy. Godparents in Renaissance and Counter-Reformation Tuscany "had no role [in naming] beyond that of transmitting to the priest and presenting before God, at a baptismal ceremony which the child's parents did not attend, the name or names that the child's parents had chosen". The only exceptions seem to have been when the godparent was of very high status, where taking his name represented a great honour. In the 1460s, King Ferdinand of Naples gave his name to a son of the Florentine ambassador Pandolfo di Messer Gioanozzo Pandolfini, and he later gave the boy gifts and paid for his education. Around the same time, a son of Piero de' Pazzi was called Renato after his royal godfather King René of Provence, who had lodged in the Pazzi residence while on a visit to Florence. Again, at the baptism of Roberto Bellarmino in 1542 "the Grand Penitentiary of the Catholic Church, Cardinal Roberto Pucci stood as his sponsor . . . and it was in honour of this very influential dignitary that he received his first name".[29]

At Quenza in Corsica, "a powerful godparent was often chosen to do him honour and to obtain his protection", but his name would not be given to his godchild, unless the main transmission duties had already been accomplished. This meant in practice that godparents only gave their names to the youngest children.[30]

Two other aspects of name transmission require brief discussion. The first is the phenomenon of same-name siblings, which some historians (Shorter, Stone) have misinterpreted by taking it out of context. It was not a specific denial of the individuality of the child but stemmed from the transmission strategies that we have outlined, from the need to use and preserve the family names in a situation of high infant mortality.

Two policies were followed here. The same name could be given to successive live children. This practice was followed in England from at least the twelfth century to the sixteenth and was characteristic of the peerage after this. A well-known example is that of the two sons of John Paston

(1421–66), who were both called John. Frequently here the homonymous siblings would be distinguished by the designation Senior and Junior or equivalents. An unusually late example provides the explicit reason for the custom. "So feeble was my constitution, so precarious my life", wrote Edward Gibbon, "that, in the baptism of each of my brothers, my father's prudence successively repeated my Christian name of Edward, that, in case of the departure of the eldest son, this patronymic appellation might be still perpetuated in the family."[31]

A particular circumstance in which this practice survived was among half-siblings, regarded perhaps as distinct sets, whose names could or even should be repeated from set to set. Among the daughters of Thomas, fourth Earl of Southampton, who died in 1667, were an elder Elizabeth and her half-sister who had been named after her. Again, in the early eighteenth century, Daniel Finch, second Earl of Nottingham, had two daughters called Mary by two marriages.

The other way to guarantee the preservation of the family names was to replace a child who died with another of the same name as soon as possible. So "in the Josselin family [in the seventeenth century] . . . two infants born within fifteen months of each other were named Ralph after their father". William Windham and Katherine Ashe, who married in 1669, had 11 children, who included two Johns and two Thomases, names repeated because of early deaths. The Sussex shopkeeper Thomas Turner recorded the death of "my little boy Frederick" in November 1774; then the birth of "Frederick (the second son of that name)" in May 1775, a baby who lived less than two months; and finally the birth of "Frederick Turner the third son of that name" in December 1776. Very many other examples could be cited going on into the nineteenth century. The custom was also followed in New England. At Hingham, Massachusetts, in the eighteenth century, names of dead children were passed on to siblings "for nearly 90 per cent of dying children with the same name as one of their parents" and for over three-quarters of those not named after a parent.[32]

A distinction is made by Beier between the practice of renaming immediately, where replacement was the priority, and after a longer interval, where commemoration of the previous child might be a more important factor, and one more "modern" in feeling. In the Grosvenor family, for example, Viscount Belgrave, their heir, had a son in 1823 called Gilbert, who died nine months later. A second son, born in 1825, was called Hugh Lupus. Only in 1833, with the birth of a third son, was Gilbert revived. Often of course here the vagaries of birth intervals and gender would determine the time interval. The first child of Mary Basset was named Honor in 1558 after her mother Lady Lisle "but only lived a few days". After that she had other children but they were all male. Not till eight years later was another daughter born to receive the name Honor.[33]

Although the desire to perpetuate names was uppermost in early modern and nineteenth-century English society and high infant mortality was usually overcome by repetition of names, a different perception of the connection between the two was possible. After a couple in a Sussex village had lost three successive babies called Helen, the neighbours explained this outcome as the result of using "the first child's name for the others". About the same time, another family "had a daughter who was named Marian because of her likeness to a dead sister. She showed signs of weakness soon after birth, and all said that she would die as the three Helens had died, because the name Marian ought not to have been used." The girl's name was therefore changed to Maude and she survived.[34] The same belief was found in the Outer Hebrides.

Naming after dead siblings was also very common in Italy and France, and for the same reasons. It is fruitless to debate in general terms whether the name "perpetuates the memory of the young child who had died", or that of the relative after whom the child had been named, or whether it was more a question of just perpetuating the name, since the whole point of the system was to bind all these elements together. The name was not autonomous, not distinct from the persons who bore it. It is similarly wrong to see any necessary incompatibility between regarding a child and its name as "part of a genealogical chain stretching forward over the generations" and affection for the child as an individual. The idea of replacement was strongly associated with that of repairing loss, even of a baby, and not simply with not dropping a stitch in the continuing pattern of family names. "We named her Cécile", wrote Mme de La Tour du Pin in 1800, "a dear name borne later by one who took her place."[35]

The second aspect is the handing on of second names as first names, which seems to have been more common in Britain than on the Continent. There was a minor fashion among the English gentry from the sixteenth century onwards for using second names as first names. For example, we have Euseby Isham of Pytchley, Northants (1540); Sir Beaumont Dixie of Bosworth, Leics (1629–92) and Sir Harbottle Grimston of Essex (1627); and in the eighteenth century, Dr Johnson's friends: Topham Beauclerk, Saunders Welch and Chauncey Lawrence.

Camden noted the novelty of the practice in 1605 and attributed it to two causes: the wish of godfathers to perpetuate their names; and, more important, the wish of parents to transmit names to heirs. This requirement was most pressing when the mother was an heiress, and, according to Cooper, it became customary to give one of the sons of an heiress his mother's maiden name as a first name – an alternative to adopting it as a second name which also happened. For example, Richard Roscarrock, a Cornish gentleman, married an heiress, Isabella Trevennor, in the mid sixteenth century, and one of their younger sons was called Trevennor. Again, the first Earl of Nottingham in the mid seventeenth century, Heneage Finch, was named after his grandmother's family, and she too was an heiress. But family names from the maternal side of the family were also used more generally. Gobert Barrington, in the early seventeenth century, was the second son of Sir Thomas Barrington and his wife, formerly Joan Gobert. Richard Gough at Myddle named his second son after his wife's family, Baddeley.

The custom continued into the nineteenth century, when it spread to the middle classes.

> Thus, the Suffolk iron manufacturer Richard Garrett named his third son Newson, his wife's family of Newson having held the farm whose forge had laid the foundations of the business. All types of economic activity and religious grouping used this naming convention: the Birmingham doctors, Bowyer Vaux and Peyton Blakistone, the Ipswich attorney, Eddowes Sparrow, the Witham miller Hoffgaard Shoobridge, the Suffolk farmer Woolnough Gross . . . [and the] Colchester confectioner, Chigwell Wire.[36]

In *The Diary of a Nobody* (1892), the Pooters' son Lupin uses his middle name which is that of his mother's family. Using the mother's family name in this way was particularly important in Scotland, where it continued into the twentieth century.

Once family names had been put into circulation as first names, they began to be used independently. This distinct development was already noted by Camden, who wrote that "surnames of honourable and worshipful families are given now to mean men's children for Christian names".[37] One of the first of these to be used as an ordinary name was Dudley. Several others followed, for example, Douglas and Sidney; Clive, at first reserved for those with some Indian connection; and in the nineteenth century Cecil, Montagu, Russell and Vernon. Noble names were especially popular. Stanley probably owed its success, however, to the fame of the explorer who died in 1904; Gordon more definitely to General Gordon, who was killed in 1885. A number of family or clan names were used in Scotland: Drummond, Graham, Leslie, Lindsay and so on; and they spread later to England. Some place-names also became first names via family names, for example Clifford, Denholm, Melville and Rodney.

This trend is found in Italy and France, but it seems to be much rarer. Poulat suggested that in France "the sense of distinction between first name and family name was too strong to allow the two to be mixed".[38] The few exceptions too seem to have a different motivation. Some are associated with godparenthood, as we have seen. Others are linked to the use of saints' names, like Chantal after St Jeanne-Françoise de Chantal, or Régis after St Jean-François Régis. After the First World War, heirs of those who had died in action without children of their own were permitted to petition the courts to add the name of their relative to their own family name. So Félix Gaillard might become Félix Gaillard d'Aimé after the name of an uncle.

Usage

Only in the modern period do we begin to have a clear picture of name usage.

The formal first name was used by the Church at the rites of passage. Otherwise it was only used by itself in the early modern period and the nineteenth century among close friends and lovers and in the intimacy of the household (along with pet or hypocoristic forms). So Swift reported to Stella in 1711 of Harley's inner cabinet meetings: "They call me nothing but Jonathan." Parson Woodforde used the first name for relatives, like his niece Nancy, and for long-established servants, like Ben, which presumably reflected his mode of address to them. Use of the Christian name was an important sign of progress in friendship. In Jane Austen's *Sense and Sensibility* (1811), Mrs John Dashwood showed her pleasure with the Miss Steeles, among other things, by calling "Lucy by her Christian name". Miss Podsnap told Mrs Lammle in Dickens' *Our Mutual Friend* (1864–5): "If we are going to be real friends . . . Call me Georgiana." First-naming also marked a crucial stage in courtship. In Trollope's *Barchester Towers* (1857), Mr Arabin switches from "Mrs Bold" to "Eleanor" before embracing his future wife. To stray beyond this narrow circle was to "presume", to be guilty of bad form, as when Mr Slope calls Signora Meroni "Madeline" prematurely.

As we shall see, second names and titles were appropriate for those more distant socially, and this remained the case into the nineteenth and early twentieth centuries. In the diaries of Ellen Peel from Denbighshire in the period 1886–1908, "the Christian names of the opposite sex were never used. One might read every word of the diary without discovering that Captain Fenwick was baptized George and Captain Bertie Reginald, though they are mentioned on nearly every page." And this reluctance to use first names even extended to close relatives among the provincial middle classes in the nineteenth century, with husbands and wives, for example, maintaining formal modes of address at least in public. The aristocracy may have been freer in this respect. Balzac notes that around 1840 the mutual use of Christian names was "a last shade of social distinction that marked off the inner circle of the aristocracy of Angoulême".[39]

The official baptismal name or names were not necessarily those used in everyday life. This can be demonstrated in France from the seventeenth century to the present day. "He was registered as Jean-Louis, but he is called Pierre-Marie", an ethnologist was told in the Bigouden. A study of the Vexin shows that only about half the men and women listed in the 1836 census bore names identical to those in the register of births. A quarter of the men were given two names at birth but only declared one, sometimes the first, sometimes the second; others with three names at birth declared only two; others with only one name at birth declared two or three; and so on. This situation was typical. The official name was especially likely to be replaced when it was very common. Individuals might also be known by different names in different contexts. At Minot "the same person may be Marcel for his in-laws; Jean for his blood-relatives; and Maurice for his age-group".[40] People might also change their names on joining specific associations or milieus, like religious communities and the armed forces. Also servants, actors and prostitutes often took or were given new names. All this was informal, but names could also be formally changed. In a case in 1623, for example, the bishop of Nantes on a visit to a parish in his diocese authorized changing the name of one of a pair of twins, both baptized Yves ten years previously, to Philippe. A secular legal process was required to do this in the nineteenth and twentieth centuries.

We have seen that hypocoristic forms were common in late medieval documents. From the sixteenth century, they fell into official disuse in French-speaking lands. At Namur, for example, they made up around 30 per cent of the corpus of names in 1500 but virtually none a century later. They were still significant in official documents at Caen in the 1560s but far less so by the 1660s, and by the 1760s they were virtually unknown. Of names in death registers at Lourdes in the 1640s, 19 per cent were in hypocoristic form: Guillaumette, Bertrandine, Jammet, and so on; but by the mid eighteenth century only about 1 per cent. A few hypocoristic names did survive, however, as proper names in different regions: Hans for Johann, Claus for Niclaus, Stoffel for Christoff, for example, in Alsace; Nofre for Onuphré, Manuel, Toni and Astasia for Stasia at Perpignan.

The decline and virtual disappearance of the hypocoristic may have been influenced by clerical directives following the Council of Trent and based on the view that such familiar forms were irreverent – we have seen that the Protestant clergy felt the same way. The general process of standardization of spelling and bureaucratic control operated in the same direction. Offical names were clearly distinguished from unofficial ones. The hypocoristic was banned from the parish register and the legal deed, though it continued in use in the family and the community.

Pet names were used for children and intimates in France through the early modern and modern periods. Medieval-style hypocoristics seem to have survived much better for women's names than for men's. Here masculine suffixes were often appended to female names: Suzon for Suzanne, Marion for Marie, Ninon for Anne. Paul Léautaud referred to his girl-friend/mistress Blanche as Blanchon in 1903. According to Robert in 1905, forms in -on for girls' names "seem to be more commonly used among the popular classes and the rural population", while forms in -ette "are more frequent in the respectable bourgeoisie". Such forms were, however, well on the decline by this time. A common replacement was "the duplication of the first syllable". In the 1840s Victor Hugo referred to his second son as Toto and was himself called by that pet name by his mistress Juliette Drouot. In the same vein, his daughter Léopoldine was Didine and Juliette herself Ju-Ju.[41]

Such names were commoner for girls than for boys. Other popular examples are Lolotte for Charlotte, Fifine for Joséphine, Loulou for Louise, and Nana for Anne.

Another common mode in rural areas, especially in the south, was to place the definite article in front of the first name or a pet version of it. At Minot, every appellation was preceded by "le" or "la" in reference: le Félix, le Noë, la Noémie. "There was also my cousin Apollonie", wrote Jules Vallès in his autobiographical novel *L'Enfant* (1879); "she was called la Polonie."[42]

The use of hypocoristic forms took longer to die in Italy. A great variety was found in the formal designations of Corsicans serving in the Genoese army in the 1560s: Antonetto, Antonietto, Antonioto; Orsaulio, Orsatello, Orsatone, Orsino. They were common too at Quenza at the start of the seventeenth century, though they had mainly disappeared by 1790. At the informal level, however, the old forms survived. The poet Giacomo Leopardi, born at Recanati in 1798, was called Giacomuccio by his sister; another brother was Pietruccio. Byron's mistress, Teresa Guiccioli, was Teresina, and her younger brother Pietro was known as Pierino. These forms were in common use for children in Calabria and elsewhere in the mid twentieth century.

Bardsley believed that in England hypocoristic forms in official usage "were practically obsolete before Elizabeth's death". This seems to be largely true, though some lower-class parents did continue to have them registered as formal names. The Bletchley parson William Cole noted in 1766 that he had baptized "the daughter of William Cooke of Eaton, whom they named Kitty at the font".[43] First names were also sometimes abbreviated in written form. Examples from the Lisle letters in the 1530s include Jo. or Jn. for John, and Ste. for Stephen. From the Willoughby circle in the early seventeenth century, we have Row. for Rowland, Phi. for Philip, Tho. for Thomas and Lett. for Lettice. Dr Johnson habitually signed himself, in private and public, Sam. Johnson. It is unclear whether these were standard abbreviations approximating to actual hypocoristic forms, as Sam. almost certainly was, or simply epistolary conveniences – to a degree idiosyncratic – like shortening common words to wd., cd., etc.

However, there is no doubt about the continuing use of hypocoristics in informal usage. A good example of usage within a circle of relatives and close friends is provided by the correspondence of Lord William Russell and his wife in the first part of the nineteenth century. He was known variously as Billikins, Billy and Bil, while she was Bessy, Bettina, Bess, Bettakina and Bet. Their children Hastings, Arthur and Odo were called Baba; Atty or Atty Patty; and Dodo or Little O; and they continued to use these childhood names among themselves into adulthood. Lord William's stepmother, Georgiana, Duchess of Bedford, was Georgy; and his brothers Tavistock, Wriothesley, John, Cosmo and Alexander were Tav or Tavy, Wrio or Rio, Johnnikins, Cosey and Ally.

Most first names of any currency had recognized hypocoristic forms. Some names attracted only one or two main forms; others had several; and there was scope for a fair degree of free inventiveness. In the first category, and all dating from the seventeenth and eighteenth centuries, were: Di (Diana); Frank and Fanny (Frances); Jim (James); Joe (Joseph); Nell (Helen); and Tony (Anthony). Other names attracted a larger number of hypocoristic forms, mainly because they were commoner names, whose bearers required to be distinguished. Examples are Aggie, Nessa, Nesta (Scots) and Nest (Welsh) for Agnes; Doll, Dora, Dodee, Dot and Dolly (modern) for Dorothy or Dorothea; Mey, Peg, Maggie (Scots), Margery, Maisie, May and Madge for Margaret; and above all the many names deriving from Elizabeth. These include Bess, Bessie, Beth, Betsy, Eliza, Elsie, Lisa (modern), Lizbeth, Lizbie, Tetty, and Tissy. It will be noted that all of these are girls' names, and they seem to have been far more prone to hypocoristic formations in the post-medieval period than boys' names. Some hypocoristic forms became independent names, like Elsie, Fanny and Margery.

English hypocoristic forms at this time were most often short versions of the full name, taking the first syllable and sometimes adding a -y or -ie suffix. The second syllable or part of the name was used much less often (Beth; Tony; Bella for Arabella). Changing the initial consonant was also comparatively rare (Nancy for Anne; Polly for Mary via Molly). Suffixes like -kin and -ot had become very rare. Doubling of syllables was also rare, though perhaps more common in the Victorian period. Maria Fagnani (1771–1856), who became the Marchioness of Hertford, was known as Mie-Mie to intimates; while Lady Louisa Hardy was Lou-Lou. One was foreign and the other had a foreign name.

Hypocoristics were especially found in the post-medieval period in certain contexts. First, they were applied to children. Many or most of the names we have cited were first given in childhood and only some survived into adult use. Secondly, hypocoristic forms could characterize intimate and special situations. In Trollope's *Barchester Towers*, Archdeacon Grantly "did not call his wife Sue more than twice or thrice a year, and these occasions were great high days", as, for example, when his sister-in-law decides to marry Mr Arabin and not Mr Slope.[44]

Thirdly, by the eighteenth century, if not before, hypocoristics, or the public use of them, had come to be seen in some circles as a provincial and lower-class trait. Congreve in *The Way of the World* (1700) had the rustic Sir Wilfull Witwoud address his fashionable half-brother as "little Tony . . . my Tantony", to the latter's mortification. Boswell noted Johnson's "tumultuous and awkward fondness" for his wife, "whom he used to name by the familiar appellation of Tetty or Tetsey". He added that the pet name was felt by Johnson's friends to be particularly "ludicrous, when applied to a woman of her age and appearance" – Mrs Johnson was fat and florid, with a large bosom. Again, in Jane Austen's *Mansfield Park* (1814), the vulgar Mr Price calls his daughters Sue and Fan, abbreviations never used in the circle of Sir Thomas and Lady Bertram. "Inappropriate" hypocoristic names became the hallmark in the nineteenth century of comical lower-class characters in fiction and real life. Charlotte Yonge related the case of a village child whose mother explained "Her name is Aspasia but us calls her Splash."[45] As Cottle noted, too, in the 1980s, there were U and non-U forms of hypocoristics. On the whole, then, the -*y* and -*ie* forms, like Reggie and Freddy, were "polite", whereas Reg, Fred, Les and Sid were not.

The inveterate nature of pet-naming is shown by the way in which it spread to second names. Queen Charlotte in the 1780s referred to her lady-in-waiting Lady Effingham as "my friend Effy". In *Pickwick Papers* (1836–7), Mrs Cluppins, trying to ingratiate herself with Mrs Bardell's boy, says "Come, Tommy, tell your dear Cluppy."[46]

Pet names shade off here into nicknames, and some of the disdain for vulgar hypocoristics stemmed from their overlap with generic nicknames deriving from first names. Certain first names attracted standard nicknames. Sam Weller observed on meeting Job Trotter: "And a wery good name it is – only one I know that ain't got a nickname to it."[47]

Other names themselves became nicknames. Jack had become the equivalent of "man", especially a man of the lower classes, by the late sixteenth century, if not earlier. So Antony, in Shakespeare's play, orders: "Take hence this Jack, and whip him." Tom, alone or in the proverbial combinations: Tom, Dick and Harry, or Tom and Jerry, fulfilled a similar function. Jimmy, from James, the commonest Scottish name after John, was used in Glasgow in recent times for "man", "especially as a vocative to a stranger". Such names were also qualified to convey more particular meanings: Jack-in-office, Cheap Jack, Tom Noodle. The often twinned English female equivalent was Gill or Jill: "There's ne'er a Jack but there's a Jill."[48]

Social classes or ethnic groups could also be designated. Hodge from Roger was used for peasants, as were Jenny and Joan for rustic women. Again, from Shakespeare, we have, from the Bastard in *King John*, "Well, now can I make my Joan a lady."[49] In later centuries, Biddy from Bridget meant an Irishwoman, or then any women. Mick or Paddy, Jock, and Taffy (from Davy) were used by the English as appellations for Irish, Scots, and Welsh men respectively.

Other names acquired more specialized meanings. A range of names was used for prostitutes or "loose" women in the early modern period: Jill, Nan or Nancy, Moll, Doll, Betty, Jenny and Kate or Kitty. Abigail was a favourite Puritan Old Testament name in the sixteenth and seventeenth centuries. For some reason in the early seventeenth century, the name became a generic term for a lady's maid. It was so used in Beaumont's *The Scornful Lady*, written about 1613, thus predating by a century the influence of Queen Anne's favourite Abigail Hill. The usage was still current around 1840. Among men, Charlie was a night watchman in the early nineteenth century; later on it came to indicate stupidity, like Cuddy from Cuthbert in Scotland. During the First World War, a Cuthbert was a man evading military service.

Nicknames from first names were also common on the Continent. In early modern and modern France, a number of popular names – Jean, Martin, Pierre – were used in proverbs and sayings to mean any man, "the man in the street". These were very common, and many dialect variations existed. Some such names were used in pairs, like Pierre and Paul, or Gautier and Guillaume.

First names were also used to designate ethnicity or region of origin, status or class, and occupation. In Italy, for example, a Michele or Michel was a German; a Pantaleone a Venetian; a Caterina a woman from Genoa or Modena. In France, Jacques was used for peasants from the Middle Ages onwards – hence *jacqueries* for peasant revolts. Pierre and Pierrot were also used for rustics. Colin, Guyot and Perrin were shepherds. Robin, at first a name for a shepherd, became the equivalent of "fool" or "buffoon", an example of a common slide from low status to low character. Servants through the sixteenth to eighteenth centuries were Gautier, Guillaume or Jacquet. Clerics were Martin. In nineteenth-century Paris an *agent de police* was called Monsieur Jules or Julot.

Again first names could also indicate qualities. Of the 200 or so words or families of words meaning "idiot" in France, about a fifth are first names. Claude, for example, was associated with stupidity, and also sometimes with deafness. This survives in the abbreviation Dodo. Jean and especially Jeannot was also a nitwit or imbecile, as were Jacques, Jacquet and Jacquot. Italian examples are Bernardo, Domenicho, Nicola and Pasquale, depending on the region. A cuckold or a jealous husband in France was "un vrai Jean", a Guillaume, or an Arnaud;[50] in Italy, a Martino or a Beniamino. Adolphe, Alphonse, Arthur and Oscar were all names in modern France for libertines or pimps. The success of Dumas *fils'* play *Monsieur Alphonse* (1873) popularized the particular meaning of that name.

Common female names were used in the same ways. In France, Marie and others referred to any woman at all. Jeanne, Jeannette, Margot and Catin were used for peasants. A Jeannette could also be a simple or silly woman; Guillemmette a sly or dissembling one, or by contrast a simpleton. Agnès had become so common a female name in the later medieval period and after that it was used at first as a generic name for any woman, and later to mean a naïve and stupid girl, as in Molière's *L'Ecole des Femmes* (1662). Agnes in various forms had the same meaning in Italy. Many names designated "light" women or prostitutes: Catin, Margot, Jeanneton and Suzon in France; Marigiovanna and Zanna in Italy.

Names were also used with qualifications. "You are neither Jeanot, nor Jean-Soul, nor Gros-Jean, nor Jean-de-l'Epine, nor Jean-Dève, nor Jean-Ridoux", a piece in the *Mercure* in 1717 proclaimed.[51] In Provence, a simple-minded man was a Jan-de-la-muelo or a Jan l'amelo. Jean-Katel was a Breton man who did women's work. Marie-couche-toi-la, Marie-mange-mon-prêt and Marie-pique-rempart were names for prostitutes.

It was always the commonest names that were used in this fashion and which took on pejorative social, ethnic and other overtones. It is also significant that hypocoristics were often used.

First names were also used to refer to whole classes of animals or birds. In France, for example, Robin was used for bulls or sheep; Guérin, Marc or Martin for rams; Raoul or Marcou for cats; Perrette for geese; Jacquot for parrots. These are all domestic creatures, perhaps humanized or personalized via this mode of naming. Animals closest to humans – dogs, horses and cows – did not usually have generic names of this kind. Their names were individual. But wild animals and birds also had generic first names. Jean and Guillaume designated wolves from the sixteenth century in Brittany and elsewhere; Martin was used for bears. A magpie was a Margot or a Jaquette, a sparrow a Philippe, a jay a Jacques or a Nicolas, and so on. Some wild animal or bird names carried over their human nicknames, for example Margot for a talkative woman and for a noisy bird. Others may have had a prophylactic effect, supposedly acting as protective euphemisms. Animal names of this kind were less common, it seems, in Britain. Philip was a name for a sparrow from the fifteenth century, Poll for a parrot from the seventeenth, while Tabby from Tabitha became a name for a cat. The fox apparently acquired the name Charlie in the 1790s, being chosen by Tory hunting squires as a way of attacking their Whig arch-opponent Charles James Fox.

Finally, the early modern and modern periods saw a process of standardization of first names. In France, patois and regional language forms were persistent, but they were gradually eliminated, first from the written name. In the Armagnac in the eighteenth century there was a disjunction between spoken and written names. The former were often regional, feminine names, for example, taking the suffix -o, while the latter were French. Already in the 1640s, only 3 per cent of written names were in the local form in Béarn. Gascon and French forms were both found at Mirande in the eighteenth century with the latter tending to supplant the former.

> Pierre had replaced Pey at the start of the seventeenth century, and only appeared in death registers along with Peyron. Peyrone, the feminine form, was still given in baptism in default of a French equivalent, Pierra appearing at the end of the seventeenth century only and Pierrette not till the start of the nineteenth century.[52]

Other names took a similar course, Guillaume replacing Guilhem, Gilles Géry, and Jean Joan or Joanot. Gascon forms survived more for girls' names than for boys'. Sometimes, as we have seen, they lacked a French substitute. There may also have been an archaism in female naming related to the greater contact of males with the outside and increasingly French world. As this suggests, bureaucratic practice meshed in with actual choices guided by social and cultural milieu and later national sentiment. The last was very probably a factor in the substitution of French for German names in Alsace in the eighteenth century and especially in the nineteenth: George for Georg, Thibault for Diebold, Antoine for Andoni.

Another bureaucratic and cultural trend affected the spelling of names. Here we may turn to England – though the phenomenon is universal. General orthographic standardization was weak before the eighteenth century, and names, in this context, were frequently spelled in a variety of ways, even when applied to the same person. In the Lisle letters as the editor notes, "John Bekynsaw, a scholar, writes William, Guyliam, Guylome and Guylyam in one short letter".[53] A young gentlewoman at court signs her own name variously Anne, Ann and An Basset. In the Barrington letters around 1630, we have Joan, Joanna or Johanna. Consistency in these matters was not achieved until the nineteenth century in private correspondence or baptismal registers. A legacy of this former orthographic uncertainty is the variation in the form of some names in modern use, for example Catherine, Catharine, Katherine, Kathryn and so on; though now parents or the bearers of the name choose one version and stick to it.

CHAPTER ELEVEN

Family names, titles and nicknames

Family names

Hereditary family names were established in much of western Europe, we have seen, by the end of the medieval period, but there were pockets of resistance and many archaic forms survived as late as this century in remoter areas and at the popular level.

In 1550, only 31 per cent of heads of households in Florence were identified by fixed family names; the rest had father's first name, with occupation, place-name or nickname. Only 5 per cent of women had family names. There were also wide social differences. In the wealthier Santa Croce district, 54 per cent of heads of households had a family name, but in Santa Maria Novella only 18 per cent. By 1630, 64 per cent of male heads of household had a family name, and 16.5 per cent of female heads; but there were still great internal discrepancies: 90 per cent of households had family names on some streets, less than 30 per cent on others. In Tuscany as a whole family names were universal in parish registers in the Chianti region by 1570, and in the Fiesole region by the early seventeenth century. But elsewhere the situation was less advanced. In the upper Mugello valley in the Appenines, family names only became universal in the second half of the seventeenth century. Similarly, in the Casentino, they appeared in the 1620s but were not completely adopted till around 1700. Always fixed second names appeared first among the élites and in agglomerations, large and small; they came in last among the poor and in areas of scattered habitat.

The situation was much the same elsewhere in Italy, with a particular delay in the south and in the islands. In Rome, second names had been commonplace among the nobility and the bourgeoisie by the later medieval period, but they did not become general until the mid seventeenth century. In the diocese of Perugia, fixed second names were usual in villages and towns by the mid eighteenth century; in the countryside, not till the end of that century. In the Romagna, family names were not established outside towns until the seventeenth or eighteenth century. Further south, "there were still persons without family names down to the most recent times".[1] At Quenza in Corsica family-name formation began in the seventeenth century and lasted over 150 years. At Bastelica, shifting patronyms were the rule through the seventeenth century. Second names appeared in the early eighteenth century, mainly for nobles and clergy; but they were not really established until the time of the French Revolution.

Family names were fixed earlier and more firmly in France, but remote and rural areas lagged behind the general movement. Second names were used in parish registers in the later department of the Haute-Garonne from the mid sixteenth century. They appeared first in the Lauragais and around Toulouse, spreading from the towns and the plain up the valleys and into the mountains through the seventeenth and eighteenth centuries. "The family name only became the principal name generally in the central Pyrenees therefore on the threshold of the nineteenth century, reaching the most isolated places even later."[2]

In the British Isles, family names were settled in England by the early modern period but not in Wales, Scotland or the islands. Common among the gentry by the seventeenth and eighteenth centuries, the second name was still absent or unusual among the lower classes in Wales, especially in areas away from English influence. In his diary, kept in the mid eighteenth century,

> William Bulkeley of Brynddu, Anglesey . . . is able to refer to persons of his own class by means of a surname or by naming [their] residence . . . [but] when he refers to servants or craftsmen or peasants, he frequently uses *ap*, or just uses the christian name; the surname does not seem to exist.

A century or so later, in 1852, the Registrar-General's Annual Report stated that "hereditary surnames" could "scarcely be said to be adopted among the lower classes in the wilder districts, where, as the marriage registers show, the Christian name of the father still frequently becomes the patronymic of the son".[3] In the same way, most people in the Highlands of Scotland had no second names or no call to use them before the later eighteenth century. Only when they were dispersed or moved away did they assume the clan names of their home districts as family names.

Always on the margins of Christian society, the Jews were a special case. Jews had dual names in the medieval period, that is a Hebrew religious or first name and a non-Jewish name, by which they were known in Gentile milieus, for example Rabbi Juda called Leon, or Ephraim called Susskind. Some of them also acquired second names in the same ways that Gentiles did. But the shifting patronymic was the most typical of these, and fixed family names were rare outside the élite through into the eighteenth century.

Hereditary family names appeared first among the Sephardim, usually formerly "converted" Jews from Spain and Portugal. In Venice in the sixteenth and seventeenth centuries, for example, Jews seem usually to have had fixed second names: Isaac Cohen, Simon Scocco, Mair Lambros; and only a few, the less well-off, had patronymics. Converted Jews who secretly returned to Judaism – they could not do this openly in a Catholic country – might take or retake Jewish names. Tristao da Costa, for example, was also known as Abraham Habibi; Filipe de Nis or Denis as Solomon Marcos. Leonardo Dona, Doge of Venice, commented in 1608:

> At home and within themselves they live as Jews. All have a name, the men and the women too, either Turkish or Jewish, by which they are called at home; but outside their houses they have a Christian name. And if you ask one of the children, "What is your name?" he will answer, "At home they call me Abraham, but in the street Francesco."[4]

However, we have seen that such double naming was characteristic of genuine Jews from early on, and it should not be taken necessarily as a sign of religious dissembling or uncertainty. It is certain that new Jewish converts changed their names, taking new "Christian" first names, but also often new second names, usually from their godfathers or sponsors. So Nathan Cohen, baptized in 1658, became Nicolò Dolfin. Others became Pisani, Cornaro, Giustinian, all distinguished patrician names. This suggests that the Jewish second name was a stigma that it was opportune to discard.

The restored Jewish community in England after 1657 was also Sephardic and of Iberian origin. The great merchants it mainly comprised all had family names: Diego Rodrigues Marques; Isaac Pereira; Fernando Mendes da Costa. Ashkenazi, who came in from the end of the seventeenth century, were Yiddish-speaking and generally much poorer. They did not have second names proper, but shifting patronymics, which became converted to Abrahams, Isaacs and Jacobs English-fashion.

The story is the same in France. The Sephardic Jews of Bordeaux, Bayonne and the Comtat had family names as a rule in the seventeenth and eighteenth centuries: Mendès, Gomès, Dasilva. As in England, they were of course Spanish and Portuguese names, "Jewish" only by association. Among the Ashkenazim of Eastern France, the situation was different. Some among the élite had fixed second names, with Lévy, Cahen or Kahn, Bloch and Weil being among the most common. But most French Ashkenazim still employed the shifting patronymic where they used second names at all. Some migrants from Alsace-Lorraine to Nantes were known in the 1770s and 1780s as "the man named Jacob", "Jacob's wife", and so on. The mayor of Metz, trying to regularize the *état-civil* in 1808, reported that nothing is more common . . . than to find a son bearing a different surname from his father, a brother from a brother, and to discover individuals having borne one name decide to take another . . . But this is nothing compared with the situation of the women: at least half of them do not themselves know what their real names are, and it is not possible to establish that they really have second names.[5]

It was this letter of an exasperated bureaucrat, to the Prefect, which prompted the imperial decree of 20th July 1808 requiring all Jews in the French Empire to adopt and declare a fixed first and second name. Such a requirement was imposed at around the same time by the governments of Austria, Prussia and Russia, as part of a general regulation of their Jewish populations. In France, Prussia and elsewhere, this was accompanied by a degree of emancipation and forced modernization.

What kinds of names did Jews adopt or have imposed on them? Patronymics could be frozen into second names, dropping the "son of" element: for example, Isaac Jacob (Alsace); Grassini or Grassino (Modena), from the Hebrew Ghershom, Gherescion or Grassin. Patronymic suffixes were common among Ashkenazim in eastern and central Europe, for example Mendelssohn or Moischewitch; but these were little used in France and Italy where such suffixes were generally absent.

Second names taken from places were especially important, reflecting the experience of migration. Both Sephardim and Ashkenazim had used such names well before 1800, though often on a nickname basis. Most old Sephardic names record places from which their bearers had been expelled or places of transit following the expulsions of the early modern period: Belmonte, Spinoza, Medina – from Spain; Florentino, Modiano or Modigliani (Modena), Finzi (Faenza) – from Italy. The oldest Ashkenazi names were also place-names: Auerbach, Epstein, Heilbronn, etc. Place-names predominated in both communities in France after 1808, for example, Milhaud, Lunel, Valabrègue in the Comtat; Durkheim (Turquem), Fould (Fulda), Dreyfuss (Trèves) in Alsace-Lorraine.

Occupational second names were rare. In Alsace-Lorraine, one finds Halphen (changer), Kaufmann (merchant), Schneider (tailor). Second names could also be taken from official positions, especially Rabbi and Cantor. Distinct here are the names indicating membership of the priestly castes, Cohen and Levi, which appear in a variety of forms. Second names from nicknames were also rare. A special category here were animal names taken from the emblems associated with particular Hebrew first names: Leib, Leibel, Léon, Lyons from the lion of Judah; Hirsch, Hersch and Herschel (hart or deer) from Naphtali; Wolf from Benjamin; and Berl, Baer, Berman from the bear of Issachar. In the ghetto of Frankfurt-on-the-Main (and elsewhere), houses were identified by signs depicting animals and other creatures and objects. These were often taken as second names, giving rise, for example, to Birnbaum (pear-tree), Engel (eagle), Schiff (boat) and, of course, Rothschild (red shield). A family of Italian Jews used the second name Rapa from their raven emblem from the fifteenth century. This name later became Rapa di Porto, from their residence in a suburb outside the gates of Mantua. When they moved to Austria, the name became Rappaport.

Along with second names already in use or developed from existing names or appellations were names foisted on Jews by officials. Registration could be hurried, difficult and confusing, and Jews might not have names ready or their choices might not be accepted. From the time of the naming legislation in German lands "date those bizarre names, which have become typically Jewish, formed by borrowing from plants and minerals".[6] Such names had to be German, part of an attempt to eliminate "old" Hebrew or Biblical names, and they were usually formed with a few elements, presumably to simplify the operation. So Blume (flower) gave Blumenfeld, Blumenberg, Blumenthal, etc.; Rose gave Rosenberg, Rosenthal, Rosenblatt; Stein gave Finkelstein, Bernstein, etc. There was also some echo here of the emblem and house-sign names. Migration spread these names to France and the English-speaking world. Some Jews without second names simply borrowed names that were already common Jewish ones, like Dreyfus, Lévy and Blum in Alsace-Lorraine. All these procedures meant that there were often relatively few Jewish second names in existence in a community, and certain names were specifically Jewish.

Though many Jewish second names were somewhat casually acquired, they could quickly become the focus for strong family identity and pride, like Gentile names. Alfred Dreyfus, for example, from a well-assimilated French family, in his fight against the wrongful accusation of treason made against him in 1894, often referred to his desire to save his family and its name from dishonour. Others with the family name Dreyfus, unrelated to Alfred, however, abandoned it during the affair, and Alfred's faithful brother Mathieu was even forced to adopt an alias for a while. This is paradigmatic of the stigma attaching to Jewish names generally in the post-Emancipation era. The Marquis de Montfanon in Bourget's novel *Cosmopolis* (1893) declares typically of the Hafners: "Their name, their faces, proclaim them to be Jews."[7]

There was a strong incentive in this situation to avoid inconvenience, discrimination and hostility by adapting or changing one's name. Meshe David Osinsky, who was born at Kurkel in the Russian Pale of Settlement around 1885, came to England in 1900. He soon started to use the name Maurice or Morris Burton, taking the second name apparently from Burton-on-Trent, which he happened to pass through in a train, and later he used the trading name Montague Burton. In 1917, he successfully applied to use this name rather than Osinsky, writing:

> I am quite satisfied that . . . publishing my name rather than the name
> of the firm under which I trade will have a most serious prejudicial

effect upon the success of my trade especially among the large number of retail traders.

It is not clear whether the prejudice was because he had already established a reputation with the name Montague Burton, or whether there was specific hostility against a foreign-sounding and Jewish name, particularly during the war. It was from about this time that he also began personally to use the new name. It is important to note here that Burton was a Zionist, very active in Jewish concerns and charities and not at all anxious to conceal his Jewishness. A number of other successful English Jewish entrepreneurs also changed their names. In England, certain "new" second names were preferred by Jews: Gordon, Harris, Lewis, Montague, Morris, Morton. Mencken relates an anecdote from the London *Jewish Daily Post* in June 1935.

> A Mrs Selby was introduced to a Mrs Levy at the bridge-table. "Are you related", asked Mrs Levy, "to the Selbys of Sydney?" "No", answered Mrs Selby, "the Sydney Selbys are Silverbergs, while we are Schneiders."

This meant of course that the new names came to attract the same antisemitic prejudice as the old. "Leopold Norfolk Gordon had a house in Park Lane", we learn in a novel published in 1905; "As may be guessed from his name, he was a Jew."[8]

In France, names were put into French forms. Alfred's father, Raphael, changed Drëyfuss to Dreyfus around 1860. Complete name changes also occurred, especially, it seems, among intellectuals. André Maurois was originally Emile Herzog; Francis de Croisset, actually from Belgium, was Franz Wiener. Much later, after the Second World War, many Jews from French North Africa "tried to dissimulate their origins by modifying their family names", but for others "it was a question rather of making their names of Hebrew or Judeo-Arabic origin conform to Francophone phonetics". There was a desire to assimilate but also a clear attachment to the family name and the history that it represented. This dual concern can also be seen in the first-name choice of North African Jews. French first names were often chosen, but they were versions of existing Jewish names and continued the traditional transmission of names within families. As Bahloul concludes, North African Jews wished "to insert themselves into Francophone culture but without forgetting the genealogical chain into which they had been born".[9]

To return to the Gentile world, second names relating to place or occupation that were still functional are found in the early modern period and later. "Names like Olaw in Flattabustare, Rasmus in Ocraquoy and Magnus in Howkenasetter . . . were still typical of Shetland in the sixteenth century." Women were still designated by place in nineteenth-century Swaledale, for

example Mary O'Kisdon. In several regions of France, the family was traditionally named after the farm where it lived. In Alsace, this was the hof-
name, so-called from the "hof" "or inalienable part of the patrimony, made
up of the house and the lands around it, which was usually transmitted to
the eldest son". Similar customs existed in the Liège region and in south-
western France. In Béarn, there were in effect two superimposed onomastic
systems: one in which the family-household was named after the house,
and a later system, in which a family name passed from father to children.
Until recently, the first was the most important, and family names derived
from house-names. In a sense, "the house transmitted its name to the person
who succeeded as its head", and this person did not need to be an heir by
blood of the previous occupant.[10]

In England, Cook was perhaps the last occupational title to hold its own
against the inherited name. Justice Shallow, welcoming Sir John Falstaff,
says: "Some pigeons, Davy; a couple of short-legged hens, a joint of mutt-
on, and any pretty little tiny kickshaws. Tell William Cook." It is still occasionally the custom for tradesmen in England to identify themselves by their
trades, for example Peter Woodcock of Norwich telephoning: "This is Peter
the painter." Such designations were also used for the better identification
of individuals. William Cole, the Rector of Bletchley, sometimes referred to
his parishioners in this manner in the 1760s, for example, "Mr Stevens the
glover on the Green" – to distinguish him from other Stevenses; "John
Garner the Tailor"; or "Jonathan Daniel's daughter Dinah". The minutes of a
meeting of the Gaelic Society of Inverness in February 1898 referred to "Mr
John Macdonald, wood merchant" – in a situation where there must have
been several John Macdonalds.[11]

We can also see name formation taking place. Gough relates that a man
known as "Welsh Franke" came to Myddle some time in the later seventeenth century from Wales.

> He lived as a plough-boy with William . . . Goslin . . . and people
> called him Franke Goslin; but when he was married [to a local
> woman] he was called to the [manorial] Court, and when the Stew-
> ard asked him his name, he said Franke. And what else? says the
> Steward. He said, Francis. Then the Steward asked him his father's
> name, and he said it was David; so he got the name of Francis
> Davis.[12]

There could not be a neater demonstration of the way in which fixed
second names met a legal or bureaucratic requirement. On the Continent,
examples may be found much later, like the rare Italian Ferrovia for a family
that lived near or worked for the railway.

All the transitional forms that we have encountered could still be found
in this later period: shifting patronymics; parents and children, and siblings,

with different second names; multiple designations; senior and junior. But two archaic modes of naming were particularly persistent: the use of the "dit" or "alias" formula; and orthographic inconsistency. Branches of the Paquay family at Malmédy used the "dit" formula on the way to adopting new second names: Quirin Paquay dit Osterman (d. 1672); Léonard Paquay le Jeune dit Léonardi (1638–1716). The form was quite common in Béarn and Gascony down to the eighteenth century; it was also found in Geneva and in French Louisiana. It continued into modern times in Belgium, being used rather like the hyphenated double second name in Britain. So a school-teacher in 1948 was called Denise Seres dit Batist, in fact "a corruption of Seresia di Batista, a noble family name of Spanish origin" found in the Antwerp region in the seventeenth century. Another example, that of the Laureys dit Tissens family that ran a restaurant at Hoeilaert, combined an established family name with a nickname.[13]

"Alias" was used in similar circumstances in England. In his will, Swift left a legacy to "Mrs Mary Swift alias Harrison", presumably a woman who had been married twice, since her mother was Martha Whiteway. The alias formula was not uncommon at Myddle in the seventeenth century, especially for Welshmen like Francis Jones alias Reece. Later and more generally it became a designation for marginal people or criminals, like "John Finnamore, alias Boswell, a vagabond fiddler" convicted of burglary in Oxfordshire in 1759; he was probably of mixed gypsy and "gorgio" descent.[14]

> "What's your name, sir?" inquired the judge [in the Bardell versus Pickwick trial].
> "Sam Weller, my lord," replied that gentleman.
> "Do you spell it with a 'V' or a 'W'?" inquired the judge.
> "That depends upon the taste and fancy of the speller, my lord," replied Sam;
> "I never had occasion to spell it more than once or twice in my life."

Here, as in other matters, Sam Weller highlighted the typical. As we have noted in connection with first names, orthographic uniformity was not achieved in England until the late eighteenth or early nineteenth century, Johnson's *Dictionary* of 1755 being an important signpost. General spelling, he declared in the Preface, had been "to this time unsettled and fortuitous".[15]

Considerable variety in the spelling of second names was found, especially at the start of the early modern period. The Lisle Letters of the 1530s may be taken as representative of their times. As their editor notes, "Arthur Lisle signs himself Lyssle, but is addressed or written of as Lile, Lyly, Lylie, Lysle, Lyssley, Lisley, Lisle, etc." The Granvilles or Grenvilles signed Graynfeld, Graynffelde or Granfyld, and were addressed as Craynfelde, Grenfild, Greenfilde, etc. Many other examples could be cited. Things had not changed much by the seventeenth century. The designer of Hatfield House around 1610 was Robert Lemyinge, Liming, Lyming or Liminge, and the clerk of the works at the New Exchange in London in 1608–9 was William Southes, Southeast, Suthes or Soothes. Swift's mother was Abigail Erick, a name also spelled, according to him, Herrick or Heyrick. Granville was still not fixed by this time. As Dr Johnson noted, George Granville, later Lord Lansdowne, who was born in 1665, also appeared as Greenville or Grenville. Much later, Admiral Sir Richard Strahan was also given the "Scottish style" Strachan in 1809; and the MP and diarist Thomas Creevey was addressed as "Crevey" in 1810.[16] Uniform spelling did not really become *de rigueur* among the upper and middle classes in England until around 1830, with the lower classes trailing behind, as Dickens suggests.

We have already noted the great orthographic variety of Scottish names, which continued into the modern period. Irish names were similarly Protean. Gaelic spelling of names was not itself uniform even in the modern period, and the linked processes of anglicization and corruption compounded the situation. This meant that for the commoner names there were always three or four variants: Ó Cathasaigh or Ó Catasaig, O'Cahessy, O'Casey and Casey; Mac Domhnaill, M'Donaill, Macdonald, Macdonnell, Donnell, for example. For less common names, or those more difficult for English people to pronounce, the versions could be far more numerous. Mac Guagain, Mac Guaicin or Mac Guaigin, itself a corrupt form of Mac Eochaidhin, could become MacQuiggan, MacGoogan, MacCookin, MacWiggan, Pigeon or Fidgeon. Mac Giola Choinnigh has 24 variants in Woulfe's list of names, and Mac Giollabhuibhe has 33.

Though there was a trend towards standardization from the end of the medieval period, "the spelling of French second names was not completely fixed until the nineteenth century".[17] Members of the élite were not consistent down to the time of the Revolution, and variation was even more marked in rural areas and areas of non-French language. In Alsace, for example, into the nineteenth century, all kinds of variations are found: in initial consonants, in vowels, in suffixes; and names were rendered into French from German and vice versa. Some names experienced a particularly large number of variant forms, for example the members of one family in a single parish between 1724 and 1809 had their family name Krähenbühl spelled 30 different ways. For France, we have some figures for the incidence of second-name spelling variation. At Rouen in the seventeenth and eighteenth centuries, 15 per cent of men's names and 20 per cent of women's had significant spelling variation; at Grisy-Suisnes (Seine-et-Marne) 16 per cent of second names had spelling discrepancies in the period from 1750 to 1765 but only 3 per cent between 1830 and 1860.

Even where second names were officially established, they might not be used locally. An English visitor to Corsica noted that "surnames have been fixed but recently, if indeed they can be said to be fixed at all . . . Even now,

though legally necessary, surnames are in practice regarded by the peasantry as an altogether secondary consideration", with Christian names and
nicknames being used instead. This situation continued in most parts of the
island down to the present day. Again, on the Aran Islands around 1900,
people were known by patronymics and/or nicknames. The schoolmaster
told Synge

> that when he reads out the roll in the morning the children repeat
> the local name all together in a whisper after each official name, and
> then the child answers. If he calls, for instance "Patrick O'Flaharty",
> the children murmur, "Patch Seaghan Dearg" [Patrick, son of John,
> plus nickname] or some such name, and the boy answers.[18]

In the Haute-Garonne before the nineteenth century, official names were
used in the parish register, as we have seen, but not in the crucial land
survey or *cadastre*.

Official and unofficial names might also be combined or varied. In the
Bigouden, naming in the mid twentieth century was still "always done by
joining first name, family name, nickname and place of residence". At Minot,
"everyone possessed three names: a family name, a first name and a nickname; according to the circumstances, they were used together or separately". In Provence, well into the nineteenth century and among the élite,

> the family name was reserved to the eldest son, younger sons
> being called by their first names. So [the poet] Frédéric Mistral [in
> French], who was a *cadet*, was actually called "Moussu Frederi"; his
> father was Mistral, his elder brother Mistralet, and his elder sister
> Mistraleto.[19]

Such declension of female names was also found elsewhere.

The relative status of the formal second name is reflected in certain
techniques and styles. An indicator of the continuing importance of the first
name as *the* name is found in early name listings. Febvre noted that in
sixteenth-century catalogues of authors, their names "are cited in alpha-
betical order not of family but of first names: all the Jacobus, then all
the Johannes, and the Paulus, and the Petrus". This style is followed in the
Roman *Index of Prohibited Books* in the early modern period. Again, in the
southern Netherlands "at the end of the seventeenth century, the clerks of
law courts and lay notaries still drew up lists of their protocols in alphabet-
ical order of first names".[20] Only with trade directories of the eighteenth and
nineteenth centuries and bureaucratic documentation from the same period
does listing by second name become predominant and then universal.

State control of naming was formally established on the Continent. As we
saw in the case of French Jews, those without "proper" second or family

names were required by law to have them. Mass migration to the cities, together with schooling, factories and conscription, multiplied the need for uniform and simple ways of identifying individuals and families, while helping to spread and impose them. This process is also reflected in usage, in family attachment to the second name, and in its standardization.

One gauge of the emphasis accorded to the second name, which we have already used for an earlier period, is the substitution of initials for first names. Initials are found in both the Paston letters of the fifteenth century and the Lisle letters of the early sixteenth century, though they are not common. By the eighteenth century, the practice of signing with initials was well established. Lord Herbert's correspondents in the 1770s and 1780s, for example, sign themselves W. Coxe, H. Dalrymple, R.M. Keith, and so on. There are some indications that at this time, the use of initials could be a sign of social inferiority. There are echoes of this in Dickens' Wilfer in *Our Mutual Friend* (1864–5). "Shy, and unwilling to own to the name Reginald, as being too aspiring and self-assertive a name", he simply signed himself R. Wilfer.[21] The general custom continued into the nineteenth and twentieth centuries, even among intimates and family members. The form was also used by women. Dorothy Osborne in the 1650s was D. Osborne and, after her marriage, D. Temple. Jane Austen in letters to her sister Cassandra in the 1790s was J. Austen. Though there may be exceptions, authors do not seem to have used initials on their books until the late nineteenth and early twentieth centuries: A.E. Housman (1896); E.M. Forster (1905); T.S. Eliot (1917). In modern Britain and Europe, the initial never clearly indicated the name as with Roman *praenomina*. It simply referred to any name or names with the right first letter or letters. It was a derivative of written culture and bureaucracy, a label attached to second names in milieus where the first name was irrelevant or unimportant.

Further contraction to initials for both names was a mark of intimacy or was used for convenience, usually the first. Dorothy Osborne addressed her husband in 1670 as "My Dearest Heart" and signed herself D.T.. Marianne Dashwood, in love with Willoughby and believing that they are to be married, signs letters to him M.D. in Jane Austen's *Sense and Sensibility* (1811–13). Friends, too, employed the contraction. Jane Welsh Carlyle in the mid nineteenth century used J.C. and J.W.C. in correspondence with those close to her. Reference to persons via initials only seems to be a modern phenomenon, deriving almost certainly from the written signature of someone in authority. An early example is that of Joseph Rowntree, who was known as J.R. at his York works in the 1880s. Here, as with initialled authors, the initials have become a kind of name, transcending their bureaucratic origins.

The use of second names in address or reference was always part of a broader system of etiquette that involved first names and titles too, and we will return to the latter. But use of the second name alone is also a guide to the latter's importance. In England, the second name alone was used from the sixteenth, but especially from the eighteenth, to the mid twentieth century, in particular circumstances. First, it was used by males to address or refer to close friends and social equals. So Lord Pembroke wrote in the 1760s to "My Dear Hamilton". Dr Johnson sometimes addressed Boswell as such, and he referred to close male friends by nicknames or second names, for example "Wilcox, the bookseller", or "poor dear Beauclerk". This practice continued until the 1960s. In Graham Greene's *The Heart of the Matter* (1948), for example, in a colonial setting during the Second World War, males of the same standing use the second name only among themselves. "Mr" or military title is used for men less closely known, by women for men in public, and by social and ethnic inferiors. Again, in Anthony Powell's *The Soldier's Art* (1966), also set at the time of the Second World War, the *arriviste* Widmerpool, a non-regular officer, complains of another officer, a regular, for his failure to adhere to the conventions in the use of rank titles:

> "I'm surprised any decent Line regiment could put up with him. They might at least have taught him not to announce himself to another officer . . . as '*Colonel* Hogbourne-Johnson.' . . . Hogbourne-Johnson is supposed to know better. The C.R.A. doesn't say, 'This is *Brigadier* Hawkins,' he says 'Hawkins here.'"

As this indicates, usage was part of a subtle code. "The question at what age, or at what degree of intimacy, one shall say Smith . . . instead of 'Mr Smith'", a guide noted in 1936, "is regulated by class distinctions fairly well defined, or by the conventions of a group, or by the nature of the occasion."[22]

Second names could be used to show social inferiority. A letter in the Lisle collection referred in 1537 to the steward of the manor of Kybworth and "Crowder, his man". Dr Thomas Eyre wrote in 1779 of the death of Lord Pembroke's land steward, "poor Adcock". Lord Pembroke himself made a nice distinction in addressing the two men who accompanied his son on the Grand Tour in the 1770s. The Reverend William Coxe, a Fellow of King's College, Cambridge, was always "Mr Coxe", while the penniless Captain Floyd, who shared his patron's military profession, was "Floyd". Servants, male and female, were often addressed by their second names, as were employees. Dover Wilson worked closely during the First World War with George Thompson, a joiner from Halifax and organizer of the Workers' Education Association in Yorkshire. "He said to me one day", Wilson relates, " 'I wish you would not call me Thompson.' I asked why not. 'Only the boss calls us by our surnames', he replied." This usage had an effect on general working-class usage. In a West Cumberland village in the 1950s, second-name usage was reserved for working men "of low prestige" within their own class.[23] Second names were also used in institutions, for other ranks in the armed forces, and for boys in schools.

Women sometimes joined in the upper-class male usage of second names for close male friends. Willoughby is so addressed in *Sense and Sensibility* by the Dashwood girls, when he is regarded as a potential or actual fiancé. But generally through the nineteenth century and the first half of the twentieth, "ladies did not address gentlemen by surname alone and were not supposed to refer to them without the courtesy title of Mr". An exception here was in addressing or referring to husbands. In a Kent will of the seventeenth century, a woman requested to be buried "near my first husband Robinson".[24] Jane Welsh Carlyle referred through the mid nineteenth century to her husband as "Carlyle". By around 1850, however, the practice was becoming either old-fashioned, provincial or lower-class.

In the seventeenth and eighteenth centuries, second names were sometimes used to refer to women. In his obituary elegy of 1627, Michael Drayton called Lady Olive Stanhope simply "Stanhope". Pepys referred to his wife's companion in 1662 as "Gosnell". In Congreve's *The Way of the World* (1700), Mrs Marwood and Mrs Fainall are sometimes referred to by second name alone. But this usage was later virtually unknown. The only exceptions were for servants, or where the woman had a doubtful reputation, or where the intention was not polite. In the second category is Lord Pembroke's reference in a letter of 1781 to the mistress of Charles James Fox: "Sir Joshua Reynolds is now painting Armstead"; or Sydney Smith's in one of 1843 to her sister: "Remember me to the Norton", that is to Caroline Norton, whose husband had brought an adultery charge against Lord Melbourne in 1836. In the third category is Lord William Russell's designation of the Princess Lieven and the Marquesa Durazzo as "the Lieven" and "the Durazzo".[25] The addition of the article was reserved to women and had a special derogatory tone. Famous actresses or singers were also dubbed in this way.

Family continuity was marked, as we have seen, via the transmission of first names, but the family name par excellence had become the second. As such, there was a primary concern to perpetuate it. This accompanied the desire, within patrilineal systems, to have a direct male heir. When Lady Lisle was believed to be pregnant in 1536, her agent Husee wished that she might have a son so "that the name survive and spring anew" and in order to advance "the name of the noble Plantagenet". The same wish was detected 240 years later in the humbler breast of the Southwark brewer, Henry Thrale, by his friend Dr Johnson. After the death of Thrale's only son, Johnson explained to Boswell that having a succession of daughters was a limited consolation: "Sir, he wishes to propagate his name." Where male heirs failed, many families took special and elaborate precautions to ensure the perpetuation of the family name and fortune through the female line. A good example is provided by the Percy family in the late seventeenth and eighteenth centuries. With the death of Jocelyn Percy, the 11th Earl of Northumberland, in 1670, the title and name became extinct and the family properties devolved upon a female child, Lady Elizabeth. When she was married for the third time to the 6th Duke of Somerset, it was a condition of the marriage that any children born of it should bear the name and arms of Percy. In the event, this condition was waived, though its aim was ultimately achieved. The 7th Duke of Somerset (who had been summoned in his father's lifetime to Parliament as a peer under the name Baron Percy) had a son, who died in his youth, which meant that the Somerset title went to a distant cousin, and a daughter, another Lady Elizabeth, who married Sir Hugh Smithson. In 1750, he succeeded to the newly revived earldom of Northumberland, and he and his wife at the same time "assumed for themselves and their heirs the surname and arms of Percy".[26]

Settlements were quite commonly used at this time "to direct inheritance through females to found cadet lines, who would perpetuate the paternal name and arms of the heiress". Changing names by heirs in these or similar circumstances was not uncommon among the British élite. For example, William Windham (III) of Felbrigg died in 1810 without children, leaving the estate to William Lukin, the grandson of his mother by her first marriage; Lukin took the name Windham on succeeding. About the same time, Jane Austen's brother Edward "took the name of Knight, with the estates left him by his father's cousin and patron, Thomas Knight".[27]

A less drastic step was for the beneficiary simply to add the new name to his own, though the new name usually became the principal one. After Sir Thomas Spencer Wilson, 6th Baronet, married the daughter of the Reverend John Maryon in 1767, acquiring the manor of Great Canfield in Essex, the name Maryon was added to that of Wilson, though the names were not formally hyphenated until the late nineteenth century. Lady Holland told her son in 1828: "Your friends the Dawsons have under Lady Caroline Damer's will assumed the name of Damer", becoming the Dawson Damers. Lady Caroline was "the sole surviving heiress of the Earl of Dorchester". As these examples indicate, the practice was at first one of the nobility and gentry, but it spread in the nineteenth century to the middle classes. It was well-established, for example, among the "intellectual aristocracy" of the later nineteenth century, studied by Annan, with the Babington Smiths, the Arnold-Fosters, the Morley Fletchers and so on. Snobbery and the wish to be distinguished were clearly factors by now. This is confirmed from the summit of Victorian society. The painter Holman-Hunt was told by Queen Victoria "We consider Hunt too ordinary a name for such an extraordinary man; we would like you to use a hyphen", which he subsequently did. By the end of the nineteenth century, the "double name" or "double-barrelled name" was a favourite target for satirists exposing middle- and lower-middle-class pretentions. In *The Diary of a Nobody* (1892), for example, we have "the young fellow Fosselton", who insisted on being called Burwin-Fosselton.[28]

More seriously, as the second name became the focus for family identity, family honour and reputation rested on it. Lady Anne Barnardiston wrote in

1641 to Sir Simonds D'Ewes in connection with the reinstatement of her step-grandson, Sir Nathaniel, to his living:

> The name of Barnardiston is and ever shall be precious to me; and if any of that name, especially the lustre of the house, should undergo justly any tart censure or incur an hard conceit amongst his neighbours, . . . it would ever much divert me, in these my declining days.

After the young Charles Burney was sent down from Cambridge in 1727 for stealing books from the University Library, his father's initial reaction was that he should change his name, so as not to dishonour that of Burney. Similar concerns were present a century later in the great Whig Russell family. Lord William Russell, a younger son, wrote to his wife in 1828 about the education of their sons: "They bear an illustrious name . . . I should be proud and gratified if my children uphold it." When Lord William later embarked on an affair with a Jewish woman in Germany, his stepmother, the Duchess of Bedford, warned him: "You must not allow yourself and others to tarnish the bright name of Russell."[29]

Though a degree of extramarital sexual behaviour was tolerated, even expected, among noble males – and females – at this time, the connection is clearly made between family reputation centred on the name and sexual honour. This was certainly present elsewhere in English society in the early modern period, and focused on women. Gough, for example, indicates the immoral reputation of a Mary Bickley by saying that she had "no better name" than her sisters. The symbolic loading of the family name persisted longest probably among the nobility, where it was anyway strongest. It was certainly draining away among the middle classes by the mid nineteenth century. Jane Welsh Carlyle told a cousin in 1842: "These [Welsh] girls in Edin[bu]r[gh] are nothing to me except in name."[30] Family names in the modern period tended to centre on the nuclear unit: the Smiths, the Joneses; while "making a name" had become an individual matter.

All of these aspects of the family name are also evident on the Continent. Name, family and renown were closely identified, especially among the nobility. To take an obvious example, when he was elevated to the cardinalate in 1622, Richelieu took his "family name for his church title" rather than the more usual title from his bishopric. He also took particular care to hand on the name via nephews and if need be sons of nieces. "Inheritance of the Richelieu title was to be . . . exclusive: those who received it were to bear the 'Sole name and none but the arms of the house of Du Plessis de Richelieu'."[31] Heirs changed their names on receiving inheritances. Honour was carried via the family name. Second names were accumulated.

The importance of the family name and its attachment to the nuclear unit is further demonstrated by the adoption of the husband's name by the wife.

The practice was normal in England at the start of the seventeenth century, according to Camden, but it was not universally followed. In parts of West Cumberland in the 1950s, it was still the "local custom" to continue "to call women by their maiden names after they are married".[32] Williams associated the custom with the coherence of the kindred, and it seems to have been characteristic of the north, including Scotland.

By the nineteenth century, among the élite, there was a further development: the denomination of a married woman in formal circumstances by both the second and the first name of her husband: Mrs John Smith. The custom of wives taking the second name remained extremely well entrenched by the mid and late twentieth century. Philip Larkin could assume in the 1950s that a potential wife would have

> . . . an instant claim
> On everything I own
> Down to my name

and muse on the "disused" status of the "maiden name" (an emblematic new term) once its erstwhile bearer had become

> . . . confused
> By law with someone else.

In fact the name change was not a legal requirement but a social convention, and one that has survived the onslaughts of feminism. According to a 1992 survey, 89 per cent of women changed their names on marriage. "Those women who do keep their maiden names are largely professionals who have secured a reputation with that name and don't want to lose recognition." Most of these women, however, only used their maiden names at work, "using their husbands' in their personal lives".[33]

Taking the husband's second name became established later on the Continent. "Most French women in the sixteenth century kept their maiden names all their lives: when necessary, the phrase 'wife of' or 'widow of' so-and-so was tacked on." In some regions, this remained the situation down to modern times. In Haute-Provence, for example, women retained their fathers' names after marriage: "The woman belongs for ever, from her birth to her death, to the lineage of her father and brothers." The same rule obtained in eighteenth-century Louisiana: "Marie Josette La Croix, who buried two husbands, is Madame Lacroix all through her adult life . . . It was not until well into the nineteenth century that American-French women lost their identities and became merely Mrs So-and-So."[34] Quite often in France itself and elsewhere through the early modern period to more recent times, either designation might be used. In the French-speaking southern Netherlands there was little uniformity in this respect in the seventeenth century, and, though by the late eighteenth century tax rolls usually listed married women and widows with their husbands' names, parish registers and censuses recorded wives with their original family names. At Minot, wives were usually known by their husbands' names by the nineteenth century, but they kept their maiden names in circulation too, as it were, if they had inherited commoning rights from their fathers. Though taking the husband's name became the rule in modern France, as in England the custom was never sanctioned by law. Indeed the Law of 6 Fructidor Year II, which remained in force into this century, discounted such a change, and married women were referred to in the *état-civil* and other official documents by their fathers' second names, sometimes using the formulae "Marie Bru épouse [or] femme Couderc", or "Marie Couderc née Bru".

Since having the family name signified belonging to the lineage and then the nuclear unit, it could not be accorded to illegitimate children. The usual recourse here, since, as Mercier put it in 1789 in his *Tableau de Paris*, they had "no father to their names", was to use the matronymic, and this indeed was taken to be a sign of illegitimate birth. A variation found in nineteenth-century Normandy was to give the child one of its mother's first names as a second name. Special names might also be used either because they were thought to be suitable, or to disguise the circumstances of the birth. The Provençal poet and mason, Mathieu Lacroix, born in 1819, was supposedly so-called because "it depicted so well the miseries and sufferings in the midst of which he would grow up",[35] being illegitimate. A disguised name was that of the daughter of Alexandre Dumas fils and Princess Naryschkin, born in 1860. She was registered under the name Colette, using a female first name as a second name, though not that of the mother.

Giving an illegitimate child its mother's name also seems to have been the preferred custom in early modern and modern England. At Myddle, for example, the illegitimate child of Elinor Hussey was called Nell Hussey, of Thomas Hall Richard Bickley after his mother. In fact, there may have been more divergence from this pattern in the past than has been supposed. The clergy and relatives might have an interest in pinning both the name and responsibility for the child on the father. At Gosforth in Cumberland, seventeenth-century parish registers reveal a number of illegitimate babies named after their fathers. In one case, a boy was named John Dickinson after the father, to which "alias Biby" – the name of the mother – was added. In Lancashire between around 1600 and around 1750, registration with the names of both parents joined by "alias" was common. In an unusual example at Myddle, the father's two names were given as baptismal names. The daughter of a man called Edge had "a bastard child" and confessed that Thomas Atcherley was its father. "At the baptizing of the child, old Edge [her father] was one of the godfathers, and he named the child Thomas Atcherley", which the minister after some hesitation accepted. A similar situation was found in some parts of Italy. In seventeenth-century Piedmont, unmarried mothers were frequently persuaded to declare the paternity of their children, who were then usually "baptized and even registered in the father's name".[36]

The father's name would also be sought and taken where he was of high status. This is nowhere more obvious than with royal bastards. Lord Lisle, the son of Elizabeth Wayte and Edward IV, was given the royal name Arthur Plantagenet. Much later, the sons of George III gave their names or titles to their numerous illegitimate offspring. The first children of Dora Jordan and the Duke of Clarence apparently had no second name immediately bestowed on them, but after 1804, they and subsequent siblings were Fitzclarences. Noble names had similar prestige. The writer Richard Savage, born in 1688, was baptized Richard Smith, Smith being the supposed name of his mother. But he later adopted the name Savage, which was that of Earl Rivers, whom he claimed to be his father. William Deane Poyntz, secretary to the British ambassador to Turin in the 1770s, was the natural son of Deane Poyntz. Among the English élite, conveying the family name to illegitimate offspring was, however, more common for daughters, since they posed no problem as far as inheritance was concerned.

A final case illustrates both a noble father's wish to give a bastard child his own name, and the practice of using invented names. In 1762, the 10th Earl of Pembroke, though married, ran off with Miss Kitty Hunter, and they had a son. "He was given the names Augustus Retnuh (Hunter reversed), and the surname Reebkomp, an anagram of Pembroke." He was subsequently informally recognized by Lord Pembroke and his family and continued to be known by and to use his strange invented name, shortened in the family to Reeb. He joined the navy, and his father wanted him to assume the Pembroke family name, Herbert, on being commissioned as Lieutenant. But Lady Pembroke resolutely opposed this proposition, and he was promoted as Lieutenant Reebkomp. The question arose again when he was promoted Captain in 1782, and as a compromise he was given the name of Montgomery.[37]

Foundlings of unknown parentage were also named in peculiar ways. At Auxerre in the later eighteenth century, most were given two baptismal names, one of which served as the second name, for example François Thomas. As with some illegitimates, it was as if they could not be given a proper second or family name. Another mode was to use the month of birth. This practice continued during the Revolutionary period, hence Cornélie Brumaire at Auxerre. Sometimes the second name recalled the place of the child's discovery. The *philosophe* D'Alembert was called Jean Le Rond, having been found on the steps of the church of St. Jean-le-Rond in Paris in 1717. An entry from the register of the parish of Saint-Julien de Lescar in Béarn followed the same principle. In October 1787 "a female infant was found on a dungheap beside the main road from Pau to Orthez" and was given the name Jeanne Marie Dominique Pauline Grand Route.[38] Abandoned children might also be called such names as Trouvé or Champi (found in a field). Institutions receiving foundlings might name them after the village from which they came, a practice found in Lower Normandy. Similar practices were found in Italy down to the early nineteenth century. Innocenti in Tuscany – from the name of the Foundlings Hospital in Florence – and Venturini in Piedmont were second names of foundlings. An official circular in 1812, applicable to the whole Napoleonic Empire, banned giving foundlings such distinctive names.

In England, foundlings were often named after the place where they were discovered. From London, we may cite Renold Falcon (1597) found in Falcon Court; Katherine Whitefryars (1627); and Harbotles Harte, "a poor child found at Hart's door in Fewter Lane" in 1611. As we have seen, the patron of the church where the child was baptized could sometimes supply its name: for example, "Roger Peeter, so named of our church" (1592). The circumstances of the birth could be generally referred to, as with John Found (eighteenth century, Plymouth); or the day of discovery used, for example, Richard Monday in Crabbe's *Parish Register* (1807). In Dickens' *Our Mutual Friend* (1864–5), Master or Mr Sloppy's name was explained by Mrs Betty Higden: "I always understood he took his name from being found on a sloppy night."[39]

Like first names, second names became standardized in the modern period, leaving orthographic and other variations behind. The process may be seen as an aspect of bureaucratization, but it also proclaimed the cultural hegemony of the prevailing nation-states.

In France, there was a general process of "francicization" of second names from the sixteenth century onwards, which ran parallel to the onset of centralization and linguistic dominance by northern French. Patois forms lingered longest in remoter regions, especially in the south. Saint-Jouan provides detailed examples from Béarn, where notaries of the Old Régime began a movement completed by fashion and the agents of the State in the nineteenth century.

Regional forms were also eliminated or altered in Britain. This is most obvious in Wales, Scotland and Ireland. Anglicization of Gaelic names in Highland Scotland occurred in three main ways. First, English or Lowland names with a similar sound might be adopted. So Mac a' Bhriuthain (son of the judge) could become Brown; Maceachran Cochrane; Gillebride Gilbert and hence Gibbon. Then names could be translated. Mac Ghille ghuirm (son of the blue lad) became simply Blue. Johnson or Johnston was substituted for Maciain; Clarke, Clark or Clarkson for Macpherson. Translating Mac into -*son* was common. Finally, the name could be shortened and/or spelled according to English style. So Macilchomhghain became Comhan or Cowan; and forms like Mackintosh, Maclean and Mackerras were used. This whole process occurred within the Highlands but received special impetus where people migrated. The poet David Mallet (*c.*1698–1765) belonged, according to Dr Johnson, to the Macgregor clan, whose members had been forced to abandon the name. His father took the name Malloch, that of a place, with which young David came to London in the early 1720s. He was advised to change it, however, since English people could not pronounce it.

Some names were proscribed in Scotland, as we have seen with the Macgregors, as a punishment for acts of rebellion, but there was no general policy of anglicization, such as was pursued in Ireland. A statute of 1465 required every Irishman living within the Pale, that is the counties of Dublin, Meath, Louth and Kildare, to take an English second name, derived from a town in England or Ireland, a colour, an occupation or an office. Official pressure to anglicize was maintained through the sixteenth and seventeenth centuries, though general acculturation was perhaps more effective within and beyond the Pale. There was no general legal ban on the O and Mac prefixes, but there was great political and cultural discouragement of their use. O'Conor Roe, for example, entered into an agreement in 1637, "in which he binds the Irish chiefs under his influence to give up the prefixes to their surnames". In the eighteenth and nineteenth centuries, the Irish Catholic élites "Englished" their names through acculturation and an inferiority complex, according to MacLysaght:

> while keeping their O's and Macs within the ambit of their own entourage (usually in the remoter parts of the country), they were so deeply conscious of belonging to a conquered nation that they frequently omitted the prefixes when dealing with Protestants, not only in legal matters but also in ordinary social intercourse . . . [So] MacDermot, Chief of the Name, though ranking as a prince among his own people and himself a prominent banker in the middle of the eighteenth century, invariably signed himself simply Anthony Dermott.[40]

As this indicates, discarding the prefix was the most obvious change of name and was very widely practised. Some names lost the O altogether, examples being Boyle, Higgins and Murphy. There were several other modes of anglicization, not always easy in practice to distinguish. At one end of the spectrum were attempts at transliteration. Irish and English versions of the same names existed from the Anglo-Norman period onwards, but most Englishing of second names of this kind was done in the later sixteenth century.

> The surname was written down more or less as it was pronounced but without any regard to the Irish spelling, which was itself inconsistent, as: O'Brien for Ó Briain; O'Callaghan for Ó Ceallagháin; O'Flanagan for Ó Flannagáin.

Though some standard forms emerged for the commonest names, this process could lead to many different English versions of the same Irish name

– we have alluded to the propensity of Irish names to great orthographic variety. The first transliteration attempts could also lead to further distortion and corruption. Mac Sheoinín, for example, was "pronounced MacKeoneen, and written MacIonyn, MacJonine, etc. in the records up to the middle of the seventeenth century". In the eighteenth century, the Mac was dropped and the form Jennings adopted. As Woulfe comments, however, in many cases the early anglicized forms were much nearer to Irish pronunciation of the time than at present. "O'Brien and O'Neill were originally pronounced O'Breen and O'Nail".[41] And the process of corruption was an internal process as well as being affected by external pressure.

Another possibility was to adopt or have imposed a similar-sounding English name. So Ó Dathlaoich might become Dolly; Ó Fionnachta Fenton via Finnerty; O'Hagan Hogg. In County Cork Ó Sealbhaigh became Shelley and in County Tipperary Shallow. There were also translations. Mac an or Ó Ghabhhhann and Mac or O Gowan became Smith; MacAnespie or Gillespie Bishop. Often the translations were incorrect. O'Heany, O'Henaghan and Mac Aneeny, all distinct names, were translated as Bird, under the mistaken impression that they incorporated the Irish "éan" for bird. Mac Aneeny was a transliteration of Mac Conaonaigh, which also took the form Conheeny, Cunneeny, and so on. This led to its being translated as Rabbit in Connaught through its resemblance to "coinín" or "coney".

There was a tendency, too, to conflate similar names via their Englished versions. So Ó Maol Sheachlainn became O'Melaghlin, which became absorbed by MacLoughlin. Mac Fhiachra, a County Galway sept, became Mac Keeghry, Keahery and finally Carey, along with at least five other names, including the Anglo-Norman Carew.

Among the élite, snobbery led some to adopt "posh" English names by one or other of these methods. So some O'Connors became Conyers; some Devlins D'Evelyns; some O'Mulligans or Mulligans Molyneux. Going one better than simply taking Englished versions of their Irish names, they picked aristocratic-sounding ones, some belonging to Anglo-Norman families.

Under the influence of general national sentiment and especially of the Gaelic League from around the 1890s, there was a reaction against anglicization. In particular, there was a return to the old O and Mac prefixes. In 1890, it has been calculated, for example, that "there were twice as many Connells as O'Connells", while by 1955 there were nine "O'Connells to every Connell". Similarly, in 1890, one-third of those registered with the name were "plain Brien", but fifty years later the name was "rarely to be found without the prefix".[42] There were some *faux pas* in this quest for national historical correctness. The Irish MacArthurs added Mac to an old Norse name that had never had it in the past, while the Gormans from County Clare and elsewhere, who had always been MacGormans, re-Hibernicized themselves as O'Gormans.

Titles

Titles were of the greatest significance in the hierarchical societies of early modern Europe and were generally used in both address and reference.

In England in the sixteenth century, "Master" was the usual title for upper-class men. All members of the élite in Ro. Ba.'s *Life of Syr Thomas More*, for example, are given this style: More himself, his sons-in-law, his friends, and members of the government and court. For the last, the title might be attached to the office: "Maister Attorney", "Maister Secretary"; otherwise it was joined to the second name. The same practice is found in the Lisle letters. In describing the dignitaries present at the arrival of Anne of Cleves on the outskirts of London in 1540, for example, an observer referred to "Master Baynton, Vice-Chamberlain", "Master Dennys, her Chancellor", "Master Carew", and so on. According to Serjeant Doderidge in 1588, "Whosoever studieth in the Universities, who professeth the liberal sciences, and . . . who can live idly and without manual labour and will bear the countenance of a gentleman, he shall be called Master." The term was still a normal form of address in the seventeenth century. A Puritan preacher who died in 1645, for instance, was known as "Master Dod".[43] The title seems also to have been in use from wife to husband, for another Puritan called in 1642 for this particular usage to be abandoned.

The abbreviation "Mr" is found in the early seventeenth century, and by the eighteenth century had ousted "Master" completely in genteel usage, relegating it to the lower orders and the young. In 1766, William Cole referred typically to a local Bletchley farmer and churchwarden, that is a man who did not belong to the gentry, as "Master Crane"; the new-born son of Lord Herbert was designated "Master Herbert" by his grandfather in 1788, an early example of a practice that would last until the twentieth century. "'Master', as a junior to 'Mister', is rather out of fashion", a hand book advised in 1936, "and is not much used except by and to servants, and in addressing letters to young gentlemen of tender years."[44]

The use of the title "Mr" was usual in Gough's *History of Myddle* for members of the clergy and gentry. The link between the title and status is shown in comments made in relation to the rise of a certain Thomas Baker. He leased Sweeney Hall and its demesnes from its owner Andrew Chambre, "who was now grown poor and would say: 'Formerly it was Mr Chambre and Tom Baker, but now it is Mr Baker and Andrew Chambre.'" In the eighteenth century, "Mr" was again the usual title accorded to all unrelated upper-class men. Parson Woodforde, for example, uses "Mr" invariably for the local élite, lay and clerical. In Boswell's *Life of Johnson*, schoolteachers, members of the Literary Club without other titles, country gentlemen, London writers, are all Mr So-and-So. But, at the same time, later in the century, the title was spreading more widely and downwards in society. Lord Pembroke recommended "Mr Wilson", a plumber, to his son in 1780; and

Parson Woodforde related in May 1790: "Mr Love the Painter dined with our folks today in the kitchen, he being painting my weather-cock."[45]

"Mr" remained the formal and polite term in the nineteenth century. When Silas Wegg in Dickens' *Our Mutual Friend* (1864–5) supposedly discovers that his employer is not entitled to his inheritance, he demonstrates the fact by omitting the "Mr" from his name: "I'm a-going to call you Boffin." As this indicates, "Mr" was an important token of respect, taken especially seriously perhaps on the margins of its range of usage. According to a later account, at a meeting of Cheltenham Chartists in the 1840s,

> somebody spoke of Tom Paine. Up jumped the chairman [an old blacksmith]. "I will not sit in the chair," he cried in great wrath, "and hear that great man reviled. Bear in mind he was not a prize-fighter. There is no such person as Tom Paine. Mister Thomas Paine, if you please."

Omission of the title could also be a sign of intimacy, as we saw in discussing second-name usage. In *Little Dorrit* (1855–7), Mr Meagles asks Arthur Clennam "for permission to address him with surname alone by way of increasing their friendship: 'We are delighted to see you, Clennam (if you'll allow me, I shall drop the Mister).'" By the twentieth century and down to the time of the Second World War, "Mr" was normally accorded to all men without other titles beyond the close circle of intimates. In the offices of the Port of London Authority before 1914, for example, "the youngest clerk was addressed as Mister. Slapdash abbreviations or nicknames were never used"; nor were first names.[46] Some eighteenth- and nineteenth-century wives addressed their husbands as "Mr", but this may have been eccentric as early as 1815. Mrs Palmer's custom in *Sense and Sensibility* of always referring to "Mr Palmer" was something of a joke.

Other male titles were used with stronger social differentiation built into them, at least for later periods. "Sir" was still attached to the names of clerics in the sixteenth century. The style persisted into the early seventeenth century, though "Master" or "Mr" was then becoming the preferred term, leaving "Sir" for knights and baronets. "Sir" was also used more generally in address to upper-class men. It was a term of respect used towards superiors or those in authority. So Lady Lisle addressed the upstart but powerful Thomas Cromwell as "Right worshipful sir" in 1533. Lady Ridgway, hoping to arrange a marriage between their children, addressed Sir Percival Willoughby in 1610 as "Right noble Sir".[47] "Sir" was also used by children addressing their fathers from the sixteenth century to the early twentieth. By the eighteenth century, "Sir" was also used among male social equals in formal situations. Dr Johnson addressed Boswell and other friends in letters as "Sir", and he frequently addressed protagonists in conversation in the same way. According to Chapman in 1936, this usage among social equals

had by then considerably declined and "Sir" in modern practice was restricted to certain very specific situations of social inequality: waiters and
others to customers or clients, and pupils to schoolmasters.

"Gentleman" following the name could be an alternative to "Master" or
"Mr". A plaintiff in the Court of Chivalry in 1638 was declared to be a
yeoman rather than a gentleman because he

> laboureth in husbandry, ordinarily with his own hands, holdeth the
> plough, maketh hay, selleth his corn at the market himself , , , and
> in the parish rates and other writings he is only written Richard
> Inckpen without the addition of "gentleman" to his name.[48]

Originally, "Esquire" was a term designating an apprentice knight, as we
have seen, but from the fifteenth century to the nineteenth it was a title
borne by members of the top layer of gentry. Around 1680, the heralds
reserved it to heirs of younger sons of nobles, heirs of knights, and *ex
officio* to sheriffs, justices of the peace, barristers at law and others. From
the later eighteenth century, the title was used more generally. The young
Lord Herbert had to be told in 1780 that it was not correct to use both
military rank and "Esquire" in writing to an officer. Here the "Esquire"
followed the name, and this style spread very generally among the middle
classes from the mid nineteenth century to the mid twentieth, surviving
longest in addressing letters. "Esquire" or "Squire" before the name was
mainly used to refer to country gentry by country people and servants. In
Sheridan's plays, for example, servants refer to Squire Acres, Squire Faulkland
and Squire Fashion. From this usage probably derives the modern demotic
and ironic "Squire" alone.

In the sixteenth and seventeenth centuries in England, "Mistress" was the
title given to women with status and authority, married and unmarried. So,
according to Ro. Ba., John More the younger married "Mistress Anne Chisacre,
a gentleman's daughter of worship in Yorkshire"; while More's daughter
after her marriage was "Mistress Margaret Roper". The title was applied to
noblewomen as well as commoners. Within families and households, the
title was used with the first name only. More referred to his wife as "Mistress
Alice"; Lady Lisle's daughters were "Mistress Katharine" and "Mistress
Bryggett".[49]

"Mistress" was already abbreviated to "Mrs" in the sixteenth century. In
the Lisle letters, we have Mrs Arundell for Mary Arundell (unmarried), and
Mrs Frances, Mrs Katharine and Mrs Anne for daughters of the family (also
unmarried). By the seventeenth and eighteenth centuries, "Mrs" had superseded "Mistress" entirely, though it was used in much the same way to
denote women of standing. By the late eighteenth and nineteenth centuries
all élite married women and many from the lower classes were "Mrs". Parson Woodforde, for example, referred to Mrs Custance, wife of the local

squire, but also to Mrs Andrews, a sick and poor parishioner to whom he sent some roast veal in 1793.

"Mrs" also continued to be used for unmarried women belonging to the élite and others of a certain status or age. In a letter to Sir Percival Willoughby in 1610, for example, Thomas Ridgeway referred to the latter's daughters as Mrs Bride, Mrs Lettice and Mrs Nell, only the first being married. When Cassandra Willoughby went as a young woman to act as housekeeper to her brother at Wollaton Hall, she referred to herself as "Mrs of Wollaton", and others called her "Mrs Cassandra". The same usage is found in the Barrington letters in the 1630s, and it persisted well into the eighteenth century and beyond. Swift wrote of Mrs Johnson and Mrs Long, both unmarried. Around 1730, Henry Hervey was wooing Mrs Kitty Aston, whom he subsequently married, while Samuel Johnson was in love with Mrs Hill Boothby, whom he did not. Johnson's stepdaughter Lucy Porter was addressed by him as "Miss", but when Boswell met her in 1775, she was Mrs Lucy Porter, "an old maid". By this time some uncertainty had appeared over the appropriateness of the titles accorded to age and spinsterhood. In Fanny Burney's *Camilla* (1796), Mrs Mittin asks:

> "Do you know, for all I call myself Mrs, I'm single?"
> 'Dear, la!", exclaimed Miss Dennel; "and for all you're so old!"[50]

"Mrs" was also adopted by actresses in the eighteenth and nineteenth centuries, whether they were married or not. In the eighteenth century, we have, for example, Mrs Cibber, Mrs Clive and Mrs Pritchard. Dora Bland first appeared on the stage as Miss Francis, but she soon took the stage name Mrs Jordan around 1780.

According "Mrs" to age and status lingered on to the later nineteenth and early twentieth centuries. Waterson notes of the housekeeper of Erdigg: "As at most large houses, her post entitled her to be referred to as 'Mrs' rather than 'Miss'" – like Cassandra Willoughby two or three centuries before. Again, M.V. Hughes recalls being taken as a child in London in the 1870s to see an old lady called Mrs Ayres.

> "Where is Mr Ayres?", I asked my mother one day, when we got out-side. "There isn't any Mr Ayres", she replied, "and there never was any Mr Ayres . . . They call her Mrs Ayres from courtesy, because she is so old."[51]

"Madam" or "Madame" had a more restricted usage. It was employed as a respectful title of address to socially superior women in the early modern period. The cleric James Harrison addressed Lady Joan Barrington in 1629, for example, as "Worthy Madame".[52] Tenants and junior relatives also used the term. A century and a half later, William Coxe addressed Lady Pembroke as "Madam" in the same way. The term was also used by children to upper-class mothers. By the later nineteenth and twentieth centuries, this title had become further restricted. It was used in letters to ladies one did not know and by shop assistants to customers, and, in the contracted form "Ma'am", to women of very high status, especially royalty.

The modern distinction between "Miss" for unmarried and "Mrs" for married women took some time to evolve. "Miss" was used for girls and unmarried women of higher status from the late seventeenth century, if not earlier. In a letter to his friend Bennet Langton in 1765, Dr Johnson sent compliments to "Miss Langton", "Miss Di" and Miss Juliet".[53] There was a clear distinction made in the usage between adult women, for whom "Miss" was attached to the second name, and children, for whom it was attached to the first. Also, as Johnson's compliments to the Langtons illustrate, the same distinction came to be made between the eldest daughter and her sisters. This is very clear, for example, in Jane Austen's *Sense and Sensibility*, where the elder sister is Miss Dashwood or Miss Steele and the younger Miss Marianne Dashwood or Miss Lucy Steele. "Miss' could also indicate social superiority at this time. Evelina in Fanny Burney's novel of 1778 is addressed and referred to by her lower-class relations, the Branghtons, as "Miss".

But to continue to call an adult women by "Miss" plus her first name was derogatory. In Congreve's *Love for Love* (1695), Miss Prue is "a silly country girl". "Miss" for an older woman also came to be associated with hopeless spinsterhood. Mrs Mittin expained her choice of "Mrs": "if one is called Miss, people begin so soon to think one an old maid, that it's quite disagreeable." Mr Wardle introduces his sister in *Pickwick Papers* (1836–7): "Miss Rachael Wardle. She's a Miss, she is; and yet she an't a Miss – eh, sir, eh?" This indicates also perhaps, as Phillipps notes for the later nineteenth century, that use of "Miss" without the name was becoming a lower-class habit, "grocerly", according to a character in a Gissing novel of 1905.[54] "Miss" continued and continues to be used formally for unmarried women (in competition lately with the uninformative "Ms"). It was also used like "Master" with the Christian name for children by nurses, servants and governesses down to the time of the Second World War. "Miss" alone now seems confined to pupils addressing or referring to schoolmistresses.

Certain other terms were used of and among the lower classes down to the end of the eighteenth century. The commonest were "Goodman" and "Goodwife", abbreviated to "Goody"; and "Gaffar" and "Gammer".

Titles were also universal on the Continent. At Strasbourg in the sixteenth century, the title denoted a person of "quality" and was used in the baptismal registers with the first name alone. "Herr, Doctor or Juncker (squire) served as appellations for members of the magistracy, clergy, upper bourgeoisie or nobility".[55] Among French immigrants to Geneva in the mid sixteenth century, various titles were used with both first and second names.

So we have "Noble Jehan Budé . . . Noble Ysabeau Monon" (1549); and "Noble et honnorable personne Pierre de Brenasses" (1550). "Honnorable homme" was also used for respectable bourgeois. "Honeste Jehan filz de honeste Michiel Seguyn" (1550) was a goldsmith from Paris; "Maistre Guillaume Senravi" (1550), a doctor of medicine from the Auvergne. Later on, for example at Saint-André-des Alpes in the seventeenth and eighteenth centuries, notaries used "Sieur" for bourgeois living nobly, for masters of the more prestigious crafts and for those who had held municipal office. "Monsieur" was used by the late eighteenth century in the same way, and was still a term for bourgeois men in the nineteenth century. It became a universal designation for men later in the nineteenth century. Here it was used formally with the second name, and in address alone.

Montaigne noted in 1580 that "women of quality are called Dames; the middling sort Damoiselles; and those of the lowest orders Dames again". Two centuries later the middle term had disappeared as a social title. Mercier noted of Paris in the 1780s that "all women are addressed as Madame, from a duchess to a flower-seller".[56] Though "Demoiselle" or "Mademoiselle" was tending to be used for young women, unmarried and married, "Madame" could also be applied to spinsters. In Italy, "Don" and "Donna" were the common titles of respect from the sixteenth century onwards, and survived in the rural south down to modern times. They tended to be replaced in the nineteenth century by "Signor" and "Signora", which became universal.

Titles (together with first and second names) provided a register of modes of address and referral that could be used to indicate subtle grades of social distance or relationship. Stendhal relates that his maternal grandfather, a member of the minor nobility of the Dauphiné and unusually a "liberal", revered Voltaire and ridiculed the royal family and the court. "He referred with disgust to *la* Du Barry [Louis XV's mistress] and the absence of the word *madame*, in the context of our usual exquisite manners, shocked me greatly." We have seen that among the Russells in the early nineteenth century first names and nicknames were commonly used, but a coolness between the Duchess of Bedford and Lady William could occasion and be reflected in a reversion to titles. So, in a letter to her stepson in 1832, the Duchess referred to "Lord and Lady Tavistock" and "Lord John", for his brothers and sister-in-law, rather than "Tavistock" and "John" or even "Tavy" and "Johnnikins". A little later the Duke wrote to Lord William in conciliatory fashion: "Tell Bessy, if I may presume to call her so". After a further breach in 1824, the Duke is back to formal terms, referring to his wife as "the Duchess". Different modes were also used in the public and private spheres, as we have made clear. Dr Johnson, for example, addressed his stepdaughter as "Dear Madam" on a letter in 1775, but inside the letter he called her "my dear love".[57]

Before the later eighteenth century, title usage reflected a largely unquestioned hierarchy. After the French Revolution on the Continent there was a brief period in which the old titles were rejected, but what then prevailed was an egalitarian bestowal of "Monsieur" and "Madame" and their equivalents on the whole population. There was no such clear-cut development in Britain. Both "Mr" and "Sir" as forms of address retained class connotations that meant that they were different from "Monsieur". But titles became negotiable within the class framework, as Fred Kitchen indicated in 1942. The gentleman farmer who

> farmed the Manor House . . . was one of the fussily important sort, and alderman and Justice of the Peace. If you wanted a favour of him, all you had to do was to pump hard on the handles at each end of his name. If you omitted the handles you drew no water.[58]

One further kind of title must be introduced to complete the picture. Kinship terms were used in address in the past to a far greater degree than now and involving a wider circle of kin. This reflects of course the greater importance of kinship ties generally and the larger scope of significant kin. We shall confine our discussion to England, where we have already encountered this phenomenon in the later medieval period.

The correspondence of the Barrington family in the early seventeenth century provides a good case-study. They were a higher gentry family from Hatfield in Essex. The senior member of the family was the widowed Lady Joan Barrington, who died in 1641. Her eldest son Thomas addressed a letter "to the honourable my very loving mother" and signed it "your most dutiful son". A younger son, John, opened a letter similarly "Dear mother" and signed "your obedient son". Siblings addressed each other as "good brother", "dearest sister" and so on, and signed accordingly. Uncles and aunts were treated in the same way by their nephews and nieces, and vice versa. So Sir John Bourchier addressed a letter "to the honourable his much esteemed ant [sic] the Lady Barrington" and signed "your firmly loving nephew". Robert Barrington referred to "my niece Mewx", and Judith Barrington to "my niece Wallop", while Elizabeth Masham, one of Joan's daughters, referred to "her uncle Altham", a relative by her mother's first marriage. "Cousin", too, was used in address and reference.

Most interesting perhaps is the usage vis-à-vis in-laws, who were assimilated to kin. Brothers-in-law were always referred to as "my brother Gerrard", "his brother Mildmay", and so on. Sir Gilbert Gerard, her son-in-law, addressed Lady Joan as "my honourable mother" and signed "your dutiful son"; Sir William Meux signed "your loving son", and William Masham opened a letter "dear mother". Lady Judith Barrington, wife of Francis, signed "your faithfully loving daughter" and referred to her sisters-in-law as "my sister Masham", "my sister Everett", and so on, using their married second names. More distant relationships might be treated in the same way. So Sir William Masham referred to "my son St. John", meaning the husband of his wife's daughter by a previous marriage. Richard Whalley addressed Lady Joan as "my honourable and most worthy sister" and signed himself "your ladyship's ever obliged weak brother", Lady Joan being the sister of his second wife. Relations by godparenthood were also addressed in the kinship idiom. Lady Mary Eliot, almost certainly a god-daughter, called Lady Joan "dear lady mother" and signed herself "your obedient loving daughter".[59]

Later in the seventeenth century, Pepys consistently refers to siblings, uncles and aunts, and cousins with the kinship title plus family name: "her sister Wight", "Uncle Fenner", my cousin Turner". The first name is attached less often to the kinship term and only occasionally the full name, as with "my Cousin Harry Alcocke". Pepys distinguished between male and female cousins, referring to "my she-cousin Porter" and "my she-Cousin Claxton".[60]

Kinship terms of address continued in use through the eighteenth and nineteenth centuries. Characters in Congreve's plays refer to "Brother Dick", "Brother Val", "Brother Antony", though he makes it clear that this is already a provincial habit. The Reverend Joseph Greene, schoolmaster and curate at Stratford-upon-Avon, wrote in the early eighteenth century of "my Aunt Daws" and "Sister Molly", and he always addressed his brother in correspondence as "Brother" and signed the same.[61] Again, Parson Woodforde always wrote "Brother John", "my Sister Clarke", "my nephew Samuel", and so on.

Siblings and cousins were addressed by kinship terms well into the nineteenth century. But, as Phillips notes, the use of "Cousin" with the second name, and more so of "Brother" or "Sister", was by the mid nineteenth century "particularly characteristic of provincial usage", as in *The Mill on the Floss*.[62] In the twentieth century, the general use of kinship terms in addressing or referring to relatives retreated to those of the second degree, and only uncles and aunts had a name attached, and this was the first not the second. By the 1960s even this usage was in decline. The family was contracting and relationships within it had become informal.

Use of sibling and parental terms for in-laws survived into the nineteenth century. In 1818, Keats called the wife of his brother George "Sister George", though her name also happened to be Georgiana, and he addressed her as "my dear sister". By the end of the century, the custom was an oddity, if Lady Monkswell is typical. She recorded in 1887 that Lord Chief Justice Coleridge, who had married a much younger woman as his second wife, addressed her mother as "Mother", to her own husband's "great amusement", though here of course age and status must have added to the incongruity of the term. The disappearance of this usage left in-laws in a titular limbo, as Firth, Hubert and Forge noted in 1969.[63]

We have seen that "Sir" and "Madam" were often used in address to parents. Dr Johnson, then aged 50, addressed his mother in a letter in 1759 as "Honoured Madam" and signed "Your dutiful son". In the early Victorian period, "Mama" and "Papa" were normally used in the upper classes. Mrs General in *Little Dorrit* observes that "Father is rather vulgar, my dear . . . Papa is a preferable mode of address." "Mammy", "Mummy", "Ma" and "Pa" were used lower down the social scale. In *Our Mutual Friend*, the *nouveau riche* Podsnaps are called "Ma" and "Pa". By the mid twentieth century, "Mummy" and "Daddy" were used by middle-class children, graduating to "Mother" and "Father" in adulthood, and "Mum" and "Dad" by working-class children and adults. "Daddy" was not a term used for fathers earlier but rather for older men generally. Fanny Burney called an older family friend in the 1770s "Daddy Crisp".[64] From the 1960s or earlier, the children of more progressive or lax parents used first names, though this was generally felt to be confusing and/or disrespectful.

There is more variety in grandparental terms. In a case-study from the 1960s, "Grandma . . . and Granny . . . made up about 70 per cent, each of about equal use. The next most popular form was Nanna (Nannie, Nan), with Grandmother, Grandmama, Grandmummy [and others] . . . all very low on the list." For grandfathers, "the most popular was Grandpa (about 40 per cent) and then Grandad . . . with about 20 per cent. Grandfather had considerably less popularity, while Grampie, Grandpop, Grandpapa and Granddaddy were used by only one or two people".[65] Most of these terms seem to be comparatively modern. Charlotte Yonge wrote in 1864, for example, that Granny had not been thought of in the 1820s.

Kinship terms were also used by extension in "fields which seem to present some analogy with family relations and statuses". The most obvious is perhaps the use of "Father", "Mother", "Brother" and "Sister" (and equivalents) for members of the clergy and religious orders. More recently, "Sister" is used for hospital nurses, while "Brother" and "Sister" are used in political and other associations to indicate solidarity and equality of status. A servant girl at Myddle in the late seventeenth century addressed an older man in the village as "Good Uncle Elks". This mode survived at the popular level, though in modern times parental terms were preferred. "The use of Dad to an elderly man and Mum or Ma to any elderly woman is common in working-class circles", Firth, Hubert and Forge noted; "this assimilates them to parental status, with its mixture of familiarity and respect."[66] Such usage was traditional ("Mother", "Daddy" and other terms being used earlier) and proclaims a real community beyond but like the family. The more recent "Grandpa" for older men is distinctly pejorative and belongs to a very different world where "youth culture" despises age. The use of "Uncle" and "Aunt" for friends of parents seems to have been limited to the middle-class in the mid twentieth century, but is again an indication of the continuing importance of the family as both model and social focus.

We have seen that religious did not as a rule change their names in the medieval period, though they had special titles such as Dom and Fra. Practice in the established orders remained unchanged, but the new or reformed orders or congregations associated with the Counter-Reformation did introduce new styles. The Reformed Carmelites made the adoption of the name of a saint or an attribute of God, Jesus or Mary a compulsory addition to the first name in 1567. Reformed Benedictine and Reformed Cistercian congregations followed the same style. Nuns at Montmartre in the early seventeenth century, for example, included la Mère Marguerite de Sainte-Gertrude and la soeur Marie de l'Incarnation. In official documents, this name was attached to the official name with the "dit" formula: la soeur Thomasse Le Queux, dite de Sainte-Cécile. Friars retained the style Brother So-and-So of such-and-such a place, but by the seventeenth century, if not before, the first name was a new name. When the Franciscan St Charles of Sezze was invested as a lay brother in 1635 at Nazzano, the Father Guardian "gave us each a name: Brother Joseph . . . ; Brother Alexius . . . ; and to me, Brother Cosmas, a name that was changed [again] at my profession [a year later] to Brother Charles . . . at the request of my mother".[67] By the nineteenth century, the Reformed Carmelite style became very common, especially for women religious. The custom of taking the name Mary plus another name – Sister Mary Alban, Sister Mary Dominic – also became common.

Noble names and titles

Noble titles formed the top layer of the social hierarchy and are a special case deserving separate treatment. We left them at the end of the Middle Ages with graded titles just established in England, though far less clearly elsewhere.

Generally across Europe only a minority of the nobility possessed titles by 1800. Titles did become more widespread from the later sixteenth century onwards as part of a process of stratification within the nobility and reflecting the establishment of the notion of a royally-created service nobility as against an independent noble caste. The process probably reached its apogee in Spain. All the Italian nobilities, save the Venetian, were modelled on the Spanish and had graded titles: Principi, Duchi, Marchesi, Conti, Visconti, Baroni and Gentiluomini. In the Duchy of Mantua in 1775, for example, there were 161 noble houses: 5 Principi, 35 Marchesi, 62 Conti, 52 untitled nobles and seven noble bourgeois. In Italy, too, as elsewhere on the Continent, noble titles were borne by all members of the family, and not simply by its head as in Britain. For example, the Leopardi children – all under 10 – at Recanati in 1808 were referred to as Conte Giacomo Tardegardo, Conte Carlo Orazio and Contessa Paolina.

There was a comparative "indifference towards noble titles in France", save for that of "Duc", always granted by the King, and "Sire", "Sieur" or "Seigneur", which seems to have been almost universal. This is almost certainly because age of nobility was such a primary concern. Old nobles were generally scornful of titles, associated with more recent '*annoblis*'. As Duclos wrote in 1769 of a family whose nobility went back to the early thirteenth century, "A Tavanes has no need of any title other than his birth." This attitude was represented in this century by Proust's Baron de Charlus. As his nephew Saint-Loup explains, he ought, when his father died,

> to have taken the title of Prince des Laumes, which his father used before he became Duc de Guermantes . . . But my uncle feels that people are rather apt to overdo the Italian Prince or Grandee of Spain business nowadays. Though he had half-a-dozen grander titles to choose from, he has remained Baron de Charlus, as a protest, and with an apparent simplicity, which really covers a good deal of pride.

By contrast, new nobles were attached to their titles and often anxious to abandon their family names. It is reported that when asked to become Secretary of State for War in 1757, the Duc de Belle-Isle, whose family's nobility and ducal status were quite recent, only agreed on condition that he should sign papers with his title and military rank and not his family name of Fouquet, as was customary.

The full title of a noble, which could list several *seigneuries*, offices held, etc., was reserved for formal documents and occasions. For example, the baptismal act of his son drawn up in 1698 refers to "le haut et puissant seigneur René, sire de Froullay, comte de Tessé, chevalier des Ordres du Roy, colonel général des Dragons de France, lieutenant-général pour le Roy dans sa province du Maine, Laval et le Perché, premier et grand écuyer de Mme la Duchesse de Bourgogne"; but he signed as René de Froullay-Tessé.[68] At the end of the eighteenth century, Stéphanie-Félicité du Crest de Saint-Aubin, Comtesse de Bourbon-Lancy, who had married Comte Brulart de Genlis, was known as Madame de Genlis. As this shows, in everyday usage short versions of names were employed. Signatures very often used the family name alone or that of the *seigneurie*; and the mode of address was "Monsieur", "Madame" or "Mademoiselle".

We have seen that noble families had taken the names of fiefs as second or family names from the eleventh century onwards. Some maintained an exclusive attachment to this name. When Jean-Baptiste d'Andelot was nominated as *bailli* of Dôle in 1564 and was asked "to put a title of a *seigneurie*" on the document of appointment, he refused, wishing to be designated solely by his family name.[69] But progressively from the sixteenth century onwards, noble and ennobled families had family names *and* the names of their main *seigneurie*. So Cardinal Richelieu's father was François Du Plessis de Richelieu, a form which his son inherited. On becoming Chancellor of France in 1624, Etienne d'Aligre received the rank of *chevalier* and added de La Rivière to his name, La Rivière being his main estate. When the

Norman family of Clérel acquired the *seigneurie* of Tocqueville in 1661, they again took the additional name de Tocqueville. This practice could lead to the accumulation of names. But it was also common for branches of families to drop the family name, replacing it with those of their *seigneuries*. So in the sixteenth century, in the house of Béthune, some took the name de Locres; in that of Estouteville, some became de Groucher and some de Criquebeuf. To prevent this, the Ordonnance of Amboise in 1555 forbade nobles or non-nobles to take any other name than their family name and enjoined nobles to sign documents with their family names and not those of their estates. Repetition of these injunctions in the seventeenth century suggests that they were not being heeded, and indeed royal letters of ennoblement, which became the only proper avenue of entry into the order, used the form of name plus *seigneurie*.

Montaigne had criticized this trend in 1580 because it undermined family continuity:

> It is a bad custom with bad effects to France to call everyone by the name of his land or *seigneurie*, and the thing in the world that does most to mix and confuse lineages. A cadet of good family, having had as his appanage an estate under whose name he is known and honoured, cannot honestly abandon it; then years after his death, however, the estate goes to a stranger, who does the same.

Family lines and ties were thus thrown into confusion, uncertainty and oblivion.[70] Montaigne was thinking of legitimate noble families, but royal legislation also had its sights on the illegitimate assumption of noble status by this means. The Ordonnance of Blois in 1575 laid down that non-nobles acquiring fiefs were not ennobled thereby, and a decree of 1614 specifically banned non-nobles from taking the names of *seigneuries* they might obtain.

The practice was common and virtually unstoppable. Marc Bloch cites an example from Normandy: the Perrotte de Cairon from Caen, whose fortune was made "in trade or office" and who by the mid seventeenth century

> adorned themselves with the title of squires [*écuyers*] and invariably had their family name followed in the documents by the name of a *seigneurie*: sieurs de Saint-Laurent, de la Guère, de Cardenville, de Saint-Vigor, de la Pigassière.

What was legitimate and what illegitimate in such social trajectories was often inextricably mixed. The Perrenot family of Ornans in the Franche-Comté, for example, rose through the law and office, and from 1527 Nicolas Perrenot "realized the great dream of bourgeois of his time, by buying an estate whose name, joined to the family name, would proclaim the success, the ascension, the passage accomplished from the middle class into the aristocracy". The name of the estate was Grandvelle. This was officially raised to a barony in 1555 and became the main name of Nicolas' descendants, who included Antoine, minister of Philip II in the Netherlands.[71]

This process, especially the illegitimate version, continued of course into the modern period. Among other examples, Balzac has the Parisian magistrate Monsieur Camusot de Marville, "who had added the name of the estate of Marville to his family name". Proust's "extremely wealthy" M. Thirion married a member of the old noble Guermantes family and "from that day onwards he called himself the Marquis de Villeparisis , , . after a little place outside Paris".[72]

In modern times, the "de" or particule was taken to be the sign above all of noble status rather than the *seigneurie*. As we have seen, the preposition "de", linking a second name to the first, originally signified either place of origin or residence or sometimes descent and was not a noble characteristic. In Béarn in the fifteenth and sixteenth centuries "de" was used generally to attach all second names whatever their nature. Elsewhere at this time the form was found among peasants, linking them to their house, farm or household, and among agricultural workers sometimes to attach them to their masters. The point is nicely underlined by names found in a list of licensed female beggars in Paris in 1424–5: Jehanne de Lannoy, Cassine de La Croix, Catherine de Pommonceaulx.

But gradually, probably because it provided the linkage with the name of the *seigneurie*, the particule did come to have a different significance. It was increasingly used by nobles and became associated in people's minds with noble status. Already in the mid sixteenth century, the particule was being adopted by those with social pretensions, and the practice was satirized by Rabelais. The "de" might be placed in front of the family name or attached to another name as if it were a *seigneurie*. In *L'Ecole des Femmes* (1663), Molière presents "a peasant called Gros-Pierre" with a small piece of land surrounded by a ditch, "who assumes the pompous name of Monsieur de l'Isle".[73] Properly ennobled persons by this time were using the particule in front of their names in addition to the name of their *seigneurie*, like the d'Aligre. The double particule thus became not uncommon. At the same time, those without *seigneuries*, or resisting the trend of taking their names, simply added the "de" illogically to their family names, like de Maistre, de Bertrand, or Pierre de Corneille, the dramatist, whose father was ennobled in 1637.

By the eighteenth century, the particule was clearly identified with the nobility. By the middle of the century, this view had penetrated Béarn. "De" disappeared from general usage and became reserved by notaries and the clergy to nobles and at a pinch important bourgeois. By the time of the Revolution the identification was so deeply rooted everywhere that many nobles dropped the particule, though this was not legally required. Alfred de Vigny recounted that, as a schoolboy in a Paris college during the First

Empire, he was bullied when he admitted to being a noble. "You have a 'de' to your name: aren't you noble?", he was asked.[74]

Noble titles and status had of course been abolished at the Revolution. Both were revived during the First Empire and the constitutional monarchies, but thereafter titles remained without legal standing, though jealously guarded by their holders. Victor Hugo noted in February 1849 during the Second Republic:

> I have received from M. le Duc de Doudeauville the announcement of the death of his mother . . . : "Mme Bénigne-Augustine-Françoise Le Tellier de Montmirail, Grande d'Espagne de première classe, veuve de M. Ambroise de La Rochefoucauld, Duc de Doudeauville", it said, despite the constitution. These people never give up.

However, nobles regained no special legal status in the first half of the nineteenth century and title usage was purely social, as Tocqueville remarked in 1840.

> Under the old French monarchy, officers were always called by their titles of nobility; they are now always called by the title of their military rank. This little change in the forms of language suffices to show that a great revolution has taken place in the constitution of society.[75]

Nevertheless, "social" ennoblement via assumption of the particule proliferated in the post-Revolutionary era to an unprecedented extent. Often the "de" was simply assumed and then used at registration of births and marriages or in other official documents with the aid of complaisant officials. Guy de Maupassant's father, for example, assumed the "de" in 1846 just prior to his marriage, had it recorded at the wedding and then passed it on to his son. Alternatively the name could be officially changed by petitioning the courts for a "rectification of one's *état-civil*" and they were very "benevolent" towards this kind of snobbery. After the First World War, people were "granted rectification if they could show that they were the heirs of a soldier killed in action without leaving children". They were then permitted to add that person's name to their own, joined by the particule. "This pious intention 'ennobled' more Frenchmen than even Louis XIV did with letters of nobility, sale of offices, and so on."[76]

In England, too, nobles had traditionally taken the name of their estates, and the association between family name and place continued into the early modern and modern periods. In some cases, the family still held the manor or estate whose name it bore, like the Roscarrocks of Roscarrock (Cornwall), the Strelleys of Strelley (Nottinghamshire), or the Noneleys of Noneley (Shropshire) – all from the seventeenth century. Otherwise gentry were known by the principal estate in addition to their different family name: for example, Henry Gage of Raunds (Northants), John Littcott of Swallowfield (Berks), or Sir Thomas Kitson of Hengrave (Suffolk) – all in the mid sixteenth century. Formally all full titles of peers included a place-name – Baron Blank of Blanktown in the county of Blankshire – and in the medieval period titles were linked to places where nobles resided or exercised authority. Noble titles taken from actual estates continued into the early modern period. So, on becoming a baron in 1712, Sir Thomas Willoughby took his title from Middleton, his estate in Warwickshire. The same custom was followed, as we have seen, in Scotland. When Dr Johnson crossed the heath near Forres where Macbeth was supposed to have met the witches, he addressed Boswell in a parody of Shakespeare: "All hail Dalblair! hail to thee, Laird of Auchinleck!" Boswell explained in his account later that he had indeed these titles or names, since not only was he heir to his father's estate of Auchinleck, but he had also "purchased some land called Dalblair; and . . . in Scotland it is customary to distinguish landed men by the name of their estates".[77]

Later on in the nineteenth and twentieth centuries, new peers seem to have picked a place with which they had some looser association. The future Lady Monkswell had decided in 1845 that, if her husband ever became a peer, he would take that name – a valley on the border of Dartmoor of which the couple were fond. As in France, this meant that nobles could have a "peerage name" that was the same as their family name, for example Curzon or Byron; or they could have two names, like "Lord Salisbury, whose surname is Cecil; [or] Lord Derby, whose surname is Stanley".[78]

With noble titles in Britain, one should again distinguish between the full and formal title and that in current use; also between usage from commoners to nobles and usage among nobles themselves. The Duke of Bedford in 1700 was William, Duke of Bedford, Marquess of Tavistock, Earl of Bedford, Baron Russell and Baron Russell of Thornhaugh, Baron Howland of Streatham, etc. In formal address, dukes were "the Most Noble Duke of", "his Grace" and "Your Grace"; other peers "the Most Noble Lord", "His Lordship" and "Your Lordship". Further honorific forms were also used. Lord Lisle was addressed by a correspondent in 1534 as "Right honourable and my singular good lord". The "honourable" remained part of noble address down to the present.

Dukes and duchesses were also referred to less formally (and later addressed) by their short titles: for example, the Duke of Bedford; other peers as Lord So-and-So, with Lady for their spouses. The short title included the place-name for dukes, but not as a rule for other peers. In the sixteenth and seventeenth centuries, further qualificatives were used, such as "my Lord of Suffolk" (1535) or "my Lord Montague" (1565). These were dropped in the eighteenth century, and they never developed into general titles as on the Continent.

Short titles were used among family and intimates as well as more generally. Lady Holland, for example, wrote to her son in 1829: "Poor Emily, M[archione]ss of Londonderry died suddenly yesterday morning."[79] Lord William Russell referred to his father in his diary around the same time as "the Duke of Bedford".

By the eighteenth century, peers and peeresses signed with a short version of their title without formal prefix and not using any second name they may have had. The first name, which had been used down to the time of the Restoration, was also suppressed – on the French model according to Charlotte Yonge. So the 10th Earl of Pembroke in the mid and late eighteenth century signed Pembroke and not Herbert, his family name. But his wife signed Elizabeth Pembroke. Similarly among the earl's correspondents and friends, the Marquess of Bristol was Bristol, the Duke of Queensberry was Queensberry, and the Duchess of Marlborough was C. Marlborough. The same form was used in reference. This usage persisted into the nineteenth century and was practised even within families. The 6th Duke of Bedford, for example, always signed Bedford, even to close relatives. Shortly before his death, he concluded a letter to his daughter-in-law in 1839 "always your affectionate Bedford"; while a nephew of the 7th Duke and Duchess referred to "Aunty Bedford."[80]

The eldest sons or heirs of peers above the rank of viscount took the family's second title as a courtesy title, a convention found from the eighteenth century if not before. So the eldest son of the Duke of Bedford was Marquess of Tavistock, of the Duke of Marlborough Marquess of Blandford, and so on. The definite article was not used with these courtesy titles, but they were employed in short form in address, reference and signature. The 7-year-old heir of the Duke of Marlborough signed himself, in a letter to his sister in 1746, "Your most affectionate brother Blandford". Where a family had further titles, the next of these would go to the heir of the heir. So Tavistock's eldest son was Russell or Baron Russell, the title coinciding here with the family name. Where a peer had no secondary title, the heir took the style Lord plus the family name. So Lord Bertie was heir to the Earl of Lindsey. These titles of heirs seem to have been treated also as first names and could be abbreviated accordingly. The early-nineteenth-century Tavistock was called Tavy, we have seen, by his relatives. In Anthony Powell's *At Lady Molly's* (1957), Erridge, heir to the Duke of Warminster, was similarly known as Erry, and another character comments "I don't even know what Erry's Christian name is."[81]

Younger sons of peers with higher titles took the courtesy title of Lord plus their first name and the family name. So the younger sons of the 6th Duke of Bedford were Lord William Russell, Lord John Russell, and so on. The younger sons of earls and all children of viscounts and barons were "the Honourable", making use of a title that had once been used for principal nobles, as we have seen.

The names and titles of knights took the form Sir John Willoughby or Francis Lovel knight, or with both indicators together: Sir Thomas Willoughby, Knight – all examples from the fifteenth and sixteenth centuries. In common parlance, the form was Sir John, Sir Thomas, and so on. Baronets, invented in the early seventeenth century, added the style or an abbreviation of it to their names. The dislike of using the initial with "Sir" is modern. Pepys referred to "Sir W. Batten", "Sir W. Pen"; Lady Wortley Montagu in 1744 to "Sir J. Cope." When Gladstone wrote to propose that the future Lord Monkswell be raised to the peerage in 1885, he addressed him as "My dear Sir R. Collier".[82] Wives of knights and baronets were Lady So-and-So – without the first name which was reserved for daughters of higher peers. Dame was used in the sixteenth century but died out.

All these complex forms served to distinguish the nobility clearly from the rest of society. Though complexity, accumulation and arcaneness were the usual modes for doing so, the opposite minimalist solution was also found. The chiefs of Scottish clans had the special privilege of using the clan name alone. "In consequence of this practice, the late Laird of Macfarlane", Dr Johnson related, "considered himself as disrespectfully treated, if the common addition was applied to him. Mr. Macfarlane, said he, may with equal propriety be said to many; but I, and only I, am Macfarlane."[83] According to Black, placing the definite article in front of Gaelic names beginning with Mac is a solecism. In similar fashion, the chief or "prince" of the Irish O'Neills was O'Neill, of the O'Donnells O'Donnell.

Another means of establishing noble exclusivity and social superiority, more marked perhaps in later periods when real noble power had waned, was the adoption of idiosyncratic pronunciation and spelling of their names. For example, the Scottish Auchinleck was pronounced Affléck, and Marjoribanks Marshbanks, and the English Cholmondeley Chumley, Gower Gore, Knollys Noles, Sudeley Sully, and Wriothesley Roxly. Cavendish, the family name of the Dukes of Devonshire, was pronounced Candish in the sixteenth and early seventeenth centuries, but this usage seems not to have survived. The same phenomenon is found in France. So Broglie from the Piedmontese Broglio was popularly pronounced Bró-yee, though the "correct" noble pronunciation was Breuil or Broille. Similarly, Castries was Castre; Croy was Crouï; Talleyrand was Talran or Tailleran; and Uzès was Uzai. Proust mocks the pleasure felt by Mlle. Legrandin, who entered the nobility by marrying a Cambremer, at being able to display this insider's knowledge:

> by virtue of the transmutation of solid bodies into more and more subtle elements, the considerable . . . fortune that she had inherited from her father, the finished education that she had received . . . all this was . . . to find its utmost sublimation in the pleasure of being able to say . . . "I shall ask you to dine to meet the Uzai."[84]

Nicknames

Nicknames or by-names had always been used as unofficial names in addition to or instead of official ones. Some, we have seen, became second names. In the modern era, once second names had become established, nicknames persisted of course, being used within communities, institutions and families. They were usually individual in origin but they could be inherited. They were also different in kind from other names by this time in that they retained a more primitive, "descriptive" function.[85] Unlike the first or family name, the nickname still records some real feature of the person named. A broad distinction may be made between nicknaming in "traditional" communal and in "modern" more restricted settings.

Scotland provides good examples of the former. In the fishing towns and villages of the north-east coast, whose populations kept themselves apart from those of the surrounding countryside, very few first or second names were in use. According to Joseph Robertson, writing in 1842, there were 25 George Cowies in Buckie, who were distinguished as George Cowie Doodle, George Cowie Carrot, George Cowie Neep, etc.. Robertson also cites the experience of a stranger seeking a fisherman called Alexander White in another village. Meeting a girl, he asked:

"Cou'd you tell me fa'r Sanny Fite lives?"
"Filk Sanny Fite?"
"Muckle Sanny Fite."
"Filk muckle Sanny Fite?"
"Muckle lang Sanny Fite."
"Filk muckle lang Sanny Fite?"
"Muckle lang gleyed Sanny Fite" . . .
"Oh! It's 'Goup-the-lift' 'ye're seeking", cried the girl, "and fat the deevil for dinna ye speer for the man by his richt name at ance?"[86]

Dorian's study of the Gaelic-speaking minority in three East Sutherland villages shows that traditional nicknaming or by-naming of this kind was still very much intact in the 1960s. In the villages just three family names accounted for between 70 and 90 per cent of the Gaelic-speakers, and first names were also repeated. This meant that official names, apart from their being associated with the alien external world, were "virtually non-functional". Instead individuals were known by by-names. By far the commonest type was genealogical, and in practice a patronymic or matronymic, since more than two generations were rarely involved. Here a person would be known by a pet version of his or her first name plus the name of their father or mother, sometimes in the genitive, for example Jessie Sarag, Jessie of Allie or Allie's Jessie. Descent could be traced via either parent and no significance seems to have been attached to which. It was "not uncommon for a family of siblings to be split down the middle, with some of the children by-named after the mother and some after the father". Less commonly, an individual could be known either by the father's or the mother's name: Hughie Jessen or Hughie Rob. Occasionally, individuals would be named after those who reared them rather than an actual parent. So Katie Elag, an illegitimate child brought up by her grandmother, had her name. Occasionally a woman might be by-named after her husband.

The second category was the nickname proper. This could be simply descriptive, referring to a physical characteristic, occupation or place of origin or residence, for example Big Bella, Jessie Cobbler or Andrew Cromarty; or it could be more obviously derisive, based on an attribute or an event, for example Johnnie Lassie (an effeminate man) or Jeannie Hen (who gabbles incessantly). A striking nickname of this type overrode the genealogical by-name, though some people had both kinds of name. Both types of by-name could be inherited and attached to a whole family. So those with the genealogical name Davie could be called the Davies, while Bumble's children, wife and grandchildren all had the by-name Bumble. Very few people had no by-name at all. This usually occurred when their family name was distinctive, or when they had two first names, a rarity. In the latter case, however, the genealogical name could be used "where identity was in doubt."[87]

Dorian stresses that the primary function of the by-name was identification, but the nickname type had further dimensions. Some of these names were offensive and could not be used in the person's presence. They were used to place people but also to put them in their place. An intermediary category could be offensive if used by acquaintances or younger people but not if used by close friends, relatives and contemporaries. They were associated with status and ranking. One may also conclude from her research that by-names or nicknames were a clear expression of community and a way of marking its boundaries. By-names and not official names were used within the communities. Outsiders and non-Gaelic-speakers who did not know the right by-names or who misused them were the objects of ridicule.

Similar by-name or nickname systems existed till recently in small communities in Ireland, the Isle of Man, Wales and England. A good example is provided by Myddle in the mid to late seventeenth century. Here, according to Gough, we have "Robert Ames, whom they call little Robert Ames"; "Black Nell"; "Great John Matthews" and "Little John Matthews"; the wife of Samuel Downton who was "called White Legs because she commonly went without stockings"; and three Eavan or Evan Joneses called Evan the Tanner, Black Evan and Eavan Soundsey.

Traditional nicknames were ubiquitous on the Continent too. Aebischer wrote that in the Fribourg countryside, for example, in the 1920s, "the family name has only an artificial life, maintained thanks to the administration and the *état-civil*; in ordinary life, it is almost totally supplanted by sobriquets or nicknames".[88] The distinction between the two name systems, national and local, was exacerbated in many areas by linguistic particularism, very marked for example in Alsace or in Corsica. Until the late seventeenth century or the eighteenth century in France, these nicknames still appeared in official documents, sometimes attached with a "dit" or "alias" formula. But from around 1700 they went underground. Often by the mid twentieth century, though still in use, they had become a subject of embarrassment or secrecy and were kept from outsiders. Zonabend relates that she only began to hear about nicknames and then to learn actual examples after she had been at Minot for a long time.

In France, as in Scotland and elsewhere, different types of by-name or nickname may be distinguished. Here we may take Dauven's study of the village of Méharicourt in the Somme in the first half of the twentieth century as exemplary. First, there were abbreviations of first names, often in the form of a doubling-up of syllables, for example Tintin for Augustin, Nonore for Eléonore. "If syllables were not doubled, then the abbreviations were generally preceded by the word 'Tchou', meaning little or son: Tchou Mile (Casimir) or Tchou Dolphe (Adolphe)." But, since there were several individuals with the same first name and the same abbreviated form of it, "a further distinguisher was often added". This could be occupational: Tchou Mile Tonji (the cooper); or a first or family name: Tchou Mile Ambroise; Tchou Mile Lhomme. Secondly, there were names of origin, for example, Achille d'Herville or Marie ed' Maucourt. Sometimes only the place-name was used, preceded by "ech", meaning "this", for example, Ech Parigou (a nursling from Paris). The place-name could also be used more generally. Ech Breton did his military service in Brittany; Ech Zoulou arrived in the village at the time of the Zulu wars.

Thirdly, there were nicknames proper, also usually preceded by "Ech", or "El" for women. Physical traits included Ech Grou (gros – large), El Gamme ed Bou (jambe de bois – wooden leg), El Rousse, and Ech Lenette or Quat'zieu (Quatre yeux – Four eyes or Specs). Moral or behavioural traits included Brin d'Vin (drunkard) and Julie Saint-Lundi (an idler who took Mondays off work). Sometimes, as this shows, the nickname was joined to the first name, and epithets could be doubled: Ech Sourd André; El Rousse Lenette. Then there were names deriving from events, including birth circumstances. Zephyr Dix-neuf was the 19th child in a family; Achille d'Ech Christ and Ech Bon Djeu carried the crucifix in religious ceremonies. Fourthly, there were occupational names, which we have already seen could be used to qualify first names, but which were also used alone, for example Ech Manchon (mason); Ech Musii (menuisier or joiner).[89]

In France (as elsewhere), some kinds of nickname were more prevalent in particular places than others. Hypocoristic forms of first names were common, for example, in the Somme, as we have seen, but also in the Doubs and Auvergne. Names taken from place of residence, farm or household were important in the Bigouden; genealogical names in Corsica and elsewhere. This relates to the functions ascribed to nicknames by social anthropologists and to the structure of the communities in which they are found.

In general, as Pitt-Rivers has argued, nicknames are a form of community control and express community values. They situate individuals within the community and they provide sanctions against deviance. So, in Minot, La Viergette (the little virgin) "had two children without being married"; elsewhere, we have seen drunkenness and idleness penalized. Such names were attached in the first place to individuals, and they could be both wounding and shameful. Here it is significant that in many places nicknames were mainly confined to men and belonged to the competitive realm of male honour and assertiveness. They were "a form of verbal aggression". They were thus almost never used in address but only in reference, in gatherings where the bearer was absent, or with lowered voices. In north-west Portugal, they were names "which are not for writing down"; elsewhere they were "bad names".[90] Where they could be used in address, as we saw in Scotland, this was only between intimates or in special circumstances.

Related to this is the more neutral function of simply signalling membership of the community. Cohen has emphasized this in connection with Southern Tuscany, where a strong sense of community identity and of local pride was evident. The use and knowledge of the local nicknames sets the village and its members apart from other neighbouring villages. Here the nickname cuts across family boundaries but forms new boundaries between the in-group and the outside world. Within the family and beyond the community, the nickname is not used. Isolation may be a factor in explaining this communal nickname function, though some form of inter-action with outside is also required. In these circumstances, nicknames "abolish social differences". But nicknaming may also demonstrate the existence of stratification or "class" distinction within a community. On the Greek island of Karpathos, for example, the rich peasants had by-names deriving from positions in the prestigious religious hierarchy; middling peasants had neutral nicknames; and pejorative names were reserved to the poor; and this kind of situation was also found elsewhere.

At "Montevarese" in Southern Italy having nicknames separated

> peasants from the bourgeoisie. Members of the lower strata of the
> bourgeoisie frequently denied that they possessed nicknames even
> if . . . [those] of their peasant ancestors were still remembered and
> maliciously repeated behind their backs.

Collective nicknames were also used for the members of a whole community or class of people, usually "out-groups". At Donnemarie (Seine-et-Marne), for example, "the forest workers or immigrants from the Perche were called Gauthiers".[91]

Some nicknames remained individual, but in traditional communities nicknames or by-names were also often inherited. This was a way of marking continuities and differences within the community, as when occupational names were still given to those who had not followed the paternal or grand-paternal profession, or when outside origin was noted in the same way down the generations. The naming system "involved the past history as well as the present situation of every individual". Most obvious, however, as in Haute-Provence and in Corsica, the continuing by-name "reinforced or reflected the emphasis on the male line" and rendered the formation of sub-groups transparent.[92] So, at Saint-André in the eighteenth century, among the Simons there were the Simon Ruiné, the Simon Gaix, the Simon Mort and so on. Here one can see how use of a restricted stock of names in fact reflected and marked a clan-type organization with sub-lineages. The naming system was a genealogical map of the community, stressing common origins and tracing descent from a limited number of ancestors. As such, it could signal marrying-groups and mark incest prohibitions.

In Corsica, there was a regular system of family nicknames or *cugnomi*, which were attached to branches of larger family groups. Like other nicknames, they derived from first names, place-names, occupations, and physical or moral traits or events. As in Bastelica, each established family comprised several *cugnomi*, the number reflecting its age and the number of its branches. The Folacci, for example, had thirteen; the Franceschini and the Vincenti seven each; and the Pittiloni six. The Franceschini included I Pupulleli (little breasts), Gli Scarponi (slippers), and I Barraconi (from a place); the Firoloni I Carcassó (marking the fact that "the ancestor concerned did his military service at Carcassonne and often talked about it"), I Ricini and I Mastro Battisti.[93]

Elsewhere, the emphasis on patriliny was less firm, as we have seen for the east coast of Scotland. In the Jura village of St. Aubin-en-Vuilly, the Ramuz, for example, were divided into the Gadi, the Briançon, the Mince and so on, some of which had derived their names from affines. In rural Catalonia, the social unit was the household or domestic group, known as the "cal" or "can". This was based on the stem family (man, wife, son, daughter-in-law and children) but could include non-kin. Each household had a name or "renom", which was borne by its members. The renom was "used either as a term of reference or address". It could be substituted "for a first name as a term of address" or it could "be linked to a first name or even to a [personal] nickname as if it were" an official family name.

> Thus Josep Vilaro from cal Bepo is addressed as Pep [nickname of Josep] or as Bepo and he is referred to as Pep del Bepo or simply Bepo. To distinguish him from his father, also called Josep, he is known as the young Bepo and his father as the old Bepo.

Young Bepo's son, called Francesc, aged 12, is known as Francesc or also as Bepo. The wife of old Bepo "is referred to as the Bepa or as María del

Bepo"; her daughter Pilar, married to the smith (ferré) "is referred to occasionally as Pilar del Bepo but most often as Pilar del Ferré". The renom was attached to the domestic group and when an individual moved from one group to another via marriage or adoption he or she adopted the renom of that new group. Renoms were "not transmitted patrilineally but via the household". Renoms derived from place-names, occupations, patronymics, nicknames and names of farms, and were still being coined very recently. But the most prominent households had kept theirs for centuries. They were in effect a kind of second name for use in the community. Official second names appear to have been imposed from outside, and their relationship to renoms remains obscure.[94]

Nicknames were important, too, in "modern" and urban societies, where they were most prominent in certain closed milieus. An example from the early modern period is provided by French "noms de guerre". All or most soldiers in the seventeenth and eighteenth centuries were given such names, probably by the sergeant or recruiting officer. "They were mentioned after the first name and the family name in official documents." There were various types. Family or first names might be used, the latter often preceded by "Saint", for example Saint Jean, Saint Louis, Saint Estienne. Places of origin were also very common, though, as with other nicknames, the place referred to might have some other connection with the person – a period of residence or a military campaign, for instance. Topographical names were also common. Direct occupational names were found, but reference to the tools of the trade were more frequent, for example La Lancette for a surgeon, or Desrasoirs for a barber. Lavocat was not an actual lawyer, but a man who could present an argument, a barrack-room lawyer. Some names referred to the soldier's past history: a previous regiment or company, like La Sarre; or a place of garrison or imprisonment, like Magdebourg or Dunkerques. Names from nature were common too, especially flowers: La Fleur, La Violette, La Rose, La Tulipe. Reference to physical traits was rare; Blondin was the commonest example here. Moral traits reflected an easy-going nature or a joie de vivre: Sans Souci, Monplaisir, Jolicoeur; or specifically military qualities: Sans Peur, Sans Quartier, Frappe d'Abord.

Till the mid eighteenth century, "noms de guerre" were like nicknames in general use, and, though they were in French and not patois, they seem to have been used as such by common soldiers, though there may have been some unofficial nicknames in circulation too. The "official" noms de guerre do not include pejorative or obscene names. Noms de guerre helped to create an esprit de corps using a familiar idiom. From the mid eighteenth century, the army bureaucratized the system. Each company had its list of names, which were allotted mechanically without attention to a man's individual character. The names in use were further sanitized and it seems that their use by soldiers declined. Corvisier sees this as a sign of the increased isolation of the French army from the general population, chiming in with other developments, notably living in barracks. In a broader perspective, the trend fits in with the general abandonment of by-names in the official world and their restriction to the private sphere.[95]

Nicknaming seems to have been universal among the élites in all countries from the sixteenth century to the twentieth. Nicknames were used within kinship groups, sets or circles, or more widely. A well-known English example is the circle which formed around Dr Johnson in the mid eighteenth century. Boswell relates that "Johnson had a way of contracting the names of his friends: as Beauclerk, Beau; Boswell, Bozzy; Langton, Lanky; Murphy, Mur; [Thomas] Sheridan, Sherry."[96] The Earl of Pembroke in the 1780s habitually referred to those politicians in office of whom he disapproved by nicknames, either of his own invention or in wider currency. Lord North, for example, was Boreas; Lord George Germaine, Minden; Lord Sandwich, Twitcher or Jemmy Twitcher. Only occasionally is the reason for the nickname made clear, as with "Single Speech Hamilton", who made a celebrated maiden speech in the House of Commons in November 1755, which lasted from 2 o'clock one afternoon until 5 o'clock the following morning.

Nicknames were again very common among the mainly noble political élite of the early nineteenth century. Thomas Creevey, for example, in his correspondence and journals constantly refers to men, but also women, by their nicknames. So, for example, Lord Palmerston was Cupid or Palmy; Lord Sidmouth, The Doctor (after his father's profession); Lord Liverpool, Jenky (from his family name Jenkinson); Lord Darlington, Niffy-Naffy; the Duke of Norfolk, The Jockey, Little Barney, Little Twitch or Scroop; while Princess Lieven was Snipe; the Countess of Darlington, The Pop; Queen Victoria, Little Vic; and Lady Jersey, Sally or Silence.

Sometimes again we learn why the names were bestowed. Lady Jersey's first name was Sarah and she was very talkative. Lord John Russell was called Pie and Thimble and, after he married a widow in 1831, The Widow's Mite, because he was so small. Poodle Byng had very curly hair. Though Creevey was especially partial to using and coining nicknames, the habit was general, and the names are found in all other private documentation of the period from the same milieus. It indicates the small size and cohesion of London "society" at the time. Nicknaming also seems to have been common among the middle classes at this time, in and out of London. Creevey recounted to his stepdaughter that Morritt, author of a work on ancient Troy, was known as "Troy" Morritt. He had a very fat brother, "and as the elder brother is called 'Troy', the other goes by the name of 'Avoirdupois' Morritt. Damned fair for the provinces!"[97]

Nicknaming survived among the various sections of the modern British élite, though it seems to have become much more restricted than it was in Creevey's time, a sign of a loss of homogeneity, of fragmentation. There was, for example, a set of names specific to the Bloomsbury circle in the period around 1910 to around 1930. Nicknaming was also characteristic of élites on the Continent. Proust, for example, noted "the mania for nick-names" among the aristocratic set associated with the Guermantes. M. de Charlus, whose name was Palamède, was called Mémé; Prince von Faffen-heim was Von; the Prince d'Agrigente was Gri-Gri; two very large noble ladies, who went about together, were Petite and Mignonne, and so on.[98]

Élites or élite sets here were a type of relatively closed group, using nicknames like slang and other forms of exclusive behaviour to reinforce their boundaries and control access. In Britain in recent times, nicknaming is found, as McClure notes, in particular kinds of social group: schools, work-places, prisons, long-stay hospital wards, the armed services, sporting fraternities and teams, occupational groups (orchestras, theatrical comp-anies), and communities belonging to socially cohesive industries like mining, ship-building or fishing. Here they fulfilled the same consolidating function, as well as others found in traditional rural communities.

"More than any other type of personal name, the nickname reflects the social power that namers exert over the named." Nicknames are often given by leaders of social groups as an exercise of power, and, as has often been noted, they are more prevalent the more closed the group is. They are, for example, much more common in boarding than in day schools. Here, as in rural communities, nicknaming is a variety of sanctioning. It is "central to the unofficial rituals of abuse and mockery, whether the object of derision is present and addressed directly, or whether absent and 'called' only in the third person". At the extreme, nicknaming may become a mode of scapegoating and humiliation, of collective bullying, which is far less obvi-ous in the traditional setting. Above all, nicknaming stigmatizes "anything uncommon – heritage, accent, appearance, attitudes", all deviations from the norm that "are experienced as in some way threatening".[99]

"But not all nicknaming is hostile; it may be deferential" or signal mem-bership of a friendship group. Here, not to have a nickname may be the excluding device, and, as with the élites which we have discussed, having a nickname and joining the group that used a set of nicknames was a sign of belonging to that special group. So, members of the crew of the royal yacht *Britannia* habitually used nicknames (in contrast to practice in the regular "Grey Navy") and people's family names might not even be known. In a newspaper article in 1995, a member of the England cricket team referred to his fellow-members via their nicknames (Hicky, Goughie, Athers, etc.) but to members of the opposing West Indies team by their full names.[100]

Types of modern nickname have been analyzed by scholars. McClure distinguishes between secondary nicknames formed from official names, and primary ones that are original and distinct from the latter. Secondary nicknames may be formed by abbreviation or suffixation of the first or second name. This includes the traditional hypocoristic like Bob, Dick or Maggy. At a more complex level, lexical substitution or word-play takes

287

place. McClure isolates four categories here, taking examples from school-children's names. First, there is substitution through partial homonymy, for example Donald to Duck; Wellington to Boots; Goulden to Wondercrisp. Secondly, there are synonyms: Dinger for Bell; Y-Front for Underwear from Underwood. Then there are antonyms: Queen(y) for King; and fourthly metonyms, for example Shotgun for Sheriff; Weed for Gardiner. There are also nicknames that go with particular family names: Dusty Miller, Foxy Reynolds, Muddy Waters or Walters, and so on. These are frequently given to adults in the work-place and are another testimony to the modern importance of the second name. As we have seen earlier with traditional examples, primary nicknames were frequently literal epithets relating to physique, like Lofty, Shorty or Tich. Metaphorical epithets were also used here, for example Carrots or Ginger for red hair; Skyscraper or Maypole for a tall thin child. And then there was a whole range of names relating to incidents and events.

Pseudonyms may be seen as a modern form of by-name. The main difference between the pseudonym and most other names, including nick-names, is that it is not given to the individual by other people but is chosen by him or her (or an agent) to replace the given name, usually in certain limited situations. Particular categories of person are most likely to use pseudonyms: criminals, especially confidence men; opponents of repressive régimes; actors; and writers.

Pseudonyms were employed as a disguise, to avoid detection and per-haps arrest and prosecution. So they were used by Catholic priests operat-ing in sixteenth-century England, or by Resistance workers during the Second World War. The first literary pseudonyms were thus employed by political writers. Five authors attacking the institution of episcopacy in 1641 used the collective pseudonym Smectymnus, made up from the initial letters of their names. Swift employed a number of pseudonyms and very rarely signed any of his work with his own name. A famous series of letters attacking the government in the 1760s and 1770s, probably written by the Earl of Shelburne, were signed: Junius. A little earlier in France, the young Arouet, having suffered exile and a spell in the Bastille for his satirical writings, adopted the name Voltaire.

The wish to avoid embarrassment or "exposure" was a factor in later or gentler environments. Cecily Fairfield explained:

> I chose the pen name of Rebecca West because when I was 18,
> I was contributing articles to a paper which, because of its radical-
> ism, my mother would not let me read and something had to be
> done about it. I chose *that* name because at an earlier age I played
> that part in Ibsen's *Rosmersholme*.[101]

Having once used the name, she was unable to drop it. Pseudonyms might also be used where a writer had another very different career. So in nine-teenth-century England, the diplomat Robert Lytton wrote novels as Owen

Meredith, and the Oxford don and mathematician Charles Lutwidge Dodgson wrote children's books and nonsense as Lewis Carroll.

Gender could also be disguised, women adopting male names much more frequently than men took women's. Several important female writers made this choice in the mid nineteenth century. Aurore Dupin, Mme. Dudevant, used the name George Sand from 1832. She had employed the name Jules Sand in collaboration with her lover Jules Sandeau and simply adapted the previous name. She wished to avoid trouble from her relations, which using her real names might have occasioned, but, more important, "obsessed by the idea that all women were slaves, she wished to escape from her destiny by using a man's name". She also wore male clothing and "from then on, she gave a masculine termination to all adjectives which she applied to herself".[102] In England, the Brontë sisters were Currer, Ellis and Acton Bell, and Mary Ann Evans was George Eliot (choices which posterity has rejected in the first but not the second case). With the Brontës, there was a wish to keep real life and authorship distinct, and a shrinking from publicity, but also a concern to be judged as writers *per se* and not as "women writers".

By the nineteenth century, moreover, the phenomenon of the positive and then more permanent pseudonym had appeared, a name chosen because it sounded better than the person's given name. This was manifested by writers (Pierre Loti, Anatole France, Stéphane Mallarmé; Mark Twain; Mark Rutherford, E. Nesbit), but more so by actors and later film stars. Some French actors and actresses in the nineteenth century favoured a shorter name, snappier, easier to remember and distinct from the normal first plus second name. So Rachel Félix was Rachel; Julie Bernat, Mme. Bernard Derosne, was Judith; and Gabrielle-Charlotte Réju was Réjane. Especially in Hollywood, the renaming of film stars followed a distinct policy. The new names had to sound glamorous, more American than the originals, and distinctive without being odd. Foreign elements were removed, particularly if they were Jewish; so Issur Danielovitch Demsky became Kirk Douglas; Julius Ullman, Douglas Fairbanks; Dino Crocetti, Dean Martin. Masculinity was also expressed via terseness. Roy Harold Fitzgerald became Rock Hudson; Marion Michael Morrison, John Wayne. Femininity was similarly expressed via euphony, with some use of alliteration, and here a certain degree of foreignness might be retained giving an exotic effect. Thus, Norma Jean Baker became Marilyn Monroe; Hedwig Kiesler, Hedy Lamarr; Dorothy Kaumeyer, Dorothy Lamour.

There was a similar desire in musicians, especially English ones, to appear more exciting by assuming foreign-sounding names. Thus, in Anthony Powell's novels, the infant prodigy violinist Carolo's real name, according to another character, "is Wilson or Wilkinson or Parker, . . . something rather practical and healthy like that. A surname felt to ring too much of plain common sense."[103]

CHAPTER TWELVE

America

Like other cultural traits, American naming practices derived from Europe and were fundamentally no different from their models. There were significant minor variations, however, in first-name choice and usage, while the assimilation of first and second names of immigrants (including Blacks) to American norms was a special feature. More recently, some American trends have impacted back on to European practice.

First names

As we have seen, the first settlers in America had an "English" pattern of first names, with John, William, Edward and so on in the lead for men, and Mary, Elizabeth and Anne for women. From the mid seventeenth century in New England, Puritan names became dominant. At Concord, Massachusetts, between 1691 and 1770, for example, the commonest male names, along with the traditional but also Biblical John and Thomas, were Joseph, Samuel, David and Timothy; and the commonest female names, along with Mary and Elizabeth, were Sarah, Abigail, Hannah and Rebecca. In New England between 1780 and 1850, however, there was a "precipitous decline in the use of Biblical (and especially Old Testament) names". For boys they fell from 75 per cent to 25 per cent and for girls from 55 per cent to 30 per cent. At Concord by 1820, "the old favourites John, Joseph, Samuel [had given way] . . . to a new set of non-Biblical choices, such as Charles, William, Frank, George, Henry, etc." At the same time "those few Biblical names still common in the 1840s such as Sarah, David, John and Joseph" had become "traditional" in New England, losing their Puritan connotations.[1] These names also spread to areas that had never been ones of Puritan influence. Benjamin and Joseph entered the top ten male names in Virginia, for example, between

1750 and 1790; and Sarah and Susanna the top ten female. A few other "new" names also entered the list of generally popular names at this time: James, brought by Scottish, and Frederick and Jacob, brought by German immigrants.

These changes reflected "a strong current of secularization" but predated the onset of major urbanization, industrialization and the "new" immigration. They have also been seen as signs of "the reintegration of rural New England [in particular] into the transatlantic middle class" via the medium of shared first names. This reconvergence with British popular culture was to a degree reversed from the middle of the century with further and often non-British immigration.[2]

The ten commonest boys' names in the USA in 1875 were, in order, William, John, Charles, Harry, James, George, Frank, Robert, Joseph and Thomas. In 1900, Samuel and Arthur had entered the list, ousting Harry and Frank. In 1925, Richard, Donald and Edward appeared (or reappeared); and in 1940 David, Ronald and Michael appeared, while Thomas reappeared. There was little change in 1950: Gary entered the list, and Charles re-entered it. 1960 saw the arrival of Mark and Steven and the re-entry of Joseph; 1970 the arrival of Jeffrey, Christopher and Brian. By 1990, Matthew, Joshua, Andrew, Daniel, Justin and Ryan had entered the list of top White male names; Brandon, Anthony, Joshua and Jonathan of non-White names. The full lists for 1995 were, for Whites: Michael, Joshua, Matthew, Jacob, Zachary, Christopher, Tyler, Brandon, Andrew and Nicholas; and for non-Whites: Christopher, Michael, Brandon, Joshua, James, Anthony, Devonte, Jonathan, William and Justin.

The ten commonest girls' names in 1875, in order, were Mary, Anna, Elizabeth, Emma, Alice, Edith, Florence, May, Helen and Katherine. Half of these had been replaced by 1900, with Ruth, Margaret, Dorothy, Mildred and Frances coming in. In 1925, Barbara, Betty, Jean and Ann(e) entered the list; and in 1940, Patricia, Judith, Carol(e), Sharon, Nancy, Joan and Sandra. Linda, Susan, Deborah, Kathleen and Karen arrived in 1950; and Kimberly, Cynthia and Lori in 1960 with a re-entry by Catherine. The list was all new in 1970, except for Kimberly: Michelle, Jennifer, Lisa, Tracy, Kelly, Nicole, Angela, Pamela and Christine. The top ten were almost entirely renewed again in 1990 for Whites with Ashley, Jessica, Amanda, Sarah, Brittany, Megan and Stephanie appearing and Katherine reappearing; and for Blacks; Brittany, Ashley, Jasmine, Jessica, Tiffany, Erica, Crystal, Danielle and Alicia. The full lists for 1995 were, for Whites, Ashley, Jessica, Sarah, Brittany, Kaitlyn, Taylor, Emily, Megan, Samantha and Katherine; and for Blacks, Jasmine, Brianna, Brittany, Ashley, Alexis, Jessica, Chelsea, Courtney, Kayla and Sierra.

The most striking feature of first-name choice in the period since 1875 is the volatility of the list of commonest names. This can be gauged generally by calculating the number of new names entering the top ten names every decade. This rose for boys' names from around one in the period 1875–1925 to two or more in the inter-war period, and then three after 1950. Comparable figures for girls' names were two in the period 1875–1925, four to five in the inter-war period, rising to a peak of nine in the 1960s. Figures for both genders for the top twenty names are in line with this.

Rapid turnover can also be seen in the fortunes of individual names. Taking boys' names, Louis, for example, was very popular from 1875 to 1900, then declined from 1925 to 1940, to become virtually unused. Michael was little used in the early twentieth century, rose quite quickly to tenth most common in 1940 and second in 1950. Michael reached top position in 1960 and remained there through into the 1990s. Christopher entered the top fifty in 1950, became fairly common through the 1950s and 1960s, and reached eighth position in 1970 and second position in 1990.

Among girls' names, Minnie was quite popular from 1875 to 1900, then virtually disappeared. Mildred similarly was in eighth position in 1900, 28th in 1925 and then became virtually unknown. Lillian was very common till 1900, but then fell off sharply. Among Smith College graduates, Wright notes "the almost total disappearance of once popular names, such as Ethel, Bertha, Charlotte, Clara, Agnes, Emma, and the sudden rise of Patricia, Lois, Betty, Constance, Priscilla, Marilyn and Suzanne" in succeeding decades. Names in "-ie", which were in favour around 1900, such as Abbie, Addie and Nellie, had also become "old-fashioned" by the 1950s.[3] Generally, again Michelle was unknown before 1950, jumped to twentieth in 1960 and then first place in 1970, after which it fell back. Karen, too, was unknown till 1950, when it suddenly reached tenth place; then it quickly declined. Ashley came from nowhere to become the commonest name for White girls in 1990 and 1995. Another recent name, Brittany, suddenly arrived as fifth for Whites and first for non-Whites in 1990, remaining very high in both categories in 1995.

The USA also experienced the phenomenon of "classic" names that retained their popularity over long periods of time. Thomas, for example, remained popular throughout the whole period from 1875, falling off only in the 1990s. William likewise was very popular from 1875 to 1970, when it went through a dip, rising to high popularity again in 1995. Both Robert and Joseph retained leading positions for a century until 1970, when they went into decline. Charles similarly was very common until 1950, then fell off, especially in the 1990s. As we have seen, many of these names were already "traditional" in 1875. Female "classic" names were also in evidence. Ann(e) was fairly steady from 1900 to 1975, though at a low level of popularity. Catherine, Elizabeth, Margaret and Laura similarly spanned the century from 1875. Helen was common through to 1950, when it fell off. As in Europe, "classic" names in the USA seem to have been favoured by the better-educated and the well-off. But "classic" names in the USA differ from those in the UK and more so France in that they retained much higher levels of popularity consistently. The same is true of some recent leading names.

Michael and Christopher, for example, retained their high level of popularity over quite long periods of time.

Both these names were in fact old names revived, and other examples may be cited, notably from the Old Testament. Joshua was not in the top fifty names before 1970, but rose to the top six in the 1990s. Rebecca was popular in 1875, then became quite rare, reviving around 1950; it entered the top fifty in the 1960s and remained in the top thirty names in the 1990s. Deborah came from further back to arrive at fifth place quite suddenly in 1950; it was at second place in 1960, at thirteenth in 1970, then fell off considerably. The revival of old names was less of a feature in the USA than in Europe, the corollary of the greater importance of "classic" names.

American first names in effect displayed divergent developments, old and new, in this and other ways. Despite a trend towards national uniformity, as in so many other areas of life, regional patterns in naming persisted. Zelinsky, for example, found a continuity in first-naming choices in New England across the whole period 1790–1970. Certain names were characteristic of the South. At the time of the First World War, Hugh, Milton and Clyde, Lucille, Josephine and Marguerite were Southern names. Old Testament names retained a special vogue in the south-western "Bible Belt" down to the 1930s. Ralph McGill, born around 1900 in rural Tennessee and himself named after Emerson, wrote that

> people in our village almost all had first names from the Bible . . .
> There was, of course, an occasional William to commemorate William
> of Orange. But the Book was the proper source of names.[4]

Dunkling's comparative tables of the top ten names in different states in 1975 reveal that significant differences remain, especially for girls' names. Louisiana and Oregon, for example, shared only five girls' names but nine boys'; Connecticut and Louisiana shared six girls' names but eight boys'; Oregon and Wyoming six girls but nine boys'.

First-name transmission in America before the nineteenth century paralleled the situation in the European countries from which settlers came. Names were passed on within families, with two models prevailing. At Hingham, Massachusetts, for example, two-thirds of first children born before 1721 "had the same first name as one of their parents". Names of grandparents were given less often to second and later children. Sharing names between brothers' sons was very rare. At the same time, the practice of passing the names of dead children to later-born siblings was common. First-naming therefore expressed a strong sense of family, but one focused on the nuclear unit rather than its multigenerational and lateral extensions.[5]

By contrast, among the Dutch settlers of Schenectady around eight out of ten "first sons or daughters born . . . between 1781 and 1800 shared the name of a grandparent". It seems that "grandparental names were allocated sequentially according to the sex and birth order of the child". The eldest son was almost invariably named after his paternal grandfather, and the eldest daughter in two-thirds of cases after her paternal grandmother. Second sons and daughters took names correspondingly from the maternal side of the family.[6] Here first-naming emphasized the sense of dynasty and wider kinship ties. This second pattern was also found in Virginia and Cape Cod in the colonial period.

At Hingham, the traditional familial pattern of first-naming declined sharply after 1820, coinciding with the introduction of "middle" names. Naming after parents and dead siblings remained significant but at a much lower and falling level. This decline is found all over the USA and can be linked to fundamental social changes. "In the midst of the continual movement which agitates a democratic community", Tocqueville wrote in 1840, "the tie which unites one generation to another is relaxed or broken; every man readily loses the trace of the ideas of his forefathers or takes no care about them." More particularly, the family became "less patriarchal and more matrifocal, less hierarchical and more egalitarian", and there was more stress on the individual both within and apart from the family.[7]

But there were important differences of pace in this development in different areas and for different groups. Naming after family members remained generally more important through to the twentieth century in the South rather than the North, and it seems to have survived best in rural rather than urban areas, among the well-to-do rather than the poor, for boys rather than girls, and among certain immigrant groups. Most important, it had become selective rather than prescriptive. In rural Kentucky, for example, around 1940, only 5 per cent of men had first names that were not family names and over 70 per cent of men "were named for their fathers". However, in the socially similar Blue Ridge country of Virginia about the same time there was a strong "tendency to disregard ancestral nomenclature in the bestowing of Christian names", though where family names were given they tended to be those of grandparents rather than parents.[8] To take an urban immigrant example, among second generation Greek immigrants in New York 68 per cent of men and 58 per cent of women were named after specific relations, and among those of the third generation 78 per cent were named after kin – mainly grandparents.

The fullest modern study is Rossi's for middle-class families in Chicago from the 1920s to the 1950s. Here kin were "the major source of the personal names for children", and 62 per cent of the sample were named after a particular relative, usually a parent or grandparent. Boys were more likely to be named after kin than girls, and elder rather than younger children. Over the period there was no overall change in the prevalence of naming children after kin as such, but there was a change in the precise pattern. In the 1920s, sons tended to be named after paternal kin and daughters after maternal kin, with a general emphasis on the former. By the 1950s, these gender distinctions had tended to disappear, and there was more of a balance between the two sides of the family, irrespective of the gender of the children. Rossi saw this development as a reflection of a decline in family solidarity across the generations and of a broader increase in "egalitarianism across age and sex lines".[9]

Besnard has queried this interpretation. He suggests that particularly by the 1950s relating first-name choice to particular kin by parents was a rationalization of choices actually dictated by fashion, a view which the breakdown of specific lineage naming would tend to confirm. And there is much evidence, going back to the nineteenth century, that parents selected names for their children from the circle of kin without following any obvious rules and that they mixed these names with other new ones. For example, the children of Lee and Helen Black of Forest Creek, Oregon, in order, were Olena Martha, born in 1906, whose first name was new and whose second was that of a paternal aunt; Lottie Myrtilla, born in 1908, again with one new name and another borne by paternal relatives; John Mappin, born in 1911, who had both names of his paternal grandfather; Ruth Edna, born in 1915, whose names were either new or from maternal kin; and Helen Isabelle, born in 1918, with her mother's name as her first name and a new "middle" name.[10] The same combination of kin names and new names in vogue continued over successive generations down to the present.

The importance of family name transmission is reflected in two other American practices: the use of "Junior" and of dynastic ordinals to distinguish sons, usually the eldest, from homonymic fathers. "Junior" was also most often attributed to the elder or eldest son. In the nineteenth century, "Junior" for the younger was frequently complemented by "Senior" for the elder man, but this mode was on the decline by the time of the Second World War. The use of "Junior" or "Jr" after the name used to be associated with the upper classes of the Eastern seaboard, but again by the time of the war had been adopted much more generally. In a school sample in the mid 1930s, 28 per cent of boys had the appellation; in a much more general sample in 1971 3.3 per cent of men, which suggests an important decline. The burden of "Junior" and the position of familial and social inferiority that it betokened was expressed with anguish by the novelist Henry James, who bore it for 40 years, placing it on the title-page of all his works up to and including *The Portrait of a Lady* in 1881. "Throughout his life Henry volubly protested against the parental failure to let him have a distinctive name and [hence] an identity of his own", and he tried to prevent his married elder brother William from perpetuating the custom with his children – without success. That this was not peculiar is indicated by a recent study, which finds a correlation between bearing "Junior" and psychiatric disorder. "A boy is named Junior in deference to the father's wish to perpetuate himself in his son, to have his son emulate him, and at the same time to retain a clearly superior role himself." This "colours and aggravates the natural conflict between father and son", causing frequent and special neuroses.[11]

Dynastic numbers seem to have been introduced in the early nineteenth century. "At the start '2nd' seems to have been only a substitute for 'Jr', but now often indicates, not the son, but the grandson or nephew of the first bearer of the name", Mencken noted in 1936. "The use of the Roman numerals II, III, etc. came much later" and these "tended to be reserved for individuals in the direct line of descent",[12] but these distinctions were not strictly followed. "Junior", "2nd" or "II" continued to be interchangeable, and the appellation "Junior" might be retained until both parents, not just the father, died. So, in El Dorado, Arkansas, George Morgan, born around 1900, had a son George Morgan Junior, still referred to as George Junior by his widowed mother. George Junior's eldest son was George Morgan III, and his eldest son George Morgan IV.

There were no equivalent appellations in use for girls. This relates to the fact that boys' names were generally more "traditional" than girls'. Studies of New York State, for example, from the 1960s to the 1980s found that the naming of boys was taken more "seriously" than that of girls. The commonest girls' names were "more likely to be of a novel or unconventional origin".[13] Where boys were given "new" names, these were likely to be old names revived, whereas girls' new names were more likely to be outside the traditional repertoire.

Fashion had long been a factor in first-naming. Naming after public figures, for example, began with the first Revolutionary heroes: Hancock, president of the First and Second Continental Congresses; Washington; and Warren, killed at Bunker Hill in 1775. By the late 1770s, "thousands" of babies were being named Franklin, Jefferson, Otis and Adams, "to be followed in due course by Hamilton, Marshall, Jackson, Harrison, Lincoln, Grant" and so on. "The most popular nomenclature relic" of the Revolutionary period, still in vogue in the 1940s, was Elmer, the name of two pamphleteers. Lee, after General Robert E. Lee, also became a very popular name among both genders following the Civil War – and not only in the South.[14] Names from literature and later the cinema also played a model role. A clear example is Bonnie, the pet name of Melanie's child in Margaret Mitchell's *Gone with the Wind* (1936) and in the subsequent film.

By the post-Second World War period, the role of fashion *per se* became predominant as religious and family influences on naming declined. The processes by which fashions were formed and spread have been little studied, however. An older pattern of top-down diffusion, found in Europe, seems to have been less important in the uncentralized and culturally diverse USA, with more room being left for "class" and ethnic preferences or differential class and ethnic exposure to an increasingly homogeneous popular culture and mass media.

All modern Western first-naming systems have divergent trends towards conformity and originality. As in older systems, a few names were very common, though now these change rapidly from decade to decade. Names occurring too frequently lose their cachet and are replaced by others. At the same time, the concentration on just a few names is lessened and the overall name stock increases. These trends are found early on in the USA and to a marked degree.

First, name stock and the phenomenon of concentration. At Concord, Massachusetts, in the seventeenth and early eighteenth centuries, the top ten male names accounted for nearly two-thirds of all choices; and comparable figures arc found elsewhere. Women's names were equally or more concentrated. By the end of the eighteenth century at Concord, the top ten male names accounted for only one-third of choices, and this again was typical. This process continued through the nineteenth and twentieth centuries. By 1975, among Princeton students, the top ten male names accounted for 34 per cent of persons, and the top ten female names for 51 per cent. Comparable figures for California were 29 per cent for men and 22 per cent for women. Over the past two centuries, the stock of first names has expanded from a few hundred to over 3,000 for both genders.

The trend towards conformity in first names has been strongly affected by the desire of successive waves of immigrants to assimilate via the use of "American" names. As Mencken noted in 1936, "the favourite given-names of the old country almost disappear in the first native-born immigrants". In Mencken's own case, he was named Henry after his father's brother of Northern Irish stock, and Louis after his German paternal grandfather. The old transmission was still operative and the old names underlay the new ones. The actual name of Mencken's grandfather was Ludwig, but "it was decided to translate it". The clergyman wrote "Louis" on the certificate in the French form, but the name was always pronounced Lewis. This process was repeated in a thousand ways for members of different immigrant groups. Among Greeks, for example, Panagiotis became Pete, Demetrios Jim, Basil Bill, Stacros Steve, Athanasios Thomas or Tom, Constantine Gus or Charles; among Slovaks, Jaroslav became Jerry, Miloslav Milo and so on.[15]

At a later stage the process of translation or adoption of a similar "American" name to the chosen original was dropped and immigrants used American names as such for their children. This seems to have occurred among those of Norwegian origin in Minnesota by the late 1930s. The commonest boys' names there were Arthur, Clifford, Clarence, Donald, Gordon and Harold, of which only the last may be related to a Norse name; and the commonest girls' names were Helen, Margaret, Ruth, Dorothy and Marion, which closely reflected the commonest female names generally at the time. Only in a very few cases did a "foreign" or non-British name enter the American repertoire of first names, for example the German Carl, the Scandinavian Karen, and possibly the Dutch Derek.

"European visitors to America in the nineteenth and twentieth centuries never wearied of expressing a mixture of horror and amusement at the wild proliferation of American names." The custom of giving unusual or invented names seems to have begun in New England in the nineteenth century (probably in the wake of Puritan nomenclature) and then to have spread elsewhere. In this century it was found especially "in the Bible Country of the South and Southwest".[16] Both Mencken and then Pyles produced lists of these names for men but especially for women, from which we can only select. Men's names include Ace, Almouth, Belvin, Cluke, Dolphus, Elvis, Flavel, Fonzo, Glore, Jamanuel, Kennis, Leandrew, Lum, Mord, Noyce, Occum, Oral, Poke, Tandy, and Vernace. Women's names include Alfa, Alsenatha, Amerette, Bashie, Brooxie, Bythella, Cementa, Chairynne, Clazene, Coita, Coweene, Daisybee, Dawnette, Dewdrop, Elmonia, Enolia, Etna, Eulice, Evannah, Flowanna, Fomby, Gamelle, Gaylene, Glassie, Groveline, Horlene, Jacel, Jeeta, Jessoise, Lalabelle, Lazella, Lonzetta, Lotolia, Luvna, Merdelle, Molvene, Myricille, Onza, Oota, Pencilla, Pheotine, Quejette, Ragine, Refolla, Seena, Teretha, Thallis, Totus, Vangele, Vomera, Weeda, Welo, Wreatha, Zelvateen, Zessie and Zippa. Such names never exceeded 15 per cent of first names overall, though in their regions of predilection they were far more important.

Some writers have associated the bestowal of such names with lack of wealth and education, and this may have been a factor in some places, for example the Blue Ridge district of Virginia and New York City, but, as Mencken noted, "some of the most extraordinary specimens on my list are taken, not from the police news in the Bible Belt newspapers, but from rosters of college students and the elegant gossip of the society columns". Those with unusual names in Oklahoma in the 1940s belonged to families of "highly reputable social standing".[17]

Another feature of the "peculiar" names of Oklahoma and elsewhere was a significant loosening-up of the normally strict rules ascribing one set of names to males and another to females. In the 1940s, Marion, Carol and Beryl were all names given to boys as well as girls. Sharon Lee and June also occurred as boys' names, while Nigel, Vincent and Tommie Joe occurred as girls'. Much more generally, diminutive male names, such as Tommie, Billie, and Bobby, became common female names, often in combinations.

Invented or novel American first names fall into certain categories. Male names were given female endings, for example Lloydine, Oscaretta, Bobbette. Some were place-names, sometimes modified: Denver, California, Texana, Arzonia. Titles were also particularly favoured: Duke, Earl, Lady, Leroy, Prince. Earl was the commonest of these.

> Another large class of non-canonical girls' names is produced by adorning old names with new and mellifluous terminations, for example Carrine, Marcelette, Olgalene, or by making collision forms of two or more, for example Gracella, Aloxuise, Hannora.

Certain suffixes recur here: -elle, -ette, -ene or -ine. There were also "novel abbreviations" like Affie, Berthie or Oshie; "rococo spellings" like Cylvia,

Dorrace, Pyrl; imaginative use of capitals and apostrophes, as in ClarEtta, De'an, E-Vetha, Lo Venia; and changes of initial like Garguerite, Maomi and Omelia, or Landrew and Terbert. There was a "breakdown of names by syllables and their reconstruction", for example Kathella, Kathann, Kathymay, that is reminiscent of the Germanic dithematic systems. There were also pure creations, like Flouzelle, Glitha, Lephair, Wheirmelda and Moonean.[18]

A number of reasons have been adduced for the choice of peculiar first names. Assuming that such names were mainly given by "educationally and culturally deprived groups such as the Southern white and negro share croppers and the so-called 'hill-billies'" (an assumption that we have seen was only partially correct), Brender related them in 1963 to the fact that such groups were prolific, with many children to name towards whom parents were indifferent, if not hostile. There is confluent evidence here that peculiar first names could be a distinct social handicap in some circumstances. But the explanation offered by Sizer for the "fanciful" names of the Blue Ridge district is much more plausible generally: "It is as if the mothers crystallize in a poetic name a fleeting dream of beauty denied them in their hard lives." She cites one such mother's own explanation: "Hit war born in th' spring, an' it war so sweet an' tender, jus' like th' buds on th' trees, so I named it Mountain Bud." Compensation for poverty, lack of sophistication, attention to birth circumstances went along with lack of external supervision. Mencken observed that Catholics were less prone to peculiar first names than Protestants, because priests insisted on a saint's name. Pyles has noted more generally that there is a strong correlation between the strange first names of the Bible Belt and the practice of adult baptism. This left parents, and especially mothers, free to select names without clerical guidance. Ironically, with post-Second World War migration, "the increasing numbers and prestige" of Baptists and other sects such as the Assemblies of God and the Jehovah's Witnesses, all of whom rejected infant baptism, led to "the decline of the Christian name" throughout the South and South-West.[19]

To these mainly negative factors should be added two positive ones. First was the desire to give a child an original, if not unique name, expressive, Pyles suggests, of the extreme individualism of American society. A Mrs Hoyette White of Oklahoma City, who named her five daughters, in the 1920s and 1930s, Wilbarine, Norvetta, Yerdith, Marlynne and Arthetta, explained: "I wanted names no one had ever had and nobody would ever want. So I made them up."[20] But here one should note that the Bible Belt, far from being a region of rampant individualism, is one where the sense of family and community is strong. One source of unusual names was family names. The traditional naming of sons with their mothers' maiden names continued and was extended to daughters. Also the new names were often formed from elements in the family repertoire. To take the White sisters again, Wilbarine incorporated her father's middle name, Wilbur; Norvetta recalled her mother's maiden name, which was North; and Arthetta derived from her father's first name Arthur. The second positive factor, so well represented by Mrs White, is an inventiveness and creativity, an exuberance and love of novelty, all characteristic of American culture.

Second or "middle" names seem to have arrived in America at the end of the eighteenth century and then to have become quickly established as normal. They seem to have been introduced among the élites, as in Europe, and then to have percolated downwards. "In the drafted army of World War I, a highly egalitarian assemblage, every American was presumed to have a middle name." In 1978, 75 per cent of the population had them. More than two first names was "most unusual". "Middle names were particularly useful . . . as mediating devices that allowed a strong sense of family to co-exist with an equally strong sense of individuality."[21] The first name followed fashion, while the middle name preserved some family tradition. Combined names, linking two first names in everyday use, became frequent, especially for girls, in the nineteenth century, and remained common in the south after this, examples being Sara Lee, Lily May, and Sue Ellen.

For men, the middle name was often initialled: Beverley R. Grayson (c.1800, Virginia); Calvin E. Stowe (mid nineteenth century, Massachusetts). According to Mencken, the custom only became widespread in the inter-war period. An analysis of Who's who and similar registers in the 1940s showed 65 per cent of the élite using this form. By this time it had spread more widely socially, however, and was a sought-after status symbol. This is confirmed by the fact that, though the initial did usually stand for an actual given name, in many cases it was a cypher – simply adopted to acquire prestige. The empty initial could be used for other reasons. In the case of President Harry S. Truman, born in 1884, the S stood for no particular name. He had one grandfather called Solomon and another called Shippe, and the S was a compromise. The use of phantom initials was so common by the time of the Second World War that both the US Army and Navy distinguished in listing personnel between initials that stood for actual names and those that did not by enclosing the latter in quotation marks or brackets. Among the Amish, all children born to a couple were given the same middle initial. In some communities this was the first letter of the mother's family name, in others that of the father's first name. Among some Amish, this initial was nearly always used with the first name in everyday life. So Isaac Z. Smoker was Iksie, and his brother Samuel Samsie; Daniel T. Esh was Dantee; and so on.

Other aspects of American usage should be mentioned. "An easy transition to the use of first names upon short acquaintance is typical American business and social practice", a social psychologist noted in 1958, "and reflects the prevailing approval of an extroverted type of adjustment." Studies of modes of address confirm this. Reciprocal title and last name: Mr Brown, were restricted by the mid twentieth century to formal settings, such as courtrooms, official meetings and gatherings; while reciprocal second name alone, which had been characteristic of some institutions, was very old-fashioned. Non-reciprocal first name and title plus second name was normal between children and adults. It was also sometimes used between inferiors and superiors at work or generally. In the South until the 1960s or after, "the white man is accustomed to call the Negro by his first name, but he expects to be called" Mr So-and-So in return.[22]

The typical American use of first names to comparative strangers was found odd by those from other more formal cultures. A Japanese Rotarian wrote in 1937 that addressing an acquaintance in this way in Japan would be considered "as somewhat coarse and of questionable taste". The custom in America seems to date from the 1920s, though there was some loosening-up on earlier formality before then. That earlier formality is evoked by Henry James, writing of New England in particular around 1825 and

the universal "Mr" of the male address. It was apparently in use with Judge Story for all his friends, for his colleagues, however familiar – a fact that we think of as throwing a light on relations, as they existed in that more straitened world, as showing how little provision, so to speak, was made for them. We see that the normal relation of intimacy, the only one at all concerned, was, rigidly, that of a man's fireside – his intimacy with his wife, his children and his Creator. The others, the outside ones, remained formal, civil, dutiful, but never could have become easy.[23]

By contrast, modern usage extended a would-be intimacy to all, eventually abandoning even those few remaining acknowledgements of social distance that we have noted.

The familiarity of first-name usage was taken a stage further in the liking for hypocoristic forms. Diminutives and pet forms were given as first names proper, for example Peggy, Flo, Mamie or Beth for girls; Ben, Phil, Josh and Dan for boys. This custom seems to have applied especially and first to girls and was found in Virginia and New England from the later eighteenth century. It became more common and widespread subsequently.

In addition, of course, where the full name had been given at birth, the pet form was actually used. Studies of college students from the 1940s to the 1970s found that most preferred the short versions of their names, while a 1941 enquiry discovered that full names were often selected by parents for their children because of their hypocoristic forms. A study of modes of address in American English in 1964 concluded that "male first names . . . very seldom occur in full form but are almost always either abbreviated or diminutized or both". The authors noted that this treatment of the formal name was much less common with women, perhaps because they often already had pet forms of names.[24]

Hypocoristic names of both kinds were more common in some places than others and seem to have been particularly characteristic of the Bible Belt, where they formed a sub-category of the unusual names of the region. Of the graduates of the University of Oklahoma in 1950, 10 per cent had names such as Arch, Benny, Cy, Guss, Hi, Newt, Ollie and Zeph. As Pyles stressed, these names were frequently formal given names, and, where they were not, they were used in the most formal circumstances, for example official announcements of births, marriages and deaths. They were also used alongside titles, such as "Hon" (for office-holders), "Rev" and "Professor". Mencken and Pyles both suggest that office-holders and office-seekers used the hypocoristic form to convey easy-going informality and "a sort of bonhomie". Speaker Rayburn of Texas was quoted in the local press in 1955 as saying (untruthfully): "I was named Sam, not Samuel. We don't believe in putting on airs in our family." More generally, Pyles suggests that the custom reflects the fact that "juvenility is highly regarded" in the USA. What had been appellations for children have become normal for adults.[25]

We should also mention here the custom, already alluded to in connection with middle names, of initialling some or all of a person's names to produce what is in effect a kind of hypocoristic name or nickname. This occurs with well-known figures, such as O.J. Simpson, and the form has been used for some presidents: F.D.R., J.F.K., and L.B.J..

Second names, titles and nicknames

Second names in America have few distinctive features beyond those occasioned by the experience of immigration and settlement. Stabilization came perhaps surprisingly late.

> Many of the conscripts rounded up for [the First World War] . . . had only the vaguest idea of the spelling of their names, and not a few were uncertain as to what their names were, but by the time they were discharged every man had a name that was imbedded in the official records, and he had to stick to it in order to enjoy any of the benefits and usufructs of a veteran.

This process was further aided in the inter-war years by the spread of life insurance, by automobile registration and then by Social Security. So "by 1940 American family nomenclature was vastly more stable than it had been in 1910, or even in 1920".[26]

Besides Black slaves, whom we will deal with separately, one other group actually acquired second names in the modern period. American Indians did not originally have fixed "family" names and their given names often changed through their lifetimes. Also they did not use their names in the modern European or American way. Kluckhohn wrote of the Navaho in 1962 that

> as long as the world of a person remains within traditional inter-personal limits, there is little need for names. Kinship terms are enough for him to address or refer to everybody and they in turn can designate him adequately.

So, on the reservation, kinship terms were used and not names and "tradit-ional Navaho consider it impolite to use a person's given name in his or her presence". But, when they were settled on reservations, the Indian Bureau had laid down that all Indians had to have fixed family names, and children entering school or adults coming into contact with the administration were allotted names "in the American fashion". Native names could be translated, for example Standing Bear, Little Cloud or Broken Nose. "Sometimes tribal names were retained as surnames . . . Wahneeta, Wayskakamick . . . , but [both] such forms were greatly outnumbered by commonplace English names" such as Jackson, Simpson, Brown or Johnson.[27]

This was an experience that native Americans shared with many immig-rants. The ten commonest family names in the USA in the late 1930s were Smith, Johnson, Brown, Williams, Jones, Miller, Davis, Anderson, Wilson and Moore. This list was virtually unchanged by 1995, and it was almost identical to the list of commonest names in the UK. Beneath the overall national listings, there are significant regional variations. In New York City, Cohen was in first place, with Murphy, Kelly, Meyer and Schwartz among the first ten. Levy was the second most common name in New Orleans. "In Grand Rapids, Michigan, in a region of heavy Dutch settlement", there are no Dutch names in the first five family names, "but the sixth is the Dutch DeVries, the ninth is DeYoung (De Jong) and the eleventh is Van Dyke".[28] Though these variations reflect different patterns of settlement and indicate the partial retention of ethnic names, they cannot do more than qualify the overall picture.

This was one in which the majority of America's vast population of immigrants from European countries sought to assimilate to the American norm generally and linguistically. In the area of names, this meant to adopt or to approximate to English names. This might occur by deliberate choice on the part of a family or individual, by the action of immigration and other officials often ignorant of foreign languages and changing the unfamiliar name they heard into something more familiar to them, or by a process of general pressure on peculiar names by neighbours, employers and others. Here first names were always more amenable to change, having a strong element of choice already there; second names were in theory invariable and changing them was of more consequence. Established Americans would have to go through some form of legal process in order to change their family names, though there were no formal barriers against doing so such as existed in some European countries. By contrast, a minority of immigrants sought to maintain a certain ethnic identity, to cling to at least part of the group and family traditions, and this might well mean retaining their original names in some shape or form. These two tendencies affected different groups in different ways at different times.

Mencken has profusely illustrated the process of assimilation to Anglo-American norms as far as second names are concerned. He notes that in 1928 only two-thirds of those with English or Welsh family names had in fact acquired them "by ancient inheritance"; the rest had borrowed them, usually as equivalents of their non-English names. More particularly, a study in 1932 indicated that only just over half the American Smiths were of British origin. "The rest are German Schmidts, Scandinavian Smeds, Czech Kovárs, Hungarian Kovácses, Syrian Haddads and Polish Kowlczyks", as well as Jews with a variety of names.[29] Mencken also cites a few classic examples of key American figures with assimilated names: General George Custer, the Indian fighter, the great-grandson of a Hessian soldier named Küster; General J.J. Pershing, the descendant of a German family named Pfoersching, who arrived in Pennsylvania in 1749; and President Herbert C. Hoover, descendant of another German immigrant to Pennsylvania, Andreas Huber.

This process of adapting second names began with the earliest settlers and affected all groups. Among Germans, "ch" and "g" tended to be replaced, Bloch becoming Block or Black; Albrecht, Albert; Steinweg, Steinway. The umlaut "met the same fate: Grün was changed to Green, . . . Düring to Deering".[30] Sometimes the spelling was changed to keep the German sound in English. So Blüm became Bloom, Reuss Royce, Friedmann Freedman, Heid Hite or Hyde, Roggenfelder Rockefeller, Kranheit Cronkite. Alternatively, the original spelling might be retained but the name's sound changed. So Roth came to be pronounced Rawth; Uhler Youler; and Werner to rhyme with Turner. Final "e"s were silenced. Then, as we have seen, there were translations, like Schmidt to Smith, Becker to Baker, and Zimmermann to Carpenter.

Slav names were even more difficult for Anglo-American tongues. Czech names, for example, might be transliterated, Zděný becoming Stenny, Hřebec Hurbick and so on. Or English names with similar sounds could be substituted: Macy for Macá, Curtis for Kuťis, Wallace for Vaľis. Matoušek became Matthews via the German Matuscheck. Some Czechs adopted Irish forms here, Projín becoming Brian or O'Brien; Otřáska O'Tracey, and Očenášek O'Shaunnessy. Names were also translated, for example Holič to Barber, Ulk to Wolf, and Zajíc (meaning rabbit) to O'Hare. A particular difficulty was presented by patronymic suffixes. The Polish -ewski and -owicz, for example, tended to be dropped. In other cases, such suffixes and prefixes might themselves become the name. Among Greek immigrants, for example,

Constantinipoulos, Serasimopoulos, etc. might all become Poulos; while Pappadakis, Pappachristides and Pappadimitracoupoulos all became Pappas.

Scandinavian "ö", "j" and "sj" were also difficult sounds and signs and were generally altered. So the Swedish Sjörgren became Shogren, Segren or Seagren; Esbjörn became Esbyorn then Osborne; Hjelms became Helms. Names were translated too: for example, Sjöstrand became Seashore, and Högfelt Highfield. Finnish names could be translated – for example Maki to Hill, Joki to River or Rivers –; or transliterated – for example, Hämäläinen to Hamlin. Others were abbreviated. Höyhtyä became Hoyt; Pitkajarvi (long lake) could be shortened to Järvi "and then changed to Jarvis . . . ; Pulkka and Pullinen [were] . . . often changed to Polk".[31]

Mencken wrote in 1936 that "of all the immigrant peoples of the United States, the Jews seem most willing to change their names", in order to avoid "the disadvantages that go with . . . their Jewishness". They sought "to conceal their origin, or, at all events to avoid making it unnecessarily noticeable". This began with the first generation of immigrants and accelerated among those established in the country. A study of over 1,000 petitioners for change of name in Los Angeles in the 1940s indicated that about half of them were Jewish, while the Jewish population in the city was only 6 per cent. Moreover, whereas non-Jews usually sought a change of name following divorce or family break-up, Jews' name changes correlated rather with upward social mobility and the wish to escape "ethnically visible names . . . perceived by their bearers to hold adverse or objectionable connotations".[32] Such considerations were not of course exclusive to Jews, though they may have felt them especially acutely.

As a result

it has . . . become impossible in America to recognize Jews by their names. There are not only multitudes of Smiths, Browns and Jones among them, but also many Adamses, Lincolns, Grants, Lees, Jeffersons and Harrisons, and even Vanderbilts, Goulds, Schuylers, Cabots and Lowells.[33]

Frequently, "English" family names were chosen that were not far removed from the original name. So Abrahams became Allen or Adams; Burstein became Burr; Finkelstein, Finn or Flint. Often, as with other groups, names were translated or transliterated. So Rosenstein became Rosestone; Blumenfeld, Bloomfield; and so on. Abbreviations were very common, too: Greenberg to Green; Rosenberg to Rose. Less drastic and to some degree the result of linguistic wear-and-tear rather than deliberation were names whose spelling became more "English" in appearance. So Cohen, Cohn or Kohn became Cone, Cowan, Conn or Coyne; Levy became Leevy, Lewis, Lewin or Lee.

Mencken suggests that the process was facilitated for Jews by the fact that they had often not had their second names for very long and had "less sentimental attachment to them" than other immigrants. It has also been argued that there was nothing Jewish or Hebrew about most of the names borne by immigrants from central and eastern Europe. A Jew might as well be called Whitehill as Weisberg, Wilson as Wolfsohn, and the habit of adapting names was traditional. Nevertheless, despite the massive onomastic assimilation that took place, many Jews retained their names in discernible form. Certain Jewish names did remain prominent in areas of dense settlement; we have seen that Cohen was a, and sometimes the, leading name in New York City. More generally, "half the Jews [serving] in the U.S. Armed Forces during World War II bore last names that were . . . recognizably Jewish".[34]

Mencken's exhaustive studies stressed the process of assimilation to Anglo-American norms on the part of immigrants. Other and mainly later studies have emphasized rather this second option: the wish and the fact of retaining some kind of ethnic identity via names, despite the very strong pressures to assimilate which were reinforced in the second and later generations. Fucilla and Campisi note that the pattern of assimilation for most Italian Americans has been one of compromise, maintaining links with the family past and with things Italian. There was rarely any attempt to conceal Italian origin and names were more often modified than totally changed. A recent study of Hungarian immigrants to Canada finds that less than 3 per cent even modify their family names except for giving up diacritical marks over vowels. It concludes that "forces stronger than linguistic pressure for conformity are at play . . . By immigrating a Hungarian severs all patriotic and family ties. His name may be the only piece of heritage left", and it may be especially important to personal and group identity as a result.[35] This surely applies to other more recent immigrant groups to North America. More generally, there has been a trend among descendants of older immigrants into the USA to revive their ethnic names, as they feel more secure perhaps in being American yet wish to proclaim their "roots".

Another factor of great importance in explaining whether or not ethnic names are retained is the degree of physical dispersal of the group concerned. Groups which stay together in "urban villages" or rural districts and thus maintain elements of the old way of life also retain their names. A study of French Louisiana in 1941 showed not only that there were fairly sharp boundaries, detectable by family names, between those of French and non-French background and language, but there were similar boundaries between original "Creole" settlers and later Acadians or "Cajuns".

A further American idiosyncrasy concerns the names of married women. The general rule in the modern period was for married women to take their husbands' family names preceded by Mrs, as in Britain. However, as Mencken noted in 1936, it was "common . . . for a woman, on marrying, to use her maiden surname as a middle name; thus Miss Mary Jones, on becoming Mrs Brown, signs herself Mary Jones Brown".[36] Occasionally the two names were hyphenated. Some ethnic groups retained different customs, notably the French settlers of the Mississippi valley, among whom married women retained their own family names until well into the nineteenth century. More recently, it has been common for women to keep their own family names on marriage for feminist reasons. This raises problems about the second or last name to be taken by the children of these marriages. A recent study for Canada indicates that using the father's last name is the commonest because it is the simplest and most convenient solution. Next preferred is to use the mother's last name as a middle name for the child, yet another example of the versatility of this term.

Beyond the universal "Mr" and "Mrs", Americans before this century used occupational titles, and Southern males were fond of militia titles, especially Colonel. Hereditary titles, European-style, were of course proscribed in the Republic. In modern times, "Mr" and "Mrs" have a somewhat tenuous existence, as we have seen. Occupational and military titles survive, and there are some groups or individuals attracted by other honorifics. The "Hon" accorded to members of Congress and past and present senior office-holders, including mayors and judges, was also, until recently, given to or taken by the leaders of important organizations and pressure groups and the editors of important newspapers; while members of certain women's organizations "prefix 'Lady' indiscriminately to either the Christian name or the surname".[37]

Additional or alternative nicknames seem to have been common in all classes and ethnic groups through the colonial and modern periods, and they present few distinctive features compared with their equivalents in Europe. They were perhaps most prevalent and most public among isolated rural communities and socially deprived groups in the great cities, mainly Blacks and Puerto Ricans recently. They were also common in institutions, including schools.

A good example of the first is provided by the Amish. A scarcity of first and second names made nicknaming here "almost . . . an onomastic necessity".[38] In addition to names relating to traits, events, occupations and places, there were abbreviated versions of the first name, often combined with an initial, as we have seen, and genealogical names. Here children were linked to parents or grandparents with or without a possessive, with matronyms being especially common, for example Nancy-John, Nancy-Jake, Suzie-Ezra; or John's Amos; or Amos' John's Amos and Sim's Suzie's Ezra (after grandfather and father and mother respectively).

In the Blue Ridge district of Virginia, where everyone in a "hollow" might have the same family name, possessive terms were also used. "For example, one woman says to another, 'Have you heered that Eas's Bennie has done married Minnie's Lilie?', or 'John's Claude is a sorry girl', or 'Ella's Pete is talkin' [courting] Howard's Mazie.'"[39] Sometimes this same device was used, as in Europe, to designate sets of descendants or sub-lineages within lineages or "clans". Among Kentucky hill people around 1940, descendants from a great-grandfather were referred to as a "generation" and were named after that ancestor, for example the "Old Dicks" among the Browns. Similarly in Mecklenburg County, North Carolina, there were Clerk Isaac and Long Creek Isaac sets of Alexanders.

Two other forms of nickname have been studied in the USA but not Europe. The ethnic epithet, analogous to the personal nickname, was particularly prevalent in the multi-ethnic USA. Allen found 186 terms for 35 groups through the nineteenth and twentieth centuries. The importance of this kind of name throws another light, or casts another shadow, on assimilationist name-changing.

Nicknames were also given to public persons or "celebrities", for example baseball players. A study of these finds that before the Second World War, when players were genuine folk-heroes devoted to the game and its values and also socially at one with their mainly working-class following, then they were given nicknames through which an intimacy between players and fans was expressed. But with the commercialization of the sport, especially from the 1960s, nicknaming fell off, indicating an alienation between players and followers. Using an index to measure the frequency of nicknames among players, Skipper traces a threefold rise from 1871 to around 1920 and then a decline, with especially marked falls in the 1950s and again in the 1970s. He suggests that a similar pattern might be found in the relationships between politicians, high-ranking military personnel and other leaders and their followings over the same period.

Black names

Black names were in many ways no different from other American names, though, like other aspects of Black culture, they had some peculiarities deriving in the first place from the experience of slavery.

Observers at the time and since were impressed by the special and supposedly "characteristic" nature of slave names. Categories noted were foreign, Biblical and Puritan, and classical names, among others. In the seventeenth and eighteenth centuries, a high proportion of slaves did have "foreign", i.e. non-English names. These were mainly French or Spanish. In Louisiana before 1800, the proportion was 87 per cent, with much lower figures – around 15 per cent on average – elsewhere. This fell very quickly in the nineteenth century to around 1 per cent, reflecting the absorption of territories formerly under foreign rule or influence.

Biblical names, like Abraham, Isaac, and Sarah, do seem to have been quite common among slaves in the nineteenth century, at a time when the general White population was abandoning them, and the two phenomena may well be linked. One also finds Puritan names, such as Charity, Patience and Prudence. Titles were also given as names, for example General or King, as were places, like Bristol, Cambridge, Alabama or Tennessee – perhaps marking where slaves were born or sold. Slaves were also named after famous people: Byron, Washington, Lafayette, Napoleon.

But contemporaries were and historians have been struck above all by the classical names borne by slaves. Fanny Kemble referred in 1838, for example, to "the tribe of black-faced heathen divinities and classicalities who make believe to wait upon us here [in Charleston] – the Dianas, Phyllises, Floras, Caesars, etc.".[40] Other not uncommon names were Cato, Pompey, Juno, Dido, Scipio and Venus. However, though conspicuous, such names were in a distinct minority. Among the names recorded by Kemble herself on her husband Pierce Butler's Georgia plantation, only 6 per cent of males and 17 per cent of females in fact had classical names.

But why were classical names given at all? First, they were in general currency in the eighteenth and nineteenth centuries, as we have seen for Europe. They were borne by White people, among whom they were also more common for women than for men. Secondly, some classical names bore a similarity to certain African names and could be used as substitutes, for example Phoebe for Phiba or Phibbi, and Cato for Keta. This might have encouraged the use of other classical names for slaves. Some writers, thirdly, have stressed the derogatory and humiliating aim of classical names, which, it is assumed, were given by owners to put slaves in their place. Kemble again wrote: "Venus . . . is a favourite name among these sable folk, but, of course, must have been given originally in derision." Writing of Jamaica, where classical names seem to have been more common than in the USA, De Camp emphasized the same factor. "It was sometimes considered a good joke to name an exceptionally stupid man Plato or Socrates or to name a sexually promiscuous woman Diana." One may also point to a parallel between the naming of slaves and that of animals. Mules in Mississippi in the 1850s had names like Cato, Pompey and so on, as well as other kinds of name shared by slaves, while hunting dogs in the Old South were called Scipio or Caesar. This mode of naming should not be read in an entirely negative way, however. Owens cites the case of a master placing a tombstone with an epitaph on the grave of a loved slave: "Cesar [sic], the Ethiopian".[41]

This brings us again to the issue of African names. "The continued use" of African names "among native-born slaves has been seen as evidence of the persistence of African culture in the New World",[42] and has sometimes been exaggerated for this reason. Puckett estimated that about 13 per cent of slaves had African names in the eighteenth century, a proportion that fell to around 1 per cent in the nineteenth, paralleling the decline of other foreign names. The proportion may have been higher, however, among names or nicknames actually used by slaves themselves rather than the names given or recognized by slave-owners. African names remained more important among free Blacks in the nineteenth century.

The commonest form of African name was the day-name, deriving from the day of the week on which a child, male or female, was born. These were common in the West African societies from which most slaves came and formed a set of 14 names. Day-names are found among African slaves in New England, Nova Scotia and the West Indies as well as in the Old South. The commonest ones recorded in the south were Quash, Squash or Quashy, born on Sunday; Cudjo, born on Monday; Quaco or Quack, born on Wednesday – all of which were male; and Cuffy, a male, and Phiba, a female, born on Friday. These names were corrupted or eroded: for example Cuffie became Coffee. They were also sometimes translated: Monday, Wednesday, Friday. Day-names are only one example of the African (but also European) custom of naming a child after the circumstances of or events relating to its birth. Some phrase names are found among early American slaves. More common were names of months: April, June, August; of times of day: Morning; or of seasons or festivals: Winter, Easter. Other names were also given, for example Sambo or Mingo; and those deriving from tribal names like Hibou from Ibo, Becky from Beke, Fantee from Fanti and Bamba. Some African names were anglicized, Andoni becoming Anthony, Nsa Henshaw and Effiom Ephraim. African names tended to become ethnic epithets of a pejorative kind and were abandoned by ex-slaves after emancipation for that reason. A few survived, sometimes as family names, like Cuff or Cuffie.

In seeking the legacy of Africa in Black naming practices, one should go beyond the survival of specific appellations, however, and look at the general approach to naming. Here, as we shall see, some Blacks demonstrated a liking for variety and a creative extravagance that are reminiscent of African culture, though, as we have seen, this tendency also existed among some American Whites.

Hypocoristic forms were particularly common among slave names in the nineteenth century. Names such as Bob, Bill, Cy, Dru, Jinny and Kit were given as formal names, and some such names appeared in a great variety of forms, for example Liz, Liza, Lize, Lizy and so on from Elizabeth. On the Butler estate in Georgia in 1839, 38 per cent of male and 40 per cent of female names were hypocoristics. Puckett has seen this as a utilitarian phenomenon. They were names "which required a minimum of effort in speaking or in writing them". They were also names that did not "convey a sense of dignity or equality; they are names that might well be used by an adult in addressing a child".[43] There is something in this, but it should be remembered also that such shortened names were in very general use at the time as everyday names, and that they became much commoner in the modern period, as unofficial and official names. They conveyed familiarity, in both senses of the word, as well as condescension.

The hypocoristic slave name should be distinguished from the alternative nickname. This seems to have fallen into two categories. First, as we have mentioned, there were nicknames used by the slaves themselves, different from the names given them by their owners and sometimes perhaps kept secret like the African names with which they may have overlapped. Then there were secondary names in general use, which fulfilled the function of identifying slaves more accurately where they had common names or on large plantations. So Kemble referred to "Old House Molly", so called "to distinguish her from all the other Mollies on the estate".[44] Here occupation might be used: Engineer Ned; Carpenter John; Headman Frank; and age and appearance were also brought into play: Old Daniel; Little Mag; Great Jenny. It is often difficult to determine whether slave nicknames fall into one or the other category, and one may guess that many names were created by slaves themselves and then became used more generally, names such as Pie-Ya, Frog, Monkey, Cooter, John de Baptist, Fat-man, Fly-Up-de-Creek and Cat-Fish, all recorded on Thorn Hill plantation in Alabama. Another way to differentiate individuals was via generalogical terms, as in White communities. So one has Katina's York, Jenny's Dolly, Henry's Tom, for example. Here the matronym was most common, though women might be attached to husbands or lovers. If he or she was moved about, a single slave might have a succession of nicknames, for example (from Esher Parish in Louisiana) Bacchus alias Hogtub alias Fat Jack alias John.

Although peculiar slave names have attracted more attention, most African slaves in fact had ordinary English names. The commonest male slave names in a Chesapeake Bay county in the mid eighteenth century were Jack, Harry, Will, Dick, Sam, Jemmy and Tom, and the commonest female ones Jenny, Kate, Bess, Moll, Judy, Beck and Nan. On the Georgia plantation described by Kemble, over 30 per cent of slaves had full English names like Margaret, Charlotte, Martin and Jacob, and most of the others had hypocoristic versions of English names. Again, as Stewart notes, the names of the slaves in *Tom Sawyer* and *Huckleberry Finn* "offer no distinction from those of the general population". Puckett indicates that there was some deliberate imitation of White names, full or contracted, mainly those of the owner's family and sometimes in the hope of receiving a gift – hence the term "gift-names".[45] This seems to be a kind of name patronage analagous to godparenthood. But the general process of assimilation, which affected all immigrants, seems to have been more important.

Slaves nearly always had just one name, a first name, with perhaps a nickname that might be joined to the first with an "alias". Second names were very rare. Jem Valiant on the Butler plantation was a mulatto. Slaves occasionally had their owners' names attached to them in lieu of second names: Leggett's Sam, Walker's Ned, John Hatcher. Names in this form were not used on the owner's own estate, but when slaves did work away from it or went missing, or if they were moved or sold. A few slaves had first names derived from owners: Boss, Bromley, Towers. These were presumably names of previous owners that had become attached to them, again in the process of moving or sale.

An underlying question in this discussion is: who named slaves? It is not easy to answer. Slaves who were bought would already have names but these could be changed. The naming of children born on plantations depended on the policy of the owners and also on what category of slave they belonged to: house or field slaves. Some owners and/or their wives clearly named their slaves. Humorous, classical or religious names may betray this control, or aspects of the pattern of naming. Few names were duplicated on the Chesapeake Bay plantations in the mid eighteenth century and names were not usually transmitted within families.

Other owners allowed slave parents to name their offspring, and we have seen that they might pick African names or imitate those of the master's family. More significantly, names were passed on within slave families. Slavery was not conducive to family life. Mother–child relations were upset by the field labour required of women, while spouses and siblings might be separated by sales. However, marriage was normal: "in most cases bondsmen selected their partners and went to great lengths to have the marriage solemnized 'officially'".[46] And some owners were reluctant to part families. It was liberal owners, who thus fostered slave families, who also left the naming of children to their parents.

Some historians have used these naming practices to measure the strength of family ties among slaves. Cody examined the transmission of names among slaves of the Gaillards in South Carolina. She found that children were named after parents and other kin. "Siblings named their children for one another, particularly brothers for brothers and sisters for sisters, suggesting the strength of same-sex sibling ties." Naming had a compensatory function here. "Frequently broken paternal and fraternal ties were symbolically mended through naming practices." Sons were much more often named after fathers than daughters after mothers, and brothers' names were preserved more than sisters'. This reflects the fact that the "owners recognized only uterine ties and the paternal relationship was more vulnerable", though there may also have been a traditional patrilineal sense. In passing on his slaves to his descendants, old Gaillard "preserved the nuclear unit of father, mother, and children under 15 . . . Beyond 15, sons were frequently dispersed and separated from their parents and their young siblings, while daughters more frequently remained with them."[47]

Cody's case study confirms Owens' more general conclusion that the slave family was not so loose and mother-orientated as has been supposed, and that slaves "often tried desperately to nurture familial affections . . . despite the potential of bondage to disrupt" them. Cody also claims that naming "reflected a strong recognition of the individual identity of each child . . . Infants were not named until several days after birth", with much thought going into the choice.[48] Naming after dead siblings was unknown. She also sheds light on the persistence, albeit as a minority custom, of peculiar or pejorative names bestowed by masters. Classical, Biblical and derogatory names were in fact largely absent among the Gaillard slaves, but, Cody argues, the presence of such names does not preclude slave choice and the use of names to record or emphasize family ties. For, once such names had been given, they might well be preserved and transmitted just because they were family names, as happened generally among European families.

"After the coming of freedom", wrote Booker T. Washington,

> there were two points upon which practically all the people on our place were agreed, and I find that this was generally true through-out the South: . . . that they must leave the old plantation for at least a few days . . . in order that they might really feel sure that they were free [and] . . . that they must change their names.

New names were symbolic of emancipation, "signs of freedom".[49] Two changes were called for here: the adoption of a second name, and the alteration or elaboration of the first.

The second names of former owners were usually avoided, though some did take the names of important planters in order to gain their patronage. Names of overseers might also be picked. Often existing first names were chosen, being treated as patronymics. Quite often names of famous people were adopted, like Lincoln, Sherman, Grant and especially Howard after the head of the Freedmen's Bureau. These were all men thought of as friendly to Blacks. Booker T. again illustrates this with his own experience. Until he went to school, he had simply been called Booker, but when the roll was called he discovered that "all of the children had at least two names . . . I was in deep perplexity, because I knew that the teacher would demand of me at least two names, and I had only one." In the event, he had a bright idea, and, when the teacher did ask "what my full name was, I calmly told him 'Booker Washington', as if I had been called by that name all my life; and by that name I have since been known". However, most freed slaves were less bold and "chose names that were simply common where they lived and thus seemed regular and proper and suitable to their station in life".[50] A study of second names in 1924 showed that 75 per cent of American Blacks bore English names, 13 per cent Irish and 12 per cent Scottish. The commonest names in order were Brown, Smith, Jones, Williams, Jackson, Davis, Harris, Robinson and Thomas, which does not differ greatly from the list of commonest second names in general. Black second names remained very fluid until conscription in the First World War and Social Security imposed regularity on them, but again we have seen that this was a more general phenomenon.

Changes of first name among ex-slaves were not always made at once but often came with the second generation. Names associated with slavery were dropped. This meant very often the "characteristic" names that we have discussed, including hypocoristics. Sometimes these were filled out instead. So Polly's Jim became Apollos James. As this shows, the link with the old name was kept. Middle names were also sometimes given. A peculiar feature was the adoption by men of a middle initial. This could relate to an actual name as with Booker Taliaferro, but more often it seems that it was an empty initial simply lending prestige to the bearer, "part of what the coloured man . . . called his 'entitles' ".[51] We have seen that this was a White practice too.

Paradoxically, those who have studied Black first names in the post-Emancipation era have concentrated their attention on unusual names, seen as distinctively Black. In fact, until recently, "the names of African Americans most often paralleled those of their White counterparts".[52] Even in the South, most Blacks had standard English first names. A study of Black college students in 1938 found that only 15.3 per cent of females and 8.4 per cent of males had unusual names. Most telling, the proportion of unusual names among Blacks varied from region to region. It was 9.9 per cent in Ohio, 10.4 per cent in the Upper South, 13.9 per cent in the Lower South, and 16.3 per cent in Oklahoma and Texas. This matched the distribution of unusual names among Whites.

Nevertheless, a minority of Blacks did give and bear names of a "highly fantastic nature". For example, a study of Rockingham County, North Carolina in 1930 provided Agenora, Audrivalus, Earvila, Eldeese, Katel, Limmer, Margorilla, Roanza and Venton Orlaydo. Some unusual Black names were African survivals. African names as such were usually rejected as slave names or ethnic epithets, for example Sambo and Quashee. Only, it seems, in the Gullah country along the South Carolina and Georgia coastline did African names proper become established and survive. In some families specific names were used: Abeshe, Agali, Bafata, Dodo, Ishi and so on, and children did not have English names. But more often the African names were nick-names, and their meanings had been lost. People continued to use them in the inter-war period "because their parents and grandparents did so".[53] At the same time and of more general significance, the Gullahs bestowed English names in African style, evoking birth circumstances and parental mood or seeking to bring children good fortune.

"In addition to the names of the months and days, the following are typical: Blossom (born when the flowers were in bloom), Wind, Hail, Storm, Freeze, Morning, Cotton (born in cotton-picking time)." There were also special names for twins and names referring to parental circumstances: Pleasant Times, Hard Times. Then there were praise names or auguratives like Fortune, Redemption, Refuge, Precious Allgood, which may have been the fruit also of religious involvement; and phrase names both religious and secular: I will Arise, Daisy Bell Rise Up, Try and See. Some names among the Gullah and found more generally as male nicknames "were patently reminiscent of West African totems or clan names": Frog, Bear, Cat-Fish, Squirrel.[54] We have encountered these among slaves. One may also detect the influence of the African notion of giving every child a completely new and unique name.

All of this is relevant to Black naming generally, though most unusual Black names clearly had little to do directly with African origins. If the style was African, it was creative and contemporary, and most names were very much of their own time and place. This is most obvious with first names after brands and modern items: Hershey Bar, Listerine, Creamola. Though taking special forms, unusual Black naming is one facet of a general American inventiveness and freedom in first-naming, already evident among the Puritans of New England and exemplified also by Bible-Belt Whites.

There is some evidence that Black names were becoming more distinctive through the first half of the twentieth century. At the Arkansas State College, later A.M. and N. College, Pine Bluff, for Black women, unusual names rose from 14.6 per cent in the period from 1900 to 1919 to 35.6 per cent in 1935. McGregory asserts that the advent of the Civil Rights movement reversed this trend, encouraging acculturation at all levels. Names then became more distinctive again in recent years. McGregory's study of Indiana found that about one quarter of girls' names were distinctive in 1965, but 40 per cent by 1980. Boys' names remained more traditional from the custom of naming them after fathers, but here too there was a clear trend towards distinctive Black names. McGregory relates this development to the disillusionment which followed the "success" of the Civil Rights movement. Among the new names used in recent years were a few with African resonance, including some after African leaders: Satonga, Lachandra, Olatunji; Jomo Kenyatta, Kwame Nkrumah.

But unusual or distinctive names are only one measurement of ethnic divergence here. Blacks and Whites also chose different names from within the "traditional" Anglo-American repertoire. In the later nineteenth and early twentieth centuries, there were names favoured by Blacks but not by Whites: Nathaniel, Isaac, Oliver, Cecil, Clifford for boys, for example; and Carrie, Rosa, Cora and Naomi for girls. Distinctive patterns of naming have remained in evidence or have been reinforced through the second half of this century. Among babies named in the early 1950s, the overlap in the commonest names for Blacks and Whites was considerable for boys: seven from the top ten and fourteen from the top twenty; but not for girls. Only three girls' names appear in both top ten lists and only eight in both top twenty lists. This disparity between Black and White popular names was maintained for girls and increased for boys. In 1990, three names appeared in both Black and White female top ten lists and eight in both top twenty lists; in 1995, the figures were three and seven. In 1990, four names appeared on both Black and White male top ten lists, and eleven in both top twenty lists; in 1995, the figures were four and nine.[55] All this indicates a clear and growing cultural divide.

CHAPTER THIRTEEN

Europe in the twentieth century

By the twentieth century, the pattern of personal naming was firmly and definitively fixed. The second, last or family name was invariable and passed from father to legitimate children. Within countries the pool of family names was closed. Some new names were introduced by immigration but these confirmed to the prevailing norms in function and often form. First and (and "middle") given names continued to be bestowed at birth and selected from an accepted repertoire, but this repertoire expanded and the rules or conventions by which names were allotted to individuals changed. Transmission of names within families gave way to the following of fashion. Only first names in this period therefore really have a history, and attention must be focused on them. The subject has been most thoroughly investigated for France.

France

The stock of first names was much greater in modern times. Around 2000 first names were in use in the 1980s. Concentration on a small number of these remained but was far less than in previous centuries. At the end of the nineteenth century the top ten names for each gender covered around 40 per cent of those named but only 30 per cent by the 1930s and subsequently. More particularly, among children born in Paris between 1946 and 1996, the ten commonest male names covered 38 per cent of boys and the ten commonest female names 26 per cent of girls. Concentration on individual names also fell off: 12.5 per cent of girls were called Marie in the 1890s and 7.5 per cent in the decade from 1900 to 1909; but none of the commonest girls' names from the 1930s onwards exceeded 4.5 per cent, with the exception of Nathalie in the 1960s with 7.1 per cent. Among boys' names, Jean was still the name of nearly 8 per cent of boys in the 1920s and early 1930s, but this figure fell to 5 per cent in the 1950s and 1960s. Other leading names then and later only reached 4 per cent or less.

The ten commonest male names for France as a whole in the decade from 1900 to 1909 were, in order, Louis, Pierre, Jean, Marcel, André, Henri, Joseph, René, Georges and Paul. Louis remained most popular till 1914, when it was ousted from first place by Jean, which remained there until 1939. Jean, Pierre and André continued to be very common through the inter-war years, with René gaining ground. Also in the inter-war period, Michel, Claude and Jacques appeared in the top ten. Michel dethroned the traditional Jean as leader around 1940, keeping first place till the 1950s. Jean tended to be replaced by composites with Jean. After the Second World War Alain took second place, followed by Gérard and Daniel. Philippe took the leading place in 1958, replacing Patrick and remaining at the top till 1970. Leaders of the 1960s were Pascal and Christophe, with Eric and Laurent. Stéphane assumed the lead in the early 1970s and Sébastien in the late 1970s. Other leading names of this decade were David, Laurent still, Frédéric and Nicolas, which assumed the lead in the 1980s, together with Julien. Others in the top five through the 1980s were Mickaël and Mathieu. The top ten male names in the late 1980s were Julien, Nicolas, Jérémy, Mickaël, Mathieu, Guillaume, Romain, Anthony, Sébastien and Jonathan. "Traditional" names and particularly Jean had survived into the inter-war period but had ultimately been replaced by "new" names, some drawn from older layers of the traditional repertoire, others from foreign sources.

The top ten female names from 1900 to 1909 were, in order, Marie, Jeanne, Marguérite, Marie-Louise, Germaine, Yvonne, Madeleine, Louise, Suzanne and Marcelle. Marie had fallen to third place by 1930, while Jeanne had taken first place. In the 1930s, Jeannine leapt to top place with Monique. Other common names of the inter-war period were Simone, Jacqueline and Yvette. Monique remained in the lead till the mid 1940s. After the war, Danielle and Michèle passed Monique, and Françoise and Nicole completed the top five. In the 1950s, Martine took the lead and for a short time Brigitte. Other very common names of the 1950s were Chantal, Catherine, and Sylvie, which became the leader in the early 1960s. Nathalie took up the lead in the late 1960s, followed by Isabelle, Sylvie and Valérie. Nathalie and Stéphanie led in the 1970s, followed by Sandrine, Christelle and Céline. Aurélie was the leader in the 1980s, followed by Emilie. The top ten names in the late 1980s were thus Aurélie, Emilie, Elodie, Julie, Audrey, Mélanie, Jennifer, Stéphanie, Céline and Amandine. There is the same pattern here of traditional names surviving into the inter-war period, but their subsequent rout is more complete than with boys' names. Some new girls' names are revivals of names popular in the past but most were quite novel or formerly obscure.

In addition to this general change in the kinds of name that were most popular, there was a much greater turnover of names in the shorter run and an increased acceleration in this turnover. This can be measured in various ways. The composition of the list of the top ten names changed with growing rapidity – first for girls, then for boys. Until 1920 only one or two names changed every five years; after the end of the Second World War three to five names changed over the same period, so that "none of the commonest first names would be found occupying that place 20 years later". Again, "the duration of life of the common first names was reduced". In the pre-industrial era, names had life-spans of centuries; in the nineteenth century, of 50 years. Pierre and André remained in vogue for the first 40 years of this century. Then Michel lasted for 30; Philippe for 20; Patrick for 15; and Sébastien for hardly ten. There was a similar pattern with girls' names, though the life-spans were generally shorter. Monique remained popular for 20 years, and more recently Sandrine and Stéphanie for only ten. By the later twentieth century, a popular name took about ten years from its first appearance to its apogee. For example, Sébastien was virtually unknown in 1966 and reached its peak in 1976; Sandrine was very rare in 1962 but very common in 1972. Moreover, names now do not fade away. After the "death" of fashionable names, they become at once old-fashioned, dated, unusable. As the lasting popularity of names in the past "marked a strong desire for (and the fact of) social continuity", so contemporary naming patterns reflect conflict or divergence between generations and rapid general social and cultural change.[1] Each generation or cohort in effect now has a distinctive name-set, which identifies and dates it.

A few names among the most common did, however, come and go more slowly, and there was a category of name among the lower levels of popularity that remained in vogue over quite long periods of time. These "classic" names were usually borne in France by members of the middle class and can be seen as "bearers of the notion of continuity", of turning to the past for security.[2] We have also noted the phenomenon of the revival of names. Some "new" names were invented in France; others were borrowed from abroad, but most often the stock of the most popular names was renewed through recourse to the past.

There were also significant changes in the style of names. Names sounding alike, with the same suffixes, were popular at the same time. In the 1920s and 1930s, for example, female names in -ette were very common: older names like Antoinette, Juliette and Henriette, but also newer coinages like Georgette, Odette and Josette. All of these suffered a sharp decline after 1945 except Bernardette, which was a name with special religious significance. Names in -ine were also popular for girls in the inter-war period: Jeannine, Jacqueline, Claudine. In the 1940s, names in -iane became common: Christiane, Liliane, Josiane. Girls' names in -ine revived in the later 1970s: Sandrine, Céline, Delphine; while names in -ie have been common more recently: Aurélie, Elodie, Mélanie. Male names have been much less affected by suffix vogues, though one finds recently Sébastien, Julien, Damien and so on.

Another stylistic feature of modern first names in France has been contemporaneous or successive variations on the same name. Patrick and Patrice came and went together in the 1950s and 1960s, as did Francis and François to be eclipsed by Franck around 1970. This in turn fell off, and around 1980 François alone remained as a "classic" name. Michel, the leading name through the 1940s and early 1950s, fell into decline in the 1960s, to be replaced by Michaël and then very strongly in the late 1970s and 1980s by Mickaël.

Most individuals were given two first names, but composite names lost ground sharply. Marie-Louise, we have seen, remained common till around 1920, but it was unusual at that time. There was then a revival of composite names in the 1940s and 1950s – mainly for boys, with the commonest being Jean-Claude and Jean-Pierre. In the period from 1940 to 1945, Jean- composites accounted for 14.4 per cent of boys. All female composites at this time were with Marie, with Marie first except in Anne-Marie. The composite form was almost totally eclipsed from the 1960s, but not quite. The commonest in the late 1980s were girls' names with Anne: Anne-Laure, Anne-Sophie. These and the rarer male examples, like Charles-Edouard, were confined to the bourgeoisie.

First names continued of course to be indicators of gender, and differences in the style and nature of male and female names continued. In general, male names were more "serious" and traditional than female names, which were more likely to be innovative and to have "elements of decoration and fantasy".[3] The repertoire of female names was also much greater than that of male names. This was in part still the result of feminization of male names. This phenomenon had diminished somewhat but remained very obvious. Suffixation, very often the mode of feminization, swelled the numbers of female names, as we have seen. At the same time, the greater concentration of girls' names, found in the nineteenth century and lasting into the twentieth, was reversed, as the predilection for Marie and its composites came to an end.

What factors influenced the choice of first names in twentieth-century France? First, as in other continental countries, name selection was regulated by law. The Law of 11th Germinal Year XI, in force for nearly two hundred years, gave control over the choice of names to the State and restricted choice to names found in the Catholic calendars of the saints and those well-known from classical antiquity. The Germinal Law was revised in 1966 to allow the use of Muslim and other calendars, and by that date registration officials had in general become liberal in their application of the law. But tolerance of names outside the canon was uneven and arbitrary. Feminized and suffixed names were normally allowed, though strictly illegal. But a name permitted in one town might be banned in another. At Dijon in 1970, for example, Vanessa was refused by the registrar, and the parents of the child had to go to court to have it registered. The Law of 9th January 1993 finally relinquished state control over naming; only names likely to cause prejudice to a child were proscribed. Alongside official state regulation in France, control was exercised by the Church. Most children were baptized until recently, and priests added saints' names where they had not already been chosen. Generally, however, these official controls over naming appear to have had little impact by themselves.

The transmission of names within families was ceasing to be an important factor in urban areas in the nineteenth century and in rural areas by the early years of this century, though it was still quite often given by parents as a reason for their choice if they were asked. Naming after godparents also declined. At Fronton, for example, the traditional system held up until the 1920s, disappearing in the 1950s. In the first two decades of the twentieth century, the first name of a godparent appeared as the first name of the godchild in 68 per cent of cases; in the inter-war period, in 25.5 per cent; but in the 1960s and 1970s in only 5 per cent. The use of godparents' names as "middle" names held up better but still went into a steep decline. In the period from 1940 to 1959, children had a godparent's name as a middle name in 38 per cent of cases; in the 1960s and 1970s in only 19 per cent.

Rather than being guided by family or religious tradition, the modern era has been characterized by "free choice" in the bestowing of first names. But this choice has in practice been constrained by the forces of fashion. First names, Besnard has argued, are in effect the essential manifestation of fashion. They are "resources whose consumption is obligatory, but which have no 'use' and cost nothing." They are not therefore influenced by "economic" considerations like other tokens of fashion such as clothes or décor. Parents wish to give a child "a name which individualizes it, and hence is not too common, but which does not saddle it either with a name that is too odd . . . The phenomenon of fashion is born precisely from this tension between originality and conformity." But more obviously perhaps than other fashionable products, first names have nearly always been used before. Their current "meanings" are "intrinsically equivocal and ambivalent".[4] They are contemporary, as fashionable products must be, but they have deep historical resonances, of which givers and bearers can be barely aware.

As we noted for the nineteenth century, French scholars have seen fashion as irreducible here, discounting some of the more obvious influences behind it. They are at pains to stress, for example, that fashions in popular names do not derive from famous holders of those names.

> The celebrity of a star (Brigitte), the popularity of a serial or a TV programme (Thierry, Sébastien, Emilie), the success of a song (Nathalie) can amplify the spread of a first name, but they cannot start it. Among the names mentioned, none was unknown; they all enjoyed a small vogue before the mediating events in question. Indeed, the fact that they were already in the air at the time explains why a singer or a producer chose them.

The effect and speed of such mediation varies. With Sébastien and Thierry it was fast; with other names it was slower, reflecting perhaps a distinction between generations. The association of a name with a "star" could also be counter-productive. Thus Brigitte Bardot had nothing to do with the initial success of Brigitte, but "her fame precipitated the fall of the name, which had become too visible and was therefore seen as too common".[5]

Another feature of the modern scene in France is the existence of guides for prospective name-giving parents. These provide information on the etymology of names, information about the saints and other famous people who bore them, and, in some cases, notions about the character and pro-spects of individuals bearing particular names. But once again these are seen to be reflections rather than makers of fashion.

Older fields of naming also became more dominated by fashion, and especially naming after saints. There appears to be a linkage between the beatification or canonization of new saints and their popularity as name models, for example that of Thérèse after the raising to the altar of Thérèse of Lisieux in 1925, or of Bernardette after 1933. But this was not a new phenomenon, and there had always been fashions in saints' names. What was new was their short-lived nature, and here they were simply reflecting the general trend.

Some investigations have been made into these broader movements of taste. Besnard and Desplanques have shown that for much of the twentieth century first names were spread by "vertical social diffusion". They were launched by the élite and especially the higher intellectual professions; they were then taken up by the intermediary professions, artisans and shopkeep-ers; then by white- and blue-collar workers; and finally by those working in agriculture.[6] For example, Sylvie was borne by 3 per cent of the daughters of the élite in the 1950s, by 2 per cent of those of the intermediary profes-sions, and by only 0.5 per cent of those of agricultural workers. Among the upper and middle classes, this name reached its apogee in the early 1960s, but among workers and those in agriculture only five years later. Again, Philippe was borne by 3 per cent of sons of the élite in the late 1940s but by only 0.6 per cent of workers. Philippe reached its high-point among the well-to-do in the 1950s, and among other social groups in the early 1960s, except for agricultural workers among whom it continued to progress until the late 1960s. The time-gap between élite and general vogues for specific common names had in fact been greatly and progressively reduced from over 30 years in the later nineteenth century to under 15 in the 1940s, and five to six in the 1960s, but it was still present into the 1970s.

Analysis also shows that new names spread outwards from the Paris region to other large cities and then to smaller towns and rural areas. This movement obliterated older regional variations in the incidence of names, still detectable down to the 1950s. It is also clear that young parents were the most sensitive to new fashionable names.

While the most fashionable names were diffused in this way down the social scale, other factors were present. Independently of fashion, the administrative, political and business élites, and still more the liberal professions, remained attached to "classic" names. They were "gilt-edged" names less likely to date than those more in vogue. The upper classes were also the first to abandon names once they had achieved great popularity. The nobility and would-be nobility showed a particular disdain for popular names, and especially for novelties like Yvette and Paulette or Josiane and Liliane in the early twentieth century and for American imports later.

From the later 1970s, the vertical model of diffusion no longer seems to hold. "None of the ten female names most common in France between 1985 and 1989 experienced a vogue with the élite, either earlier or at the same time"; while among the equivalent male names only three did so. Now "certain first names remain confined to the upper reaches of society (Antoine, Guy, Béatrice, Odile, for example); others appear simultaneously in nearly all groups but only develop fully in lower-class milieus". Still others are primarily lower-class names, for example those imported from the USA like Cindy, Jennifer, Anthony and Gregory. This pattern is paradigmatic of general social and cultural structures in the late twentieth century.

> Social cleavages were expressed in the past essentially by gaps in the realization of preferences for the same objects, in conformity with the model of hierarchical diffusion. Recently, they tend to be expressed in the choice of different objects . . . The disappearance of the vertical diffusion of tastes does not therefore signify their homogenization

but rather their fracture into discrete spheres.[7] We saw this process happening also in the USA between Blacks and Whites, but it is clearly more general. Naming practices also demonstrate that this social and cultural polarization involves groups or classes; it is not an atomization into wholly individual choices, though that tendency may also be present. The role of the mass media, moreover, seems to be deflected by the presence of distinct groups or classes, which reduce its homogenizing tendency or adapt it to their different and divergent needs.

First-naming also throws light on the acculturation of immigrants. A study of Hmong immigrants from Laos looks at children born in France to mainly naturalized parents between 1977 and 1993. The Hmong are a minority group in Laos, without classes or castes. In their homeland, individuals were given two names: a child's name at birth and an adult's name, bestowed when a man became a father. The child's name was usually novel and unique. It nearly always had a clear meaning and was chosen from certain lexical fields: those of the domestic and agricultural sphere; those of the body and clothing; that of ritual and myths; and that of the natural world.

There were also augurative or wish-names. Names given to girls and boys were of the same type and often overlapped. The child's name was nearly always one word, more often concrete than abstract. Adult names were given by the parents-in-law. The lexical field of choice was wide, and, though similar, child and adult names were distinct.

There were five kinds of choice among Hmong immigrants. First was the use of Hmong names only, representing 27 per cent of the sample. This represented continuity with the past, though the child's name was transliterated for French usage, and more children had two-word than one-word names, a departure from the native pattern. Secondly, only French names might be given, an option adopted by only 0.4 per cent. Thirdly, Hmong adult names were given to children. This was the most popular option, representing 32 per cent. Names actually given in Laos were used, but also new names in the traditional form, which showed a great deal of inventiveness. A reason for this option was the fact that the child's name could not be changed in France at adulthood. The opportunity was also taken to escape the control traditionally exercised by the in-laws. Here change and adjustment were taking place in the new environment but within Hmong and not French culture. The fourth option was to give one Hmong and one French name. In about half the cases, the Hmong name was not registered, however, only the French. This bi-cultural option was chosen by 19 per cent. Finally, in the fifth option, a name was invented which made some kind of sense in both cultures, for example Nkauj deb shi neeg (Lady far away from life), which became Goldelle Shining in French.

The case-study shows that in the circumstances of immigration and cultural shift, not to say shock, the system of nomination is radically altered, but not simply in the direction of taking over the host culture's system. This forms a contrast with the example of European immigrants to the USA but is closer to that of native Americans, where the cultural gap was similarly wide. Among the Hmong, immigrants tended to be atomized as individuals; families became nuclear; work had a proletarianizing effect. All of this was reflected in the naming practices. Names became more singularized; wider kin and community controls over naming weakened. There were also contradictory tendencies, arising from continuing existence in two cultures. There was "a desire for an extreme singularization in the Hmong register along with the wish to conform and assimilate in the French register".[8] But this is also an echo of a general dichotomy in the modern French situation, as we have seen.

Other studies focus on mixed marriages. Two contrasting models exist among ethnically mixed couples in modern France. Cambodian Khmer–French couples give French names to their children with the aim of facilitating their social integration. Naturalized Cambodians may even take new French names as adults. Cambodian identity is retained but via other cultural features and not through names which could be socially prejudicial.

French–Algerian couples, however, experience a more fraught situation, dominated by issues of stigmatization via names and of cultural betrayal. For them, two contradictory demands have to be met: to avoid the discriminatory effect for their children of belonging to a despised group; and not to completely deny the ethnic identity that the mixed marriage has itself put in question. One way round this dilemma is to choose neutral "international" names, such as Sonia or Nadia. About half the female children in the sample from the late 1980s studied by Streiff-Fenart had such names. Also names could be used that were alike in French and Arabic, for example Rémi and Rahmi, Cédric and Sadi. Always names that were obviously Christian or Muslim were avoided. Another way was to use double first names, one French, one Arabic. Where the husband was Algerian, the Arabic name came first but was again usually not a traditional Arab or Muslim name but one that was more neutral or ambiguous, like Samy, Karim or Malik.

Naming was of special importance for Algerians. They had traditionally had Islamic names and to take a French name was in some ways to change sides in a situation of more or less open conflict. Then a mixed marriage had dire effects for an Algerian family. A son marrying out deprives the family of the chance to marry a daughter or makes it very difficult. The pain and upset is to some extent repaired or a complete break avoided, if the child of the marriage has a name that can be construed as ethnically Algerian by his relatives. On the other hand, the name or first name must not proclaim the child's belonging to what is an out-group in France too strongly, or it will suffer.

Britain

Though it has not been so thoroughly studied, the overall situation in Britain was probably very similar to that in France.

The name stock seems to have expanded through the twentieth century, while concentration declined. In the 1970s, the top ten boys' names in England and Wales accounted for 36 per cent of the relevant male population, and the top ten girls' names for 20 per cent. The percentage was significantly lower in Scotland, among some religious groups, especially Roman Catholics, and among Blacks.

The ten commonest boys' names in England and Wales in 1900 in order were William, John, George, Thomas, Charles, Frederick, Arthur, James, Albert and Ernest, in the main a "traditional" list. Robert, Ronald and Kenneth replaced Ernest, Charles and Arthur in 1925. In 1935, Brian, Peter, Michael, Alan and David entered the top ten; in 1950, Stephen, Paul and Graham. Andrew, Mark, Ian and Gary appeared in 1965, together with Richard. In 1975, Matthew, Daniel, Christopher and Darren came in. There were no new names in the 1985 list, though the order changed and some names from previous years re-entered. The top ten names in 1995 in order were Daniel, Thomas, Matthew, Joshua, Adam, Luke, Michael, Christopher, Ryan and Jack.

The ten commonest girls' names in England and Wales in 1900 were Florence, Mary, Alice, Annie, Elsie, Edith, Elizabeth, Doris, Dorothy and Ethel. Only three of these can be called "traditional". In 1925, Joan, Joyce, Kathleen, Irene, Betty and Eileen entered the list, and Margaret reappeared. In 1935, Shirley, Jean, Patricia, Sheila, Doreen, Sylvia and Barbara entered the list; and in 1950, Linda, Christine, Carol, Jennifer and Janet, while Susan and Ann reappeared. The 1965 list was totally new except for Susan, with Trac(e)y, Deborah, Julie, Karen, Alison, Jacqueline, Helen, Amanda and Sharon. The 1975 list was again virtually a new start with eight newcomers: Claire, Sarah, Nicola, Emma, Joanne, Rachel, Lisa and Rebecca. Laura, Gemma, Kelly, Victoria and Katherine appeared or reappeared in 1985. The full list for 1995 was Rebecca, Amy, Sophie, Charlotte, Laura, Lauren, Jessica, Hannah, Jade and Emma.

There is the same decline of "traditional" names as in France. John, for example, which remained at first or second place until 1950, dropped out of the top ten by 1965, out of the top twenty by 1975, and out of the top fifty by 1995. New boys' names in England and Wales, however, were over-whelmingly Biblical, with three from the Old Testament in the 1995 list – all in a resolutely secular age. Old Testament names were also important among most recent new girls names, which were otherwise more miscellaneous, with nineteenth-century revivals alongside real novelties. American influence seems clear in all this. It also demonstrates once again how names have lost old and acquired new meanings, for names like Adam, Joshua and Daniel are almost certainly not perceived as Old Testament names.

The lists of commonest names in Scotland were significantly different through the first half of the twentieth century. In 1935, only four of the names on the English top ten list for boys figured on the Scottish equivalent and only three of the English girls' names. Common names in Scotland without the same vogue in England and Wales included Alexander, Andrew and Ian for boys, and Annie, Isabella, Helen and Janet for girls. Some distinctively Scottish names were later exported, like Janet, Fiona, Lindsey and Leslie. Traditional names, especially for boys, were used far more extensively in Scotland down to 1960 than "in any other English-speaking country".[9] By the 1970s, the pattern of Scottish first names had largely con-verged with that in the rest of Britain.

We have seen that older names were revived. In Scotland, Wales and Ireland, this could take a "nationalist" or ethnic form. Some such names were invented like the Scottish Fiona. Welsh ethnic names included Aled, Bleddyn, Dafydd, Emyr, Gwilym and Wyn for boys, and Angharad, Bronwen, Eluned, Mair and Sian for girls – a mixture of Welsh versions of established "foreign" names and Welsh names proper.

By the first half to the twentieth century, most Irish names were of "foreign", not Irish, origin. Woulfe gives figures of 80 per cent for men's and 90 per cent for women's names in the 1920s. Among the commonest male names in the 1950s were John, Patrick, Michael, James, William, Thomas and so on. The great popularity of Patrick and Michael was then "comparatively recent".[10] There was a deliberate attempt to revive old Irish first names from the 1920s. In 1923 Woulfe published a guide for parents listing both old Gaelic names and Irish versions of other names. As a result and for other reasons, ethnic names had become much more common by the 1970s, names such as Donal, Eamon, Dermot and Sean; or Ciara, Deirdre, Eilis, Rois and Siobhan. Some of these have entered the general British repertoire. New names were also introduced to Ireland through the medium of Catholicism, for example Bernadette and Philomena.

There was the same acceleration in the turnover of popular names in Britain as in France. This can be measured from Dunkling's lists for England and Wales. Between 1800 and 1900, the turnover in the top ten male names was small, one or two every 25 years. A more rapid movement began in the twentieth century with four names changing between 1900 and 1925, and eight between 1925 and 1950. The rate of change per decade for male names was 1.6 between 1900 and 1925; 3.2 between 1925 and 1950; 3.3 between 1950 and 1965; 4 between 1965 and 1975; 2 between 1975 and 1985; and 6 between 1985 and 1995. There was thus a doubling of the rate of change in the second quarter of the century, with an especially rapid turnover from 1925 to 1935; some slowdown in the 1950s and early 1960s; then a much more rapid turnover from 1965 to the present with some slowing of the rate between 1975 and 1985.

Girls's names remained comparatively stable until 1850, but change then set in, with five names changing between 1850 and 1875; four between 1875 and 1990; eight between 1900 and 1925; and nine between 1925 and 1950. The rate of change by decade was greater, and greater earlier, for girls than for boys. Two per top ten changed between 1850 and 1875; 1.6 from 1875 to 1900; 3.2 from 1900 to 1925; and 3.6 from 1925 to 1950, with a high of 7.0 in the decade from 1925 to 1935. Between 1950 and 1965, the rate rose to 6, and between 1965 and 1975 to 8. There was some slowdown between 1975 and 1985, as with boys, but a return to 7 in the decade from 1985 to 1995.[11] Girls' names were thus changing rapidly a quarter of a century before boys'. The inter-war period was one of accelerated change for both genders. The pattern of popular name change also fits into the general pattern of cultural change in the 1960s and 1970s, followed by some reaction in the 1980s and further change in the 1990s.

The process of turnover can also be seen by looking at individual names. Here again the life-span of popular names shortened over time. For example, Albert was already the 20th most popular boys' name in 1850. Its popularity increased through the second half of the nineteenth century, reaching its height in 1900. It was still fairly common in 1925 but suffered a big fall by 1935 and still more by 1950; it then became uncommon and then almost unknown in the 1970s and after. Ronald was rare in 1900; rose suddenly to popularity in the inter-war years; fell fairly rapidly through the 1950s and 1960s; and was virtually unknown from the 1970s. Gary or Garry appeared around 1930; it rose to popularity very quickly in the 1950s, reaching its peak in 1965; it then declined, though still fairly common through the 1970s and 1980s. Darren only appeared in 1960, enjoyed a sudden rise in the later 1960s, reached its apogee in the yearly 1970s, and then fell off. The rough time-span has gone from a century to 30 or 40 years to around 15.

Girls' names followed the same pattern in more accentuated form. Gladys, for example, appeared as the 11th most popular name in 1900, starting from nowhere; it was still popular in 1925; then it suffered a catastrophic fall, becoming very rare in the 1950s and then unused. Patricia followed a similar path. It was very rare in 1900, quite common in 1925, rose suddenly to the fourth commonest name in 1935, remained very popular through the 1950s and early 1960s, then suffered a rapid fall, becoming virtually unknown in the 1980s and 1990s. Jacqueline appeared in the early twentieth century but was extremely uncommon; it rose suddenly in the late 1940s, 1950s and early 1960s to peak in 1965 at seventh place; it then suffered a sudden fall and by 1975 was relatively uncommon again. Linda was very rare through the first three decades of the century, then rose at an unprecedented rate from almost nothing in 1935 to second place in 1950; its popularity survived till the mid 1960s, when it went into decline, and by the 1980s it was virtually unused. More recently, Gemma appeared in the mid 1950s, remained very rare till the mid 1970s, then rose very quickly in the 1980s, reaching sixth place in 1985; after this it declined. Here the time-span was already around 30 years at the start of the century and fell to ten years.

We also find in Britain the phenomenon of the "classic" name, though as in the USA this seems to exist at a higher level of popularity than in France. Examples are Richard, which remained common throughout the twentieth century, with a high-point in 1965 at tenth place; Robert, similarly popular through the century, with a high-point in the 1950s; and Stephen or Steven, which was very popular through from the 1950s to the early 1970s, but which never fell below a certain level. There are also "classic" girls' names, though generally they had less following than boys'. Examples are Catherine or Katherine, whose level of popularity altered very little through the century; Helen, which rose to a peak of popularity in 1965; and Mary, which declined steadily from 1900 but which only became an unusual name after 1970. Once again this illustrates the more "traditional" character of boys' names.

As we have noted, "new" boys' names were often Biblical revivals. Two clear examples are Andrew and Matthew. Andrew was little used before 1935, but rose rapidly from the late 1940s to become the third commonest name in 1965. It has suffered some decline since but was still fairly common in 1990. Matthew was rare before 1960, when it began to rise; this rise accelerated in the 1970s and 1980s, and the name was in second and third place in 1985 and 1995 respectively. Revived names among girls often had a nineteenth-century flavour. Emma, for example, was a very popular name in the mid nineteenth century. It then fell into decline, reviving quite suddenly in the 1970s; it was in fourth place in 1975 and remained in the top ten in 1985 and 1995. Charlotte was very popular in 1800 and remained so into the mid-Victorian period. It was then eclipsed, not reviving until the 1970s and reaching fourth place in 1995. Rebecca had a very similar history. It was very popular at the start of the nineteenth century, fell off from around 1850, was virtually unused from 1900 to the 1960s, and then rose quickly through the 1970s, reaching the top ten in 1975 and first place in 1995.

All of this meant subjectively that names were increasingly "dated". Particular names, especially for women, placed them in time. So girls born before 1920 might be Bertha, Flora or Gladys; those born in the 1920s Daisy, Dora or Ethel; those born in the 1930s Audrey, Enid or Daphne. Karen, Jennifer, Jacqueline and Sandra belonged to the 1950s and 1960s; Dawn, Kerry and Lorraine to the 1970s. Individuals were thus "landed" very often with names that became unfashionable in their lifetimes and which they could not easily discard. The generation gap and the speed of cultural change were made palpable. At the same time, a new layer of meaning was attached to names, an evocative element of nostalgia. Thus G.S. Fraser in "Christmas Letter Home", written during the Second World War, readily evoked pre-war innocence via the use of names:

> And Bunny and Stella and Joyce and Rosemary
> Chattering on sofas or preparing tea,
> With their delicate voices and their small white hands.[12]

As all this indicates, the traditional modes of transmission had given way to the reign of fashion. British evidence suggests, however, that parents still had reasons for their choices of names for their children. This is conveyed in H.E. Bates' popular novel *The Darling Buds of May* (1958):

> Pop drove happily . . . thinking of his six children and the splendid
> . . . names he and Ma had given them . . . There was a reason for
> them all. Montgomery, the only boy, had been named after the
> general. Primrose had come in the Spring. Zinnia and Petunia were
> twins and they were the flowers Ma liked most. Victoria, the youngest
> girl, had been born in plum-time,

while the eldest girl, Mariette, was named after Queen Marie-Antoinette. Other more objective data confirms this view. In letters to Dunkling, parents often asserted that there was a conscious reason behind their choice: naming after family, the influence of books and films, avoiding names that were too common, birth circumstances, choosing a name that "went" with the family name. A survey in the 1970s reached the same conclusions. Where parents gave reasons for their choice, 40 per cent referred to liking the sound of the name, 38 per cent to a family connection, and 20 per cent to a well-known person from the past or present bearing the name. Like Besnard, however, Dunkling believed that the choice came first and the reasons afterwards, and he cites a parent who acknowledged the influence of fashion re his or her choice of Matthew: "Probably a few years ago I would never have dreamed of using this name, but simply from the fact that it has become popular one gets used to the sound of it and eventually likes it."[13]

As in France, the determinants of fashion are unclear. Why, for example, were flower names like Rose, Lily, Violet and Daisy, common at the end of the nineteenth century, to be followed by jewel names, such as Pearl, Ruby and Beryl? Media influence is an obvious factor to turn to, at first literature, then films and television. Ethel was the name of the heroine of Thackeray's *The Newcomes* (1855) and of that of Charlotte Yonge's *The Daisy Chain* (1895); Gladys similarly figured in the titles of two romantic novels at the end of the nineteenth century. More recently, Deborah was the name of two popular film actresses. Tracy, a diminutive for Teresa, was the first name of the character Tracy Samantha Lord, played by Grace Kelly in the film *High Society* (1956). But in all these and similar cases, it seems that the media acted only as amplifiers for names that already had some following. One must explain, too, the principle of selectivity involved. Why are some heroes, heroines and stars imitated, but not others? As Dunkling points out, neither Winston, Errol nor Elvis had any appreciable impact on nomenclature in the lifetime of their famous holders or posthumously. Victoria "was rarely used in Britain . . . during the queen's reign", but it did become popular later in this century. Media usage could also put a blight on a name. George Robey's song "Archibald, certainly not" "seems to have had a highly detrimental effect on the name's image",[14] while Eric similarly became a derogatory name in reaction to Dean Farrar's novel of that title published in 1858. Here again, however, one suspects that there must already have been something about the name in order for it to be treated in this way.

Names clearly belong, too, to broader cultural movements. A good example is the Celtic revival of the late nineteenth and early twentieth centuries. We have already referred to the revival of ethnic first names in Ireland and Wales, which began at this time, but England was also affected. The Irish Deirdre dates from the early twentieth century. Doreen, Eileen and Maureen also began their vogue around the same time, the last remaining popular till the 1950s. Sheila, a phonetic form of the Irish and Scottish Sile, itself a form of Celia, was also very popular in Britain from the 1920s to the 1950s. Welsh female names include Enid and Gladys, which we have already encountered.

Also at work here was the taste for foreign or foreign-sounding names, again most often for girls. An early example was the German Linda introduced in the late nineteenth century. More recently, there has been a vogue for French versions of names that already exist in English: Denise, Diane, Nicole; and for Scandinavian names: Greta, Karen, Kirsten and Ingrid. Such names might at first be truly exotic like Anastasia McLaughlin in Ulster celebrated by Tom Paulin. Her father's

> . . . trade was flax and yarns, he brought her name
> With an ikon and *matrioshka* – gifts for his wife
> Who died the year that Carson's statue was unveiled.[15]

But those that survived soon became common currency, the strangeness in them domesticated.

Within these ambiences, names took on complex and changing meanings, standing for social stereotypes. Dunkling supplies an interesting compilation of these from literary sources. According to G.B. Stern, who herself was given the name around 1890, Gladys, then a fashionable "pretty" name, "from 1910 onwards . . . was frequently disowned as the type of name associated with that slightly giggling girl of fiction, fond of cheap scent, high heels and whispering in corners". A guide to girls' names written in 1900 described Mildred as "an extremely pretty old Anglo-Saxon name", but a character in Somerset Maugham's *Of Human Bondage* (1915) refers to it as "an odious name . . . so pretentious". Again, in Andrea Newman's *A Bouquet of Barbed Wire* (1969), the question is asked: "Monica . . . what image does that conjure up? The hockey-field. The swimming bath. The gymnasium. Tennis courts and netball and lacrosse."[16]

More recent surveys have quantified such insights. According to one undertaken in the late 1970s, "Christopher is expected to be fair-haired, tall and charming", "Gloria is expected to be blonde and outgoing", "Mary . . . to be gentle", and so on.[17]

Like other fashions, first names seem mainly to have descended the social scale and to have moved from the centre to the periphery, though some local idiosyncrasies remained in the modern era. Imitation and following the fashion also had connotations of liberation and the achievement of equality. For a rising family of farm-working origin, the Ashbys, in the Cotswold village of Tysoe in the 1880s and 1890s, "names from the eighteenth century, Mestor and Robert and Dinah seemed associated with a mean, marred past that was left behind, and were set aside in favour of Elsie and Wilfred and Daisy". Much later in West Cumberland, new names like Brian, Vincent, Geoffrey, Celia, Patricia, Daphne and Hilary appeared in the late 1940s and 1950s. Similar to names appearing in the quality newspapers, these new names were "apparently inspired by motives of prestige". A very similar trend is detectable in urban working-class milieus at around the same time. At Bethnal Green, for example, there was a break with "the inheritance of names" after the end of the Second World War, and new names like Glenn, Gary, Stephen and Nicholas for boys, and Marilyn, Carol, Gloria and Linda for girls, were introduced. This was symptomatic of the penetration of the local community by cultural influences from outside.

> The popular press, the cinema, the radio and now the television have put new models, drawn from other classes and other parts of the world, before local people, creating new aspirations and new ideals.[18]

Little or no research has been carried out specifically on the diffusion of first names in Britain, but there are pointers that confirm this view. In the 1970s, for example, certain names achieved popularity first among birth notices in *The Times*, an élite newspaper, and only later more generally. Thus Benjamin was 14th in the *Times* list in 1971 but did not figure in the general top 50 list; Daniel was 20th in *The Times* but 41st in the whole country; Emma was 3rd in *The Times* and 23rd in the whole country; and Rebecca was 7th in *The Times* and 20th generally. By 1975, Benjamin was 29th in the whole country, Daniel 8th, Emma 4th, and Rebecca 12th. "One can only conclude that *Times* readers were proving to be leaders of fashion."[19] However, by this time, if not earlier also, this process seems to have involved only some kinds of name. Upper- and middle-class parents disliked new names, and the trends which they set were in revivals.

There is no doubt that certain names at any given time were more used by and associated with certain classes than others. This may have become more obvious recently in Britain as in France, but it is not a new phenomenon by any means. Jane Duncan wrote of Scotland around 1910:

> My family had a code of rules about . . . Christian names. Roughly, these names fell into three classes: (a) names for people like us: Janet, Elizabeth, Catherine, Isobel, Duncan, George, John (b) names for the gentry: Victoria, Alexandra, Lydia . . . Edward, Torquil, Anthony . . . (c) names silly and outlandish: Gladys, Wendy, Muriel . . . Victor, Barry, Robin . . . it was quite in order for the gentry to take a notion to call a girl Jean, although this name was truly the property of people like us, for the gentry had all sorts of licence, but it would not have been the thing for me to have been named Eleanor or Eve.[20]

Later the *Times* lists in the 1970s show a similar divide between the upper middle class and those below them. Traditional names such as James, Edward or William were all more common in *The Times* than among the population as a whole. Upper- and middle-class parents were more susceptible to the old-world charms of girls' names like Emma, Louise and Charlotte, though these were all later imitated by the lower classes, as we have seen. The *Times* lists also showed a tendency to avoid new working-class names. By 1971, for example, Darren was the seventh most popular name in England and Wales generally and it was tenth in 1975, but it never figured in the *Times* lists. Similarly, Tracey, Sharon, Joanne, Lisa, Julie, Karen, Deborah, Kelly and Kerry "have all been used very much less by readers of *The Times* . . . than by . . . parents generally". The avoidance was deliberate. Dunkling reports receiving many letters from middle-class parents, in which "one detects . . . a strong reaction against modern first names such as Craig, Darren, Scott, Shane, Warren and Wayne for the boys, Beverl(e)y, Cheryl, Gaynor, Hayley, Kelly, Kerrie, Lorraine, Mandy and Trac(e)y for the girls. Such names were thought and said to be 'vulgar'."[21]

How far did these new names represent an American invasion, as is often supposed? Here we need to consider the convergence or divergence between popular names in the USA and Britain generally, as well as overall traffic between the two countries. In fact there was progressive divergence from the end of the nineteenth century. Of the top 20 male names in England and Wales in 1875, 16 figured among the top 20 in the USA. Taking 25-year periods, this overlapping number fell to 13 in 1900, 12 in 1925, 8 in 1950, 11 in 1975 and 8 in 1995. The divergence for girls' names was established earlier. Only 11 of the British top 20 figured in the comparable American list in 1875, and only 8 in 1900; but this figure then remained constant at 8 or 9. For girls' names in recent times, however, the divergence has been much greater as far as the top ten names are concerned. In 1975 only three of the British top ten figured in the American list, and in 1995 only one.

Some names then were peculiar to or much commoner in one of the two countries. In 1950, for example, Brian, Colin, Graham, Keith and Barry were British, and Thomas, Richard, Gary, Mark, Daniel and Gregory American. In 1995, Adam, Ashley and Luke were British, and Jacob, Brandon and Cody American. The same pattern is even more obvious for girls' names. In 1950, Jennifer, Janet, Pamela and Sheila were British; Deborah, Sharon, Donna and Cynthia American. In 1995, Rebecca, Sophie, Chloe, Jade and Gemma were British; and Brittany, Taylor, Megan and Elizabeth American.

Influence and movement of names across the Atlantic was a two-way process, with England and Wales being the dominant cultural partner in the nineteenth century and the USA by the later twentieth century. Among boys' names, the USA took Alfred from Britain at the end of the nineteenth century, and Harold in 1925. The USA also borrowed Ronald, Dennis and Kenneth in 1950. Movement the other way was rare before 1975. Then Paul and Lee (mainly a girls' name in the USA) entered the British top 20, but Brian, Jeffrey and Eric entered the US top 20 from Britain at the same time. Only by 1995 was the balance clearly with the USA, Britain borrowing Jack,

Daniel, Thomas, Benjamin, Aaron and Stephen, while the USA took from Britain Nicholas, William and Jonathan.

Traffic in girls' names was sparse before the Second World War. Britain borrowed Lilian in 1925, and Sarah and Martha were revived in the USA following British example in 1900 and 1925. In 1950, however, US predominance was clear, with Britain adopting Ann, Jacqueline and Linda. In 1975, Joanne, Helen, Karen, Trac(e)y and Deborah were in the British top 20, all previously popular American names. To offset this, Jennifer, Heather and Christine entered the US top 20. In 1995, Britain had borrowed Amy and Laura, with no corresponding American adoption. In measuring cultural exchange, one should note that independent innovation and revival were found on both sides. Most names that were "borrowed" were already established; they simply had their popularity greatly boosted.

Of course, in Britain, as in France, most people had two given names, though one of them, usually the "middle" name, was dormant, rarely used. Middle names in effect are "almost a separate nomenclature". They are sometimes used to preserve family names (first or second), or to try out new names, especially for boys. They are also 'used to put old names out to grass'. Many traditional names survive mainly as middle names. "Ann(e), especially, is now [1995] used ten times as a middle name for every one use as a first name."[22]

Finally, to first-name usage. J.B. Priestley commented in 1934 on the fact that an elderly middle-class employer, visiting ex-workers to give them food-tickets, was addressed by all of them by his first name: "Nothing better illustrates the genuine and deep-seated democracy of Lancashire than this practice", which he also found in the Potteries. But this was already part of a more than local tendency, and the environment in which first names could be and were used greatly expanded again in the second half of the century. This happened within the circle of kin. Among London middle-class families studied in the 1960s, children were beginning to drop "Uncle" and "Aunt" titles and use first names only, and some did this with parents, too. Firth, Hubert and Forge note that

> to call a person by his name, as distinct from his kin relation, is to remove an indicator of appropriate social behaviour. This is particularly relevant in the English system, in which by convention juniors traditionally used kin terms in addressing their seniors, who for the most part used first names in return.

The new habit could therefore be seen as "disrespectful", a threat to authority, again a manifestation of democracy of a kind.[23]

The wider extension of first-name usage among colleagues, on first acquaintance and within the ambience of the media, American-style, may be seen in part in the same light. It signals the abolition of social distinctions, a rejection of hierarchy and formality, a would-be feeling of equality. But, as critics have pointed out, it can also be felt as an invasion of the intimate circle by those who do not really belong there, a means of promoting an instant and false friendliness without going through the series of nominal registers that used to pave the way.

Italy

Concentration on the most popular names was at comparable levels in modern Italy to modern France and Britain and represented the same fall from earlier levels. In the 1980s, the top ten male names accounted for 30.5 per cent of men and the top ten female for 25 per cent of women. In Italy there was a marked discrepancy between concentration on first first names and on "middle" names, the latter being very much lower.

The ten commonest male names in the 1980s were, in order, Giuseppe, Giovanni, Antonio, Mario, Luigi, Francesco, Angelo, Vincenzo, Pietro and Salvatore; and the ten commonest female ones Maria, Anna, Giuseppina, Rosa, Angela, Giovanna, Teresa, Lucia, Carmela and Anna Maria. Both lists are far more "traditional" than their French and British equivalents. This chimes in with the fact that regional variations seem to have been far more important in Italy, a sign of late unification and the persistence of real cultural diversity in different parts of the country. Some names belonged to particular regions and had little following elsewhere, unless there were special reasons for this. Salvatore, as we have seen, was a Sicilian name, especially common in the provinces of Catania and Palermo, but it had been spread elsewhere by migration, especially to the industrial regions of the north. There was a similar pattern with other Sicilian names like Carmine, Gaetano, Carmela and Rosalia. There was also a noticeably uneven pattern of incidence by region for universal names with no exclusive local links. Margherita, for example, was commonest in Piedmont; Paola and Sergio in the Veneto; Battista in Lombardy.

Sicilian names were religious names, and this was a general Italian feature: 57 per cent of male and 58 per cent of female names overall were religious, mainly the names of saints. Including middle names, nine out of ten Italians had a religious name, whose religious meaning was probably still significant. This reflects the continuing importance of Catholicism in Italian life. Two other historical forms also remained salient in Italy: hypocoristics and composite names. Names like Gianni, Beppe and Dino were in common use and were sometimes given as formal first names. Composite names with Giovanni were especially common: Giovan Battista and its variants, Giovan Paolo, Gio Maria, and so on.

The corollary of this was the comparative rarity of "new" and foreign names. De Felice placed 8 per cent of names in the 1980s in the foreign category (mainly German), and under 0.5 per cent for men and 2 per cent for women in the "modish" category. Another peculiarity of modern Italian names is "the extension of male and female names to the opposite gender".[24] So not only were male names feminized in the familiar way, but female names were masculinized, producing names like Emilio, Anno, Tereso, Rosario and Concetto. Here, it seems, religious concerns overrode any sense of male distinctness.

We have no studies of the history of first-naming over the last century in Italy nor of the diffusion of names more recently, but it seems very likely that this apparent conservatism derives both from the political and religious situation that we have alluded to and from the strength of family loyalties. Transmission of names within families was still probably operative in recent times, halting the inroads of fashion. It is possible, too, that style, to which Italians are so attached, was allowed to reign in clothes, décor and so on, while nomenclature was preserved as a bastion of continuity.

Conclusion

Having traced the history of personal naming over more than two millennia, what general conclusions can we draw?

First, naming practices go through a limited number of long-term phases. The Roman *tria nomina* develop in the Republican period and survive into the Empire to be replaced for most classes by a Latin single-name system. With the fall of Rome, this gives way – but not at once – to a Germanic single-name system, in which names are composed of specific elements and in which originally each person has a distinct name. Only in the central medieval period is a second name introduced, which becomes a fixed family name from around the fourteenth century, though this process is delayed for much of the peasantry until later. Once fixed from the medieval period, second names survive unchanged down to the present. Christianity had little impact on naming practices until the same central medieval period when naming after the universal saints became very common. This greatly reduced the name stock and introduced the phenomenon of concentration: very many people shared very few names. The modern Christian first name plus hereditary family name is the norm from this time. Further first or middle names were added from the seventeenth and eighteenth centuries. The rhythm of these changes was influenced by external factors which we will discuss, but it immediately suggests a periodization somewhat at odds with traditional schemes. Roman and Latin influence persisted well after the fifth century. The decisive changes and the formation of our modern system came in the central medieval period, and, once formed, the new system did not change through the early modern and modern centuries with their upheavals. It merely spread through society and experienced minor modifications.

Overall one is struck by the continuities within and beyond these movements. Some names like Mary and John in their various forms have been in

continuous use throughout the Christian era. Once the "Christian" repertoire proper was established in the central medieval period, it remained in force down to this century. Even in our present fashion-led situation, most first names are still either Graeco-Roman, Biblical or saints' names, and "new" names are revivals from this old stock. Our family names or surnames were almost certainly fixed before the sixteenth century and have been passed down the generations from that time. This all embeds each individual and each family, wittingly or not, in a historical milieu and reflects a deep continuity in our culture.

Names place the individual in his or her family, community, gender and class. Here the fixing of the family name marks a crucial stage in the history of family structure that has often been ignored. Earlier systems, like the Germanic leading names, had associated individuals with looser kindreds; the hereditary second name marked the advent of patriliny. At first the context was the noble line, but later it was the bourgeois and peasant small family. At the same time, other naming practices, like inherited nicknames, pointed to the survival of larger dispersing clans. The subordination of individual to family and its concerns is demonstrated by the custom of transmitting names. These clearly indicated birth order and role within the family as well as underlining continuity with the ancestors. Traditional nicknames also signalled membership of communities, where individuals and families were securely placed and supervised.

Most names also indicated the gender of their bearers, but a significant feature of personal naming from Roman times to the present has been the formation of female names from male names. Roman women bore feminized versions of their father's *gentilicium*; medieval and early modern women suffixed versions of the names of male saints; and modern women's names have not by any means broken with this pattern. Though medieval and modern names were never the precise status indicators that Roman names were, they nevertheless retained an important class dimension, which was reinforced until recently by the use of titles. Today the pattern of first names betrays class and ethnic divergence in the face of egalitarian rhetoric and supposed cultural homogenization.

Personal naming also reflects the growing complexity of society and State. Kinship terms or single names, possibly nicknames, may have been adequate for use within families or small communities, but in the expanding towns of medieval and then modern Europe further means of identification proved necessary. The expanding State and its legal/judicial system also needed to identify individuals more clearly, to attach them to property, to tax and recruit them, to prosecute them. Only in the modern era, however, was compulsion applied in this area.

The Church also had a bureaucratic interest in names, having its own fiscal and legal systems in the medieval period and after and controlling registration in early modern times. However, the decisive influence in the

Christianization of names came from below, as a popular movement, rather than from above. This important aspect of the Christianization of the populations of western Europe was a medieval phenomenon and not one associated with the reforms set on foot in the sixteenth century. The impact of the Reformation was locally important but not of the same order.

In recent times, the choice of first names has been freed from the constraints of family and religion, but few parents take full advantage of this freedom. Naming is now determined by fashion, and the child is named as an individual with a name that is shared with thousands or tens of thousands of others. Modernity is marked by standardization with the semblance of individualism. The rapid turnover of first names also means that individuals are placed in time via their names in a way that they were not in the past. Then the traditional name linked a person to social structures that were permanent or slow–moving; now the name system is largely detached from these structures, though the same name may be used paradoxically and may act as a marker of rapid change.

Notes

Preface

1. Bloch (1964), I, p. vii.
2. Hyde, p. 120.
3. Pitt-Rivers (1976), p. 321.
4. Gardiner, p. 1.
5. Jullian, p. 42.
6. Nicolaisen (1978), pp. 40 and 42; Nicolaisen (1976), p. 142.
7. Nicolaisen (1976), p. 151.
8. Nicolaisen (1980), p. 41.
9. Zelinsky, pp. 748–9.
10. Nicolaisen (1986), p. 140.
11. Mauss, p. 134.
12. Zonabend (1980b), p. 12.
13. Bateson, p. 228.

Chapter 1

1. MacMullen (1982).
2. Appian, I, pp. 20–1.
3. Mommsen, I, p. 31.
4. Livy, Book VI, Vol. III, pp. 262–7.
5. Fustel de Coulanges, p. 106.
6. Livy, Book VI, Vol. III, pp. 262–3.
7. Nicolet, p. 50.
8. Kajanto (1977a), p. 66.
9. Propertius, pp. 316–17.
10. Pliny the Elder, Book XVIII: 10, Vol. V, pp. 194–7.
11. Livy, Book VII, Vol. III, pp. 386–9.
12. Suetonius, Penguin, p. 153.
13. Livy, Book II, Vol. I, p. 261.
14. Suetonius, Penguin, p. 209; and Loeb, II, pp. 87–8.

15. Livy, Book VII, Vol. III, pp. 470–3.
16. Livy, Book VI, Vol. III, pp. 366ff.
17. Cicero, *Letters to his friends*, III, pp. 308–9; Wiseman, p. 258.
18. Fustel de Coulanges, pp. 108–9.
19. Syme (1986), p. 19.
20. Kajanto (1977a), p. 66.
21. Finley, p. 131.
22. Schulz, I, p. 86.

Chapter 2

1. Livy, Book XXX, Vol. VIII, p. 536.
2. Cicero, *Pro Plancio*, pp. 422–3.
3. Tacitus, *Annals*, Penguin, pp. 195 and 284.
4. Cicero, *Letters to his friends*, Book III: vii, I, pp. 192–5.
5. Juvenal, *8th Satire*, Loeb, pp. 160–1.
6. Cicero, *Pro Sulla*, pp. 334–9.
7. Adams, pp. 150 and 158.
8. Hopkins (1983), p. 55.
9. Cicero, *Pro Brute*, cit. Gelzer, p. 32.
10. Keppie, pp. 43–4.
11. Hopkins (1978), pp. 124–5.
12. *Dict. d'Archéol. chrét. et de Liturgie*, 12:2, Col. 1487.
13. Varro, II, pp. 378–9.
14. Weaver (1972), pp. 2–3 and 46.
15. Varro, II, pp. 388–9.
16. Gordon, p. 98.
17. *Ibid.*, p. 97.
18. Momigliano, p. 14.
19. Kajanto (1968), p. 529.
20. Alföldy, pp. 294–5.
21. Weaver (1964), p. 315.
22. *Dict. d'Archéol. chrét. et de Liturgie*, 6:1, Col. 104.
23. Varro, II, pp. 436–7.
24. Cicero, *Letters to his friends*, I, pp. 166–7, 210–11 and 432–3.
25. Juvenal, *1st Satire*, Penguin, p. 66.
26. Pliny the Younger, *Letters*, Book 3: XIV, Loeb, Vol. I, pp. 212–15.
27. Treggiari, pp. 85–6.
28. Suetonius, Loeb, II, p. 139.
29. Treggiari, p. 234.
30. Cit. Millar, p. 144.
31. Hopkins (1978), p. 116.
32. Weaver (1972), pp. 2–3.
33. Weaver (1986), p. 147.

Chapter 3

1. Sherwin-White, p. 409.
2. Caesar, *The Gallic War*, Book I:47, pp. 76–9.

3. Pliny the Younger, *Letters*, Penguin, p. 207.
4. Ramsay, p. 205.
5. Badian, p. 258.
6. *Select Papyri* (ed. Hunt & Edgar), V: 112, Vol. I, pp. 304–7.
7. Condurachi, p. 297.
8. Garnsey & Saller, pp. 20ff.
9. Polybius, Book VI: 52–6, Vol. III, pp. 384ff; Momigliano, pp. 29–30 and 48.
10. Brunt, p. 162.
11. Purcell, in Boardman, Griffin & Murray, pp. 182–3.
12. Balsdon, p. 155.
13. Millar, p. 197.
14. Daux, p. 406.
15. Toutain, pp. 194–5.
16. Pflaum (1977), p. 318.
17. Bénabou, p. 577.
18. Toutain, pp. 191–2.
19. Balsdon, p. 151.
20. Box, II, p. 180.

Chapter 4

1. Cameron (1985), p. 173.
2. Le Glay, p. 273.
3. *Dict. d'Archéol. chrét. et de Liturgie*, 6:I, Cols. 1016–17.
4. *Ibid.*, Col. 1017.
5. Statistics compiled from lists in Jones, Martindale & Morris, *Prosopography* I; Martindale, *Prosopography* II.
6. Ausonius, I, pp. 66–7.
7. Duval, p. 454.
8. MacMullen (1964), p. 50.
9. Hopkins (1965), p. 13.
10. Ausonius, I, pp. 134–5.
11. Arnhem, pp. 68–9.
12. Ausonius, I, pp. 2–3.
13. Cagnat, p. 53.
14. Cit. Cameron (1985), p. 173.
15. Pflaum (1970), pp. 175–6.
16. *Ibid.*, pp. 184–5.
17. Kajanto (1966), pp. 20–1.
18. Kajanto (1963), p. 48.
19. Acts 1:23 and 13:1, *The New English Bible*.
20. Kajanto (1966), pp. 42–3.
21. *Ibid.*, pp. 56 and 59.
22. Suetonius, Penguin, pp. 275 and 130.
23. Martindale, *Prosopography*, II, pp. 79–80.
24. Apuleius, *The golden ass*, Book IX: 17, pp. 424–5.
25. Ramsay, p. 207.
26. *Dict. d'Archéol. chrét. et de Liturgie*, 7:1, Col. 635.
27. *Ibid.*, 12:2, Col. 1494.

28. *Ibid.*, 7:1, Col. 636.
29. Kajanto (1963), pp. 100–1.
30. Marrou, pp. 432–3.
31. Kajanto (1963), pp. 110 and 107.
32. *Ibid.*, pp. 110ff.
33. Marrou, pp. 432–3.
34. Eusebius, p. 311.
35. Kajanto (1963), p. 94.
36. *Dict. d'Archéol. chrét. et de Liturgie*, 12:2, Col. 1511.
37. Pietri, p. 442.

Chapter 5

1. Duchesne, Vols. I–III.
2. James, p. 25.
3. Poly & Bournazel, p. 232.
4. Longnon, I, p. 267.
5. Serra (1924–6), pp. 543ff.
6. Lazard (1974).
7. Bergh, pp. 190–1.
8. Barley, p. 5, citing Schramm.
9. Morlet (1968–85), I.
10. Cit. D'Arbois de Jubainville, pp. 89–90.
11. Gregory of Tours, *History of the Franks*, II, 37; IV, 25; X, 29; VII, 32 (pp. 153–4, 219, 549 and 415); Woolf (1939), pp. 197–8.
12. Cit. D'Arbois de Jubainville, pp. 54–6.
13. Barley, p. 6.
14. *Anglo-Saxon Chronicle*, pp. 14–15.
15. Cit. Stenton (1924), p. 169.
16. Woolf (1939), pp. 15–16.
17. Charles-Edwards, pp. 28–30.
18. Not all -*ing* place-names designate kindreds; some relate to individuals and some to topographical features.
19. Bede, I, Book 2, Ch. IX, Loeb, pp. 246–7.
20. *Ibid.*, I, Book 2, Ch. I, Loeb, pp. 200–3.
21. Barley, pp. 2–5 and 13–15.
22. Schmid (1978), pp. 42–3.
23. Werner (1978), pp. 149–50.
24. Depoin, pp. 554–5.
25. *Ibid.*, pp. 546–7.
26. Werner (1977), p. 26.
27. Fichtenau, p. 39.
28. Depoin, p. 548.
29. Cit. Poly & Bournazel, p. 90.
30. Bonnassie (1975), I, p. 280.
31. Poupardin, pp. 76–7.
32. Bouchard (1988a), pp. 5–6ff.
33. Bouchard (1988b), p. 3.
34. Cit. Jane Martindale, pp. 38–9.

35. Werner (1978), pp. 151–2.
36. Schmid (1978), p. 161.

Chapter 6

1. Morlet (1985), p. 546.
2. Bergh, p. 156.
3. Constable, p. 272.
4. Weis, p. 579.
5. Knowles, Brooke & London.
6. MacBain (1897), p. 307.
7. Calculated from Pacaut, Annexe I, pp. 149–54.
8. Bede, I, Loeb, pp. 428–31; II, pp. 12–13.
9. *Anglo-Saxon Chronicle*, p. 124.
10. Calculated from *Rolls and registers of Bishop Oliver Sutton*, VII.
11. Calculated from Leccisotti.
12. Aebischer (1924), p. 113.
13. *Millénaire monastique*, I, p. 269; Morand, Ch. II.
14. Bourin & Chareille, I, p. 150.
15. Wollasch, pp. 183–90.
16. Weis, p. 579.
17. *Rouleaux des morts*, pp. 177ff.; *Liber Vitae . . . Winchester.*
18. Knowles, Brooke & London.
19. Knowles, pp. 64 and 84.
20. John of Salisbury, *Historia pontificalis*, p. 85.
21. Southern (1953), p. 137.
22. Southern (1970), p. 238.
23. The full list in Ullmann, pp. 372–6, has been used.
24. La Roncière (1990), pp. 63–4.
25. Duffaut, I, p. 186.
26. Fisher, p. 152.
27. Michaelsson (1927–36), I, p. 69; Maître (1964), p. 39.
28. Bede, II, Loeb, pp. 224–9.
29. Aebischer (1928), p. 95.
30. Kempers, p. 75.
31. *Diaries of Buonaccorso Pitti and Gregorio Dati*, pp. 115ff., 126ff. and 134ff.
32. Kedar, pp. 444–5.
33. Beech, p. 95.
34. Bourin, p. 245.
35. Bloch, p. 67.
36. La Roncière (1983), pp. 48–9.
37. Biget, pp. 311 and 319.
38. Morlet (1968–85), II, p. 83.
39. Poly & Bournazel, p. 112.
40. Waley, p. 189.
41. Le Pesant, p. 53.
42. P. Beck (1980), p. 265.
43. Waley, p. 188.
44. Cit. Fucilla, pp. 3–4.
45. Cit. Bardsley, p. 6.

Chapter 7

1. Michaelsson (1927), p. 74.
2. Aebischer (1924), p. 167.
3. Bourin, pp. 234–5.
4. Berger (1953), p. 112.
5. Whitelock, p. 152.
6. Reaney (1967), p. 309.
7. MacLysaght (1964), p. 9.
8. Woulfe, p. xx.
9. Saint-Jouan, III, p. 287.
10. Cit. Holt (1982), p. 17.
11. Vasari, I, p. 98.
12. Heers (1974), p. 106.
13. Matarazzo, *Chronicles*, p. 260.
14. Cit. Reaney (1967), p. 222.
15. Giraldus Cambrensis, *Speculum duorum*, pp. 78ff.
16. Morgan & Morgan, p. 47.
17. Blottière, I, p. 36.
18. Insley (1982), p. 94.
19. Vasari, II, pp. 14–16.
20. Brucker (ed.) (1971), pp. 150, 195 and 13.
21. Cit. Woulfe, p. xxiii.
22. Kneen, p. xxii.
23. McKinley (1980), p. 52.
24. Musset (1976), pp. 94–5; Musset (1977).
25. Duby, p. 60.
26. Higounet (1968), p. 577.
27. Canestrier, p. 139.
28. Heers (1977), pp. 38–40.
29. Holt (1982), p. 21.
30. Black, p. 27.
31. Bouchard (1979), pp. 45–7.
32. Saint-Jouan, III, p. 280.
33. Holt (1982), p. 31.
34. Bonenfant & Despy, p. 34.
35. Bouchard (1979), p. 45.
36. Holt (1982), p. 22.
37. Duby, p. 145.
38. Holt (1972), p. 25.
39. Holt (1982), p. 15.
40. Saint-Jouan, IV, p. 54.
41. Vallet (1961), p. 148.
42. Lot, p. 220.
43. Mestayer, p. 12.
44. Homans, pp. 196 and 442.
45. Hilton, p. 30.
46. Redmonds (1972–3), p. 171.
47. Bois, p. 69.
48. Lebel (1939), pp. 105–6.

49. Vasari, II, p. 116.
50. Quantin, p. 126.
51. Higounet (1953), p. 7.
52. McClure (1979), p. 175.
53. McKinley (1969), p. 55.
54. Lopez, p. 15.
55. Clark (1982–3), II, p. 73.
56. Langland, *Piers Plowman*, Passus V, 226, p. 43.
57. H. Leyser, p. 148.
58. Thrupp, p. 170.

Chapter 8

1. Clanchy, p. 99; McClure (1982), p. 92.
2. Clark (1982–3), II, pp. 66–7.
3. Tengvik, p. 10; Wagner, p. 150; cit. Scott Thomson, p. 225.
4. Valéry, pp. 241–2.
5. Grendi, pp. 275–6; Vasari, I, pp. 125, 199 and 202; Baxandall, pp. 159 and 118–19.
6. Vasari, I, pp. 134 and 158.
7. Insley (1982), p. 93; Morgan & Morgan, p. 14.
8. Dante, *Inferno*, XIX, pp. 70–1; Toubert, pp. 700–1.
9. Gigot, p. 732.
10. *Liber Vitae Ecclesiae Dunelmensis* (1841), p. 109.
11. Lopez, p. 8; Toynbee, p. 105; F.W. Kent, pp. 255–6.
12. Prat, p. 203.
13. D'Alauzier, p. 192.
14. Cit. Poole, p. 10.
15. Cit. Clanchy, p. 31; Zimmermann, pp. 292–3; Bourin and Chareille, 2, p. 310.
16. Reichert, cit. Michaelsson (1927–36), I, p. 310; Bourin and Chareille, 2, p. 316.
17. Vallet (1961), pp. 280–1.
18. Nicholas, p. 278; Saint–Jouan, IX, pp. 131–8.
19. Bloch, p. 69; Michaelsson (1927–36), I, p. 188.
20. Bouchard (1979), pp. 47–8.
21. Cit. MacBain (1897), p. 282; Elwyn Williams, p. 57; McKinley (1990), pp. 39–40.
22. John of Salisbury, *Historia pontificalis*, p. 46.
23. MacLysaght (1957), pp. 160–1; MacLysaght (1964), p. 12.
24. Cit. Martine, pp. 16–17; MacBain (1897), p. 314.
25. Black, p. xxxviii.
26. Herlihy, pp. 178–80; Goldthwaite (1968), pp. 69ff.
27. Chojnacki (1973), p. 62; Matarazzo, *Chronicles*, pp. 47 and 55.
28. F.W. Kent, p. 254; D. Kent, p. 169.
29. Grendi, pp. 281 and 249; Heers (1974), p. 107.
30. Heers (1977), p. 149.
31. *Ibid.*, p. 54.
32. Toubert, pp. 701 and 711.
33. Saint-Jouan, VI, pp. 225ff.
34. Vasari, II, pp. 105, 310ff., 273–80 and 307; Gwyn A. Williams, p. 279.
35. Bourin & Chareille, 2, p. 218.

36. Morgan & Morgan, p. 12.
37. Nègre, p. 60.
38. Cit. Cooper, p. 260.
39. Camden, p. 153; Homans, p. 187.
40. Schneider, p. 127.
41. Herlihy, p. 96; Vasari, I, pp. 191–2; *Chester Mystery Cycle*, p. 129.
42. Nègre, p. 59.
43. Duby, pp. 75–6.
44. Grohmann, p. 111.
45. Machiavelli, *Castruccio Castracani*, p. 166.
46. Shakespeare, *The Merchant of Venice*, Act II, Sc. 2, p. 38.
47. Wagner, pp. 104–5.

Chapter 9

1. Warion, p. 147.
2. Dupâquier et al. (1987), p. 44.
3. Neveux, pp. 132–3.
4. Vallet (1961), p. 120.
5. Dupâquier, pp. 137–8.
6. Burguière (1980), p. 41.
7. Canestrier, p. 149.
8. Charles of Sezze, *Autobiography*, p. 205; Klapisch-Zuber (1985a), p. 303.
9. Woulfe, p. 7; MacLysaght (1957), p. 41.
10. Cit. Bardsley, p. 44; cit. D.S. Smith, p. 544.
11. Montaigne, *Essais*, Book 1, Ch. XLVI, "Des Noms", I, p. 308; Camden, p. 56.
12. Cit. Bardsley, pp. 185–8.
13. Gough, *The History of Myddle*, p. 147; Boswell, *The life of Samuel Johnson*, II, p. 53; Camden, p. 56; Winstedt, I, p. 66; Kilvert, *Diary*, 26 February 1870, p. 12.
14. Dodge, p. 473; Stewart (1948), p. 119.
15. Stewart (1948), p. 119.
16. Fischer, pp. 220–2; 1 Samuel, 7:12.
17. Cit. Stewart (1948), pp. 133–4.
18. Mencken (1978), II, pp. 467–8.
19. Fauvel, p. 105.
20. Denis (1977), p. 348; Kintz (1984), pp. 232 and 236–7.
21. Hale, pp. 151–2.
22. These samples have been compiled from the three volumes of the *Livre des habitants de Genève*.
23. Balzac, *A bachelor's establishment*, p. 138.
24. Holman-Hunt, *My Grandmothers and I*, p. 164.
25. Woodforde, *Diary*, 27 March 1765, p. 30.
26. Chandos, *History of the Willoughby family*, p. 18; Shakespeare, *Pericles*, Act III, Sc. 3, p. 44.
27. Burckhardt, p. 149.
28. Boswell, *The life of Samuel Johnson*, II, p. 156.
29. Camden, p. 56; Forster, pp. 1–2.
30. Nikonov, p. 180.
31. Montaigne, *Essais*, I, pp. 308–9; La Bruyère, *Les Caractères*, IX, 23, p. 244.

32. Dauzat, p. 65.
33. Shakespeare, *Love's labour's lost*, Act V, Sc. 2, p. 186; Camden, p. 103; Withycombe, p. 172; Wortley Montagu, *Letters*, 9 October 1757, pp. 482–3.
34. Dupâquier et al. (1987), p. 84.
35. Morgan & Morgan, pp. 19 and 22–3.
36. Houth-Baltus (1956), p. 39.
37. Yonge, pp. 385–6.
38. Bernet, pp. 247–8.
39. Bianchi (1982), p. 228; Dommanget, pp. 326–8.
40. P.M. Jones, p. 250.
41. Michaëlsson (1927–36), I, p. 66.
42. Taine, *Histoire de la littérature anglaise*, IV, p. 209.
43. Sterne, *Tristram Shandy*, pp. 48ff.; Sheridan, *St. Patrick's Day, Plays*, p. 104; Austen, *Mansfield Park*, p. 211.
44. Withycombe, p. 14; Blakiston, pp. 210 and 191.
45. From the Crowder/Woodward genealogies traced by Norman and Sarah Crowder.

Chapter 10

1. Livi Bacci (1972), pp. 324–5.
2. Dupâquier et al. (1987), p. 29; Warion, p. 148; Delord, p. 92; Goursaud, II, p. 306.
3. Camden, pp. 57–8; cit. Withycombe, p. xxxi.
4. W.M. Williams, p. 229.
5. Yonge, p. 465; Dunkling (1978), pp. 33–4.
6. *Diaries of Buonaccorso Pitti and Gregorio Dati*, pp. 127–8; cit. Maurois (1953), p. 28.
7. Camden, pp. 57–8; Klapisch-Zuber (1985a), p. 288; Klapisch-Zuber (1984), pp. 42–3.
8. Schnapper, pp. 19–20; cit. Migliorini, p. 17.
9. Gresset, p. 210; Sangoi, p. 72; Maître (1967–8), p. 412.
10. Souque, p. 72.
11. Collomp (1980), p. 54; Zonabend (1979), p. 60.
12. Zonabend (1980b), p. 12.
13. Zonabend (1980a), pp. 235–6.
14. Fine, p. 114.
15. Sturdy, p. 180.
16. cit. F.W. Kent, p. 46.
17. Klapisch-Zuber (1985a), pp. 299 and 301–3.
18. Ettori, p. 53; Sorbier, pp. 177–81.
19. Canestrier, p. 149; Ettori, p. 53.
20. Macfarlane, p. 88.
21. Elwin, p. 20.
22. Johnson, *Lives of the poets*, II, pp. 289–90.
23. Dante, *Paradiso*, Canto XV, p. 189; Cornford, p. 173.
24. Dauzat, p. 56.
25. Duby & Duby, p. 63.
26. Brun, p. 39; Jolas et al., p. 13.

27. Fine, pp. 110ff.
28. Burguière (1980), pp. 30–2.
29. Klapisch-Zuber (1985a), p. 288; Brodrick, p. 3.
30. Ettori, p. 53.
31. Gibbon, *Autobiography*, pp. 20–1.
32. Beier, p. 209; Turner, *Diary of a Georgian Shopkeeper*, pp. 83–4; D.S. Smith, p. 546.
33. *Lisle Letters*, p. 515.
34. Clodd, p. 137.
35. Burguière (1984), p. 34; D.S. Smith, p. 546; La Tour du Pin, *Memoirs*, p. 338.
36. Davidoff and Hall, p. 222.
37. Camden, p. 150.
38. Maître (1967–8), p. 421.
39. Swift, *Journal to Stella*, pp. 193–4; Austen, *Sense and sensibility*, p. 214; Dickens, *Our mutual friend*, p. 139; Trollope, *Barchester Towers*, pp. 530 and 284; Askwith, p. 26; Balzac, *Lost illusions*, p. 65.
40. Segalen, p. 67; Zonabend (1979), p. 67.
41. Léautaud, *Journal*, 22 October 1903, p. 51; Robert, pp. 79–80; Hugo, *Lettres à Juliette Drouet*, pp. 27, 67 and 107.
42. Vallès, *L'Enfant*, p. 59.
43. Bardsley, p. 82; Cole, *Diary*, p. 145.
44. Cit. Phillipps, pp. 152–3.
45. Congreve, *The way of the world, comedies*, p. 415; Boswell *The life of Samuel Johnson*, I, p. 52; cit. Withycombe, p. 34.
46. *Pembroke Papers*, II, p. 359; Dickens, *Pickwick Papers*, p. 648.
47. Dickens, *Pickwick Papers*, p. 213.
48. Shakespeare, *Antony and Cleopatra*, Act II, Sc. 13, p. 137; Dunkling (1978), pp. 75–6; Swift, *A complete collection of genteel and ingenious conversation, prose works*, XI, p. 256.
49. Shakespeare, *King John*, Act I, Sc. 1, p. 14.
50. Peterson, p. 83.
51. Cit. Peterson, p. 66.
52. Houth-Baltus (1956), pp. 35–6.
53. *Lisle Letters*, p. 39.

Chapter 11

1. Lopez, p. 8.
2. Blaquière, p. 107.
3. Morgan & Morgan, p. 15; cit. Reaney (1967), p. 317.
4. Cit. Pullan, p. 208.
5. Cit. Mendel, pp. 54–5.
6. Roblin (1950), pp. 297ff.
7. Paul Bourget, *Cosmopolis*, p. 20.
8. Sigsworth, p. 29; Aris, p. 127; Mencken (1936), p. 501; cit. Weekley, p. 54.
9. Bahloul, pp. 63–4 and 66.
10. Geipel, p. 165; Denis (1984), p. 314; Jakobi et al., p. 71.
11. Shakespeare, *King Henry IV, Part 2*, Act V, Sc. 1, cit. Weekley, pp. 4–5; Cole, *Bletchley diary*, pp. 51–2 and 81; MacBain (1900), p. 152.

12. Gough, *History of Myddle*, p. 110.
13. Vincent (1958), pp. 195–6 and 200.
14. Swift, Will, in *Prose Works*, Vol. XI, p. 411; Winstedt, II, p. 23.
15. Dickens, *Pickwick Papers*, p. 483; Johnson, *Prose and poetry*, p. 302.
16. *Lisle Letters*, p. 39; Stone, pp. 64 and 98; *Creevey papers*, pp. 95–7 and 133.
17. Dauzat, p. 148.
18. Barry, p. 79; Synge, *Aran Islands*, p. 109.
19. Segalen, p. 64; Zonabend (1979), p. 51; Benoît, p. 188.
20. Febvre (1941), p. 36; Helin, p. 22.
21. Dickens, *Our mutual friend*, pp. 32–3.
22. Anthony Powell, *The soldier's art*, p. 31; Chapman, p. 239.
23. *Lisle Letters*, p. 377; *Pembroke Papers*, I, p. 353; Dover Wilson, p. 83; W.M. Williams, p. 218.
24. Phillips, p. 14; Gittings, p. 87.
25. *Pembroke Papers*, II, p. 117; Sydney Smith, *Letters*, p. 315; Blakiston, pp. 92–3.
26. *Lisle Letters*, pp. 299 and 201; Boswell, *Life of Johnson*, I, p. 632; *Syon House*, p. 27; Heywood, pp. 68–9.
27. Cooper, pp. 228–9; Jane Austen, *Letters*, p. 23 (editor).
28. Lady Holland, p. 91; Holman-Hunt, p. 29; Grossmith & Grossmith, *The diary of a nobody*, p. 151.
29. Cit. Hexter, pp. 212–13; Blakiston, pp. 162 and 380–1.
30. Gough, *History of Myddle*, pp. 207–8; Carlyle, *Letters*, p. 98.
31. Marvick, pp. 90 and 245.
32. W.M. Williams, p. 81.
33. Philip Larkin, *The less deceived*, pp. 16 and 60; Baker.
34. Davis, p. 71; Collomp (1980), p. 44; McDermott, p. 30.
35. Mercier, *Tableau de Paris*, p. 156; Camproux, p. 218.
36. W.M. Williams, p. 82; Gough, *History of Myddle*, p. 123; Cavallo & Cerutti, p. 92.
37. *Pembroke Papers*, I, p. 33 and *passim*.
38. Saint-Jouan, IX, p. 138.
39. Bardsley, p. 234; Dickens, *Our mutual friend*, pp. 199 and 201.
40. MacLysaght (1957), p. 16.
41. Woulfe, p. 36; MacLysaght (1957), pp. 187–8.
42. MacLysaght (1957), pp. 17 and 62.
43. *Lisle Letters*, p. 361; cit. Wagner, p. 112; Haller, p. 59.
44. Cole, *Bletchley diary*, p. 55; Chapman, p. 241.
45. Gough, *History of Myddle*, pp. 158–9; *Pembroke Papers*, II, p. 48; Woodforde, *Diary*, p. 377.
46. Dickens, *Our mutual friend*, p. 653; cit. E.P. Thompson, pp. 838–9; cit. Phillipps, p. 144; cit. McClure (1981), p. 63.
47. *Lisle Letters*, pp. 52–3; Chandos, *History of the Willoughby Family*, pp. 74–5.
48. Cit. Wagner, pp. 113–14.
49. Ro. Ba., *Life of Syr Thomas More*, pp. 131, 137 and 57; *Lisle Letters*, pp. 263–4 and 414.
50. Chandos, *History of the Willoughby family*, pp. 125 and 127; Boswell, *Life of Johnson*, II, p. 575; cit. Hemlow, p. 268.
51. Waterson, pp. 91–2; Hughes, *A London child*, p. 84.
52. *Barrington family letters*, pp. 70–1.
53. Boswell, *Life of Johnson*, I, p. 323.

54. Congreve, *Comedies*, p. 272; cit. Hemlow, p. 268; Dickens, *Pickwick Papers*, p. 51; Phillipps, pp. 157–8.
55. Kintz (1984), p. 231.
56. Montaigne, *Essais*, I, p. 344; Mercier, *Tableau de Paris*, p. 31.
57. Stendhal, *Vie de Henri Brulard*, pp. 87–8; Boswell, *Life of Johnson*, I, p. 574.
58. Cit. Snell, p. 164.
59. *Barrington family letters*, *passim*.
60. Pepys, *Diary*, 1662.
61. J. Greene, *Correspondence*, p. 27 and *passim*.
62. Phillipps, p. 163.
63. Houghton, *The life and letters of John Keats*, p. 92; Monkswell, *A Victorian diarist*, p. 142; Firth, Hubert & Forge, pp. 330–2.
64. Boswell, *Life of Johnson*, I, pp. 206–7; cit. Dunkling (1977), p. 34; Hemlow, p. 67.
65. Firth, Hubert & Forge, p. 325.
66. *Ibid.*, pp. 303–4; Gough, *History of Myddle*, p. 121.
67. St Charles de Sezze, *Autobiography*, pp. 43 and 60.
68. Du Puy de Clinchamps, p. 53; Forster, p. 10; Proust, *A la Recherche*, 4, pp. 73–4; cit. Cordonnier, p. 72.
69. Febvre (1970), p. 223.
70. Montaigne, *Essais*, I, pp. 308–9.
71. Bloch (1952), I, pp. 142–3; Febvre (1970), pp. 83–4.
72. Balzac, *Le Cousin Pons*, p. 33; Proust, *A la Recherche*, 5, p. 403.
73. Cit. Weekley, p. 140.
74. Vigny, *Journal d'un poète*, p. 408.
75. Hugo, *Choses vues 1849–69*, p. 130; Tocqueville, *Democracy in America*, p. 529.
76. Du Puy de Clinchamps, pp. 109–10.
77. Boswell, *Journal of a tour to the Hebrides*, p. 83.
78. Pyles, p. 136.
79. Lady Holland, p. 97.
80. Blakiston, pp. 431 and 505.
81. *Pembroke Papers*, I, pp. 22–3; Powell, *At Lady Molly's*, p. 31.
82. Monkswell, *A Victorian diarist*, pp. 119–20.
83. Johnson, *Prose and poetry*, p. 780.
84. Proust, *A la Recherche*, 7, pp. 305–6.
85. Barley, p. 14.
86. Cit. Black, p. xxxi.
87. Dorian, *passim*.
88. Aebischer (1923), p. 107.
89. Dauven, *passim*.
90. Zonabend (1979), pp. 69–70; Gilmore, p. 687; Pina-Cabral (1984), p. 150; Foster, p. 119.
91. Zonabend (1979), p. 71; Brögger, p. 92; Dauzat, p. 100.
92. Segalen, p. 75; Collomp (1980), pp. 56–7; Collomp (1984), pp. 175–6.
93. Martin-Gistucci, I and II.
94. Iszaevich.
95. Corvisier, II, pp. 851–61, 985 and 1049–57.
96. Boswell, *Life of Johnson*, I, p. 485.
97. *Creevey Papers*, p. 468 and *passim*.

98. Proust, *A la Recherche*, 6, pp. 97 and 170–1.
99. McClure (1981), pp. 65 and 70–1; Morgan, O'Neill & Harré, pp. 71 and 75–6.
100. McClure (1981), pp. 71–1.
101. Cit. Marble, p. 219.
102. Maurois, pp. 131–2.
103. Powell, *Casanova's Chinese Restaurant*, p. 24.

Chapter 12

1. Dumas, pp. 201 and 203.
2. *Ibid.*, p. 203.
3. Wright, p. 168.
4. McGill, pp. 47–8.
5. D.S. Smith, p. 548.
6. Tebbenhoff, pp. 569–71.
7. Tocqueville, *Democracy in America*, p. 296; Fischer, p. 231.
8. Wyatt-Brown, pp. 124–5; Sizer, pp. 36–7.
9. Rossi.
10. *Diary of Mary Louisa Black*, Appendix C.
11. Edel, p. 58; Plank (1971), p. 133.
12. Mencken (1936), p. 520; Mencken (1978), p. 501.
13. Lieberson and Bell, p. 519.
14. Mencken (1978), pp. 469 and 471.
15. Mencken (1936), p. 505.
16. Fischer, p. 232; Mencken (1978), p. 468.
17. *Ibid.*, pp. 496–7; Pyles, p. 144.
18. Mencken (1978), p. 494; Stewart (1979), p. 38.
19. Brender, p. 8; Sizer, p. 35; Pyles, pp. 150–1 and 154–5.
20. Pyles, p. 152.
21. Stewart (1979), p. 30; Mencken (1936), p. 518; Fischer, p. 231.
22. Hartman (1958), p. 293; Brown & Gilman, pp. 267–8.
23. Mencken (1978), p. 525; Henry James, *William Wetmore Story*, I, p. 37.
24. Brown and Ford, p. 236.
25. Pyles, pp. 153 and 145.
26. Cit. Mencken (1978), p. 461.
27. Cit. Fiske, p. 76; Mencken (1978), p. 445.
28. Mencken (1936), p. 401.
29. *Ibid.*, pp. 477–8.
30. *Ibid.*, pp. 482–3.
31. *Ibid.*, pp. 492–3.
32. *Ibid.*, p. 497; Broom et al., pp. 33ff.
33. Mencken (1936), p. 498.
34. *Ibid.*, p. 501; Kaganoff, p. 72.
35. Nogrady, p. 438.
36. Mencken (1936), p. 517.
37. Pyles, p. 140.
38. Mook, p. 111.
39. Sizer, p. 34.

40. Kemble, *Journal*, p. 40.
41. *Ibid.*, p. 245; De Camp, p. 142; Owens, p. 14.
42. Cody, p. 198.
43. Puckett (1938), pp. 38–9; Puckett (1937), p. 478.
44. Kemble, *Journal*, p. 201.
45. Stewart (1979), p. 37; Puckett (1937), p. 485.
46. Owens, p. 193.
47. Cody, pp. 194ff.
48. Owens, p. 208; Cody, p. 202.
49. Washington, *Up from slavery*, p. 17.
50. *Ibid.*, p. 26; Mencken (1978), pp .447–8.
51. Washington, *Up from slavery*, p. 18.
52. McGregory, p. 390.
53. Puckett (1938), p. 43; cit. Mencken (1978), pp. 514–15.
54. Cit. Mencken (1978), pp. 514–15; Paustian, p. 187.
55. Figures taken from lists in Dunkling (1977), p. 156; Dunkling (1995), pp. 50 and 54.

Chapter 13

1. Desplanques, p. 69; Bozon, p. 89.
2. Bozon, p. 93.
3. *Ibid.*, p. 91.
4. Besnard (1991), pp. 56–7; Besnard (1979), p. 347; Bozon, pp. 95–6.
5. Bozon, pp. 92–3; Besnard (1991), p. 59.
6. Besnard (1991), p. 58; Desplanques, p. 74.
7. Besnard & Grange, pp. 278–9.
8. Hassoun.
9. Dunkling (1977), p. 203.
10. MacLysaght (1957), p. 40.
11. Figures computed from Dunkling (1995), pp. 47–8 and 51–2.
12. Selwyn (ed.), p. 39.
13. Dunkling (1995), pp. 45 and 78.
14. Dunkling (1995), p. 45; Dunkling (1978), pp. 21–2.
15. Paulin, *The strange museum*, p. 26.
16. Dunkling (1978), p. 103; Dunkling (1995), pp. 93ff.
17. Morgan, O'Neill & Harré, p. 19.
18. Ashby, pp. 209–10; W.M. Williams, p. 80; Young and Willmott, p. 25.
19. Dunkling (1977), p. 175.
20. Cit. Dunkling (1995), pp. 92–3.
21. Dunkling (1977), p. 180; Dunkling (1995), p. 80.
22. Dunkling (1995), p. 27.
23. Priestley, *English journey*, p. 279; Firth, Hubert & Forge, pp. 304–5.
24. De Felice (1982), p. 187.

Glossary

arrondissement	French administrative division
augurative	intended to bring good fortune
cadet	younger son
dithematic	comprising two elements; a type of Germanic name
état-civil	official registration of births, marriage and deaths in France; status deriving therefrom
etymological	relating to origin or meaning of word or name
hagionymy	naming after saints
homonym	having the same name
hypocoristic	derived version of a name, either shortened or with suffixes
lexical	relating to a word, i.e. having a meaning
matronymic	additional name after mother
noms de guerre	nicknames of soldiers
onomastic	to do with names
patrilineal	of descent traced in the male line
patronymic	additional name after father
polyonomy	the practice of having many names
prefix	syllable(s) added to beginning of word or name
primogeniture	system of inheritance in which the eldest son takes all or the bulk of the estate, etc.
robe	division of French nobility comprising magistrates and officials
sept	subdivision of clan
sibling	brother or sister
suffix	syllable(s) added to end of word or name
syncopis	removal of letters or syllables

Bibliography

Part I   Ancient Rome

(a)   Primary

Appian. *Roman history*, I, trans. Horace White (London and Cambridge, Mass.: Loeb Classical Library, 1912 and 1964).

Apuleius. *The golden ass*, ed. S. Gaselee (London and New York: Loeb, 1928).

Ausonius [2 vols], ed. H.G. Evelyn White (London and Cambridge, Mass.: Loeb, 1919 and 1968).

Caesar. *The Gallic War*, trans. H.J. Edwards (London and Cambridge, Mass.: Loeb, 1917 and 1963).

Cicero. *De inventione*, trans. H.M. Hubbell (London and Cambridge, Mass.: Loeb, 1949).

Cicero. *Letters to his friends* [4 vols], trans. W. Glynn Williams (London and Cambridge, Mass.: Loeb, 1927–54).

Cicero. *Pro Plancio*, trans. N.H. Watts (London and New York: Loeb, 1923).

Cicero. *Pro Sulla*, trans. C. Macdonald (London and Cambridge, Mass.: Loeb, 1976).

Eusebius. *The history of the Church from Christ to Constantine*, trans. G.A. Williamson (Harmondsworth: Penguin Books, 1965).

Juvenal. *The sixteen satires*, ed. and trans. Peter Green (Harmondsworth: Penguin, 1967).

Juvenal and Persius, ed. G.G. Ramsay (London and Cambridge, Mass.: Loeb, 1918 and 1961).

Livy [14 vols], trans. B.O. Foster et al. (London and Cambridge, Mass.: Loeb, 1919–59).

The New English Bible, New Testament (Oxford and Cambridge: OUP and CUP, 1961).

Pliny the Elder. *Natural History* [10 vols], trans. H. Rackham et al. (London and Cambridge, Mass.: Loeb, 1938–63).

Pliny the Younger. *Letters*, ed. and trans. Betty Radice (Harmondsworth: Penguin, 1963).

Pliny the Younger. *Letters and panegyrics* [2 vols], trans. Betty Radice (London and Cambridge, Mass.: Loeb, 1969).

Plutarch. *Parallel lives* [11 vols], trans. Bernadotte Perrin et al. (London and Cambridge, Mass.: Loeb, 1914–26).

Polybius. *Histories*, III, trans. W.R. Paton (London and Cambridge, Mass.: Loeb, 1923 and 1966).

Propertius, trans. H.E. Butler. (London and Cambridge, Mass.: Loeb, 1912).

Select Papyri, I, ed. A.S. Hunt & C.C. Edgar (London and Cambridge, Mass.: Loeb, 1952).

Suetonius [2 vols], trans. J.C. Rolfe (London and Cambridge, Mass.: Loeb, 1914).

Suetonius. *The twelve Caesars*, trans. Robert Graves (Harmondsworth: Penguin, 1957).

Tacitus [5 vols], trans. C.H. Moore & John Jackson (London and Cambridge, Mass.: Loeb, 1930–7).

Tacitus. *The Annals of Imperial Rome*, ed. and trans. Michael Grant (Harmondsworth: Penguin, 1956).

Varro. *De Lingua Latina* [2 vols], trans. R.G. Kent (London and Cambridge, Mass.: Loeb, 1938 and 1967).

(b)   Secondary

Adams, J.N. Conventions of naming in Cicero. *Classical Quarterly* **NS 28**, pp. 145–66, 1978.

Alföldy, G. L'onomastique de Tarragone. See *L'Onomastique latine*, 1977, pp. 293ff.

Arnhem, M.T.W. *The senatorial aristocracy in the later Roman Empire* (Oxford: Oxford University Press, 1972).

Axtell, H.L. Men's names in the writings of Cicero. *Classical Philology* **10**, pp. 386–404, 1915.

Badian, E. *Foreign clientelae (264–70 BC)* (Oxford: Oxford University Press, 1958).

Balsdon, J.P.V.D. *Romans and aliens* (London: Duckworth, 1979).

Bénabou, Marcel. *La résistance africaine à la romanisation* (Paris: Maspéro, 1976).

Boardman, John, Jasper Griffin & Oswyn Murray (eds). *The Oxford history of the Roman world* (Oxford: Oxford University Press, 1991).

Box, Herbert. Roman citizenship in Laconia. *Journal of Roman Studies* **21**, pp. 200–14 and **22**, pp. 165–83, 1931–2.

Broughton, T.R.S. *The Romanization of Africa Proconsularis* (Baltimore and London, 1929).

Brunt, P.A. The Romanization of the local ruling classes in the Roman Empire. See Pippidi (ed.), 1976, pp. 161–73.

Cagnat, René. *Cours d'Épigraphie latine*, 4th edn (Paris, 1914).

Cameron, Alan. The date and identity of Macrobius. *Journal of Roman Studies* **56**, pp. 25–38, 1966.

Cameron, Alan. Polyonomy in the late Roman aristocracy: the case of Petronius Probus. *Journal of Roman Studies* **75**, pp. 164–82, 1985.

Chase, George Davis. The origin of Roman praenomina. *Harvard Studies in Classical Philology* **8**, pp. 103ff., 1897.

Chastagnol, André. L'onomastique de l'album de Timgad. See *L'Onomastique latine*, 1977, pp. 325–37.

Cheesman, G.L. *The Auxilia of the Roman Imperial Army* (Oxford: Oxford University Press, 1914).

Condurachi, E.M. La Costituzione Antoniniana e la sua applicazione nell'Impero Romano. *Dacia* 1958, pp. 281–316.

Daux, Georges. L'onomastique romaine d'expression grecque. See *L'Onomastique latine*, 1977, pp. 405–17.

Dean, L.R. *A study of the cognomina of soldiers in the Roman legions* (Princeton, 1916).

Dictionnaire d'archéologie chrétienne et de liturgie [15 vols], Dom Fernand Cabrol and Dom Henri Leclercq (eds) (Paris: Letouzey, 1924–53).

Duff, A.M. *Freedmen in the early Roman Empire* (Oxford: Oxford University Press, 1928).

Duval, Noël. Observations sur l'onomastique dans les inscriptions chrétiennes d'Afrique du Nord. See *L'Onomastique latine*, 1977, pp. 447–56.

Etienne, R. et al. Les dimensions sociales de la Romanisation dans la peninsule ibérique des origines à la fin de l'Empire. See Pippidi (ed.), 1976, pp. 95–107.

Finley, M.I. *Aspects of antiquity: discoveries and controversies* (London: Chatto and Windus, 1968).

Fustel de Coulanges, N.D. *The ancient city* (New York: Doubleday, 1960; original edn 1864).

Garnsey, Peter & Richard Saller. *The Roman Empire: economy, society and culture* (London: Duckworth, 1987).

Gelzer, Matthias. *The Roman nobility* (Oxford: Basil Blackwell, 1969; original edn 1912).

Gilliam, J.F. Dura rosters and the *constitutio Antoniniana. Historia* (Wiesbaden) **14**, pp. 74–92, 1965.

Gordon, M.L. The nationality of slaves under the early Roman Empire. *Journal of Roman Studies* **14**, pp. 93–111, 1924.

Gougenheim, G. Les sobriquets latins. *Revue Internationale d'Onomastique* **5**, pp. 131–8, 1953.

Halkin, Léon. *Les esclaves publics chez les Romains* (Brussels, 1897).

Hopkins, Keith. Elite mobility in the Roman Empire. *Past and present* **32**, pp. 12–26, 1965.

Hopkins, Keith. *Conquerors and slaves, sociological studies in Roman history 1* (Cambridge: Cambridge University Press, 1978).

Hopkins, Keith. *Death and renewal, sociological studies in Roman history 2* (Cambridge: Cambridge University Press, 1983).

Jones, A.H.M., J.R. Martindale & J. Morris. *The prosopography of the later Roman Empire, I, AD 260–395* (Cambridge: Cambridge University Press, 1971).

Kajanto, Iiro. On the problem of "names of humility" in early Christian epigraphy. *Arctos* **NS 3**, pp. 45–53, 1962.

Kajanto, Iiro. *Onomastic studies in the early Christian inscriptions of Rome and Carthage* (Helsinki: Acta Instituti Romani Finlandiae II: 1, 1963).

Kajanto, Iiro. *The Latin cognomina.* Helsinki: Societas Scientiarum Fennica, Commentationes Humanorum Litterarum **36:2**, 1965.

Kajanto, Iiro. *Supernomina, a study in Latin epigraphy.* Helsinki: Societas Scientiarum Fennica, Commentationes Humanarum Litterarum **40:1**, 1966.

Kajanto, Iiro. The significance of non-Latin cognomina. *Latomus* **27**, pp. 517–34, 1968.

Kajanto, Iiro. Women's praenomina reconsidered. *Arctos* **7**, pp. 13–30, 1972.

Kajanto, Iiro. Of the chronology of the cognomen in the Republican period. See *L'Onomastique latine*, 1977a, pp. 63–70.

Kajanto, Iiro. Of the peculiarities of women's nomenclature. See *L'Onomastique latine*, 1977b, pp. 147–59.

Kajanto, Iiro. The emergence of the late single name system. See *L'Onomastique latine*, 1977c, pp. 421–30.

Keppie, Lawrence. *Understanding Roman inscriptions* (London, 1991).

Le Glay, Marcel. Remarques sur l'onomastique gallo-romaine. See *L'Onomastique latine*, 1977, pp. 269–77.

Leon, H.J. The names of the Jews of Ancient Rome. *Transactions of the American Philological Association* **59**, pp. 205–24, 1928.

MacMullen, Ramsay. Social mobility and the Theodosian Code. *Journal of Roman Studies* **54**, pp. 49–53, 1964.

MacMullen, Ramsay. The epigraphic habit of the Roman Empire. *American Journal of Philology* **103**, pp. 233–46, 1982.

Marrou, H.I. Problèmes généraux de l'onomastique chrétienne. See *L'Onomastique latine*, 1977, pp. 431–3.

Martindale, J.R. *The prosopography of the Later Roman Empire*, II, AD 395–527 (Cambridge: Cambridge University Press, 1980).

Millar, Fergus. Epictetus and the Imperial Court. *Journal of Roman Studies* **55**, pp. 141–8, 1965.

Momigliano, A. *Alien wisdom: the limits of hellenization* (Cambridge: Cambridge University Press, 1975).

Mommsen, Theodor. *The history of Rome* [5 vols] (London: Richard Bentley, 1894).

Nicolet, Claude. L'onomastique des groupes dirigeantes sous la République. See *L'Onomastique latine*, 1977, pp. 45–59.

L'Onomastique latine, Colloques internationaux du Centre National de la Recherche Scientifique, 1975 (Paris, 1977).

Pflaum, H.G. Titulature et rang social sous le Haut-Empire. In *Recherches sur les structures sociales dans l'antiquité classique, Caen 1969* (Paris: Editions du Centre National de la Recherche Scientifique, 1970), pp. 159–85.

Pflaum, H.G. Spécificité de l'onomastique romaine en Afrique du Nord. See *L'Onomastique latine* (1977), pp. 315–24.

Pietri, Charles. Remarques sur l'onomastique chrétienne de Rome. See *L'Onomastique latine*, 1977, pp. 437–45.

Pippidi, D.M. (ed.). *Assimilation et résistance à la culture Greco-Romaine dans le monde ancien*, Travaux du VIe Congrès International d'Etudes Classiques, 1974 (Bucarest and Paris, 1976).

Pulgram, E. The origin of the Latin *Nomen Gentilicium*. *Harvard Studies in Classical Philology* **58/9**, pp. 163–87, 1948.

Ramsay, Sir William Mitchell. *The cities of St Paul: their influence on his life and thought* (London: Hodder and Stoughton, 1907).

Rawson, Beryl (ed.). *The family in ancient Rome: new perspectives* (London: Routledge, 1986).

Reinhold, M. Usurpation of status and status symbols in the Roman Empire. *Historia* (Wiesbaden) **20**, pp. 275–302, 1971.

Sanders, Gabriel. Les Chrétiens face à l'épigraphie funéraire latine. See Pippidi (ed.), 1976, pp. 283–99.

Schulz, Fritz. Roman registers of births and birth certificates. *Journal of Roman Studies* **32**, pp. 78–91 and **33**, pp. 55–64, 1942–3.

Sherwin-White, A.N. *The Roman citizenship* (Oxford: Oxford University Press, 1973).

Solin, Heikki. Die innere Chronologie des Römischen Cognomens. See *L'Onomastique latine*, 1977a, pp. 104–38.

Solin, Heikki. Die Namen der Orientalischen Sklaven in Rom. See *L'Onomastique latine*, 1977b, pp. 205–10.

Solin, Heikki & Olli Salomies. *Repertorium nominum gentilium et cognominum Latinorum* (Hildesheim and Zurich, 1988).

Syme, Ronald. Imperator Caesar: a study in nomenclature. *Historia* (Wiesbaden) **7**, pp. 172–88, 1958.

Syme, Ronald. *The Augustan aristocracy* (Oxford: Oxford University Press, 1986).

Taylor, Lily Ross. Freedmen and freeborn in the epitaphs of Imperial Rome. *American Journal of Philology* **82**, pp. 113–32, 1961.

Thylander, Hilding. *Etude sur l'epigraphie latine* (Lund, 1952).

Thylander, H. La dénomination chez Ciceron dans les lettres à Atticus. *Opuscula Romana, Acta Instituti Romani Regni Sueciae* **18**, pp. 153–9, 1954.

Toutain, J. *Les cités romaines de la Tunisie, essai sur l'histoire de la colonisation romaine dans l'Afrique du Nord* (Paris, 1896).

Treggiari, Susan. *Roman freedmen during the late Republic* (Oxford: Oxford University Press, 1969).

Weaver, P.R.C. *Cognomina ingenua*: a note. *Classical Quarterly* **58** (**NS 14**), pp. 311–15, 1964.

Weaver, P.R.C. *Familia Caesaris: a social study of the emperor's freedmen and slaves* (Cambridge: Cambridge University Press, 1972).

Weaver, P.R.C. The status of children in mixed marriages. See Rawson (ed.), 1986, pp. 145–69.

Wiseman, T.P. *New men in the Roman Senate 139 BC–AD. 14* (Oxford: Oxford University Press, 1971).

Part II   The Middle Ages

(a)   Primary

Alberti, Leon Battista. *The family in Renaissance Florence* (*I libri della famiglia*), trans. R.N. Watkins (Columbia, South Carolina, 1969).

Alberti, Leon Battista. *I primi tre libri della famiglia* (Florence, 1946).

Anglo-Saxon Chronicle, trans. G.N. Garmonsway (London and New York: Dent and Dutton, 1972).

The Anglo-Saxon missionaries in Germany, being the lives of SS. Willibrord, Boniface, Sturm, Leoba and Lebuin, ed. and trans. C.H. Talbot (London and New York: Sheed and Ward, 1954).

Bede. *Ecclesiastical history of the English nation* (London and New York: Dent and Dutton, Everyman, 1910).

Bede. *Opera historica*, ed. J.E. King (London and Cambridge, Mass.: Loeb, 1930 and 1971).

Chester Mystery Cycle, ed. David Mills (East Lansing: Colleagues Press (Medieval Texts and Studies, 9), 1992).

Dante. *Inferno* (London: Dent, Temple Classics, 1929).

Diaries of Buonaccorso Pitti and Gregorio Dati, two memoirs of Renaissance Florence, ed. Gene Brucker (New York: Harper, 1967).

Documents relating to the Manor and Soke of Newark-on-Trent, ed. M.W. Barley et al. (Nottingham: Thoreton Society (16), 1956).

Giraldus Cambrensis. *Speculum duorum or a mirror of two men*, ed. Yves Lefèvre and R.B.C. Huygens (Cardiff: University of Wales Press, 1974).

Gregory of Tours. *History of the Franks*, trans. Lewis Thorpe (Harmondsworth: Penguin, 1974).

John of Salisbury. *Historia pontificalis*, ed. Marjorie Chibnall (London: Nelson, 1956).

Kalendar of Abbot Samson of Bury St. Edmunds and related documents, ed. R.H.C. Davis (London: Camden Society (3rd series, 84), 1954).

Langland, William. *Piers Plowman*, ed. J.A.W. Bennett (Oxford: Oxford University Press, 1972).

Liber Vitae Ecclesiae Dunelmensis (Leeds: Surtees Society (13 and 136), 1841 and 1923).

Liber Vitae, Register and Martyrology of the New Minster and Hyde Abbey, Winchester, ed. Walter de Gray Birch (London and Winchester: Hampshire Record Society (5), 1892).

Machiavelli. *Castruccio Castracani*. In *The Prince* (London and New York: Dent and Dutton, Everyman, 1908).

Matarazzo, Francesco. *Chronicles of the City of Perugia 1492–1503*, trans. E.S. Morgan (London: Dent, 1905).

Oldest English Texts, ed. Henry Sweet (London: Early English Text Society (Original Series 83), 1885).

Paston Letters [3 vols], ed. James Gairdner (London, 1872–5).

Recueil des Actes des Ducs de Normandie de 911 à 1066, ed. Marie Fauvoux (Caen: Mémoires de la Société des Antiquaires de Normandie (36), 1961).

Rolls and registers of Bishop Oliver Sutton, VII, ed. R.M.T. Hill (Lincoln: Lincoln Record Society (Publication 69), 1975).

Rouleaux des morts du IXe au XVe siècle, ed. Léopold Delisle (1866).

Shakespeare. *The Merchant of Venice*, ed. John Russell Brown (London and New York: Methuen, Arden edn, 1964).

Vasari, Giorgio. *Lives of the artists* [2 vols], trans. George Bull (Harmondsworth: Penguin, 1987).

Vespasiano da Bisticci. *Memoirs*, trans. W.G. and E. Waters (London: Routledge, 1926).

(b)   Secondary

Adigaud des Gautries, Jean. *Les noms de personnes Scandinaves en Normandie de 911 à 1066* (Lund: Nomina Germanica 11, 1954).

Aebischer, Paul. Sur l'origine et la formation des noms de famille dans le Canton de Fribourg. *Biblioteca dell' Archivum Romanicum* (Geneva) Series II, **6**, pp. 1–112, 1923.

Aebischer, Paul. L'Anthroponymie wallonne d'après quelques anciens cartulaires. *Bulletin du Dictionnaire Wallon* **13** (3–4), pp. 73–168, 1924.

Aebischer, Paul. Essai sur l'onomastique catalane du IXe au XIIe siècle. *Anuari de l'Oficina Romanica* (Barcelona) **1**, pp. 43–118, 1928.

Aebischer, Paul. Les origines de la finale -i des noms de famille italiens. *Onomastica* **1**, pp. 90–106, 1947.

Bardsley, Charles W. *Curiosities of Puritan nomenclature* (London: Chatto and Windus, 1880).

Barley, Nigel F. Perspectives on Anglo-Saxon names. *Semiotica* **11**, pp. 1–31, 1974.

Baudot, M. Destin des noms divins en onomastique. In *Proceedings of the 13th International Congress of Onomastic Sciences, Cracow 1978*, (Warsaw), I, pp. 165–80, 1981.

Baxandall, Michael *Painting and experience in fifteenth-century Italy* (Oxford: Oxford University Press, 1988).

Beck, James. *Masaccio, the documents* (New York: J.J. Augustin, Harvard University Center for Italian Renaissance Studies 4, 1978).

Beck, Patrice. Noms de baptême et structures sociales à Nuits (Bourgogne) à la fin du Moyen Age. *Bulletin Philologique et Historique*) (1980), pp. 253–66.

Beck, Patrice. Les noms de baptême en Bourgogne à la fin du Moyen Age. In *Le prénom, mode et histoire*, Jacques Dupâquier et al. (eds) (Paris, 1984), pp. 161–5.

Beech, George T. Les noms de personne poitevins du 9e au 12e siècle. *Revue Internationale d'Onomastique* **26**, pp. 81–100, 1974.

Bennett, Judith M. Spouses, siblings and surnames: reconstructing families from medieval village court rolls. *Journal of British Studies* **23**, pp. 26–46, 1983.

Berganton, M.F. *Le Dérivé du nom individuel au Moyen Age en Béarn et en Bigorre, usage officiel, suffixes et formations* (Paris: Editions du CNRS, 1977).

Berger, Roger. Les anciens noms de famille d'Arras: anthroponymie et lexicologie. *Annales de la Fédération Historique et Archaeologique de Belgique* **35**, pp. 107–21, 1953.

Berger, Roger. *Le nécrologie de la Confrérie des Jongleurs et des Bourgeois d'Arras (1194–1361)* II (Arras, 1970).

Bergh, Åke. *Etudes d'anthroponymie provençale*, I, *Les noms de personne du Polyptique de Wadalde* (Göteborg, 1941).

Biddle, Martin (ed.). *Winchester in the Middle Ages: an edition and discussion of the Winton Domesday* (Oxford: Oxford University Press, 1976).

Biget, Jean-Louis. L'évolution des noms de baptême en Languedoc au Moyen Age (IXe–XIV s.). *Cahiers de Fanjeaux* **17**, pp. 297–341, 1982.

Binns, Alison. *Dedications of monastic houses in England and Wales 1066–1216* (Woodbridge: Boydell Press, 1989).

Black, George F. *The surnames of Scotland: their origin, meaning and history* (New York: New York Public Library, 1946).

Bloch, Marc. Noms de personne et histoire sociale. *Annales d'Histoire Economique et Sociale* **4**, pp. 67–9, 1932.

Blottière, Jean. Surnoms et patronymes du XIe au XIIIe siècle dans le Vexin Français, le Pinserais et le Mantois. *Revue Internationale d'Onomastique* **25**, pp. 31–44, 1973.

Bois, Guy. *The transformation of the year One Thousand* (Manchester: Manchester University Press, 1992).

Bonenfant, P. & G. Despy. La noblesse en Brabant au XIIe et XIIIe siècles. *Moyen Age* **64**, pp. 27–66, 1958.

Bonnassie, Pierre. Une famille de la campagne barcelonaise et ses activités économiques aux alentours de l'An Mil. *Annales du Midi* **76**, pp. 261–303, 1964.

Bonnassie, Pierre. *La Catalogne du milieu du Xe à la fin du XIe siècle* (Toulouse: Publications de l'Université de Toulouse-Le Mirail, 1975).

Bouchard, Constance B. The structure of a twelfth-century French family: the Lords of Seignelay. *Viator* **10**, pp. 39–56, 1979.

Bouchard, Constance B.. The origins of the French nobility: a reassessment. *American Historical Review* **86**, pp. 501–32, 1981.

Bouchard, Constance B.. Patterns of women's names in royal lineages, ninth–eleventh centuries. *Medieval Prosopography* **9**(1), pp. 1–32, 1988a.

Bouchard, Constance B.. The migration of women's names in the upper nobility, ninth–twelfth centuries. *Medieval Prosopography* **9**(2), pp. 1–19, 1988b.

Bougard, Pierre & Maurits Gysseling. *L'impôt royal en Artois (1295–1302), Rôles du 100e et du 50e présentés et publiés avec une table anthroponymique.* (Louvain and Brussels: Onomastica Neerlandica, 1970).

Bourin, Monique (ed.). *Genèse médiévale de l'anthroponymie moderne I* (Tours, 1990).

Bourin, Monique & Pascal Chareille (eds). *Genèse médiévale de l'Anthroponymie moderne* II [2 vols] (Tours, 1992).

Brattö, Olof. *Studi di antroponimia fiorentina, il libro di Montaperti (An. MCCLX)* (Göteborg, 1953).

Brattö, Olof. *Nuovi studi di antroponimia fiorentina, i nomi meno frequenti del libro di Montaperti (An. MCCLX)* (Stockholm and Göteborg, 1955).

Brattö, Olof. *Liber Extimatianum (Il Libro degli Estimi MCCLXIX)* (Göteborg: Göteborgs Universites Årsskrift (62:2), 1956).

Broëns, Maurice. L'anthroponymie du haut Moyen Age dans les pays soumis au rayonnement de Toulouse. *Revue Internationale d'Onomastique* **7**, pp. 217–24, 1955.

Broëns, Maurice. L'anthroponymie gotique du IVe au Xe siècle et ses rapports avec l'anthroponymie franque. *Acta Salmanticensia* **11**(2), pp. 243–60, 1958.

Brucker, Gene A. The Medici in the fourteenth century. *Speculum* **32**, pp. 1–26, 1957.

Brucker, G. (ed.). *The society of Renaissance Florence* (New York: Harper Torchbooks, 1971).

Cam, Helen. Pedigrees of villeins and freemen in the thirteenth century. In *Liberties and communities in medieval England* (Cambridge: Cambridge University Press, 1942), pp. 124–35.

Camden, William. *Remains concerning Britain* (Wakefield: EP Publishing, 1974; original edn 1605).

Cameron, K. Bynames of location in Lincolnshire subsidy rolls. *Nottingham Medieval Studies* **32**, pp. 156–64, 1988.

Canestrier, P. Prénoms et noms de famille dans le comté de Nice depuis le XIe siècle. *Revue Internationale d'Onomastique* **3**, pp. 139–51, 1951.

Carnoy, Albert. *Origines des noms de famille en Belgique* (Louvain, 1953).

Carr, A.D. The making of the Mostyns: the genesis of a landed family. *Transactions of the Honourable Society of Cymmrodorion* (1979), pp. 137–57.

Carrez, H. Particularités physiques et noms de personne dans la région dijonnaise. *Annales de Bourgogne* **9**, pp. 97–131, 1937.

Carrez, H. Particularités du domicile et noms de personne dans la région dijonnaise. *Annales de Bourgogne* **10**, pp. 7–46, 1938a.

Carrez, H. Le vocabulaire de l'alimentation et les noms de personnes dans la région dijonnaise. *Annales de Bourgogne* **10**, pp. 173–88, 1938b.

Carrez, H. Noms de personne féminins dans la région dijonnaise du XIIe au XVe siècle. *Annales de Bourgogne* **14**, pp. 85–129, 1942.

Carrez, H. Surnoms évoquant des infirmités portés dans la région dijonnaise du XIIe au XVe siècle. *Onomastica* **1**, pp. 41–51, 1947.

Castellani Pollidori, Ornella. Nomi femminili senesi del secolo XIII. *Studi Linguistici Italiani* **2**, pp. 46–64, 1961.

Cesarini-Sforza, L. Per la storia del cognome nel Trentino. *Archivo Trentino* **25**, pp. 97–108 and 193–219; **26**, pp. 72–102 and 185–200; **27**, pp. 45–64; **28**, pp. 13–73 and 191–236, 1910–13.

Charles-Edwards, T.M. Kinship, status and the origins of the Hide. *Past and Present* **56**, pp. 3–33, 1972.

Chojnacki, Stanley. In search of the Venetian patriciate: families and factions in the fourteenth century. In *Renaissance Venice*, J.R. Hale (ed.) (London, 1973), pp. 47–90.

Chojnacki, Stanley. Dowries and kinsmen in early Renaissance Venice. *Journal of Interdisciplinary History* **5**, pp. 571–600, 1975.

361

Clanchy, M.T. *From memory to written record: England 1066–1307* (London: Edward Arnold, 1979).

Clark, Cecily. People and languages in post-Conquest Canterbury. *Journal of Medieval History* **2**, pp. 1–34, 1976.

Clark, Cecily. Women's names in post-Conquest England: observations and speculations. *Speculum* **53**, pp. 223–51, 1978.

Clark, Cecily. The early personal names of King's Lynn: an essay in socio-cultural history. *Nomina* **6**, pp. 51–71; **7**, pp. 65–89, 1982–3.

Clark, Cecily. English personal names ca.650–1300: some prosopographical bearings. *Medieval Prosopography* **8**, pp. 31–60, 1987a.

Clark, Cecily. Willelmus Rex? vel alius Willelmus? *Nomina* **11**, pp. 7–33, 1987b.

Clark, Cecily. A witness to post-Conquest English cultural patterns: the *Liber Vitae* of Thorney Abbey. In *Studies in honour of René Derolez*, Simon-Vandenbergen (ed.) (Ghent), pp. 73–85, 1987c.

Colman, Fran. The name-element Aedel- and related problems. *Notes and Queries* **226**, pp. 295–301, 1981.

Constable, Giles. The *Liber Memorialis* of Remiremont. *Speculum* **47**, pp. 261–77, 1972.

D'Alauzier, L. Relève de noms de personnes à Capdenac au XIIIe siècle. *Revue Internationale d'Onomastique* **3**, pp. 190–6, 1949.

D'Arbois de Jubainville, H. *Etudes sur la langue des Francs* (Paris, 1900).

Dauzat, Albert. *Les noms de personne, origine et evolution*, 4th edn (Paris: Delagrave, 1950).

De Beauvillé, G. Les noms de famille de France tirés des noms de métiers, de charges et de dignités. *Revue Internationale d'Onomastique* **5**, pp. 45–59; **6**, pp. 53–65, 137–42, 221–34 and 301–13; **7**, pp. 59–72 and 147–59, 1953–5.

Depoin, J. De la propriété et de l'hérédité des noms dans les familles palatines. *Revue des Etudes Historiques* (1902), pp. 545–57.

Dewindt, E.B. *Land and people in Holywell-cum-Needingworth, structures of tenure and patterns of social organisation in an East Midlands village 1252–1457* (Toronto, 1972).

Duby, Georges. *The chivalrous society* (London: Edward Arnold, 1977).

Duby, Georges & Jacques Le Goff. *Famille et parenté dans l'Occident médiéval*, Actes du Colloque de Paris 1974 (Rome: Ecole Française de Rome, 1977).

Duchesne, Abbé L. *Fastes episcopaux de l'ancienne Gaule* [3 vols] (Paris, 1894–1915).

Duffaut, H. Recherches historiques sur les prénoms en Languedoc. *Annales du Midi* **12**, pp. 180–93 and 329–54, 1900.

Dumville, David N. The Anglian Collection of royal genealogies and regnal lists. *Anglo-Saxon England* **5**, pp. 23–50, 1976.

Dumville, David N. Kingship, genealogies and regnal lists. In *Early medieval kingship* P.H. Sawyer & I.N. Wood (eds) (Leeds, 1977), pp. 72–104.

Dupont-Ferrier, G. Les prénoms et les noms à Paris du XIIIe au XVIe siècle. *Bulletin de la Société de l'Histoire de Paris et de l'Ile-de-France* **69–70**, pp. 28–9, 1945.

Dyggve, H.P. *Onomastique des trouvères* (Helsinki: Annales Academiae Scientiarum Fennicae, Series B XXX, 1934).

Ekwall, Eilert. Variation in surnames in medieval London. *Humanistika Vetenskapssamfundets i Lund Årsberättelse* **45**, pp. 207–62, 1944.

Ekwall, Eilert. *Early London personal names* (Lund, 1947).

Ekwall, Eilert. *Studies on the population of medieval London* (Stockholm, 1956).

Ekwall, Eilert. *English place-names in -ing* (Lund: Acta Reg. Societatis Humaniorum Litterarum Lundensis 6, 1962).

Elkins, Sharon K. *Holy women of twelfth-century England* (Chapel Hill: University of North Carolina Press, 1988).

Elwyn Williams, D. A short enquiry into the surnames in Glamorgan from the thirteenth to the eighteenth centuries. *Transactions of the Honourable Society of Cymmrodorion*, (1961), pp. 45–87.

Emery, Richard W. The use of the surname in the study of medieval economic history. *Medievalia et Humanistica* **7**, pp. 43–50, 1954.

Feilitzen, Olof von. *The pre-Conquest personal names of Domesday Book* (Uppsala, 1937).

Feilitzen, Olof von. Some unrecorded Old and Middle English personal names. *Namn Och Bygd Ars* **33**, pp. 69–98, 1945.

Feilitzen, Olof von. Notes on some Scandinavian personal names in English 12th-century records. *Anthroponymica Suecana* **6**, pp. 52–68, 1965.

Feilitzen, Olof von. Some Old English uncompounded personal names and bynames. *Studia Neophilologica* **40**, pp. 5–16, 1968.

Feilitzen, Olof von & Christopher Blunt. 1971. Personal names on the coinage of Edgar. In *England before the Conquest: studies in primary sources presented to Dorothy Whitelock*, Peter Clemoes & Kathleen Hughes (eds) (Cambridge: Cambridge University Press, 1971), pp. 183–214.

Fenouillet, Félix. *Les noms de famille en Savoie* (Chambry, 1919).

Feuchère, Pierre. La noblesse du nord de la France. *Annales* **6** (1951), pp. 306–18.

Fichtenau, Heinrich. *The Carolingian Empire* (Oxford: Basil Blackwell, 1957).

Fisher, J.D.C. *Christian initiation: baptism in the medieval West* (London: SPCK Alcuin Club Collection 47, 1965).

Flechia, G. Di alcuni criteri per l'originazione de'cognomi italiani. *Accademia Nazionale dei Lincei*, Classe di scienze morali, storiche e filologiche **3** (1878), pp. 609–21.

Flom, G.T. Alliteration and variation in Old Germanic name-giving. *Modern Language Notes* **32** (1917), pp. 7–17.

Flutre, L.F. *Table des noms propres avec toutes leurs variantes figurant dans les romans du Moyen Age écrits en français ou en provençal* (Poitiers: Centre d'Etudes Supérieures de Civilisation Médiéval, 1962).

Forssner, Thorvald. *Continental-Germanic personal names in England in Old and Middle English times* (Uppsala, 1916).

Fossier, Robert. La Noblesse picarde au temps de Philippe le Bel. In *La Noblesse au Moyen Age, XIe–XVe siècles*, Philippe Contamine (ed.) (Paris: Presses Universitaires de France 1976), pp. 105–27.

Franklin, Peter. Normans, saints and politics: forename-choice among fourteenth-century Gloucestershire peasants. *Local Population Studies* **36**, pp. 19–26, 1986.

Fransson, Gustav. *Middle English surnames of occupation 1100–1350* (Lund: Lund Studies in English 3, 1935).

Fucilla, Joseph G. *Our Italian surnames* (Evanston, Illinois, 1949).

Gabotto, F. *Storia della Italia occidentale nel Medio Evo*, I (Turin, 1911).

Geipel, John. *The Viking legacy: the Scandinavian influence on the English and Gaelic Languages* (Newton Abbot, 1971).

Gewin, J.P.J. Vaste Regels bis Naamgering in de Vroege Midde Middeleeuwen. *Anthroponymica Onomastica Neerlandica* **12**, pp. 29–68, 1961.

Gigot, Jean-Gabriel. La fixation des noms de personnes en langue vulgaire au XIIIe siècle. *Actes du 89e Congrès National des Sociétés Savantes (1964), Bulletin Philologique et Historique*, (1967), pp. 725–33.

Giry, A. *Manuel de Diplomatique* (Paris, 1894).

Given-Wilson, C. & Alice Curteis. *The Royal bastards of medieval England* (London: Routledge, 1984).

Goldthwaite, Richard A. *Private wealth in Renaissance Florence, a study of four families* (Princeton, 1968).

Goldthwaite, Richard A. *The building of Renaissance Florence: an economic and social history* (Baltimore and London: Johns Hopkins Press, 1980).

Gourvil, F. Noms "héroïques" dans l'anthroponymie bretonne. *Acta Salmanticensia* **11**(2), pp. 217–31, 1958.

Grendi, Edoardo. Profilo storico degli alberghi genovesi. *Mélanges de l'Ecole Française de Rome (Moyen-Age–Temps Modernes)* **87** (1975), pp. 241–302.

Grohmann, Alberto. *L'imposizione diretta nei comuni dell'Italia centrale nel XIII secolo, La Libra di Perugia del 1285* (Rome: Collection de l'Ecole Française de Rome (91), 1986).

Gysselin, M. & P. Bougard. *L'Onomastique calaisienne à la fin du 13e siècle. Anthroponymica Onomastica Neerlandica* **13**, 1963.

Harvey, Barbara. *Living and dying in England 1100–1540: the monastic experience* (Oxford: Oxford University Press, 1993).

Heers, Jacques. *Le clan familial au Moyen Age: étude sur les structures politiques et sociales des milieux urbains* (Paris: Presses Universitaires Françaises, 1974; English edn, Amsterdam, 1977).

Heinzelmann, Martin. L'aristocratie et les évêchés entre Loire et Rhin jusqu'à la fin du VIIe siècle. *Revue d'Histoire de l'Eglise de France* **62** (1976), pp. 75–90.

Herlihy, David. *The social history of Italy and Western Europe, 700–1500: collected studies* (London: Variorum Reprints, 1978).

Higounet, Charles. Mouvements de population dans le Midi de la France du XIe au XVe siècle d'après les noms de personne et de lieu. *Annales* **8** (1953), pp. 1–24.

Higounet, Charles. Le groupe aristocratique en Aquitaine et en Gascogne (fin Xe–début XIIe siècle). *Annales du Midi* **80** (1968), pp. 563–79.

Hilton, R.H. *The English peasantry in the later Middle Ages* (Oxford: Oxford University Press, 1975).

Hjertstedt, Ingrid. *Middle English nicknames in the lay subsidy rolls for Warwickshire* (Uppsala: Studia Anglistica Upsaliensia 63, 1987).

Holt, J.C. Politics and property in early medieval England. *Past and Present* **57** (1972), pp. 3–52.

Holt, J.C. *What's in a name? Family nomenclature and the Norman Conquest* (Stenton Lecture 1981) (Reading: University of Reading, 1982).

Homans, George C. *English villagers of the thirteenth century* (New York: Norton, 1975; original edn 1941).

Hughes, D.O. Kinsmen and neighbors in medieval Genoa. In *The Medieval City*, Harry A. Mistkimin et al. (eds) (New Haven, 1977), pp. 95–111.

Insley, John. Regional variation in Scandinavian personal nomenclature in England. *Nomina* **3** (1979), pp. 52–60.

Insley, John. Lancashire surnames. *Nomina* **6** (1982), pp. 93–8.

Jacobsson, Harry. *Etudes d'anthroponymie lorraine, les Bans de de tréfonds de Metz (1267–1298)* (Göteborg, 1955).

James, Edward. *The origins of France, from Clovis to the Capetians, 500–1000* (New York, 1982).

Jensen, Gillian Fellows. *Scandinavian personal names in Lincolnshire and Yorkshire* (Copenhagen, 1968).

Jensen, Gillian Fellows. The names of the Lincolnshire tenants of the Bishop of Lincoln c 1225. In *Otium et Negotium, Studies in Onamatology and Library Science presented to Olof von Feilitzen* (Stockholm, 1973), pp. 86–95.

Jones, P.J. Florentine families and Florentine diaries in the fourteenth century. *Papers of the British School at Rome* **24** (1956), pp. 183–205.

Jönsjö, Jan. *Studies on Middle English nicknames*, I (Lund: Lund Studies in English (55), 1979).

Kedar, Benjamin Z. Noms de saints et mentalité populaire a Genes au XIVe siècle. *Moyen Age* **73** (1967), pp. 431–46.

Kempers, Bram. *Painting, power and patronage: the rise of the professional artist in Renaissance Italy* (London: Allen Lane, 1987).

Kent, Dale. *The rise of the Medici: faction in Florence 1426–1434* (Oxford: Oxford University Press, 1978).

Kent, F.W. *Household and lineage in Renaissance Florence: the family life of the Capponi, Ginori and Rucellai* (Princeton, 1977).

Kneen, J.J. *The personal names of the Isle of Man* (Oxford: Oxford University Press, 1937).

Knowles, Dom David. *The religious orders in England*, III, *The Tudor Age* (Cambridge: Cambridge University Press, 1959).

Knowles, Dom David, C.N.L. Brooke & V.C.M. London. *The heads of religious houses, England and Wales 940–1216* (Cambridge: Cambridge University Press, 1972).

La Roncière, Charles de. Orientations pastorales du clergé, fin XIIIe–XIVe siècle: le témoignage de l'onomastique toscane. *Comptes-Rendus de l'Académie des Inscriptions et Belles-Lettres* (1983), pp. 43–65.

La Roncière, Charles de. 1990. A monastic clientèle? The abbey of Settimo, its neighbours and its tenants (Tuscany, 1280–1340). In *City and countryside in late medieval and Renaissance Italy, essays presented to Philip Jones*, Trevor Dean & Chris Wickham (eds) (London and Ronceverte: Hambledon Press, 1990), pp. 55–67.

Lancaster, Lorraine. Kinship in Anglo-Saxon society. *British Journal of Sociology* **9** (1958), pp. 230–50 and 359–77.

Langlois, Ernest. *Table des noms propres de toute nature compris dans les Chansons de Geste* (Paris, 1904).

Lazard, Sylviane. Les noms de personne dans les papyrus ravennates du VIe siècle. *Studi Mediolatini et Volgari* (1973), pp. 7–38.

Lazard, Sylviane. Tradition ancienne et influence chrétienne dans l'anthroponymie ravennate du Xe siècle. *Actes du 99e Congrès National des Sociétés Savantes* (Besançon), Philologie et histoire I (1974), pp. 445–54.

Lazard, Sylviane. Evénements historiques et anthroponymie à Rimini de la fin du VIIe au milieu du Xe siècle. *Onoma* **22**, pp. 1–15, 1978.

Le Pesant, Michel. Les noms de personne à Evreux du XIIe au XIVe siècles. *Annales de Normandie* **6**, pp. 47–74, 1956.

Lebel, Paul. Notes d'anthroponymie bourguignonne. *Annales de Bourgogne* **11**, pp. 93–120, 1939.

Lebel, Paul. *Les noms de personne en France* (Paris: Que sais-je?, 1946).

Leccisotti, Tommaso. *Monte Cassino* (Abbey of Monte Cassino, 1987).

Leeson, Francis. The development of surnames, II: locative surnames in West Sussex. *Genealogists Magazine* **16**, pp. 536–46, 1971.

Lefftz, Joseph. Origine et repartition des noms de famille en Haute Alsace. *Revue d'Alsace* **97**, pp. 81–90, 1958.

Levillain, L. Les Nibelungen historiques et leurs alliances de famille. *Annales du Midi* **49**, pp. 337–408, 1937.

Lewis, A.R. The Guillems of Montpellier: a sociological appraisal. In *Medieval Society in S. France and Catalonia* (London: Variorum, 1984), pp. 158–69.

Leys, O. La substitution de noms chrétiens aux noms préchrétiens en Flandre occidentale avant 1225. *Acta Salmanticensia,* Filosofia y Letras **11**(1), pp. 403–12, 1958.

Leyser, Henrietta. *Medieval women: A social history of women in England 450–1500* (London: Weidenfeld and Nicolson, 1995).

Leyser, K. The German aristocracy from the ninth to the early twelfth century, a historical and cultural sketch. *Past and Present* **41**, pp. 25–53, 1968.

Lipman, V.D. *The Jews of medieval Norwich* (London: Jewish Historical Society of England, 1967).

Longnon, Auguste (ed.). *Polyptique de l'abbaye de Saint-Germain-des-Prés* (Paris: H. Champion, 1895).

Lopez, R.S. Concerning surnames and places of origin. *Medievalia et Humanistica* **9**, pp. 6–16, 1955/6.

Lot, Ferdinand. De l'origine et de la signification historique et linguistique des noms de lieux en -ville et en -court. *Romania* **59**, pp. 199–246, 1933.

Loyd, Lewis C. *The origins of some Anglo-Norman families* (Leeds: Publications of the Harleian Society 103, 1951).

Loyn, H.R. Kinship in Anglo-Saxon England. *Anglo-Saxon England* **3**, pp. 197–209, 1974.

Lund, Niels. Personal names and place-names: the persons and the places. *Onoma* **19**, pp. 468–85, 1975.

MacBain, A. The old Gaelic system of personal names. *Transactions of the Gaelic Society of Inverness* **20**, pp. 279–315, 1897.

MacBain, A. Early Highland personal names. *Transactions of the Gaelic Society of Inverness* **22**, pp. 152–68, 1900.

McClure, Peter. Surnames from English place names as evidence for mobility in the Middle Ages. *Local Historian* **13**, pp. 80–6, 1978.

McClure, Peter. Patterns of migration in the late Middle Ages: the evidence of English place-name surnames. *Economic History Review* 2nd Series **32**, pp. 167–82, 1979.

McClure, Peter. The origin of the surname *Waterer*. *Nomina* **6**, p. 92, 1982.

McKinley, R.A. *Norfolk surnames in the sixteenth century* (Leicester: Leicester University Press, 1969).

McKinley, R.A. *Norfolk and Suffolk surnames in the Middle Ages* (London and Chichester: English Surnames Series, 1975).

McKinley, R.A. Social class and the origin of surnames. *Genealogists Magazine* **20**, pp. 52–6, 1980.

McKinley, R.A. *A history of British surnames* (London: Longman, 1990).

MacLysaght, Edward. *Irish families: their names, arms and origins* (Dublin: Hodges Figgis & Co., 1957).

MacLysaght, Edward. *More Irish families* (Galway and Dublin, 1960).

MacLysaght, Edward. *A guide to Irish surnames* (Dublin: Helicon, 1964).

Maillard, François. Noms de personnes du Lyonnais en 1307. *Bulletin Philologique et Historique* **60**, pp. 735–70, 1964.

Maillard, François. Les noms de personnes à Cluny en 1309. *Revue Internationale d'Onomastique* **22**, pp. 195–212, 1970.

Martindale, Jane. The French Aristocracy in the early Middle Ages: a reappraisal. *Past and Present* **75**, pp. 5–45, 1977.

Matthews, C.M. *English surnames* (London: Weidenfeld and Nicolson, 1966).

Mélanges de l'Ecole Française de Rome, Moyen Age, "Genèse médiévale de l'anthroponymie moderne: l'espace italien", **106**(2), pp. 313–736, 1994.

Mestayer, Monique. Les Lieux-dits Chez N dans le canton de Saint-Amant-de-Boixe. *Nouvelle Revue d'Onomastique* **1**, pp. 11–15, 1983.

Michaëlsson, Karl. *Etudes sur les noms de personne français d'après les Rôles de taille parisiens (Rôles de 1292, 1296–1300, 1313)* [2 vols] (Uppsala: Uppsala Universitets Årsskrift, 1927–36.

Michaëlsson, Karl. Quelques observations sur le nom d'Agnès. *Studier I Modern Sprakvetenskap* **11**, pp. 1–41, 1931.

Michaëlsson, Karl. Les noms d'origine dans le Rôle de taille parisien de 1313. *Goteborgs Högskolas Årsskrift* **36**, pp. 355–400, 1950.

Millénaire monastique du Mont Saint-Michel. [3 vols] (Paris, Lethielleux, 1967–71).

Moisl, Hermann. Anglo-Saxon royal genealogies and Germanic oral tradition. *Journal of Medieval History* **7**, pp. 215–48, 1981.

Moisy, Henri. *Noms de famille normands étudiés dans leurs rapports avec la vieille langue et spécialement avec le dialecte normande ancien et moderne* (Rouen and Paris: Bulletin de la Société des Antiquaires de Normandie VII, 1875).

Montorsi, William. *La "Matricola Popolare" di Cremona del 1283* (Cremona: Annali della Biblioteca Governativa e Libreria Civica di Cremona (13), 1960).

Morand, Edmond. *L'Abbaye de Saint-Amable de Riom* (Clermont-Ferrand, 1930).

Morgan, T.J. & Prys Morgan. *Welsh surnames* (Cardiff: University of Wales Press, 1985).

Morlet, M.-T. Etudes d'anthroponymie occitane, les noms de personne de l'obituaire de Moissac. *Revue Internationale d'Onomastique* **9**, pp. 269–82; **10**, pp. 31–51; **11**, pp. 193–207, 1957–9.

Morlet, M.-T. Les noms de personne à Eu du XIIIe au XVe siècle. *Revue Internationale d'Onomastique* **11**, pp. 131–48 and 174–82; **12**, pp. 62–70, 137–48 and 205–19, 1959–60.

Morlet, M.-T. Les noms de personne à Amiens au XIVe siècle. *Bulletin Philologique et Historique*, (1960–1), pp. 527–52.

Morlet, M.-T. *Etude d'anthroponymie picarde, les noms de personne en Haute Picardie aux XIIIe, XIVe, XVe siècles* (Amiens, 1967).

Morlet, M.-T. *Les noms de personne sur le territoire de l'ancienne Gaule du VIe au XIIe siècle* [3 vols] (Paris: Editions du CNRS, 1968–85).

Morlet, M.-T. 1985. Les noms de personne dans les registres de comptes de l'Hotel-Dieu de Soissons au XVe siècle. In *L'Onomastique, témoin de l'activité humaine*, G. Taverdier (ed.) (Fontaine-lès-Dijon, 1985), pp. 283–305.

Musset, L. L'aristocratie normande au XIe siècle. In *La noblesse au Moyen Age*, P. Contamine (ed.) (1976), pp. 71–96.

Musset, L. Aux origines d'une classe dirigeante: les Tosny, grands barons normands du Xe au XIIIe siècle. *Francia* **5**, pp. 45–80, 1977.

Nègre, Abbé E. Les noms de personne à Rabastens (Tarn) à la fin du XIVe siècle, d'après le Livre de l'Arc. *Revue Internationale d'Onomastique* **8**, pp. 59–76, 1956.

Nicholas, David. *The metamorphosis of a medieval city: Ghent in the age of the Arteveldes 1302–1390* (Lincoln and London: University of Nebraska Press, 1987).

Olivieri, Dante. I cognomi della Venezia Euganea, saggio di uno studio storico-etimologico. *Biblioteca dell'Archivum Romanicum* (Geneva), Serie II Linguistica **6**, pp. 113–272, 1923.

Ortali, G. La famille à Bologne au XIIIe siècle. See Duby & Le Goff (eds), 1977, pp. 205–23.

Pacaut, Marcel. *Louis VII et les élections épiscopales dans le royaume de France* (Paris, 1957).

Poly, Jean-Pierre & Eric Bournazel. *The feudal transformation 900–1200* (New York and London: Holmes and Meier, 1991).

Poma, Cesare. *Cognomi italiani formati da verbi che indicano azione* (Città di Castello, 1914).

Poma, Cesare. Fallaci apparenze in cognomi italiani. *Archivo Glottologico* **18**, pp. 353–61, 1919.

Poole, Austin Lane. *Obligations of society in the XII and XIII centuries* (Oxford: Oxford University Press, 1946).

Postles, D.A. Personal naming patterns of peasants and burgesses in late medieval England. *Medieval Prosopography* **12**(1), pp. 29–56, 1991.

Postles, D.A. The baptismal name in thirteenth-century England: processes and patterns. *Medieval Prosopography* **13**(2), pp. 1–52, 1992.

Poupardin, René. Les grandes familles comtales à l'époque carolingienne. *Revue Historique* **72**, pp. 72–95, 1900.

Prat, René. Etude d'anthroponymie sur deux villes de Quercy. *Revue Internationale d'Onomastique* **3**, pp. 201–9, 1951.

Prati, A. Composti imperativi quali casati e soprannomi. *Revue de Linguistique Romane* **7**, pp. 250–64, 1931.

Quantin, Gérard. Les noms de personne de la paroisse Saint-Hilaire de Reims au XIVe siècle. *Revue Internationale d'Onomastique* **6**, pp. 121–35, 1954.

Raftis, J. Ambrose. *Warboys: two hundred years in the life of an English medieval village* (Toronto, 1974).

Rajna, Pio. L'onomastica italiana e l'epopea carolingia. *Romania* **18**, pp. 1–69, 1889a.

Rajna, Pio. Gli eroi brettoni nell'onomastica italiana del secolo XII. *Romania* **18**, pp. 161–85, 1889b.

Rajna, Pio. Altre orme antiche dell'epopea carolingia in Italia. *Romania* **26**, pp. 34–73, 1897.

Rajna, Pio. Il Casato di Dante. *Studi Danteschi* **3**, pp. 59–88, 1921.

Reaney, P.H. Pedigrees of villeins and freemen. *Notes and Queries* **197**, pp. 222–5, 1952.

Reaney, P.H. Notes on the survival of Old English personal names in Middle English. *Studier I Modern Sprakvetenskap* **18**, pp. 84–112, 1953.

Reaney, P.H. *The origin of English surnames* (London: Routledge, 1967).

Redin, Mats. *Studies on uncompounded personal names in Old English* (Uppsala, 1919).

Redmonds, George. Problems in the identification of some Yorkshire filial names. *Genealogists Magazine* **17**, pp. 205–12, 1972.

Redmonds, George. Surname heredity in Yorkshire. *Local Historian* **10**, pp. 171–7, 1972–3.

Reuter, T. (ed.). *The medieval nobility: studies on the ruling classes of France and Germany from the 6th to the 12th century* (Amsterdam, 1978).

Robinson, Fred C. The significance of names in Old English literature. *Anglia* **86**, pp. 14–58, 1968.

Russell, Josiah C. Mediaeval Midland and Northern migration to London, 1100–1365. *Speculum* **34**, pp. 641–5, 1959.

Saint-Jouan, R. de. Le nom de famille en Béarn et ses origines I–XI. *Revue Internationale d'Onomastique* **2**, pp. 121–41, 199–218 and 278–90; **3**, pp. 45–58, 131–8, 211–29 and 285–300; **4**, pp. 45–59, 131–8, 221–30 and 289–302, 1950–2.

Schmid, Karl. "De Regia Stirpe Waiblingensium", remarques sur la conscience de soi des Staufen. See Duby & Le Goff (eds), 1977, pp. 49–56.

Schmid, Karl. The structure of the nobility in the earlier Middle Ages. See Reuter (ed.), 1978, pp. 37–59 [original 1959].

Schneider, Jean. La ville de Metz aux XIIIe et XIVe siècles (Nancy, 1950).

Schramm, Gottfried. Namenschatz und Dichtersprache (Göttingen: Vandenhoeck und Ruprecht, 1957).

Scott Thomson, Gladys. Family background (London: Jonathan Cape, 1949).

Searle, W.G. Onomasticon Anglo-Saxonicum, a list of Anglo-Saxon proper names from the time of Bede to that of King John (Cambridge: Cambridge University Press, 1897).

Seltén, Bo. Some notes on Middle English by-names in independent use. English Studies 46, pp. 165–81, 1965.

Seltén, Bo. Early East-Anglian nicknames, "Shakespeare" names (Lund: Scripta Minora, Regiae Societatis Humaniorum Litterarum Lundensis, 1969).

Seltén, Bo. The Anglo-Saxon heritage in Middle English personal names, East Anglia 1100–1399 [2 vols] (Lund: Lund Studies in English, 1972–9).

Seltén, Bo. Early East-Anglian nicknames, Bahuvrihi Names (Lund: Scripta Minora, Regiae Societatis Humaniorum Litterarum Lundensis, 1975).

Serra, G.D. Cognomi canavesani (Piemonte) di forma collettiva in -aglia, -ata, -ato. Dacoromania 3, pp. 523–49, 1923.

Serra, G.D. Sulla continuità dell'onomastica latina-romanza nei nomi propri canavesani (e piemontesi). Dacoromania 4, pp. 517–640, 1924–6.

Serra, G.D. Nomi personali femminili piemontesi da nomi di paesi e città famose nel medioevo. Rivista Filologica 1, pp. 85–98, 1927.

Serra, G.D. La tradizione Latina e Greco-Latina nell'onomastica medioevale italiana. Göteborg: Göteborgs Högskolas Årsskrift 40(2), 1950.

Sisam, Kenneth. Anglo-Saxon royal genealogies. Proceedings of the British Academy, (1953), pp. 287–348.

Skeat, W.W. On the survival of Anglo-Saxon names as modern surnames. Transactions of the Philological Society 7, pp. 57–85, 1907.

Smart, Veronica. Moneyers' names on the Anglo-Saxon coinage. Nomina 3, pp. 20–8, 1979.

Smith, A.H. Early northern nick-names and surnames. Saga-Book of the Viking Society 11(1), pp. 30–60, 1934.

Smith, A.H. English place-name elements (Cambridge: English Place-Name Society 25, 1956).

Southern, R.W. The making of the Middle Ages (London: Hutchinson, 1953).

Southern, R.W. Western society and the Church in the Middle Ages (Harmondsworth: Penguin, 1970).

Stenton, F.M. Personal names in place-names. In Introduction to the Survey of English place-names, A. Mawer & F.M. Stenton (eds) (Cambridge: English Place-Name Society, 1924), 1, Part 1, pp. 165–89.

Stenton, F.M. The historical bearing of place-name studies: the place of women in Anglo-Saxon society. Transactions of the Royal Historical Society 4th Series 25, pp. 1–13, 1943a.

Stenton, F.M. Anglo-Saxon England (Oxford: Oxford University Press, 1943b).

Stowell, W.A. Old-French titles of respect in direct address (Baltimore, 1908).

Ström, Hilmer. Old English personal names in Bede's History, an etymological-phonological investigation (Lund: Lund Studies in English 8, 1939).

Tengvik, Gösta. *Old English bynames* (Uppsala: Nomina Germanica 4, 1938).

Thrupp, Sylvia L. *The merchant class of medieval London (1300–1500)* (Ann Arbor Paperbacks, 1976).

Thuresson, Bertil. *Middle English occupational terms* (Lund: Lund Studies in English (19), 1950).

Tits-Dieuaide, M.J. Un exemple de passage de la ministérialité à la noblesse, la famille de Wesemael (1166–1250). *Revue Belge de Philologie et d'Histoire* **36**, pp. 335–55, 1958.

Toubert, Pierre. *Les structures du Latium medieval, le Latium méridional et la Sabine du IXe siècle à la fin du XIIe siècle* I (Rome: Ecole Française de Rome, 1973).

Toynbee, Paget. *A dictionary of proper names and notable matters in the works of Dante*, revised C.S. Singleton (Oxford: Oxford University Press, 1968).

Trautz, Fritz. Noblesse allemande et noblesse anglaise, quelques points de comparaison. See Duby & Le Goff (eds), 1977, pp. 63–81.

Tucat, J. Les prénoms béarnais d'après le Dénombrement des feux de 1385. *Bulletin de la Société des Sciences, Lettres et Arts de Pau* 3rd series **7**, pp. 60–75, 1947.

Ullmann, Walter. *A short history of the Papacy in the Middle Ages* (London: Methuen, 1972).

Valéry, Paul. *Masters and friends* (Princeton, 1968).

Vallet, Antoine. Les noms de personne du Département de la Loire. *Acta Salmanticensia, Filosofia y Letres* **11**(1), pp. 259–68, 1958.

Vallet, Antoine. *Les noms de personne du Forez et confins au XIIe, XIIIe et XIVe siècles* (Lyon: Société d'Edition "Les Belles Lettres", 1961).

Vercauteren, F. Une parentèle dans la France du Nord aux XIe et XIIe siècles. *Moyen-Age* **69**, pp. 223–45, 1963.

Vincent, Auguste. Les noms de lieux dans les noms de famille de Belgique. *Bulletin de la Commission Royale de Toponymie et de Dialectologie* (Brussels) **20**, pp. 211–34, 1946.

Vincent, Auguste. *Les Noms de famille de la Belgique* (Brussels, 1952).

Violante, Cinzio. Quelques caractéristiques des structures familiales en Lombardie, Emilie et Toscane au XIe et XIIe siècle. See Duby & Le Goff (eds), 1977, pp. 87–147.

Wagner, A.R. *English Genealogy* (Oxford: Oxford University Press, 1960).

Waley, Pamela. 1988. Personal names in Siena, 1285. In *Florence and Italy: Renaissance Studies in Honour of Nicolai Rubinstein*, Peter Denley & Caroline Elam (eds) (London: Westfield Publications in Medieval Studies 2, 1988), pp. 187–91.

Weis, Beatrice. Répartition des noms de personnes en Alsace au XIIe siècle selon les porteurs et leur situation sociale. In *Proceedings of the XVIth International Congress of Onamastic Sciences*, Jean-Claude Boulanger (ed.) (Quebec: Les Presses de l'Université Laval, 1990), pp. 577–83.

Werner, K.F. Liens de parente et noms de personne, un problème historique et méthodologique. See Duby & Le Goff (eds), 1977, pp. 13–40.

Werner, K.F. Important noble families in the kingdom of Charlemagne, a prosopographical study of the relationship between king and nobility in the early Middle Ages. See Reuter (ed.), 1978, pp. 137–202.

Whitelock, Dorothy, Scandinavian personal names in the Liber Vitae of Thorney Abbey. *Saga-Book of the Viking Society*, **12**, pp. 127–53, 1940.

Williams, Gwyn A. *Medieval London: from commune to capital* (London: Athlone Press, 1963).

Wolff, Philippe. La noblesse toulousaine: essai sur son histoire médiévale. In *La Noblesse au Moyen Age*, P. Contamine (ed.) (1976), pp. 153–74.

370

Wollasch, Joachim. A Cluniac necrology from the time of Abbot Hugh. In *Cluniac Monasticism in the Central Middle Ages*, Noreen Hunt (ed.) (London: Macmillan, 1971), pp. 143–90.

Woolf, Henry Bosley. The naming of women in Old English times. *Modern Philology* **36**, pp. 113–20, 1938a.

Woolf, Henry Bosley. The personal names in *The Battle of Maldon*. *Modern Language Notes* **53**, pp. 109–12, 1938b.

Woolf, Henry Bosley. *The old Germanic principles of name-giving* (Baltimore: Johns Hopkins, 1939).

Woulfe, Patrick. *Irish names and surnames* (Dublin: M.H. Gill & Son, 1923).

Zimmermann, Michel. Les débuts de la "Révolution Anthroponymique" en Catalogne (Xe–XIIe siècles). *Annales du Midi* **102**, pp. 289–308, 1990.

Part III   Modern Times (and Introduction)

(a)   Primary

Austen, Jane. *Letters* (London: John Lane, 1925).

Austen, Jane. *Mansfield Park* (London: Everyman, 1906; original edn 1814).

Austen, Jane. *Sense and sensibility* (London: Everyman, 1906; original edn 1811).

Balzac, Honoré de. *A bachelor's establishment* (*La Rabouilleuse*) (London: Weidenfeld and Nicolson, 1951; original edn 1842).

Balzac, Honoré de. *Le Cousin Pons* (Paris: Nelson, 1956; original edn 1847).

Balzac, Honoré de. *Lost illusions* (London: John Lehmann, 1951; original edn 1837–43).

Barrington family letters 1628–1632, ed. Arthur Searle (London: Royal Historical Society, Camden Fourth Series, 28, 1983).

Boswell, James. *Journal of a tour of the Hebrides* (London: Collins, 1955; original edn 1785).

Boswell, James. *The life of Samuel Johnson* (London: Everyman, 1906; original edn 1791).

Bourget, Paul. *Cosmopolis* (Paris, 1893).

Burney, Fanny. *Evelina* (London: Everyman, 1909; original edn 1778).

Carlyle, Jane Welsh. *Letters*, ed. Trudy Bliss (London: Gollancz, 1949).

Chandos, Cassandra, Duchess of. *The continuation of the history of the Willoughby Family* (Eton: The Shakespeare Head Press, 1958).

Charles of Sezze, St. *Autobiography*, ed. Leonard Perotti (London: Burns & Oates, 1963).

Cole, Rev. William. *The Blecheley diary 1765–67*, ed. F.G. Stokes (London: Constable, 1931).

Congreve, William. *Comedies* (London: World's Classics, 1925).

Crabbe, George. *Poetical works* (Edinburgh: Gall and Inglis, 1854).

Creevey Papers, ed. Sir Herbert Maxwell (London: John Murray, 1905).

Diary of Mary Louisa Black in 1865 (Medford, Oregon, 1989).

Dickens, Charles. *The life and adventures of Nicholas Nickleby* (London: Chapman and Hall, 1890; original edn 1838–9).

Dickens, Charles. *Our mutual friend* (Oxford: Oxford University Press, 1952; original edn 1864–5).

Dickens, Charles. *The posthumous papers of the Pickwick Club* (Oxford: Oxford University Press, 1948; original edn 1836–7).

Douglas, Norman. *Old Calabria* (London: Martin Secker, 1915).

Dover Wilson, John. *Milestones on the Dover Road* (London: Faber, 1969).

Drayton, Michael. *Minor poems*, ed. Cyril Brett (Oxford: Oxford University Press, 1907).

Evans, George Ewart. *The horse in the furrow* (London: Faber, 1960).

Gaskell, E.C. *The life of Charlotte Bronte* (London: Everyman, 1908; original edn 1857).

Gibbon, Edward. *Autobiography (memoirs of my life and writings)* (London, 1962).

Gough, Richard. *The history of Myddle*, ed. David Hey (Harmondsworth: Penguin, 1981).

Greene, Graham. *The heart of the matter* (London: Heinemann, 1948).

Greene, Rev. Joseph. *Correspondence 1712–1790*, ed. Levi Fox (London: HMSO, 1965).

Grossmith, George & Weedon. *The diary of a nobody* (London: Everyman, 1940; original edn 1892).

Holland, Elizabeth, Lady. *Elizabeth, Lady Holland to her son 1821–1845*, ed. the Earl of Ilchester (London: John Murray, 1946).

Holman-Hunt, Diana. *My Grandmothers and I* (London: Hamish Hamilton, 1960).

Houghton, Lord. *The life and letters of John Keats* (London: Everyman, 1969; original edn 1848).

Hughes, M.V. *A London child of the 1870s* (Oxford: Oxford University Press, 1977).

Hugo, Victor. *Choses vues 1849–1869* (Paris: Gallimard, 1972).

Hugo, Victor. *Lettres à Juliette Drouet* (Paris: Pauvert, 1964).

James, Henry. *William Wetmore Story and his friends* [2 vols] (London: Thames and Hudson, 1903).

Johnson, Samuel. *Lives of the English poets* [2 vols] (London: Everyman, 1910; original edn 1779–81).

Johnson, Samuel. *Prose and poetry*, ed. Mona Wilson (London: Hart-Davis, 1963).

Kemble, Frances Anne. *Journal of a residence on a Georgian Plantation in 1838–1839*, ed. John A. Scott (London: Cape, 1961).

Kilvert's Diary 1870–1879, ed. William Plomer (London: Cape, 1944).

La Bruyère. *Les Caractères ou Les Moeurs de ce siècle* (Paris: Hachette, 1923; original edn 1687–94).

La Tour du Pin, Madame de. *Memoirs*, ed. Felice Harcourt (London: Century Publishing, 1969).

Larkin, Philip. *The less deceived, poems.* (Hessle: The Marvell Press, 1955).

Léautaud, Paul. *Journal of a man of letters 1898–1907*, trans. Geoffrey Sainsbury (London: Chatto and Windus, 1960).

Lieven-Palmerston Correspondence 1828–1856, ed. Lord Sudley (London: John Murray, 1943).

Lisle Letters, ed. Muriel St. Clare Byrne (Harmondsworth: Penguin, 1985).

Livre de l'Académie de Genève (1559–1878), I, Le Texte, ed. S. Stelling-Michaud (Geneva, 1959).

Livre des habitants de Genève, ed. Paul-F. Geisendorf [2 vols] (Geneva: Travaux d'Humanisme et Renaissance (26 and 56), 1957–63.

Livre des habitants de Genève 1684–1792, ed. Alfred Perrenoud and Geneviève Perret (Geneva and Paris: Droz and Champion, 1985).

McGill, Ralph. *The South and Southerners* (Boston: Atlantic – Little Brown, 1959).

Mercier, Louis Sebastien. *The picture of Paris before and after the Revolution (Le Tableau de Paris).* (London: Routledge, 1929).

Mistral, Frédéric. *Mémoires et récits* (Raphèle-les Arles: Marcel Petit, 1980).

Monkswell, Mary, Lady. *A Victorian Diarist*, ed. E.C.F. Collier (London: John Murray, 1944).

Montaigne, Michel de. *Essais*, I (Paris: Editions Garnier, 1962).

Osborne, Dorothy. *Letters to Sir William Temple, 1652–54* (London: Everyman, 1914).

Paulin, Tom. *The strange museum* (London: Faber, 1980).

Pembroke Papers, letters and diaries of Henry, Tenth Earl of Pembroke and his circle 1734–94, ed. Lord Herbert [2 vols] (London: Cape, 1942–50).

Pepys, Samuel. *Diary* III, 1662, ed. Robert Latham & William Matthews (London: G. Bell and Sons, 1970).

Powell, Anthony. *At Lady Molly's* (London: Fontana, 1969; original edn 1957).

Powell, Anthony. *Casanova's Chinese Restaurant* (London: Fontana, 1970; original edn 1960).

Powell, Anthony. *The soldier's art* (London: Fontana, 1968; original edn 1966).

Priestley, J.B. *English journey* (London: Heinemann, 1934).

Proust, Marcel. *Remembrance of things past (A la Recherche du Temps Perdu)*, trans. C.K. Scott Moncrieff [12 vols] (London: Chatto and Windus, 1941).

Randell, Arthur. *Sixty years a Fenman* (London: Routledge, 1966).

Ro. Ba. *The life of Syr Thomas More*, ed. E.V. Hitchcock and Mgr P.E. Hallett (London: Early English Text Society 222, 1950).

Selwyn, Victor (ed.). *The voice of war: poems of the Second World War* (Harmondsworth: Penguin, 1996).

Shakespeare, William. *Antony and Cleopatra*, ed. M.R. Ridley (London: Methuen, Arden, 1965).

Shakespeare, William. *King John*, ed. E.A.J. Honigmann (London: Methuen, Arden, 1967).

Shakespeare, William. *Love's labour's lost*, ed. R.W. David (London: Methuen, Arden, 1951).

Shakespeare, William. *Pericles*, ed. F.D. Hoeniger (London: Methuen, Arden, 1963).

Shakespeare, William. *Romeo and Juliet*, ed. Brian Gibbons (London: Methuen: Arden, 1980).

Sheridan, Richard Brinsley. *Plays* (London: Everyman, 1906).

Smith, Sydney. *Selected letters*, ed. Nowell C. Smith (Oxford: World's Classics, 1956).

Stendhal. *Vie de Henry Brulard* (Paris: Editions Garnier, 1953).

Sterne, Laurence. *The life and opinions of Tristram Shandy gentleman* (Oxford: World's Classics, 1951; original edn 1759–67).

Swift, Jonathan. *Journal to Stella*, ed. Harold Williams [2 vols] (Oxford: Oxford University Press, 1948).

Swift, Jonathan. *Literary essays, prose works* XI (London: Bohn's Standard Library, 1907).

Synge, J.M. *The Aran Islands* (Oxford: Oxford University Press, 1979; original edn 1907).

Tocqueville, Alexis de. *Democracy in America*, ed. Henry Steele Commager. (Oxford: World's Classics, 1946; original edn 1835–40).

Trollope, Anthony. *Barchester Towers* (London: Nelson, no date; original edn 1857).

Turner, Thomas. *The diary of a Georgian shopkeeper*, ed. G.H. Jennings (Oxford: Oxford University Press, 1979).

Vallès, Jules. *L'Enfant* (Paris: Garnier-Flammarion, 1968).

Vigny, Alfred de. *Journal d'un poète* (Paris: Nelson, no date).

Washington, Booker T. *Up from slavery* (Oxford: World's Classics, 1945; original edn 1901).

Woodforde, James. *The diary of a country parson 1758–1802*, ed. John Beresford (Oxford: Oxford University Press, 1978).

Woolf, Virginia. *Diary*, ed. Anne Olivier Bell and Andrew McNeillie [5 vols] (London: Hogarth Press, 1977–84).

Wortley Montagu, Lady Mary. *Letters 1709–1762* (London: Everyman, 1906).

(b)   Secondary

Akinnaso, F. Niyi. Names and naming principles in cross-cultural perspective. *Names* **29**, pp. 37–63, 1981.

Allen, Irving Lewis. Personal names that became ethnic epithets. *Names* **31**, pp. 307–17, 1983.

Allen, L. et al. The relation of first name preference to their frequency in the culture. *Journal of Social Psychology* **14**, pp. 279–93, 1941.

Annales de Démographie Historique 1972.

Arcamone, Maria Giovanna. Naissance et décadence des noms de personnes en Italie entre le Moyen Age et les temps modernes. In *Proceedings of the XVIth International Congress of Onomastic Sciences 1987*, Jean Claude Boulanger (ed.) (Quebec, 1990), pp. 131–9.

Aris, Stephen. *The Jews in business* (Harmondsworth: Penguin, 1973).

Ashby, M.K. *Joseph Ashby of Tysoe 1859–1919* (Cambridge: Cambridge University Press, 1961).

Askwith, Betty. *A Victorian young lady* (Wilton: Michael Russell, 1978).

Bagley, Christopher & Louise Evan-Wong. Psychiatric disorder and adult and peer group rejection of the child's name. *Journal of Child Psychiatry* **11**, pp. 19–27, 1970.

Bahloul, Joëlle. Noms et prénoms juifs nord-africains. *Terrain* **4**, pp. 62–9, 1985.

Baker, Emily Laurence. For richer, for poorer, in your name or in mine. *Guardian*, Women, 2 June 1993, p. 12.

Barrett, Richard A. Village modernization and changing nicknaming practices in northern Spain. *Journal of Anthropological Research* **34**, pp. 92–108, 1978.

Barry, John Warren. *Studies in Corsica, Sylvan and social* (London, 1893).

Bates, Real. Stock, caractéristiques et mode de transmission des prénoms dans une population traditionnelle, l'exemple du Canada sous le régime français. In *Proceedings of the XVIth International Congress of Onomastic Sciences* (1990), pp. 163–75.

Bateson, Gregory. *Naven* (London: Wildwood House, 1980; original edn 1958).

Beaumaire, Frantz. Exposé historique et juridique de la particule DE comme preuve de noblesse. *Revue Internationale d'Onomastique* **5**, pp. 31–44, 1953.

Behrens, C.B.A. *Society, government and the Enlightenment: the experiences of eighteenth-century France and Prussia* (London: Thames and Hudson, 1985).

Beier, Lucinda McCray. *Sufferers and healers: the experience of illness in seventeenth-century England* (London: Routledge & Kegan Paul, 1987).

Bennett, Michael. Spiritual kinship and the baptismal name in traditional European society. In *Principalities, powers and estates*, L.O. Frappell (ed.) (Adelaide: University Union Press, 1979), pp. 1–13.

Benoît, Fernand. *La Provence et le Comtat venaissin, arts et traditions populaires* (Avignon: Aubanel, 1975).

Bering, Dietz. *The stigma of names: antisemitism in German daily life 1812–1933* (Ann Arbor: University of Michigan Press, 1992).

Bernard, H. Russell. Paratsoukli: institutionalized nicknaming in rural Greece. *Ethnologia Europaea* **2**, pp. 65–74, 1968–9.

Bernet, Jacques. Les prénoms républicains sous la Révolution française: l'exemple du district de Compiègne. See Dupâquier et al. (eds), 1984, pp. 247–53.

Besnard, Philippe. Pour une étude empirique du phénomène de mode dans la consommation des biens symboliques: le cas des prénoms. *Archives Européennes de Sociologie* **20**, pp. 343–51, 1979.

Besnard, Philippe. 1984. De la sous-exploitation des prénoms dans la recherche sociologique. See Dupâquier et al. (eds), 1984, pp. 51–9.

Besnard, Philippe. Le choix d'un prénom, actualité de la méthode durkheimienne. *Recherches Sociologiques* **3**, pp. 53–60, 1991.

Besnard, Philippe. The study of social taste through first names: comment on Lieberson and Bell. *American Journal of Sociology* **100**, pp. 1313–17, 1995.

Besnard, Philippe & Guy Desplanques. *Un prénom pour toujours, la côte des prénoms hier, aujourd'hui et demain* (Paris: Balland, 1986 and 1988).

Besnard, Philippe & Cyril Grange. La fin de la diffusion verticale des goûts? (Prénoms de l'élite et du vulgum). *Année Sociologique* **43**, pp. 269–94, 1993.

Bialor, Perry A. What's in a name? Aspects of the social organization of a Greek farming community related to naming customs. In *Essays in Balkan Ethnology*, William G. Lockwood (ed.) Kroeber Anthropological Society 1967.

Bianchi, Serge. Manifestations et formes de la déchristianisation dans le district de Corbeil. *Revue d'Histoire Moderne et Contemporaine* **26**, pp. 256–85, 1979.

Bianchi, Serge. *La Révolution culturelle de l'An II* (Paris: Aubier, 1982).

Blakiston, Georgiana. *Lord William Russell and his wife 1815–1846* (London: John Murray, 1972).

Blaquière, H. Du prénom au surnom, l'évolution des noms de famille du XVIe au XIXe siècle sur le territoire de l'actuel département de la Haute-Garonne. *Revue Internationale d'Onomastique* **21**, pp. 105–8, 1969.

Blin, M.E. Prénoms auxerrois de l'An II. *Annales de Bourgogne* **16**, pp. 269–70, 1944.

Bloch, Marc. *Les caractères originaux de l'histoire rurale française* [2 vols] (Paris: Armand Colin, 1964; original edn 1931).

Bolgar, R.R. *The classical heritage and its beneficiaries* (Cambridge: Cambridge University Press, 1954).

Bozon, Michel. Histoire et sociologie d'un bien sumbolique, le prénom. *Population* **42**, pp. 83–97, 1987.

Breen, Richard. Naming practices in western Ireland. *Man* **NS 17**, pp. 701–13, 1982.

Brender, Myron. Some hypotheses about the psychodynamic significance of infant name selection. *Names* **11**, pp. 1–9, 1963.

Brodrick, James. *Robert Bellarmine, saint and scholar* (London: Catholic Book Club, 1961).

Brôgger, Jan. *Montevarese, a study of peasant society and culture in southern Italy* (Bergen: Universitetsforlaget, 1971).

Broom, Leonard et al. Characteristics of 1107 petitioners for change of name. *American Sociological Review* **20**, pp. 33–9, 1955.

Brown, Roger & Marguerite Ford. 1964. Address in American English. In *Language in culture and society*, Dell Hymes (ed.) (New York: Harper and Row, 1964), pp. 234–44.

Brown, Roger & Albert Gilman. The pronouns of power and solidarity. In *Style in language*, Thomas A. Sebeok (ed.) (New York: The Technology Press of MIT and John Wiley, 1960), pp. 253–76.

Brun, J.P. Les noms de famille, prénoms et surnoms à Chanousse et à Montjay, diocèse de Gap. *Revue Internationale d'Onomastique* **29**, pp. 36–43, 1977.

Brunschvicg, Leon. Les Juifs de Nantes et du pays nantais. *Revue des Etudes Juives* **19**, pp. 80–142 and 294–305, 1889.

Burckhardt, Jacob. *The civilization of the Renaissance in Italy, an essay* (London: Phaidon, 1944; original edn 1860).

Burguière, André. Un nom pour soi, le choix du nom de baptême en France sous l'Ancien Régime. *L'Homme* **20**, pp. 25–41, 1980.

Burguière, André. Prénoms et parenté. See Dupâquier et al. (eds), 1984, pp. 29–35.

Burns, Michael. *Dreyfus: a family affair 1789–1945* (New York: HarperCollins, 1991).

Busse, Thomas V. Nickname usage in an American high school. *Names* **31**, pp. 300–6, 1983.

Campisi, Paul J. Ethnic family patterns: the Italian family in the United States. *American Journal of Sociology* **53**, pp. 443–9, 1947–8.

Camproux, Charles. Surnoms d'enfants naturels, Lacroix. *Revue Internationale d'Onomastique* **4**, p. 218, 1952.

Cassato, Umberto. *Gli ebrei a Firenze nell'eta del Rinascimento* (Florence, 1918).

Cavallo, Sandra & Simona Cerutti. Female honor and the social control of reproduction in Piedmont between 1600 and 1800. In *Sex and gender in historical perspective*, Edward Muir & Guido Ruggiero (eds) (Baltimore and London: Johns Hopkins, 1990), pp. 73–109.

Chapman, R.W. *Names, designations and appellations* (Oxford: S.P.E. Tract No. 47, 1936).

Chitty, Erik. Naming after godparents. *Genealogists Magazine* **16**, pp. 47–9, 1969.

Clifford, James L. *Young Samuel Johnson* (London: Heinemann, 1955).

Clodd, Edward. *Tom Tit Tot, an essay on savage philosophy in folk-tale* (London, 1898).

Cody, Cheryll Ann. Naming, kinship, and estate dispersal: notes on slave family life on a South Carolina plantation, 1786 to 1833. *William and Mary Quarterly* **39**, pp. 192–211, 1982.

Cohen, Eugene N. Nicknames, social boundaries and community in an Italian village. *International Journal of Contemporary Sociology* **14**, pp. 102–13, 1977.

Collinson, Patrick. *Godly people: essays on English Protestantism and Puritanism* (London: Hambledon Press, 1983).

Collomp, Alain. Le nom gardé, la dénomination personnelle en Haute-Provence aux XVIIe et XVIIIe siècles. *L'Homme* **20**, pp. 43–61, 1980.

Collomp, Alain. Un stock de prénoms dans deux groupes de villages de Haute-Provence de 1630 à 1770. See Dupâquier et al. (eds), 1984, pp. 169–76.

Cooper, J.P. Patterns of inheritance and settlement by great landowners from the fifteenth to the eighteenth centuries. In *Family and inheritance: rural society in western Europe 1200–1800*, Jack Goody et al. (eds) (Cambridge: Cambridge University Press, 1976), pp. 192–305.

Cordonnier, Paul. Une origine possible des prénoms civiques. *Annales Historiques de la Révolution Française* **30**, p. 70, 1958.

Cornford, James (ed.). *The Book of Common Prayer with historical notes* (London: S.P.C.K., no date).

Corvisier, André. *L'armée française de la fin du XVIIe siècle au ministère de Choiseul, Le Soldat*, II (Paris: Presses Universitaires de France, 1964).

Cottle, Basil. *Names* (London, 1983).

Croix, Alain. *Nantes et les pays nantais au XVIe siècle, étude démographique* (Paris: SEVPEN, 1974).

Cyncynatus, M. et al. Monsieur Dupont s'appelle Martin et son prénom est Jean. *Economie et Statistique* **35**, pp. 49–53, 1972.

Darlu, Pierre et al. Quelques statistiques sur la distribution des patronymes en France. *Population* **52**, pp. 607–34, 1997.

Dauven, Lucien. Les sobriquets à Méharicourt (Somme). *Revue Internationale d'Onomastique* **2**, pp. 59–66, 1950.

Davidoff, Leonore & Catherine Hall. *Family fortunes: men and women of the English middle class, 1780–1850* (London: Hutchinson, 1987).

Davis, N.Z. *Society and culture in Early Modern France* (London: Duckworth, 1975).

De Camp, David. African day-names in Jamaica. *Language* **43**, pp. 139–49, 1967.

De Felice, Emidio. *I cognomi italiani* (Bologna, 1980).

De Felice, Emidio. *I nomi degli Italiani* (Rome, 1982).

Delord, J.-F. Les prénoms à Fronton (Haute-Garonne) du XVIe siècle à nos jours. See Dupâquier et al. (eds), 1984, pp. 85–98.

Delsart, H.M. *Marguérite d'Arbouze, Abbesse du Val-de-Grâce 1580–1626* (Paris: Lethielleux, 1923).

Denis, M.-N. Noms et prénoms en Alsace au XVIIIe et au XIXe siècles. *Annales de Démographie Historique*, pp. 343–53, 1977.

Denis, M.-N. Usage des prénoms dans l'Alsace rurale aux XVIIIe et XIXe siècles. See Dupâquier et al. (eds), 1984, pp. 311–19.

Desplanques, Guy. Les enfants de Michel et Martine Dupont s'appellent Nicolas et Céline. *Economie et Statistique* **184**, pp. 63–83, 1986.

Dillard, J.L. The West African day-names in Nova-Scotia. *Names* **19**, pp. 257–61, 1971.

Dillard, J.L. *Black names* (The Hague, 1976).

Dinn, Robert. 1990. Baptism, spiritual kinship, and popular religion in late medieval Bury St. Edmunds. *Bulletin of John Rylands Library* **72**, pp. 93–106, 1990.

Dodge, D.K. Puritan names. *New England Quarterly* (October 1928), pp. 467–75.

Dommanget, Maurice. Débaptisation collective de prénoms. *Annales Historiques de la Révolution Française* **24**, pp. 326–8, 1952.

Dondaine, Colette. Quelques aspects de l'anthroponymie franc-comtoise. In *L'Onomastique*, G. Taverdier (ed.) (1985), pp. 270–3.

Doppagne, Albert. De quelques usages anthroponymiques actuels en Belgique francophone. In *L'Onomastique*, G. Taverdier (ed.) (1985), pp. 277–81.

Dorian, Nancy C. A substitute name system in the Scottish Highlands. *American Anthropologist* **72**, pp. 303–19, 1970.

Du Puy de Clinchamps, Philippe. *La noblesse* (Paris: Presses Universitaires de France, 1968).

Duby, Georges & Andrée. *Les Procès de Jeanne d'Arc* (Paris: Gallimard-Julliard, Collection Archives, 1973).

Dumas, David W. The naming of children in New England, 1780–1850. *New England Historical Genealogical Register* **132**, pp. 196–210, 1978.

Dunkling, Leslie Alan. *First names first* (London, 1977).

Dunkling, Leslie Alan. *Scottish christian names* (Edinburgh, 1978).

Dunkling, Leslie Alan. *The Guinness book of names*, 7th edn (London: Guinness, 1995).

Dupâquier, Jacques. Naming-practices, godparenthood, and kinship in the Vexin, 1540–1900. *Journal of Family History* **6**, pp. 135–55, 1981.

Dupâquier, Jacques et al. (eds). *Le prénom, mode et histoire* (Paris, 1984).

Dupâquier, Jacques et al. *Le temps des Jules, les prénoms en France au XIXe siècle* (Paris: CNRS, 1987).

Edel, Leon. *Henry James: the untried years 1843–1870* (London: Rupert Hart-Davis, 1953).

Elwin, Malcolm. *The strange case of Robert Louis Stevenson* (London: MacDonald, 1950).

Embleton, Sheila M. "But what will you call the children?" In *Proceedings of the XVIth International Congress of Onomastic Sciences*, 1990, pp. 245–54.

Emmanuelli, R. Note sur les prénoms corses au XVIe siècle. *Bulletin de la Société des Sciences Historiques et Naturelles de la Corse* **93**, pp. 29–40, 1973.

Ervin-Tripp, S.M. Sociolinguistic rules of address. In *Sociolinguistics*, J.B. Pride & Janet Holmes (eds) (Harmondsworth: Penguin, 1972), pp. 225–40.

Ettori, Fernand. Des noms de baptême aux noms de famille, Anthroponymie et société dans la communauté de Quenza au XVIIe siècle et au XVIIIe. *Etudes Corses* **17**, pp. 51–67, 1989.

Fauvel, Daniel. Choix de prénoms et tradition familiale: Pays de Caux, 1600–1900. See Dupâquier et al. (eds), 1984, pp. 99–108.

Febvre, Lucien. Ce qu'on peut trouver dans une série d'inventaires mobiliers, de la Renaissance à la Contre-réforme: changements de climat. *Annales d'Histoire Sociale* **3**, pp. 41–54, 1941.

Febvre, Lucien. *Philippe II et la Franche-Comté* (Paris: Flammarion, 1970; original edn 1912).

Finch, Mary E. *The wealth of five Northamptonshire families 1540–1640* (Oxford: Northamptonshire Record Society (19), 1956).

Fine, Agnès. Transmission des prénoms et parenté en Pays de Sault, 1740–1940. See Dupâquier et al. (eds), 1984, pp. 109–25.

Fink, Carole. *Marc Bloch: a life in history* (Cambridge: Cambridge University Press, 1989).

Firth, Raymond (ed.). *Two studies of kinship in London* (London: Athlone Press, 1956).

Firth, Raymond, Jane Hubert, Anthony Forge. *Families and their relatives: kinship in a middle-class sector of London* (London: Routledge & Kegan Paul, 1969).

Fischer, D.H. Forenames and the family in New England: an exercise in historical onomastics. In *Generations and change, genealogical perspectives in social history*, Robert M. Taylor & Ralph J. Crandall (eds) (Macon, Georgia, 1986), pp. 215–41.

Fiske, Shirley. Rules of address: Navajo women in Los Angeles. *Journal of Anthropological Research* **34**, pp. 72–91, 1978.

Forster, Robert. *The House of Saulx-Tavanes, Versailles and Burgundy 1700–1830* (Baltimore and London; Johns Hopkins, 1971).

Foster, George M. Speech forms and perception of social distance in a Spanish-speaking Mexican village. *Southwestern Journal of Anthropology* **20**, pp. 107–22, 1964.

Fox, J.R. Structure of personal names on Tory Island. *Man* **192**, pp. 153–5, 1963.

Fox, Robin. *The Tory Islanders, a people of the Celtic Fringe* (Cambridge: Cambridge University Press, 1978).

Gardiner, Alan. *The theory of proper names, a controversial essay* (Oxford: Oxford University Press, 1954).

Germain, Jean. Les prénoms à Namur (Wallonie) de la fin du XVe au XVIIe siècle. In *Proceedings of the XVIth International Congress of Onomastic Sciences* (1990), pp. 273–86.

Gilmore, David D. Some notes on community nicknaming in Spain. *Man* **NS 17**, pp. 686–700, 1982.

Gittings, Clare. *Death, burial and the individual in Early Modern England* (London: Routledge, 1988).

Goujard, Philippe. Le stock de prénoms en Pays de Caux 1686–1795. See Dupâquier et al. (eds), 1984, pp. 203–7.

Goursaud, A. *La Société rurale traditionnelle en Limousin,* II (Paris: Maisonneuve et Larose, 1977).

Gresset, Maurice. Les prénoms dans le monde judiciaire comtois aux XVIIe et XVIIIe siècles. See Dupâquier et al. (eds), 1984, pp. 209–22.

Guibeaud, Jean. Étude sur les noms de baptême à Perpignan de 1516 à 1738. *Bulletin d'Histoire et de Philologie Comparée* (1897), pp. 339–487.

Haas, Louis. Social connections between parents and godparents in late medieval Yorkshire. *Medieval Prosopography* **10**(1), pp. 1–21, 1989.

Habbe, Stephen. Nicknames of adolescent boys. *American Journal of Orthopsychiatry* **7**, pp. 371–7, 1937.

Hale, John. *The civilization of Europe in the Renaissance* (London: HarperCollins, 1993).

Haller, William. *The rise of Puritanism* (New York: Columbia University Press, 1938).

Hartman, A.A. Criminal aliases: a psychological study. *Journal of Psychology* **32**, pp. 49–56, 1951.

Hartman, A.A. Name styles in relation to personality. *Journal of General Psychology* **59**, pp. 289–94, 1958.

Hassoun, J.P. Le choix du prénom chez les Hmong au Laos puis en France. *Revue Française de Sociologie* **37**, pp. 241–71, 1995.

Helin, Etienne. La dénomination des personnes dans quelques régions de la Belgique francophone. See Henry (ed.), 1974, pp. 20–31.

Hemlow, Joyce. *The history of Fanny Burney* (Oxford: Oxford University Press, 1958).

Henry, Louis (ed.). *Noms et prénoms, aperçu historique sur la dénomination des personnes en divers pays* (Dolhain: Ordina Editions, 1974).

Hexter, J.H. *On historians* (London: Collins, 1979).

Heywood, Valentine. *British titles: the use and misuse of the titles of peers and commoners* (London: 1951).

Holberton, Paul. *Palladio's villas, life in the Renaissance countryside* (London: John Murray, 1990).

Houdaille, Jacques. Prénoms les plus fréquents dans quelques communes d'après les listes nominatives de 1836. *Population* **37**, pp. 663–9, 1982.

Houdaille, Jacques. Les prénoms des Protestants au XVIIe siècle. *Population* **51**, pp. 775–8, 1996.

Houston, Thomas J. & F.C. Sumner. Measurement of neurotic tendency in women with uncommon given names. *Journal of General Psychology* **39**, pp. 289–92, 1948.

Houth-Baltus, Madeleine. Les prénoms des habitants de Mirande au XVIIe et au XVIIIe siècles. *Revue Internationale d'Onomastique* **8**, pp. 31–42, 1956.

Houth-Baltus, Madeleine. Les noms de personne en Armagnac. *Acta Salmanticensia* **9**(1), pp. 295–321, 1958.

Hubler, Lucienne. De Pierre à Jeremie ou l'influence de la Réforme sur le choix des prénoms, Vallorbe, 1569–1650. *Etudes de Lettres* (Faculté de Lettres, Université de Lausanne) **4**(3), pp. 21–37, 1980.

Hyde, J.K. *Literacy and its uses: studies on late medieval Italy* (Manchester: Manchester University Press, 1993).

Iszaevich, Abraham. Household renown: the traditional naming system in Catalonia. *Ethnology* **19**, pp. 315–25, 1980.

Jakobi, L. et al. Transmission des noms et réconstitution des généalogies, influence de coutumes en Béarn. *Biométrie Humaine* **11**, pp. 69–79, 1976.

Jardin, André. *Tocqueville, a biography* (New York: Noonday Press, 1988).

Jolas, Tina et al. "Parler famille". *L'Homme* **10**, pp. 5–26, 1970.

Jones, P.M. *The peasantry in the French Revolution* (Cambridge: Cambridge University Press, 1988).

Jullian, Camille. Quelques remarques sur l'anthroponymie gallo-romaine. *Revue des Etudes Anciennes* (1919), pp. 40–2.

Kaganoff, Benzion C. *A dictionary of Jewish names and their history* (London: Routledge, 1978).

Kintz, J.-P. Anthroponymie en pays de langue germanique, le cas de l'Alsace, XVIIe–XVIIIe siècles. *Annales de Démographie Historique* (1972), pp. 311–17.

Kintz, J.-P. Société luthérienne et choix des prénoms à Strasbourg, XVIe–XVIIe siècles. See Dupâquier et al. (eds), 1984, pp. 231–7.

Klapisch-Zuber, C. Constitution et variations temporelles des stocks de prénoms. See Dupâquier et al. (eds), 1984, pp. 37–47.

Klapisch-Zuber, C. The name "Remade": the transmission of given names in Florence in the fourteenth and fifteenth centuries. In her *Women, family and ritual in Renaissance Italy* (Chicago and London: University of Chicago Press, 1985a), pp. 283–309.

Klapisch-Zuber, C. Compérage et clientèlisme à Florence (1360–1520). *Richerche Storiche* **15**, pp. 61–76, 1985b.

Klein, Paul. Les changements de noms en Israël. *Revue Internationale d'Onomastique* **3**, pp. 301–13, 1951.

Kolonitskii, B.I. "Revolutionary names": Russian personal names and political consciousness in the 1920s and 1930s. *Revolutionary Russia* **6**, pp. 210–28, 1993.

Lane, Frederic C. *Venice, a maritime republic* (Baltimore and London: Johns Hopkins, 1973).

Laplatte, C. Commentaire de la loi du 3 avril 1950 sur la francisation des noms et prénoms étrangers. *Revue Internationale d'Onomastique* **3**, pp. 119–29, 1951.

Lavender, Abraham D. United States ethnic groups in 1790: given names as suggestions of ethnic identity. *Journal of American Ethnic History* **9**, pp. 36–66, 1989.

Lawson, E.D. Men's first names, nicknames, and short names: a semantic differential analysis. *Names* **21**, pp. 22–7, 1973.

Lawson, E.D. Women's first names: a semantic differential analysis. *Names* **22**, pp. 52–8, 1974.

Léon, Monique. Of names and first names in a small French rural community: linguistic and sociological approaches. *Semiotica* **17**, pp. 211–31, 1976.

Lévi-Strauss, Claude. *The savage mind* (London: Weidenfeld and Nicolson, 1972).

Lieberson, Stanley & Eleanor O. Bell. Children's first names: an empirical study of social taste. *American Journal of Sociology* **98**, pp. 511–54, 1992.

Livi Bacci, M. Quelques problèmes dans le couplage des données nominatives en Toscane. *Annales de Démographie Historique* (1972), pp. 323–31.

Livi Bacci, Massimo & Lorenzo Del Panta. Identification des individus à partir du XVIIe siècle en Italie. See Henry (ed.), 1974, pp. 83–93.

McClure, P. Nicknames and petnames: linguistic forms and social contexts. *Nomina* **5**, pp. 63–76, 1981.

McDermott, John Francis. French surnames in the Mississippi Valley. *American Speech* **18**, pp. 26–32, 1943.

Macfarlane, Alan. *The family life of Ralph Josselin, a 17th-century clergyman* (Cambridge: Cambridge University Press, 1970).

McGregory, Jerrilyn. Aareck to Zsaneka, new trends in African American onomastics. In *Proceedings of the XVIth International Congress of Onomastic Sciences* (1990), pp. 389–96.

Maître, J. La Fréquence des prénoms de baptême en France. *Année Sociologique* **15**, pp. 31–74, 1964.

Maître, J. Problèmes épistemologiques posés par une sociologie du baptême. *Epistemologie Sociologique* **5**, pp. 397–429, 1967–8

Malone, Kemp. Meaningful fictive names in English literature. *Names* pp. **8**, 1–13, 1957.

Marble, Annie Russell. *Pen names and personalities* (New York: Appleton, 1930).

Martine, Roddy. *Scottish clan and family names, their arms, origins and tartans* (Edinburgh, 1987).

Martinetti, Joseph. Etude de la diffusion de huit patronymes dans l'espace insulaire. *Etudes Corses* **29**, pp. 115–44, 1987.

Martin-Gistucci, M.G. Surnoms de famille dans le village corse de Bastelica. *Revue Internationale d'Onomastique* **23**, pp. 31–47 and 105–21, 1971.

Marvick, E.W. *The Young Richelieu* (Chicago and London: University of Chicago Press, 1980).

Maurevert, Georges. De la particule "de" et de la particulomanie. *Mercure de France* (December 1916), pp. 603–35, and (January 1917), pp. 35–61.

Maurevert, Georges. Le particule et le Marquisat de Guy de Maupassant. *Mercure de France* (October 1926), pp. 224–8.

Maurois, André. *Lélia: the life of George Sand* (London: Cape, 1953).

Mauss, Marcel. *Oeuvres* 2 (Paris: Editions de Minuit, 1974).

Meigs, Peveril 3rd. An ethno-telephonic survey of French Louisiana. *Annals of the Association of American Geography* **31**, pp. 243–50, 1941.

Mencken, H.L. *The American language, an inquiry into the development of English in the United States*, 4th edn (1936).

Mencken, H.L. Bulletin on "Hon". *American Speech* **21**(2), pp. 81–5, 1946.

Mencken, H.L. *The American language*, Supplement II (New York, 1978).

Mendel, Pierre. Les noms des Juifs français modernes. *Revue des Etudes Juves* **90**, pp. 15–65, 1950.

Migliorini, Bruno. *Dal nome proprio al nome comune* (Florence: Biblioteca dell' Archivum Romanicum, Serie II Linguistica, 13, 1968).

Minois, Georges. *Les religieux en Bretagne sous l'Ancien Régime* (Luçon: Editions Ouest-France, 1989).

Minton, A. Some aspects of the form of personal names, dropping of preultimate given names. *American Speech* **33**(2), pp. 35–45, 1958.

Molin, Jean. Les noms de baptême à Nogent L'Artaud de 1668 à 1797. *Actes du Congrès National des Sociétés Savantes* (Section d'Histoire Moderne et Contemporaine) **103**, pp. 253–67, 1978.

Mook, Maurice A. Nicknames among the Amish. *Names* **15**, pp. 111–18, 1967.

Moore, A.W. *Manx names*, 2nd edn (London: Elliot Stock, 1903).

Morgan, Jane, Christopher O'Neill & Rom Harré. *Nicknames, their origins and social consequences* (London: Routledge, 1979).

Mulon, Marianne. Petites communes et grands hommes. *Historia* **428**, pp. 64–5, 1982.

Mulon, Marianne. Anthropotoponymes, appropriations, commémorations. In *Proceedings of the XVIth International Congress of Onomastic Sciences* (1990), pp. 15–39.

Nadal, Jordi. La dénomination des personnes en Catalogne depuis le XVIIe siècle. See Henry (ed.), 1974, pp. 51–6.

Needham, Rodney. The system of teknonyms and death-names of the Penan. *Southwestern Journal of Anthropology* **10**, pp. 416–31, 1954.

Neveux, Hugues. Les prénoms masculins à Caen (1568–1775). *Annales de Normandie* **31**, pp. 115–145, 1981.

Nicolaisen, W.F.H. Words as names. *Onoma* **20**, pp. 142–63, 1976.

Nicolaisen, W.F.H. Are there connotative names? *Names* **26**, pp. 40–7, 1978.

Nicolaisen, W.F.H. Onomastic dialects. *American Speech* **55**, pp. 36–45, 1980.

Nicolaisen, W.F.H. The structure and function of names in English literature. *Studia Anglica Posnaniensia* **18**, pp. 139–52, 1986.

Nikonov, V.A. The personal name as a social symbol. *Soviet Anthropology and Archaeology* **10**, pp. 168–95, 1967.

Niles, Philip. Baptism and the naming of children in late medieval England. *Medieval Prosopography* **3**(1), pp. 95–107, 1982.

Nogrady, Michael. Treatment of Hungarian names in Canada. In *Proceedings of the XVIth International Congress of Onomastic Sciences* (1990), pp. 433–9.

Orgel, Samuel Z. & Jacob Tuckman. Nicknames of institutional children. *American Journal of Orthopsychiatry* **5**, pp. 276–85, 1935.

Origo, Iris. *The last attachment: the story of Byron and Teresa Guiccioli as told in their unpublished letters and other family papers* (London: Cape and John Murray, 1949).

Origo, Iris. *Leopardi: a study in solitude* (London: Hamish Hamilton, 1953).

Owens, Leslie Howard. *This species of property: slave life and culture in the Old South* (Oxford: Oxford University Press, 1976).

Partridge, Eric. *The Penguin dictionary of historical slang* (Harmondsworth: Penguin, 1972).

Paustian, P. Robert. The evolution of personal naming among American Blacks. *Names* **26**, pp. 177–91, 1978.

Peterson, Axel. *Le Passage populaire des noms de personne à l'état de noms communs dans les langues romanes* (Uppsala, 1929).

Pettegree, Andrew (ed.). *The Reformation of the parishes* (Manchester: Manchester University Press, 1993).

Phillipps, K.C. *Language and class in Victorian England* (Oxford: Basil Blackwell, 1984).

Pina-Cabral, João de. Nicknames and the experience of community. *Man* **NS 19**, pp. 148–50, 1984.

Pina-Cabral, João de. *Sons of Adam, daughters of Eve, the peasant worldview of the Alto Minho* (Oxford: Oxford University Press, 1986).

Pitt-Rivers, Julian A. *The people of the Sierra* 2nd edn (Chicago and London: Chicago University Press, 1971).

Pitt-Rivers, Julian A. Ritual kinship in the Mediterranean: Spain and the Balkans. In *Mediterranean family structures*, J.G. Peristiany (ed.) (Cambridge: Cambridge University Press, 1976), pp. 317–34.

Plank, Robert. Names of twins. *Names* **12**, pp. 1–5, 1964.

Plank, Robert. The use of "Jr." in relation to psychiatric treatment. *Names* **19**, pp. 132–6, 1971.

Plumb, J.H. (ed.). *Studies in social history* (London: Longman, 1955).

Price, Richard & Sally. Saramaka onomastics: an Afro-American naming system. *Ethnology* **11**, pp. 341–67, 1972.

Prinet, Max. Changements de nom de famille autorisés par François Ier. *Revue du Seizième Siècle* **5**, pp. 21–7, 1920.

Puckett, Newbell Niles. Names of American Negro slaves. In *Studies in the science of society presented to Albert Galloway Keller*, G.P. Murdock (ed.) (New Haven: Yale University Press, 1937), pp. 471–94.

Puckett, N.N. American Negro names. *Journal of Negro History* **23**, pp. 35–48, 1938.

Pullan, Brian. *The Jews of Europe and the Inquisition of Venice, 1550–1670* (Oxford: Basil Blackwell, 1983).

Pyles, Thomas. *Selected essays on English usage* (Gainesville: University Presses of Florida, 1979).

Quilgars, H. Une procédure de changement de prénom au XVIIe siècle. *Annales de Bretagne* **21**, pp. 290–1, 1905–6.

Ralph, Elizabeth & Mary E. Williams (eds). *The inhabitants of Bristol in 1696* (Bristol: Bristol Record Society, 1968).

Reinius, Josef. *On transferred appellations of human beings chiefly in English and German* (Göteborg, 1903).

Rennick, Robert M. The Nazi name decrees of the 1930s. *Names* **18**, pp. 65–88, 1970.

Robert, C.M. *Phraséologie Française* (Gröningen: Wolters, 1905).

Roblin, Michel. Quelques remarques sur les noms de famille des Juifs en Europe Orientale. *Revue Internationale d'Onomastique* **2**, pp. 291–8, 1950.

Roblin, Michel. Les noms de famille des Juifs d'origine Ibérique. *Revue Internationale d'Onomastique* **3**, pp. 65–72, 1951.

Rossi, Alice S. Naming children in middle-class families. *American Sociological Review* **30**, pp. 499–513, 1965.

Roth, Cecil. *A history of the Jews in England* (Oxford: Oxford University Press, 1964).

Rutman, Darret B. & Anita H. "In nomine avi": child-naming patterns in a Chesapeake county, 1650–1750. In *Generations and change*, Robert M. Taylor & Ralph J. Crandall (eds) 1986 pp. 243–65.

Samuel, Raphael (ed.) *Miners, quarrymen and saltworkers* (London: Routledge, 1977).

Sangoï, J.C. La Transmission d'un bien symbolique: le prénom: Bas-Quercy 1750–1872. *Terrain* **4**, pp. 70–6, 1985.

Schnapper, Dominique. Essai de lecture sociologique. See Dupâquier et al. (eds), 1984, pp. 13–20.

Schücking, Levin L. *The Puritan family* (London: Routledge & Kegan Paul, 1969).

Schwarzfuchs, Simon. *Napoleon, the Jews and the Sanhedrin* (London: Routledge, Littman Library, 1979).

Scott, H.M. (ed.). *The European nobilities in the 17th and 18th centuries* [2 vols] (London: Longman, 1995).

Segalen, Martine. Le nom caché, la dénomination dans le pays bigouden sud. *L'Homme* **20**, pp. 63–76, 1980.

Severi, Carlo. Le nom de lignée, les sobriquets dans un village d'Emilie. *L'Homme* **20**, pp. 105–18, 1980.

Sigsworth, Eric M. *Montague Burton, the tailor of taste* (Manchester: Manchester University Press, 1990).

Sire, P. La Révolution française et les prénoms. *Folklore de l'Aude* **2**, pp. 286–93, 1939.

Sizer, Miriam M. Christian names in the Blue Ridge of Virginia. *American Speech* **8**, pp. 34–7, 1933.

Skipper, James K. The sociological significance of nicknames: the case of baseball players. *Journal of Sport Behavior* **7**, pp. 28–38, 1984.

Smith, Daniel Scott. Child-naming practices, kinship ties, and change in family attitudes in Hingham, Massachusetts, 1641 to 1880. *Journal of Social History* **18**, pp. 541–67, 1984–5.

Snell, K.D.M. Deferential bitterness: the social outlook of the rural proletariat in eighteenth- and nineteenth-century England and Wales. In *Social orders and social classes in Europe since 1500*, M.L. Bush (ed.) (London and New York: Longman, 1992), pp. 158–84.

Sorbier, P.A. *Dix ans de magistrature en Corse* (Agen, 1863).

Souque, Henri. Les noms de baptême à Lormont au XVIIe siècle. *Annales du Midi* **90**, pp. 71–81, 1978.

Spitzer, Leo. Suffixes masculins dans les prénoms féminins français. *Romanic Review* **37**, pp. 127–49, 1946.

Stewart, George R. Men's names in Plymouth and Massachusetts in the 17th century. *University of California Publications in English* **7**(2), pp. 109–37, 1948.

Stewart, George R. *American given names, their origin and history in the context of the English Language* (New York, 1979).

Stone, Lawrence. *Family and fortune, studies in aristocratic finance in the 16th and 17th centuries* (Oxford: Oxford University Press, 1973).

Streiff-Fenart, J. *Les couples franco-maghrébines en France* (Paris: Editions L'Harmattan, 1989).

Sturdy, D.J. *The D'Aligres de la Rivière, servants of the Bourbon State in the 17th century* (Woodbridge: Boydell Press, Royal Historical Society 48, 1986).

Syon House (Derby: English Life Publications, 1992).

Taine, Hippolyte. *Histoire de la littérature anglaise*, I (Paris, 1905).

Tavuchis, Nicholas. Naming patterns and kinship among Greeks. *Ethnos* **36**, pp. 152–62, 1971.

Taylor, A.J.W. The significance of "darls" or "special relationships" for Borstal girls. *British Journal of Criminology* **5**, pp. 406–18, 1965.

Tebbenhoff, Edward H. Tacit rules and hidden family structures: naming practices and godparentage in Schenectady, New York 1680–1800. *Journal of Social History* **18**, pp. 567–85, 1984–5.

Tesnière, Michel. Deux siècles de prénoms dans une famille normande. *Revue Internationale d'Onomastique* **24**, pp. 131–50, 1972.

Tesnière, Michel. *Vie et mort des noms de famille* (Paris: Pamphlet, 1979).

Thompson, E.P. *The making of the English working class* (Harmondsworth: Penguin, 1968).

Tomalin, Clare. *Mrs Jordan's profession* (London: Viking, 1994).

Tonkin, Elizabeth. Jealousy names, civilised names: anthroponymy of the Jlao Kru of Liberia. *Man* **NS 15**, pp. 653–64, 1980.

Toury, Gideon. Surnames and their substitutes. In *Semiotic theory and practice II*, Michael Herzfeld & Lucio Melazzo (eds) (Amsterdam and Berlin: Mouton de Gruyter, 1988), pp. 1143–52.

Trevelyan, Raleigh. *A hermit disclosed* (London: Longman, 1960).

Varro, Gabrielle & Djaffar Lesbet. Le Prénom révélateur. In *Générations issues de l'immigration*, G. Abou-Sada & H. Millet (eds) (Paris: Arcantère, 1986), pp. 139–53.

Vernier, Bernard. La circulation des biens, de la main-d'oeuvre et des prénoms à Karpathos. *Actes de la Recherche en Sciences Sociales* **31**, pp. 63–87, 1980.

Vernon, Anne. *A Quaker business man, the life of Joseph Rowntree 1836–1925* (London: Allen and Unwin, 1958).

Vincent, Auguste. L'emploi de *dit* dans les noms de personnes. *Bulletin de la Commission Royale de Toponymie* **32**, pp. 195–216, 1958.

Voth, H.R. Hopi proper names. *Field Columbian Museum Publication* (Chicago) 100, Anthropoligical Series **VI**(3), pp. 67–81, 1905.

Wallman, Sandra. Preliminary notes on "soprannomi" in a part of Piedmont. *Studi Piemontesi* **2**, pp. 126–32, 1973.

Warion, Roland. Nommer à Fours. See Dupâquier et al. (eds), 1984, pp. 145–57.

Waterson, Merlin. *The servants' hall, a domestic history of Erddig* (London: Routledge, 1980).

Weekley, Ernest. *The romance of names* (London: John Murray, 1914).

Wells, F.L. & Helen R. Palwick, Notes on usage of male personal names. *Journal of Social Psychology* **31**, pp. 291–4, 1950.

Wieschoff, H.A. The social significance of names among the Ibo of Nigeria. *American Anthropologist* **43**, pp. 212–22, 1941.

Williams, W.M. *The sociology of an English village* (London: Routledge & Kegan Paul, 1964).

Winstedt, E.O. Notes on English Gypsy christian names. *Journal of the Gypsy Lore Society* 3rd Series **1**, pp. 64–90 and **2**, pp. 16–39, 1921–2.

Withycombe, E.G. *The Oxford dictionary of English christian names*, 3rd edn (Oxford: Oxford University Press, 1977).

Wright, Warren. Fashions in girls' names at Smith College. *Names* **2**, pp. 166–8, 1954.

Wrigley, E.A. *Identifying people in the past* (London, 1973).

Wyatt-Brown, Bertram. *Southern honor, ethics and behavior in the Old South* (Oxford: Oxford University Press, 1982).

Yonge, Charlotte M. *History of christian names*, 2nd edn (London, 1884).

Young, Michael & Peter Willmott. *Family and kinship in East London* (Harmondsworth: Penguin, 1957).

Youngson, A.J. (ed.). *Beyond the Highland Line, three journals of travel in 18th-century Scotland* (London: Collins, 1974).

Zelinsky, Wilbur. Cultural variation in personal name patterns in the eastern United States. *Annals of the Association of American Geographers* **60**, pp. 743–69, 1970.

Zonabend, Françoise. Jeux de noms, les noms de personne à Minot. *Etudes Rurales* **74**, pp. 51–85, 1979.

Zonabend, Françoise. *La Mémoire longue, temps et histories au village* (Paris: Presses Universitaires de France, 1980a).

Zonabend, Françoise. Le nom de personne. *L'Homme* **20**, pp. 12–17, 1980b.

Index

(*Common first names are listed in their main English form with other variants indicated but not separately indexed.*)

Venice 117, 121, 140, 155, 161, 167, 179, 215, 239, 244, 272
Vercauteren 83
Vespasian 19, 24, 34, 39, 58
Vexin 124, 125, 189, 190–1, 211, 216, 234
Victor 40, 41, 60, 98, 99, 102, 189, 210, 212, 235, 331
Victoria (Victoire) 189, 210, 212, 219, 325, 328, 331
Victoria, Queen 214, 255, 286
Vigny, Alfred de 275–6
Villon 153
Virginia 290–1, 294, 298, 299, 301, 307
Visconti 108
Voltaire 209, 288
Vosges 218

Wakefield 139
Wales 117, 123, 127–8, 131–2, 134, 155, 164, 174, 207, 243, 248, 249, 325
Walsingham 143
Walter (Gautier, Walterus) 89, 90, 107, 125, 126, 134, 138, 148, 150, 152, 154, 157, 172, 176, 214, 239, 283
Warboys 105, 107, 110, 117, 157, 158
Washington, Booker T. 313
Weaver 33
Weller, Sam 238, 249
Wessex 74, 76, 100
West, Rebecca 288
Whitelock 116
widows 128, 153, 172, 175, 177
Wilkes, John 196
William (Guglielmo, Guillaume, Willelmus, etc.) 84–5, 86, 89, 90, 106, 107, 108, 109, 113, 114, 119, 124, 125, 127, 128, 134, 139, 147, 148, 150, 152, 154, 156, 157, 158, 159, 160, 162, 163, 165, 171, 172, 178, 190, 195, 197, 211, 213, 214, 226, 231, 236, 239, 240, 241, 248, 250, 255, 268, 269, 290, 291, 292, 293, 317, 324, 326, 331, 333
Williams, W.M. 213, 257
Willibrord 94, 97
Willoughby, family and circle 190, 202, 217, 236, 264, 266, 279
Wilson 203, 253, 255, 263, 306
Winchester 91, 94, 96, 97, 107, 116, 122, 144, 159, 173
Windham 231, 255
Wingfield 217
Withycombe 190
women's names 15–18, 52, 54, 60, 72, 74, 75, 83–4, 88, 89, 90, 91, 105, 107, 108, 114, 118, 128, 131, 132, 149, 172–7, 198, 207–8, 221, 235, 240–1, 254, 319
Woodforde, Parson 201, 227, 234, 263, 264, 265, 270
Woulfe 117, 262, 326
Wriothesley 236, 279
Wulfstan 76
Wynfrith 94, 97

Yonge, Charlotte 208, 214, 218, 238, 271, 278, 329
York 143, 158, 172, 196, 217
Yorkshire 122, 136, 139, 155, 156, 195, 206, 253
Yves 89, 140, 205, 235

Zaccaria 157
Zelinsky xii, 293
Zimmermann 160
Zonabend xii, 282